CorelDRAW® X7:
The Official Guide

About the Author

Gary David Bouton (Central New York) is an award-winning CorelDRAW illustrator and author of hundreds of expert design and drawing tutorials. He's written almost 30 books on topics—this is his seventh on CorelDRAW—along with books on Photoshop, vector illustration packages, and software programs used to edit video, create and render 3D models, and produce Hollywood-style special effects. For McGraw-Hill Education, Gary has written *Xara Xtreme 5: The Official Guide* and co-authored *Photoshop CS4 QuickSteps*. He is a former Madison Avenue art director and has been a professional illustrator for 35 years. He currently runs a full-service design graphics firm where he designs logos, photorealistic product realization, and computer animations. Gary has also served on Corel's CorelDRAW feature review board and was a finalist in the Corel World Design contest.

About the Technical Reviewer

William Schneider (Athens, Ohio) currently teaches computer graphics and digital photography in the School of Visual Communication at Ohio University. He was a finalist in the annual Corel World Design Contest on two occasions and has written numerous magazine articles about photography and computer artwork. William's photographs and graphical designs have also been published in a number of venues, including *Italian Renaissance Art: A Source Book*, for which he created hundreds of illustrations and photographs. When not working at the computer or printing in the darkroom, William likes to woodwork and ice skate.

CorelDRAW® X7:
The Official Guide

Gary David Bouton

New York   Chicago   San Francisco
Athens   London   Madrid   Mexico City
Milan   New Delhi   Singapore   Sydney   Toronto

Cataloging-in-Publication Data is on file with the Library of Congress

McGraw-Hill Education books are available at special quantity discounts to use as premiums and sales promotions, or for use in corporate training programs. To contact a representative, please visit the Contact Us pages at www.mhprofessional.com.

CorelDRAW® X7: The Official Guide

1 2 3 4 5 6 7 8 9 0   DOC DOC   10 9 8 7 6 5 4

ISBN   978-0-07-183314-1
MHID   0-07-183314-5

Sponsoring Editor Roger Stewart	**Technical Editor** William Schneider	**Production Supervisor** George Anderson
Editorial Supervisor Patty Mon	**Copy Editor** LeeAnn Pickrell	**Composition** Cenveo Publisher Services
Project Editor LeeAnn Pickrell	**Proofreader** Paul Tyler	**Illustration** Gary David Bouton and Cenveo Publisher Services
Acquisitions Coordinator Amanda Russell	**Indexer** Rebecca Plunkett	**Art Director, Cover** Jeff Weeks

Contents at a Glance

Contents

Part I Student Orientation Weekend

Part III   Working with Object Tools for Art and for Business

CHAPTER 7   Choosing (and Understanding) the Right Path Tools 165

CHAPTER 8   Exploring Special Shapes, Connectors, and Other Office Automation Helpers 187

Part VI Creating the Illusion of a 3D Composition

Part VII Special Effects in CorelDRAW

Part VIII   Bitmaps and Photos and How to Use CorelDRAW Graphics Suite to Work with Them

Part IX   Getting Your Work in the Public Eye

CHAPTER 23   Professional Output: A Primer on Prepping Your Work for Print . . . 591

CHAPTER 24   Basic HTML Page Layout and Publishing 625

Foreword

With more than 25 years of development, CorelDRAW Graphics Suite is a complete and professional collection of graphics products. Combining an extensive toolset for illustration, page layout, typography, photo editing, and so much more, CorelDRAW X7 provides everything creative professionals and aspiring designers need to turn their ideas into amazing pieces of art. Learning tools remain a very important part of that creative journey, so we're pleased to bring you the new *CorelDRAW X7: The Official Guide*.

Having the tools at your fingertips is one thing, but being able to make the most out of them and achieve the professional results you want requires practice and great learning resources. In addition to CorelDRAW's vast collection of training videos and online documentation, the ongoing partnership between McGraw-Hill Professional, author Gary David Bouton, and Corel Corporation gives you the book you need to make the most of CorelDRAW X7. Covering everything from text in a composition, to working with shapes, object tools, and effects, this guide will show you how to become a CorelDRAW power-user, giving you tips and tricks to make you highly productive.

Congratulations to our *Official Guide* author, Gary David Bouton, for providing such a high-quality book packed with references, insights, and detailed help. As you go through each chapter, you'll find invaluable information for both beginners and graphics professionals alike.

On behalf of everyone on the CorelDRAW team at Corel Corporation, thank you very much for choosing CorelDRAW Graphics Suite X7 and for expanding your product knowledge with this latest edition of *CorelDRAW X7: The Official Guide*.

Happy CorelDRAWing!
Gérard Métrailler
Vice President, Product Management, CorelDRAW
Corel Corporation
Ottawa, Ontario, Canada
August 2014

Acknowledgments

- *To Roger Stewart*   A very realistic man helped us get this manuscript past the finish line and into your hands. I want to thank Roger—my second book with him—for the patience, the candidness, and for using a very human set of bearings that were instrumental in our efforts. Thank you, Roger, you helped me make my thoughts into a book.
- *To Amanda Russell*   Oh, Woman of Infinite Patience, I need to thank you for managing to be encouraging, diligent, forceful, and charming—all at the same time. You're a delight to work with and perhaps someday you'll teach me how to read a Production spreadsheet. ;)
- *Project Editor LeeAnn Pickrell*: This is about the billionth book that LeeAnn and I have worked on, and because we're on different coasts we might never meet face to face, but we know each other well enough professionally to work together and produce outstanding work. Thanks again and again, LeeAnn.
- *Technical Editor William Schneider*—*Professor* Schneider, actually, but he lets me call him Bill because he pities my life. Bill and I go *wayyyy* back as a couple of Corellians who entered the World Design Contest that Corel Corporation puts up yearly. And we've worked with the earliest CorelDRAW version right up to the one you're using today. Bill has more than edited my work for accuracy; you should know that he *wrote* several passages in this book. Thanks Bill, and I'll try to send you something better than an ice cream voucher when this thing winds down.
- *Barbara Bouton*, for the use of her photography in this book's tutorials.
- *Nick Wilkinson*, for portions of his original manuscript on VBA.
- *Production Supervisor George Anderson*: Thanks to George and his staff for creating a wonderful layout of this book's interior, both printed and as an eBook.
- *Tony Severenuk at Corel Corporation*: Thanks to Tony for his technical support and explanations of the more mystical CorelDRAW features.
- *Corel Product Manager Gérard Metrailler*: I need to thank this man in print because it felt as though Gérard were standing right next to me while I wrote this book, except for moments when I felt he was in the kitchen looking for snacks. Seriously, you cannot write something that demands as much concentration as this book

does, and Gérard answered my questions and provided me with media usually at a moment's notice. I thank you, Gérard, as I thank Corel's engineers for an outstanding product. I hope I did you all proud.

- Special thanks to Ross Blair and M. E. Volmar for pointing out the errors in the version X6 book. Boy is my face red, but thanks again, and you'll see that any older content in this book (there is *not* a lot) reflects your diligence.

Introduction

When I first got a glimpse of CorelDRAW Creative Suite X7 back in late 2013, I said to myself "Gosh!" (or something *like* Gosh!). "This thing is larger yet terser than previous versions; they've simplified the UI and made it more intuitive; it sports the look of Windows 8..." Thanks, Corel Corp.; how am I supposed to make all this good stuff fit in this book? Then it dawned on me—this is the *CorelDRAW X7 Official Guide*, not the online Owner's Manual, not a cheat sheet; it has always been a way to guide you through the program, to get active and hands-on with tutorials...and all of a sudden, the vision of this book became one of simplicity, getting down to brass tacks, an all-meat, no-fat tome, just like the CorelDRAW program itself.

What you're going to get out of this new edition is an approach to CorelDRAW without definitions, a well-rounded education in color and vector graphics without going nerd, and hopefully some inspiration that will lead to original, stunning work that looks as though you sweated the details a lot more than you really did. Version X7 can help bring your ideas to life a lot faster than with previous versions, and all you need is a little guidance. A *guide* would do the trick, wouldn't it? You know, like an *Official Guide*?

Okay, the proof is in the pudding. If I'm to make good on my promise of a fortified, no-nonsense book (well, there's a *little* nonsense in it), I should stop writing this Introduction and we should both be getting to the Good Stuff beyond these obligatory beginning pages. Here's a summary of what's in store.

How This Book Is Organized

One of the wonderful things about a book, including eBooks, is how patient they are with you. You're encouraged to progress at your own speed, and if you're in luck, the book is organized in such a way that you can dive in at any point and come up the richer. I feel very strongly that you have a powerful book in your hands. I encourage you to "pick and choose" through this summary to find an open door through which you can easily find other rooms through other doors, and when you've had you fill, you can bookmark (or not) a section and revisit it later.

- **Part I** is a greeting meant for both first-time and more experienced Corellians, and Chapter 1 sets the tone and pace with a walk-through of new and changed features. You'll be pleasantly surprised with what you see and will use and how

CorelDRAW is more tightly integrated with the Web than ever. Resources that couldn't possibly fit on a disc are yours in a click, and Corel keeps the media fresh with community offerings, and Corel's own, ever-changing set of fonts, patterns, and other content. You'll also dive right into the deep end of CorelDRAW with a guided set of steps to create your first piece of commercial art (if you're new to the program).

- **Part II** is a whirlwind of informational goodies that you'll want to know before you create your first drawing. You'll get the lowdown on how to set up multi-page documents and how to use a feature that creates instant shapes for you. You'll get lessons on rotating and shrinking things and a general education on how to keep all the neat stuff you're going to create and download in an arrangement that provides you with what you want, when you want it.

- **Part III** leans toward help for the novice artist who sits down at a computer at a small to medium business and is expected to design a poster or flyer by the end of the day. Impossible? Let's be optimistic and get into the details on special shapes you can transform just by dragging on them and how to use connectors for professional flowcharts. When you've gained a sense of confidence, Chapter 9 is your key to CorelDRAW design basics, getting a little hands-on with some of the more robust and complex features in CorelDRAW. Hint: It's worth it!

- **Part IV** will get your fonts, your grammar, and especially your spelling (just trying to be fnnny here) to look as polished and professional as your artwork. Part IV delves into your choice of fonts for different occasions, using CorelDRAW's proofing tools and just a little Desktop Publishing. A picture says a thousand words, and you want them to be good-looking, *meaningful* words!

- **Part V** is the one you might want to read first! You know all those paths you draw? This section shows you all the options for filling a closed path and how to make an ordinary outline into a stunning one with CorelDRAW's bevy of calligraphy and features that pepper a line with vegetables, candy, you name it. This part is about anything *but* how to draw a simple line.

- **Part VI** takes your drawing into another dimension. If you're into sci-fi, there's a signpost up ahead; your next stop...extrude tools, bevel tools, perspective features...anything that deserves to be 3D is at your command once you read through this part.

- **Part VII** (that's "Part 7" if you're not into Roman numerals) shows you the Distortion tools (there *have* been additions since X6) and how to mess up a perfectly good rectangle in seconds! Learn how to use the Node tool, too, so you can expertly modify any object. Create complex compositions that will serve as elegant borders for coupons and get a taste for importing bitmaps and melding them into a vector composition. You're going to make an advertisement that looks like it belongs in a magazine.

- **Part VIII** is all about photos and how to use and edit them in CorelDRAW and the under-advertised PHOTO-PAINT, also a part of Corel's CGS bundle. See how to retouch a photo—a tricky task and a lot more complicated than painting a mustache on your aunt Wilma. Learn what you can and cannot do with images by discovering the basic and not so basic virtues and limitations of computer art that doesn't use vectors.

- **Part IX** (pronounced "icks") is where the author, editors, and tech support at Corel Corporation must draw this book to a close. Fortunately, it's all about publishing: getting that hard work you do into the public eye, either through traditional printing or posting to the Web. Let your friends, family, and prospective clients see what you can do after finishing this section of our book.
- **Online Bonus Chapter** shows you how to design a typeface using CorelDRAW and how to export your very own TrueType font. Imagine making and distributing a font that has your company logo to everyone in your department. You'll learn the steps in this online PDF document and become font savvy in a jiffy.

Tutorial and Bonus Content: Where to Find It

Tutorial

Tutorials are scattered around this book like so many peanut shells on the ground after a circus. Many of these Tutorials will go better and more smoothly, and better demonstrate a technique or principle, if you have a working file loaded in the drawing window, so we've provided you with several. At the beginning of a chapter, you'll be directed to download a zip file that accompanies the written tutorials. Open the file you were asked to download, and you'll be all set to follow and work along. To get the tutorial files, go to the following URLs:

- **www.mhprofessional.com/bouton**   Here you'll find the book's tutorial files to download.
- **www.theboutons.com**   This is a mirror site for the files. Go to the top page, and you can't miss the conspicuous, obnoxious, but superbly designed *CorelDRAW X7 Official Guide* Download icon.

Additionally, the author has supported tutorial and bonus files at TheBoutons. com since he began writing *The Official Guide* with version X4 in 2008. If you visit The Boutons' website, you can browse previous book pages and discover links to previous user content such as additional PDF chapters, blank scenes to which you can add your own logos using CorelDRAW's Perspective tool, Gary's handcrafted typefaces, and a seamless texture or three.

The shorter this Introduction is, the more space there is to teach you, so enough with the front of the book. Start thumbing through the pages, find some of the Good Stuff, put on some smooth jazz, because Led Zep is classic but not Tutorial Music, and let's begin.

PART I

Student Orientation Weekend

1 Welcome! What's in Store, and What's New

If you've just upgraded to CorelDRAW X7 from X6, you're going to be in for a thrill. All your dreams have just come true. This version has all the power and features of X6, but the interface has been reworked so you'll find it extremely intuitive to use, regardless of what you're doing or where you're looking. If you're new to CorelDRAW but have experience with drawing programs, you're in for the treat of the century, because everything is easy, intuitive to discover, and virtually everything that has to do with drawing is right at your cursortip. If you're totally new to CorelDRAW, do *not* hold your breath or take a deep gulp or anything! CorelDRAW is feature-rich without being overwhelming, and once you understand the conventions covered in this chapter, finding the Pen tool's going to be as easy as finding your favorite ballpoint in the coffee mug designated for writing tools on your desk.

Let's call this chapter "The Pre-Party." Here, you'll get warmed up, confident, and ready to take off in The Main Event chapters to follow.

If You're New to Vector Drawing Programs

If you've been using CorelDRAW since its beginnings around 1990, you can skip ahead here—this section is for people who were recently gifted with their first copy of the Suite, or just became curious about what this CorelDRAW thing is everyone talks about.

What Vector Drawing Is and Isn't

If you purchased the CorelDRAW Suite in expectation of retouching your great-grandparents' wedding photo, CorelDRAW would not be the program to use, but happily Corel PHOTO-PAINT *is,* and it's part of the Suite. The Graphics Suite contains two major programs that cover the two primary types of computer graphics—vector and bitmap—and the difference is worth a little explaining. Let's begin with bitmap graphics because they are more common in email, on the Web, and in printing than vector graphics.

Bitmap Images

Bitmap images, such as those you take with your mobile phone or other device, are also called *resolution-dependent* images, because they contain a fixed number of picture elements called *pixels*. All the visual information that you can save in a digital photo—a bitmap image—is taken at the time you snap the photo; you cannot increase or decrease the size of the image without introducing distortion. This is because bitmap images, by their nature, shrink in dimensions you'd measure with a ruler when you increase their resolution. Bitmap images also become greater in printable size when you decrease their resolution, which is something you can do in PHOTO-PAINT, and this is covered in later chapters. The key to understanding some of the unflexibility of bitmap images is that inverse, unchangeable relationship between measured size and the number of pixels per unit of measured size (resolution). The amount of detail always depends on the size of the bitmap image.

Often in desktop publishing, the terms *resize* and *resample* are used to describe, respectively, the shrinking of an image *without changing the number of pixels,* and—quite differently—resizing, or "blowing up," a bitmap, which does, in fact, distort the original image information. Figure 1-1 shows an original *high-resolution* image at left. You can make out the phrase on the coffee mug and every detail looks crisp and well defined. This is because the *resolution,* the number of picture elements per inch, is very high. At right is a *low-resolution* image of the same coffee cups. You've probably seen this *pixelation* effect when you've zoomed in very close to a bitmap. The elements are more predominant than the image they are supposed to represent; you will get this sort of unwanted effect if you don't capture a scene at high resolution and also if you're handed a low-resolution image and expected to do something meaningful with it.

You'll learn to work with bitmap images later in this book; a good generalization to remember is that bitmap images require *a paint program* to edit and create, whereas vector illustrations are the product of a vector *drawing program,* which is covered in the following section.

Vector Imaging

Twenty years ago, vector drawing programs required concentration and a little patience because computer processors had a fraction of the power that we enjoy today. One of the most notable characteristics of drawing programs is the "undo-ability" of your composition. For example, when a painter paints a masterpiece, it's also a "set piece"; it's laborious and sometimes impossible to make corrections or enhancements to the painting because the paint is dry and the deed is done. But vector drawing programs let you move objects around, decide and redecide on the color, position, and size of any element on the page.

Resolution: 300 pixels per inch   Resolution: 72 pixels per inch

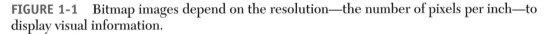

FIGURE 1-1   Bitmap images depend on the resolution—the number of pixels per inch—to display visual information.

A vector drawing has two elemental characteristics: all the objects you create have a shape—an outline often called a *path*—and an interior that you might choose to fill with any of a number of CorelDRAW's exotic collection of fills. This illustration demonstrates how a vector drawing program makes an outline and a fill visually meaningful. The design is made up of a thick white outline around the circles and a Fountain Fill that is a red-to-orange linear gradient.

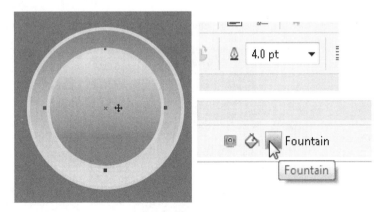

This might come as a surprise, but CorelDRAW is updating your monitor with *bitmap information* every time you create or edit something on a page: there have

been very few vector monitors still in existence since the 1970s; they were like oscilloscopes, and it was nearly impossible to create something beautiful or even interesting on them. So CorelDRAW deals in math, specifically *geometry,* when you make a design using the tools, and these geometric (and other) calculations can be indefinitely updated and refined, and part of the beauty of working with vector graphics is that you can scale a drawing up or down to any required size, and the elements in the composition remain crisp and scaled to perfectly represent what you originally created.

Here's an example of the flexibility you have when you create a vector design; in Figure 1-2 at left, you can see the Simple Wireframe view of the drawing from Figure 1-1. Not much to it, right? But when you assign this object a fill and an outline type (in this case, solid white) as in the middle image, it takes on a character and becomes what we commonly call "art." Now at right, this is the same set of circles with a square background, but the fill has been changed to vector artwork from the Corel CONNECT collection. Yes, you can fill a vector design with *other* vectors, and you can even change an outline to a dotted line in different styles and even an outline style that looks like a brush stroke. All the creativity you can imagine in CorelDRAW is a matter of defining an object and then using an interesting outline style and a novel object fill.

The Vector Sky's the Creative Limit!

By now you're imagining that bitmap images are the sole medium of photographic artwork, whereas vector artwork is limited to shapes that might make a good pie chart or something. Rubbish and not at all; for over 20 years, CorelDRAW artists have been testing the creative bounds of this constantly evolving program, and everything from photorealistic artwork to menus, to catalogs, and even physical license plates are designed in CorelDRAW every day.

View | Simple Wireframe   Identical paths, but different outline styles and fills

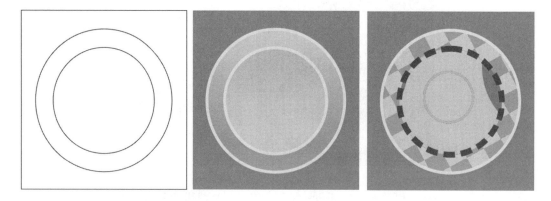

FIGURE 1-2   The underlying geometry of your CorelDRAWing can be simple. Then you dress up the object with fantastic fills and outline styles.

Open *a pear.cdr* from the Chapter 1 download file if you like and then choose View | Simple Wireframe from the menu. Figure 1-3 shows both the vector drawing in wireframe and at a different size, and on the left, you can see the original image the drawing was based on. You can also see the advantage of the vector illustration over the bitmap version when a large copy is needed. At left, there is noticeable pixelation when the bitmap version is enlarged, but when it's visually represented as a collection of objects with different colors and transparency values, all CorelDRAW has to do is calculate the final scale of the elements, and the resolution-independent artwork retains all the visual value of a smaller version.

You're going to have the time of your life with CorelDRAW X7, just as soon as you get an intellectual handle on the tools, the interface, and other goodies that you can add to your designs!

Right now is a good time for novices and experienced CorelDRAW users alike to get a gander at what's new in this version...

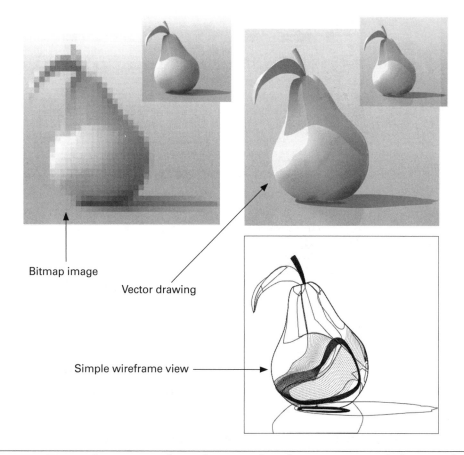

Bitmap image

Vector drawing

Simple wireframe view

FIGURE 1-3   Vector drawings can have the warmth and attractiveness of a bitmap photo when you learn how CorelDRAW's tools work.

Corel CONNECT: Your First Stop

After you've installed your software, or on first launching CorelDRAW (or PHOTO-PAINT), you'll see a box onscreen that asks you to sign into your Corel Account or to Create An Account. Corel CONNECT is a thorough implementation of what is called in tech magazines "cloud computing." In PlainSpeak, Corel has put a community of users at your fingertips. You'll have access to new fills (and other content) that Corel and other users create through CONNECT and your account. Having an active Internet connection (a fast one is best) is vital to a pleasant and rewarding CorelDRAW user experience.

There are two types of accounts. The Standard Membership is totally free and guarantees that you have all the fonts and clipart and other media that used to come with a physical delivery of a program on disc. The Premium Membership requires a monthly subscription fee, and as you'd expect, you get a lot more goodies with Premium. When you start or exit a Corel program, you're offered the subscription option. The following illustration shows you the box that you *really* should fill out and *not* dismiss by closing.

You're Welcomed Before You Enter CorelDRAW

Once you've filled in the registration data, CorelDRAW's splash screen appears before the program opens. And before CorelDRAW opens, you're welcomed by a screen overlain on the workspace. Owners of previous versions know about the Welcome

Screen, but new to version X7 is the number of choices you have—Corel Corporation has laid out a rich table of contents—from which you can choose to watch tutorial videos before getting down to work and set up the workspace to suit your needs.

Let's take a look at your options. Figure 1-4 shows the Welcome screen. As you can see, a main window explains or shows the item you've clicked in the left column.

- **Get Started**   This icon shows the most common options to pick from when you want to start a drawing or open one you've saved. You can find these options under the File menu, and you can also start a new document and override the Welcome screen by clicking the New document icon (the page icon at the far left) on the program's Standard bar.
- **Workspace**   When you click this icon, you're given the choice of starting a Lite workspace; it has fewer calories than Regular, and I'm just kidding—it offers a very limited Toolbox and other features, and you might want to "hold back" on

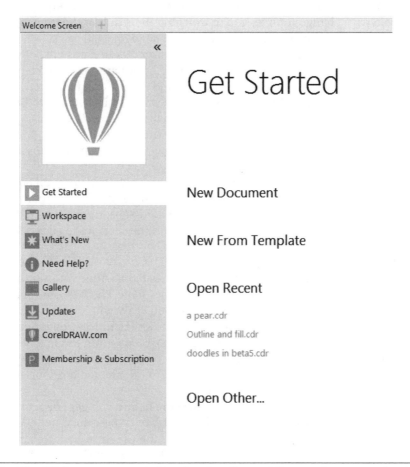

FIGURE 1-4   The Welcome screen is Destination Central for starting a new drawing, doing research, choosing an interface, and getting software updates.

using all the new features because you have this book to guide you. The Classic and Default interfaces are similar, except the Classic interface will remind experienced users more of previous versions. Under the Advanced category, you can set up CorelDRAW to make Desktop Publishing or Illustration features more prominent and accessible. Finally, under the Other heading, you can even set up CorelDRAW to remind you of Adobe Illustrator if you're coming to CorelDRAW from that or a similar program.

- **What's New**   Here, you can learn about new features in a well-written, fairly comprehensive but brief document, which is displayed in the center of the screen when you click this icon.
- **Need Help?**   Clicking this icon unravels a brief list of resources you can access online and directly within the interface to get up and running. Corel offers a very useful collection of video tutorials on the basics.
- **Gallery**   Here, you can enjoy images created by other CorelDRAW users, many of them contestants in Corel's annual art contest. The gallery is updated frequently; remember that you're cloud computing with CorelDRAW, so when a web page changes online, you're watching the result of those changes, so you might want to visit the Gallery often to see newly posted work.
- **Updates**   Clicking here lets you make certain that updates are delivered to you and your software. It's a good idea to put a checkmark next to both options listed so you're in the know about CorelDRAW and other Corel updates.
- **CorelDRAW.com**   This option tells you how to get in touch with Corel's community—clicking the icon doesn't actually take you to CorelDRAW.com but merely gives you the URL. At CorelDRAW.com, you can share your experiences, get great tips and tricks, and find interesting reading from the pros and other community members.
- **Membership & Subscription**   This is another chance to get on board with the Standard or Premium service. Don't take this option lightly; without creating an account and thus getting your free Standard Subscription, you'll be at a loss for fills, fonts, and other media that you'll definitely want to access from within CorelDRAW.

Finally, if the Welcome screen becomes unwelcome after your tenth or eleventh visit to CorelDRAW, you can uncheck the Always Show The Welcome Screen At Launch checkbox at the bottom left. Then, CorelDRAW will always begin with a bare-bones menu. This can be a little disorienting, however, unless you realize that to put CorelDRAW into action, you need to either choose New from the File menu (or New from Template, or Open a previously saved document), or click the New button on the Standard bar. Doing this brings CorelDRAW to life, the toolbox tools aren't dimmed anymore, and life is good.

There's just one more eensy matter to settle before you get down to work for the first time: CorelDRAW needs you to tell it what *type* of new document you'd like it to create for you. The following illustration shows the Create A New Document dialog, and just like the Welcome screen, at the lower left you can check the Do Not Show This Dialog Again checkbox, so you don't see this dialog every session—but you really should let it appear all the time. Why? Because without this dialog, you'll start a new document *all the time* with default settings, and this will play havoc with page size and color settings. CorelDRAW is quite color-sensitive. For example, a document set up for RGB color mode will look hideous if you try to print it with commercial CMYK inks. An explanation of your choices is in order right here.

- **Name**   Any time you save a document, you can name it. But by naming the document at the beginning of a session, all you need to do is press CTRL + S at any time, and CorelDRAW saves your document (by default) to the Documents folder in Windows.

Tip   Once you change the saved location for files (D:\My DRAW files), CorelDRAW remembers that location, and subsequent art will be saved to the folder you specified.

- **Preset Destination**   This option can be a confusing and potentially misleading set of words to the newcomer! A *destination* in computer graphics terms is "where the design you draw will ultimately be displayed." Your work could be going to a commercial printer, to a website, or anywhere that colors in your document might display incorrectly. It's often best to set the Preset Destination to Default RGB from the drop-down list. In addition to the Web and Default RGB options, your other choices are mostly CMYK color-based and are onscreen simulations of subtractive CMYK pigments. Your screen might be inexplicably dull—especially the color palette—if you choose a workspace that displays in the CMYK color space.

- **Size, Width, and Height boxes**   These options are where you set your page size. Your page size can be changed at any time from within CorelDRAW, but it's nice to get this one out of the way before getting creative. You'll see a units box to the right of these fields, so if you're accustomed to millimeters instead of inches, or typographer's picas, choose the unit you need here. You can also click the little icons of pages to specify Landscape (wide) or Portrait (tall) page orientation.

- **Number Of Pages**   You can add, subtract, and reorder a multiple page document at any time in CorelDRAW, but if you know here and now that you're going to create a font, or a leaflet, you can specify the number of pages you want for the file.

- **Primary Color Mode**   The color mode of a graphics file has a great impact on how you work and how colors are printed or, conversely, on how they're displayed on a web page (which is viewed on an RGB monitor). You can choose RGB or CMYK from the drop-down list; if you've never sent a file to a commercial printer, you should choose RGB color mode because RGB is the way human beings perceive color. RGB color mode is predictable; it's like looking at any other scene in the real world.

- **Rendering Resolution**   Here's that irritating "resolution" word again! What this value means is how many dots you want the printer (or other output device) to use to render your work to paper. The default, 300 dots per inch (dpi), is quite high, and chances are, if you work at home, you've got the document set up to as much as a home inkjet or laser printer can render. However, if you don't intend to render at all, but instead want to export a design as a bitmap for email attachments, 72 or 96 dpi is fine. In this instance, the "dots" are actually pixels; for example, 96 pixels per inch has been a typical screen resolution for years. If you're outputting to a web page, you might want to consider 72 pixels per inch because this is the resolution web professionals render their graphics to in 2014. And if you're sending a bitmap copy of your work to a friend with a high-resolution tablet, consider rendering to 300 dpi because high-resolution screens are becoming more and more popular.

- **Preview Mode**   Without question, choose Enhanced. It's the maximum viewing quality; it won't slow down your work unless your computer is using a processor from an ATM bank machine; and there's a reason, discussed later in this *Official Guide,* for the other viewing quality modes.

- **Color Settings**   Digest this set of explanations slowly. Take your time; this *Guide* has got nowhere to go, and color management is a vital feature that protects the way your artwork looks when printed.

    The first three settings will work just fine at their defaults for most people in the Western Hemisphere. *Profiles* are a collection of settings that make up the optimal "environment" for a graphics file as it is sent to a printer or other rendering device (such as an imagesetter, a high-resolution printing device). The *RGB Profile* for an RGB color space in which you design something is, by default, sRGB, which is terrific for most inkjets because most of them today are calibrated to the sRGB color space, and sRGB (sometimes called *small*RGB) is the color space of the Web. The *CMYK Profile,* by default, is U.S. Web Coated (SWOP, or Specifications for Web Offset Printing) v2. This set of color characteristics is quite common, so, in theory, if you do work for output by a commercial printing house, the final print should look something like your original RGB image in CorelDRAW onscreen. Countries in Europe and the Pacific Rim have other standards to choose from in the drop-down list. The *Grayscale Profile* really has only one parameter that could be adjusted and that is Dot Gain (at 20%, a very generous compensation). *Dot gain* is the compensation a commercial printer uses when printing black ink on any number of different types of paper, all with different rates of absorption. In principle, if you make the halftone dots in the printing plates (or in the direct-digital process) a specified amount *smaller,* the ink will spread (gain) just the right amount to make the halftone copy of your art look good on the page.

The fourth option under Color Settings is *Rendering Intent,* and it is misunderstood by 11 out of 10 people. Seriously, this term means you need to choose between four well-established conversion processes when your artwork uses colors that cannot be expressed using the combination of *C*yan, *M*agenta, *Y*ellow, and blac*K* pigments. In essence, your monitor uses red, green, and blue light to show you what you've drawn, whereas printing uses different colors. As a result, RGB color with a larger color space than CMYK has colors CMYK inks can't express accurately; therefore, something needs to be done—and it's called *color conversion*—so your CMYK print looks more than vaguely like what's on your monitor! The four choices are

- **Relative Colorimetric**   This setting is all-around probably the best conversion for most of your CorelDRAW drawings and even photographs you import to a CorelDRAW document. Relative colorimetric doesn't preserve the whitest whites (the *White Point*), but instead shifts all colors and all brightnesses to the nearest colors that the CMYK color space can express. *Relative* does clip (exclude) certain colors that are widely out of range, so two different reds, for example, in your onscreen original, might be forced to render as the same red. The relationship of one color to another is preserved during this conversion, however, so the human eye's brain sees this conversion as well-balanced and even very close to the onscreen original. It's also a good choice for commercial printers to pull a color proof of work before a large press run.

- **Absolute Colorimetric**   The White Point and Black Point, unlike Relative, is preserved in Absolute Colorimetric rendering intent. This guarantees that highly identifiable colors (such as Coca-Cola red and Federal Express purple) are reproduced accurately, at the expense of shifting other colors. If you need specific color accuracy for certain colors, this is your choice.

- **Perceptual**   This rendering intent takes the entire expressible range of colors (the *gamut*) available from one device (such as your screen), and compresses it to fit with the gamut of the destination device (such as an inkjet printer). The result is that all the colors in the print have shifted somewhat, even if only one or two colors were out of CMYK's range (gamut), but the relationship between all colors is preserved. If you're obsessed with color accuracy, this wouldn't be your first choice of conversion methods, but if you're most concerned with the relationship between the original colors—grass green contrasted against sky blue in a photo for example—you'd choose this method.

- **Saturation**   This setting is for highly stylized comic-bookish artwork, charts, graphs, and any time you're free to totally forget about color accuracy and relationships between colors in a document. When you just need garish hues on a page to make a sales pitch or to accurately render a Marvel Comics hero in uniform, this is your option.

Finally, you can and probably should save your Custom settings. Do this by clicking the little 3.5" floppy disk icon next to the Preset Destination option and then giving the Preset a unique name.

Now that you have a new blank page onscreen, it's time to choose your tools for creating your future masterpiece. All of which deserves its own section, as follows.

The CorelDRAW Application Window

The application window is mainly what you see when CorelDRAW is open. The "Big Deal" in version X7 is that the application *interface* has been extensively updated and simplified so you can almost work at the speed of thought. Predictability and intuitiveness are the foundation of this version, and you'll immediately notice that version X7 has the Windows 8 look and feel. *Drawing windows* (sometimes called *document windows*) contain the drawing page or pages that hold the graphics and other content you create. Even when no drawing windows are open, the application window provides access to certain command menus, toolbars, the Toolbox, dockers, the Status bar, and the color palette.

It's ridiculous and unnecessary to provide a figure here that lists every single element in the application window. Corel Corporation has done a terrific job of doing this task in the Owner's Manual. This *Official Guide* provides you with the quickest way from point A to Point B, and, therefore, Figure 1-5 points out both new and key features you'll want to understand if you're just beginning to work with vector graphics. CorelDRAW obeys Microsoft Windows conventions, so if you know that a page icon means "new document," a floppy disk means "save," and so on … and that CTRL + P means print, and you have CTRL + S, CTRL + C, CTRL + V, and many of the other standard File and Edit menu commands down, you're way ahead of the game. The application window is mapped out and labeled in Figure 1-5, with explanations to follow.

- **Tabbed document interface**   One innovation experienced users will immediately notice is the tabbed drawing windows. You can have more than one drawing window (sometimes called a *document window* in other applications) open in the application window, but only one can be active at a time. The specific settings you see displayed on the toolbar, Property bar, dockers, and other application window interface elements are those that are assigned to the currently active drawing window. They change if you make another drawing window active, by clicking on the desired drawing window.

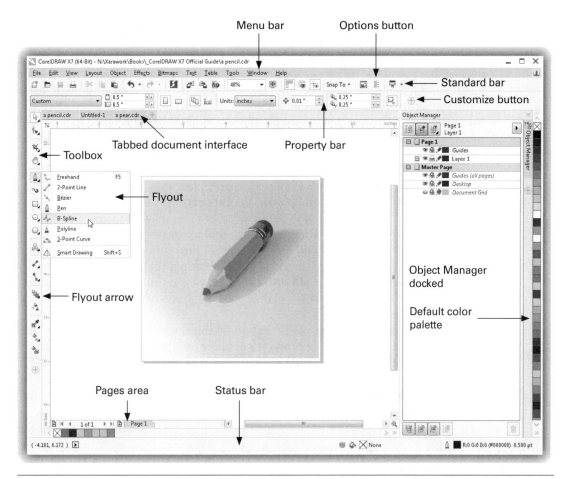

FIGURE 1-5   The CorelDRAW application window provides a highly organized, intuitive workspace.

> **Tip**   This new tabbed document arrangement isn't a hard-wired feature. If you're used to seeing documents side by side so you can drag a selection from one document to the other, drag the title bar of the document off the tab, and it will float in the drawing window. You can also choose Window | Tile Horizontally or Tile Vertically to see more than one document at a time.

- **Menu bar**   Although CorelDRAW has a standard menu bar, common to almost all Windows programs, what's in the menu is extraordinary, delightful, and important to creating complex artwork. Working left to right, it's a fair generalization that the leftmost menu items have to do with arranging shapes, viewing complexity onscreen, and other important workaday commands, but no flashy graphics effects. The center of the menu bar is where you'll find effects—effects you can apply to imported images (but not as easy or as refined as retouching in PHOTO-PAINT) and desktop publishing goodies under the Text menu. Toward the right, you'll find commands to change global settings, color controls, and commands that make the dockers appear. *Dockers* are panels that can float in the drawing window or be docked directly to the left of the vertical color palette. Dockers provide options for an effect or a tool that cannot be fully listed in a menu command. You might call them miniature dialog boxes for a function.

- **Standard bar** The bar that lies across the interface, below the menu bar, provides very basic controls, some of which are under the File and Edit menus. You can start a new document, go to Options (where just about everything in CorelDRAW can be modified), import and export content, and undo the last move you didn't want to make.

- **Property bar** Unlike the Standard bar, the Property bar is *context-sensitive;* what's offered on it changes based on the current tool you've selected. For example, let's say you've chosen the B-Spline tool for drawing some open paths. On the Property bar, you can add arrowheads, set the outline width, and set other functions specific to paths and closed objects. Choosing the Pick tool results in controls for Nudge distance, positions of selected objects, and your choice of units. If you're ever at a loss for what a tool does, or how to modify it, your first stop should be the Property bar.

- **Toolbox** The column docked to the left of the interface when you first open this new version is called the Toolbox, and it's actually another toolbar in the sense that you can undock it and let it float above the workspace, and you can use the new Customize feature to add or remove items from it to suit your work needs. In general, the editing tools are toward the top of the Toolbox, shape creation toward the center, and special effects and outline/fill properties are toward the bottom.

Note If you're not a designer and want to use CorelDRAW for graphs and charts—for technical purposes—you'll find connector drawing tools, almost magical shape creation and table tools, toward the center of the Toolbox within groups that contain similar tools for drawing.

- **Flyout** What an umpire calls at a ball game, and I've wanted to use that joke for three versions of this book now. Seriously, the Toolbox is just too small to offer all the features that it does, so tools with similar or related functions are grouped with a single tool icon on top of the rest of the group. When you want a tool in the group that is not the top tool, you click + hold on the flyout arrow (see next) to expand the group, release the mouse button, and then click the desired tool.

- **Flyout arrow** This is the precise point on a tool group icon—the triangular tick mark at the bottom right of the icon; you must click + hold to get the flyout with the rest of the group tools to appear.

- **Object Manager docked** Figure 1-5 shows one of the panels in CorelDRAW called a *docker.* Here, the docker is opened, yet docked to the right of the interface. Dockers are covered in this book as a specific feature (such as the Lens Effect docker) is discussed, but generally, the docker itself, not the features within it, is brought to the workspace in a 1-2 move: First, you choose Window | Dockers and then click the docker you want to access. Some dockers have shortcut keys (such as Object Properties, which is ALT + ENTER), whereas others need to be called the long way, although you can set a shortcut key of your own via Tools | Options | Workspace | Customization | Commands. The docker appears at the right edge of the interface. Second, you open the docker and perhaps even move it about. To undock and float a docker, you click + drag the docker's title bar from the right window edge into the drawing window. You can also dock a docker in various other places in the interface. If you drag it around the edges of the drawing window, eventually a dark preview rectangle appears; you halt movement at that point and release the mouse button. Dockers have a common close button to the right of their title bar, and to retract and expand a docker, you click the title bar while it is docked in its original position in the interface.

The reason why the Object Manager docker is shown here, and not, for example, the Fillet/Scallop/Chamfer docker, is because CorelDRAW offers drawing layers, and it is from this docker that you can arrange, hide, lock, and create new layers, a *very* important feature in CorelDRAW for complex drawings.

- **Default color palette**   There are many ways to fill an object with a solid color in CorelDRAW, but the fastest is to use the convention that many graphics programs offer; you'll see a set of swatches, vertically, at the far right of the interface. To apply a color to an unselected shape, you left-click + drag a swatch (called a *color swatch*) on top of the object on the page and then release the mouse button. To fill a selected object, you left-click a swatch. The color palette is determined when you create a new document (by choosing the color mode), and colors are covered in Chapter 15 in this *Guide*. Clicking the down arrow at the bottom of the palette scrolls the colors up to reveal hidden ones and the arrow at top does the inverse. Clicking right-facing arrows at the bottom of the palette expands the palette to reveal all the colors on the palette.

Tip To change the path's outline color in an object, you right-click instead of left-click on a color swatch.

- **Customize button**   New to version X7, Quick Customize appears when you click this plus-sign button on the Property bar—and every chosen tool changes your Property bar items—and the Toolbox. First, you're greeted with a flyout box that has a checkmark next to every tool (and any function on the Property bar); you can select or unselect any tool, and consequently the tool is hidden, but not deleted, from the toolbar. Additionally, should you choose to click the Customize button on the flyout and then navigate in the Options box to Commands, you can choose a feature in CorelDRAW and then drag its icon to the Toolbox or the Property bar, as shown in Figure 1-6.

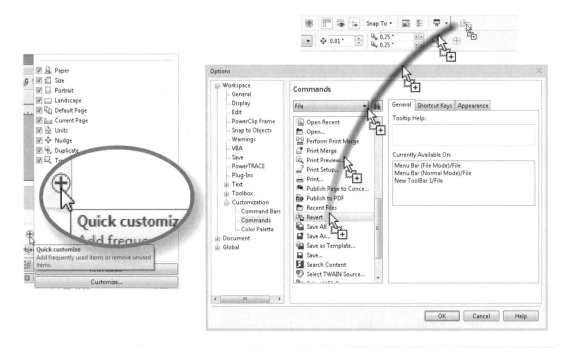

FIGURE 1-6 The Quick Customize feature makes the workspace and your toolset as individual as your own work preferences.

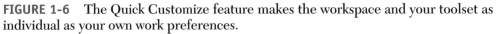

Tip With Quick Customize and other personalization features that you can perform on the program, you might make an unwanted modification, or 2, or 15, to CorelDRAW and now you don't like the way it works (or doesn't work!). Now, *think about this advice carefully*: Exit the program, and then while you launch CorelDRAW again, hold F8 to reset the program to its factory defaults. Factory defaults might *overwrite* any *wanted* modifications you've made, so this is a *last-ditch* effort to get up and running with CorelDRAW again.

- **Options button** The Options button on the Standard bar eliminates the need to sift through the menu or remember the shortcut (CTRL+J). Options is the key to the castle in CorelDRAW; it's where you can adjust virtually everything in the program, so having this button in plain sight is a boon to users.
- **Pages area** In this area, you can add pages to your current document, delete pages, and reorder pages in your multipage document. These commands and more can be executed as menu commands from the Layout menu. If you want an *overview* of your book, manual, pamphlet, or other multipage document, you don't do this in the Pages area but instead from View | Page Sorter View, where you can drag and drop pages to reorder them.

Tip You will run into a number of predictable UI elements in CorelDRAW, such as number boxes, radio buttons, and others that are featured in many Windows programs. However, spinner buttons might be new to you. *Spinner buttons* can do one of several things. *Command* buttons perform commands instantaneously, but *toggle* buttons control (and indicate) a specific feature's On and Off states, using a *pressed* or *not pressed* appearance. Generally, a *pressed* state indicates On, whereas the *not pressed* state indicates Off. *Shortcut* buttons open dialogs to further options, whereas *selector* buttons open lists of preset selections. *Spinners* (also known as *spin boxes*) are similar to combo boxes; they're used to specify values by typing or using mouse actions. Single clicks on the up and down arrow buttons increase *or* decrease the values incrementally, but you can *also* click-drag on the divider between the two arrow buttons, up to increase or down to decrease the value. See the following illustration.

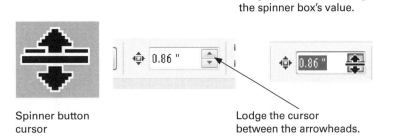

Drag up or down to change the spinner box's value.

Spinner button cursor

Lodge the cursor between the arrowheads.

Note Left-handed artists are not uncommon; if you're a southpaw, the order of your mouse buttons is not defined in CorelDRAW, but instead in the operating system's Control Panel | Mouse. Just mirror the instructions in this chapter: if a step tells you to left-click, it's the right mouse button, and vice versa.

Corel CONNECT in the Workspace

Earlier, the importance of registering with CorelDRAW to get a free Standard account was mentioned, and here's the reason why. Corel CONNECT has been with the Graphics Suite for several versions, but it's mature now and fully integrated with the software. When you have an active Internet connection, all you need do is click on the button on the Standard bar, as shown in this illustration, and Corel CONNECT commences.

Using Your Universal Connection

Integrating media from a remote server across the Internet with content you've created and stored on your hard drive is quite easy now. After you've launched Corel CONNECT, the Connect docker features appear: the Connect box and the Tray, an additional docker you can reveal by clicking its icon at the top right in the Connect docker. You might want to drag the Tray docker (by its title bar) away from its docked position and reposition it horizontally at the bottom of the interface; see the following illustration. By doing this, you can browse the Corel CONNECT media, drag anything you like to the Tray to make it a local copy (and not on the Internet), and still have room to see the page and work on your composition.

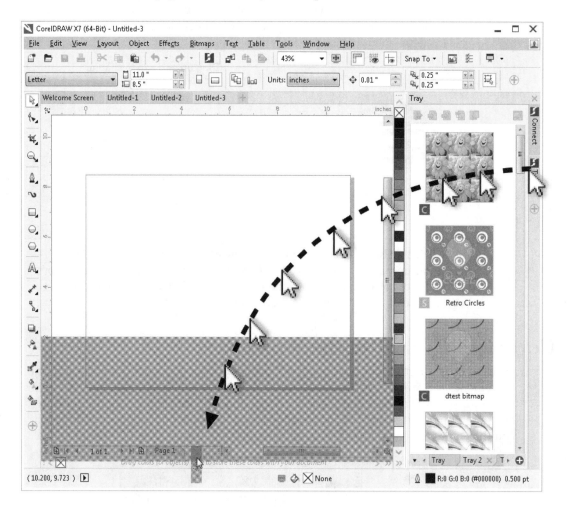

Here's a brief run-through (let's call it a Tutorial) of how you download and install a Corel typeface using CONNECT and the Tray docker.

Tutorial   CONNECTing to Media Using Corel CONNECT

1. With CorelDRAW open, first click the sign-in icon at the far right of the menu bar. Sign in to access content on Corel CONNECT.
2. Click the Corel CONNECT icon on the Standard bar, and then wait a moment until the connection is established.
3. Let's say you want to browse the collections for a new typeface. In the Libraries area, click the arrow to the left of the Content Exchange icon to expand the folder.
4. Click the Fonts title, and then double-click OpenType-Latin to dig down one level.
5. From here, you can browse any of the alphabet title folders. Let's say you're in dire need of the Balloon Xtra Bold font; you double-click the folder marked "B," and it expands in the window to show all the typefaces that begin with *B*. See the following illustration.

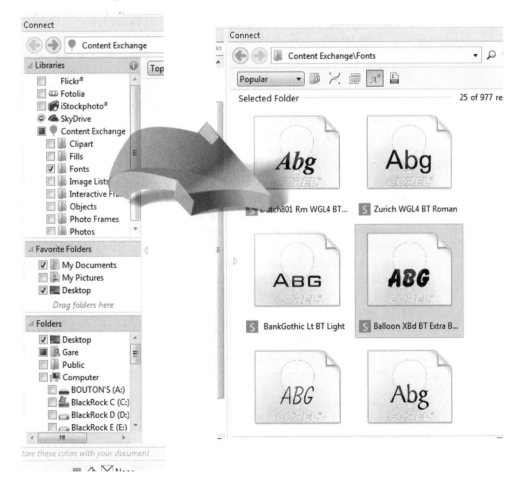

6. Right-click over the Balloon XBd BT Extra Bold icon and then choose Install from the pop-up menu.

7. Let's experiment with the Tray docker now. If the Connect docker is too narrow to show all the icons, the Show/Hide Tray button at the far right will be hidden. An easier way to get the Tray to display is by choosing Window | Dockers | Tray.

8. Let's move the Tray docker so it's more of a tray and not a shelf in the interface! Click-drag the Tray docker by its title and drag it toward the bottom of the interface. When you see a medium gray rectangle toward the bottom of the interface, this is your cue to release the mouse button, and the Tray affixes itself to below the drawing window.

9. The Tray is where you can keep media—fonts, bitmap fills, just about any media—and you can add additional Trays to categorize your downloads. The actual media is still in its original location; Corel content is still on the Web—it's only referenced on the Tray—but the user files that you might add to a Tray are in their local location on your hard disk.

The content that you subscribe to is always on Corel's website (it's "in the cloud"; don't worry about its physical location). When you add media to a Tray, what you see is a reference to the file that's still on Corel's server, and only when you drag the media into the drawing page (or install it, as is the case with typefaces) does a transaction occur. Then the media is on your hard drive(s) for keeps. Your own files that you might add to a Tray are not on Corel's servers (in the cloud); user files remain on your hard drive(s)—and that's why this "cloud computing" can be very convenient if you don't think about where your files "really" are.

Tip It's easy to identify Corel content that is Standard from those items that are only available to owners of Premium subscriptions. Standard content thumbnails are marked with a small *S* within an orange block, and Premium media is marked with a *P* within a blue block. If you don't have a Premium membership, you can see the thumbnails, but cannot access Premium files. The letter *C* within a green block means this is part of the Corel Community Exchange, a fellow member created and uploaded it, and usually these are free to download. In exchange, you might want to give the content a rating, similar to liking something on Facebook.

Figure 1-7 demonstrates a practical use of the Tray docker; several textures have been chosen and placed in the Tray to keep these "Favorites" separate from the other massive content in Corel's Content Exchange. In this figure, one of the Standard content fills is being referenced to the Tray, where it will then be handy for filling the illustration in the drawing window.

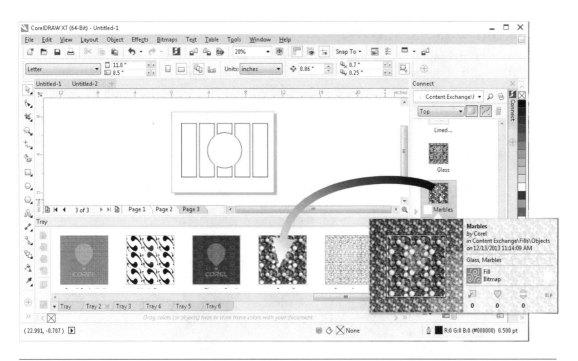

FIGURE 1-7   Collect Premium membership, Content Exchange, and Standard fills, fonts, and content on your own hard drive, and create different Trays to keep the content organized.

Depending on the type of media, a right-click might offer options to Install, Apply, or another command. In the illustration here, the object in the drawing window is selected, and all the artist needs to do is right-click on the thumbnail in the Tray and then choose Apply to fill the design.

For experienced users, you'll find the new workflow will allow you to arrive much faster at a graphical idea, and new users will feel right at home with the intuitive UI properties.

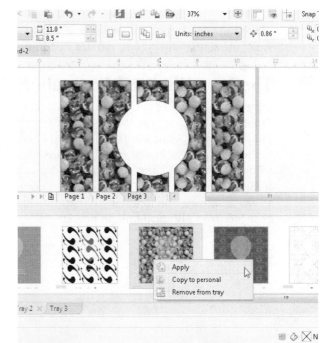

So What Else Is New?

Corel Corporation coded many enhancements to previous versions of CorelDRAW in the spirit of "logical evolution." As one example, the Shape tool has been used for many versions in combination with the Reduce Nodes slider on the Property bar to eliminate excess nodes along a path, especially when the path has been created using Power Trace on a poor-quality bitmap. The evolution in version X7 is you now have a local tool *in addition to* Power Trace; it's called the Smooth tool and you drag over a selected path *only* where you want excess nodes removed, as shown here in the illustration.

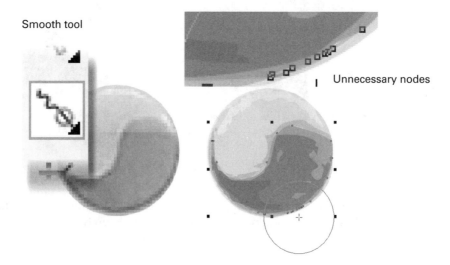

Smooth tool

Unnecessary nodes

The following sections will familiarize new and experienced users with some of the new and important design features in X7. You should read the What's New? Welcome screen document, too, for last-minute changes in the program.

The New Elliptical Fountain Fill

Gone is the Radial Fountain Fill type. In fact, the drop-down list is gone on the Property bar to give way to a faster set of buttons to change Fountain Fill types. Moreover, there is an additional control handle on Fountain Fill objects; in addition to the Start and End color handles, there is a circular handle that can set the angle of a linear fountain fill and also the roundness of an Elliptical Fountain Fill type. The color handles can still be used for positioning and rotating the fountain fill (also called a *color gradient*). The following illustration shows you how a radial fountain fill is changed to an elliptical one, in one step.

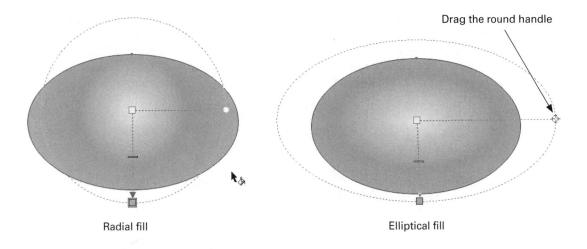

Drag the round handle

Radial fill   Elliptical fill

Color Node Pop-Ups

Because both transparency and fountain fills in version X7 can have multiple control points (called *nodes*), mousing all the way over to the color palette and the Property bar every two seconds can get to be a real chore, especially if you use a large monitor. Corel has addressed this by creating a pop-up color-picking panel that offers transparency and full color controls when your cursor is on the color or transparency node of an object.

As you can see in the following illustration, the pop-up appears as a slender bar with a color flyout at left and a transparency slider at right. When you click the Node Color picker button (at left in the illustration), you're presented with every imaginable way to choose a color; the various color models and even an eyedropper tool are at your disposal for changing the current color node's value.

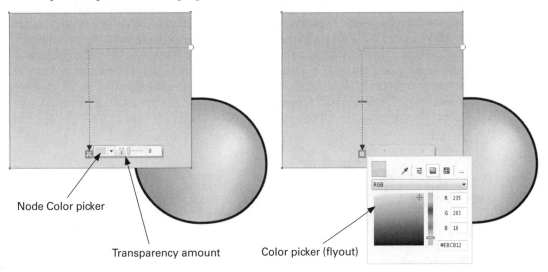

Node Color picker

Transparency amount   Color picker (flyout)

When the pop-up is active, it makes no difference whether you are working on node color editing or transparency editing; you can edit either property. In this illustration, you can see that after the colors in the fill in the previous illustration were adjusted, the transparency value of the bottom color node was edited, making an object (which has CorelDRAW's Mesh fill) placed behind it partially visible.

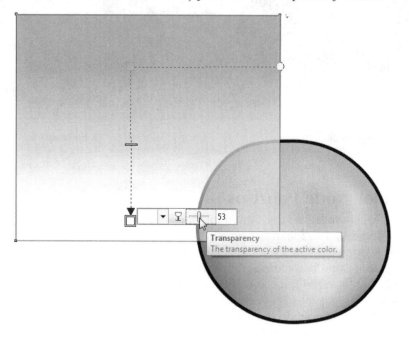

The Smart Fill Tool

The Smart Fill tool behaves a little like the Intersection Shaping command and a little like an auto-fill utility. When you have two or more overlapping shapes, you can click on their intersecting area with the Smart Fill tool, and a new shape is created and filled. You can determine the solid fill color on the Property bar and an outline color. You will achieve more interesting and artistic effects if you click the tool around objects that overlap and have no fill, but filled shapes that overlap will result in some new objects, too. The illustration here demonstrates what the tool creates. You do not need to have an object selected to apply this tool.

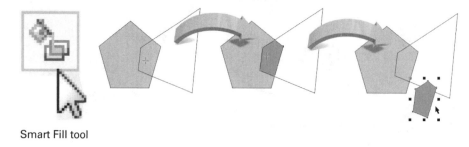

Smart Fill tool

Quick Response Codes in CorelDRAW

The Barcode Wizard is now the Edit | Insert Barcode command and it's even easier than before to put a barcode on the page, as long as you know the numerical value for an item. And right below this command is the new Insert QR Code command.

One of the neat things about Corel's implementation of the QR Code feature is that you can design the QR code, the look of it, while you code the data into it. You can add a simple drawing and personalize the QR code object so people without scanning software can still appreciate your advertising to a certain extent.

PDFs to Go

As commercial printing has embraced the Portable Document Format (PDF) for printing jobs, Corel has made it easy and fast to export your work to PDF by placing a Publish To PDF button on the Standard bar. You have access to all the properties of your document from within the Publish dialog—when you click the Settings button in the Publish To PDF dialog—and you can still export to PDF the traditional way, but this is a convenient, handy improvement to the interface.

You could call this chapter "foreshadowing," but this literary device is usually reserved for novels you buy at the airport, and not technical tomes. Kidding aside, there are a lot of pages under your right thumb, and it's all good stuff. Your next stop is to look under the hood and kick the tires of this brand new model, as your guided tour of X7 becomes more hands-on and pretty productive considering it's only the second chapter!

2 The Roadmap to Features and Productivity in CorelDRAW

To say that CorelDRAW is a drawing program is like saying Mount Everest is rather tall—it's a phenomenal understatement. In addition to the drawing tools, you also have filters and panels (*dockers*) that offer everything from color samples to the revamped Align and Distribute Object feature. You'll find effects for bitmap imports, typography tools for desktop publishing—in fact, there's so much to explore, it could fill a book. Specifically, *this* book.

To make the most of your valuable time, there are many ways to perform just about everything in X7, and there *are* hard ways and easy ways. Guess which way you'll learn in this chapter? There aren't secrets or mysteries to unravel with CorelDRAW. There's just stuff you might not know how to find or to use. Let's get down to some serious exploration of fun features in this new version right now.

The CorelDRAW Workspace

Once CorelDRAW has loaded and you've specified a default document, the sheer wealth of options and tools can make a beginner (and many experts!) feel more than a little intimidated and lost. You have more help than you might imagine, though, beginning a drawing. Suppose you want to change the page size or hide all the guides you dragged from the rulers? Or suppose you need a more detailed explanation of the B-Spline tool you're about to use? You can refine, redefine, and customize your document and your view of the document with a few well-placed clicks, and you always have a tutor right within the workspace, covered in the sections to follow.

The Page Shadow: It's a Command Control

Although the *page shadow*—the medium gray trim around the right and bottom of the drawing page in the drawing window—might seem like an artistic interface embellishment, it's actually a shortcut to all the options one could ask for specific to the page. What is the orientation you want for the page? What rendering resolution do you need (for printing and when you import bitmaps)? Although some page layout options are available on the Property bar, by using the Pick tool, you can double-click the page shadow to open the Options dialog. From there, you can access the Page Size tab, which is a comprehensive resource, shown in Figure 2-1.

Now that you know how to get to the Page Size options at lightning speed, let's breeze through a short tutorial that demonstrates how useful they can be.

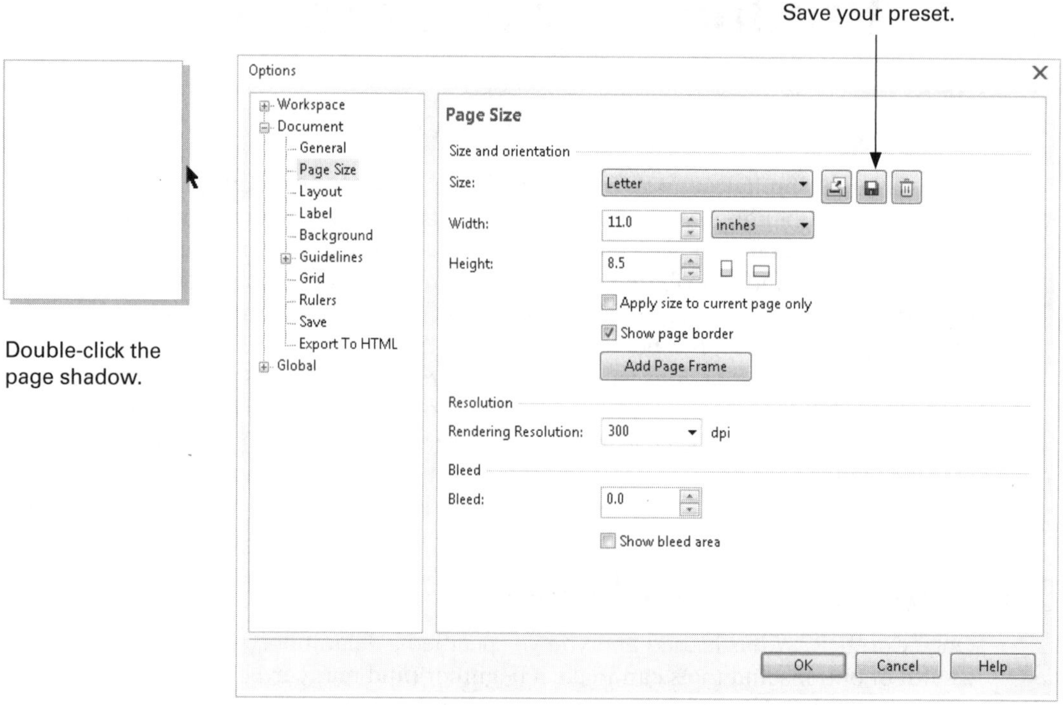

Save your preset.

Double-click the page shadow.

FIGURE 2-1   The quickest way to access all options for the drawing page is to double-click the page shadow with the Pick tool.

Tutorial Defining and Saving a Custom Page Size

1. In a new document, using the Pick tool, double-click the page shadow. The Page Size Options dialog appears.
2. Bear with us Americans for a moment; the default page size you saw in Figure 2-1 is measured in inches and has a default page size of 8½" by 11". Let's make a square page; type **8.5** in the Width field that says "11".
3. Let's also pretend that this is a multipage document, and you only want the first page to be square. Put a checkmark in the Apply Size To Current Page Only checkbox. (Because you've moved from one field to the next, the 8.5 value you typed in the Width field in step 2 has now been accepted. Occasionally, you'll find a Windows program that requires you to press ENTER to confirm a text or numerical entry. Not X7.)
4. Say you want to design something that is *exactly* 8½" by 8½". Well, a page frame would expedite this need, so click the Add Page Frame button. You now have an exactly 8½" square object on Layer 1, Page 1, with no fill and a black outline that exactly matches the page edges.
5. Let's say you're growing weary of this supervised experimentation, and you want to conclude this mini-tutorial. Save this custom page layout by clicking the floppy disk button shown in Figure 2-1. In the Custom Page Type dialog, type an evocative name in the text field, such as **square 8.5**. Click OK to exit the dialog, click OK to return to the page, and you're done.

Try out your new page preset now. Create a new document, and then with the Pick tool, go to the Property bar and click the Page Size drop-down list. As you can see in the following illustration, the preset created in the previous tutorial is right there, and if you choose it, a square page appears in the drawing window and the document has the other page attributes you declared in the tutorial.

Page Options on the Property Bar

Don't be fooled by the terms *Page Type* or *Page Size* when it comes to options specific to your current document in CorelDRAW. You have control over more cool and useful things than you'd imagine if you just switch to the Pick tool for a moment to display the properties on the Property bar, which is *contextual*, just as the right-click pop-up menu (also called *the context menu*) is.

Figure 2-2 shows the right-most controls on the Property bar when the Pick tool is the active tool; the bar has been split so you can see a larger detail of it in this book.

The following section explains the purpose of and, at times, an inspired use of the features; they can save you time and frustration if you know why Corel put them there.

- **Dimension num(ber) boxes** These are numerical entry fields for the units you've selected for the current page size. Although an abbreviation for the units follows the numerical entry, you don't have to type, for example, the double-prime character (") denoting inches to enter a value—CorelDRAW adds it in there after you put the cursor in a different field because the software understands you've specified inches when you created a new document. Therefore, you can change the page size at any time in a document, merely by typing in a new value. Only when you're done resetting the values should you press ENTER to confirm the current entries.

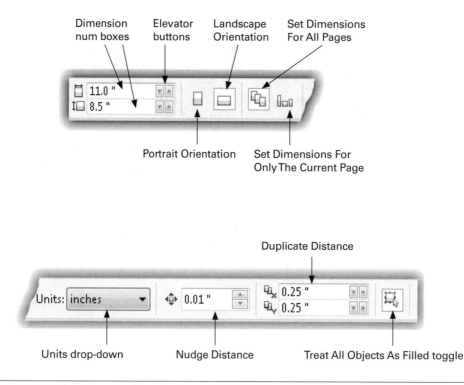

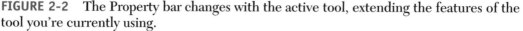

FIGURE 2-2 The Property bar changes with the active tool, extending the features of the tool you're currently using.

Tip Even though there is a Units button on the Property bar for changing, for example, centimeters to inches, if you type an abbreviation for a value into a num box after typing the number value—and then press ENTER or move your cursor to a different field—CorelDRAW will enter the value with the new unit and then return the num box display back to the original units. Here's a specific example: suppose your document is set up for inches and a coworker pokes his head into your cube and tells you the boss wants the width of the document to be 3 feet, as improbable as that seems. In the Width num box, you type **3 ft**, press ENTER, and the document is 3 feet wide now. Then Width num box returns to inches for units and reads 36.0".

- **Elevator buttons**   Most of the time in CorelDRAW, where there's a num box, there are *elevator buttons* directly to the right of the fields. You click the up arrow button to increase the current value and click the down arrow button to decrease the current value in the corresponding box. For the Dimension boxes, the value (in inches) for increasing or decreasing the amount is 0.05".

Note If you put your cursor directly between the up and down elevator buttons on any of these *combo boxes* (a box that accepts both manual number entry and clicking/ dragging on elevator buttons), you'll see that the cursor has changed to a two-way arrow with a divider in between the arrows. Drag up or down to *significantly* change the value of a nudge, or a page dimension, or any value box that features elevators buttons.

- **Portrait and Landscape Orientations**   With a simple click of either of these buttons, you rotate your page by 90 degrees. A wide page becomes a tall one, and vice versa. *Portrait* is tall and *landscape* is wide.
- **Set Dimensions For All Pages**   You should only click this button *after* you've set a new page size. Then, all the pages in your multipage document are identical in orientation and size.
- **Set Dimensions For Only The Current Page**   If you've made a different-sized page, perhaps for printing scrapbook content, and want only this page uniquely sized, click this button while viewing the page. All other pages will remain the same size.
- **Units drop-down**   Clicking this button reveals a drop-down list of units, from which you change all features that display and use units. For example, if your current unit of measurement in X7 is inches, and for some whimsical reason you choose Feet from the Units drop-down, a standard US letter page size will be displayed as .917' tall instead of 11". Similarly, if you had a Nudge Distance set on the Property bar of 1 inch, the distance displayed will be the same absolute value, but it will now read 0.083' now.
- **Treat All Objects As Filled toggle**   A *toggle* is just a fancy computer term for an "on/off switch," but this feature itself is a genuine boon to artists, especially if you're used to Illustrator and being able to select objects just by touching their edge. When switched (*toggled*) on—the icon has a slim outline around it (see the

following illustration—you can use the Pick tool to click-drag to move an unfilled object by dragging on its edge or anywhere in its unfilled interior.

Default state: Feature is toggled on. You can click-drag anywhere on the shape from its outline to its interior, whether it's filled or not. Outline around icon tells you the state is active.

Inactive state: Feature is toggled off by clicking it. You can't click-drag from the interior of an unfilled object.

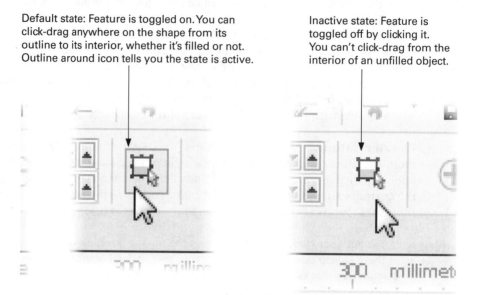

This option is terrific when you want to keep an object unfilled but the outline width is so thin the object is hard to select. Figure 2-3 shows a side-by-side comparison of dragging the left, unfilled object. In CorelDRAW, you see both the current position and the original position of an object you drag. Micro-hint: the object you're moving is in "preview" mode and you'll see a thin blue outline in the workspace instead of the original colored-outline.

- **Nudge Distance**   The keyboard arrow keys can be used to move a selected object by a predefined distance, called the *Nudge Distance,* although you can also shove, push, and propel a selected shape, depending on the distance you specify in this box. Alternatively, you can use the elevator buttons to nudge an object up, down, and across in increasing increments of 0.05" per arrow key click. This feature is useful for moving an object out of the way, and then returning it to its original position when you've finished editing some other object.

 Note   You can push two arrow keys simultaneously to nudge an object diagonally. What's really happening is CorelDRAW is understanding two sequential commands, but for you, the effect is a diagonal move and it can save time.

- **Duplicate Distance**   When you need to copy an object or group of objects, pressing CTRL+C and then CTRL+V gets you there; the copy rests precisely on top of the original you selected. However, you can simply press CTRL+D to duplicate your selected object(s), and use these fields to offset where the copy appears. Positive values you type in these fields place the duplicate up and to the right of the original.

Treat All Objects As Filled, turned off   Treat All Objects As Filled, turned on

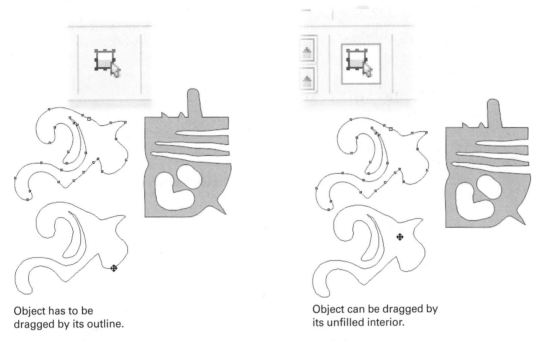

Object has to be   Object can be dragged by
dragged by its outline.   its unfilled interior.

FIGURE 2-3   Moving unfilled objects is simple in CorelDRAW: you toggle the Treat All
Objects As Filled button on the Property bar.

> **Tip** Using CTRL while pressing a Nudge Distance arrow key is called a *micro-nudge*, a
> fraction of the Nudge Distance determined by what you specify in Tools | Options |
> Workspace | Document | Rulers tab. If you hold SHIFT, this is called *super-nudging*,
> and it's a multiple of the Nudge Distance, again, set on the Rulers tab of Options.
> Options is easily accessed by clicking the Options icon on the Standard bar
> (covered later in this chapter).

Can You Give Me a Hint?

The Toolbox has an unbelievable number of tools, and many of the tools are only
the top face of a tool group flyout—the pen tools, the edit tools, and the effects tools
all contain several different neighboring tools on their respective flyouts. Suppose
you want to draw a freeform shape and are unsure which tool is the best to use?
Click + hold on the Curve tool group (tools that produce curves, mostly pen tools) to
reveal the flyout and then choose a tool.

But which tool will be best for your goal? Let's say you want to create a shape
consisting of both arcs and straight lines. Several drawing tools are suitable for your
task. Let's suppose that you choose the Bezier Pen tool, a good overall choice for

drawing. Now, there are only two drawing techniques you use with the Bezier Pen tool, but you're not sure what they are.

Select Help | Hints, and as soon as you click a tool on the Toolbox to choose it, the Hints docker is at the ready with a succinct explanation of the workings of the tool, as shown in Figure 2-4.

CTRL, ALT, and SHIFT Are Your Friends

The modifier keys CTRL, ALT, and SHIFT are used by many programs to extend a command; even the simple Windows Copy command uses a modifier key, CTRL, for CTRL + C. In CorelDRAW, you should learn to reach reflexively for a modifier key when using a tool to change its function.

Although no two tools are the same in X7, these modifier keys serve some common functions:

- **CTRL**   An abbreviation for *Control,* you should think of this term as similar to *Constrain.* For example, when using the Rectangle tool, if you hold CTRL while you drag, it constrains the dimensions of the object to a perfect square. Similarly, if you put an object into Rotate/Skew mode (you click with the Pick tool on an object that's already selected), and you hold CTRL while you drag on a rotation handle, the rotation is constrained to the number of degrees you've specified in Options | Workspace | Edit. You can also constrain node control handles while you're drawing by holding CTRL. This is useful for creating objects whose node angles are all identical.

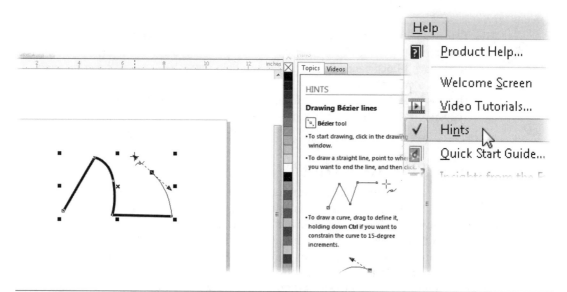

FIGURE 2-4   When you want to learn the basics of a tool or feature quickly, use the Hints docker.

- **ALT** You might think of this key as offering ALT(ernatives) to the basic command you're executing or tool you're using. For example, when dragging with the Bezier tool, you usually wind up with curved path segments, but if you hold ALT while click + dragging, a straight line segment is the result. ALT is not as common a modifier key as CTRL or SHIFT, but the point is that when you believe a tool or command has more than one way to work, try out these three keys before stopping your work to find help.
- **SHIFT** SHIFT might be thought of as "add to." When using the Pick tool, SHIFT-clicking on objects adds to your current selection of objects. When drawing shapes with object tools such as the Polygon, Ellipse, and Rectangle tools (and others), holding SHIFT before you click-drag draws the object from its center outward instead of from the corner.

And remember that modifiers can also be used in combination. So if you hold CTRL + SHIFT while you click-drag a rectangle, the rectangle is drawn from its center outward and it is also constrained to a square at the same time.

Choosing Tones from the Color Swatches

On the color palette, you have many choices of colors with the default palette, but you will have still more variations of these colors by using a simple technique. Although digital color is an additive process, when contrasted against the subtractive color process of painting with traditional pigments, we still use the term *tone* to mean the lightness or brilliance characteristic of a color. The way tones were traditionally mixed was to add white (producing a *tint*) or to add black (producing a *shade*). In X7, you have a much faster and more accurate way to refine your chosen color swatch before you apply the color to a shape. In the following illustration, you can see that a selected object and the Pick tool is over a color swatch; the trick is to click and then hold on the color swatch, and a tones mini-palette appears. While holding, move your cursor over to the mini color swatch you want, and then release the mouse button to apply the color to the selected object.

Click+hold a color swatch to get the tone flyout.

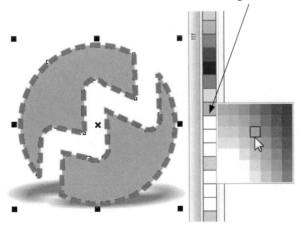

Surprises When You Right-Click and Use the Wheel

If you're using the traditional mouse for drawing in CorelDRAW, there's more power to tap into when you understand what right-clicking and setting up the mouse wheel does. Let's take these hardware features one at a time. Digitizing tablet users can use the same power by using pressure and the buttons on their stylus.

Tap into the Power of the Right-Click Menu

It's called various names by different companies, but for ages Windows has supported a pop-up menu, alternatively called a *context* or *contextual menu*. What it does is a lot more important than what it's called! *Contextual* means that the menu commands on this pop-up menu change, depending on which tool is currently chosen. As an exercise, choose the Pick tool and then right-click over an empty area of the drawing page. The menu gives you commands for undoing the last edit, creating a new object, and other commands specific to helping you out when you're using the Pick tool. If you right-click over an empty page area (not an object or an effect), you'll see only commands useful when you use the Pick tool.

Here's something particularly important when used in combination with the Shape tool: you can turn selected nodes and path segments from straight and sharp to smooth and curved, respectively. Figure 2-5 shows the context menu when

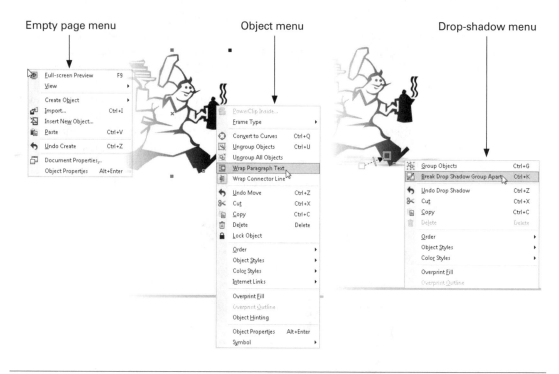

FIGURE 2-5 The right-click menu serves you up commands pertinent only to the area or object over which you click.

right-clicked over an empty page area, over an object, and over an effect, in this case, a drop-shadow.

If you can't remember, find, or think of the command you need while drawing, right-click, even with a drawing tool active. Chances are the command you need is right there on the menu.

Dropping a Copy of a Selected Object

When using the Pick tool, left–mouse button dragging moves a selected object, but right–mouse button dragging can do something entirely different, especially when you use the right–mouse button drag in combination with the other button, other keys, and the SPACEBAR. Here are the three methods for making a copy—and several copies—without using the Copy and Paste, Duplicate, or Step And Repeat commands:

- *Right-click + drag, release, use the pop-up menu.* If you're just getting the hang of using a point-and-click device, this is the most sure-fire way to copy an object quickly. See the following illustration.

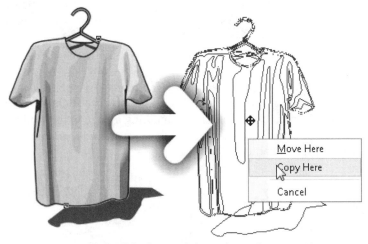

Right click+drag and then release the
mouse button to reveal a pop-up menu.

- *Left click + drag, then click both buttons, then release.* This is the traditional CorelDRAW "drop a copy" technique, and if you get used to this series of maneuvers, it's perhaps the fastest way to position the copy precisely while creating it. See the next illustration.

Left click+drag, then tap both mouse buttons, then release.

- *Hit the* SPACEBAR *key repeatedly while left + dragging a shape to make several copies.* This method for duplicating the selected object (or objects, or groups of objects) is not only a quick method for populating a page with duplicates, but it's also silly fun. Try it with a simple shape such as a rectangle, and before you know it, you have a page of confetti—or shirts:

Left-button drag: every time you press the SPACEBAR, a duplicate is placed.

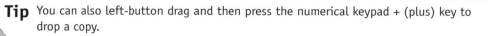

Tip You can also left-button drag and then press the numerical keypad + (plus) key to drop a copy.

Page Navigation: Panning and Zooming the Smart Way

There are dozens of shortcut keys in CorelDRAW, and you can also set your own (explained in Chapter 1). There are only a handful, however, that you'd really be wise to commit to memory, and they are listed later in this chapter. One of the CorelDRAW shortcuts that is good but not critical to remember is this one.

While you are using any tool (*except* the Text tool), pressing SPACEBAR toggles you to the Pick tool and another SPACEBAR press returns you to the last-used tool. Many users remember that H is the shortcut for the Pan tool, and after using the tool, a press of the SPACEBAR toggles the current tool to the Pick tool. You can elect to ignore memorizing the shortcut for the Hand tool (although it's easy to remember) if you merely remember that the wheel on your pointing device—usually a mouse—serves as both an immediate panning and zooming tool:

- If you press down on the mouse wheel while dragging, you temporarily toggle to the Pan tool and you can drag your view of the document window in any direction you see fit, as shown here.

Press the wheel while dragging to pan the document view in the window.

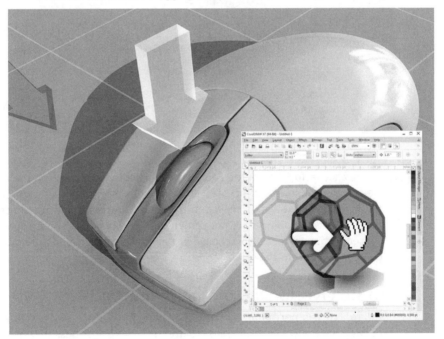

- If you roll the mouse wheel away from you, causing a clockwise rotation of the wheel, you zoom into the current document. If you roll the mouse wheel toward you, you zoom out. Additionally, when you zoom in, you can direct the zoom point by hovering your cursor over the desired area of the document—many programs that offer zoom don't do this. See the following illustration.

Pull it toward you to zoom out.

Roll the mouse wheel away from you to zoom in.

Use the cursor to point to the zoom-in area.

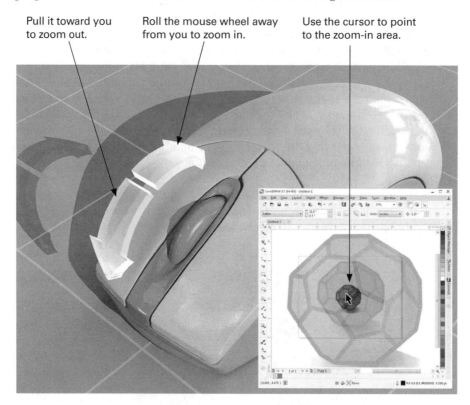

Tip If you choose To Fit from the Zoom Levels dialog, you're taken to the closest view in the window that includes all drawn objects. Now, if you zoom in or out, the objects will always be viewed in the center of the window. If you choose a zoom level when objects are not centered in view, and don't first choose To Fit, subsequent zoom levels you choose or type in the combo box will not display all objects centered in the view.

Not to Be Overlooked on the Standard Bar...

The Standard bar is a permanent screen element (unless you deliberately detach it and/or hide it); it always displays the same features regardless of which tool you choose. Corel Corp. has reworked and simplified the Standard bar in version X7 to bring you the most needed features at a click. Therefore, you'll have to dig through the menu commands less often, and seldom have to interrupt your work for "Adventure Time."

The section calls out and describes some of the features you'll want to familiarize yourself with, as shown in Figure 2-6:

- **Import**   If you're new to computer graphics, Import, at least as far as CorelDRAW is concerned, means *to bring a copy of something into the drawing window and the original has not been touched.* Adobe Illustrator, just for reference, calls this action *placing* a file. This is *not* the same action as opening a CorelDRAW file, although you can import a CDR file. The long way to this command is on the File menu: File | Import. Opening and copy the CDR file is the easier way. CorelDRAW comes with an exceptional collection of import filters, both for text and graphics files, so bringing in a text document you need to lay out and a JPEG photo for a brochure are as easy as pie carried out to three decimal places.
- **Export**   This is the opposite of importing something, but exporting is not the same as saving a file. CorelDRAW has extensive export filters—*including* exporting objects as typefaces (read the Bonus Chapter on making your own fonts). For example, if you need a PNG file made from your Corel drawing, you can do so in the Export dialog, where you can also choose a resolution (see Chapter 1) and whether you want transparency supported. When you export, you're *not* sending

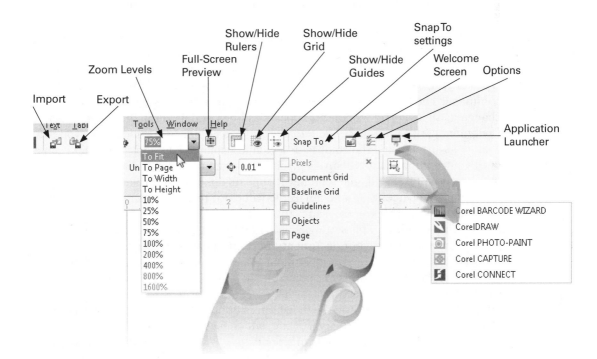

FIGURE 2-6   The Standard bar is always at the top of the UI to provide you with common and necessary command shortcuts.

your Corel artwork *original* anywhere; it's a copy, usually in a different file format, that is leaving the drawing window.

- **Zoom Levels** This combo box offers preset resolutions, and you can also type a custom value in the field (and then press ENTER). The maximum zoom level is 264,583 percent, and the minimum is 1 percent. You'd be hard-pressed to exceed those levels of magnification in your work, and at each extreme it's very difficult to navigate and see objects.
- **Full-Screen Preview** Clicking this button removes the entire UI and presents your drawing at whatever magnification you had before clicking the button. This feature is great for making a presentation and for taking uncluttered screen captures. Although in Full-Screen Preview you can see the printable page and its drop shadow, guidelines and the grid will not display. A click anywhere returns you to the UI and your work.
- **Show/Hide Rulers** This button toggles on and off to display and hide the rulers on the top and left of the drawing window border.

Tip You can move the rulers anywhere in the drawing window by SHIFT+dragging a ruler. The rulers still hide and show when you use the Show/Hide Rulers button, but you need to restore them to their default locations manually if you move them around the drawing window—there is no specific "restore" command for ruler position.

- **Show/Hide Grid** When in View | Pixels display mode, this button toggles the visibility of the different grid on and off, although a grid can continue to Snap To objects you move around, even if the grid is visibly hidden. CorelDRAW has three types of grid, and you choose which one to hide and display via the View | Grid command. The *Document grid* is the default grid in all documents, and you can change its spacing and whether it appears as lines or dots through the Options | Document |Grid command. The *Baseline grid* has no line/dot options, but you can change its spacing and the color with which it displays. The *Pixel grid* is not visible until you've imported a bitmap—a pixel-based graphic. You can set the color, the opacity of the Pixel grid, and whether it appears onscreen after you've zoomed in more than 800 percent, an unchangeable value, for reasons apparent when you're at 800 percent and all you can see is the grid!
- **Show/Hide Guides** This setting shows/hides any guidelines in a template or guides you've added to your document; this button has no effect, naturally, if there are no guidelines in your document. There is another way to hide Guides if you have the Object Manager open. You click the Show/Hide eye icon for the Guides entry on the Object Manager list.
- **Snap To settings** This drop-down list offers options to make each interface object become magnetic ("sticky") or not, which is useful when you want to enable the stickiness of the pixels in a photo you imported, or the guides, or the grid, or other objects. In general, you probably don't want *any* item enabled for Snap To if you're simply drawing things freehand and have no need for precision in creating nodes or moving an object.

- **Welcome Screen**   In case you need to watch a video right away, or you disabled the Show Welcome Screen At Startup option, this button is your handy access to the Welcome Screen; see Chapter 1 for details on this screen.
- **Options**   The Options dialog is the nerve center for customizing both the way your documents behave and look, but also how CorelDRAW behaves and looks. This is probably the most important dialog you'll need for overriding default settings, and therefore this button is a welcome alternative to hunting for the command in the main menu (it's under Tools, who would have known?)—or memorizing CTRL + J.
- **Application Launcher**   Although Corel CONNECT has its own button on the Standard bar (it's called *Search Content*), this drop-down list affords access right within CorelDRAW to all the other modules included in the X7 Graphics Suite.

Caution   You'll notice that CorelDRAW is listed in the Application Launcher list, although you're working in CorelDRAW so ostensibly you've already launched it. You can launch another session, or two, or five of the same program, but just because you *can*, doesn't mean you *want* to. Saved versions of open documents become impossible to manage, and your computer's memory resources might not appreciate your testing how many copies of CorelDRAW you can load before you get the Blue Screen of Death.

Shortcut Keys You'll Want to Memorize

Here's the short list of important key combos, modifiers, and other shortcuts in X7 that you'll want to memorize. If you do, before long, CorelDRAW will seem more transparent, and the only thing you'll need to concentrate on is the work itself. This list is organized by task first, followed by what you press and/or click.

Task	Shortcut
To move an object upward by one level in the stack of objects on a layer...	CTRL+PAGEUP
To move an object to the front of a layer...	SHIFT+PAGEUP
To move an object to the top of all layers (you're actually moving the object to a new layer)...	CTRL+HOME
To move an object downward by one level in the stack of objects on a layer...	CTRL+PAGEDOWN
To move an object to the back of a layer...	SHIFT+PAGEDOWN
To move an object to the bottom of all layers...	CTRL+END
To display the Object Manager, in case you can't memorize the options, or elect to move objects manually...	CTRL+SHIFT+M
To convert a text object or other object possessing advanced properties (such as a Polygon object) to a simplified set of paths and curves...	CTRL+Q

Task	Shortcut
To break apart a compound object, one made up of two or more different paths within one object such as a donut or the letter B...	CTRL+K
To join two or more objects together to create a compound single object...	CTRL+L
To toggle from your current tool to the Zoom tool...	F2
To zoom your view of the page out, without choosing a new current tool...	F3
To repeat the last-accessed command...	CTRL+R
To start a new document without bothering (much) with the Create A New Document dialog ...	CTRL+N and press ENTER

And the Shape tool is one of the most-used and most important editing tools in CorelDRAW; here are some guides and shortcuts to using the Shape tool:

- When you're working with the Shape tool, to add a node to a path, double-click the path, or press the + (plus) key on the numeric keypad.
- When you've selected the Shape tool and clicked a node, press the – (minus) numeric keypad key to delete the node. Alternatively, you can then right-click and choose Delete (with a special icon telling you the node and not the entire shape will be deleted). Remember that when you do delete a node in an object, the neighboring path segments will resize and change to represent the new geometry. This is good advice: if you're going to delete a node, first convert or make sure the surrounding path segments are straight lines so the overall object shape doesn't change significantly.

Finally, if you've drawn an outline that has no fill because the path is open or the object is unfilled, and you want to turn the outline path into an object, press CTRL + SHIFT + Q. This is an exceptionally cool feature for making elegant objects that couldn't be filled as a series of paths, as shown here:

Eight disconnected lines

Convert line to object, press CTRL+K to break apart and add different fills and effects.

The Terms Global vs. Local

This section is a brief one, intended to familiarize you with the terms *global* and *local* as they apply to Options in CorelDRAW. A *global* change, as expected, changes everything; specific to CorelDRAW, a global change refers to how much memory you want dedicated to CorelDRAW out of your computer's memory pool, your printer settings (how CorelDRAW addresses your printer), managing the filters CorelDRAW has to load and offer (text import and export, JPEG import and export, and so on), and other program "housekeeping-related" issues. Global settings have an impact on the way you work, but mostly don't alter or help what it is you're designing. Global settings aren't "creative" settings. Global resources are also persistent ones. For example, the library of colors you find on the color palette are global resources; they're available to you with each and every document.

Local resources are objects and settings specific to a document, and the local settings you make can disappear unless you *save* your document. Where you added guidelines to a document, a specific symbol you've created (is local but can be made global), the current nudge distance ... these are all *local* settings.

Additionally, the Options dialog is quite specific about where the local and global settings are changed. Document (which means local) and Global are both featured as main entries on the Options tree in the left panel.

> **Tip** You can open more than one document window showing the same document, so you can work on one document in multiple windows. Choose Window | New Window. Both windows are "live," so you can edit in either of them and all the changes you make editing in one window will also appear in both windows. To switch views, click the title bar of the document window.

A Brief Anatomy Lesson on Dockers

Dockers are panels—palettes—where many different commands and controls related to specific tasks are grouped together in one handy location. Dockers put more of Corel's power right at the tip of your cursor without forcing you to dig through lots of dialog boxes or flit between various toolbars and menus. In general, if you display a docker such as Window | Effects | Extrude, you might initially think it's just a duplication of what's on the Property bar when the (interactive) Extrude tool is your current tool. It's not, however, and here's the important difference: you can work on refining the extrude properties of an extruded shape indefinitely when the Extrude docker is open or minimized—it's simply *there*; you set it down on the counter, but you didn't put it away, in a manner of speaking. In contrast, when you use the Extrude tool to work with the Extrude features on the Property bar, you will lose those features if you need a different tool for a moment because the Property bar is context-sensitive—it offers commands specific to the current tool. In the following illustration, you will see all the features found that are needed to refine an extrude on a unique docker.

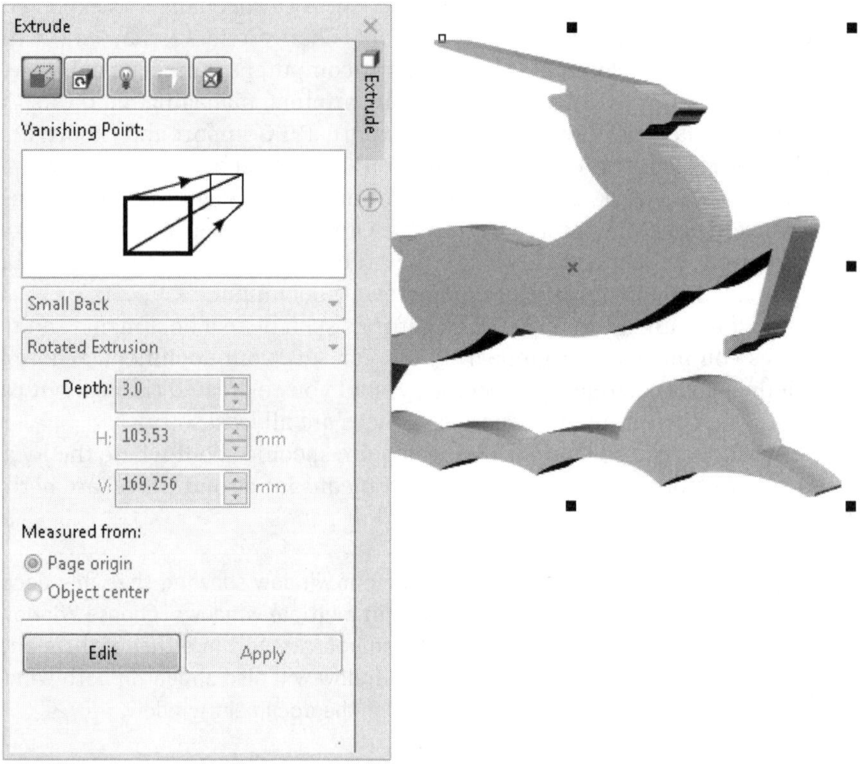

These controls can be anchored to the edge of the screen and reduced to tabs by clicking the active docker's tab (not its title bar). You can tear them off (*undock* them) and float them right next to where you are working in the interface. You can make your own groups of commonly used dockers. And, if you have a multimonitor setup, you can even drag them out of the application window and stick them on a different monitor so you have the maximum amount of space for your drawing window. It all begins on the Window | Dockers menu.

Opening, Moving, and Closing Dockers

Dockers can be opened using shortcut keys (if your memorized list isn't complete!), through menu commands, or through toolbars. For example, to open the Contour docker, choose Window | Dockers | Effects | Contour, or press CTRL + F9.

Dockers open to their last-used screen position and state, either docked or undocked. While *docked,* they are, by default, attached to the right side of your application window. Alternatively, dockers can be positioned on the left side of the screen or anchored on both sides of the screen with your document window in the middle.

While *undocked,* dockers float above the document window and can be positioned anywhere on your monitor screen(s). Docked or floating is *not* an all or nothing choice; you can have some dockers docked and some floating at the same time. The only situation you *can't* have is more than one copy of a specific docker open at one time.

Nested (Grouped) Dockers

When more than one docker is open, they often appear *nested,* meaning that multiple dockers overlay each other on the right side of your application window. While dockers are nested, clicking their individual title bars or name tabs brings them to the front of the interface.

A very quick way to build your own group of floating dockers—new to version X7—is to begin with one docker: display it by using the Window | Dockers command. Drag it by its tab into the drawing window to float it. Then click the Quick Customize button at bottom right of the floating docker. As you can see in the next illustration, the Quick Customize button offers an incredible wealth of additional, docking palettes.

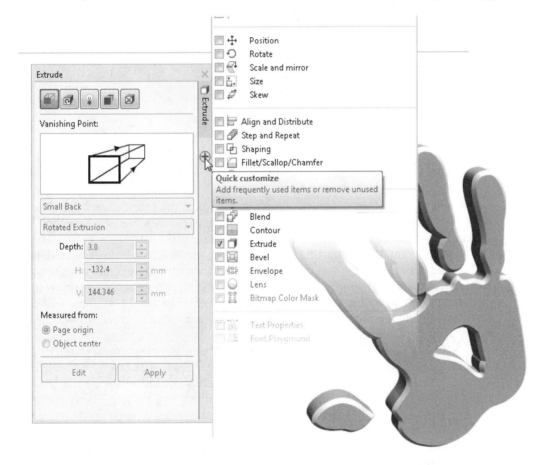

By default, the new docker you checked appears in the right-side, docked position. You then click + drag the docker by its tab (not its title bar) and then drop it into the right column where the first floating docker's tab is located. See the following illustration.

Drag the tab, not the title, to the grouped tabs area.

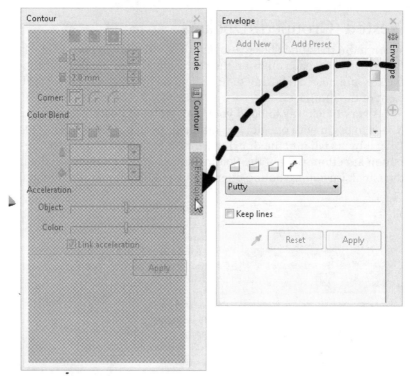

To separate a docker when it's nested, you perform the reverse operation. You drag the tab away from the group until you see a gray preview box of where the docker is going to land.

Finally, if you want to maximize your drawing window area but still keep docked and nested dockers handy, you click any tab, and the entire collection of dockers collapses to a neat row of titled tabs. To access any of the dockers once again, you click the tab of the docker you need and the group extends again with the selected docker open and the others tabbed in the right column, an improvement over docker behavior in previous versions of CorelDRAW.

It's Reality Check Time now: you bought this book as your guide to CorelDRAW X7, so it's a safe bet that you want to learn how to (a) draw, (b) draw with CorelDRAW, and (c) not have to read 14 chapters before getting to some of the "good stuff." Fair is fair, and Chapter 3 puts you into the thick of it. You're going to draw a fairly complex drawing in CorelDRAW, even if you've never owned a previous version or used a vector drawing program before. If this sounds unlikely, you'll be proven wrong shortly, because the author will sit invisibly on your shoulder, call out commands, and explain why the tools you're asked to use are the quickest and best ones to use.

C'mon—it'll be as thrilling as when you borrowed dad's car when you were 11!

3 Diving into CorelDRAW! Your First Professional Composition

Whether it's a tech book (*this* is a tech book), or an engaging work of fiction like a detective novel, a good author will bait you for the first few chapters and then BANG! You're off and running on a high-speed adventure by Chapter 3. In short, in a tech book, this departure from a standard teaching method is called "Learning by *doing*."

Even if you're an intermediate-level user, you have to admit that the drawing in Figure 3-1 is pretty rich in detail and perspective.

This chapter is going to take you step by step, process by process, through reproducing this scene, and along the way, you'll become more familiar, not only with the location of the tools you might use most often, but also how they work together in a synergy that produces outstanding artwork in the time it takes to read a chapter in a book!

So let the author be your co-pilot from here on in and you do the steering. It's going to be an exciting and educating journey all the way from File | New to File | *Definitely* Save! Okay, that's not a menu item, but you *will* be pleased with how far you get in this amazing program with a minimum of coaching.

Working with the Star Tool to Build a Pattern

As you saw in the first figure, the child's ball is decorated with stars, all the same color, but of different sizes and angles of rotation. Additionally, the pattern of stars displayed on a curved surface really should distort outward a little at the center, perfectly in keeping with the roundness of an actual ball. This is a step you'll address later in this chapter. For now, in the following steps, you'll grow acquainted with one of the Shape Tools group, the Star tool, and then you'll move on to editing a star, duplicating it, and eventually making a fill for the ball illustration. Follow along here.

FIGURE 3-1   By following along in this chapter, you'll have a ball.

Tutorial Making the Background: Putting the Star Tool to Work

1. You'll use the Rectangle tool first to create a background because you won't
   be able to see very light yellow stars against a white background to edit them!
   Choose the Rectangle tool from the Toolbox (or press F6), and then while holding
   CTRL (to constrain what you draw to a perfect square), drag diagonally until the
   rulers tell you the square is about 4", and then let go of the mouse button.

2. On the color palette, click a light blue color to fill the square with solid color.
   Pastel Blue is a good choice, and if you have tooltips enabled and you hover over
   the collection of blues, a callout confirming the color is Pastel Blue appears.

3. It's star time. The Shape Tools group is directly beneath the Ellipse tool on
   the Toolbox. Any time you see a tick mark at the lower right of an icon, that
   means it's part of a group and there are other tools in the group to access if

you click-hold on the top icon. So click-hold and then move your cursor over to the Star tool to choose it.

4. As with the Rectangle tool, holding CTRL will constrain the star shape you'll click-drag to be perfectly symmetrical. Marquee-drag a star about 1/5th the size of the rectangle, within the rectangle now.

5. Click the yellow color on the color palette, docked to the right of the interface to fill the star with a solid fill.

6. By default, objects are created with a black outline, a very thin width, and no fill. The outlines on the star and the background shape aren't very artistic-looking, so choose the Pick tool (the top tool on the Toolbox), select the blue background, and then right-click on the "X" color swatch, as shown in the following illustration. Then remove the outline around the star in the same way. This illustration shows you a summary of steps 1–6. Here, the star has a white outline around it just so you can see it better in this book. It will actually have a thin black outline when you draw it.

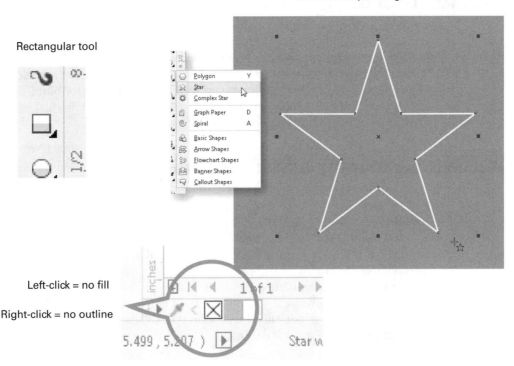

Hold CTRL as you drag.

Rectangular tool

Left-click = no fill

Right-click = no outline

7. Save the file by pressing CTRL + S, and then find a location on your hard drive where it won't get lost. *Don't* close the file; we've hardly *begun*!

Tweaking the Star Object

Like many "special" objects that are fast and convenient to create in CorelDRAW, the Star tool produces objects that can be modified at any time—even after you close the program and open it a week later (don't do this now). Star objects have two unique properties. First is the capability to change the number of points or sides—from 5 to 11, for example—at any time, even if you extrude the star. The other special property, which you'll use next, is the degree of sharpness the points of the star have. When you first create a star shape, it has a value of 53, which is the sort of star shape you see on military craft and a third-grader's report. For this chapter, it will look a little more fun and lighthearted if the stars on the ball are slightly inflated and a bit cartoonish. Therefore, you'll decrease the Sharpness value before you get into duplicating and populating the blue background with stars. Here are two different approaches to modifying the star.

Tutorial Reshaping a Star: Technique 1

1. After click-dragging the star while holding CTRL, filling the star with solid yellow, and removing the outline width, put your cursor between the elevator buttons next to the Sharpness area on the Property bar.
2. Drag downward until the star looks a little puffed up, or you've arrived at a Sharpness value of about 36, by dragging between the elevator buttons in the downward direction. Hang on; there's also a manual way to do this, which involves getting to know another tool in CorelDRAW.

Tutorial Reshaping a Star: Technique 2

1. Choose the Shape tool, the top tool in the Editing group, just below the Pick tool on the Toolbox.
2. Drag one of the convex nodes along the outline of the star slightly outward, as shown in Figure 3-2. You don't have to hold CTRL while doing this manual edit; there is no way to turn the star into a spiral or anything. The Shape tool is often used to change the appearance of "special" objects in CorelDRAW. For example, a rectangle produced with the Rectangle tool (and not hand-drawn) can have curved corners if you pull on their corner nodes with the Shape tool. As you grow more experienced with CorelDRAW, the Shape tool will become your tool of preference for editing.

Making a Pattern of Stars

Let's think about how this star pattern should be designed. Stars of the same size, rotational value, and spacing would make a boring kid's toy, one they'd soon abandon and go back to their Xbox. So let's take this opportunity to make a visually interesting pattern by unevenly spacing duplicates of your plump star.

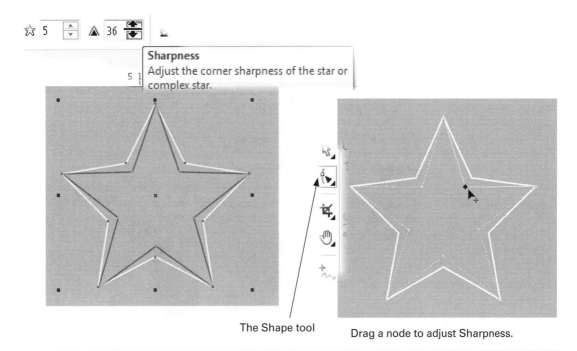

The Shape tool   Drag a node to adjust Sharpness.

FIGURE 3-2   There are (at least) two different ways to stylize a star produced with the Star tool.

You're going to learn the now-classic "drop a copy" technique for duplicating and moving objects, and you'll do a little proportional scaling along the way. You put these moves together, and no one will suspect that all the stars in the pattern on the ball began as one single copy.

Ready?

Tutorial   Creating More Stars than a Hollywood Agent

1. With the Pick tool, drag the star you just modified to a different location on top of the light blue background. It can go a little outside of the background rectangle if you're artistically inclined to add a little chaos to this ball's design. This is step "a" in the following illustration.
2. When you arrived at the location where you want a duplicate of the star, don't release the left mouse button—and tap the right mouse button. This drops a copy of the original where your cursor is currently located. This is callout "b" in the next illustration.

3. Release both mouse buttons and the operation is complete—"c" in this illustration. You can do this as many times as you like, but let's instead learn some steps to make the distribution and spacing a little more random.

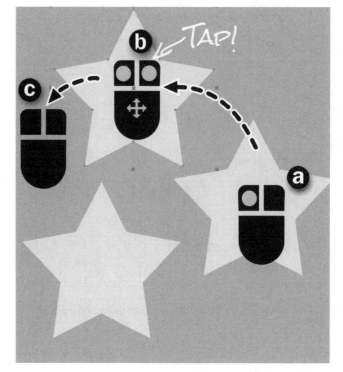

4. Press CTRL + S, and keep the document open.

Okay, it's on to refining and completing the pattern for the ball. Again, you can "drop a copy" or move a star so it's slightly outside of the background rectangle because the areas outside will be clipped eventually by a circle shape, representing the ball. Let's give scaling and rotation features a workout next.

Tutorial Rotating and Scaling to Populate the Pattern Area

1. By the time you've dropped more than three copies of the star shape, you'll be running out of room on the background to make an intricate pattern! With the Pick tool, select one of the stars so you can see the eight bounding-box handles, and then drag one of the corner handles—*not* the ones at 3, 6, 9, or 12 o'clock—

toward the center of the star, as shown in the next illustration. CorelDRAW provides a preview of what the final size of the scaled star will be; when you think it's an artistically appropriate size, release the mouse button, and you've scaled the star.

Drag a corner handle of the star toward its center.

Tip When you grab a corner handle to scale an object, the position of the scaled object changes—it moves to the corner opposing the control handle you're manipulating. If you'd like to scale an object from its center inward so its final position is the same as before scaling, hold SHIFT and drag any corner control handle.

2. Let's try the rotation feature in CorelDRAW now, so all the stars don't look like clones of each other, even though they are. When an object is not selected, there's no screen element around it. When you select it (with the Pick tool), you'll see eight little dots bounding the selection, bounding-box handles, and you just used them in step 1. Now, when an object is selected and you click on it, rotation handles appear at the corners and skew handles appear at top, bottom, left, and right. So click to select one of the stars right now, and then click the selected star to make the rotation handles visible.

3. Click-drag any of the four rotation handles to rotate the selected start, as shown in the following illustration.

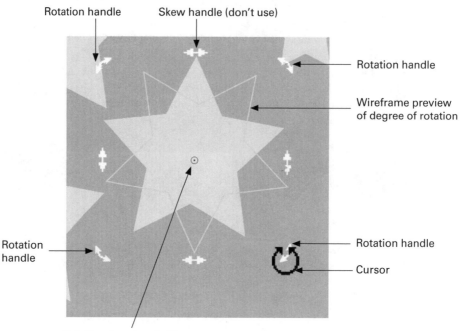

Rotation handle

Skew handle (don't use)

Rotation handle

Wireframe preview of degree of rotation

Rotation handle

Rotation handle

Cursor

Rotational center of object

4. Okay. That's all you need to know to make about 14 stars of different sizes, at different distances apart (this is called *distribute*, and it's a feature in CorelDRAW's Object menu covered in Chapter 6), and at different degrees of rotation. Press CTRL + s, go get a refreshing beverage of your choice, and then read on to see how to turn a bunch of stars into a bulging bunch of stars. Like the balls on the star, except without the ball.

Shaping Operations and Combining Objects

Grouping objects requires very few brain cells: the shortcut is CTRL + G. However, in the steps to follow you don't want to group the stars, leaving them as distinct objects, more or less like 14 passengers on the same bus. Instead, you want to perform the Weld operation, available on the Property bar when more than one object is selected. This operation combines all the paths that make up the stars into one path whose components just happen to have spaces between them. This effect is sort of like the letter *o* when you type it. O is a combination of two circles that don't touch one another.

The reason why you're going from star-maker to welder will become evident after you've taken a few more steps.

Tutorial   ## Trimming the Stars
to the Background and Beyond

1. With the Pick tool, try to marquee-select (diagonally drag the cursor while holding the mouse button) only the stars on the page. If you see a small origin marker, or node, on the background rectangle, that means it's selected, too, a natural mistake during precision work. To retain the selection of the stars but to deselect the rectangle, hold SHIFT and then click the background rectangle. You might notice a message on the Status bar at the bottom of the workspace that "*x* Objects Selected on Layer 1" has decreased by 1, which is both a confirmation and a reassurance.

2. On the Property bar, click the Weld button, shown here in the illustration. If you look closely at your screen, you'll see little *origin markers* (*nodes*) on each star. This means you've welded them all and that this galaxy of stars is now one discontinuous (meaning there are spaces between its single shape) object.

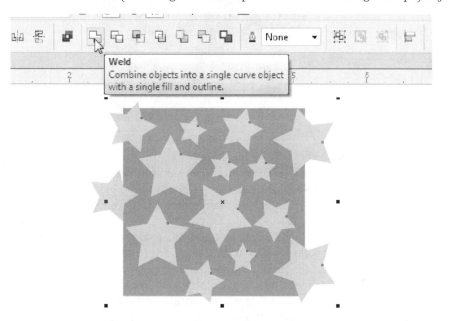

3. Let's get rid of the star portions that lie outside of the rectangle background now; they won't be featured in the final composition. Select the background rectangle using the Pick tool, and then press CTRL + C (Copy) and then CTRL + V (Paste), and you now have a duplicate resting on top of all the other shapes. When you paste, the order of the new object is always on top of the others, unless you paste to a different layer (explained in Chapter 6).

4. With the rectangle still selected, hold SHIFT (to additively select) and click on the star object; you should see a few places where the welded stars stick outside of the top rectangle. With both objects selected, click the Intersect button on the Property bar, as shown in this next illustration.

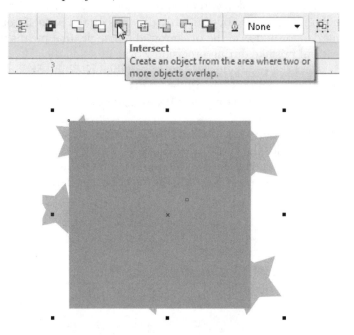

And apparently nothing has happened, but this is because, by default, when you command CorelDRAW to create an intersection between two or more objects, it does so, but it also leaves behind the original objects (unless you use the Object | Shaping Docker, which can do very obvious and destructive editing).

5. First, with the Pick tool, select and delete the top blue rectangle. This leaves the original welded stars, with the intersection result underneath. So click on any stars that lie outside the box, and then press DELETE. This next illustration shows what the intersection object looks like when it's moved away from the background—but this is only an illustration—not a step—so don't move the Intersect shape! All parts outside of the duplicated rectangle have been removed.

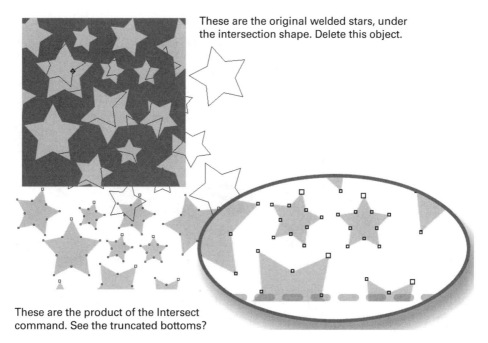

These are the original welded stars, under the intersection shape. Delete this object.

These are the product of the Intersect command. See the truncated bottoms?

6. Choose File | Save, and probably refill that glass with another refreshing beverage. The heavy-duty stuff is coming up next.

An Introduction to Enveloping Objects

The Envelope tool/docker (CTRL + F7) is perhaps the most sophisticated feature in any graphics program boasting the same basic features. You can turn any shape or group of shapes into Goofy Putty (we're not allowed to use the actual brand name here). You can stretch and twist at a number of control bounding nodes; this feature is not destructive. You can remove an Envelope at any time when the tool is active by clicking the Property bar's Clear Envelope button.

In this next set of steps, you won't be working with the core feature of the Envelope tool—the control points—but you *will* use a preset—Circular—to make the stars conform to a round beach ball you haven't created yet. You will in this section, but stars come before balls except in the dictionary.

Tutorial   Enveloping and Trimming the Welded Stars

1. With the Pick tool, select the intersected, welded stars.
2. Choose the Envelope tool from the Effects flyout group on the Toolbox. You'll immediately notice a bounding box with several control nodes, but don't touch them.
3. On the Property bar, click the Preset List drop-down at the far left and then choose Circular. Figure 3-3 shows steps 2 and 3 in sequence and you have to admit the Circular envelope preset makes the stars look pretty darned cool!

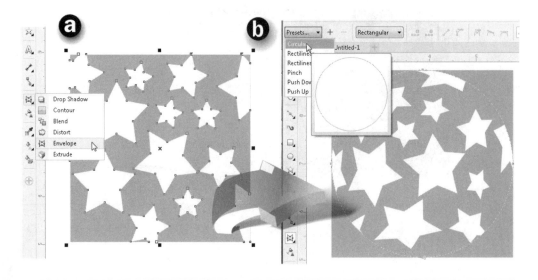

FIGURE 3-3   Use the Circular preset with the Envelope tool to make a "fisheye lens" treatment out of any group of CorelDRAW vector shapes.

4. You need to drag two guides out of the rulers now to establish the exact center of the background square, so you can create a circle on top of it and so the stars finally get their well-deserved and much-anticipated ball. First, select the background rectangle; you'll see a very small "x" in the center—this is the absolute center mark for both the rectangle and the stars...because the star-welded shape was intersected with a copy of the background so they're both equal (more or less) in orientation and size.

5. Drag from the vertical ruler over to the little "x". You now have a vertical guide for the center of this composition.

6. Because you dragged a guide out of a ruler, the rectangle became deselected, so select it again. Now drag a horizontal guide to the little "x" from the top horizontal ruler. See the illustration here.

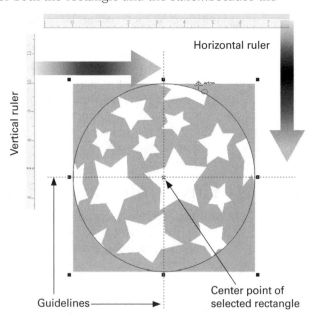

7. Choose the Ellipse tool from the Toolbox; put the cursor at the intersection of the two guides in the center of the square; and then while holding CTRL + SHIFT, drag away from the center, in any direction, until the circle produced is just a fraction smaller than the background rectangle, as shown in this illustration. In this instance, CTRL constrains the ellipse to a perfect circle and SHIFT makes the direction of the oval created begin at the center point and expand outward.

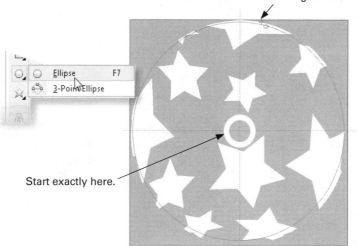

8. Choose the Eyedropper tool from the Toolbox (a; see Figure 3-4), and click to sample the background rectangle for its exact color. The eyedropper cursor now turns into a paint can (b), ready to fill the next object you click over.
9. Click over the circle you created in step 7, being careful not to position your cursor on any part of the stars object. Now, the stars are hidden by the filled circle, but this is as planned.
10. Choose the Pick tool, select the blue background rectangle, and then press DELETE (or CTRL + X).
11. With the Pick tool, select the blue circle, and then on your keyboard, press CTRL + PAGEDOWN (c). This is a shortcut command for Object | Order To Back Of Layer. Now the stars are on top of the circle. Be sure to remove the outline around the circle by right-clicking the No Outline swatch on the local color palette at the bottom of the page or the global one on the color palette docked to the right of the interface. Figure 3-4 shows all of this graphically.
12. Press CTRL + S as usual!

Adding Shading to Your Composition

The perspective and choice of colors and the general shape of the beach ball are all fine and in place. However, the quality of lighting is missing from this scene, and *lighting*—highlights and shading (and sometimes shadows)—has been a quality of classic painting for centuries. And you didn't buy CorelDRAW to become anything less than a classic modern-day master now, did you?

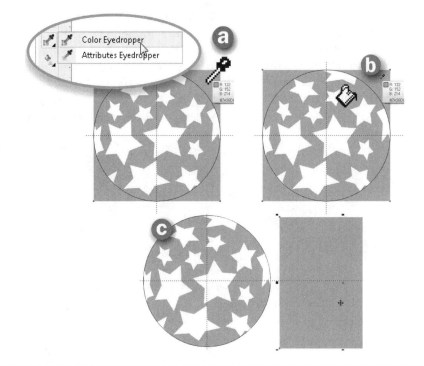

FIGURE 3-4 Pick up the color of the background, and apply it to the shape that contains the stars.

The first thing you'll do is make a significant change to the blue beach ball solid color by overlaying a tinted circle and using X7's enhanced Transparency features—it's only proper that if the ball has shading, the stars should, too. Even experienced CorelDRAW users should follow along here—in X7 it's easier than ever to set up a very complex fountain fill.

Tutorial Adding Lighting to the Beach Ball

1. With the Pick tool, click any part of the blue background, and then press CTRL + C (Copy) and CTRL + V (Paste). The stars are once again hidden by a duplicate of the blue beach ball shape.

2. Choose the Transparency tool from the Toolbox. Drag from about 11 o'clock to 4 o'clock, as shown in Figure 3-5. You'll notice that the sphere appears to be solid at top left, and the stars are appearing at bottom right, where the Transparency Linear fill type is 100% transparent. Figure 3-5 should get you acquainted with the elements, the controls, and *why you're getting the results*

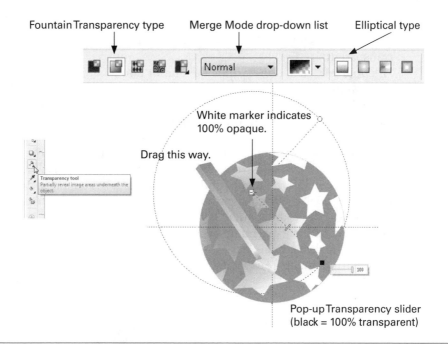

FIGURE 3-5   Drag the Transparency tool just as you would the Fill tool, to set an initial linear progression from a start color (or opacity) to an end point with different values.

from these steps that you are, which is the most important part of this tutorial and of this book. The next stop is the Property bar and a little assistance from the pop-up Transparency slider to create dramatic changes in this piece.

3. Although a duplicate of the result of the following steps can be seen at right in Figure 3-6, you do not have to move or duplicate the object currently on top of your blue circle with the stars on top. First, click the Elliptical Fountain Transparency button on the Property bar; the transparency values will be precisely wrong. Let's make corrections here.

4. Change the Merge Mode from Normal to Multiply. Doing this will intensify the shading you're going to perform.

5. The color node markers along the axis of a transparency fill are represented by white as totally opaque, black as totally transparent, and shades of gray as partial transparency. Click the beginning color node marker, let the Node color picker appear, and then drag its little slider all the way to the right, making the marker black, and making the beginning point of an elliptical (in this case, circular) transparency totally transparent.

6. Click on the end marker, the point you dragged to, and then on the Node color picker menu set the value to **0**, all the way to the right, making this area totally transparent.

7. Ask yourself, "What on Earth is the author doing here!?" Bear with him: You *add* transparency nodes by double-clicking the transparency line—that dashed guy that connects the Start and the End points. Double-click a point close to the end point, let the pop-up menu appear, and then drag its slider to anywhere from 12 to 0. Do you see what's happening? The bottom transparent area will serve as "rim lighting," making the beach ball look even that much rounder, a trick artists have used for centuries to make palace facades look more opulent and the royal family's children's faces look less flat.

8. One more double-click above the previous (0 value) marker. Give this new transparency marker about a **31%** value.

9. Don't be afraid to experiment and move the markers along the transparency handle (the dashed blue guy) to increase or decrease contrast between neighboring transparency values. See Figure 3-6.

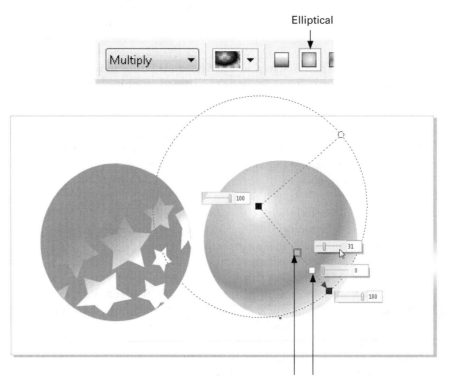

FIGURE 3-6 The ball will get its color detail from your drawing. It will get its tonal detail from this transparent object overlay.

10. Let's assume you didn't move the duplicate circle to which you applied these various transparency values at different intervals. You should have a fairly dimensional illustration, like the one shown here.

Tip Don't be afraid to—in fact, by all means do—reposition the beginning and end points of the transparency overlay if the beginning point isn't at upper left and the end at about 5 o'clock. The rest of the composition depends on this lighting direction. Shadows and other elements need to be in synch and not contradict one another.

Adding Highlights and a Shadow

The beach ball doesn't look as shiny as new ones do, so the solution to illustrating this is to use a circular transparency inside of a circle whose size is larger than the end point of the transparency. The visual effect is that the highlight is feathered.

1. With the Ellipse tool, drag an ellipse at the upper left of the ball, as shown in the illustration following step 3. You can and should remove the outline width and fill the ellipse with pure white.
2. Choose the Transparency tool, drag it across the white ellipse, but do not let the beginning or end point of the fountain fill go outside of the ellipse. Select Screen from the Merge Mode drop-down on the Property bar.
3. Increase the size of the Ellipse using its control handles and the Pick tool if necessary. In the following illustration, you can see, at left, the solid ellipse and, at right, the ellipse with the Elliptical transparency applied. The white outline is there simply to demonstrate the bounds of the ellipse when it has no outline width and its transparency handles stay within the ellipse outline. At far right, you can see the somewhat phony effect caused when you don't keep

the transparency handles inside the outline of the object. What is supposed to be a soft highlight looks like a frosted glass oval with its outer dimensions clearly visible.

4. A good way to intensify this highlight without doing any amount of recalculation of values, midpoints, or any of that other jazz is to simply, now, select the highlight ellipse with the Pick tool, and then press CTRL + C, then CTRL + V. The following illustration shows you duplicates of the ovals above the ball for comparison's sake.

Blending Yourself a Cast Shadow

CorelDRAW X7 has its own Shadow tool, and it's covered in Chapter 18, but for now let's try a manual technique for making a shadow beneath the ball. This ball is going to be resting on the floral pattern provided in the *Pattern for Floor.cdr* file. And as shadows go, they are never 100 percent opaque in real life. The solution? At least the one in this chapter? You're going to create a small dark ellipse at partial opacity and put it almost underneath and to the right of the beach ball, and then create a larger ellipse that eventually will be 100 percent transparent. Then you'll blend the two so there is not only a highly photorealistic off-center shadow beneath the ball, but, in some areas, you'll be able to see the floor pattern. *Don't* get the idea that this is the last chapter in this *Guide* you'll need to read before becoming CorelDRAW Master (or Mistress) of the Galaxy. But what you're going to accomplish *is* pretty sophisticated and exceptionally cool:

Tutorial   Making a Cast Shadow with Blends

1. With the Ellipse tool, create a small ellipse to the right of the ball. Give it about **88%** black color and a solid transparency of about **94%**. With the ellipse selected, right-click over the No Color Swatch (the guy with the "X") to remove the outline. You achieve solid transparency by clicking the Uniform Transparency button at left on the Property bar.

2. Press SHIFT + PAGEDOWN to put the ellipse behind the ball in order of elements on this page.

3. Make a much bigger ellipse (see the illustration following step 4), and give it a **30%** black fill and about a **75%** solid transparency. Remove its outline as you did with the smaller ellipse in step 1.

4. With the larger transparent object selected (which might be a challenge without going to View | Wireframe!), press SHIFT + PAGEDOWN for the sake of a correct transparency-enabled blend to put this ellipse to the very back of the drawing page. A dashed outline has been added to the larger, nearly invisible object in the following illustration so you have a reference as to where the ellipses go.

5. Choose the Blend tool from the flyout group above the Transparency tool, and then drag from the nearly invisible large ellipse to the small one, as shown in Figure 3-7. At left, you can see the Blend tool being applied to the two ellipses—you'll notice a white node marker at each end of the blend line and

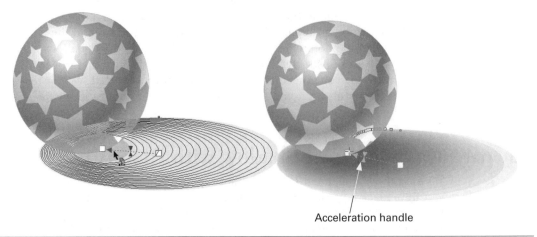

Acceleration handle

FIGURE 3-7   You have a lot of power and control over shadow-making when you choose to combine blends with transparency.

a pair of acceleration handles in the center of the line. These handles perform a "preference" of one end of the blend over the other, and the effect when you drag the handles toward the ball is that darker tones become visible, whereas at the outskirts of the cast shadow, there is a gentle drop off in color and opacity, which looks quite natural and photorealistic.

6. Press CTRL + S!

Tip Even while two objects are blended together, the start and end objects can be moved. You might have to go to Wireframe view to select one of the objects, but once you do, you can create fine or coarse changes to the shape of your blend object. You can also experiment with different fills for the two objects to fine-tune the shadow's appearance.

Adding a Background and a Floor in Perspective

Let's do the floor first because it's an exciting adventure into the Perspective tool. And there aren't a lot of exciting tech books out here. Select and copy the pattern from the *Pattern for Floor.cdr* document, and then paste it into the ball composition. Then follow along.

Tutorial   A Starry Ball Sitting on a Floral Rug

1. If the author messed up in building these files and the pattern is on top of the ball, press SHIFT + PAGEDOWN to put the pattern to the back of the layer. Now, we're talkin'.

2. The shadow might be too light against the pattern, or too dense, and if this is the case, select one of the control objects—perhaps the inner one is

responsible for the shadow's imperfection—and then double-click the Fill icon toward the right of the Status bar, the one that has a red slash through it because it can't figure out a solid color within a Blend group. This displays the Edit Fill box. In real time, you can lighten the percentage of black of the chosen control object and accept the change only when the Blend result looks good onscreen. See the following illustration.

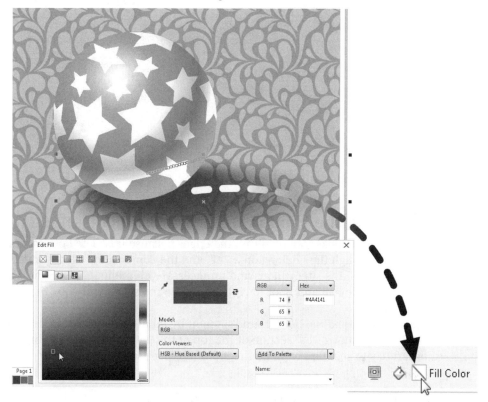

3. With the pattern selected, choose Effects | Add Perspective and four black squares (handles for you to manipulate) appear around the four corners of the group of objects.

 Note Vector fills, new to version 7, will not accept the Perspective command, and bitmaps distorted as significantly as you're going to distort them would make them suitable for confetti but not art components. However, the author designed one of four tiles to create this large pattern as a vector shape, not a bitmap fill. As a result, you can do whatever you want in terms of distorting it.

4. This step is really easy and marginally fun: with the Shape tool, pull the bottom two control handles of the perspective floor away from each other, and then drag the top two handles nearer to each other, but not by a lot, because by this tutorial's conclusion, you'll frame the piece and don't want bizarre empty

triangles peeking through the background. See the following illustration for reference. And ignore the page border entirely.

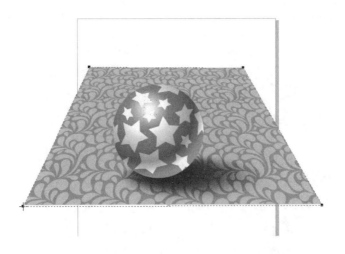

Completing the Composition with Embellishments

The composition looks rough around the edges because it *is*! The bottom edges of the floor look as though they belong on a 747, and the composition ideally should be in portrait mode, all the superfluous and unnecessary elements hidden, and a simple frame around the ball and floor to truly complete the scene and your first project in this *Guide*.

Let's first extend the background's height by taking a black rectangle that fits over the ball and the narrowest section of the top of the pattern. And then you'll use linear transparency to seamlessly blend the top of the pattern's end with gentle light falloff.

Tutorial   Framing Your Composition

1. With the Rectangle tool, draw a tall, moderately wide rectangle that covers the ball entirely and obscures the top of the pattern. Remove any outline width or color, and make it **90%** or **100%**, so it sort of reminds you of that monolith in *2001: A Space Odyssey*.
2. Take the Transparency tool and drag downward on this rectangle. Now comes the challenging part: you need to make the exact point at the top edge of the pattern **100%** opaque and then let the opacity gently fall off so you can clearly see the ball with no shadow casting on it. Today is your lucky day, though: you can select both the ball's components and its shadow and then press CTRL + PAGEUP to lift the order of the ball and shadow above the transparent rectangle without affecting the pattern. The following illustration shows all the action.

Linear Transparency is 100% opaque where the top of the pattern ends.

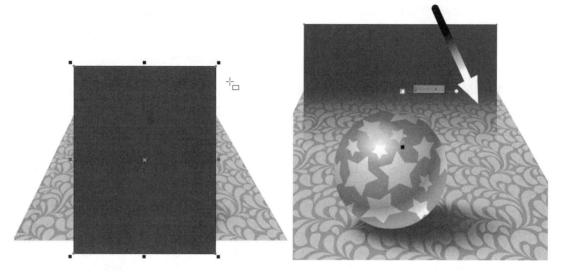

3. A frame around the piece is a no-brainer at this point; you already know how to use the Rectangle tool. However, and this is a big however, there's a new feature you're not familiar with yet (unless you're a Corel Pro, in which case don't soil this one for the others): the PowerClip feature. A PowerClip puts things you select into another object, and the effect is like a door that's open, but can be moved around without anything spilling out of the closet. With the Rectangle tool, draw a rectangle around only those areas you want to be visible in your finished piece. A good option is 16 points and is used here with a dull bluish-green outline color.

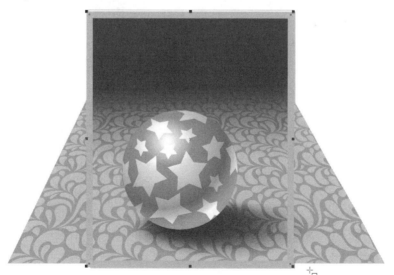

4. Press CTRL + A to select all. The frame is going to be the PowerClip container so you don't want it in this selection. With the Pick tool, SHIFT + click on the frame to exclude it from the selection.

5. Choose Object | PowerClip | Place Inside Frame. A gargantuan Monty Pythonesque arrow appears and you click the frame object. And *bang*! All your hard work is perfectly framed with no unwanted areas sticking outside of the frame. And all your hard work should now look like Figure 3-1 at the beginning of this chapter.

You've done well. You should use Corel Capture to make a copy of this and email it to everyone in your address book to prove you're getting results out of X7 and this *Guide*. This might be anticlimactic (or a *denouement,* as my editors like to call it), but Chapter 4 is not the 350mph, "I don't know what I'm doing but it's sure fun!" chapter that this has been. We need to shift back into first gear and get your hands around page size, working with multi-page documents and setting up guides—horizontal, vertical, and everywhere in-between. You can't go printing your finest artwork if it's larger than the default page size of your printer, now can you?

Believe it or not, this test drive has shown you a lot of essentials to getting the most out of this program, so sit tight, lay off the caffeine for a few hours, and the incline we're going to take to get to our destination isn't quite as vertical from here on up!

PART II

Getting Started with CorelDRAW X7

4   Working with Single- and Multi-page Documents

You have an idea for promoting your product or service; you have your graphics, and you have some body copy and a snappy headline in mind. The next step is to define the dimensions within which you express your promotional idea. And this is where an understanding of CorelDRAW's Guides comes in handy.

Do you need a flyer, or perhaps a four-page booklet? This chapter covers the beginning of any graphics project: setting up pages in CorelDRAW. You'll learn about layout styles, page dimensions for your screen and for printing, page reordering, and in the process, gain a good working knowledge of what you need to do—and what you can tell CorelDRAW to do—to create a page that suits your ideas.

Note Download and extract all the files from the Chapter04.zip archive to follow the tutorials in this chapter.

Setting Up Your Document Page

Every new file you create has its own set of *page properties* that have two attributes: *physical* properties and *display* preferences. The *physical properties* refer to the size, length, and color of each page as you'd define a physical page in the real world. *Display preferences* control how page values are *viewed*. Let's begin with the most common options and then move on to the more specialized features.

Controlling Page Size and Orientation

If you've unchecked the Always Show The Welcome Screen At Launch checkbox, the default size of a new document is CorelDRAW's default, which might depend on the language version of CorelDRAW you use. For this US author, it's US Letter, 8 1/2" by 11", but this can be changed. The quickest route for document size change is through the Property bar while the Pick tool—and no objects—are selected. The Property bar features options for setting your page to standard-sized pages, custom sizes, and orientation, as you can see in Figure 4-1. If you have a multi-page document, the Property bar also has ways to change all pages at once or only the currently visible page.

The Paper Type/Size and orientation options control the format of your document. When you have a specific format for a design you need to print, the following sections cover the options available to you in CorelDRAW.

Paper Type/Size

To make sure your CorelDRAW page matches the paper in your printer, clicking a Paper Type/Size option from the Property bar is the quickest method. From the drop-down box, you can choose Letter, Legal, Tabloid, or other common sizes. Once you've made a selection, the dimensions are automatically entered as values in the Page Width and Height boxes on the Property bar. If you have a limited need for different

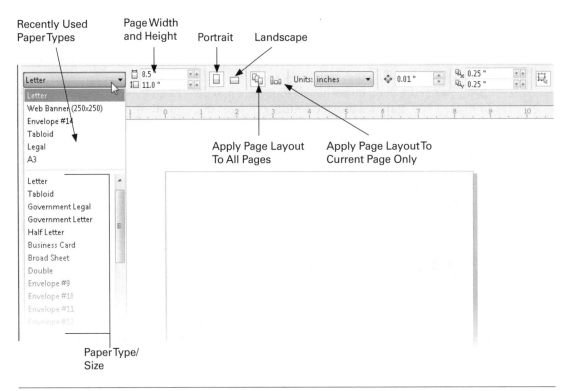

FIGURE 4-1 You change page size and orientation by using the Property bar.

paper sizes, click the Edit This List button at the bottom of the drop-down list, and you can delete seldom-used sizes: click Delete Page Size in the Options box.

- **Page Width and Height**   You are not limited to a page size that's the same as the paper in your printer; page width and height values can be freely adjusted to match just about any paper size. For a custom page size, type specific values directly into the Page Width and Height boxes, and then press ENTER.
- **Landscape/Portrait Orientation**   Clicking either Portrait or Landscape on the Property bar while using the Pick tool (with no objects selected) sets the page orientation. If the page width you enter is less than the page height entered, the orientation is automatically set to Portrait, and vice versa for Landscape. Changing from one orientation to the other automatically switches the values in the Page Width and Page Height fields.
- **All Pages/Current Page**   You can create a document up to 999 pages long, with different pages set to any size or orientation. The All Pages and Current Page buttons operate in "either/or" fashion—like the orientation buttons—so you can set the page size either for all pages in your document at once (the default) or only for the current page. To set only the current page to be different from the others in your document, click the right of these two buttons on the Property bar (directly to the left of the Units drop-down) and set your new page size and orientation as needed. Other pages in the document aren't resized when you choose this option.

 Note   If you've unintentionally removed a page size you need later, you can re-create it. Click the Paper Type/Size drop-down list on the Property bar, then choose Edit This List. Create, name, and save the page in the Options | Page Size box.

Page Viewing Options

With CorelDRAW at its default settings, when you select File | New, you'll see a rectangle in the workspace. This rectangle represents your document page in height and width. However, what you *won't* see is how your page will be printed to a personal printer or to a commercial press. Whenever you print a page, you'll see two areas called the *printable area* and *bleed area*, and you can add nonprinting guidelines to provide a page preview ... so objects and text at the edges of your work don't get partially printed. You certainly want these features visible when designing for print; the grippers on printers often prevent edge-to-edge prints. To have CorelDRAW add Bleed and Printable Area (*safety*) guides to your page, press CTRL + J, and then choose Document | Guidelines | Presets; check Printable Area and Bleed Area, as shown in next illustration. The bleed area extends to the edge of the page, and this is correct for personal printers; see the following Note.

Note   A *bleed* is the part of the printed image that extends beyond the edge of the page. When printing to a personal printer, there is no bleed because bleed is only relevant when a page on a commercial press is trimmed to final book size. For example, if a commercial press uses 12"×14" paper and the final trim size is 8½"×11", you could set up a bleed area of 10"×13" to make a design extend to the edge of the page the audience reads.

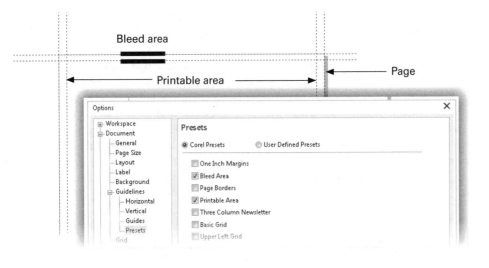

 Note If you are printing to a borderless photo printer, your printable area will be the same size as your page border.

The Printable Area and Bleed Area properties depend on the printer options you choose in the Print dialog; this is a new, streamlined location for print preferences in version X7. You can press CTRL + P (File | Print) to access the printer you want to choose along with basic options on the General tab. The Preferences button, as with most Windows programs, takes you to the native print driver options, which is, for example, dependent on Canon's inkjet features, not Corel. To check out the trim, image positioning on the page, and other options, click the Layout tab.

> **Tip** Setting a bleed amount is done using the Tools | Options | Document | Page Size area, using the Bleed num box. The bleed amount can be defined anywhere between 0 (which is the exact edge of your page) and 900.0 inches (which is silly). Be sure to put a check in the Show Bleed Area box before clicking Apply so you can see how your document is set up onscreen.

Controlling Page Background Color

To specify a page background color for your document, choose Tools | Options | Document | Background. Also, there's a convenient button on the Standard bar that opens the Options dialog. By Default, No Background is chosen in this box.

> **Tip** You can skip the step of going to the main menu to choose Tools to get to Options. The Options button is located on the Standard bar (which means it's always visible), with a tiny picture of checkmarks on it.

- **Solid** Choose this option and a color from the selector to specify any uniform color as the page background. Click More in the color selector to use a color picker in different color models (RGB, CMYK, and so on), a mixer, or a specific color palette. Also, you can use the Eyedropper tool to the left of the More button to choose *any color anywhere on your monitor;* the Eyedropper can leave CorelDRAW's program window. This means that if CorelDRAW's UI is not maximized, you can use the Eyedropper to sample the color of an icon on your desktop! Once a color has been chosen, the page background is set to that color, but the bleed area and the workspace are not.
- **Bitmap** Choose this option to use a bitmap as the page background. Click the Browse button to open the CorelDRAW Import dialog, and locate and choose a bitmap. Background bitmaps are tiled as many times as needed to fill the page. You can also scale the number of repeating tiles by clicking the Custom Size radio button and entering values. The best bitmaps to use for patterns are ones that have been designed to tile seamlessly. In Figure 4-2, you can see a completed design you'll work with in a moment. *Swimwear Sale.cdr* uses a muted ocean waves pattern, one of several you can use in the downloaded zip archive, to add a subtle graphical theme to the sale flyer. The Bitmap option is terrific for creating several different signs or stationery that contains different text but must be tied together in a theme. You can, for example, create different text on layers such as "Swimsuit Sale," "Vacation Sale," and "Inflatable Theme Toy Sale," and then print the various signs by hiding all but one layer for printing. You can't accidentally move the background, and this technique is quick to set up when you have 12 different messages that need a common background.
- **Source** The Source options let you establish an external link to the bitmap file or store a copy of it internally with your CorelDRAW document file. Choose Linked to maintain an external link or Embedded to store the bitmap with your document. While Linked is selected, the file path to the bitmap is displayed,

FIGURE 4-2 Use a bitmap as a background for your design and text.

and the bitmap itself must be available to CorelDRAW during printing. This option is very useful when you need to conserve on saved CorelDRAW file sizes; additionally, you can modify the background bitmap in PHOTO-PAINT or Painter, and then reload the edited bitmap in the future.

- **Bitmap Size** This field contains "either/or" radio buttons. If you choose Default Size, the background appears on the page because the bitmap's original dimensions allow it to tile as many times as needed to fill the page. However, if you want a smaller bitmap as the background (more tiles), you click the Custom Size button. The Maintain Aspect Ratio option is checked by default; you probably don't want the bitmap background to look smooshed or stretched—with Maintain Aspect Ratio turned on, all you need to do is enter one value in either the H or V field, and CorelDRAW automatically fills in the remaining field. Note that bitmaps are resolution dependent, unlike vector drawings. Thus, you can usually scale a bitmap down, but don't try to enlarge it because the bitmap will go through something called *resampling,* and blurriness is often the result. Remember: scale down = yes; scale up = no.

- **Print And Export Background**   Use this option to control whether the page background you've added to your document page is included when exporting your drawing files or when you print the document. It's available when either Solid or Bitmap is selected for the page background; by default, it's active.

Open *Swimware Sale.cdr* now, and work through the Background options to change the waves background to something else you prefer for the piece.

Tutorial   Changing a Background Bitmap

1. If you haven't already extracted the contents of the zip archive for this chapter, do so now, and create a folder for the PNG images and place them there.
2. With *Swimwear Sale.cdr* open, choose Tools | Options | Document | Background.
3. Notice that the Bitmap button is chosen (there is already a bitmap as the background), and that the bitmap is embedded. This means that unless you own the bitmap on your hard drive, the next step will forever overwrite this *waves screened.png* file, something to consider when you embed a bitmap. Often, you might find it useful to simply externally link the bitmap background so you don't have to remember whether you have a spare copy of the image. Click Browse now to locate the folder of PNG files from Step 1.
4. Choose one of the PNG files, or you could choose your own image. With the file selected, click Import.
5. You can't preview the imported image as it will look; you can only click OK now to see how the new background has affected the composition. Before doing this, though, try setting the Custom Size to something other than the default. If you're using one of this chapter's example bitmaps, try setting the Height and Width to **3"**. Click OK and the layout has a new background.
6. Optionally, you can open the Object Manager (Window | Dockers | Object Manager), and click the Visibility icon for the "Swimwear" layer so the little eye icon is closed. This clears everything from the page except the background image and the logo at top. Now you can design a different flyer using the same background bitmap and logo by clicking, for example, "Vacations" to set the current layer.

Alternatively, when you want to perform variations on a page layout, see Chapter 6 for the details on working with Master Layers.

Tip   If a bitmap background appears to have a white seam in an area, this is a visual effect of the bitmap trying to blend (*anti-alias*) with the page itself, which is white. If you zoom in and out, the thin white edge will disappear because at certain viewing resolutions the anti-alias blending matches the resolution of the tiling bitmap background. The design *itself* will print with no visible white edges; this is simply a page viewing issue.

Using Layouts and Labels

The Property bar is used to set up basic page and paper sizes and orientation, but designers often need to lay out designs for items such as labels, booklets, tent cards, and greeting cards *that are printed on standard size paper.* These items are definitely *not* laid out like a single-page flyer. Happily, CorelDRAW provides specialized layouts that are just a few clicks away, so you don't have to sit at your workstation all day folding paper to try to figure out exactly where the fold lines are and where the text needs to be upside down. These timesavers are not on the Property bar—you need to open the Options dialog to select the one you need from the Layout drop-down box.

Choosing Specialized Layouts

On the Layout page of the Options dialog, you can choose from seven specialized layouts for your document, including Full Page, Book, Booklet, Tent Card, Tri-Fold Brochure, Side-Fold Card, and Top-Fold Card.

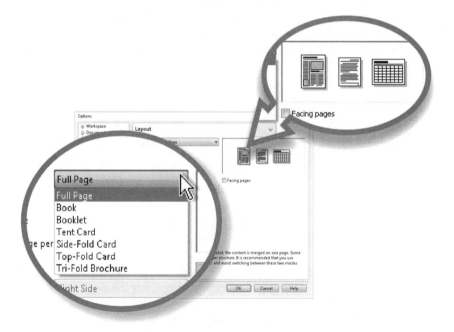

Choosing one of these layout styles instantly divides the current document page size into horizontal and vertical pages, based on the preview supplied in the dialog.

- **Full Page** This layout style is the default for all new documents, and it formats your document in single pages, like those shown in the previous illustration.

- **Book**   The Book layout format, shown right, divides your document page size into two equal vertical portions, and each portion is considered a separate page. When printed, each page is output as a separate page.

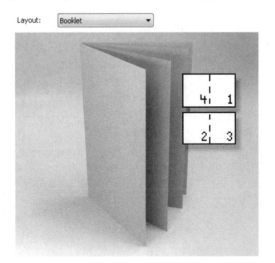

- **Booklet**   In a similar arrangement to the Book layout, the Booklet layout format divides your document page size into two equal vertical portions. Each portion is considered a separate page. When printed, however, pages are paired according to typical imposition formatting, where pages are matched according to their final position in the booklet layout. In a four-page booklet, this means page 1 is matched with page 4, and page 2 is matched with page 3, as shown here.

- **Tent Card**   The Tent Card layout format divides your document page size into two equal horizontal portions, although each portion is considered a separate page. Because tent card output is folded in the center, each of your document pages is printed in sequence and positioned to appear upright after folding.

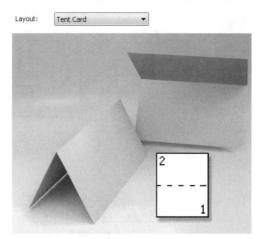

- **Side-Fold Card**   The Side-Fold layout format divides your document page size into four equal parts, vertically and horizontally. When printed, each document page is printed in sequence, and positioned and rotated to fit the final folded layout. Folding the printed page vertically and then horizontally results in the correct sequence and orientation.

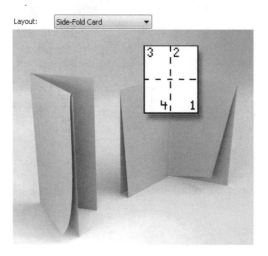

- **Top-Fold Card**   Like the Side-Fold layout, the Top-Fold layout format also divides your document page size into four equal parts, vertically and horizontally. When printed, each document page is printed in sequence, and positioned and rotated to fit the final folded layout.

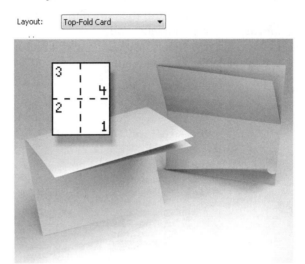

- **Tri-Fold Brochure**   Set your page orientation to Landscape using File | Print Setup, and you then have the ideal layout for travel brochures and restaurant tabletop stand-up menus. You can print both sides for a total of six panels, with live space measuring about 3½" wide and 8" high on the end panels.

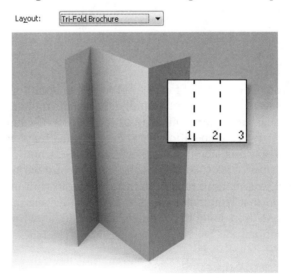

Using Preformatted Labels

CorelDRAW has a comprehensive collection of label formats for preformatted paper stock, from vendors such as Avery, Ace, and Leitz. To use most of these label formats, your document page should be set up for Portrait orientation. Once you've clicked the Labels entry under Document in the left column, the Size page turns into the Label page, offering access to the label collection. After you've selected a specific label format, the preview window shows its general layout and indicates the number of rows and columns available, as shown here.

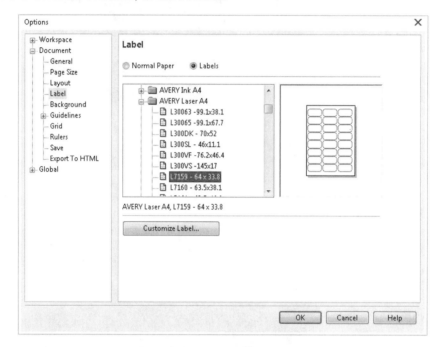

After you choose a label format and return to your document, each of your document pages will represent an individual label. You'll need to add the exact number of pages to accommodate all of your labels. If you don't see the exact manufacturer for your specific label type, you can create your own from scratch or base it on an existing label format (see Figure 4-3). Choose an existing label from the list of label types; click Customize Label; set the number of rows and columns; and set the label size, margins, and gutters according to your own label sheet. Once you've created the format, you may save your label by clicking the plus (+) button next to the Label Style drop-down list or delete a selected label from the list by clicking the minus (–) button.

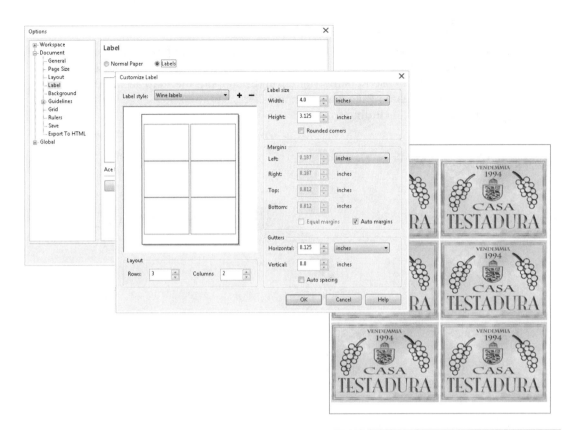

FIGURE 4-3   If you don't find the label you need, modify an existing label using the Customize Label options.

Naming Pages

Whenever a new document is created, CorelDRAW automatically creates the names, such as "Page 1," "Page 2," and so on. These default page names can be customized using several different methods.

When creating web page documents—where each document page is a separate web page—adding a unique name to the page creates a title for the exported page. When your document is printed, page names can also be printed in the margins, can indicate the contents of the page, and can provide other page-specific information.

Tip   Use the PAGE UP (previous page) or PAGE DOWN (following page) keyboard keys for fast navigation.

Using the Rename Page Command

Use the Rename Page command to assign a unique name to pages. Choose either Layout | Rename Page, or (more quickly) right-click the Page tab of your document window and then choose Rename Page from the pop-up menu to access the command. The Rename Page dialog, shown here, can rename a page with a name of up to 32 characters, including spaces.

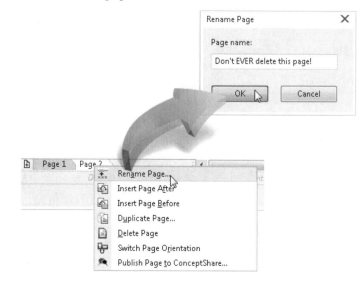

Save Details with Your File

Document Properties is a CorelDRAW feature that provides details about a document you save without having to type in the margins. To access Document Properties—to both enter and view information—right-click on a blank part of the page. In addition to typing yourself little reminders, Document Properties is also a convenient method for tagging designs you export to JPEG and other bitmap file formats. As you can see in Figure 4-4, the same information you type in Document Properties is available to Windows users when they right-click your image in a file folder and choose Details.

 Note Users who don't own CorelDRAW cannot access Document Properties info you've embedded in a native CDR file by right-clicking. The solution to this problem is to make them buy CorelDRAW!

Navigating a Multi-page Document

To go to different pages in a document, click a Page icon at the lower left of the document window. If the page isn't in view, you can scroll to locate it, or (for lengthy documents) open the Go To Page dialog, shown next, by clicking between the Next

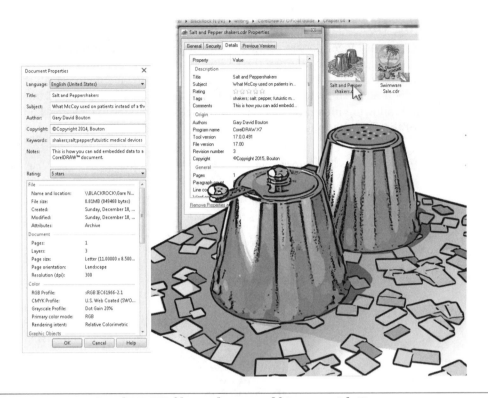

FIGURE 4-4   Save your CorelDRAW files and exported bitmaps with Document Properties metadata.

Page and Previous Page buttons at the lower left of your document window. It's the field that lists the pages, "2 of 4," for example; the field turns light blue when you click on it. You can move quickly to a specific page in your document with this feature.

Click here to open the Go To Page dialog.

Using the Object Manager

The Object Manager docker offers the advantage of mass-editing page names from within a single docker. To open the Object Manager, choose Windows | Dockers | Object Manager. Once the docker is open, you want to be able to see all the pages in your document, so first make sure the Layer Manager View (the third button at top— see the following illustration) is set to All Pages, Layers, And Objects. Then click the first of the three buttons at top, Show Object Properties.

The Object Manager is easily docked to the right edge of the UI, but you might accidently close it on occasion, and it's a pain to go through three menu levels to fetch it again. Try this instead: there is no key combo for Object Manager, so open Options (the shortcut is a button on the Standard bar and also the keyboard combo is CTRL+J), and then go to Workspace | Customization | Commands. In the Commands area, there's a drop-down you want to set to Object. Scroll about ¾ down the list until you find Object Manager. Click the Shortcut Keys tab and then insert your cursor in the New Shortcut Key field and then *hold* (do *not* type!) CTRL, keep holding CTRL, then hold ALT, then hold M. *As soon as the shortcut appears in the box, release* the keys, don't go to sleep on them—make a definitive and quick entry or multiple entries will go into the field. Click Assign, click OK, and you're done. Object Manager is easy to remember with the *M* you used in the shortcut, and in no time, you'll be able to call up the docker in its floating state, all ready to use.

In this view, all page and object names are displayed. To rename any page (or any object), click once directly on the page title to select the page you want to name or rename, click a second time to highlight the page name text, then type a name, and finally press ENTER. Page names appear in the Page tabs at the lower left of your document window, accompanied by a numeral indicating the page's order in your document, as shown in the following illustration.

Tip To see more (or less) of the pages of your document in the Page tab area of your document window, click-drag on the vertical divider between the Page tabs and the horizontal scroll bar.

Click-drag to expand/reduce the Page tab area.

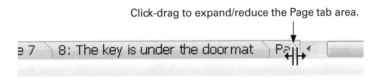

Page Commands

There are several ways to add and delete pages from a document; using menu commands, shortcuts while holding modifier keys, and certain page views are three methods. However, quick is best, and in this section, you'll see the most convenient way as well as methods that are easiest to remember. You can decide for yourself which best suits the way you work.

Inserting Pages and Setting Options

From the main menu, choose Layout | Insert Page to open the Insert Page dialog, which has a host of options for specifying your new page properties and where you would like to add the new page in relation to your existing pages. Look ahead to Figure 4-5 to get a better visual on the explanation to come.

Enter the number of pages needed in the Insert box, and choose to add them either Before or After your current page, or between specific pages in your document using the Page box. You are not limited to the orientation or size of your current page when you add pages, unlike the constraints imposed by traditional printed books and magazines!

Tip To quickly add a new page to the beginning or end of your document, go to the first or last page and click the plus (+) symbol on the left or right of the page buttons at the lower left of your document window. To add a page before or after your current page, right-click the Page tab to the right of these buttons, and choose either Insert Page Before or Insert Page After from the pop-up menu.

Deleting Pages

Deleting document pages can be done by choosing Layout | Delete Page from the main menu; you can delete one or more of the existing pages in your document. By default, the dialog opens to display the current page as the page in the Delete Page box, shown at right, but you may select any page before or after your current page if you choose. To delete an entire sequence of pages, click the Through To Page option, which enables you to delete all pages in a range between the page specified in the Delete Page box through to any page following your current page. Pay careful attention to the word "Inclusive" after the last page number: if you type, for example, 10 when you want to delete pages 1–9, well, oops—there goes your day unless you press CTRL + Z immediately! See the Insert Page and Delete Page dialogs in Figure 4-5.

Tip To delete the current page, right-click the page name on the Page tab, and then choose Delete Page from the popup menu. *There is no confirmation* when you delete a page, so make sure you've had your second cup of coffee in the morning before doing this.

Moving and Duplicating Pages

You're going to create such fantastic content in CorelDRAW that you might not even want to delete it. Instead you might want to move and/or copy pages. To move a page, use a click-drag action on the Page tab to drag it to a new position. To copy a page—*and all its contents*—thus creating a new page order, hold CTRL while click-dragging the Page tab, dragging the page to a new position. You can see this in the next illustration. CorelDRAW does not duplicate the name of a user-named page; you'd wind up with

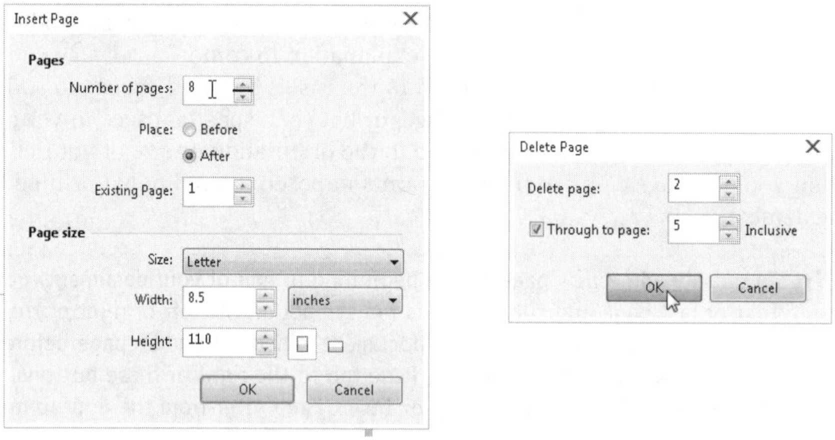

FIGURE 4-5 The Insert Page and Delete Page dialogs let you add and delete pages at various points in your document.

an organizational nightmare if it did, so it's a good practice to name a duplicate page after you've created the copy.

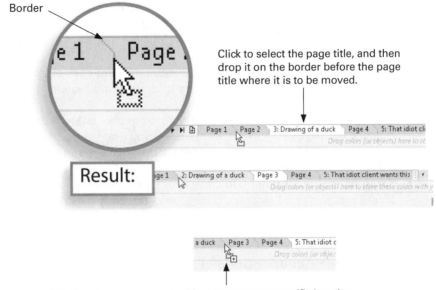

CTRL+click-drag to copy a page and its contents to a specific location.

Using the Page Sorter

Page Sorter is a view that provides you with a broad look at your document and all its pages. In this view, you can add, delete, move, or copy pages in a single view. You can also change the Paper/Type Size and the page orientation of all the pages or just selected pages. A CorelDRAW document can contain pages of different sizes, which can be very handy when you are designing matching business cards and letterhead or other similarly related materials. To open your document and all its pages in Page Sorter view, choose View | Page Sorter View. Page Sorter displays all pages in your document.

Tip Using Page Sorter, you can export either your entire document or only selected pages quickly. Click to select the page you want to export and choose File | Export, or click the Export button in the Standard bar to open the Export dialog. To export only specific pages, click the option to Export This Page Only, which, by default, is not selected. Exporting is *not* to be confused with *saving*; exporting pages is usually done to get your work into bitmap format, Adobe Illustrator file format, or Corel Media Exchange (CMX).

In Page Sorter view, a single click selects a page. Holding SHIFT while clicking pages enables you to select or deselect contiguous multiple pages. Holding CTRL while clicking enables you to select or deselect noncontiguous pages. The following actions enable you to apply page commands interactively to single or multiple page selections, as seen in Figure 4-6.

- **Move page(s)** To move a page and change its order in your document, click-drag the page to a new location. During dragging, a vertical I-beam appears, indicating the insertion point for the page or the first page of the selected sequence of pages.
- **Add page(s)** To add pages to your document, right-click any page and choose Insert Page Before or Insert Page After from the pop-up menu to insert a page relative to the selected page.
- **Copy page(s)** To copy pages—and their contents—hold CTRL while click-dragging the page to a specific location. During dragging, a vertical I-beam appears, indicating the insertion point for the page copy or the first page of the selected sequence of pages.
- **Name or rename a page** To add a new name or change an existing page name, click the page name below the page to select it; click a second time to highlight the page title, and enter a new name; then press ENTER. You can also rename a page by right-clicking a specific page and choosing Rename Page from the pop-up menu to highlight the page name for editing.
- **Change page size/orientation of all pages** In Page Sorter view, the Property bar displays typical page property options for applying standard or custom page sizes and changing the orientation between Landscape and Portrait.

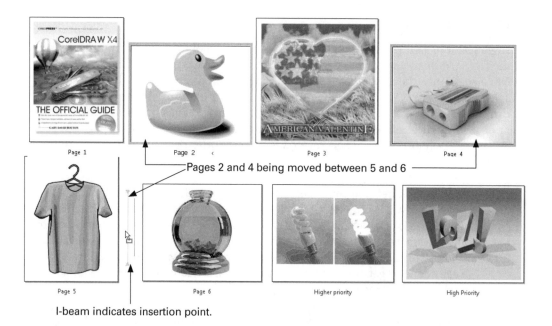

FIGURE 4-6 Page Sorter enables you to manage your document pages interactively while viewing all page properties.

If you want to change the orientation of *all* of the pages in the document, click the Apply Page Layout To All Pages button on the Property bar and *then* click either the Portrait or the Landscape button to change all pages to that orientation.

• **Change page size/orientation of selected pages** If you only want to change the orientation of some of the pages, click the Apply Page Layout To Current Page button. Then select the pages you want to change, and click the Portrait or Landscape button to change the page(s) to the desired orientation as shown.

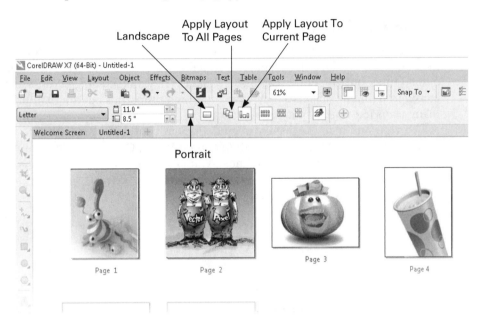

Changing the orientation in Page Sorter view not only changes the view, but also changes how the pages themselves are oriented in the document. As you can see above, the first and last pages have drawings that look better in Portrait view; you CTRL-click pages 1 and 4 in this example, click the Current Page button, and both the Page Sorter view and the pages themselves are reoriented. If you want to rethink this dynamic change, repeatedly pressing CTRL + Z (Edit | Undo) to restore your document.

Exiting Page Sorter view is easily done; click the Page Sorter View button. Any changes applied while in the Page Sorter are applied to your document.

Tip To exit the Page Sorter view and immediately go to a particular page in your document, double-click the page.

Working with Guidelines and Guide Layers

Now that you have a handle on page setup, multi-page particulars, and page dimensions, it's time to turn to perhaps the first thing you *put* on a page: a guide. Guides help you design with accuracy and give you a perspective on a composition so you save time second-guessing where items should be in relation to one another.

CorelDRAW's page guides, dynamic guides, and objects you put on guide layers don't print. Guides are just like the blue pencils some of us used on drafting tables before computer graphics. With today's digital tools and electronic guidelines, you have the precision only a computer application such as X7 can offer, plus the same speed and ease with guides as any object you draw on a page.

The following sections are the operator's manual for guides: how to use them and how to customize them.

Using Guidelines

Guidelines placed on your document page extend between the top, bottom, left, and right edges of the document window. Guidelines appear as vertical and horizontal dashed lines, but guidelines can also be *rotated*. In CorelDRAW, *guidelines* are considered unique objects—they have their own properties but are manipulated in many ways like objects you draw.

To view and hide the display of guidelines in your document window, right-click a blank area of the page and then choose View | Guidelines. By default, a new document doesn't have any guidelines—you need to create them, which is shown next. To have objects *snap* to the guidelines you create, choose Snap To | Guidelines on the Standard bar, as shown here.

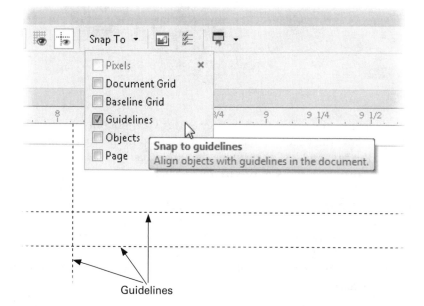
Guidelines

Manipulating Guidelines

The following steps guide you (pun notwithstanding) through the tasks you'll need most often when working with guides:

- Make sure the rulers are visible; they're where many of the guides live. With the Pick tool selected, and no objects selected, right-click and then choose View | Rulers. Then, using any Toolbox tool you like, click-drag beginning on a ruler, and release the mouse button anywhere in the workspace. Although dropping a guide on the page is most useful, you can certainly create a guide on the pasteboard area to measure and align objects not currently placed on the page.

- To move a place guide, you need to select the Pick tool. Then hover the cursor over the guide you'd like to move; when the cursor turns into a double-headed arrow, you're all set and all you need to do is to click and drag the guide.
- If you want to eliminate a guide, hover over it with the Pick tool until you see the double-headed arrow cursor (to indicate you've selected it), click the guide to confirm the guide is "in focus" in the interface, and then press DELETE or CTRL + X.
- If you need a guide that travels diagonally, you create a guide first. Next, click it to select it, and then click a second time, and you'll see a center and rotation handle. One of the neat things about rotating a guideline is that you can move its center point before dragging on the rotation handles to, for example, rotate a guide around the corner of a shape you have on the page. You move a slanted guideline exactly as you do a perfectly horizontal or vertical guide—you click-drag it to reposition it. In the illustration of the light bulb, where the design needs shafts of light emanating from a center point, that is *not* the default center of a guide that's put into slant mode. No problem; you change the center of rotation, and then drag a rotation handle clockwise or counterclockwise. See the illustration; it should shed some light on guidelines. Sorry.

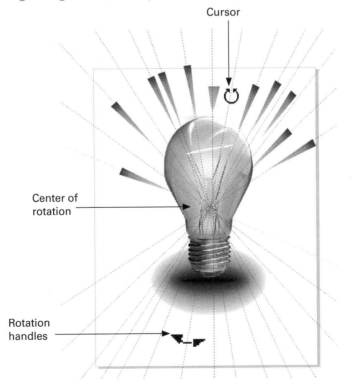

Cursor

Center of
rotation

Rotation
handles

> **Tip** Treat guides like any other object on the page. You can move and rotate several guides by SHIFT-selecting them. You can also drop a copy of a guide, like you do to duplicate objects.

Controlling Guideline Properties

If you place several guidelines at an exact spacing, you manage all guidelines via Tools | Options | Documents | Guideline. Separate subsections are here for controlling the vertical, horizontal, and slanted guidelines. You can also right-click either of the rulers, choose Guidelines Setup, and a Guidelines docker appears. Additionally, while a guideline is selected in a document, you can open the Guidelines docker by clicking the Guidelines button on the Property bar.

> **Tip** You can also double-click a guide in the drawing workspace using the Pick or the Shape tool to display the Guidelines docker.

The engineers at Corel have simplified the process and centralized your options for guidelines placement, all through the Guidelines docker. You first choose Horizontal or Vertical Guides from the drop-down list; the Y box becomes active; and you type in a value, then press Add. Remember, the Y measurement is, by default, the same as the rulers: values increase from bottom to top. You also have a lock option. You can change a guide's value on the page by typing in a new value after you've clicked the guide in the list and then click the Modify button. Additionally, at any time, your cursor can "step out of the box"; you can make a manual adjustment and that adjustment is reflected in the inches value on the Guidelines docker's list. Try it out; it's quite a cool new feature in X7.

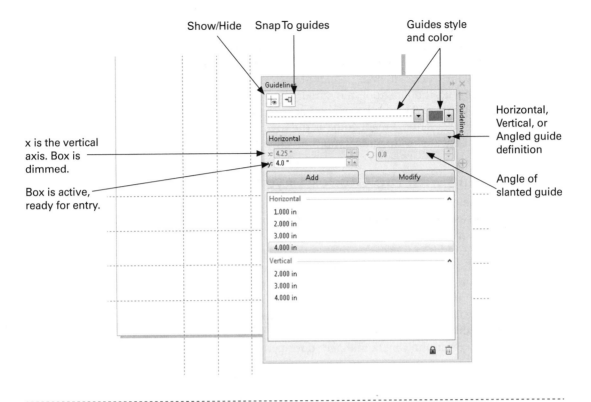

Show/Hide   SnapTo guides

Guides style and color

x is the vertical axis. Box is dimmed.

Horizontal, Vertical, or Angled guide definition

Box is active, ready for entry.

Angle of slanted guide

Tip Changing the color and style of guidelines is quite handy, for example, if you're designing a series of medium blue rectangles. You'd certainly want to choose a contrasting color for the guides!

Adding, Deleting, and Moving Guidelines

You can adjust guides using the Guidelines docker's Modify feature. The list below the main area on this docker contains the position of the existing guidelines on your document page. Here are steps to perform common tasks:

1. To create a new guideline, first choose Horizontal or Vertical from the button drop-down. Now, enter a value in the Horizontal, Vertical, or Angled num box according to the position where you want the new guideline to be created. Then click the Add button. A new guideline is created where you want it.
2. To move an existing guideline, click it in the list, type the new value in the x or y num box, and then click the Modify button. The selected guideline has moved, and on the list, you can see its new location is correctly entered.
3. To delete a specific guideline, select it in the list, and then click the Trashcan button at lower right on the docker. The selected guideline is gone from the page, and as you see the page from your current view, your document is immediately updated.
4. To remove all guidelines in the list, marquee-select all the entries on the list, and then click the Trashcan button.

Locking and Unlocking Guidelines

All guidelines are editable by default; you can move or delete them using the Pick tool. But occasionally a guide that moves accidentally is as welcome as a friend holding your ladder sneezing accidentally. You can lock guidelines simply by selecting the guide with the Pick tool; the cursor should turn into a double-headed arrow straddling the guide, and then you choose Lock Object from the pop-up menu when you right-click. Unlocking a guide is the inverse process of locking one. With the Pick tool, right-click over the guide and then choose Unlock Object from the context menu.

Working with the Guides Layer

Guides belong to a special layer—named Guides on the Object Manager—reserved just for these assistants. To view the layers in your document, open the Object Manager by choosing Window | Dockers | Object Manager. There are two Guides layers: if you click the Guides (All Pages) entry on the Object Manager list under Master Page, every guide you create will be featured on this page and on every page you create in the future in this document. On the other hand, every new page, including the first page, comes with its own Guides layer, and guides specific to a layer will not show on other pages. By default, all guidelines on the Guides layer are set as Visible, Non-Printable, and Editable. You can change any of these by clicking the symbols to the left of the Guides layer in the Object Manager docker, as shown here:

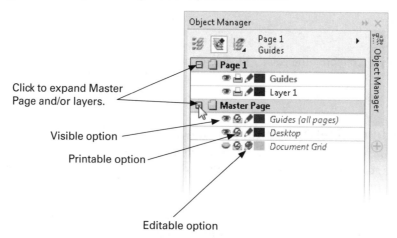

Click to expand Master Page and/or layers.

Visible option

Printable option

Editable option

To set all options for a layer at once—including the display color of objects on the Guides layer in the Object Manager docker, right-click the layer name, for example, the Guides layer, and then choose Properties from the pop-up menu. Doing this opens the Guides Properties dialog to reveal further options.

Make an Object a Guideline

You can make almost any drawing shape into a guideline. Going the other way around, you can also turn a guide into a drawing object, and moving any guideline to a drawing layer automatically makes it a printable object. You use the Object Manager docker to move objects between layers. Moving any object to the Guides layer makes a guideline, with all the same properties as a typical guideline, except it doesn't have to be a *line*—spirals and trapezoids make useful guides. After an object becomes a guideline, anything you draw in its proximity snaps to it, as long as the Snap To Guidelines option is active. Think of the artwork you can clean up and refine when you're tracing over the original with a drawing tool that snaps to the original.

To move an object to the Guides layer, follow these steps:

1. Create or select at least one drawing shape that you want to use as a guideline.
2. Open the Object Manager docker by choosing Windows | Dockers | Object Manager.
3. Expand the tree directories in the Object Manager docker to locate both the Guides layer on the Master Page and the shape you want to make into a guideline so both are in view.
4. In the Object Manager docker, click-and-drag your shape icon (not the shape on the page) from its current page and layer to on top of the Guides layer title on the Master Page. As you drag, your cursor changes to an arrow pointing at representations of layers, indicating the shape's current position as it is dragged. You then release the mouse button and the operation is a success. The following illustration also shows a "before and after" of a star shape when it's moved to the Master Page Guides layer. Unlike guidelines you drag from rulers, the look of a user-defined guide doesn't have the dashed lines; it's a solid line with no fill.

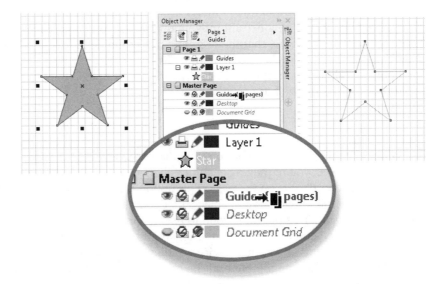

Generally, after moving a shape to the Guides layer, it's a good practice to lock the layer. A guide that moves when you don't intend it to is as useful as putting a stepladder on a pair of roller skates.

The New Alignment and Dynamic Guides Docker

Corel Corp. has made a dramatic change and improvement to Dynamic Guides, adding Alignment and Margins between aligned objects as an additional perk in X7. You'll find the Alignment and Dynamic Guides docker under Windows | Dockers. The docker actually has three areas of functions—Alignment, Guides, and Margins—and you can enable all of them (although your screen might become cluttered with data you don't need), or uncheck one or more of the functions to use only what you need. The following sections take you through the features and the buttons and also how and why you'd use these features, by way of example.

Alignment Properties on the Docker

Before moving forward, do *not* mistake the Alignment feature on this docker for the Align and Distribute docker (CTRL + SHIFT + A). The Alignment and Dynamic Guides docker is a manual feature—it reports to you and offers suggestions but it does *not* align things *for* you. It's a really sophisticated ruler, not a pocket calculator as analogies go.

Figure 4-7 shows the Alignment features in action. To begin at the beginning, you must check the box for Alignment Guides on the docker before you can do anything with the Alignment and Dynamic Guides docker.

Okay, the author is trying to renovate North Carolina Avenue by adding affordable housing (a $200 house fits most people's budgets). The goal here is to align the house at the bottom right of the *housing.cdr* file (open it and try this yourself). By simply using only the Alignment features—Margins and Dynamic Guides are disabled—you don't have to hold CTRL to constrain movement and all you do is drag up and a little to the left until you can see that the chimney hasn't moved horizontally at all as it's moved up vertically—the dashed light-blue alignment guide demonstrates this when your object is aligned, and the guide disappears if your object is moved off-alignment, or you release the mouse button.

Figure 4-7 also shows the option buttons in the Alignment Guides area, and they're new...and important, so a little time will be devoted to their function right here.

- **Object Centers**   Click this button if you want these temporary guides to appear when the object you're moving becomes aligned, vertically or horizontally, with the center of other objects on the page. This option is really good for quickly making an accurate distribution of several objects that you need to equally space apart.
- **Object Edges**   This option is good to use in combination with Object Centers, so you can see exactly where in relationship to another your desired object lays. In the case of aligning a square with another square, you will see two guides, one indicating top-edge alignment and the other indicating bottom alignment.
- **Individual Objects in a Group**   When you need to align grouped objects, it's not necessary to ungroup them and then use either the Alignment and Dynamic

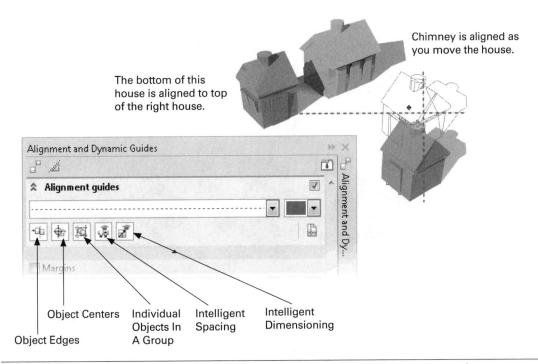

The bottom of this house is aligned to top of the right house.

Chimney is aligned as you move the house.

Object Edges

Object Centers

Individual Objects In A Group

Intelligent Spacing

Intelligent Dimensioning

FIGURE 4-7 The Alignment and Dynamic Guides docker helps you in precise design measurements and placements, and it disappears when you're done.

Guides or the Align and Distribute dockers. Nope: you use the Pick tool to CTRL + click the lucky object to be aligned to something else in the drawing, and then move it around until the temporary guides tell you that your object is now realigned, as shown in this illustration.

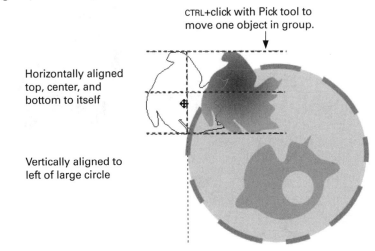

CTRL+click with Pick tool to move one object in group.

Horizontally aligned top, center, and bottom to itself

Vertically aligned to left of large circle

Group of three weird objects

- **Intelligent Spacing** This feature is sort of like an equidistant distribution function. In the illustration here, you can see that the diamond is selected and the goal is to place it an equal distance between the club and the spade. You'll see these unique divider guides when the object is in the desired position, and the Intelligent Spacing option even tells you onscreen what the distance is between objects, in this case the x-spacing (horizontal) is 0.115 inches. Naturally, if you have units set up to a value other than inches, Intelligent Spacing will report picas, centimeters, and so on.

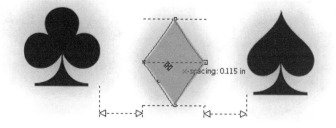

- **Intelligent Dimensioning** Ordinarily, you'd want to hold CTRL to proportionately scale a selected object larger or smaller, but this is unnecessary when you've selected an object and clicked the Intelligent Dimensioning button. Open *Brochures.cdr* and give this a try. The left pamphlet is smaller than the one at right; also they are identical copies of each other. Suppose your boss unreasonably demands (at a quarter to five) that the left pamphlet be the same size as the larger one at right. No problem; as shown in this illustration, you click the Intelligent Dimensioning button in the Alignment Guides area of the docker, and then with the Pick tool, you drag any corner control handle away from the center of the tiny pamphlet. Once the special blue guides appear for either the height or the width, you can release the mouse button and both objects are identical out to three decimal places.

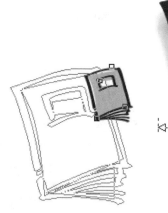

w: 2.288 in

Adding Margins to the Mix

Aligning things can be an exciting sport, especially on rainy days, but artistically, there are often times when you need to not only align objects, but also add space—a margin—between the objects. And this is where the Margins area of the Alignment and Dynamic Guides docker comes into play.

Like the alignment options, margins can be set to any color and be dashed or solid in appearance, so there's zero chance that what you're aligning will be the same color as these guides. The feature is simple to use and to explain: You should have Object Edges and/or Object Centers enabled in the Alignment Guides area first or the margins won't be awfully relevant to your aligning efforts. Enable Margins you want between the aligned objects. Pick one of the objects and then start dragging it toward the other object. See the following illustration; it can't hurt. You'll see by the alignment guides when the tops and or bottoms are aligned, but then you'll see markers, shown in the next illustration, that tell you when you've reached the desired margin between the objects.

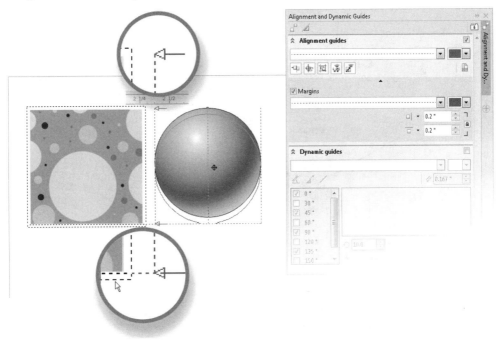

Dynamic Guides

Okay, this is the weird and wonderful part of the Alignment and Dynamic Guides docker. Dynamic Guides can actually help you draw technically accurate objects because your cursor snaps to the nearest of angles that you enable on the docker.

Figure 4-8 shows the bottom portion of the docker where all the Dynamic Guides features are located. Let's run them down, and along the way you'll see illustrations demonstrating some of the creative uses of Dynamic Guides.

- **Default angle increments**   You have a number of degrees, spread out in 15 degree increments, that you can use (or not use by unchecking their boxes) when the Dynamic Guides feature is enabled. This means that every time you draw a straight line (let's say you use the Polyline tool), end the path segment, and begin another, when you come to a 15 degree or 30 degree angle relative to the angle of the first path segment—CorelDRAW pops up onscreen info called a tool tip, informing you that you are beginning this next segment from the edge of the preceding one, the number of degrees off the original path's orientation, and how far you're traveling away from the end of the first path.

Note   Tooltips only pop up when the Show Tool Tips button in the Dynamic Guides area is active.

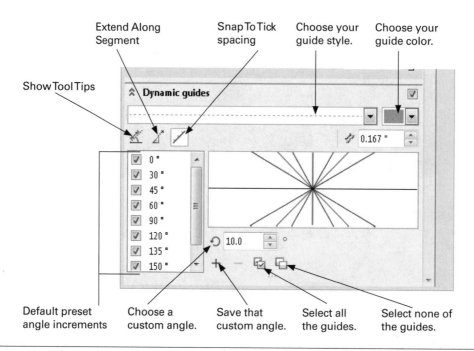

FIGURE 4-8   The revamped Dynamic Guides can be one of the most useful upgrades for CorelDRAW users who need architectural precision.

- **Extend Along Segment** Without needing to pull a guide out of a ruler and rotating it so it's perfectly aligned with a path you've drawn, you can activate Extend Along Segment, and the temporary Dynamic Guide will keep you on the straight and narrow, as shown here.

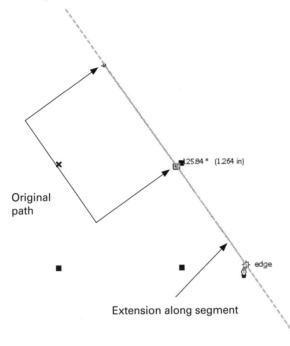

Original path

25.84 °   (1.264 in)

edge

Extension along segment

- **Snap To Tick spacing** There are invisible tick marks when you drag a path segment; you'll "feel" some resistance when you use your mouse to pull the onscreen cursor a specific distance. Tick spacing is found in the Alignment and Dynamic Guides docker. First, click the right-most icon, and then the num box becomes active for Tick Spacing tweaks. You enable and disable this feature by using this button on the docker.
- **Creating a custom angle and saving the custom angle** You might find that 15 degree increments aren't what you need—for example, to make a five-sided polygon (yeah, yeah, you could use the Polygon tool, but play with me here), you'd need an angle of 72 degrees, not to be found on the preset list. So you type in this value, click the + button to add it to the list, and off you go.

If you have any doubt that Dynamic Guides can make quick work of shapes that are exceptionally complicated, check out this next figure. It was created entirely using Dynamic Guides at default preset values and paying attention to how long each segment was using the tooltips.

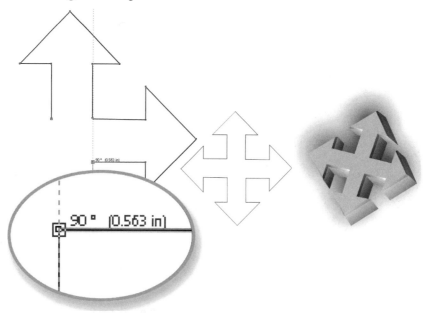

Page definition, sorting pages, margins, bleeds, and enough other options have been discussed in this chapter to fill a book! Now that you know how to set up a page, how about filling it with some artwork? Chapter 5 takes you through how to create and modify basic shapes and how to transform them—scale, rotate, move, all that good stuff. Page setup meets page content right around the corner of the next page.

5 Creating Basic Shapes and Applying Transformations

You have to begin *somewhere* with the DRAW part of CorelDRAW—and *this* is the chapter. The creative process within this program usually follows: you build objects that you then customize and refine through fancy fills and elegant outlines covered in later chapters. Therefore, you need to know the steps to create simple geometric shapes and the basic editing moves to create exactly the shape you want to fill and stroke.

 Note Download and extract all the files from the Chapter05.zip archive to follow the tutorials in this chapter.

Using the Rectangle Tool and Property Bar

The Rectangle tool is simple enough to use, but it doesn't just create a four-sided, right-angle polygon—it creates a rectangle that has *special properties* in CorelDRAW. You'll find the Rectangle tool in the Toolbox; you can quickly select it by pressing the F6 shortcut key.

 Note Rectangles drawn with the Smart Drawing tool have special editing properties, too. See Chapter 8.

The Rectangle tool gives you the option to apply corner "roundness" based on a percentage value. Roundness can be set either manually by dragging a corner with the Shape tool—the most common technique experienced Corellians use—or by using the Property bar's Corner Roundness option, which is available when a rectangle is selected. By default, you round all four corners equally and together. However, if you unlock the Edit Corners Together toggle button, you can manually enter different values for each of the four corners, as discussed in the following section. There are several more features for changing the shape of a rectangle object that are reversible (no destructive changes are made) on the Property bar. Figure 5-1 shows the features and some of the results you can achieve with this seemingly basic shape-creation tool.

Tip You can also choose the Rectangle tool while any shape creation tool is selected (the Ellipse tool, for example) by right-clicking a blank space on the document page and choosing Create Object | Rectangle from the pop-up menu.

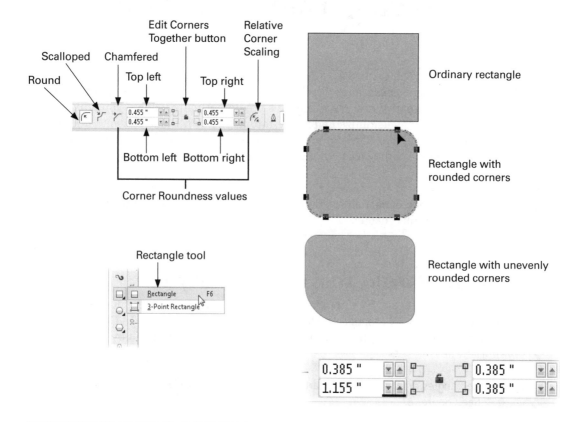

FIGURE 5-1 The Rectangle tool creates shapes that can be modified—and then returned to their original state at any time.

Drawing a Rectangle

To create a rectangle, choose the Rectangle tool from the Toolbox, and click-diagonal-drag in any direction to define its corner positions, as shown here. The act of click-dragging begins by defining the first two legs; as you drag, the corner positions can be redefined, depending on where your cursor is on the page; and then before you release the mouse button, you've defined the position for the remaining rectangle corners and you've built the remaining sides.

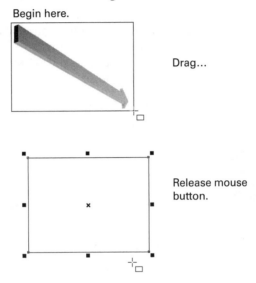

Begin here.

Drag...

Release mouse button.

While the Rectangle tool is selected, notice that the cursor is a crosshair with a small rectangle shape at its lower right. As you click-drag using the cursor, you'll also notice that the Status bar and Property bar show the coordinates, width, and height properties of your new object shape.

Setting Rectangle Corner Properties

Corner Roundness is one of three different effects you can apply and dynamically edit when you're into rectangles. Corner Roundness, as well as the Scallop and Chamfer corner styles, can be applied to a rectangle from a value of 0 to about one-half the overall length of one of its sides. If you think about this one, a 2" rectangle *can't* have more than a 1" rounded corner on each side! The Corner Roundness amount can be changed anytime while the shape remains a native rectangle, that is, as long as it has not been converted to curves. By typing **0** into any of the size boxes while the rectangle is selected, you remove the corner style. Corner Roundness, Scallop, and Chamfer can be set uniformly for all corners (the default) or independently when the Edit Corners Together lock option is in the unlocked state.

Tip Double-clicking the Rectangle Tool button in the Toolbox instantly creates a rectangle border around your current document page.

While a rectangle is selected, use any of the following operations to change corner properties according to your needs:

- Click the type of corner style you want on the Property bar, and then either type in the size for the corner values or drag the elevator buttons up or down to adjust the size of the corners.
- Set your rectangle's corners manually using the Shape tool, by first unlocking the Edit Corners Together toggle button, and then CTRL + dragging any corner control point away from its corner (toward a side that makes up the rectangle). Enabling Edit Corners Together causes all corners to be rounded or scalloped an equal amount by dragging on any of the control points.
- Use the Object Properties docker by pressing ALT + ENTER, clicking the Rectangle tab, and then editing any property you so choose.

Figure 5-2 shows rectangles with different types of corners; this is an ideal feature for building interesting signs, borders, and frames for documents.

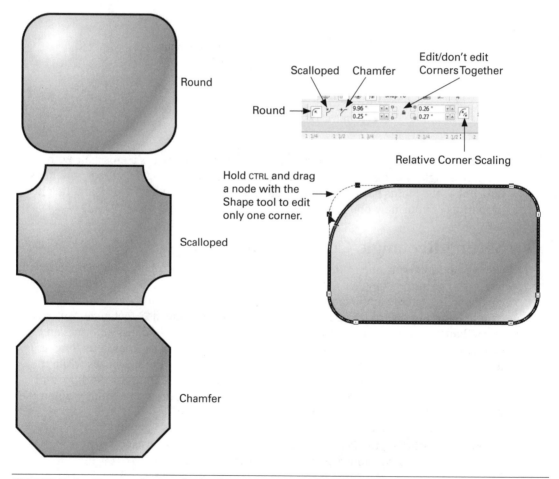

FIGURE 5-2 Rectangles can have almost any type of corner you can imagine.

Creating 3-Point Rectangles

If you want to create a rectangle and rotate all in one fell swoop, you can use the *3-Point Rectangle tool.* You'll find it grouped with the Rectangle tool in the Toolbox.

Using this tool, you can draw new rectangles at precise angles, as shown in Figure 5-3. The rectangle you create is a native rectangle shape, so you can round its corners and manipulate it as you would any other shape.

To create a rectangle using the 3-Point Rectangle tool, you click-drag—clicking sets the first point of the rectangle and the subsequent distance you drag determines both the angle and length of the rectangle. As soon as you release the mouse button, you move your cursor (*without* clicking—this is called *hovering*) to determine the height of the rectangle. A final click seals the deal and you now have a rectangle whose corners you can round and perform other operations on.

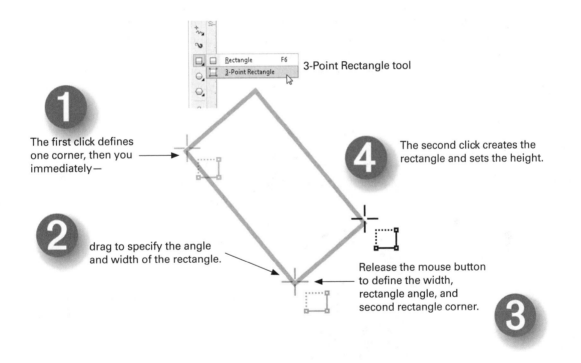

FIGURE 5-3   Draw new rectangles at precise angles with the 3-Point Rectangle tool.

Using the Ellipse Tool and Property Bar

Ellipses are a staple of commercial design work. Essentially an ellipse is a circular shape that is not perfect. The Ellipse tool can be used to draw both circles and ellipses, but in CorelDRAW, an ellipse shape has additional, special properties, just like a rectangle can be a round-cornered rectangle. Ellipse shapes can be edited to create dramatically new shapes while retaining their elliptical properties. In contrast, a shape you might draw that *looks* like an oval, using the Bezier tool, for example, will have no special properties and always remains an oval.

Ellipses are easy enough to draw with the Ellipse tool and can be set in several different states: as an oval or circular closed-path, pie wedge, or arc. Pie wedges are the portions of an ellipse—like a single slice of a pie or, conversely, a whole pie with a slice removed. Arc shapes are open paths, exactly like pie wedges, except the two straight line segments are missing.

To create an ellipse, choose the Ellipse tool, shown in Figure 5-4, from the Toolbox or press F7, followed by a click-drag in any direction.

While the Ellipse tool is selected, the Property bar shows ellipse-specific options, shown in Figure 15-4, that enable you to control the state of your new ellipse shape before or after it has been created. Choose Ellipse, Pie, or Arc. A complement is reserved for pie and arc shapes: for example, if you specify a 15-degree pie wedge,

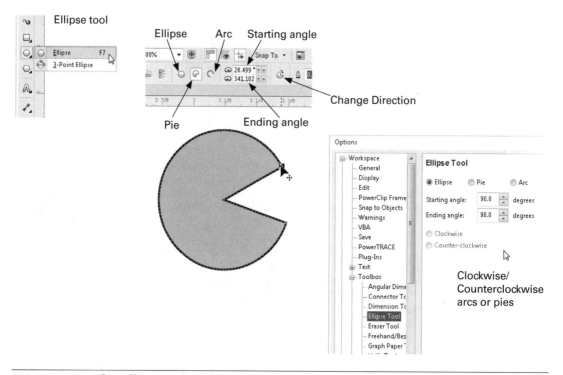

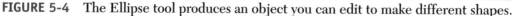

FIGURE 5-4 The Ellipse tool produces an object you can edit to make different shapes.

clicking the Change Direction icon changes the shape to a 345-degree wedge. Additionally, if you want a Pie or Arc to travel in a different path direction, double-click the Ellipse Tool icon on the Toolbox, which takes you to Options, where you can choose clockwise or counterclockwise path directions. Figure 5-4 shows your options and the features on the Property bar when the Ellipse tool is selected.

Tip You can also choose the Ellipse tool while any tool is selected by right-clicking in an empty space on your document page and choosing Create Object | Ellipse from the pop-up menu.

Drawing an Ellipse

Let's walk before running; before creating pie and arc shapes, let's create circles and ovals. Start with these brief steps.

Tutorial   # Round One with the Ellipse Tool

1. Choose the Ellipse tool (F7) and use a click-diagonal-drag action in any direction. As you drag, an outline preview of the shape appears. An ellipse shape has two overlapping control nodes (so onscreen it looks like only one node); if you drag down and left or right, the nodes will be located at 12 o'clock. Conversely, if you drag up and left or right, the control nodes will be located at 6 o'clock.
2. Release the mouse button to complete your ellipse shape creation.

Controlling Ellipse States

All ellipses have two control points (*nodes*—a start and an end) that overlap each other and are visible when the ellipse is selected. When these control points are separated, they create either a pie or an arc state, and each control point determines either the *starting* or *ending angle* of the pie or arc.

You can separate these control points either by using Property bar options or by dragging the points using the Shape tool. Dragging *inside* the ellipse's shape creates the Ellipse Pie state. Dragging *outside* the shape creates the Ellipse Arc state, as shown here.

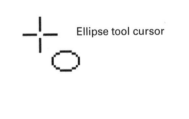

Ellipse tool cursor

Dragging inside creates a pie shape.

Dragging outside creates an arc shape.

Tip Even though pies and arcs appear as if sections or path parts are missing, the portions are still there. They're just hidden from view.

To draw a new pie or arc without drawing an oval-shaped ellipse first, click either the Pie or Arc button on the Property bar before you start drawing. You can also switch any selected ellipse between these states using these buttons. By default, all pies and arcs are applied with a default starting angle of 0 degrees and a default ending angle of 270 degrees. Starting and ending angles are based on degrees of rotation from –360 to 360 degrees; this is counterclockwise in orientation.

Creating 3-Point Ellipses

The *3-Point Ellipse tool* is the key for creating ellipses while setting a rotation angle (perfect circles show no possible rotation angle; we're talking *ovals* here). You'll find it grouped with the Ellipse tool in the Toolbox, as shown in Figure 5-5. This tool's operation is very much like the 3-Point Rectangle tool.

You can create ellipses at precise angles without needing to create and then rotate an existing one, as shown in Figure 5-5. The shape you create is still an ellipse with all associated properties, such as optional pie and arc states.

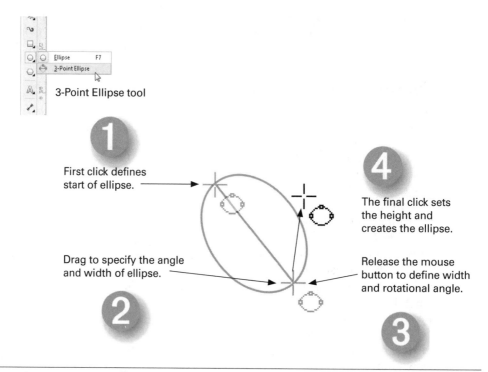

1 First click defines start of ellipse.

2 Drag to specify the angle and width of ellipse.

3

4 The final click sets the height and creates the ellipse.

Release the mouse button to define width and rotational angle.

3-Point Ellipse tool

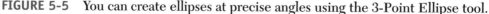

FIGURE 5-5 You can create ellipses at precise angles using the 3-Point Ellipse tool.

To create an ellipse using the 3-Point Ellipse tool, choose the 3-Point Ellipse tool, click to set the beginning point of the ellipse, and then drag to specify its width and rotational angle. Release the cursor and then position your cursor where you want the maximum height of the oval defined. Click, and your ellipse is complete.

Using Polygons and the Property Bar

The *Polygon tool* (the shortcut is Y) is unique to the category of vector drawing software; competing applications offer a polygon tool, but CorelDRAW's Polygon tool produces shapes *that can be edited*—making dynamic changes, just like CorelDRAW rectangles and ellipses. The shapes you create with the Polygon tool can have as few as 3 or as many as 500 points and sides; by default, all polygon sides are straight paths. You'll find the Polygon tool, together with the Star, Complex Star, and other group tools, in the Toolbox. While the Polygon tool is selected, the Property bar offers the number of sides for the polygon you'll draw.

Drawing and Editing Polygons

Many of the tricks to creating symmetrical, complex shapes with the Polygon tool lie in the *editing* of them. Read the Shape tool section in Chapter 7 before getting too involved with the Polygon tool because you really need to know how to use the Shape tool in combination with the Property Bar to make the most of a polygon shape.

To create a default polygon, you use the same click-diagonal-drag technique as you use with the Rectangle and Ellipse tools. This produces a symmetrical shape made up of straight paths. Because you'll often want a shape more elegant than something that looks like a snack food, it helps to begin a polygon shape by holding SHIFT and CTRL while dragging: doing this produces a perfectly symmetrical (not distorted) polygon, beginning at your initial click point and traveling outward. Therefore, you have the shape positioned exactly where you want it and can begin redefining the shape.

Here, you can see the Polygon tool cursor and a symmetrical default polygon. Because the Polygon tool can be used to make star-shaped polygons, there are nodes that govern the outer points of the star, and then there are "inner" nodes in between the points that control the curves between points. When you edit a polygon, the position of these points can be reversed. These nodes have no control handles because they connect straight path segments. However, in the following tutorial, you'll get a jump start on advanced shape creation and really get down in very few steps to creating a dynamite polygon shape through editing.

Polygon tool

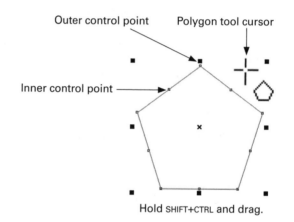

Outer control point   Polygon tool cursor

Inner control point

Hold SHIFT+CTRL and drag.

Here is a brief tour of how to create and then edit a polygon to design any symmetric object you can imagine—and a few unimaginable ones.

Tutorial   Reshaping a Polygon

1. Choose the Polygon tool from the Toolbox. Before you do anything else, set the number of sides to **12** on the Property bar.
2. Hold CTRL to constrain the shape to a symmetrical one, and then click-diagonal-drag on the page. Release the mouse button after you have a polygon that's about 3" wide.
3. To better see what you're doing, left-click over the color palette with the polygon selected to fill it. By default, polygons are created with a small stroke width and no fill.
4. Choose the Shape tool from the Toolbox. Click any of the control points on the polygon to select it, but don't drag yet. Hold CTRL and then drag outward, to constrain the movement of the cursor so the polygon doesn't take on a lopsided appearance (although you can create interesting polygons by dragging in any way without holding CTRL). You should have a star shape now, as shown here.

5. Notice that on the Property bar you now have a lot of icons that control how line segments pass through nodes and whether the segments are straight or curved. Click any line segment that makes up the polygon; your cursor should have a wiggly line at lower right, as shown here, meaning that you've clicked a line. Then click the Convert To Curve button on the Property bar, converting not only the line, but also all the lines in the polygon that are symmetrical to the chosen line, to a curve. Or perhaps more simply, use the same command by right-clicking a point and using the pop-up contextual menu.

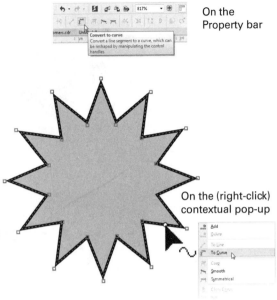

On the Property bar

On the (right-click) contextual pop-up

6. You'll now see two control handles. They lay exactly on the segment that appears to be a line but now has curve possibilities. First, click an inner or outer original node along the polygon path, as shown next. This reveals the handles. It is now possible to create a curve by dragging on the segment *between* the control handles. Doing this, as you can see here, creates a very interesting and complex symmetrical shape, and you can now see the control lines and handles for the curve segment much more easily and can manipulate the control handles to further embellish your creation.

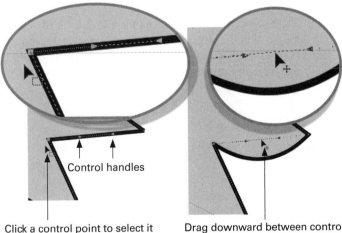

Control handles

Click a control point to select it and reveal the control handles.

Drag downward between control handles to curve the segment.

FIGURE 5-6 Here are shapes you can create using a polygon object and the Shape tool.

Figure 5-6 shows but a few creative examples of polygon editing: from gears to those vinyl flowers you put over shower stall cracks; you have immense design power at your disposal with the Polygon tool.

> **Tip** After editing a polygon, you can change the number of sides. For example, you've created a 12-petal flower polygon, and then decide you want only 8 petals. You select the edited shape with the Pick tool and then decrease the number of sides using the elevator buttons to the right of the values box on the Property bar.

Stars and Complex Stars

You have variations on polygons at the ready in CorelDRAW, in the same group as the Polygon tool. The Star tool can be used to create pointy polygons with anywhere from 3 to 500 points. The Complex Star tool creates a number of combined polygons to make a star shape; you can create interesting symmetrical shapes by filling a complex star—the result contains both filled and vacant polygon areas as the component paths intersect one another.

Working with the Star Tool

The Star tool produces objects by using the click-diagonal-drag mouse technique; CTRL-SHIFT-dragging creates symmetrical stars beginning at the initial click point traveling outward.

On the Property bar, when the Star tool is selected, you'll see options for the number of points for the star and the "pointiness" (*sharpness*) of the resulting object—how severe the indents are between points. At a setting of 1, the star object is not at all pointy—you'll see that it looks quite like a Polygon tool object. So, if you can make a star using the Polygon tool, why would you ever choose the Star tool? The answer is because when using the Star tool the geometric structure of a star shape is always perfectly symmetrical. Although you can use the Shape tool to tune the sharpness of a Star tool object's points manually, the angle between points is always consistent. In the illustration here, you can see a Star tool object compared with a Polygon tool object that has been clumsily edited. You can't perform this goof with the Star tool; its interior angles are always mirrored and symmetrical.

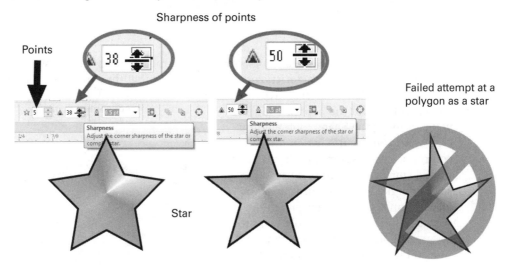

Using the Complex Star Tool

Think of the kaleidoscope images you enjoyed as a child (or still do) when you choose the Complex Star tool—because with only an edit or two using the Shape tool, you can create mesmerizing symmetrical shapes, unlike with any other tool in CorelDRAW.

To use the tool, you know the drill if you've read this far! You click-diagonal-drag to create a shape; by default, the complex star has 9 points of a value of 2 on a 1- to 3-point sharpness scale (available to define on the Property bar, as shown in the following illustration).

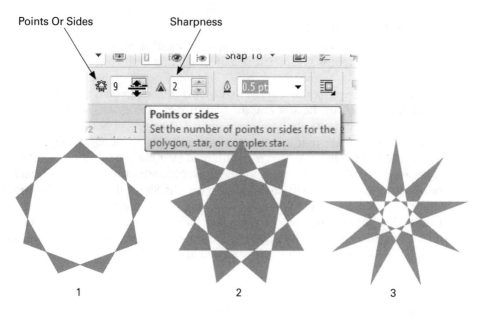

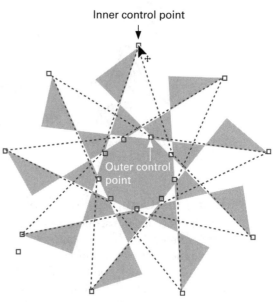

CTRL, SHIFT, and CTRL + SHIFT perform the same modifiers as they do with other shapes. One unique characteristic of complex stars is that they have two control points: one for the inner, negative space, and one for the points. When you edit using the Shape tool, holding CTRL constrains your edits on the control points to symmetry, but if you want a spiral treatment of a complex star, don't hold CTRL and drag any way you like on both the inner and outer control points. You'll probably want to assign a fill to a complex star as your first edit because unfilled complex stars aren't as visually interesting. The illustration here shows what you can create by moving the inner control point to outside the outer control point. Imagine the snowflake patterns you can build; and like snowflakes, no two complex stars are alike.

Next, you can see other examples of simply playing with the Shape tool on a complex star object. Also try assigning a wide white outline property to a complex star as a property to create still more variations.

Using the Spiral Tool

With the Spiral tool (press A as the keyboard shortcut), you can create circular-shaped paths that would be tedious, if not impossible, to create manually. Spiral objects are composed of a single open path that curves in a clockwise or counterclockwise direction. They can also be designed to expand in even segment distances or in *increasing* distances as the spiral path segments travel away from its center (called a *logarithmic* function). You find the tool in the Toolbox, grouped with the Polygon and Basic Shapes tools.

The Spiral tool options share space on the Property bar (shown next) with options for the Graph Paper tool and include Spiral Revolutions, Symmetrical, and Logarithmic Spiral modes, and a Spiral Expansion Factor slider.

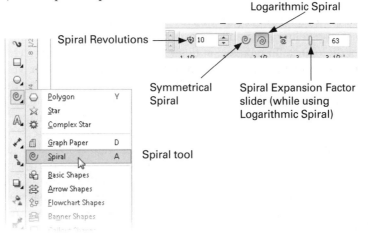

The objects you can create can have between 1 and 100 revolutions, each of which is equal to one complete rotation around its center point. The direction of the revolutions is set according to the click-diagonal-drag action you take when creating the initial shape, as shown here...

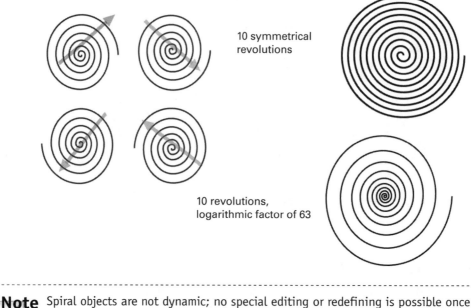

10 symmetrical revolutions

10 revolutions, logarithmic factor of 63

Note Spiral objects are not dynamic; no special editing or redefining is possible once the spiral has been created. This means you must set their properties before they are created. Other than your using the Pick or Shape tool to edit their size or shape, spiral objects are a "done deal."

By default, all new spiral objects are set to Symmetrical. If you choose Logarithmic, the Spiral Expansion Factor slider becomes available. Here's how the options affect the spiral objects you can create:

- **Symmetrical vs. Logarithmic**   A symmetrical spiral object appears with its spiral revolutions evenly spaced from the center origin to the outer dimensions of the object. To increase or decrease the rate at which the curves in your spiral become smaller or larger as they reach the object's center, you may want to use the Logarithmic method. The term *logarithmic* refers to the acceleration (or deceleration) of the spiral revolutions. To choose this option, click the Logarithmic Spiral button on the Property bar before drawing your shape.
- **Logarithmic Expansion option**   While the Logarithmic Spiral tool is selected, the Spiral Expansion slider is available—as well as a value field you can type into—and you can set this rate based on a percentage of the object's dimensions. Logarithmic Expansion may be set from 1 to 100 percent. A Logarithmic Expansion setting of 1 results in a symmetrical spiral setting, whereas a setting of 100 causes dramatic expansion. If you need a shape that is reminiscent of a nautilus, increase the Logarithmic Expansion to 50 or so.

Using the Graph Paper Tool

The Graph Paper tool (the shortcut is D) is used to create a grid containing hundreds (even thousands) of rectangles—an emulation of graph paper. Graph paper is invaluable in chart-making as well as artistic uses. You'll find the Graph Paper tool, shown here, grouped with the Polygon and Spiral tools. This tool's options on the Property bar let you set the number of rows and columns for your new graph paper object. As with the Spiral tool, you must set options *before* drawing your graph paper object; a graph paper object cannot be edited dynamically.

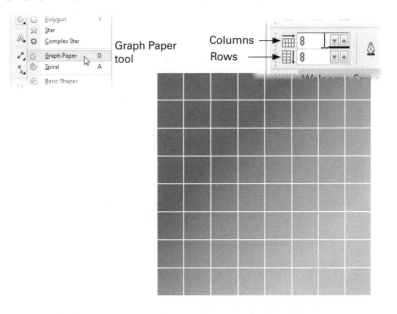

Tip   The rectangles in a Graph Paper group are, in fact, *native rectangles*; you can ungroup the rectangles (CTRL+U) and then make scallop and rounded rectangles on each and every one of the graph paper component objects.

Let's explore one of the many creative ways to create and use the group of rectangles that the Graph Paper tool builds for you. This next assignment uses the Add Perspective Effect to make a dimensional chessboard beneath a drawing of chess pieces, and one or two tricky editing techniques, but you're guided step by step all the way. Watch how you can dramatically improve the look of a composition just by using the Graph Paper tool and some minor editing.

Tutorial   Power-Drawing a Grid with Graph Paper

1. Open *Chess set.cdr*. A drawing has been created for you, and your assignment is to put a chess board behind the drawing. Choose Window | Dockers | Object Manager if it's not docked and visible now. The chess pieces are on a locked

layer and the layer titled "Make chess board here" should be the current editing layer. Click this layer title on the Object Manager list if it isn't chosen.

2. Select the Graph Paper tool from the Toolbox or press D to select it.

3. Using Property bar options, set the number of rows and columns to **8** for your new graph paper object.

4. Using a click-diagonal-drag action, hold CTRL and drag to create the new object. Release the mouse button when the graph paper is about 7" high. See the following illustration.

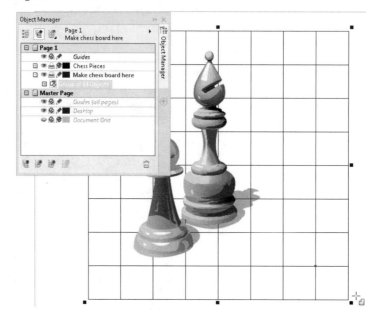

5. Look at the Status bar; it tells you that a group of 64 objects is selected. All the graph paper objects can take on a new fill and outline color in one fell swoop: click a medium gray color swatch on the color palette, and then right-click white to make the outlines white.

6. The white grouting that the outlines represent on this chessboard are a little too thin. No problem: with the grouped objects selected, set the outline width to **2** points now. This is a feature new to version X7: the ability to set the outline width of grouped objects directly from the Property bar.

7. Choose Effects | Add Perspective. You'll see a red dashed outline with four control points surround the group, but it's not editing time yet to apply a perspective.

8. Select the Pick tool, and then click the selected graph paper object to reveal the rotate and skew handles. While holding CTRL to constrain rotation, rotate the grouped rectangles by 45 degrees. By default, CorelDRAW constrains rotation to 15° increments; therefore, two points of resistance as you CTRL + drag does the trick.

9. Choose the Shape tool (F10); the grouped shapes again feature the perspective control points.

10. Choose the top control point and then drag it down until you have a chessboard in perspective. You will know when you've dragged enough—the chess pieces drawing will visually fit right into place.

Hold CTRL and rotate 45 degrees.   Use the Shape tool to drag the top node down.

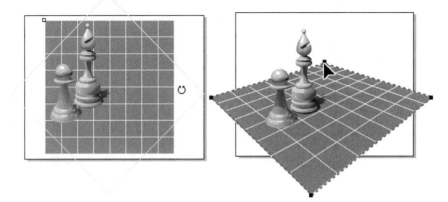

11. Optionally, with the grouped chessboard in its final perspective aspect, press CTRL + U (Object | Group | Ungroup Objects). Fill every other rectangle with a lighter color; doing this enhances the look of the chessboard, the overall illustration, and also lets the cast shadows from the chess pieces become more apparent.

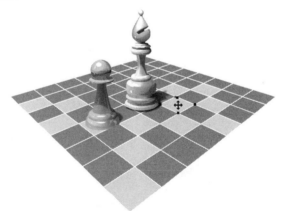

 Tip Holding CTRL while you drag constrains the shape of the graph paper object, but not the cells in the graph. Therefore, you could, for example, create a five-row, two-column graph whose overall proportions are square, but the cells within the graph paper object would be distorted to rectangles.

Converting Shapes to Curves

Any of the shapes discussed in this chapter can be converted to curves by using the Object | Convert To Curves command (CTRL+Q). Using this command removes any dynamic-editing properties. For example, an ellipse shape many be converted to a pie or arc (and vice versa); but after it is converted to curves, you'll no longer have the option of turning the object into a pie wedge. The same applies to rectangles, polygons, and so on. With the exception of the Undo command, once an object is converted to curves, there is no way to return the object to its dynamically editable state.

Using the Convert Outline To Object Command

Many of the shapes covered in this chapter, the spiral in particular, are shapes that have outline properties but no fill. So what do you do, for example, if you want a gradient-filled spiral? The Object | Convert Outline To Object command converts any shape's outline properties to a closed path. To apply the command to a selected object, choose Object | Convert Outline To Object, or use the shortcut: CTRL + SHIFT + Q. Once the outline is converted, the resulting closed path looks exactly like the shape of the original, except it can be filled because it's not an outline, but instead a closed path object whose shape is based on an outline.

When an outline is converted to an object, CorelDRAW performs a quick calculation of the Outline Pen width applied to the object and creates a new object based on this value. When applying this command to objects that include a fill of any type, a new compound-path object is created based on the outline width. If the object includes a fill of any type, the fill is created as a new and separate object applied with an outline width and color of None. When you're converting open paths, only the path itself is created as a single outline object of the path according to the Outline Pen width applied. Figure 5-7 shows a spiral shape with a thick black Outline Pen width that is converted to outline using the command.

Original with 16-point outline applied   New fountain-filled object based on the outline

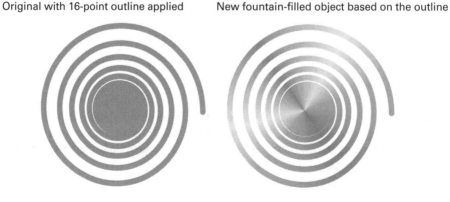

FIGURE 5-7 When an object is converted to an outline, CorelDRAW performs calculations that create a new object.

Things are certainly shaping up now, aren't they? You've learned how to create basic shapes, how to edit them to create scores of original and visually interesting items. This isn't the half of it. In Chapter 6, you'll learn to move, rotate, scale, and put your new objects anywhere you like on the page, on a new layer, in a group, and on a bus to Cleveland. Okay, that might be stretching a joke as well as the length of the book. Arranging and organizing objects is your next destination, and you'll find it to be a moving experience.

6 Arranging and Organizing Objects

When you create or import an object, it's might not be *exactly* where you want it on the page. Or the position might be fine, but the object's a little too large. It might also be rotated by a few unwanted degrees, or it's part of a group or on the wrong layer—you get the picture. This chapter covers the techniques to use in CorelDRAW to *transform* objects—both the manual approach and pinpoint precise numerical entry approach are covered. You'll soon have the skills to compose elements on a page the way you want them, and then you can stop cursing at the cursor.

> **Note** Download and extract all the files from the Chapter06.zip archive to follow the tutorials in this chapter.

Basic Object Selection

The Pick tool—by default, the tool at the top of the Toolbox—can move, scale, or create other transformations when you click an object to select it and then drag to move the selection, for example. Use the SHIFT key as the modifier when you're selecting things on a page; you *add* to your existing selection by SHIFT + clicking other objects. If you've selected an object unintentionally, SHIFT + click on the object (that's already selected) to deselect it.

With one or more items selected, you'll notice that information about the selected shapes is displayed on the Status bar. The other workspace area to watch is the Property bar, which shows the position and size of the selection and offers options relevant to the tool being used, such as the number of degrees to rotate the selected object(s). Also, if you press ALT + ENTER when something is selected, the Object

Properties docker provides you with not only details about the object, but also the opportunity to quickly *change* many of the object's properties.

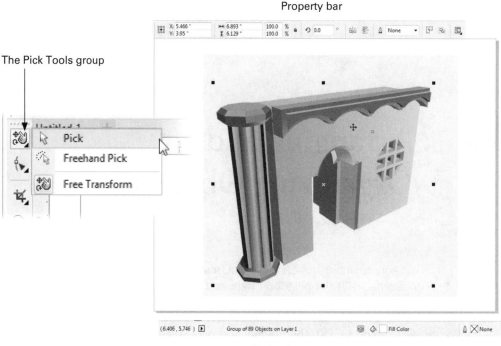

Property bar

The Pick Tools group

Status bar

Pick Tool Selections

The Pick tool can be used for at least two things, the most important of which are to choose an object or several objects and to create a *change* in the selected object(s) by moving it and adjusting its selection handles.

Clicking an object once selects it. While an object is selected, *selection handles* appear—the eight black markers surrounding the object, as shown in Figure 6-1. Additionally, depending on the type and properties of an object, you'll see *nodes* at various areas around the object, which indicate the first node in an object path or subpath (of combined vector objects) when a vector object is selected or the edge of an object when a bitmap is selected. A small *X* marker appears at the centermost point of the object, indicating its center origin. This origin can be moved and is quite useful for defining a center of rotation for an object, and it's discussed later in this chapter.

Note Nodes are edited using the Shape tool, covered in Chapter 9. The Pick tool has no effect on nodes.

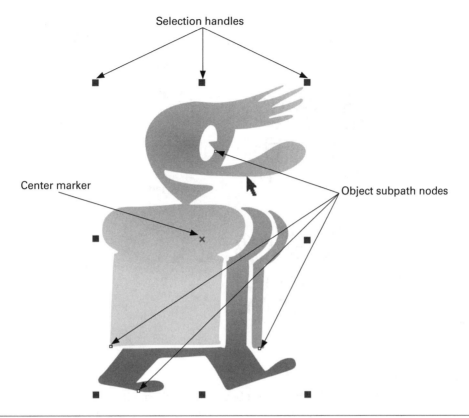

FIGURE 6-1 Select any object with a single click using the Pick tool.

Tip Occasionally you'll create a shape with an outline stroke that's very narrow and has no fill, but you're having trouble selecting the darned thing with the Pick tool. You're in luck because, by default, Treat All Objects As Filled is turned on. You don't need to select the outline because with this option, you can click on an empty interior and the object is selected anyway. If you don't care for this option, go to the Options dialog (CTRL+J) and select Workspace | Toolbox | Pick Tool from the tree at left. Clear the Treat All Objects As Filled checkbox, and then click OK to close the dialog.

Picking and Freehand Picking

The Freehand Pick tool is located in the Pick Tools group, and both new and experienced CorelDRAW users might want to give this selection tool a try; the Freehand Pick tool behaves exactly like the (regular) Pick tool after an object is selected, so you can move or perform other transformations without switching tools.

The main difference between these tools is that with the Pick tool, you must click-drag to define a rectangle that the desired objects are completely within. The Freehand Pick tool is used more like a shape creation tool than a rectangle creation tool; you can click-drag around objects, selecting some and avoiding others, regardless of how closely the objects neighbor one another. The illustration here visually demonstrates the different properties of the Pick and Freehand Pick tools.

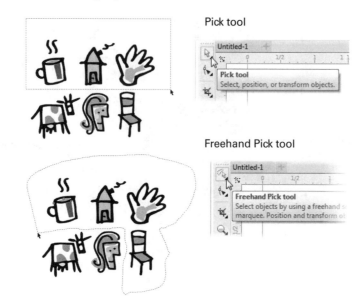

Selection Techniques

You can use mouse and keyboard combinations while navigating through a collection of objects and for selecting more than one object at a time using the Pick tool. Many of these object-selection techniques can also be used in combination with each other. Here's how to select more than one object in one fell swoop:

- **SHIFT-clicking to select**   Holding the SHIFT key while clicking an unselected object adds it to your current selection. This also works in the reverse: holding SHIFT while clicking a selected object *deselects* the object. This technique works with both the Pick and Freehand Pick tools.
- **Marquee-selecting objects**   To select all objects in a specific area, use the (regular) Pick tool and click-drag diagonally to surround the objects; a dashed blue outline representing the rectangular area being selected appears until you release the mouse button. When you do so, all object shapes completely within the area you define are selected.
- **Holding ALT while marquee-selecting**   If you come to CorelDRAW from Adobe Illustrator, you can use the convention of selecting objects by merely touching a shape in a marquee-selection technique. Holding the ALT key as the modifier while click-dragging to marquee-select a specific area selects all objects within— and even ones whose *edge* you touch. Holding SHIFT + ALT while marquee-selecting causes the reverse to occur, deselecting any objects that are already selected. There is also a option (Tools | Options | Workspace | Toolbox | Pick Tool and then click Treat All Objects As Filled) that saves you from holding ALT all the time.

- **Pressing TAB to select next object** Suppose you have a bunch of objects in a document, but some of them overlap, and you're getting nowhere by attempting to click the one you need. Pressing the TAB key alone while the Pick tool is active selects a shape and selects the next single object arranged directly behind your current selection (whether or not it overlaps the current object). Holding SHIFT while pressing the TAB key selects the single object arranged directly in front of your current selection. This tabbing action works because each new object created is automatically ordered in front of the last created object. Tabbing cycles through single object selections on a page, whether you have a current object selected or none at all. The key is to begin tabbing *after* you've chosen the Pick tool.
- **ALT + click to select objects covered by other objects** To select an object that is ordered in back of and hidden by other objects, hold the ALT key while the Pick tool is selected and then click where the object is located. Each time you ALT + click with the Pick tool, objects that are ordered farther back in the stack are selected, enabling you to "dig" to select hidden objects.

The Pick Tool's Shape Tool State

If you're getting an idea that the Pick tool has a host of hidden features, you're right. One of these is its alternate state—the temporary Shape tool state. The Pick tool can temporarily act like the Shape tool while a single object is selected and when held over object nodes, but this isn't its normal behavior, and you need to first enable this feature in Options; choose Workspace | Display and then check Enable Node Tracking.

The temporary Shape tool state lets you move object nodes without changing tools, conveniently giving you control to modify selected characters in a line of Artistic Text, to edit open and closed paths, and to modify an ellipse, star, polygon as star, graph paper object, and even a bitmap. The next illustration shows Enable Node Tracking in action. When the Pick tool is outside of a shape it looks like an arrow cursor. After an object is selected and the tool is over an object node, however, the tool changes to the Shape tool and you can move nodes.

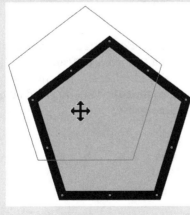
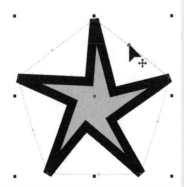

Pick tool moving selected object

Pick tool in Shape tool state selecting object with object node selected and moving node

Tip Although you can select nodes with the Pick tool when Enable Node Mapping is active, you can't perform editing operations other than moving a node. To create curves from straight path segments and work with node control handles, you need to use the genuine Shape tool.

Selecting Objects by Type

So far, you've learned to select any objects on or off your page. But you can also select objects by their type (such as text objects, guidelines, and path nodes), using commands from the Select All menu, shown in the following illustration. Shown here all text objects are selected, and CorelDRAW is being very clever; it didn't select the "O" or the "a" because they are drawings and not text. You can extrude, add a perspective, and put any type of fill you like on text, and *it's still text*. See how effortless sifting through a page of objects can be? Each time you use a command, a new selection is made (and any current selection of objects becomes *not* selected).

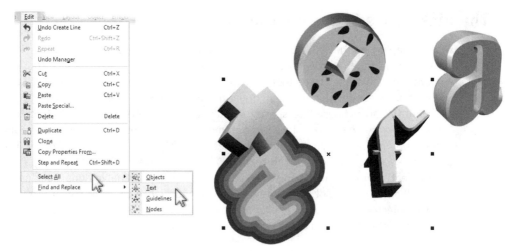

Caution You can't select what's locked or hidden. Check the status of layers with the Object Manager if an object is apparently welded to the page. Also, click an immovable object and if its selection handles are tiny lock icons, right-click over it and choose Unlock Object from the pop-up contextual menu. Any and all objects can now be locked on an object-by-object basis in X7.

Here's how to use each of the commands:

- **Select All Objects**   Choosing Edit | Select All | Objects selects all objects in your current document window. Quicker is the CTRL + A keyboard shortcut, which accomplishes the same thing and is easy to remember.

Tip Double-clicking the Pick tool in the Toolbox instantly selects all visible objects in your current document window view.

- **Select All Text**   Choosing Edit | Select All | Text instantly selects all text objects both on and off the current document page. Both Artistic and Paragraph Text objects are selected after using this command (unless they have been grouped with other objects, in which case they are ignored). Text objects that have effects (such as Contour or Extrude effects) also are selected using this command.
- **Select All Guidelines**   Guidelines are actually a class of document page objects, different from objects you draw, but objects nonetheless. To select all guidelines on your document page, choose Edit | Select All | Guidelines. Selected guidelines are indicated by a color change (red, by default). To select guidelines, they must be visible and cannot be locked; probably the fastest way to unlock or unhide a bunch of guidelines is to double-click one using the Pick tool to display the Guidelines docker. The Guidelines docker has options for locking/unlocking and hiding/revealing existing guides. If guidelines you've placed merely aren't visible on your page, and you're sure you laid some down in your last session, try choosing View | Guidelines.

Tip Guidelines can be created using a click-drag action from your ruler onto your document page. Rulers can be displayed and hidden via a neat new button on the Standard bar, directly to the right of the View Full Screen button.

- **Select All Nodes**   You can have the Shape tool or the Pick tool (which will magically change into the Shape tool) and an object selected (closed or open paths qualify) when using this Select command. Choose Edit | Select All | Nodes to select all the object's path nodes. For a quicker method in the same situation, use the CTRL + A shortcut when either the Pick tool (which changes to the Shape tool) or the Shape tool is your current tool. Special CorelDRAW objects, such as rectangles, ellipses, and polygons, can't be selected this way because their shapes are defined dynamically by "control points" instead of nodes.

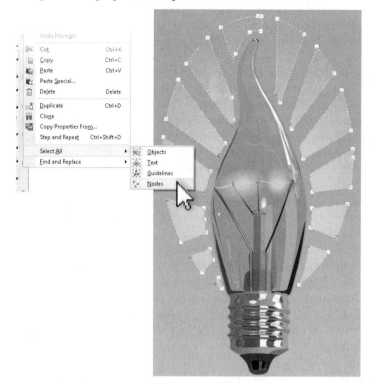

Tip Shapes are often made up of two or more paths that are combined. To select all the nodes on a combined path, first select the object and then double-click the Shape tool on the Toolbox.

Moving Objects

When moving objects, it's important to lift using your legs and position yourself carefully to avoid back injury. However, moving objects in *CorelDRAW* is a lot less stressful and heavy. You basically have two options to move objects directly: using the Pick tool and dragging, or using the keyboard arrows to precision nudge objects in any of the four directions.

Tip For information on moving and transforming objects, see the section "Applying Precise Transformations," later in this chapter.

Using the Pick Tool

Holding the Pick tool over certain areas of a selected object activates the tool's positioning cursor, as shown in the illustration. This means a click-drag action on the area will move your selected object(s) in any direction. As you drag your object, you'll see a preview outline, indicating its new position. When you release the mouse button, the move is complete.

Preview outline

Positioning state of Pick tool cursor

Tip   If you're having difficulty selecting and/or moving an object because it's too small, you can increase your view magnification using the Zoom tool or use the keyboard nudge keys, covered next.

Using Nudge Keys

As an alternative to using the Pick tool, you can also move selected objects by a distance you specify by nudging using your keyboard arrow keys. To nudge a selected object, press the UP, DOWN, LEFT, or RIGHT arrow key. Your object will be moved by the nudge value specified on the Rulers page of the Options dialog. You can customize the Nudge distance by opening the Options dialog (CTRL + J), clicking to expand the tree directory under Workspace and Document, and clicking to display the Rulers options page, as shown here:

Nudge increment options

> **Tip** You have eight possible directions in which to nudge your artwork. In addition to using an arrow key, you can also press two neighboring keys—such as LEFT and UP—to perform a *diagonal* nudge.

Using nudge keys, you can perform moves according to the Nudge value or by larger or smaller values. These are referred to as *Super* and *Micro nudges.* Like "normal" nudges, these values are set on the Rulers options page. Here are the techniques for using Super and Micro nudges:

- **Super nudge**   This action moves a selected object in larger increments than a normal nudge. To use Super nudge, hold SHIFT while pressing the UP, DOWN, LEFT, or RIGHT arrow key on your keyboard. By default, this moves your selected object by twice the default value for a "normal" nudge distance, although as you can see in the preceding illustration, you can change that 2 to a larger value in the Super Nudge num box.
- **Micro nudge**   The pint-sized version of a typical nudge is the Micro nudge, which moves your object in smaller increments. To use Micro nudge, hold CTRL while pressing the UP, DOWN, LEFT, or RIGHT arrow key on your keyboard. By default, Micro nudges move the selected object by one-half the default nudge distance, but again, this value's in the Micro Nudge num box and you can make it even smaller.

Transforming Objects

A *transformation* is any type of object shape or position change, short of actually editing the object's properties. This includes changing an object's position, size, skew, and/or rotating or reflecting it. Dragging an object directly in a document is more intuitive than precision transformations—but both approaches have their own special advantages. In this section, you'll learn how to apply transformations using both techniques.

Transforming Objects Using the Cursor

For the intuitive method, the Pick tool is what you need to transform objects by the simple act of click and dragging. Depending on the type of transformation you need to apply, you can click-drag any of the four, black, square selection handles that surround the selected object or group of objects to change an object's size *proportionally*—by width only and by height only. Dragging any middle selection handle or side handle scales the object *disproportionately*—"smush" and "stretch" are the more common terms for disproportionate scaling, as shown in Figure 6-2.

During transformations, CorelDRAW keeps track of the object's transformed size, position, width, height, scale, and rotation angle. CorelDRAW remembers your object's original shape from the time it was created, regardless of how many transformations have been applied to it. You can remove all transformations and restore the object to its

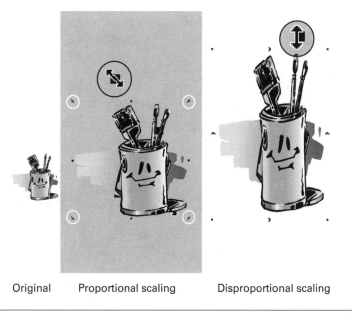

Original   Proportional scaling   Disproportional scaling

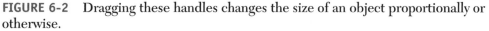

FIGURE 6-2   Dragging these handles changes the size of an object proportionally or otherwise.

original state in a single step: choose Object | Transformations | Clear Transformations to return your object to its original shape immediately.

While transforming objects, you can constrain certain shape properties by holding modifier keys. Here are the effects of holding modifier keys for constraining a transformed object's shape:

- **To change object size (scale)**   Click-drag any corner handle to change an object's size *proportionally,* meaning the relative width and height remains in proportion to the original object's shape. Hold ALT while dragging any corner selection handle to change an object's shape *disproportionally,* meaning width and height change, regardless of original proportions.
- **To change width or height only**   Click-drag any side, top, or bottom selection handle to change the size of the object in the drag direction. Hold SHIFT while doing this to change the width or height from the center of the object, or hold CTRL while dragging to change the width or height in 200-percent increments.

Tip   When transforming an object using the Pick tool on any of the object's control handles, click the right mouse button during the transformation and then release both mouse buttons to "drop a copy." The active object you're dragging becomes a copy, applying the transformation to a duplicate, not the original. This technique is a quick and easy way to mirror a duplicate and make symmetrical compositions.

You can also rotate or skew an object using Pick tool states that become available after you click a selected object a second time—you click an object that is *already* selected once to display rotation and skew controls around the object. This action causes an object (or group of objects) to look like the illustration of the 45 here, an ancient analog sound device best known to listeners who know who Little Anthony and the Imperials were.

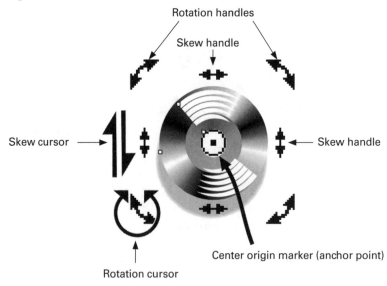

Rotation handles

Skew handle

Skew cursor →

Skew handle

Center origin marker (anchor point)

Rotation cursor

You control the point around which objects are rotated or skewed, by *moving* the center origin marker or anchor point of an object or group of objects. Your cursor will change to display either the rotation or skew cursor when held over a corner or side handle. A good creative example of offsetting the original center of an object is covered in the following tutorial, where you'll make a circular pattern from a group of objects.

Tutorial   Off-center Object Rotation to Create a Design

1. Open *Pattern Ding.cdr*. The page has guidelines that you'll use and a single grouped object, the source for the radial pattern you'll build.
2. With the Pick tool, click the object to select it, and then click the selected object (again) to put it into rotational and skew mode.
3. Drag the center rotation origin to the intersection of the guidelines.
4. Click-drag the top right (bent double arrowhead) handle downward until the light blue object preview is slightly overlapping the original object.
5. Before releasing the mouse button, press the other mouse button, and then release both buttons to "drop a copy" of the original object. Unless you've configured your mouse or other pointing device to accommodate left-handers, the primary mouse button is the left one, and the button you click briefly to drop a copy is the right one.
6. Repeat steps 4 and 5 with the copy of the object, working clockwise until you've made a circle from copies of the pattern, as you can see in this next illustration.

Note   If steps 4 and 5 seem like a lot of manual effort and you accept the idea that computers are supposed to be time-savers, instead of repeating the steps, you can use Edit | Repeat (CTRL+R) to quickly rotate and copy the rest of the grouped objects.

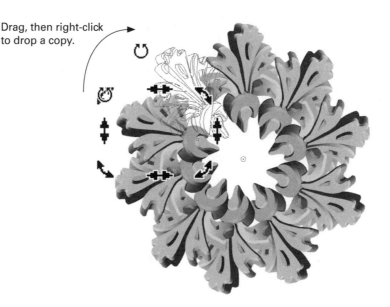

Drag, then right-click
to drop a copy.

Tip To flip a selected object quickly, either vertically or horizontally, use the Mirror Vertical and Mirror Horizontal buttons on the Property bar while using the Pick tool.

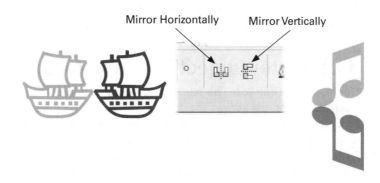

Mirror Horizontally   Mirror Vertically

Using the Free Transform Tool

The *Free Transform* tool is the middle ground between controlling transformations entirely with mouse gestures and the hands-off controls of the Transformations docker. When you use the Free Transform tool, the Property bar offers four transformation modes: Free Rotation, Free Angle Reflection, Free Scale, and Free Skew, as shown here, performing the Free Angle Reflection, to mirror the drawing's original location and left-to-right orientation.

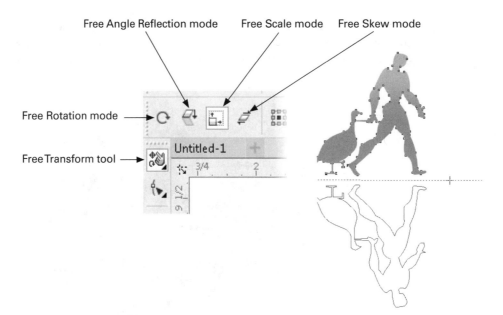

Free Angle Reflection mode   Free Scale mode   Free Skew mode

Free Rotation mode

Free Transform tool

To transform a selected object in one of these four modes, click to select the mode, and then use a click-drag action on your object. A live preview of the new object's shape appears. While using Rotation or Angle Reflection modes, a reference line appears as you drag to indicate the object's angle transformation from its original state.

Using the Free Transform tool and then applying a little transparency can yield compositions that contain believable reflections. The Free Transform tool works with bitmaps as well as native CorelDRAW vector objects.

Copying Effects with the Attributes Eyedropper Tool

In addition to properties such as outline color, and effects such as perspective (covered in later chapters), you can copy transformations between objects using the Attributes Eyedropper tool. To do this, choose the tool, have both the objects in view, and then click the Transformations button on the Property bar. Then check the individual properties you want to sample. For example, if you want to copy the scale of an object to a different object, put a check in the Size box in the Transformations list, making sure no other transformations, effects, or properties are checked. Click OK to close the flyout and save your choices. You now click the Attributes Eyedropper tool over an object whose scale you want to apply to a different object; the cursor turns into a paint bucket shape and you click over the target object to apply the transformation. The cursor will remain a bucket until you either click the Select Object Attributes button on the Property bar or you change tools. Because of the persistent state of the apply (the paint bucket cursor) transformations, you can click over several *objects* with the cursor until you've finished your work and no longer need the tool.

There are limitations to what the Attributes Eyedropper tool can copy and apply:

- You need to be careful to select the attributes you need copied and applied to other objects; the Properties, Transformations, and Effects drop-down selectors can, for example, copy a single color and then apply it to a single object, but the Attributes Eyedropper cannot sample several colors in a group and apply them in order to another group or single object. What it can do with grouped objects, however, lies in the Transformations list. If you pick Scale, and then sample from a group of object and apply the tool to a single object or group, the large objects will indeed scale in proportion to the source group of objects.
- You can copy an attribute and apply it to a contour object because CorelDRAW sees this as one object. Similarly, a PowerClipped group of objects is seen as one object, as is an extruded shape. Blend objects are seen as two (or more) objects, so don't try applying an attribute to blend objects.

In the following set of steps, you'll get a better idea of the power of applying copied attributes. You're going to rotate a drawing of a knife (a PowerClipped group of shapes) and its shadow based on the angle of rotation of a different piece of flatware in the composition. Dig in!

Tutorial Straightening Objects via Attributes

1. Open *Table Setting.cdr*. Now, understand that the trick to unrotating the knife and its shadow lies in the fact that it was originally rotated, and CorelDRAW can read the information about the previous transformation. You cannot duplicate a transformation using an object that has had no transformation to begin with.
2. Choose the Attributes Eyedropper tool from the Toolbox. Click the Transformations drop-down list on the Property bar and then check only Rotation. All other boxes should be unchecked, including those in the Properties drop-down box.
3. Click the fork.
4. When the cursor is a paint bucket, click exactly over the knife. You'll see, as shown in Figure 6-3, that the knife almost magically straightens itself. By the way, you could also choose Object | Transformations | Clear Transformations to accomplish this with a selected object, but the Attributes Eyedropper proves faster a lot of times.
5. Click over the shadow of the knife and consider yourself a perfect host now.

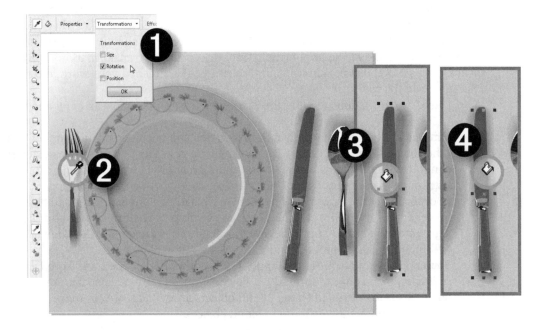

FIGURE 6-3 Sampling and pasting attributes is a quick way to change scores of elements dramatically in a composition.

Applying Precise Transformations

The Transformations docker is terrific for applying multiple transformations with a single command. The docker has five Transformation buttons: Position (Move), Rotation, Scale And Mirror, Size, and Skew, as shown in this fantastic illustration. To open the Transformations docker, choose Window | Dockers or choose Objects | Transformations, and then click any submenu command and the entire docker appears docked to the right edge of the drawing window. The docker has been detached in the illustration here.

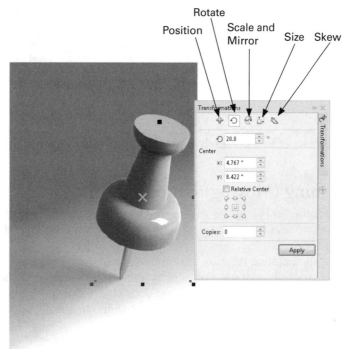

For all transformations, the procedure is the same: click the button for the type of transformation, enter the values you need, and then click the Apply button in the docker to transform the selected object(s). In this section, you'll learn what each area does for you and the options offered for each.

 Note Options in the Transformations docker vary by transformation type. In the illustrations shown in the next few pages, examples show only the specific transformation being discussed.

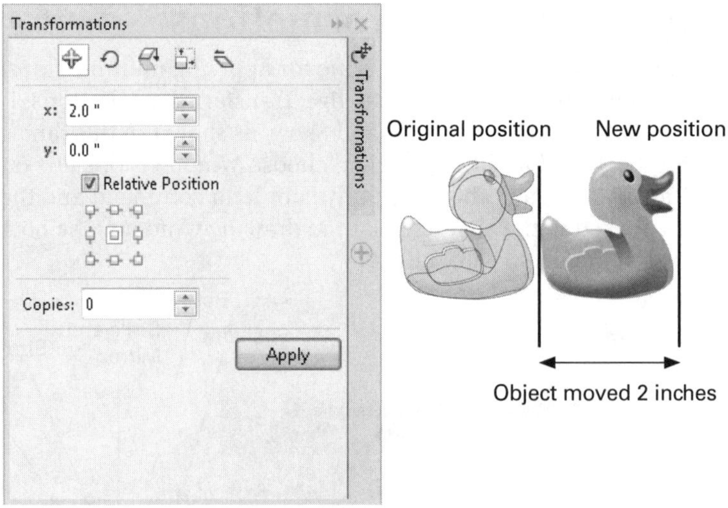

FIGURE 6-4 This object was precisely moved by applying a Position transformation.

Positioning (Moving) Objects

Options for the Position page will move your object selection a specified distance, either *horizontally* (x) or *vertically* (y), to a specific point on your document page, as shown in Figure 6-4.

While the Relative Position option is selected, entering new values and clicking the Apply button moves your objects by a specified distance. If the Relative Position option is *not* selected, you'll be moving your object to a specific location, for example, if you type **11** in the x (horizontal) field and then click Apply, your object moves to the 11" mark on the horizontal ruler.

If you specify a value greater than zero in the Copies field, and use the Relative Position option, you create a duplicate object every increment of the x value you've typed in.

Rotating Objects

On the Rotation page, you can enter exact angles of rotation based on degrees and in default increments of 5 using the spin boxes. Here, you see two very different results when using relative and absolute positioning and two copies of the tea kettle.

Set location on
the object for
transformation

Tip The ornament you turned into a flower earlier in this chapter could have been created using the Rotation transformation, an off-center location for the object's transformation point, and several copies specified.

Entering negative values rotates an object clockwise, whereas positive values cause counterclockwise rotation. Selecting the Relative Center option lets the object be rotated around its center marker position. By default, the marker is at position $x = 0$ and $y = 0$—at the object's geometric center. Entering new values has the same effect as moving the center marker position with the Pick tool, but with the advantage of mathematical precision. When Relative Center is not selected, the x and y values represent fixed page coordinates for the center of rotation.

Tip You can change the initial transformation point on an object by first clicking any of the nine mini-boxes above the Copies field. So, for example, if you want an object to rotate by 15 degrees, making seven copies, but commence the process from the lower left of the object's bounding box, you first click the lower-left mini-box. This Windows 8 minimalist look makes it a little hard to see what you're doing: the selected mini-box takes on an outline box around it when selected instead of taking a checkmark, but if you need this feature, this is a fast and easy option.

Scale and Mirror Objects

The Scale And Mirror transformation has features for entering precise changes in object size. You can also flip the object either *x* or *y,* and/or simultaneously, by clicking one of the two mirror buttons, as shown here.

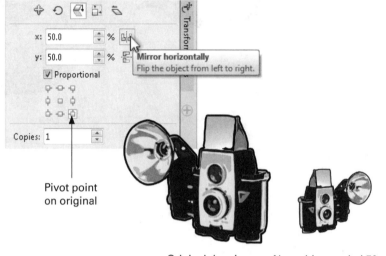

Pivot point
on original

Original drawing   New object scaled 50 percent
and mirrored horizontally

When the Proportional option is selected, width and height scaling operations are locked to each other. This means that scaling the width or height by a given percentage value causes the adjacent value to be calculated automatically to preserve your selected object's original proportions. When the Proportional option is unselected, your object's new horizontal and vertical scale values are unlinked, meaning you can apply scaling commands to either the width or height, independent of each other. Remember that the final position of any copies is determined by which of the mini-boxes above the Copies field you selected before clicking Apply.

Sizing Objects

This transformation type gives you the option to change either the *x* and/or *y* measure of an object selection based on the values entered. For example, entering **2** inches in the Width box and clicking the Apply button scales the selected object to a width of two inches. When the Proportional option is not selected, the width and height values can be changed independently. While it's selected, both width and height values are linked and calculated automatically to alter the size of the object proportionally.

Precision Skewing

The term *skew* means to change the position of two sides of a shape in a parallel fashion while leaving the other two sides alone; *slanting* is a more common synonym for "skew." The Skew transformation also gives you the chance to apply both vertical and horizontal skew independently or simultaneously by entering degree measures, in turn, transforming the object either x or y. As with rotation commands, negative degree values produce clockwise skews, whereas positive values cause counterclockwise skews. Choosing the Use Anchor Point option lets you specify left, center, right, top, bottom, sides, or corner points as the point around which your objects are skewed, as shown here, by choosing the Use Anchor Point option. The skewed copy more or less looks like a cast shadow of the original symbol, doesn't it?

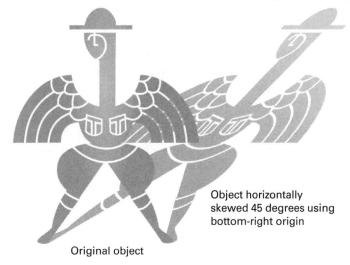

Object horizontally
skewed 45 degrees using
bottom-right origin

Original object

Controlling the Order of Things

How your objects are ordered is another consideration when organizing drawing objects in a composition. The order of objects determines whether an object appears in front of—or behind—another object. Your page and the pasteboard (the area surrounding your document page) are always the *backmost* point, whereas your screen is always the frontmost point. All objects are layered between these two points.

When overlapping objects are ordered, they appear in front of or behind each other, according to their order. As you create each new object, it is put in front of all existing objects *on the current document layer*. Changing the object order lets you rearrange overlapping objects without changing their position on the page. To do this, CorelDRAW has a series of order commands that let you shuffle the order of objects in various ways. You'll find them in the Object | Order submenu, but you can also apply them using shortcut keys or the To Back Of Layer and To Front Of Layer buttons, available toward the far right on the Property bar, when an object is selected.

Note The *hierarchy* of object ordering on a layer is very different than *object layers*. Although layers each have their own collections of objects that can be ordered in a sequence, the layers *themselves* can *also* be ordered. This means that if you're trying to control the ordering of two or more objects, check the Status bar to make sure they're on the same layer.

Here's how each of the object order commands works:

- **To Front** This command shuffles your selected object(s) to the very front of the current layer. Press SHIFT + PAGE UP or choose Object | Order | To Front to apply it. The To Front command is also available as a Property bar button when an object is selected.
- **To Back** This command shuffles your selected object(s) to the very back of the current layer. Press SHIFT + PAGE DOWN or choose Object | Order | To Back to apply it. The To Back command is also available as a Property bar button while an object is selected.
- **Forward One** This command shuffles your selected object(s) forward by one in the object order of the current layer. Press CTRL + PAGE UP or choose Object | Order | Forward One to apply it.
- **Back One** This command shuffles your selected object(s) backward by one in the object order of the current layer. Press CTRL + PAGE DOWN or choose Object | Order | Back One to apply it.
- **In Front Of** This command is interactive and puts your selected object directly in front of any object you specify in the current layer order. A targeting cursor will appear, and you use it to choose which object to shuffle your selection in front of. Choose Object | Order | In Front Of to apply it.
- **Behind** This command also causes a targeting cursor to appear, enabling you to specify which object you want your object selection to be shuffled behind in the object order on the current layer. Choose Object | Order | Behind to apply it.
- **Reverse Order** This command effectively shuffles the order of your selected object so that it's in the reverse of its current order on the layer. Front objects become back objects and vice versa. For example, if your objects were numbered 1, 2, 3, and 4 from front to back, applying this command would reorder them to 4, 3, 2, and 1. Choose Object | Order | Reverse Order to apply it.

Tip When changing object order using the Reverse Order command, grouped objects are considered a single object, so their relative order in the group will be preserved. To reorder objects within a group, you'll need to ungroup (CTRL+U) the objects first before applying the command.

Working with Views of a Document's Depth: Layers

CorelDRAW's layer feature provides invaluable ways not only to organize but also to view complex drawings. You can create several layers and move shapes among layers. You can also name layers, control their order and appearance, change object ordering within layers, group objects, and quickly see object information. One immediate advantage to adopting layers in your composition work is that you can hide layers; suppose you have a lot of objects that need labels, and you need to print the objects with and without the labels. Put all the labels on a layer, hide the layer, print just the objects, then unhide the layer and make a second print!

Exploring the Object Manager

The Object Manager docker is your resource for viewing layer content and using layer options. With the Object Manager, you can perform a whole range of actions: navigate document pages, create and name layers, select and move objects among layers, and set layers as editable, printable, and visible. To open the Object Manager docker, choose Windows | Docker | Object Manager. As mentioned in Chapter 4, a keyboard shortcut such as M is a good idea to assign to the Object Manager, unless you want it docked to the workspace window for all of time.

The Object Manager shows a listing of the layers, each accompanied by options and a flyout menu. A Master Page also appears and includes default layers for controlling guides, the desktop, and grid objects. If more than one page is in a document, you can specify whether you want odd, even, or all pages in the file to have Master Pages; more on this later in the chapter. Figure 6-5 shows a drawing and what the Object Manager reports for this composition. There is only one page; the drawing was created on two layers on Page 1, and you can see a main entry below Layer 2 that indicates a group of 10 objects. Actually many more objects make up the notepad illustration, but they are in subgroups within the entry that says 10 objects— as far as the Object Manager goes, you need to expand all the + boxes to see what really exists in the drawing aside from grouped objects, whose number is unknown

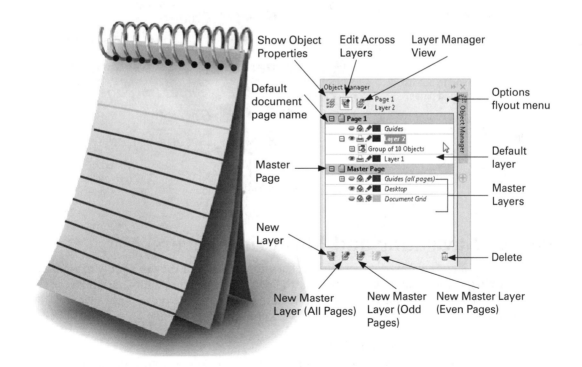

FIGURE 6-5   View information, and also name and alter it with the Object Manager.

until you look. As you dig through the groups on the Object Manager, you will see individual entries named curve, rectangle, polygon...the Object Manager is quite explicit about objects in groups, making locating an object a much easier task than in most other drawing programs.

> **Note** Master Pages for odd- and even-numbered pages in a multi-page document make page numbering and special elements belonging to a facing page easier than ever to compose.

Navigating Pages, Objects, and Layers

The best way to use the Object Manager docker to navigate through your document, select layers, and control layer options is by experimenting yourself; the following steps are a guide. You'll learn exactly how these operations are performed; look at the next illustration, which shows a default layer structure for a new document.

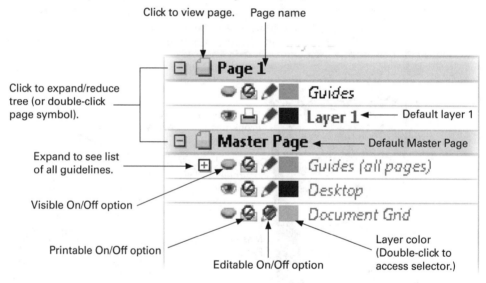

Tutorial Navigating and Mastering Layers

The next steps have no right or wrong execution, but rather they're simply exploration steps to get you comfortable working with layers. This is why an illustration has already been created for you; you just work the steps and see how any of several techniques can be applied to your own work, future and present.

1. Open *Alarming.cdr* in CorelDRAW.
2. Open the Object Manager docker: Window | Dockers | Object Manager. Look at the status of the layers. The background—the pattern fill of the clocks is locked

so it cannot be moved at present. Also, there's a layer on top with a default name, and it's hidden, which also means it's locked. Investigate a little now; unhide the top layer to see what's inside.

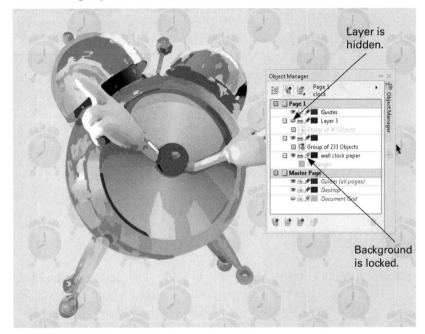

3. Okay, the author is trying to be funny here. And hopefully succeeding. The layer contains a third hand, yet within the context of an alarm clock, it's really a second hand. It's possible now to select the group of objects on Layer 3 by clicking them with the Pick tool, and if you click a second time, you can rotate the hand by dragging the rotation handles, and turn time itself back to Chapter 1. Click twice (slowly, don't double-click) on the name of Layer 3 on the Object Manager, and then type a name in the field that's more descriptive than "Layer 3" for future reference. Try **extra hand**, because why not?

4. Double-click the extra hand layer title to open its contents. The hand is several grouped objects, and they can be moved to the "clock" layer. First, rename the group: click twice on the "Group of 36 objects" and then type **third hand** in the field. Notice that control nodes are visible when a group or a single object is selected. Press (SHIFT + F2) to Zoom To Selected. Selecting items from the Object Manager is an easy way to select and then zoom into an object you want to work on.

5. Double-click the "clock" layer title to open it, and then drag the "third hand" group below the layer title, but above the "Group of 233 objects" entry. Layers

have a hierarchy, and if you put the group below the "Group of 233 Objects," the third hand would be hidden from view by the 233 other objects.

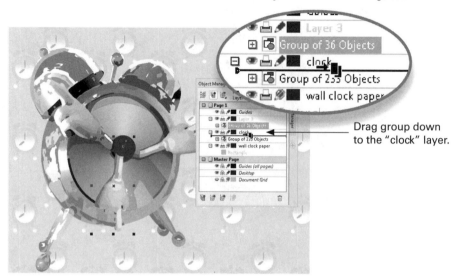

Drag group down to the "clock" layer.

6. Double-click the "extra hand" layer title. This action produces precisely nothing, which indicates that there is nothing nested within the layer. So it's okay to delete it—with the layer title highlighted, click Delete (the trash icon). Poof.

Caution There is no confirmation box with the Delete trash icon; it's similar to pressing the keyboard DELETE key. Be careful how you use it. To undo an inadvertent deletion, you need to click the workspace to put the document (and not the Object Manager) "in focus," and then press CTRL+Z (Edit | Undo).

7. Similarly, the background is expendable in this composition. Click the "wall clock paper" layer title to select it. Notice the trash icon is dimmed—this is because the layer is locked; you can confirm this by trying to move the clock pattern with the Pick tool. Click the Lock or Unlock pencil icon with the red slash over it to make the layer editable, and then click the Delete button.

Tip Every object, down to single objects, on the Object Manager's list can be renamed. Consider giving a very important object a custom name in your own work. Then, at any time, you can locate the object by conducting a search with the Edit | Find And Replace feature, or just by scrolling through the list of objects.

8. Create a new layer by clicking the New Layer button. Name it and then drag its title to the bottom of the layer stack on this page.
9. Lock the clock layer.

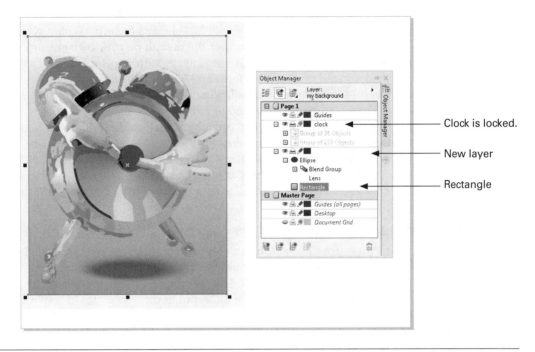

FIGURE 6-6   Working with layers takes full advantage of CorelDRAW's search capabilities and makes it easy to modify only certain elements in a complex drawing.

10. Click the new layer highlighted on the Object Manager list, choose the Rectangle tool from the Toolbox, create a rectangle as a background for the clock, and then apply a fill. Figure 6-6 shows a linear gradient fill (covered in Chapter 12) and a blend with transparency added to the new background layer—see Chapter 14 for the scoop on blends and contours.

Using Object Manager Editing and View States

Objects can be on different layers, and you can edit across layers in CorelDRAW. Create a new file that has objects on, let's say, three layers to better learn through example about the editing and view states of CorelDRAW layers. Open the Object Manager docker. You'll see three view state buttons at the top of the docker—that's where information about viewing and editing behavior are set. Clicking each button toggles its state on or off. Each button has the following effects:

Tip   You can use the Combine, Group, or Convert To Curves command on objects in the Object Manager docker by selecting the objects, right-clicking them, and choosing a command from the pop-up menu.

- **Show Object Properties** Click the Show Object Properties button to set whether you want to view a detailed name for a layer's contents (color, type of object, and so on), or just the name, either the default or your own custom name.
- **Edit Across Layers** Click the Edit Across Layers button to set whether objects can be selected, moved, and copied between layers. While cross-layer editing is disabled, objects appear grayed out, allowing only objects on your current page layer and/or the desktop to be selected or edited. While cross-layer editing is enabled, you can select, move, or edit any object on an unlocked layer.
- **Layer Manager View** The Layer Manager View button toggles your view to show only your document's layers. When working with complex drawings that have many pages, layers, and objects, using this view can make managing layer properties a lot easier. In this state, all page and object information is omitted.

Controlling Layer Properties

Using the Layer Properties dialog, you can control specific properties for each layer. To access these options, right-click a specific layer in the Object Manager docker and choose Properties from the pop-up menu. You can access properties directly from the pop-up menu or display a modeless dialog for defining the properties of a specific layer. There is a minor difference between using the dialog and the pop-up: the pop-up (right-click) menu has the Delete, Cut, Copy, and Paste commands. However, in X7, you can now rename layers in the Layer Properties dialog in addition to the Object Manager.

Options in this dialog control the following layer properties:

- **Visible** This option enables you to toggle the view state of a layer between visible or hidden. You can also control the visibility of objects on a layer by clicking the Eye symbol to the left of the layer name.
- **Printable** This option toggles the printing state of objects on the layer on or off. You can also set whether layer objects are printable by clicking the Printer symbol beside the layer in the Object Manager docker to toggle the printing state of objects on the layer.

 Note Nonprinting layers will also not export. If you need objects selected on a nonprinting layer to be included when exporting, you need to turn on the layer's Printable option.

- **Editable** Use this option to lock or unlock all objects on a layer. While a layer is locked, its objects can't be edited (or even selected), which is a little different than the Lock (object) command. You can also set whether layer objects are editable by clicking the Pencil symbol beside the layer in the Object Manager docker to toggle the editing state of objects on the layer.
- **Master Layer(s)** You can have layers for odd, even, and all pages in the Master Page entry on the Object Manager docker. You can create a new Master Layer,

and you can also drag an existing layer from a page to the Master Page entry. Changing a layer to a Master Layer makes it part of the Master Page structure. Any objects on a Master Page appear on all pages. For details on working with Master Pages and Master Layers, see the next section.

- **Layer Color** This selector sets the color swatch as it appears in the docker listing directly to the left of a layer name, for easy recognition. Layer Color also determines object colors when viewed using Normal or Enhanced views while the Override Full Color View option is selected. You set the color coding for a layer by double-clicking the color indicator next to a layer name to open a typical color selector menu and then clicking any color from the drop-down color picker.

Working with Master Page Layers

Whenever a new document is created, a *Master Page* is automatically created. The Master Page isn't a physical page in your document, but instead a place where document objects can be placed so they appear on every page of your document. Objects on a Master Page layer are visible and printable on every page in your document, making this an extremely powerful feature. For example, placing a text header or footer or a company logo on a Master Page layer is a quick and easy way to label all the pages in a pamphlet or brochure.

Moving any object onto a layer on the Master Page makes it a Master Page object and causes it to appear on each page. Let's try out this feature:

Tutorial Working with Master Page Items

1. Open the Object Manager docker by choosing Window | Dockers | Object Manager.
2. Click the New Master Layer (All Pages) button—the second in the row of buttons at the bottom of the docker. A new layer is automatically added to the Master Page with the default name "Layer 1."
3. With this new Master Layer as your current layer (click the entry to make sure it's selected), create the object(s) you wish to appear on every page in their final position and appearance. By creating the object while the Master Layer is selected, the object automatically becomes a Master Layer object. You can also move objects from other pages onto the Master Layer by click-dragging them in the docker list from their position under a layer name to the Master Layer name.
4. Click to select the new Master Page object(s) on your document page. Notice that you can still select, move, and edit it. To toggle the lock or unlock state of your Master Layer objects, click the Edit button (the pencil symbol) beside the Master Page in the docker. Locking prevents any accidental editing of the Master Page objects.
5. Add pages to your document by clicking the + button at the lower left of the workspace. As you browse through the pages, you'll see the same object on all pages.

Several default layers already exist on your document's Master Page for controlling special items that appear in your document, such as Guides, Grids, and Desktop. These layers have the following purposes:

- **Guides Layer** This is a global layer for guides you create; if you click the Guides (all pages) entry on the Object Manager to select it, and then drag a guide onto the page, all pages in the document will display this guide. If you need a guide on only one page, you choose that Guides entry on the page you're working on, drag a guide from the rulers, and that guide belongs to that page and is not a Master Page item.

Tip You can move a local guide, a guide you created on a page, to the Master Guides entry on the Object Manager to make it global—it will then appear on every page of your document.

- **Document Grid** This controls the appearance of grid lines. You can control the grid color and visibility, but you can't make the Grid Layer printable, nor can you change its editable objects or add objects to that layer. Options in the Document Grid Properties dialog enable you to control the grid display color and to gain quick access to the Grid page of the Options dialog by clicking the Setup button in the dialog. To open the Document Grid Properties dialog, right-click the Document Grid under the Master Page in the Object Manager docker and choose Properties from the pop-up menu.

Tip Document Grid visibility can be toggled on or off by clicking its eye icon on the Object Manager docker.

- **Desktop Layer** This is a global Desktop, the place outside of your drawing page. If you want to keep objects handy but don't want to print them on your page, drag the object to this entry on the Object Manager. If you put an object on the Desktop from a layer, you can't hide it or keep it from printing, but if it's explicitly placed on the Master Desktop, you can hide it, keep it from being edited, and keep it from printing.

Hopefully, this chapter has shown you how to transform not only objects, but also your skill level with CorelDRAW. You now know how to move, scale, rotate, and perform other operations on page objects and their duplicates. You also know how to both manually transform and use the dockers and other features for precise moving and alignment of the elements you need for a terrific design. Chapter 7 takes you into *creating* these shapes that you now know how to move; you put Chapters 6 and 7 *together,* and your family's going to start missing you because you'll be having too much fun designing to sit down for regular dinners!

PART III

Working with
Object Tools for Art
and for Business

7

Choosing (and Understanding) the Right Path Tools

If you thought learning to create basic shapes and modifying them in Chapter 5 was a fun learning experience, hold on: basic shapes will basically get your work only so far. CorelDRAW's path building and editing tools are at your disposal, so you can create *exactly* what you envision. The Curve Tools group on the Toolbox has tools that make any shape you can imagine (and some you *can't*) a snap to design. In the following sections, you'll work through the *editing* process of lines and their nodes, so now you don't have to draw something that's *close* to what you need. This chapter is the DRAW part of CorelDRAW. Incidentally, the Artistic Media pen is no longer part of this Curve Tools group; it has its own icon on the Toolbox, and the Smart Drawing tool is covered in Chapter 8 because it's of enormous use to novices whose jobs require them to become graphic designers instantly. *Experienced* users will enjoy Chapter 8, too!

Note Download and extract all the files from the Chapter07.zip archive to follow the tutorials in this chapter.

Sidling Up to CorelDRAW X7's Curve Tools

The most basic shape you can draw in CorelDRAW (and any vector drawing program) is a *line*: a line is a path that passes through at least two *points,* called *nodes* in CorelDRAW. A line is actually a mathematical equation, and as such, it doesn't necessarily have an outline color or width, and it doesn't even have to be a *straight* line. However, a line *does* have a *direction*—the direction in which you draw the line. This might seem obvious, but vectors *do* have a direction, and you can end up with arrowheads on the wrong end of a line and all sorts of unwanted stuff if you fail to remember the basic properties of a vector graphic.

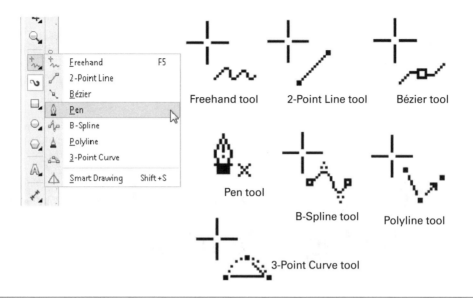

FIGURE 7-1 For visual reference while you work, each of the different drawing tools has a unique cursor.

You can assign a line scores of different properties: arrowheads, a dashed outline around clip-out coupons, solid colors, and varying widths. Joining the beginning and ending points of a line (a path) closes the path. If the beginning doesn't meet the endpoint, the shape is called an *open path*.

CorelDRAW X7's Curve tools are task-oriented; although they all produce paths, your choice of tool(s) for a task depends on what you want to draw. For example, do you need an object whose curves are flawless—like those of a physical French curve? This task calls for the B-Spline tool. You can also "mix and match"; you can begin an object with one tool and finish it with a different tool—your choices depend on the object you want to create. Some of these tools work similarly so it's best to become acquainted with what the different cursors *look* like, as shown in Figure 7-1.

How to Fill an Open Path

When you draw a path and the beginning and ending points don't meet, you have an *open path*, and ordinarily you cannot apply a fill to its interior. But you can *indeed* fill an open path—just like in Adobe Illustrator—when you know how to turn on this option.

To change DRAW's behavior so all open paths are filled—so you don't need to close the path first—follow these steps:

1. Open the Options dialog; just click the button on the Standard bar.
2. Expand Document, and click General to display the associated options on the right side of the dialog.
3. Click the Fill Open Curves option to select it, and click OK to close the dialog.

After choosing this option, the open paths you draw can have an interior area.

How to Draw in CorelDRAW

Although you can use the Artistic Media tool and its variants to "paint" in CorelDRAW—this nicety is covered in Chapter 13—right now, we're talking technique and proficiency with vector shapes made of straight lines and curves connected by nodes. In the Curve Tools group, you'll find CorelDRAW's path and node creation pens; you can use them for both accuracy and artistic expression, and they each have varying degrees of ease of use that correspond directly to their power.

Drawing with the Freehand and Polyline Tools

The *Freehand* and *Polyline tools* share a common function, giving you the freedom to draw as if you were sketching by freehand on a physical sketch pad, but the tools work in slightly different ways. Sketched lines can create a single open or closed vector path. Both tools are located in the Toolbox grouped with other line-creation tools.

For mouse users and stylus users alike, click-dragging initially produces a Start node for a path segment and then, when you release the mouse (or stylus) button, a node is placed, setting the end of the path segment. To use these tools:

1. Begin by selecting the Freehand tool.
2. You can create a continuous line by click-dragging a path shape. As soon as the mouse button is released, the line is complete, as you will see at left in Figure 7-2.
3. To *extend* this path—to *add* a path segment after the first segment's End node—you position your cursor over either the Start *or* End node (the cursor now features a tiny bent arrow), and to continue with a freeform path, just start click-dragging again.
4. Now, let's say you want to extend this path with a straight line segment or two. Instead of click-dragging on the End node of the previous segment, you click and then release the mouse button; the cursor turns into a little line segment icon; and at whatever point you want to end this segment, you single-click.
5. If you want to keep going with straight line segments, don't just click an End node and move your cursor; *double-click* an End node and you are now creating a new line segment that is joined to the previous line segment by a node.
6. To create a path that only has straight lines, you single-click, and then move the cursor and double-click each time you want the line segment to end and a new one to begin. Figure 7-2 shows the result at right, along with what the cursors look like and do depending on the position of the cursor over the page or the path. Do not freak out at the apparent complexity of this figure! It's a map to the treasure of mastering the Freehand tool.

The Polyline tool, on the other hand, can be used similarly to the Freehand tool, except only a single click adds a node and you can continue to add path segments.

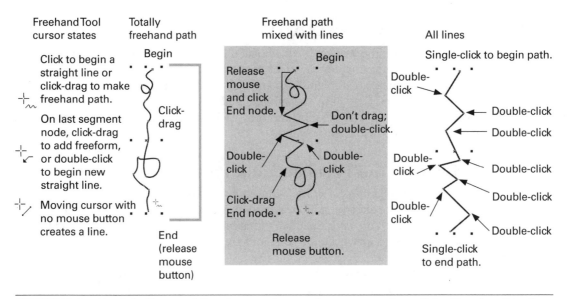

FIGURE 7-2 Straight lines and freeform paths are the strong points of the Freehand tool.

You'll notice that when you click-drag with the Polyline tool, your curves appear smoother, and this, like the Freehand tool, might serve digitizing tablet users the most. See the following illustration.

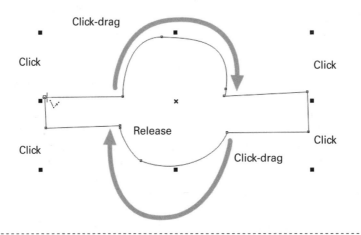

 Note A single-click using either the Freehand or the Polyline tool at the beginning of a path closes the path. It then becomes an object that can be filled, extruded, and perhaps even sold as fine art.

The Polyline tool has an *extended* function that lets you draw straight lines, mixed with perfectly circular arcs if you single-click the end of a straight line segment, hold ALT, release the mouse buttons and move the cursor position (this is called *hovering*), and then single-click. The next illustration shows that with a minimum of patience and a good idea in your head, you can easily create French-curve-like abstract objects. If you want your work to be an open path, double-click when you're done with the pen.

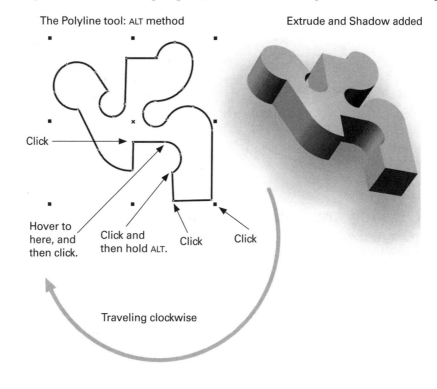

The Polyline tool: ALT method

Extrude and Shadow added

Click

Hover to here, and then click.

Click and then hold ALT.

Click

Click

Traveling clockwise

Tip   You can use the Property bar options to make any open path begin with an arrowhead; make the line—open or closed—into a dashed line, and change the stroke width.

Using either of these tools, you can control the smoothness of path shapes drawn using click-drag actions by adjusting the Freehand Smoothing option on the Property bar *before* drawing your path. You can control smoothness after *drawing* a path by selecting nodes with the Shape tool and then using the Reduce Nodes slider. Reduce

Nodes has a range between 0 and 100 percent; lower values apply less smoothing, and higher values apply more smoothing, as shown here.

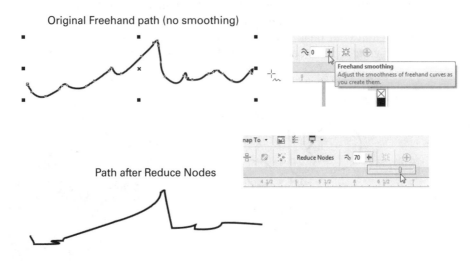

Original Freehand path (no smoothing)

Path after Reduce Nodes

Drawing Arcs with the 3-Point Curve Tool

The *3-Point Curve tool* (Figure 7-3) was created for artists to build perfectly smooth arcing line segments, with complete control over the direction and steepness of the curve between two points. First, you hold-drag the tool to set a straight line that

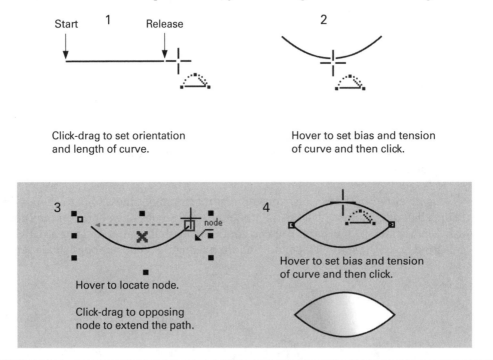

FIGURE 7-3   The 3-Point Curve tool makes difficult shapes easy to draw.

defines the angle of the curve. This sets the start and end points for the curve. Then you release the mouse button and hover the cursor to define the slope and degree of the curve; you're provided with an onscreen preview until you decide and click a point and thus create the curve. Here, you can see the process, as well as how to extend the curve with a second segment to close the path so it can be filled. This is the basis for the tutorial to follow where you'll create flower petals on an almost-completed illustration.

The terms *angle*, *slope*, and other common words don't adequately describe the characteristics of a curve to anyone other than a geometry professor. This might help: these are two additional, slightly nerdy, yet highly accurate terms describing the characteristics of a curve:

- **Bias**   When you draw an imaginary straight line through the endpoints of any curve, *bias* describes which of the two endpoints the curve leans toward.
- **Tension**   Similarly, when a straight line runs through the two points that define a curve, tension describes how closely or how far the curve's farthest point is from the line.

The following illustration shows examples of tension and bias. When you click any path's control point (a node) with the Shape tool, the curve's node sets the tension and bias, while the control handles address the heading of the path—the vector direction in which the path is going.

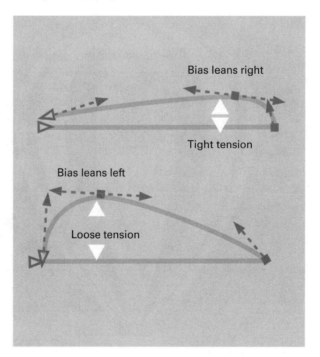

You'll quickly discover that part of the power of the 3-Point Curve tool is its usefulness in building a series of connected arcs; you can design French curves and ornamental borders by designing a 3-point curve, positioning your cursor over the endpoint until you see the cursor signifying an extension of the last-drawn curve, and then building another 3-point curve.

In the following tutorial, you'll create a cat's eye object that will serve as both a leaf and a flower petal to complete an illustration.

Tutorial 3-Point Curves and Closed Objects

1. Open *Simple Flower.cdr*. The white outlines are where the petals should be drawn and this overlay is on the Guides layer, which is locked. The center of the flower is on a layer above the current layer, and it and the background illustration are on locked layers so you can't move anything accidentally.

2. With the 3-Point Curve tool, click-drag across any of the guides, beginning at one point of the petal guide and ending at the other. Release the mouse button, and then hover below the line until the curve basically matches the curve of the guide. Then click to make the 3-point curve.

3. Hover over the right node of the curve until your cursor features an arrow and the word "node"; then click-drag to the opposite point on the underlying curve to extend this original curve. Release the mouse button when the cursor signifies that it's over the second point with a tiny arrow.

4. Hover and let the curve arc upward until it matches the underlying curve guide and then click. You now have a closed path that can be filled. See the image on the left of Figure 7-4.

Right-click while dragging to drop a copy

Object center

FIGURE 7-4   You can create smooth, connecting arcs quickly using the 3-Point Curve tool.

5. With the Interactive Fill tool, drag from left to right over the petal object. Then drag a brown color swatch from the color palette to the left (the Start color) marker, and finally, drag-and-drop a yellow-orange color swatch to the right (the End color) marker.

6. With the Pick tool, click the selected object once more to put it into rotational mode, and move the object center marker to the center of the brown object—the disc florets of the author's attempt at a Black-Eyed Susan.

7. Drag the top-right selection handle down; before releasing the mouse button, tap the right button to drop a copy of the object on to another unfilled guide object. The process is shown in Figure 7-4 at right.

8. Repeat Step 7 until you have all seven petal guides filled with duplicates of your object.

9. Drag a petal to another position, and then tap the right-mouse button while holding the left button to create a duplicate in the position where it's required (then release both buttons). Rotate it into position and fill it with a linear gradient of two different shades of green. Save your work and water it about every two to three days. The finished drawing is shown here.

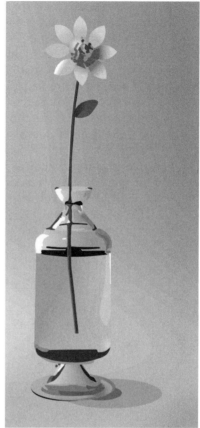

Drawing with the 2-Point Line Tool

This is the most self-explanatory tool in the Pen Tools group: you click-drag at any point on the page, and when you release the mouse button, the line is completed. Although this might seem like a "toy tool" compared to the others, it's actually quite useful for creating callouts in technical manuals, and it was used extensively in this book. Create a 2-point line, add an arrowhead, end of task.

Using the Bézier and Pen Tools

The *Bézier tool* and the *Pen tool* are variations on the same theme of drawing connected curves and straight segments through the action of first clicking to set a path point, and then either dragging to define a curve behind the click point or clicking (no dragging) to define a straight path segment behind the click point. You'll find these tools grouped together with other line-drawing tools.

One of the less obvious differences between the two tools is that the Pen tool offers a "look ahead" point when you draw with it: before you click or click-drag a point, the proposed path between the point before you click and the previous (already defined) point on the path is shown in light blue. Although control handles (those guys sprouting off the nodes, discussed later in this chapter) are displayed when a curve is defined with the Pen tool.

The Pen tool doesn't afford you as much control steering the shape of the curve as the Bézier pen tool. The Bézier tool always requires a click-drag mouse gesture to produce curves, whereas the Pen tool lets you hover your cursor before clicking to set the preceding curve in an object's path segments. When you're just beginning with CorelDRAW, the Pen tool provides a preview of the next segment you'll create, and after you gain some experience, you might want to skip the previews, pick up some drawing speed, and use the Bézier tool.

Pen tool   Bézier tool

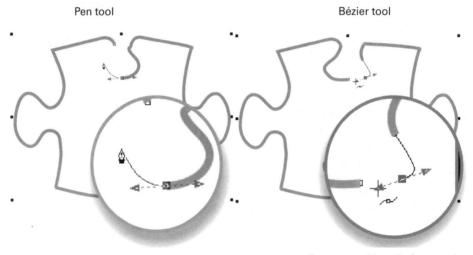

Hover cursor between previous click and next click to see a "look ahead" at the path you're drawing.

Drag control handle from node created when click-dragging.

Getting a Handle on Béziers

Both the Bézier tool and the Pen tool can create curves between two nodes whose connection to a neighboring node is smooth and symmetrical. You'll see control handles on smooth, symmetrical nodes when you click one using the Shape tool. These handles are used for intuitively reshaping the curve.

You can also create straight path segments between curves using the Bézier tool. *Click-dragging* creates smooth curves that have smooth connections between segments, whereas clicking without dragging sets a path point that is not smooth—if you click again in a different location, you'll get a straight path segment.

Because straight line segments and curve segments share so much fundamental anatomy, there is almost no distinction between the terms *line* and *curve* in the discussions in this chapter. The shapes of Bézier lines are controlled, in part, by node properties and the position of curve handles. Two paths can have nodes in the same relative page position, but have completely different shapes, as shown here.

Same node positions

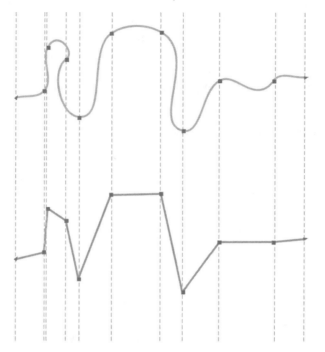

Nodes and Control Points

When a vector path describes an arc, *nodes* (points) connect a start and ending point, and the nodes have *control handles,* at the end of which are *control points* (also referred to as *nodes),* the screen element you use to manipulate curves. The number of control handles and points depends on the segment connected by each node. For example, an arc (a curve) connected to a straight line segment has one control handle visible and it controls the slope of the curve segment. When two curve segments are connected, you'll see two control handles if you click the connecting node with the Shape tool; this node can have different connection properties (cusp or smooth—described later in this chapter). A straight path segment can be described as two nodes connecting the segment, and the control handles for the nodes coincide in position with the node itself. For all intents and purposes, the control handles can't be seen; they become visible when the segment is changed to a curved segment: the control handles appear on the segment, and you can move them away from the launch point of the curve and then freely manipulate the slope of the curve by dragging the control points.

Nodes can be defined as cusp, smooth, or symmetrical by using the Shape tool in combination with the options on the Property bar, as shown in the next illustration. *Cusp* nodes can be used to create a discontinuity in direction between two line segments; in English, the two segments connect in a nonsmooth fashion. Think of the moon being on the cusp; it's crescent shaped, and this is the sort of shape you can create using cusp node connections. *Smooth* nodes cause the path slope and direction to align on either side of a node; their relationship is in 180-degree opposition, which has the effect of creating a smooth transition at the node point itself. Control handles surrounding a smooth node may be unequal distances from the node. *Symmetrical* nodes are not only smooth, but the control handles are an equal distance from the node. You'll immediately appreciate the effect of a symmetrical node; when you drag one control point away from a node, the opposing control handle moves an equal distance from the node in exactly the opposite direction. The artistic effect is that the two joined path segments take on an almost circular appearance, which is very useful for technical illustration work.

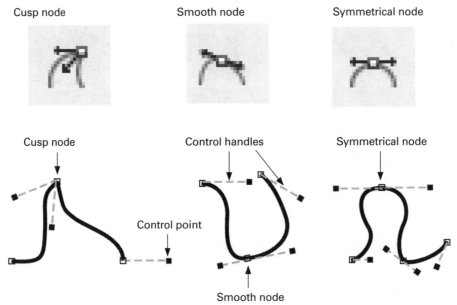

Drawing Conventions for the Bézier and Pen Tools

Both of these tools are used to create *compound paths* (segments connected by a common node) by combining a series of clicks or click-drags, but each is used in slightly different ways for different results. Using either of these tools, single-clicks define new node positions joined by straight segments. Curve segments are created by clicking to define the node position and then *dragging* to define the curve shape. Click-dragging in succession creates a continuous curved path shaped by multiple nodes and off-the-curve control handles. While using the Bézier tool, each click-drag defines and completes the curve segment. However, while using the Pen tool, the cursor remains active, and a preview of the next curve segment appears, so you can define both the curve shape and the next node point. Double-clicking ends the series of path segments.

Tip   When drawing with the Bézier tool, hold CTRL as you click to constrain new node positions to align vertically, horizontally, or within constrained angles relative to the last created node position. Holding CTRL while dragging curve handles constrains their angles to 15-degree increments relative to the last node created.

Let's try a new drawing method.

Tutorial   Drawing Curves and Straight Line Segments

1. Choose either the Bézier tool or the Pen tool and use a single-click action to define the first node position of your path. Click again to define a second point somewhere else on your page. The two nodes are now joined by a straight line.

2. Using the click-drag mouse technique, click to define your next node position, but continue dragging in any direction. As you drag, the second and third nodes are joined by a curved line.

3. If you choose the Bézier tool, you'll notice that two control handles appear joined by a dotted line. The point you are dragging is the control point that steers the control handle. The farther you drag the control point from the node, the larger the arc of the curve. Release the mouse button and notice that the control handles remain in view. Your path is complete unless you'd like to move a node or refine the position of its control points some more.

4. If you choose the Pen tool, you'll notice that a preview of your next curve appears as you move your cursor, which remains active until the next node is defined. To specify a node as the last in the path, use a double-click action to define the current node as the last point.

5. Using either tool, click your cursor directly on the first node you defined. This action closes the path and automatically joins the first and last nodes.

Editing Bézier Paths

All lines are controlled by properties of the nodes they include, which are edited using the Shape tool (F10). You'll find this tool, shown here, grouped with the Smooth, Smear, Twirl, Attract, Repel, Smudge, and Roughen tools.

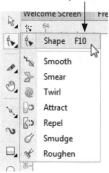

Shape tool

Using the *Shape tool,* you can change node positions and curve shapes by click-dragging the nodes and their control points, or by directly click-dragging on a path segment. While using the Shape tool, icons appear on the Property bar when one or more nodes are selected; you can select several nodes to change by marquee-dragging them or SHIFT-clicking a few.

These icons are used to set node attributes to cusp, smooth, and symmetrical, to join nodes and break nodes to create individual path segments, and to create straight lines from curves (and vice versa) when you've selected a segment or a node connecting segments. The bevy of functions on the Property bar provides exceptional control and flexibility in your design work. In short, you should *get to know the functions* for the Shape tool. The options are called out in Figure 7-5.

Obviously, being able to alter the connections between line segments is an important aspect of creating sophisticated artwork! Each of these buttons changes the selected nodes, lines, and curves in specific ways. The following is a description of what the options do and what they're called.

- **Shape Tool Selection Mode** You can marquee-select nodes the way users always have, by click-dragging a rectangular shape around the nodes you want to select, or Freehand style, which produces a lasso-like marquee you can use to be careful and exacting about which nodes in a group you want to edit. Using Freehand style, you might also want to use SHIFT to add to selected nodes.
- **Add/Delete Selected Nodes** These buttons give you the power to add new nodes to a curve or delete selected nodes after you've drawn a path, using the Shape tool and clicking at specific points on a path. To add a node, click any point

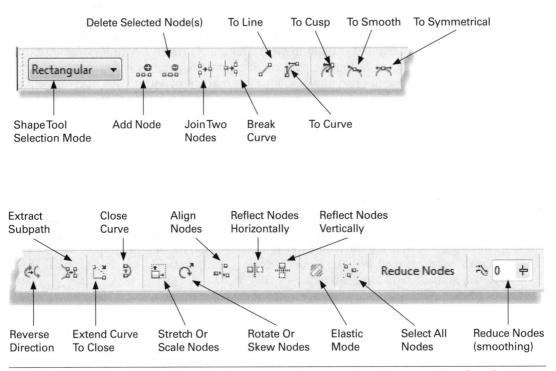

FIGURE 7-5 The Property bar offers you comprehensive control over path and node properties.

on a line to highlight the new position and then click the Add Node button. You can also add a new node to a line by clicking one or more nodes and then clicking the Add Node button to add a node midpoint between the selected node and the next node on the path. To delete a node, click to select it with the Shape tool and click the Delete Node button. You can also marquee-select (drag diagonally with the Shape tool to create a rectangle surrounding the nodes) and then delete all the selected nodes in one fell swoop. Pressing the minus (–) key on your numeric keypad or your DELETE key also deletes selected nodes.

Tip   Clicking an insertion point along a path with the Shape tool, and then pressing the plus (+) key on your numeric keypad might be a quicker way to add a node. You can also double-click anywhere on a path segment to add a node.

- **Join Two Nodes/Break Curve**   When two unconnected nodes on an open path are selected, for example, when the start point is close to the endpoint, pressing the Join Nodes button connects them to create an unbroken path. On single paths, only the unjoined Start and End nodes may be joined. On *compound paths* (paths that aren't necessarily close to one another, but have been joined using the Object | Combine command—CTRL + L is a shortcut worth memorizing), the Start and End nodes selected on two existing—but separate—paths can also be joined. While a single node is selected or while a specific point on a segment is clicked, pressing the Break Curve button gives you two unjoined nodes, breaking a closed path into an open path.

Tip   Unjoined paths are not the same as separate objects. Two paths, for example, can be located nowhere near each other on a page and yet still be part of a single path. If you want to break a path into its component subpaths, you first select the nodes using a marquee-select technique with the Shape tool, click the Break Curve button, and then choose Object | Break Curve Apart. CTRL+K is the shortcut, and it's another shortcut you'll want to commit to memory.

- **Line To Curve/Curve To Line**   These two buttons are used to toggle the state of a selected straight line to a curve state, and vice versa. A single click with the Shape tool selects a line or curve indicated by a black marker on the line. When curves are converted to lines, the path they follow takes on a shortcut: "the shortest distance between two points." When converting a straight line to a curve, the path remains the same shape, but control handles appear directly on the "line," and the quickest way to make the control points visible is to drag on the line to force it into a curve shape.
- **Extend Curve To Close**   For this command to be available, you must have both the Start and End nodes of an open path selected (marquee-select the points, or SHIFT + click to select them both). Under these conditions, clicking the Extend Curve To Close button joins the two nodes by adding a straight line between them, closing the path.

- **Auto-Close Curve** While selecting an open path, clicking this button joins the Start and End nodes to form a closed path by adding a new straight line between the two nodes. Although similar to Extend Curve To Close, depending on the closeness of the Start and End path nodes, you might not even see a visible straight line connection. You can also join the endpoints of a selected curve using the Close Curve option on the Object Properties docker's Curve tab. Press ALT + ENTER to open object properties. The Start and End nodes don't even have to be selected to use the Object Properties' method.

- **Reverse Curve Direction** While selecting a curved path on a line, clicking this button changes the direction of the path. By doing this, the start point of the path becomes the endpoint (and vice versa). The results of using this command button are most noticeable when the start or end of the line or path has been applied with an arrowhead, meaning the arrowhead is applied to the opposite end of the line or path. You may also notice subtle changes in the appearance of line styles applied to a path after using this option.

- **Extract Subpath** This option becomes available only when a compound path is selected. After clicking the Extract Subpath button, the selected path is separated from the compound path, converting it to a separate path. Using this command on a compound path composed of only two different paths is essentially the same as using the Break Apart command. It's more useful when you need to extract a specific path from a compound path made up of three or more paths.

- **Stretch Or Scale Nodes** This powerful CorelDRAW feature is not available in competing applications. When at least two nodes on a path are selected, clicking Stretch Or Scale Nodes allows the transformation between nodes using their relative distance from each other vertically, horizontally, or from center. Eight selection handles become available, just like selecting an object using the Pick tool, and you can use a click-drag action from any corner or side selection handle toward or away from the center of the node selection. Holding SHIFT constrains the stretch or scale operation from the center of the selection. For example, if you draw a cartoon portrait of a man in profile, you could select the nose nodes, and enlarge the fellow's nose without significantly affecting any other curve segment in the drawing.

- **Rotate Or Skew Nodes** Similar to Stretch Or Scale Nodes, when at least two nodes on a path are selected, clicking the Rotate Or Skew Nodes button lets you rotate and skew the selected nodes; this is a great feature for refining a shape just a little and also for creating more dramatic appearance changes (see the following illustration). Eight selection handles become available, enabling you to use a click-drag action from any corner selection handle to rotate the nodes in a circular direction either clockwise or counterclockwise. Dragging from any side handle enables you to skew the node selection either vertically or horizontally.

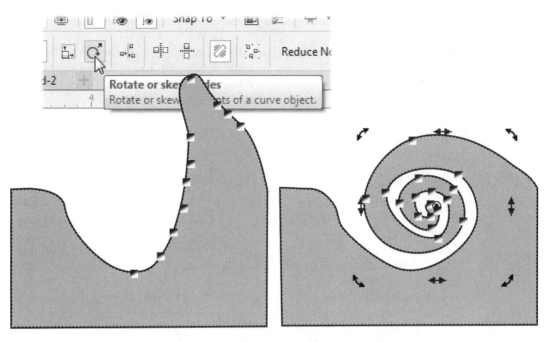

- **Align Nodes**   When two or more nodes are selected, clicking this button opens the Align Nodes dialog, from where you can choose the Align Vertical or Align Horizontal options that automatically align your node selection accordingly. In addition to these options, while only the Start and End nodes of an open path are selected, you can also choose to align control points. This has the effect of moving the two endpoints of the line to overlap each other precisely. This command is wonderful for quickly sketching a zig-zag (perhaps for an illustration of a saw blade), and then in one step, aligning the nodes to create a precise illustration.
- **Reflect Nodes Horizontally/Vertically**   These two buttons become available when two or more nodes are selected. You use these options to move nodes using nudge keys (the up, down, left, and right keys on your keyboard) or click-drag actions in opposite directions.
- **Elastic Mode**   With this command, you move selected nodes according to their relative distance from each other; the effect is like experimenting with a rubber band. For example, while a collection of nodes is selected, dragging one of the nodes causes the others to be dragged a shorter distance in relation to the node that is being dragged. While Elastic Mode is off, all the selected nodes are moved equal distances. Try this option to add a more organic feeling to a drawing you feel looks a little too studied and stiff; it adds expression to a path.
- **Reduce Nodes**   When you use this command, CorelDRAW evaluates the overall shape based on the nodes you've selected, deletes nodes that deviate from a predictable course along the path, and then repositions the remaining nodes—the effect is to smooth the curve. To use this feature, select the nodes controlling the segments you want to smooth and drag the Reduce Nodes slider control position toward 100. As you drag the slider, the shape of the curves is smoothed and you'll notice superfluous nodes disappear from the curve. This option is helpful

for smoothing lines drawn using the Freehand tool with either the mouse or a digitizing tablet stylus.

- **Select All Nodes** This button selects all the nodes in a path (or compound path) using one click. It's a great feature for users who aren't expert with the marquee-select dragging technique yet. You may also select all the nodes in a path with the Shape tool by holding CTRL + SHIFT and clicking any node on the path.

Are you ready to text drive the Shape tool? Follow along here.

Tutorial Editing Paths with the Shape Tool

1. Choose the Ellipse tool (F7) and create an ellipse of any size. Convert the ellipse shape to curves (CTRL + Q) to create a closed path with four nodes joined by four curved lines.
2. Choose the Shape tool (F10). Notice that the Property Bar now features all the line and node command buttons. Click the Select All Nodes button to select all nodes on the path.
3. With the nodes still selected, click the Add Node button (or press the + button on your numeric keypad). Notice that four new nodes are added midpoint between the four original nodes.
4. Click any of the segments once and click the Convert Curve To Line button. The curve is now a straight line, and the curve handles have disappeared.
5. Click a node on one of the other existing curves, drag either of the curve handles in any direction, and notice how they change the shape of the path.
6. Using a click-drag action, click near the middle of the curve segment and drag in any direction. As you drag, the curve handle positions at either end both move, and the shape of the curve is changed accordingly.
7. Click any node on the path to select it and click the Make Node Smooth button. Drag the curve handle of this node in any direction. Notice that when the curve handle is dragged, the opposing nodes move in perfect 180-degree opposition to each other, sort of like a really, really small teeter-totter. Click the Make Node A Cusp button and then perform the same action. Notice that the lines on either side of the node can be curved in any direction independently of each other.
8. With this node still selected, click the Break Curve button to split the path at this point. Although it may not be obvious, two nodes now exist where the original node used to be. Drag either of these nodes in any direction to separate their positions. The nodes are now control points because they break the path to form beginning and endpoints.
9. Select one of these nodes, hold SHIFT while clicking the other, and click the Extend Curve To Close button. Notice the curve is now closed again, while the two nodes have been joined by a straight line.
10. Undo your last action (CTRL + Z) to unjoin the nodes and, while they remain selected, click the Align Nodes button to open the Align Nodes dialog. If they aren't already selected, click to select all three options (Align Horizontal, Vertical, and Control Points) in the dialog and click OK to align the points.

Notice that they are positioned to overlap precisely. Click the Join Two Nodes button on the Property bar. Your path is now closed, and the nodes are joined.

11. Hold SHIFT and click to select two or more nodes on your path. With your nodes selected, click the Stretch Or Scale Node button and notice that eight selection handles appear around your node selection. Hold the SHIFT key (to constrain from center) and drag one of the corner handles toward or away from the center of the selection. All node positions are scaled relative to each other's position, and the lines joining the unselected nodes also change shape.

12. With the nodes still selected, click the Rotate Or Skew Nodes button on the Property bar. Notice that eight rotate and skew handles appear around your selection. Drag any of the corner rotation handles either clockwise or counterclockwise to rotate the nodes. Notice that they are rotated relative to their current position, and the lines joining the unselected nodes also change shape.

The preceding tutorial is only a sampling of what can be accomplished when editing nodes using the Shape tool. You'll want to invest some quality time practicing your editing skills using all the available node-shaping command buttons because the payoff is better artwork—artwork that's closer to what you have in your head—and in the long run, you'll save time creating wonderful pieces.

Controlling Freehand and Bézier Tool Behavior

The options to control how the Freehand and Bézier tools create the curves and lines you draw are set in the Freehand/Bézier Tool pane of the Options dialog, shown next. To access these options, click the Options button on the Standard bar. Then expand the tree subdirectory under Toolbox, and click Freehand/Bézier Tool. The *quick* way to get to this box, however, is to double-click the Freehand or Bézier tool buttons after choosing them from the Curve Tools group.

Here's how the options work:

- **Freehand Smoothing** The Freehand Smoothing option lets you to set the default value of the Freehand Smoothing option on the Property bar while drawing with the Freehand tool. Smoothing may be set based on a percent within a range between 0 (minimum smoothing) and 100 (maximum smoothing). This option is largely redundant with the Freehand Smoothing option available on the Property bar when a curve and the Shape tool are selected.
- **Corner Threshold** This option is for setting the default value for corner nodes when drawing with the Freehand or Bézier tool. Lower values make nodes more likely to be set to cusp nodes, and higher values make them more likely to be smooth nodes. The range may be set between 1 and 10; the default is 5.
- **Straight Line Threshold** This option pertains to how the shapes of lines or curves are created when drawing with the Freehand tool. Lower values make nodes more likely to be set to straight lines, whereas higher values make them more frequently curved. The range may be set between 1 and 10; the default is 5.
- **Auto-Join** This option sets the behavior of the Freehand or Bézier tool while drawing closed-path objects. This value represents the distance in pixels your cursor must be when clicking *near* the first node of a newly created path to close the path automatically. Auto-Join can be set anywhere within a range between 1 and 10 pixels; the default is 5 and is probably the best overall choice for the large screen resolutions we all have today.

Working with Compound Paths

Compound paths have at least two separate paths (either open or closed) composing a single shape. To examine an example of a compound path, use these steps:

1. Choose the Text tool (F8), click once to define a text insertion point, and then type an uppercase Q character. You can assign the character any typeface you like; the more ornamental the character, the more obvious the compound path will be. This character shape, shown in the illustration, has combined two paths: one represents the "positive" space and one represents the "negative" space shape.

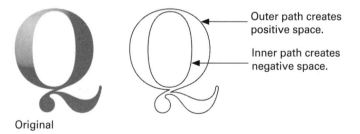

Outer path creates positive space.

Inner path creates negative space.

Original

2. While the text object is selected, convert it to curves (CTRL + Q). The Status bar now indicates the object is a Curve on Layer 1.

3. Change your view to Wireframe; choose View | Wireframe.
4. Press CTRL + K (Object | Break Curve Apart). With the Pick tool, click one of the shapes and drag to move it; clearly the two paths are now separate. You have just converted a compound path featuring two subpaths into two individual objects, as shown here.

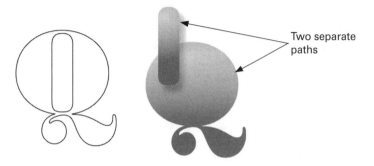

Two separate paths

Combining Objects

When separate objects are combined, they behave as a single object. When two or more closed paths are combined, they form positive and negative spaces within the object. Applying a fill to this type of object fills the positive shapes, but the negative shapes remain clear, as shown here. The Combine command does this: choose Object | Combine, or use the CTRL + L shortcut. You can also click the Combine button on the Property bar, or choose Combine from the pop-up menu.

Original objects   Combined objects

Combining objects that normally feature unique properties—such as rectangles, ellipses, polygons, and perfect shapes—permanently converts them to curves.

Breaking Paths Apart

You can separate the individual paths in a compound path using the Break Curve Apart command (CTRL + K). This command is available when a compound path composed of at least two subpaths is selected. (Using the Extract Subpath command button on the Property bar also does this, but only for the *selected* path.)

Converting Objects to Curves

Converting special types of objects to curves—such shapes auto-created with the Rectangle and Ellipse tools—frees them to be manipulated with the Shape tool as if they were ordinary paths. Choose Object | Convert To Curves; press CTRL + Q; click the Convert To Curves button on the Property bar; or right-click the object and choose Convert To Curves from the pop-up menu.

Converting an object to curves removes any special editing properties; text loses its editability as text and rounded rectangles can no longer be edited to refine the curvature of the rounded corners. Converting to curves applies to polygon, ellipse, and Artistic Text objects, and certain effects objects such as envelopes and perspective effects.

In this chapter, you've seen that there are different tools for creating paths, but the results are more or less always the same; objects have path segments and nodes, and paths can be open or closed. You've also learned how to edit paths using the Shape tool. You'd be well served to bookmark this chapter; CorelDRAW's drawing and editing tools have a lot of power, and this chapter can be a good reference in the future. After all, the program isn't called CorelFILL or CorelRECTANGLE—*drawing* is what good artwork and vector design is all about.

8
Exploring Special Shapes, Connectors, and Other Office Automation Helpers

Not everyone is a born artist. However, if you've been unfortunate enough to demonstrate some artistic abilities in a small- to medium-size business—and your boss catches wind of this—you might be moved to the rank of what's sometimes called "Accidental Art Director."

This chapter is the Corel version of a nonartists' Rescue Kit. As you unpack and read through this chapter, you will gain experience with the features most sought by your business: tables, clean and crisp dimensioning callouts for tech work, banners, perfect polygons, even though you just learned how to use a mouse last week.

Seriously: CorelDRAW is so all-encompassing as a Creative Suite that it includes something for just about every need. And this chapter is "All Business"—with a healthy serving of Fun as you've come to expect from these Guides.

 Note Download and extract all the files from the Chapter08.zip archive to follow the tutorials in this chapter.

CorelDRAW's Smart Drawing Tool

Even if you use a graphics tablet and stylus, you're still drawing freehand, and using a mouse introduces still more flubs when it comes to freehand drawing. Fortunately, the Smart Drawing tool takes the guesswork out of drawing polygonal and rounded objects—in a nutshell, you click-drag *an approximation* of what you intend, tune the options for the Smart Drawing tool based on your first drawing, and in a jiffy you have a precise object with the proportions you need. Pictured next on the Toolbox, the Smart Drawing tool instantly translates rough drawings into shapes you'd usually consider drawing with the Rectangle tool or Ellipse tool—or with other tools that require more effort and skill.

When the Smart Drawing tool is selected, the Property bar displays Shape Recognition Level and Smart Smoothing Level options (shown next) for setting the sensitivity CorelDRAW uses to translate your roughs into precise shapes.

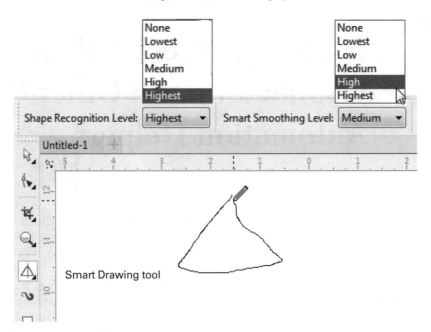

You control how precisely your sketch shape is translated into a precise shape by setting these options:

- **Shape Recognition Level**   This option determines how precisely your sketched shape is matched to a recognizable shape. You can set it to one of five levels, ranging from Lowest (sketched shapes are not easily recognized) to Highest (sketched shapes are easily recognized), with Medium being the default; None turns off the feature.
- **Smart Smoothing Level**   After you've completed a sketch by releasing the mouse button, a level of node smoothing is applied to make object recognition more, or less, precise. This option gives you total control over the smoothing action, much in the same fashion as using the Reduce Nodes spin box on the Property bar when a path is selected with the Shape tool. Choose from five options ranging from Lowest (less smoothing applied) to Highest (more smoothing applied), with Medium as the default; None turns off the feature.

Tip You can control the delay time interval between the moment you release the mouse button and stop drawing to the moment CorelDRAW determines a recognizable shape. By reducing the delay time, you can sketch several separate lines or shapes one after the other, and CorelDRAW then recognizes them as a single compound path. Double-click the Smart Drawing tool icon on the Toolbox to open Options. The Drawing Assistance Delay slider can be set between 0 and 2.0 seconds. The longer you set the delay time, the more time you'll have to keep drawing before CorelDRAW steps in to assist you.

Try the following steps to get an immediate leg up on drawing flawless objects.

Tutorial   CAD: CorelDRAW-Assisted Drawing

1. Choose the Smart Drawing tool and use a click-drag action to sketch the shape of a square or rectangle. Try to keep the sides of the shape vertical and horizontal as you draw; if the square shape looks like a melted ice cube, don't worry. When you release the mouse button, CorelDRAW automatically translates your sketch into a rectangle shape.
2. Choose the Pick tool next and check your status bar display. The shape you sketched is specified as a Rectangle, and the Property bar shows options associated with shapes created with the Rectangle tool, including the rounded-corner options. Try dragging a corner node to make the rectangle a rounded-corner rectangle.
3. Choose the Smart Drawing tool again, and sketch the shape of an oval or circle. Try to keep the shape parallel to the page orientation, although CorelDRAW can also intelligently refine a sketch of an oval that's rotated. On releasing the mouse button, CorelDRAW translates your sketched shape into an ellipse shape.
4. Choose the Pick tool and check your status bar. The shape you sketched is specified as an Ellipse, and the Property bar shows options associated with shapes created with the Ellipse tool, such as the Ellipse, Arc, and Pie properties.

Tip You can alter your sketched shapes on-the-fly using the Smart Drawing tool to backtrack and erase the path you're drawing. Hold SHIFT as the modifier key to reverse and erase. Release the SHIFT key to resume sketching normally.

The shapes you draw also have special editing properties:

- Rectangles and ovals produced by using the Smart Drawing tool become CorelDRAW objects, with the same editing properties as the objects you draw with the Rectangle and Ellipse tools.
- Trapezoids and parallelograms produced with the Smart Drawing tool become Perfect Shapes, explained in a moment.

- Other shapes you draw—triangles, arrows, stair-steps, and so on—become regular curved objects, but the Smart Drawing tool intelligently smooths out curves and straightens nearly straight line segments.
- *Perfect Shapes* are a special category of CorelDRAW objects, and they have special properties. They feature "glyph" nodes (by default, a red-filled diamond)—which are different from regular nodes along a path. These nodes—covered in the next section—can be manipulated to modify the shape without destroying any of its unique geometric properties. See Figure 8-1.

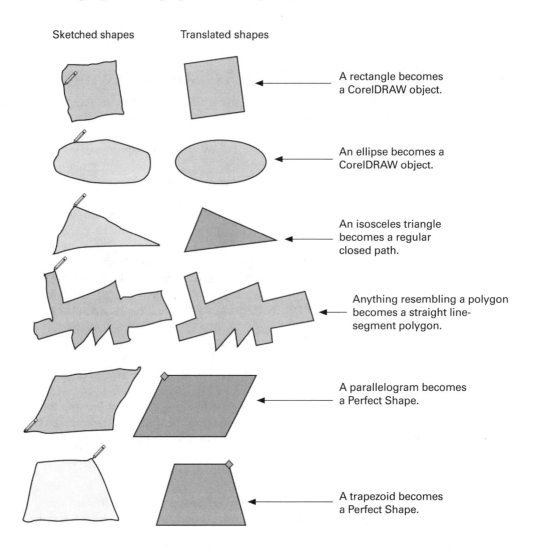

FIGURE 8-1 Perfect Shapes retain their properties even when you extensively edit their appearance.

Try these next steps to create variations on the basic appearance of a Perfect Shape.

Tutorial   Reshaping a Perfect Shape

1. Using the Smart Drawing tool, sketch the shape of a trapezoid. (Refer to Figure 8-1. In a trapezoid, two sides are parallel and the other two sides converge.) On releasing the mouse button, CorelDRAW translates your sketch into a Perfect Shape.
2. Choose the Pick tool and then look at the Status bar. The shape is identified as a Perfect Shape, a special category of shape. Use the Shape tool next to click-drag the glyph node. You'll see that the parallel sides remain parallel, and the converging sides slope away and toward each other. By duplicating this Perfect Shape, you can edit with the Shape tool and create an array of trapezoids, all different in appearance but all editable indefinitely, and all retain the geometric structure of a Perfect Shape.

The Smart Drawing tool helps you quickly draw and translate a variety of sketched shapes into different, geometrically flawless shapes more efficiently than using multiple tools. Each of the translated shapes has its own special properties, which you'll learn in detail in the sections that follow.

Using Perfect Shape Tools

CorelDRAW gives you the power to create objects called *perfect shapes*. This group of tools (see the following illustration) helps you to draw shapes, many of which would be a challenge to draw manually and some of which can be dynamically edited.

Perfect Shapes often feature one or more control points called *glyph nodes*. These nodes allow you to edit specific parts of a specially formatted object dynamically, according to the shape's design. For example, the shape representing a dog-eared page features a single glyph node that enables you to set the diameter of the inner ellipse, leaving the outer diameter unchanged, or a glyph on a beveled rectangle shape enables you to set the bevel depth, as shown in Figure 8-2.

In Figure 8-2, you see a group of Basic Shapes tools beneath the Graph Paper and other manual shape tools (covered in Chapter 5). Once you've selected a specific Perfect Shape tool, a collection of shapes becomes available on the Property bar. Choose a specific type of shape from the Property bar Perfect Shapes flyout selector, shown here, *before* drawing.

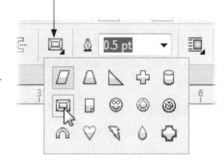

Click the Perfect Shapes button to open the flyout selector.

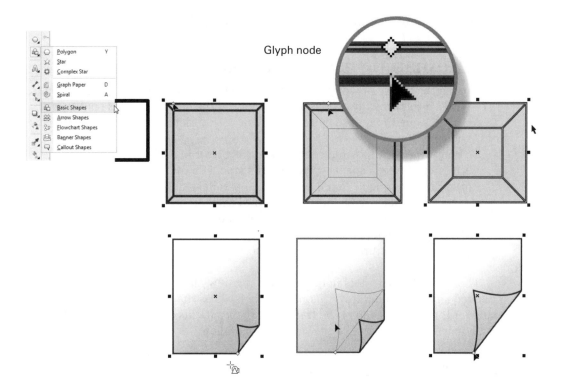

FIGURE 8-2 Glyph nodes can be used to control specific parts of these specially formatted objects.

> **Note** As you work through the shapes, you will see that not all the presets have glyph nodes, and thus do not offer variations once created using glyph nodes. The shapes in the Flowchart Shapes group, for example, are not adjustable Perfect Shapes. If you need to adjust a preset shape manually, you're better off selecting it and then pressing CTRL+Q to convert the shape to a curve, which makes the preset shape infinitely editable with the Shape tool.

Walk through these simple steps to arrive quickly at a level of perfection in your CorelDRAW design work.

Tutorial Creating Perfect Objects

1. Choose a Perfect Shape tool by clicking the Toolbox flyout and selecting a category.
2. On the Property bar, click the Perfect Shape selector and choose a symbol. Use a click-drag action to define a size and position. For all symbol types, except Callout, the direction of your click-drag won't matter because the symbols are created using a fixed orientation. For Callout shapes, the direction of your click-drag determines the object's orientation.

3. Once your shape has been created, you may notice it includes one or more glyph nodes that control certain symbol properties. In cases where more than one glyph node exists, the nodes are color coded. To position a glyph node, use a click-drag action directly on the node itself.
4. Once your object has been created and any glyph node editing is complete, your other Basic Shape properties (such as outline and fill) can be changed in the usual way. For example, you can change the width or height of your new shape using the selection handles available.

Editing Glyph Nodes

Glyph nodes are edited in similarly to the control points on a polygon. As they are moved, the glyph nodes often have the effect of resizing, changing proportion, or dynamically moving a certain part of an individual symbol. Complex symbols can include up to three color-coded glyph nodes.

To explore glyph node editing, take a moment to try this:

1. Choose the Banner Shapes tool from the Shapes group on the Toolbox.
2. On the Property bar's Perfect Shapes flyout button, click it to expand the list and then choose the second preset shape.
3. Using a click-diagonal drag action, create a new shape on your page. Notice the shape includes two glyph nodes—one yellow, one red.
4. Click-drag the yellow glyph node up or down to reposition it several times. Notice its movement is horizontally constrained; as it is moved, the vertical width of each portion of the banner changes.
5. Click-drag the red glyph node left or right to reposition it several times. Notice its movement is vertically constrained; as it is moved, the horizontal width of each portion of the banner changes to match your movement, as shown in Figure 8-3.

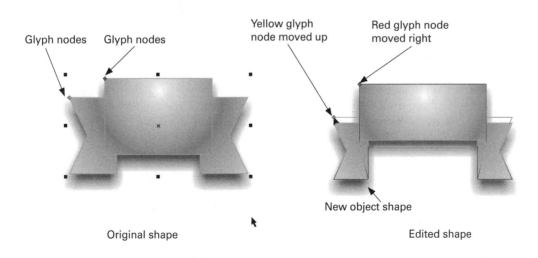

FIGURE 8-3   When movement is vertically constrained, the width of each portion of the banner changes.

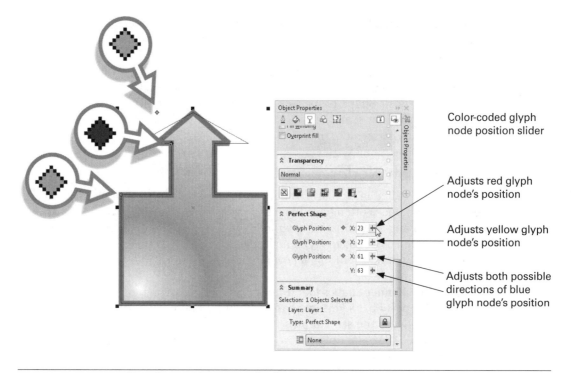

Color-coded glyph
node position slider

Adjusts red glyph
node's position

Adjusts yellow glyph
node's position

Adjusts both possible
directions of blue
glyph node's position

FIGURE 8-4 Use the Object Properties docker to edit glyph nodes.

Glyph nodes can be edited using both the Perfect Shape tool you used to create the shape and the Shape tool (F10). You can also edit glyph nodes by using the Object Properties docker for a selected Perfect Shape, as shown in Figure 8-4. This docker offers precise control over glyph node position; just right-click your shape and choose Object Properties from the pop-up menu or press ALT + ENTER. Depending on the Perfect Shape you've selected, the Object Properties docker might display one, two, or more controls.

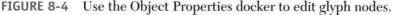

Tip You can adjust the glyph nodes of the Perfect Shapes you create using either the tool you used to create the shape (you can edit a selected Perfect Shape arrow with the Banner Shapes tool) or the Shape tool (F10) at any time in the future.

Using the Dimension Tools

If you need to annotate a drawing or an imported bitmap image with dimensions or labels calling out, for example, different parts of a machine, you'll want to use the Dimension tools, which are expressly for this purpose. The lines you create with the four Dimension tools will tag the bracketed area with units of measurement of your choice and they dynamically update when you scale them. The 3-Point Callout tool is for adding text to a wide selection of arrowhead lines; you can choose a line style for the connector as well as a width, a type of arrowhead, and any style of typeface that you have installed on your system. The text labels for callouts are also upright regardless of whether you rotate the line, and a Callout Control line can be edited at any time with the Shape tool (F10).

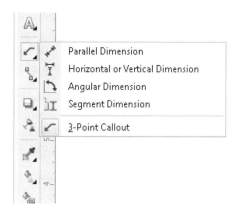

When a Dimension tool is selected, the Property bar displays options to specify the style, precision, and unit values of your displayed dimensions, and to control the display and appearance of the labeling text, as shown in Figure 8-5 and detailed in the following list.

- **Dimension Style**   This option is used to set Decimal, Fractional, or Standard measuring conventions; the default is Decimal.
- **Dimension Precision**   This option is used to set a level of precision. When using Decimal as the measuring style, you can specify precision up to ten decimal places. When using Fractional, you can specify precision using fractions up to 1/1024 of a selected unit measure.
- **Display/Hide Units**   This is a toggle button. If you don't want units appended to a dimension, leave the button turned off before you create a dimension line. Alternatively, you can click the dimension line itself—not the dimension numbers— to change the visibility of the units. If you accidentally click the text instead of the units, you'll get the option to change the font and other text-related options.
- **Dimension Units**   This option specifies the measurement unit with which to display your text labels. You can choose any of the unit measures supported by CorelDRAW.
- **Prefix/Suffix For Dimension**   With this feature, you can enter your own text so it appears before and after the text label for your dimension line. For example, you can specify a style of merchandise, such as "Plastic" or a "Children only"– sized garment. Prefix and suffix text may be any character you want and may be applied before or after the dimension line has been drawn.

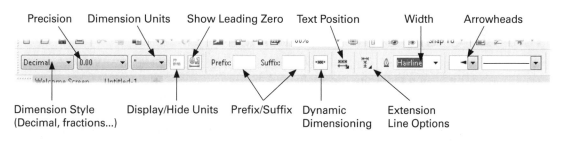

FIGURE 8-5   The Property bar offers specific modifications to your Dimension lines.

- **Show Leading Zero** When a dimension has a value of less than 1, a tenth of an inch, for example, you can add a 0 before the decimal, or choose to leave it off by toggling this button (the nondepressed state). If you have a series of columns of dimension lines, adding the leading zero will help keep the values aligned to the left or right.
- **Dynamic Dimensioning**   This option lets you specify whether your measurement values are updated automatically as the size of the dimension line is changed. By default, this option is turned on for all new dimension lines. If you plan on resizing or changing the scale of your drawing after creating the dimension lines, disabling this option freezes the values being displayed so they remain fixed, whether your dimension lines are resized or not.

Tip If, for some reason, resizing a drawing applied with dimension lines causes the measured values to change, you can right-click the dimension line and choose Break Dimension Apart from the pop-up menu as a workaround.

- **Text Position drop-down**   To specify a position for the text labels applied to your dimension line, choose one of the options from the Text Position drop-down list. Choose from top-centered, middle-centered, or bottom-centered for Auto, Vertical, Horizontal, or Callout dimension lines.
- **Extension Line Options, Arrowheads, and Width**   These are covered in the "Working with Callouts" section.

Checking Out Dimension Lines

The following steps walk you through the techniques used to build dimension lines. Let's pretend in the *Urn While You Learn.cdr* file that the drawing of the antique urn is to size: it's 6¾" tall if it existed in the real world. Your assignment is to respond to an antique dealer who wants to know the overall height of the urn, the height of the neck, and the angle of the bottom decal on the bowl of the urn, as measured from the tip of the bowl where it meets the neck. Moreover, she wants the drawing marked with fractional values and thinks metric amounts are for nerds and scientists. People go a little overboard when it comes to cataloguing antiques, but your success is ensured because you have these steps to guide you.

Tutorial   Using Dimension Lines

1. Open *Urn While You Learn.cdr*, and then select the Horizontal or Vertical Dimension tool from the Toolbox.
2. On the Property bar, set the Dimension Style to Fractional.
3. Click-drag from the top of the urn to its bottom, where you release the mouse button. With this tool, direction is set to vertical or horizontal by the direction in which you first drag.

4. Move the cursor to the left without holding either mouse button. Doing this defines a position for the control text, so make sure your cursor position is not over the urn drawing.
5. Click. You're done and the number value is called out now.
6. Choose the Parallel Dimension tool; the neck of the bottle is slightly slanted, so this is the appropriate measuring tool.
7. Click-drag from the top of the neck (below the lip) to the part that joins the neck with the bowl; release the mouse button at this point.
8. Move the cursor to the right, away from the drawing, and then single-click to add the dimension line and number value.
9. Choose the Angular Dimension tool.
10. Click-drag from the junction of the neck and bowl, and release the mouse button when your cursor is to the left of the bottom decal on the bowl.
11. Move your cursor to the right so it touches the right side of the decal.
12. Click. You're not finished yet. You now have the opportunity to set the position of the arc. Move your cursor toward or away from the vertex of the two angular lines, and then click.
13. The measurement probably will not be readable, with the black text against the dark urn. No problem: with the Pick tool, select the number value and then click the white color swatch on the color palette. Figure 8-6 shows the completed assignment.

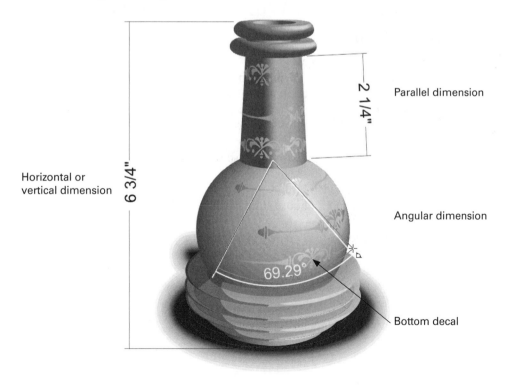

FIGURE 8-6   Use dimension lines to annotate drawings and images quickly and accurately.

Segment Dimensions

Whether you need to discover a value for technical comparison's sake, or want to make sure a part of a personal illustration is an exact length, the Segment Dimension tool is your ticket. This tool measures the distance between nodes on a path, whether the nodes are on a straight line or a curve.

To use this tool, first select a line in your composition with the Pick tool. Choose the Segment Dimension tool, and then marquee-select the two nodes you want to discover the distance between. Move the cursor away from the selection to create handles that bound the selected nodes and then click.

An Exercise in Dimensioning to Scale

All of the preceding information and examples are fine in theory; now, you're going to put the theory into practice in the next tutorial. Let's say you've been handed a CorelDRAW document with a photo in it. Your boss—or any other person who is intimidating—wants the parts of the toy water pistol called out, but here's the catch: the image of the water pistol is *not* 1:1. So how does one measure all the parts of a 7½" long toy that is 5¾" on the CorelDRAW page?

As follows!

Tutorial Drawing Scale, Windows Calculator, and Dimension Lines

1. Open *The Neptune Soaker.cdr*.
2. Choose the Horizontal or Vertical Dimension Line tool and drag it from the beginning of the body of the water pistol to the right and then release the mouse button at the end of the water plug—the yellow piece of plastic to the left of the red cap. Write this value down.
3. The boss says the body is 7½". In this example, the body length should be 5.76". You launch Windows Calculator (or use the physical home version in your workshop). 5.76/7.5 = 1.302. This is the value that this document's drawing scale must be adjusted.
4. Right-click over a ruler, choose Ruler Setup, and then in the Ruler Options box, click Edit Scale.
5. Page Distance should be **1** inch. Type **1.302** in the World Distance field, and then click OK to apply this new scale. See Figure 8-7.
6. Use the Horizontal, Vertical, Parallel, or the Angular Dimension tools to measure anything asked of you in this, or your own, drawing.

Actual size is 7.50"   7.5/5.76 = 1.302

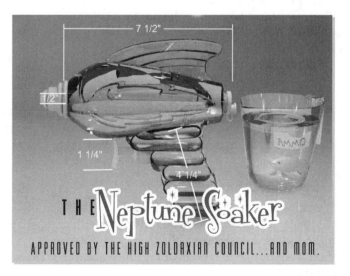

FIGURE 8-7   Adjust the World Distance scale to make measuring areas in photos and drawings accurate to scale.

When Fractional styles are combined with reassigning line and fill colors for text, you'll have a highly detailed, picture perfect presentation for the manufacturing department and even print ads, as shown here.

Working with Callouts

When using the 3-Point Callout tool, you produce two elements: a line composed of two segments (the Callout, as it's displayed on the status bar), and the control text. Callouts are not bound to an object—they can be moved anywhere on the page—but the text and the line are linked and are not moved independent of one another. You have a number of options on the Property bar when the tool is active and also when a callout is selected (after one has been drawn):

- **Callout Line Width**   By default, you always begin a callout with a Hairline width in blue. It's not such a good idea to adjust the width before drawing a line, because doing so triggers an attention box that asks whether you want the default line width—for any object you draw, not just callouts—to be changed. Instead, create your callout, and *then* adjust the width while the callout is selected. Because the callout belongs to the general class of line objects in CorelDRAW, you can change the color of the callout line by right-clicking a color swatch on the color palette while the line is selected.
- **Start Arrowhead**   This drop-down list will seem familiar if you've ever applied an arrowhead to a line using the Property bar. The same basic styles are available as they are on the Start Arrowhead collection. You can even use an arrow *tail* for a callout.
- **Line Style**   Like any other line you draw with the Pen or other drawing tool, the callout can be solid, dashed, a series of dots—choose a style by clicking the pop-up box and then click a style thumbnail.
- **Callout Shape**   You set the style for the callout text from this pop-up list of presets. The symbol doesn't affect the font—it's a style; a rectangle bounding the text, a straight line butted above or below the text; the symbols add an element of polish to your presentation.
- **Callout Gap/End Size**   Sets the distance between the tail of the callout line and the beginning of the text, when None is chosen as a preset shape for the callout text. If you use a circle or other shape, this spin box sets the size of the circle, box, or other shape that surrounds the text.

After creating a callout, you can select the text with the Pick tool, right-click to choose Object Properties from the contextual menu pop-up, and use the newly enhanced and redesigned Object Properties docker to edit all aspects of the text, from font to size to color. You can even apply a gradient fill to your text right from the Object Properties docker (if you want your text to be illegible).

To use the 3-Point Callout tool:

1. Click-drag to create a point where you want the callout to end (the node will eventually have the arrowhead). Move the cursor to where you want the "elbow" of the callout line and then click.
2. Move your cursor to where you want to place the control text and then click.
3. Begin typing the callout text.

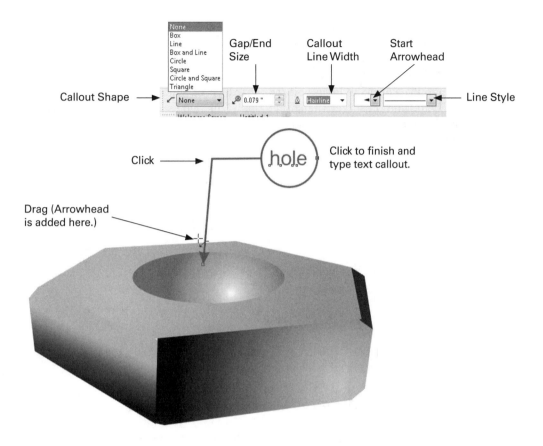

The Connector Tools

The Connector Tools group is almost so self-explanatory, it's not necessary to cover how they work here. Connector lines come in one straight segment, a right-angle, and a rounded right angle, and there's also an Edit Anchor tool, shown in the illustration here, to modify the exact location of the connector line relative to the object (or group of objects) to which the line is anchored.

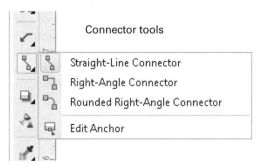

There are more uses in everyday work for Connector tools than you might imagine. Everything from mapping genealogy, to org charts, to seating arrangements at receptions—these all need text in boxes and some sort of connecting line to establish relationships. The marvelous thing about DRAW's Connector tools is that once you've connected two objects, regardless of where you move an object, the connector line preserves the connection. This makes arranging and laying out complex hierarchical maps and charts a snap. Next, the author is building his own genealogy chart.

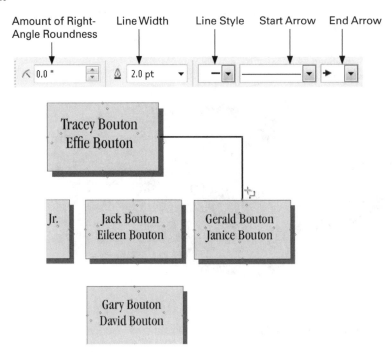

As with dimension lines, set connector line properties—arrowheads, line widths, colors, and others—after you've created the connector line.

Tables

With CorelDRAW's Table tool tucked into the Toolbox, you no longer have to struggle to present tabular data neatly and attractively in your documents. Creating data sheets or directories or displaying spreadsheet data no longer hinges on setting up elaborate networks of guidelines or paragraph text blocks with a generous handful of tab and column settings thrown in. Drag out a table with the new Table tool, or import a table from your word processor or spreadsheet program, and you're all set to use CorelDRAW's tools to make the data look good.

Creating a Table

You can create a new table with either the Table tool in the Toolbox or from the Create New Table command on the Table menu. If you use the Table tool to create the table, you can click-drag to position and size the table exactly where you want the table to be inserted. If you create the table using the menu command, the table will be inserted in the center of the document. In either case, you can drag the table to a new position or resize it just as you would any other object, such as a rectangle that you create with Toolbox tools.

Using the Proper Tool for the Job

Customizing a table happens on several levels: the entire table, a single cell, a range of cells. The content you place inside a cell, such as text or graphics, is controlled with the same tools and settings that would affect the content if it were not inside a cell. Which tool is active, and what you've selected with that tool, if anything, determines what customization options are available to you at that moment from the Property bar or the menus.

Table Options When the Pick Tool Is Active

With the Pick tool, click anywhere in or on the table to select the entire table. You can use the Pick tool to select, move, resize, stretch, skew, or rotate the entire table. When the Pick tool has been used to select the table, the following commands and options appear on the Property bar, as shown in Figure 8-8. These options apply to the entire table.

The table's position on the page and the overall dimensions of the table use the same common entry fields on the left of the Property bar that other objects such as rectangles or polygons use. Other important options are as follows:

- **Number Of Columns And Rows in the table**   Use the top control to enter the number of rows you want your table to have and the bottom one to enter the number of columns you require. You can change these entries at any time. For example, if a table currently has 2 columns and 2 rows, entering **4** in the column field and **6** in the row field immediately reconfigures the table so it contains the new number of columns and rows. If you reduce the number of columns or rows, they are removed from the bottom up and from the right to the left. Any content you have in the columns and rows is lost, so do this with aforethought!
- **Background**   Choose a uniform color for all the cells from this drop-down list. You can also accomplish the same thing by choosing a color from the color palette.
- **Edit Fill**   If you've given the table a background fill, you can go directly to the Edit Fill dialog by clicking this icon. By default, tables are filled with a Uniform fill. If you want your table to have any *other* fill type, such as Fountain or Pattern fill, you can choose it right from the Edit Fill dialog box, a feature new to X7.
- **Border**   "Border" refers to the outline of each cell and the table as a whole. You can show or hide the interior cell outlines and/or combinations of the top, bottom, left, and right sides of the table.

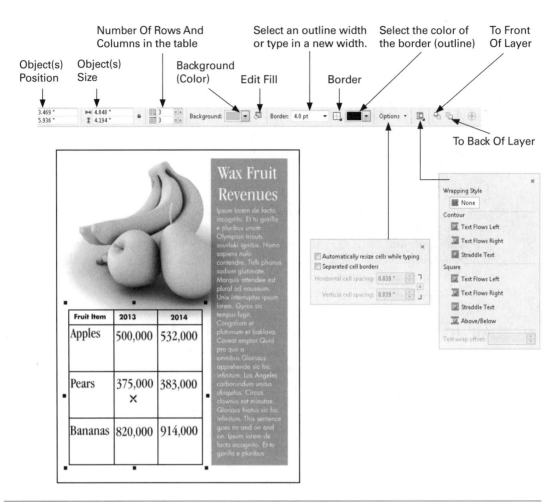

FIGURE 8-8 Use the Property bar to customize the look of a table.

- **Border Outline Width** This field applies a point outline width to the entire table, a cell (CTRL + click to select one), or to the border specified in the Border drop-down.
- **Options** The options that can be set here are Automatically Resize Cells When Typing and Separated Cell Borders. The former is useful when the amount of content you need to enter in each cell is not uniform. Enabling this prevents your content from overflowing and moving out of view. The latter option lets you space out your cells horizontally and vertically so each cell is still contained in the table but is not in immediate proximity to the adjacent cell.
- **Wrap Text** This important option determines how *Paragraph Text* flows around the table and how close the Paragraph Text box can get to the table—this option has nothing to do with the text content of the table. Tables are objects; text can be made to flow around them or over them or under them. Artistic Text is not affected by the Text Wrap setting.

- **To Front Of Layer and To Back Of Layer**   These icons become available if another object is layered on top of or below the table. Clicking these icons changes the position of the table in the stacking order.

Table Options When the Shape Tool Is Active

When you want to select a single cell or multiple cells in a table, use the Shape tool. To select a single cell, click in it with the Shape tool. To select adjacent cells, click-drag across the row(s) or column(s) that you want to select. To select nonadjacent cells, hold the CTRL key and click in the cells you want to select. Diagonal blue lines shade the cells you've selected. These lines are an onscreen visual indicator and not an actual fill.

Once cells are selected with the Shape tool, you can use the options available to you on the Property bar, as seen in Figure 8-9, to customize the cells. The attributes

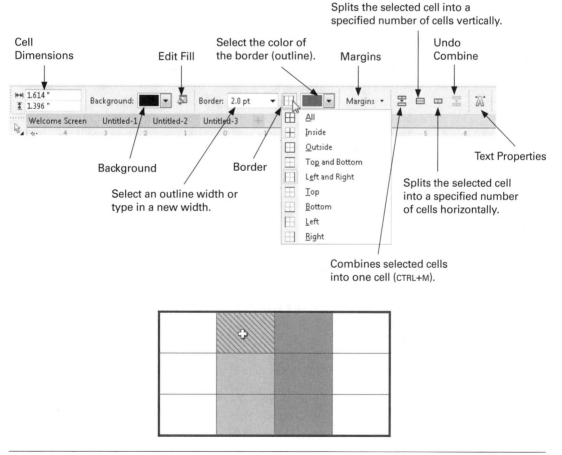

FIGURE 8-9   These options are available for customizing your tables when the Shape tool is active.

you apply to cells override any you set for the table. The first control group on the left now will set the dimensions of the selected cells as opposed to those of the entire table. The Background and Border options work the same as before, but making changes with them now only affects the selected cells. New to the Property bar are the Margins drop-down, which sets the top, bottom, left, and right margins within the cell's bounds, and a group of controls to merge or split the selected cells into fewer or more cells.

You can also use the Shape tool to select an entire column or row. With the Shape tool click the left border of the table next to the row you want to select. When the cursor turns into a small arrow, click again to select that row, or click-drag to select additional adjacent rows. To select columns, click the top table border over the column you want to select, wait for the arrow to appear, and click again to select the column, or click-drag to select additional columns.

To select nonadjacent rows or columns, follow the preceding procedure, but hold the CTRL key and then click next to or over the rows and or columns you want to select.

Editing a Table When the Table Tool Is Active

You use the Table tool to create a table by click-diagonal dragging in your document, but you can *also* use it to edit the table once it is created. Right-clicking in a table row, column, or cell, and choosing the appropriate option from the Select menu in the context menu, is a quick way to select a single row, column, or cell. To select the entire table, choose Table from the Select command on the pop-up menu.

The Table tool can also be used in the same way the Shape tool is used to select multiple columns and rows, but it is easier to use the Shape tool and avoid the possibility of creating a table instead of a selection.

You can insert or delete columns or rows from your table by clicking in a row or column and then choosing Delete | (Row or Column) from either the Table menu or the right-click context menu. You can insert a row or column by right-clicking at the juncture between two existing rows or columns, and then choose Insert | (whatever you like from the submenu) from the contextual pop-up menu.

Working with Text and Graphics in a Table

Entering text in a table is easy; just use the Table tool to click in a cell and enter text using any text entry method. You can type text directly into the cell, import text from the File menu or from the Edit Text Box dialog (CTRL + SHIFT + T), or paste text into the cell from the Clipboard.

Text in tables is handled as Paragraph Text and can be proofed, edited, and formatted in the same ways. If you want to draw a Paragraph Text box within the table cell, you can do so by click-dragging the Text tool in the cell. Artistic Text can also be typed directly in a table cell, but in general you might have a harder time editing and working with it than Paragraph Text.

You can paste any graphic into a cell, but which tool you use to select the cell that will hold the graphic makes a huge difference. If you use the Shape tool to select the target cell, the graphic will be pasted into the center of the cell as a graphic object. If you use the Table tool to select the cell and then paste the graphic into the cell, the graphic will be pasted in as an inline graphic whose size matches that of the default or current font size being used in that cell. This operation can take some time if the size reduction is great.

Once a graphic object has been placed in a cell using the Shape tool, you select it by clicking it. You can then use the control handles to resize, rotate, and skew it. You can even extrude it if you like. If you want to move the graphic to another cell, select it with the Pick tool and drag it into a different cell in the table. You can drag a graphic *out* of a table, but you cannot drag a graphic into a table. However, if the graphic was placed using the *Table tool*, the object can be modified (scaled and so on) using the Type tool. When you place a graphic with the Table tool, the Pick tool will be of no assistance in working with the graphic.

Converting a Table to Text

A table can be converted into a single Paragraph Text box at any time by selecting the table and then choosing Table | Convert Table To Text from the menu. The Convert Table To Text dialog that appears offers you the option to separate the contents of each cell with a delimiter—a comma, a tab, a paragraph, or the character of your choice. If you choose to separate the cell contents with a comma, a tab, or one of your own choice, each row of cells will be saved to a paragraph with the individual cell contents separated in that paragraph by the delimiting character you choose. If you choose to separate cell contents by paragraph, you will get a paragraph for each cell.

Converting an Existing Text to a Table

Existing Paragraph Text can be converted into a table in a process that is basically the reverse of the process outlined in the previous section. Select the text you want to convert, and choose Table | Convert Text To Table from the menu. From the Convert Text To Table dialog, choose the delimiter you've used to break up the text into the chunks that you want to go into each cell. CorelDRAW analyzes the selected text and guesses what will work best as a delimiter. Because commas and tabs are frequently used within a section of text, as delimiters, they might create many more cells than you were expecting. At the bottom of the dialog, you can see how many rows and columns it is going to create. If the number sounds wrong, cancel and go back to your original text in a text editor or a word processor. Mark the end of each piece of text you want transferred into a cell with some other character—an asterisk or a tilde, for example. Then choose User Defined and enter the character you choose as a delimiter into the field.

This chapter has demonstrated that CorelDRAW can lend you as much—or as little—automated assistance as you need to get an assignment finished. That's one of the neat things about this program; just about every arena of business, or level of experienced artist, can find what they need easier than ever in this version, and do what everyone wants to do—reach your goal!

Chapter 9 catapults you from object creation to some creative and advanced object *editing*. See how to subtract one shape from another (this is great for drawing bolts and washers), how to perform some welding on a car, and how to put a chicken back into an egg. Is Chapter 9 going to be seriously educational or out-and-out *fun*!?

The answer is: *yes*.

9

Editing Objects and Rearranging Paths

Let's say you've drawn an object and you're fairly pleased with it, *except* for that little corner you couldn't draw *just* right. This chapter shows you various techniques to massage that almost-perfect shape into *exactly* the shape you've envisioned. Because every object you draw on a page can be broken down into rectangles, ovals, path segments, and so on, this chapter covers the tools and features for doing exactly this: breaking down shapes, combining them, subtracting a little of this, and adding a little of that. Often, arriving at the design of your dreams can be realized by creating an approximation of the shapes you seek. Then, with a pull and a tug here and there, you'll get your desired results faster than by creating the drawing from scratch. You'll also see in this chapter that you can add visual complexity and embellishments through editing, which would be hard to achieve using other methods.

Note Download and extract all the files from the Chapter09.zip archive to follow the tutorials in this chapter.

Shaping and Reshaping Objects

You have a choice of two places to begin when you want to edit an object: you can use Property bar commands, or you can use the hands-on approach; both are covered in this chapter. Both approaches will serve you well, and your choice largely depends on what you need to edit, and then what type of operation is required.

CorelDRAW has great shaping commands to speed the object-creation process, such as Trim, Weld, Intersection, and Boundary. You'll also find three other shape commands at your disposal: Simplify, Front Minus Back, and Back Minus Front. In the next section, you'll learn exactly how to use these commands to shape and reshape your objects. Before getting into the specifics, though, let's take a look at where you can find these commands in X7.

Shaping Commands and the Property Bar

X7's Property bar includes shaping command buttons that let you shape selected objects instantly. These Property bar options are available only when at least two objects are selected—and the shaping commands are available whether or not the objects are positioned to overlap. The Property bar shaping buttons are shown here.

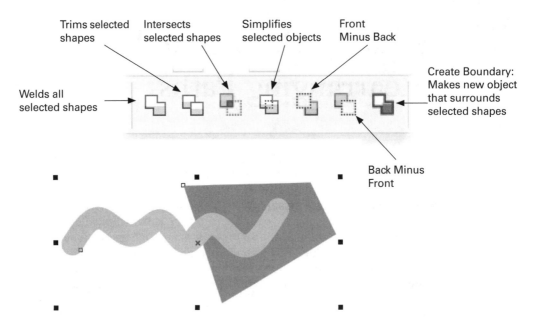

Source and Target Objects

When using Property bar shaping buttons, shapes are subtracted, added, and so on, but the original objects go away. To keep your original objects, use the Shaping *docker*, which offers options to specify that the *source object* (the one performing the operation—the "scissors") and/or the *target object* (the object receiving the operation—the "paper") should remain after shaping.

When using the Shaping docker and the Weld and Intersect operations, you have an additional helper: the Intersect With or the Weld To button at the bottom. When only one object is selected, naturally it's hard for CorelDRAW to perform these operations. The idea behind this option is that if you have several objects nestled closely together (making a target object hard to select), you click the Weld or the Intersect button, your cursor changes to a unique shape, and you then click the desired target object to complete the operation, as shown in the next illustration.

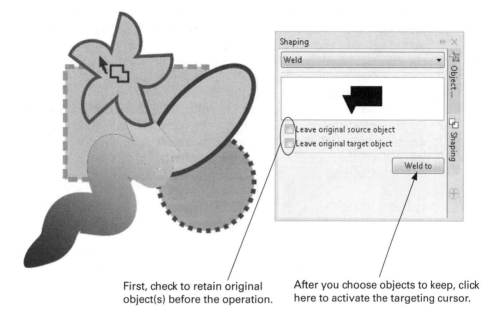

First, check to retain original
object(s) before the operation.

After you choose objects to keep, click
here to activate the targeting cursor.

Now that you know where to find the buttons to launch these commands quickly,
let's examine what you can do with them. The following list explains the results of
applying each command to at least two selected objects:

- **Weld**   The *Weld* command creates a new shape based on the outline shape of two
  (or more) overlapping objects, as shown at right. You can specify via the Shaping
  docker whether the *original* shapes remain on the page.

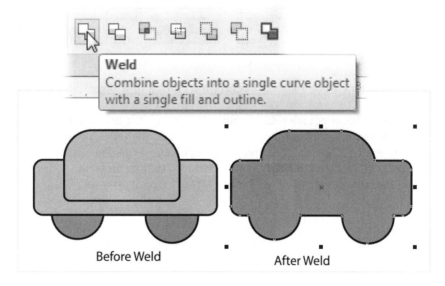

Before Weld

After Weld

This illustration shows a couple of circles and two modified rectangles with rounded edges. The car is going to be welded (because that's the way cars are manufactured), and the image at right is the result of how the different colored objects weld together. Not only did the Weld operation create a single object, but it also gave the resulting object the *color* of the *bottom-most* object, the wheels. This is important to know when welding objects.

- **Trim**   The *Trim* command removes any area of the backmost object that overlaps the frontmost object, as shown here—the rectangle used in this operation is *not* deleted and has been moved to make the result more obvious. No color change takes place; the back object does not inherit the front object's color, transparency, or any other trait.

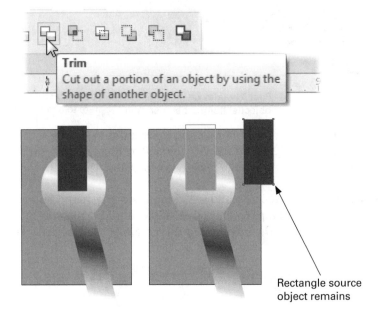

Rectangle source object remains

- **Intersect**   The *Intersect* operation creates a new object based on the overlapping areas of two or more objects. The original objects remain on the page, and the result is not obvious because the new object is in the same position as the overlapping parts of the original objects. In the following illustration, the square was on the bottom, and the resulting object takes on the color of the bottom object. Intersect is a great operation for creating difficult crops of complex objects. The new sun shape would make a nice logo for a tanning salon!

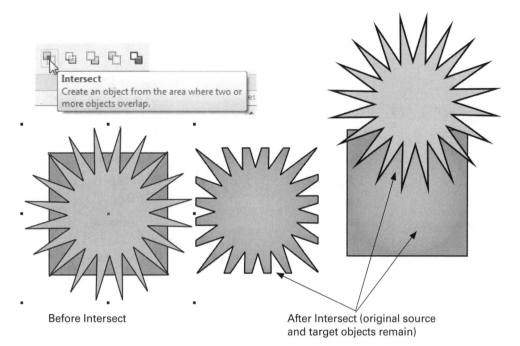

Before Intersect

After Intersect (original source
and target objects remain)

- **Simplify** The *Simplify* command removes all hidden areas of objects that "underlap" foreground object. This command is great for simplifying an intricate drawing, and it can also make a design that otherwise might not print to PostScript print just fine. A different order and arrangement of objects will give you slightly different results.
- **Front Minus Back** When two or more shapes are selected, applying the Front Minus Back command removes the hidden area of the object in back from the shape in front. When more than two shapes are selected, it removes all portions where the shapes in back are overlapped by the object in front, leaving only the object in front remaining, as shown in the center of the next illustration.
- **Back Minus Front** This shaping command works in reverse of Front Minus Back. While at least two shapes are selected, applying the Back Minus Front command removes the portions of the shape layered in front from the shape in back. When more than two shapes are selected, it removes all portions where the shapes in front overlap the shape in back, leaving only the shape in back

remaining. The following illustration shows the results of Front Minus Back and Back Minus Front, when applied to two objects, in the same front-to-back order.

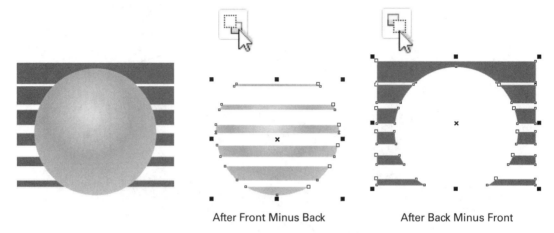

After Front Minus Back   After Back Minus Front

- **Create Boundary** This operation is similar to Weld, except it leaves the target objects on the page. Also, if there are empty spaces between objects, Create Boundary ignores them when making the combined single object. Here is an example of several selected objects and, below them, the resulting shape. By default, the new object has no fill and is ordered on top of the target objects. Just click a foreground color on the color strip, and the new object will become immediately apparent.

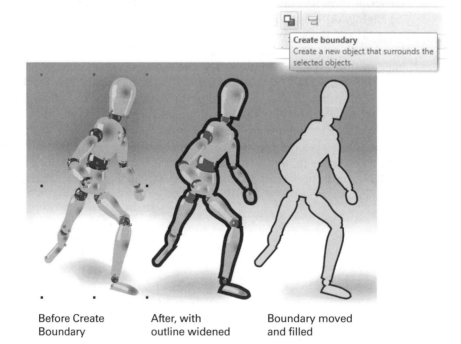

Create boundary
Create a new object that surrounds the selected objects.

Before Create   After, with   Boundary moved
Boundary   outline widened   and filled

Working Examples of Object Shaping

If you've seen some stunning CorelDRAW creations and said to yourself, "Wow, that must've taken the artist ages to do all that work," nope, it probably didn't: the artist put *object shaping* to work. The following example shows just three of thousands of creative possibilities for shaping operations.

Figure 9-1 shows an example problem and a solution using the Trim operation. The chicken came first and then the need to make the chicken look as though it's sitting in the broken eggshell. The chicken drawing is composed of several grouped sub-objects; the Trim operation trims all objects in a group. Work through the next set of steps to see how the Trim operation saves a lot of the manual effort needed to edit dozens of objects to visually integrate the chicken drawing into the scene. All the shapes required to perform the tasks have been added for you; just focus on using the Trim operation.

FIGURE 9-1   Creating the illusion that something is inside or behind some other object is usually a job for the Trim operation.

Tutorial Trimming a Chicken

1. Open *Chicken.cdr*. The goal is to position the toy chicken drawing so it looks as though it's peeking out of the half-shell at right.
2. With the Pick tool, drag the chicken group of objects and position them so the lower half of the chicken lies over the eggshell.
3. Choose Object | Shaping | Shaping to display the Shaping docker.
4. Select the dashed outline shape. The Pen tool is idea for drawing such a shape, if you were designing this composition from scratch. The blue dashed outline is only to call attention to the object in this example—the shape can be any outline color or style.
5. Choose Trim from the drop-down list on the docker. Put a check next to Leave Original Target Object so a copy of the whole chicken remains in the drawing. Why spoil a perfectly good drawing?
6. Because only one object is selected, you now click Trim on the Shaping docker to then prompt the docker to query you on what you want trimmed.
7. With the special cursor, click over the chicken.
8. With the Pick tool, move the lower (whole) chicken out of the way to see the results. Try a click-drag over the wing.

Embellishing Corners and Object Node Editing

Subtracting and adding objects is only the beginning of your adventures in making a shape that's approximately what you had in mind to exactly what you envision. The following sections introduce you to a trio of effects on the Fillet/Scallop/Chamfer docker, and a tool that can change the corners or the line segments that connect object corners. This is going to tickle your imagination, or at least give it a good massage.

Fillet/Scallop/Chamfer

Display the Fillet/Scallop/Chamfer docker by choosing it from Window | Dockers. With this docker, you can truncate the sharp corners of an object you draw.

- **Fillet**   Rounds the corners of an object.
- **Scallop**   Trims a semicircle from the corner of an object.
- **Chamfer**   Lops a straight angle off a corner at an angle perpendicular to the interior angle of the corner.

Tip None of the tools on this docker can alter a curved path segment. A shape that consists of straight paths is the best one to use with this feature; objects that combine curved and straight segments will only be affected along the convergence of two straight path segments.

When Fillet/Scallop/Chamfer evaluates sharp direction changes along a path, it "rounds off" the point of a convex area toward the inside of the path and adds to concave areas. This feature is terrific for quickly building elegant objects such as furniture pieces and machine parts and simply nice ornaments for a desktop publishing document. Enter a positive value in the Radius field (or use the elevator buttons on the docker), and you'll see a faint outline preview in your document. Click Apply when you're happy with the preview. Fillet/Scallop/Chamfer is a destructive operation, unlike the Shaping operations, so if you want to keep your original object, duplicate it before using this docker.

Figure 9-2 shows the effects of the Fillet/Scallop/Chamfer docker on the same zig-zag object created with a single-click and the Pen tool. Because the Radius of this trimming effect is measured in page units, it's usually a good idea to keep rulers visible in your document, and to refer to them to achieve the exact degree of corner truncation you need.

Down and Dirty and the Shape Tool

Up 'til now in this chapter, you've learned how to reshape objects using docker features and menu commands. But the Shape tool in CorelDRAW gets right to the heart of object editing; it's used to

- Connect the beginning and ending nodes of a path to close the path, so it becomes an object you can fill.
- Add nodes to an object so you can alter part of the object's outline.

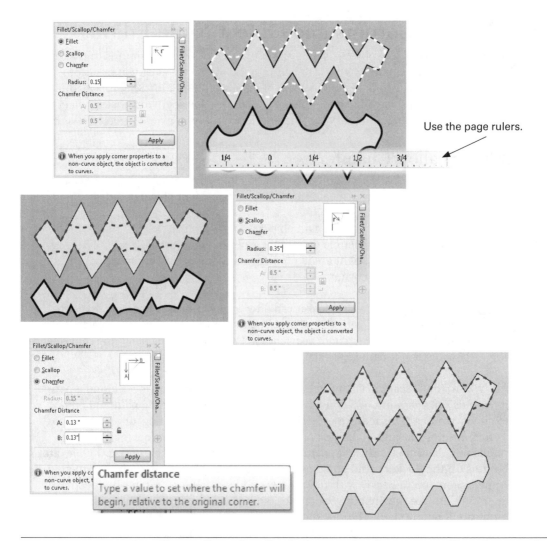

FIGURE 9-2 Use the Fillet/Scallop/Chamfer docker to take the corners off an object with intricacy and classic style.

- Remove (delete) nodes to smooth out a very rough object.
- Move nodes to alter the shape of an object.
- Change a straight line—a standalone, or a line that's part of an object—to a curve.
- Change the amount of curve in a curve segment.
- Make the node that joins two curves in an object sharp, smooth, or even symmetrical.

> **Note**   The Shape tool responds differently and creates different effects depending on the type of object on which you use it. The examples in this section use the Shape tool in combination with ordinary objects consisting of nodes and path segments. Text handling with the Shape tool is covered in Chapter 10, and special objects such as those drawn with the Ellipse and other preset shape-creation tools can be modified using the Shape tool, and the directions in Chapter 5.

You might say that the Shape tool is to editing what any of the Pen tools are to drawing. The Shape tool is covered in other chapters during tutorials, but right now it's time for a taxi driver's tour of what you can do with the Shape tool and what the results look like. Follow along in this whirlwind exhilarating (but hardly overwhelming!) series of participatory events in tutorial style.

Tutorial   Reshaping Objects with the Shape Tool

1. Open the *Shape tool playground.cdr* file, which contains example objects to work with. Pan over to the strange (and open) path marked with a bulleted "1".
2. Select the path with the Pick tool and then try to fill the shape by clicking a color swatch on the color palette. Nothing happens, right? This is because the path is almost, but not quite, closed. Zoom into the upper-left corner of the shape, and, if necessary, to see where the start and endpoints are, go to View | Wireframe.
3. Choose the Shape tool from the Toolbox (the group directly below the Pick tool), and while the shape is selected, click-drag on either end of the shape, and then drag the node over to the opposing node. When your cursor looks like the one shown in this illustration, the shape will be closed when you release the mouse button.

4. Now, what gives with the dull purple fill in this newly closed object? Aha—this is *another* trick found in CorelDRAW: the author closed the shape, filled it, and then reopened it in preparing this CDR file, and CorelDRAW remembers the fill for a previously closed object.

5. Let's move on to the red rectangle to the right of the closed object. You can tell this is a rectangle and, as such, has editing properties we do not seek using the Shape tool—just select the object, look at the status line, and the Status bar says it's a rectangle. The object needs to be converted to a simpler object, one with no special editing properties, so with the rectangle selected, press CTRL + Q (Object | Convert To Curves)

6. With the Shape tool, double-click a point on the top-center line of the rectangle. To remove this point, you can double-click on this node and it disappears, but don't do this now—it's enough right now that you simply *know* this technique. Now the closed rectangular series of straight paths has five nodes that can each be moved. But let's explore a little more.

7. Press the plus (+) key on your keyboard. Surprise! A new node has been generated, and its position on the top path segment is equidistant between the first node you added and the left-corner node.

8. Try pressing the + keyboard key a few more times until you have about eight nodes.

9. With the Shape tool, marquee-select the new node at left on this top line. Then, while holding SHIFT to additively select, select every other new node across the top of the rectangle's line. See the illustration following step 10.

10. Press the DOWN ARROW key on your keyboard several times, to nudge the selected nodes down, until your shape looks like the one shown in this illustration.

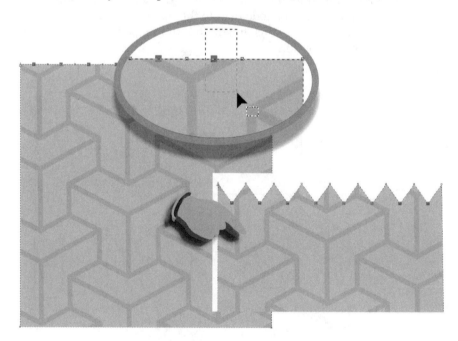

11. For the grand finale to our mini-tutorial, select the star shape at right in the document, and then press CTRL+Q to convert this polygon shape (that has special editing properties when the Shape tool is used) into an ordinary shape composed of straight paths and nodes connecting the lines.

12. With the Shape tool, marquee-select all the nodes, and then click the Convert To Curve button on the Property bar. It's okay to look ahead to the following illustration, where the button is called out. You could also have right-clicked and chosen To Curve from the pop-up menu, but it's good to learn more than one technique for accomplishing a CorelTASK!

13. The path segments have control handles on them. Technically, they are now curves, but they aren't curve-shaped because all you've done is add control handles—you haven't moved the handles to create curves. Fortunately, you can easily make all the control points force the handles to become in opposition to one another, and what this does is...oh, just watch! Click the Smooth Node button now, and you'll probably see something like a form of aquatic sea life.

Convert To Curve

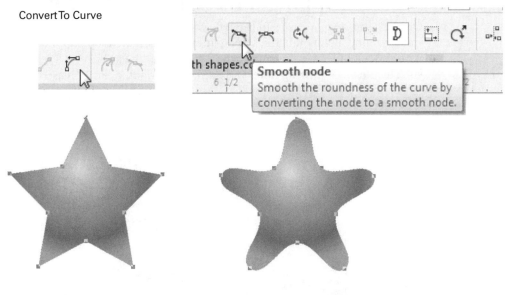

Smooth node
Smooth the roundness of the curve by converting the node to a smooth node.

Note The Shape tool, used to *edit nodes* and *control points* and *control handles*, deserves more than the cursory documentation provided in this chapter. For more details on editing control points, changing node properties, and making straight paths into curved ones, check out Chapters 7 and 17. Or if you have the time, why not read the whole book? ☺

Hiding Object Exteriors Using PowerClips

CorelDRAW PowerClips change the appearance of a shape by *hiding* certain areas of its exterior using a different shape. This, unlike other reshaping operations, is completely nondestructive, and the clipping object can release the inner clipped object(s) at any time. Consider the usefulness of PowerClips: You can hide most of an object from view and put other objects behind the PowerClip. You can play with a dozen possible scenarios for the composition you have on a page and never commit to any of them, unlike trimming an object.

To give you a sense of the creative power of PowerClips, follow these steps with a document whose objects have already been created for you. The assignment is to put a design on the bottom of a flower vase, stencil-style, so parts of the vase's original color still show through in different regions. It's not hard work when you're familiar with PowerClips.

Tutorial   PowerClipping a Design onto an Object

1. Open *Flower and Vase.cdr*. To the left, you'll see a grouped pattern with transparency. Below it is the same pattern with an envelope applied to make the pattern look bulged, as it would when viewed on the surface of a round shape such as the vase drawing here. In Figure 9-3 at right, over the vase is a thin

Original semitransparent group

Enveloped semitransparent group. *Use this one.*

Clipping object

FIGURE 9-3   Using a PowerClip can simulate the painted texture on an object.

yellow outline shape that is a fairly accurate trace over the vase. This is your PowerClip shape for the pattern—it will hide all shapes outside of it. If you'd like to experiment with the non-enveloped grouped pattern with the Envelope tool, see Chapter 14, which provides additional documentation on this feature.

2. Select the bottom pattern with the Pick tool, and then drag it over so it's on top of the yellow outline object, making certain that all parts of the pattern overlap the outline. You don't want gaps in the pattern as it's displayed on the vase.

3. Choose Object | PowerClip | Place Inside Frame.

4. A huge arrow becomes your cursor. Click the cursor over the yellow outline and the pattern scoots inside the container object.

5. The container object is now selected, and new to version X7, a control bar appears below the PowerClip object, with buttons and a flyout menu that include all the commands you'd otherwise have to go to the Object menu to access. More about these after the tutorial.

6. Right-click over the No Fill color swatch on the color palette to remove the outline, or, alternatively, choose None for the Outline Width from the drop-down list on the Property bar. See Figure 9-4.

Although the preceding example shows how to mask the exterior of a group of shapes, a PowerClip container can also have an outline width, color, and fill. In any case, the nondestructive property of PowerClips will serve you in a number of design situations.

Right-click to remove the outline of the PowerClip.

FIGURE 9-4   Let empty areas in patterns and other complex drawings show through a PowerClip object.

Figure 9-5 shows the mini toolbar and the flyout mentioned in the tutorial. The commands are described here.

- **Edit PowerClip** This button takes you to a unique view of your document, where the contents of the PowerClip are available for you to rotate, reposition, scale, recolor, and even create a new shape that you put inside the outline of the "frame"—the container shape as represented in this Edit state. When you're done editing, you'll see a single icon below the PowerClip called Stop Editing Contents; click it and you're done adjusting the PowerClip.
- **Select PowerClip Contents** You can rotate, scale, and move the contents of the PowerClip after using this command, but the contents always stay *inside* the PowerClip object. Attempting to move the contents outside the container will hide them. This command is terrific; for example, if the pattern in the preceding flower vase tutorial didn't line up exactly the way you wanted it to with the vase, you can fix it.

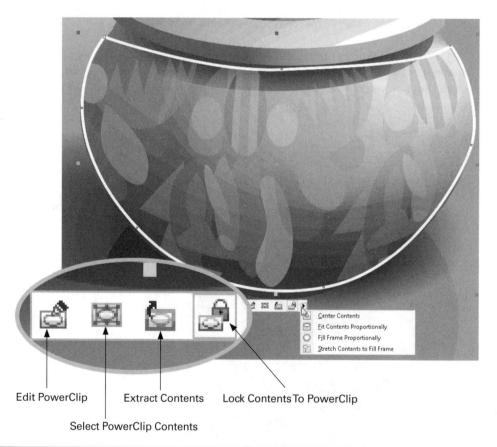

FIGURE 9-5 In CorelDRAW X7, many menu commands can be easily accessed through a context-sensitive mini-toolbar right next to where you're working.

- **Extract Contents**   This command takes the objects out of the PowerClip container. The container now features an "x" through it, indicating it's an empty PowerClip frame, and the objects on your page have no relationship to one another. If you want to do some editing on your formerly contained objects and then put them back inside the PowerClip shape, however, drag the first one (if there's more than one object you extracted), and then drop it inside the boundaries of the PowerClip object. You can put other objects back inside the PowerClip, but you need to hold the letter *w* on the keyboard before letting go of the mouse button to bind the second, third, or other object to the interior of the PowerClip.
- **Lock Contents To PowerClip**   This is an ambiguous name for the function. If you use this command, in its unlocked state, the objects inside the container object are "nailed" to the drawing page, and by moving the container object, you are changing what parts of the inner objects are seen. In its locked state, the contained shape(s) travel wherever you move the PowerClip container object. Use this command if the contained objects are the right size and in their ideal relative positions, but the container object isn't where it should be on the page.

On the flyout of this floating mini-toolbar are four almost self-explanatory commands. *Center Contents* completely reveals the contained objects within the frame (the container shape), which is handy when you've edited the contents in such a way that you can no longer see a specific object. *Fit Contents Proportionally* resizes the contents so all objects can be seen, none are completely outside of the frame, and no disproportionate scaling (commonly called "smooshing") is performed. Similarly, *Fit Frame Proportionally* increases the size of the contained shapes until each shape occupies the same volume within the container. Sometimes, to perform this operation, shapes might disappear outside the frame object to retain everything's proportions.

Finally, *Stretch Contents To Fill Frame* distorts the shapes "inside" the PowerClip and usually gives you a pattern within that is a consistent combination of objects and the frame (container) color if it originally had one. With this option, imagine a rectangular bounding box that encompasses the container; the contained objects are scaled to fit within the bounding box, not the PowerClip container itself.

Cutting with the Knife Tool

The Knife tool functions like a knife you'd use in the real world—except you can run with it and it requires no sharpening—and feels quite natural to use. You begin by hovering over an object area where you want to begin the cut; your cursor changes its appearance to signify it is ready; and then you click-drag to the end of the cut, or the other side of the object. The result is two separate closed objects. As with many of CorelDRAW's tools, SHIFT and CTRL can be used as modifier keys that add precision to your cuts as you work with the Knife. You'll find the Knife tool in the Toolbox grouped together with the Crop, Virtual Segment Delete, and Eraser tools, shown here.

Crop	
Knife	
Virtual Segment Delete	
Eraser	X

Types of Cuts with the Knife Tool

There are three ways to cut a shape with the Knife Tool, and each one requires a different keyboard/mouse technique.

- **Straight cuts**   If you want to slice an object into two separate shapes, as you'd do with a workshop saw, to produce straight lines along the sides of both objects, you aim the cursor on the near side of the object, hover until it changes from an angled cursor to an upright one, click, release the mouse button, and then click on the far side of the object, as shown in Figure 9-6.
- **Freeform cuts**   This technique can be used, for example, to quickly create an illustration of a sheet of paper roughly torn in half. You hover the cursor until it

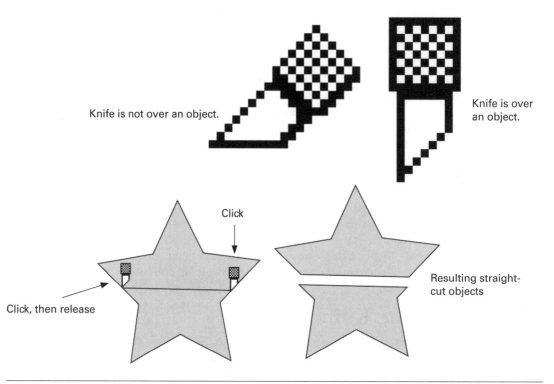

FIGURE 9-6   Click, release, and then click to create a Knife tool straight cut.

turns upright, click-hold on the near side of the object, and then drag until you reach the far side of the shape, as shown here.

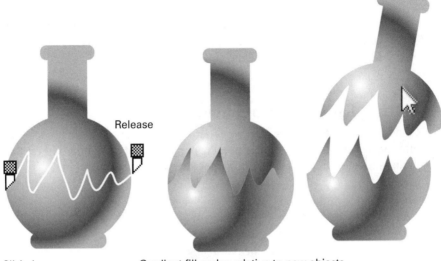

Release

Click-drag   Gradient fill scales relative to new objects.

- **Bézier cuts**   If you need to guide the Knife tool to make smooth jigsaw-like cuts, you hold SHIFT, and then click-drag points, beginning at the near side and completing the cut at the far side, as shown in the following illustration. Notice that not only do the cut result objects inherit the original shape's fill, but also this applies to all types of fills, including gradients. The shapes in this figure each have a gradient start and endpoint inherited from the original shape, and if you choose the Interactive Gradient tool, you can adjust each object's gradient directly and come up with a visually interesting jigsaw puzzle composition or other complex drawing.

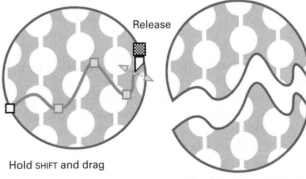

Release

Hold SHIFT and drag

Pattern fill retains original
scale and position.

Naturally, if you have a specific cut in mind, you'll get the best results using the shaping operations, and you cannot edit a Bézier cut's path as you make the cut, but the Knife tool does provide fast and easy results.

Tip If you hold both SHIFT and CTRL while click-dragging to make a Bézier cut, you constrain the direction of the path to 15-degree increments for more predictable results along the edge of the cut.

Setting Knife Tool Behavior

Using the Knife tool gives you just what you'd expect—several objects out of a single one. However, you do have the two Property bar options shown here. Each of these options toggles on and off to suit a specific cutting requirement.

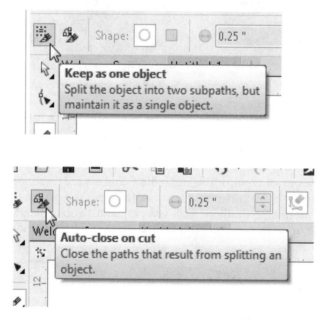

- **Auto-Close On Cut mode** This option, on by default, sets the Knife tool to create closed-path objects following any style of Knife tool cutting. If you turn this option off, the Knife tool divides an object into two open paths and removes any fill. This mode is good for breaking a closed shape into open paths. To use it, you don't drag with the Knife tool; instead click a near point and a far point.
- **Keep As One Object mode** This option is inactive by default; if you enable it, the Knife tool cuts an object, but the result is a combined path—in other words, you don't get two separate objects. This option is useful on occasions (for creating characters in typefaces, for example), but is probably not a mode you'd use every day.

Using the Eraser Tool

The Eraser tool, shown next, completely removes areas of selected objects you click-drag over—just like a real art eraser, but without the stubble landing in your lap. The Eraser comes in two different shapes, and you can define the size by using the Property bar. You'll find it in the Toolbox grouped with the Knife, Virtual Segment Delete, and Crop Tools.

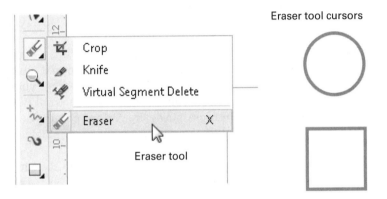

Eraser tool cursors

Eraser tool

Working with Eraser Operations

With this tool, you can remove portions of shapes in four ways:

- **Double-clicking**   When you double-click a selected shape, you remove an area that is the shape of the cursor. Therefore, if you double-click a lot with the circular cursor, you can quickly design a slice of Swiss cheese.
- **Single-click two points**   If you single-click, move your cursor, and then click a second time, the Eraser tool erases a straight line through the selected object.
- **Click-drag**   This is the most common method of erasing, and the results are totally predictable and usually look like hand-painted strokes. If you click-drag, you erase the area you've dragged over on a selected object.

 Note   Grouped objects cannot be erased with the Eraser tool. However, if you CTRL-click an object in a group to isolate it temporarily, you can indeed erase part of the object.

- **Click, hover over a different area, and then press TAB**   This technique creates several connected straight-line segments, and after you get the hang of it, it will feel like you're painting with an eraser. You'll quickly produce phenomenally expressive and complex drawings.

Walk through the following tutorial to see the power of this hover-TAB erasing technique and make it your own.

Tutorial Power Erasing

1. Open *Don't Litter.cdr*, an incomplete international symbol that tells the audience, "Put refuse in the appropriate place; don't be a pig." The orange areas are guides for you; they're locked on the Guides layer.
2. Select the main object. Choose the Eraser tool and then set the nib style to rectangular by clicking the default nib style (the circle) on the Property bar. For this example, set the nib size to about .18".
3. Single-click at the top left of the wastebasket guide. Move your cursor over to the bottom left of the wastebasket guide, but don't click. Notice as you move the Eraser tool that a path preview follows the cursor.
4. Press TAB, but *don't click* your mouse button. Notice that a new erasure appears between the first single-click point and the point where you pressed TAB.
5. To define a third point, move your cursor to a new point (without clicking the mouse button) and then press TAB again. A third point is defined, and the path between the second and third points is erased. Now single-click to end the progressive erasing feature.
6. When you're done with the wastebasket, set the nib style to round, and then add limbs to the thoughtful international guy. Use the TAB technique, for example, to extend a forearm from the guy's shoulder. Once this segment has been erased, double-click where you think his hand would be to extend the erasure. Single-click to end an erasure. Figure 9-7 shows the work in progress.

Single-click

The TAB key defines points; single-click defines the end.

FIGURE 9-7 Press TAB to define intermediate points between your first and last erase path points to create connected, straight-line erasures.

Setting Eraser Tool Properties

Set the width and shape of the Eraser tool using Property bar options, as shown next. You can also control the complexity of the removed shape, the number of path segments, and the connecting nodes created during an erase session. These properties significantly affect the shape of erased object areas.

Tip As with most of the Toolbox tools, you can get to the options for the Eraser in Options by double-clicking the button on the Toolbox.

Eraser Width

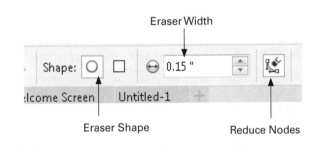

Eraser Shape   Reduce Nodes

Tip Use the keyboard to change the cursor size while you erase. Press the UP and/or DOWN ARROW keys on your keyboard while click-dragging, and the result can be a tapered brush. After you release the mouse button, the Eraser tool resets to its original size, so you don't have to worry about starting out a new erase stroke with a yard-wide tip!

Enabling the Reduce Nodes option (also called the *Auto-Reduce Nodes Of Resulting Objects* in the Eraser tool options) lets you reduce the complexity of erased area shapes at the price of what's usually trivial inaccuracy. The importance of removing unneeded nodes is twofold: first, fewer nodes along paths makes editing easier and provides more predictable results. Second, too many (and we're talking hundreds of thousands of nodes) can occasionally fail to print to older PostScript printing technology. Depending on the shape, the speed at which you erase an area, and the shape of the Eraser cursor, you might produce 45 or 125 nodes when you make a complex erasing stroke. This option is better than having none, but Reduce Nodes also requires the artist's vigilant eye to ensure the feature is doing what you want it to be doing with your artwork.

Using the Virtual Segment Delete Tool

The Virtual Segment Delete tool is used to delete specific portions of objects, specifically, overlapping areas. Additionally, this tool removes portions of an object's path where they intersect paths of *other* overlapping objects.

To use this tool to delete path segments where an object intersects itself, follow these quick steps:

1. With the Freehand tool, draw a path that loops around and crosses itself.
2. With the Rectangle tool, create a rectangle that overlaps a little of the freeform path you drew in step 1.
3. Choose the Virtual Segment Delete tool.
4. Let's see how much of the rectangle remains when you click its top segment. Hold your cursor over the segment to delete—you don't need to have the objects selected to use this tool. You'll notice the cursor becomes upright when you hover over an eligible segment. Now click. As you can see in this illustration, the fill of the rectangle disappears because it's not a closed path any more. But the segments that do remain are inside the freeform shape.

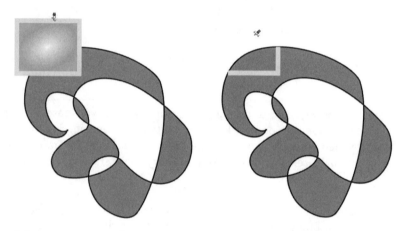

After deleting portions of a path with this tool, what remains is either an open curve with just one path, or a compound curve with two or more subpaths. For example, if the object you're deleting segments from is a closed path, deleting one segment will result in an open curve. Deleting a segment from a rectangle, ellipse, or polygon object will convert the resulting shape to curves and remove the dynamic object properties. To delete segments that are hidden behind an overlapping object, temporarily set its Fill to None.

Cropping an Illustration

The Crop tool, located in the same group as the Knife and Eraser tools, brings a bitmap effect to vector drawing. If you have experience with Corel PHOTO-PAINT or another photo-editing program, you are already familiar with a crop tool: you select an area within a photo, perform a command such as clicking inside the crop area, and the area outside the crop is deleted and the image is resized.

The Crop tool in CorelDRAW behaves exactly like an image editor's crop tool. Objects do not have to be grouped; you just drag a rectangle around the area of your design you want cropped, double-click inside the proposed crop area, and all object areas outside the crop box are deleted. In Figure 9-8, at left, you can see a photo for a housewares catalog, but at the last minute, the store wants the white mug out of the scene. The Crop tool is dragged around the desired area, and then you double-click inside the crop area to alter the imported image permanently.

This is a powerful and potentially very destructive tool, but fortunately you can work with the crop box *before* cropping: you can drag a *corner* crop box handle before cropping to resize the crop proportionately; dragging a *middle* handle disproportionately resizes the crop area. Additionally, once you've made a proposed crop, clicking, then clicking again inside the box puts the box in rotation mode, and you can actually crop a diagonal shape such as a diamond. If you want to cancel a crop operation, press ESC—or click the Clear Crop Marquee button on the Property bar and the crop box goes away.

This chapter has taken you through several processes by which you can create minor and big-time alterations to just about anything you draw; additionally, many of the operations apply to bitmaps you bring into the workspace. Use the command that best suits the task you have in mind, and use your judgment as to which operation will get you to your goal fastest. Personal computers are productivity enhancers: there's no need to labor over something when CorelDRAW and your PC can do it for you in less time.

Now that you have one, or two, or a dozen shapes on your drawing page, let's mix them up with some honest-to-gosh text: a headline here, a little body copy there. Shapes and words live together; practically no one publishes an image-only website, and Chapter 10 of this *Guide* gets you into the language of typography and the features in CorelDRAW that make your keyboard a professional communications tool.

FIGURE 9-8   The Crop tool removes all areas of every object that lies outside the crop box.

PART IV

Working with Text in a Composition

10 Paragraph Text, Artistic Text, and When (and How) to Use Them

CorelDRAW is a great facilitator of communication and self-expression, and that includes text as well as graphics. This chapter gets you started with the Text tool and other CorelDRAW type features. You'll learn how to work with them to make your thoughts and ideas inviting and clear. Text and graphics go hand in hand in presentations, and as you'll see on the following pages, you have the necessary tools at your disposal.

Note Download and extract all the files from the Chapter10.zip archive to follow the tutorials in this chapter.

CorelDRAW's Text Tool

All text you want to enter on a page in CorelDRAW is created with the Text tool, the tool with an *A* as its icon in CorelDRAW's Toolbox. To begin, click its button in the Toolbox or press F8. If there's *already* text on the page, double-clicking the text with the Pick tool switches the current tool to the Text tool and gives you an insertion point for adding text. The Text tool cursor is a small crosshair with an *A* below and to the right, which becomes an I-beam (a text-editing cursor) when it's over a text object. You click anywhere on the page or the pasteboard to create an insertion point and then start typing.

> **Note** Text copied from the Clipboard can be pasted when the Pick tool is your current tool. Usually, unformatted text—text from a TXT file you copied from (Windows) Notepad, for example—will import as Paragraph Text. Text copied from a word processor will import as a document object; double-clicking the object offers in-place editing exactly as you'd edit a WordPerfect or Word document. Choose Edit | Paste Special when pasting clipboard text to ensure that the correct formatting and original fonts are used. Use the Text tool's I-beam cursor to insert pasted text. To reselect the Pick tool while the Text tool is selected, press CTRL+SPACEBAR—for all other tools, press either SPACEBAR or CTRL+SPACEBAR.

When you use the Text tool, you can produce two different types of text objects in a document: Artistic Text and Paragraph Text. In Figure 10-1 is a layout that uses Artistic Text in combination with the Text | Fit Text To Path command—the path is hidden in this illustration. The smaller body copy text uses Paragraph Text; the top paragraph wraps around the top of the image using a CorelDRAW Envelope (see Chapter 17). Artistic Text and Paragraph Text have different properties, but both are added to a document using the same Text tool. Artistic Text, because of the way it's produced in a document, is easy to reshape and distort—you'll find it simple to do artistic things with it, such as creating a company logo. Conversely, Paragraph Text is optimized for

Did you ever have one of those days? Or perhaps *three* or *four* of those days...all in a row? You know, when the stars are aligned to form a cosmic pick-axe, pointing at the back of your head?

Life Amounts To One Big Juggling Act!

When it doesn't rain, and it doesn't pour—but it feels more like the next Ice Age, you *can* take control of your schedule *and* your life, with the amazing new best-selling book, ***Exploring Your Inner Self-Consciousness***. Learn to become a more dynamic, forceful, and irritating individual with what remains of your friends and loved ones!

FIGURE 10-1 Artistic Text and Paragraph Text have different attributes, and each is suited for different text treatments in a design.

longer amounts of text, and it's a great text attribute for quickly modifying columns of, for example, instructions, recipes, short stories, and so on. In short, Paragraph Text is best used for several paragraphs of text in a composition whereas Artistic Text should be reserved for headlines and just a few lines of text you might want to curve along a path, extrude, or do something else unique and fancy with.

Although there are similarities between Artistic and Paragraph Text, you're best off using one or the other depending on the type of text element you want in your design.

Entering and Editing Artistic Text

Artistic Text is best for illustration headlines, callouts, and other occasions when you want to create text with a special effect such as extrusion, an envelope, text on a path, and so on. To add a line of Artistic Text to a document, with the Text tool, click an insertion point and then type your phrase; alternatively, after clicking an insertion point you can press CTRL + V to paste any text you have loaded on Windows' Clipboard. To create several lines of Artistic Text, press ENTER when you want to skip to a new line and then continue typing. By default, all Artistic Text is set in Arial, 24 point; later in this chapter you'll see how to change the default font.

Artistic Text is also easy to convert to curves so you can modify a character in a word: for example, Microsoft's logo has a tick missing in the second "o". To duplicate this effect (but not Microsoft's logo), you begin with Artistic Text for the company name, press CTRL + Q (Object | Convert To Curves), and then edit away using the Shape tool. Artistic Text can be fine-tuned using the features on the Property bar when the text is selected using either the Pick tool or the Text tool. The options are shown in Figure 10-2.

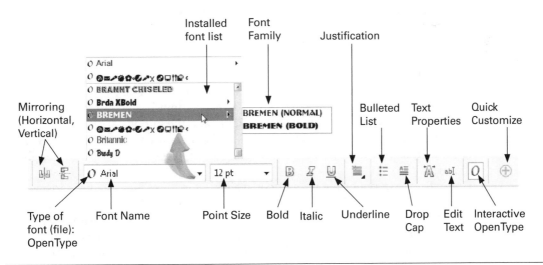

FIGURE 10-2   Use the Property bar to make Artistic Text look exactly the way you want it.

Note All the options covered in the following section are also available on the redesigned Object Properties docker, covered later in this chapter.

- **Mirroring (Horizontal and Vertical)** In addition to creating special effects, the Mirroring buttons are also useful when, for example, you want to print a T-shirt transfer with your company name. The name needs to be reversed (mirrored horizontally) to print on the transfer paper, so the unreversed print on the T-shirt reads correctly (or at least without the need for a mirror).
- **Type of font (file)** To the left of the font name in the Font Name drop-down list is an icon signifying what file format the chosen font uses: OpenType, Type 1, or TrueType. This option is nice when you're sorting your fonts in Bitstream Font Navigator or the Fonts utility in Control Panel.
- **Font Name, Font Family** The font name is the name of the typeface. By default, you're using Arial 24 point. You change fonts in a new document by selecting the text you've typed with the Pick tool and then choosing a different font from the Font Name drop-down list. If a font has family members, you'll see a right-facing triangle to the right of the font name when the drop-down list is extended; choose it by hovering above the triangle to reveal the flyout and then click the family member you want to use. You can also perform a speed-search by clicking the current name in the Font Name drop-down and then typing the first few letters of the font you want. The drop-down list immediately scrolls to the right neighborhood of installed fonts, making your selection a fast and effortless one. Note also that on the Font Name drop-down list, at the top, above the divider bar, are the fonts you've chosen recently for previous documents and even from previous CorelDRAW sessions.
- **Point Size** Text has traditionally been measured in points; with current digital typeface technology, the measure is 72 points to the inch. Artistic Text used as a printed headline can be anywhere from 18 points for a flyer headline to 72 points for a newspaper headline to 300 points and up for headlines that fairly scream at the reader.
- **Bold and Italic** These buttons on the Property bar are shortcuts to formatting a whole line of text or only selected characters as bold and italic members of the typeface shown in the Font Name box. If a specific font has no family members, CorelDRAW *doesn't* "fake" a bold or italic look, and the buttons are dimmed. If you need an italic treatment of a font that has no italic family member, a quick fix is to use the Transformation docker, and then set Skew to about –12 degrees to apply to the Artistic text.
- **Underline** An underline is an effect available for every font you have installed— you click the button when text is selected and CorelDRAW renders an underline. You can modify the style of the underline by highlighting the underlined text and choosing Object Properties. Then, in the Character area of the Object Properties docker, you click the Underline flyout and choose the type of style you prefer.

Note Underlines are great for professional documents, particularly legal ones, but an underline isn't the cleverest way to emphasize a phrase in an advertisement. Use a bold font instead, or a colored outline, or a gradient fill to attract attention artistically. Although underlines are effects, they're very real and if you convert an underlined phrase to curves (CTRL+Q), the underline becomes a simple, four-node object.

- **Justification**   Also called "Horizontal Alignment" in balloon help. This drop-down offers options for aligning lines of text. Although Justification serves you best when using long columns of Paragraph Text, applying, for example, Center Justification to two or three lines of Artistic Text gives it a more polished look. By default, there is no Justification for newly entered Artistic Text, but for all intents and purposes, it is left-justified text. Full Justification creates a splendid, professional look for columns of Paragraph Text, but tends to look awkward for multiline headlines. Left Justification is quite common and acceptable in desktop publishing, and Right Justification should be reserved for extreme design circumstances in Western countries because we read text from left to right. There is a slight difference between Full and Forced Justification, your last two choices on the drop-down list. *Full justification* ensures that both the left and the right margins are flush to an imaginary line at the width of the text column. *Forced justification* creates the same flush left and right column edges, but it also creates extra space between words and characters if a line has only a few characters. In the illustration here, you can see an awkward presentation of a few lines. You might actually *want* a wide character-spacing effect and to do this, you put a soft return at the end of a line (press SHIFT + ENTER).

Full Justification

Force Justification

Also called "Horizontal Alignment" in balloon help. This drop-down offers how lines of text are aligned relative to one another. Although Justification will serve you best when using long columns of Paragraph Text, Artistic Text takes on a more polished look, too, when you apply, for example, Center justification to two or three lines. By default, there is no Justification for newly-entered Artistic Text, but for all intents and purposes, this is left-justified text. Full Justification creates a splendid, professional look for columns of Paragraph Text, but tends to generate an awkward look for two or three line headlines. Left Justification is quite common and acceptable

Also called "Horizontal Alignment" in balloon help. This drop-down offers how lines of text are aligned relative to one another.   Although J u s t i fi c a t i o n will serve you best when using long columns of Paragraph Text, Artistic Text takes on a more polished look, too, when you apply, for example, Center justification to two or three lines. By default, there is no Justification for newly-entered Artistic Text, but for all intents and purposes, this is left-justified text. Full Justification creates a splendid, professional look for columns of Paragraph Text, but tends to generate an awkward look for two or three line headlines. Left

- **Text Properties** This button appears on the Property bar when you select the Text tool. Clicking this button displays the Text Properties docker. The Text Properties docker is very similar to the top area of the Object Properties docker. Essentially, anything you need to do to customize one or more characters in a text string, you can do using the features on the Text Properties docker. You can access the features of the Text Properties docker by clicking the button when text is selected with the Text tool and Pick tool or by pressing CTRL+T when the Shape tool is the active tool.

- **Interactive OpenType** Explained shortly, Interactive OpenType shows alternative characters in highlighted OpenType text you've typed. OpenType fonts sometimes contain scores of custom characters that are very hard for average users to access and add to text. The Interactive OpenType button shows and hides alternatives, allowing a one-click addition of special characters when a specific OpenType font contains them.

- **Edit Text** This button displays a text editing box, which also appears when you click the Text tool on text that has an effect applied such as an envelope or an extrude. CorelDRAW is designed with text-editing flexibility in mind, so to transform text using just about any feature—and to allow the text to still be editable—you work in a proxy box so you don't have to start over when you make a typographic error.

- **Bulleted List** With text selected (with the Pick tool) or highlighted (using the Text tool), clicking the Bulleted List button creates a bulleted list from your text, using a standard bullet symbol, a hanging indent for the text, and a new bullet wherever you've inserted a hard return in Paragraph Text. This button is inactive when using Artistic Text. This feature is covered in Chapter 11.

- **Drop Cap** By default, when Paragraph Text is highlighted and this button pushed, a three-line-tall drop cap is auto-created. Options to adjust the drop cap's height, spacing, and whether a hanging indent is used or not is found on the Text menu. This feature is covered in Chapter 11.

- **Quick Customize** Although technically not a part of the Text Properties features, if you want to add or remove a button on the Property bar when the Text tool is active, clicking this button will do the job.

Options for Formatting Characters

The Text Properties docker takes the place of other UI features in previous versions, and includes more comprehensive options to change selected characters. If you're new to CorelDRAW, you can change Artistic Text characters in three different ways:

- Use the Shape tool in combination with the Property bar. This method gives you control over character positioning, rotation, and other properties as covered in the next section.

- Use the Text tool or the Shape tool in combination with the Character section of the Object Properties docker. Using this method gives you more options and thus more control than the Property bar. Using Object Properties with characters is covered later in this chapter.

- Use the Text tool, the Shape tool, or the Pick tool (which works but you cannot select individual characters) in combination with the Text Properties docker. The same comprehensive options are on the Text Properties docker and in the Character area of Object Properties, but for experienced users this feature might be easier to remember by its historic shortcut, CTRL + T.

Use the Property Bar to Change Characters

As you can see in Figure 10-3, you have some options when using the Shape tool to select characters, but a more complete set of options when highlighting a character with the Text tool and then clicking the Text Properties button on the Property bar. For quick and simple reformatting, use the Shape tool, and for extensive reworking of your Artistic Text, use the Text tool. You have additional options for lines running under, over, and through selected characters, and if, for example, you've used the Character section in Object Properties to put a Double Thin Underline beneath your text, you can remove this underline later using the Property bar while character nodes are selected using the Shape tool. Character nodes appear black when selected (as shown in Figure 10-3), and your cursor is a clear indication that you're editing text with the Shape tool and not an object path node.

Tip When a character node is selected with the Shape tool, you can drag the character any which way. You don't *have* to rely on the Offset numerical entry fields on the Property bar to create offset changes.

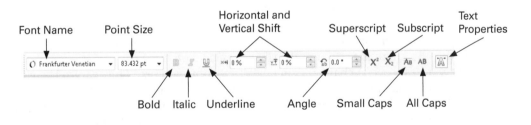

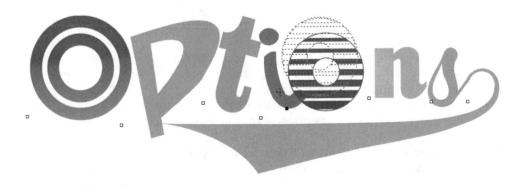

FIGURE 10-3 Format and reformat text characters using the Character Formatting box and the Property bar.

Selecting and Moving Characters with the Shape Tool

To select arbitrary characters in an Artistic Text object, select the Text object with the Shape tool (F10)—the cursor changes to the Shape tool pointer with an *A* next to it. With the Text object selected in this way, a small, empty box (a *control handle*) appears at the lower-left corner of each and every character.

- To select any character, click its control handle using the Shape tool. To select nonconsecutive characters, hold SHIFT (*not* CTRL as you'd expect) while clicking. You can also marquee-drag around the nodes you want to select with the Shape tool. With the control handles selected, you can modify the text formatting, fill, outline, and position of those characters.

- To move one or more characters selected with the Shape tool, click-drag one of the selected control handles. Alternatively, you can nudge the selected characters with the keyboard arrow keys. It's generally a good idea to keep the characters you move horizontally aligned: hold CTRL while dragging—vertical moves do not accept the CTRL key for constraining movement.

- Moving characters with the Shape tool changes their Horizontal and Vertical Shift values. You'll see new values in the Character Offset fields on the Property bar. Moving characters with the Shape tool is handy for manually adjusting the position of characters visually to improve *kerning,* or intercharacter spacing. It's also useful if you own a "bum font," a poorly coded digital typeface in which certain characters neighboring other characters are too tight or too loose.

Using the Object Properties and Text Properties Character Options

Everything you can do with the Shape tool in combination with the Property bar for editing characters within a text string, you can also do on the Object Properties docker by selecting one or more text characters with the Shape tool *or* the Text tool. Additionally, there is an area in the Character field on the docker where you can quickly access special characters in OpenType fonts you use. This feature is *not* the same as the Insert Character docker, discussed later in this chapter. Many of the OpenType typefaces you find today, both commercial fonts you buy and ones that come with Windows and other applications, are capable of holding far more than the 256 characters that TrueType fonts used to offer. CorelDRAW uses and organizes OpenType data to give you custom fractions, special ligatures, alternate characters, and other professional typesetting features when a specific font holds the special data.

Whenever you need to change a character in an Artistic Text string, select the character's node with the Shape tool or highlight the character with the Text tool, and then right-click and choose Text Properties (or press CTRL + T), and all the character options are displayed. Here's a minimal guided tour of where character formatting features have been relocated and a brief example of how to use ligatures (characters that are specially linked together) in text. Refer to Figure 10-4 as you read on:

1. **The Underline button flyout**   You can choose among six different Underline styles for a selected character or word. Remember: a tick mark at the lower right of a button means more options are available on the button's flyout. You click the button to reveal the flyout and then select your choice.

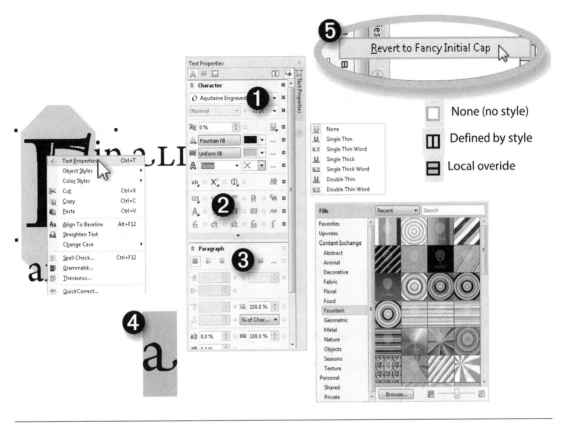

FIGURE 10-4 The Text Properties docker is your single source for formatting text highlighted with the Text tool.

2. **The OpenType typography features area** If you've chosen an OpenType character or phrase (there should be a bluish "O" to the left of the font name), and the OpenType was designed with special characters, you can do some professional and fancy stuff with your text on a page. As explained shortly, when a character, word, or phrase is highlighted, you'll see some or all of the fifteen options turn black in this area, which means CorelDRAW has checked out your font, and yes, it does have, for example, the capability to build custom fractions (such as 5/16), or ligatures such as a dotless *i* to the right of a lowercase *f*, which looks a lot more professional and is easier to read than the stem of the *f* banging into the dot on the *i*. If none of the options turn black, your OpenType font doesn't have any special features.

Tip Regardless of whether the Object Properties docker is visible, when you highlight OpenType with the Text tool, you can click the Interactive OpenType button on the Property bar. You'll see a small downward-facing triangle at the bottom of the highlighted text; by hovering over it, a flyout reveals alternative OpenType characters, if any, and you choose them by clicking a flyout selection. To hide options and the flyout triangle, click the Interactive OpenType button to return it to its off state.

3. **Advanced options**   The down triangle on the bar below the OpenType features reveals offset and rotation features when you click it—these are the same features presented on the Property bar when you select a character node with the Shape tool. You'll have an option for Overline, and the option to specify overprinting if you send this document to commercial printing and a character or other object has both a fill and an outline width.

4. **Background fill**   Characters you've selected can have a solid, fountain fill, or other type of fill behind them. The effect is like highlighting passages on a printed page. Any background fill will take up the entire font character height (which usually exceeds the height of capital letters in a font) plus the line spacing. Therefore, you can create background fills for characters that are seamless with the following line of text that has a background fill.

5. **Style modifications**   Because the Object Properties docker is integrated— and objects are treated the same as text—everything on the page can be styled, the styles can be overridden with the Object Properties docker features, and this docker can also change your restyled object back to its original styled self again. If you see an empty gray square to the right of any feature on the Object Properties docker, it means the selected text (or object) has not been styled in any way; it's an unstyled object. When you see a pastel-colored vertically divided square to the right of a property, the text is styled—and you might want to think twice about modifying your work. If you have modified a styled piece of text, you can change it back to its original style by clicking the Local Override icon and then choose Revert To Style.

Walk through these steps to discover the ease and power of working with Object Styles. Let's imagine that you worked with a Paragraph Text frame months ago to achieve a beautiful antique look with a custom color and a drop cap. You just received a multidollar contract to work on Ensign Doug's Hot and Spicy Rum, and the label for a bus stop poster needs to carry a legend on the bottle label. You think your fancy text you previously created would work well in this assignment, so your task in this tutorial is to create a Style from your saved text and then apply the Style to the text that goes on the poster.

Tutorial   Using Object Styles with Paragraph Text

1. Open *Ensign Doug's rum.cdr*. You'll see that in addition to the JPEG image on the page, there is some text above it in Arial, and a Paragraph Text block to the left, nicely formatted in Times New Roman, which contains a passage from the US Bill of Rights Amendments. If you have a more elegant, perhaps antiqued typeface than Times, select the Paragraph Text now with the Pick tool and then choose your ideal font from the drop-down list on the Property bar.

2. Choose Windows | Dockers | Object Styles. If you remember the keyboard shortcut to Graphic and Text Styles from previous versions of CorelDRAW, it's still the same: CTRL + F5.

3. With the Paragraph Text selected (using the Pick tool), right-click and then choose Object Styles | New Style Set From. You're choosing to define an entire

style set and not simply a style because the Paragraph Text has formatting and also a unique color you want to define and apply shortly to the Ensign's text.

4. On the New Style Set From dialog, type the name of this new Style Set in the text field, and notice that in the future, you can display the Object Styles docker right after you define a style by checking the box in this dialog. Click OK and your screen should look like the illustration here.

5. On the Object Styles docker, you'll see a new entry below the Style Sets heading on the docker. Select the text above the advertisement, as shown here, and then click the Apply To Selected button. Applying two defined styles to a different object is that easy, and this updated docker can spare you minutes of work (minutes are considered *hours* in Internet time!) over using the Attributes Eyedropper tool.

6. In the following illustration, you can see the result of your work. This feature is well worth investigating in your spare time because it will *save* you time. You'll note a little added touch or two to the text; you'll see how to put an envelope around text and other objects in Chapter 17—this is why the text looks as though it's *on* the label and not simply on top of the image.

Here's a working example of using OpenType features—the fast and professional way. In Figure 10-5, the author went to some professional expense and bought the Rennie Mackintosh collection of typefaces from ITC in OpenType file format. He choose these fonts because he's designing text for a print ad featuring the furniture of the famous Arts and Crafts designer, and as you can see in this figure, the font and the furniture are quite similar. The *fi* characters in "The finish" look awkward, but happily, when the whole phrase is highlighted and the Object Properties docker is open, a down arrow appears below the highlighted text, offering alternative character choices. There are not a lot of features in this OpenType font, but the *fl* and *fi* ligatures and a special picture glyph or two are supported. If your OpenType font has a special character, CorelDRAW will find it for you.

Tip Try typing a line of text, and then using Gabriola, an OpenType that comes with Windows 7 and later. You'll see that just about all the options for OpenType light up on the docker, and several prestyled combinations are offered when you click the down triangle below the text.

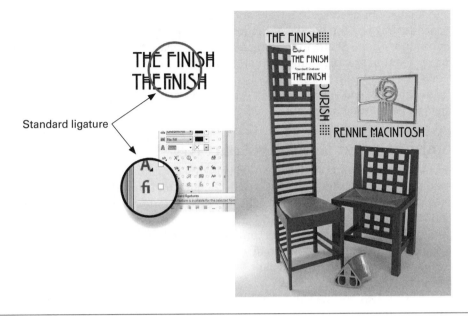

FIGURE 10-5   Use OpenType features on the Object Properties docker to access characters you couldn't otherwise.

Adjusting Spacing with the Shape Tool

When an Artistic Text object is selected with the Shape tool, two additional handles appear at the lower-left and lower-right corners of the object, as shown in the following illustration. These two handles modify the line spacing and character spacing for the entire block in one go.

To increase or decrease the word and character spacing between words only, hold SHIFT while dragging the handle at the lower-right corner of the selected text object right or left with the Shape tool. To increase or decrease the line spacing (also the before-paragraph spacing), drag the handle at the lower-left corner of the selected text object down or up with the Shape tool.

You can view and edit all spacing values modified with the Shape tool in the Paragraph Formatting box.

Combining and Breaking Apart Artistic Text

You can combine several Artistic Text objects into a single Artistic Text object; you select all the Artistic Text objects with the Pick tool, and then choose Object | Combine or press CTRL+L. Each Artistic Text object starts a new paragraph in the new Artistic Text object.

The Artistic Text objects are combined *in the order in which they are selected*—if you select several objects in one go by dragging a marquee around them, they will be selected from front to back. Artistic Text objects that do not contain spaces are combined onto a single line. If any of the selected objects is *not* an Artistic Text object, all the Artistic Text objects will be converted to curves and combined with the non–Artistic Text object.

Tip   If the text doesn't combine in the order you want or expect, you can reverse the stacking order of the original Artistic Text objects by choosing Object | Order | Reverse Order. This trick will not work, however, if the text has already been combined (changed from editable text to ordinary path objects).

To break apart Artistic Text, choose Object | Break Artistic Text, or press CTRL+K. With multiline Artistic Text objects, this command results in one Artistic Text object for each line or paragraph from the original object.

Also, using the Break Artistic Text command on single-line Artistic Text objects results in one object for each word. And breaking apart single-word Artistic Text objects results in a new object for each character.

Converting Artistic Text to Curves

Many effects can be applied directly to Artistic Text, but you might want to apply effects that cannot be applied as a "live" effect to editable text. Artistic Text objects occasionally need to be converted to curves. Choose Object | Convert To Curves, or press CTRL-Q. Text that has been converted to curves is *no longer editable with the Text tool*. Text converted to a plain object with paths and control nodes is a good way to begin creating logos.

Entering and Editing Paragraph Text

The biggest difference between Artistic Text and Paragraph Text is that Paragraph Text is held in a container—a frame—so *you don't directly edit*, for example, the width of characters in a Paragraph Text frame simply by yanking on a bounding box handle with the Pick tool. The next illustration shows at top duplicate Paragraph Text frames; they're easy to differentiate from Artistic Text; even when not selected, Paragraph Text frames have a dashed outline around them—a Paragraph *frame*. The version at top right has been scaled so it's wider than at left. The lines of text flow differently but *the characters themselves* remain unchanged, as does the spacing between characters and words. At bottom, the same text has been entered as Artistic Text and then a bounding box handle was dragged to the right using the Pick tool. What happens is that the characters themselves are stretched. That's the biggest difference between Paragraph and Artistic Text: if text doesn't have a frame, then you're scaling the text.

The Pick tool modifies the container for Paragraph Text.

The Pick tool directly modifies Artistic Text.

Once you get the hang of working with Paragraph Text (and the following sections are your guide), you'll find this type of text indispensable for business designs, and your brochures will look as slick as can be.

To create a Paragraph Text object, choose the Text tool from the Toolbox, and then click-drag diagonally to create a rectangle into which you'll enter the text. The click-hold + diagonal-drag technique (commonly called a *marquee-drag*) is the way to create a paragraph block. A paragraph block is just a container. It can be filled with text you type, or you can fill it immediately with loaded text. The sample text inside the Paragraph frame is simply a placeholder; it disappears after you've added your own text. Paragraph Text frames have resizing handles as well as kerning and leading handles (Artistic Text features these as well), discussed later in this chapter. You can fill a Paragraph Text frame with text in one of three ways:

- *Type in the frame.* You'll probably want to run spell-check (Text | Writing Tools | Spell Check or press CTRL-F12) when you're finished typing, because only three people on Earth have perfect spelling from memory, and one of them was your third-grade teacher. Don't disappoint her.

- *Paste from the Clipboard.* You'll see a dialog before you can paste if you press CTRL + V, or choose Edit | Paste (and Edit | Paste Special). Here, you can choose to keep or discard the formatting of the text on the Clipboard.
- *Import a text file.* Depending on the text file type, you might be prompted to install a compatibility pack, especially for older MS-Word documents. With a broadband connection, the process takes about three minutes; you don't have to quit CorelDRAW; and you can paste after the compatibility program is installed. By contrast, a plain TXT file with no font or paragraph attributes will import perfectly after you choose an import style from the Importing/Pasting Text dialog.

The frame you drag for imported Paragraph Text might not accommodate the amount of text. As a result, the *overflow* text is hidden; in this case, the frame is a dashed red outline instead of black. To reveal the text, you drag down on the "windowshade handle"—the small square tab, bottom-center, on the text frame; when there's hidden text, the handle has a down arrow at its center.

You always have the option to *link* Paragraph Text frames. Instead of spoiling a design by increasing the size of a frame, you can create a second, third, or any number of additional frames, and then flow the excess text into the new frames as you create the frames. You can move the linked frames around in your design, and the *content* (the *meaning* of the typed text within Paragraph Text) remains in perfect order. For example, if you need to break a paragraph into two frames in the middle of, "Now is the time for all good people to come," you do this, and in the future if you need to resize the first Paragraph Text frame, the excess words "pour" into the second frame, regardless of its position on the page. This is too neat to simply describe with words, so let's create linked text frames in the following steps.

Tutorial Creating Linked Paragraph Text Frames

1. In a word processor or plain text editor, copy some existing text to the Clipboard; it doesn't matter what the text is. Highlight a few paragraphs and then press CTRL + C.
2. In CorelDRAW, choose the Text tool and then perform a diagonal-drag to define a Paragraph Text frame. Try to make the frame smaller than the text on the Clipboard (eyeball it).
3. Insert your cursor in the frame and then press CTRL + V to paste the Clipboard text. If you copied from a word processor, CorelDRAW will flash you the Import/Pasting Text box where you have the option to retain the formatting (if any) created in the word processor—font choice, point size, justification, and tabs are all text-formatting attributes. Go with it; click the Maintain Fonts And Formatting button and then click OK.
4. Click the bottom-center text handle (the box with the black triangle arrow) and your cursor is now loaded with all the text that was hidden from view because your frame is smaller than the text you pasted into it. Your cursor takes on a new look, as shown in the following illustration.

Ipsum lorem de facto incognito. Et tu
gorilla e pluribus unum. Olympian
triouts souvlaki ignitus. Homo sapiens
nolo contendre. Telli phonus sodium
glutimate. Marquis attendee est plural
ad nauseum. Unix incognito. Et tu
gorilla e pluribus unum. Olympian
triouts souvlaki ignitus. Homo sapiens
nolo contendre. Telli phonus sodium
glutimate. Marquis attendee est plural
ad nauseum. Unix interruptus ipsum
lorem. Gyros sic tempus fugit.
interruptus ipsum lorem. Gyros sic
tempus fugit. Congolium et plutonium
et baklava. Caveat emptor.Quid pro
quo a omnibus. Glorious apprehende
sic hic infinitum. Los Angeles
carborundum unitus Mercedes. Circus
clownus e minutae. Glorious hiatus sic
hic infinitum. This sentence goes on
and on and on. Ipsum lorem de facto
Ipsum lorem de facto incognito. I

Click to load the cursor with
Paragraph Text overflow.

5. Click-hold + drag diagonally to create a new, linked text frame. The excess text from the first frame automatically flows into the new frame, as shown here. A light blue line with an arrow indicates the relationship between the text in the first and the second frame (this screen element does not print, don't worry). Try repositioning the two frames now using the Pick tool. Then try resizing the first frame. Dynamically, the second frame takes the overflow from the first frame.

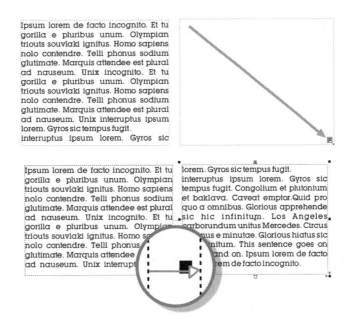

Wrapping Text Around Other Shapes

You can apply text wrapping to shapes in CorelDRAW so any Paragraph Text placed close to the shape will flow *around* the shape instead of over or under it, as shown in the examples in Figure 10-6.

All you need to do is superimpose some Paragraph Text on an object. First, you select the object (but not the text); then press ALT + ENTER to display Object Properties and click the icon directly to the right of Outline Width on the Property bar—Tooltips will tell you it's the Wrap Text drop-down and you're all set to do some text-wrapping, as shown here:

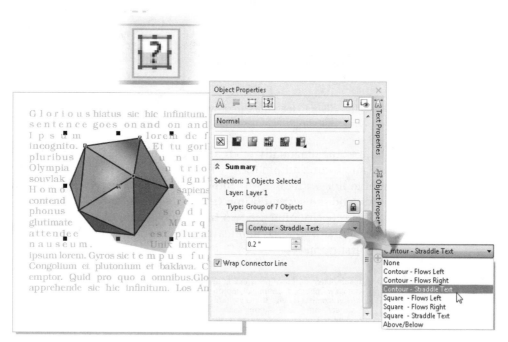

Text conforms to a shape in two different ways:

- **Contour wrapping** The text is wrapped a line at a time *around* the outline of the shape.
- **Square wrapping** The text is wrapped around an imaginary rectangle that bounds the shape with the wrap (its *bounding box*).

In either case, the text can be made to flow down the left or right of the object, or to straddle it (flow down both sides). Square wrapping also supports Above/Below where no text flows to the sides of the object.

To apply Contour-Straddle, right-click the shape and select Wrap Paragraph Text from the pop-up menu. To set a different wrapping type, select it from the Summary tab of the Object Properties docker (ALT + ENTER is the shortcut). Then set the margin distance, which is the gap between the outline or bounding box of the shape and

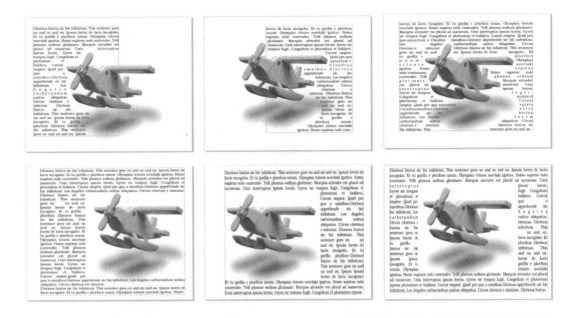

FIGURE 10-6   There are six contour and square text-wrapping options available and one nonwrapping option (None).

the Paragraph Text wrapped around it. The *Seaplane example for text wrapping.cdr* is provided in the Zip archive for this chapter in case you'd like to practice a little.

Fitting Text to Curve

Wrapping text around an object has its alter ego: putting text inside a shape, so it looks as though the text itself forms a shape. And there's a third variation called Fit Text To Curve—you can have Artistic Text follow an arc, a freeform line, and an open or closed shape, and you have options for the style in which the text follows your line.

Pouring Text into a Shape

The simplest way to form text so it appears to have a geometry other than rectangular is to first create a shape, copy some text to the Clipboard if you don't have a message in mind, and then carefully position your Text tool just inside the line of the shape (perhaps 1/8th of a screen inch inside) until the cursor turns into an I-beam with a tiny text box at its lower right. Then click to start typing, or click and then press CTRL + V to paste your Clipboard text. Text inside a shape is Paragraph Text and it obeys all the Paragraph Text–formatting conventions covered in this chapter and Chapter 11.

In this next illustration, you can see sample Paragraph Text at left; it's been copied to the Clipboard, and then the Text tool has been placed close to the white ellipse; it makes no difference whether the container object is selected. When the cursor changes to the one shown in this illustration, start typing, or in this case, press CTRL + V, and then format your text, and probably assign the container outline no color and no width to complete the illusion.

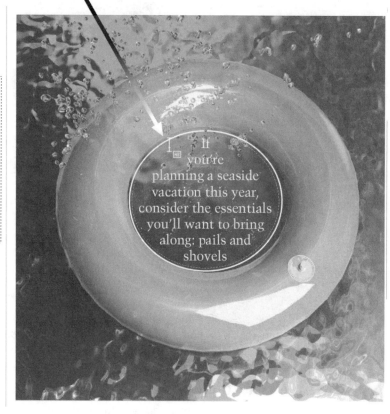

If you're planning a seaside vacation this year, consider the essentials you'll want to bring along: pails and shovels make the construction of sandcastles a lot easier, bringing a (con't.)

 Note *Orange Innertube.cdr* and *Yield sign.cdr* are in the Zip archive you downloaded. You can use them for practice, pouring text into the predefined shapes in the files.

One popular treatment for text "bound" to an object is the arc of text. You apply this treatment by first creating the arc shape (a circle usually works well) and then, instead of clicking inside the shape, you hover above the shape until your Text tool cursor becomes an I-beam with a tiny swooping curve beneath it.

Follow these steps to flow text in a semicircle:

Tutorial   Text Along a Curve

1. Open *Toon Valley Milk cartoon.cdr*. The graphic of the cow could use some text revolving around the outer circle.
2. Create a circle using the Ellipse tool.

3. With the Shape tool, drag the Ellipse node away from the center of the circle to create an open arc. Adjust each node until you have an arc centered above the cartoon. See Chapter 9 if you're unfamiliar with editing CorelDRAW objects.

4. With the Text tool, position the cursor just above the outline of the circle, and then click an insertion point and begin to type. The text follows the curve. What you type is up to you, but **Toon Valley Farms** is a solid starter for text to support the graphics that involve a cow and could go on to stardom on a milk carton!

5. If the text isn't aligned to your liking, use the Offset spin box on the Property bar to correct it.

6. If you want the text to be a little off the curve, use the Distance From Path spin box.

7. If you want a truly wild and interesting style—a treatment—of the text, such as a 3D ribbon look, check out the drop-down list at left on the Property bar. Click any of the styles to apply them. The arc still has an outline, but it takes one right-click on the X in the color palette to fix that. Figure 10-7 shows an example of the finished label, and how you can place it over a photo—covered in Chapter 16.

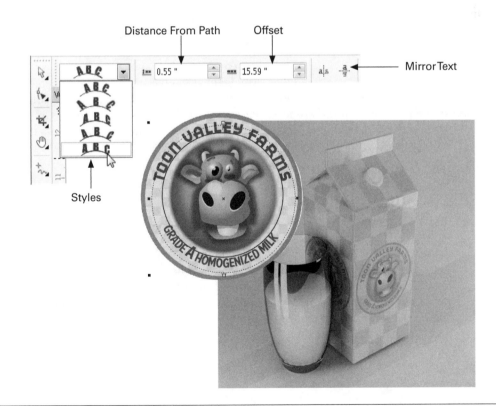

FIGURE 10-7   Use Fit Text To Curve to make your message a flowing one.

Tip Don't overlook the Mirror Text button when fitting text to a curve. If you want text arcing in a semicircle beneath a graphic—as the text at the bottom of the logo is in Figure 10-7—text can't be fit to a lower arc in a graphic without mirroring the text vertically and horizontally first.

Embedding Objects into Text

Graphic objects and bitmaps can be embedded into blocks of Artistic and Paragraph Text—in the layout profession, this is called an *inline graphic.* Embedding objects is a great way to add special symbols to text, such as logotypes, bullet points, or horizontal separators, or, for instructional graphics, mouse cursor images.

You embed an object into text in two ways:

- **With the Clipboard** Copy or cut the object to the Clipboard (CTRL + C or CTRL + X), click the Text tool in the text where you want the object to be placed, and paste the object (CTRL + V).
- **Drag-and-drop** Select the object with the mouse, and then drag it with the *right* mouse button to the position in the text where you want it to appear—a vertical bar between characters in the text indicates where the object will be placed. Release the mouse button and select Copy Into Text or Move Into Text from the pop-up menu.

Embedded objects are treated as "special characters"—they can be selected only with the Text tool or the Shape tool. To resize an object after embedding it, select it and set its point size on the Property bar as if it were a typographic character.

To delete an embedded object, select it with the Text tool and then press DELETE.

Using the Insert Character Docker

CorelDRAW, via Text | Insert Character (CTRL + F11), removes the guesswork in locating a character or symbol in any font you have installed. When you choose this command, the Insert Character docker appears, and you can insert a character in two ways:

- **As text** If you need, for example, a fancy bullet that is inline in existing text in your document, you can drag the symbol or bullet from the visual list of available characters for a specifically chosen font (from the Font list drop-down), and then hover your cursor near the location in the sentence or word where the character should go. When your cursor turns into a vertical beam, release the mouse button and the character is inserted.

New to version X7 is a context-sensitive drop-down list, a button titled simply Entire Font. Depending on the typeface you've chosen, clicking this button can help you focus and narrow the selection of glyphs in the preview window that you drag into the line of text. For example, Arial contains almost 1,000 characters, but you only want a character that pertains to currency. So you click the button, put a check next to Currency, and the symbols for Euros, Yen, a generic currency glyph, the British pound, the American dollar, and so on, are displayed, removing hundreds of visual distractions from your search.

Using the Symbol Manager

Now that you've located the perfect symbol for a design by using the Insert Character docker, save the symbol so you can reuse it in the future—then you won't have to hunt for it again! Here, the Symbol Manager (CTRL + F3) under Windows | Dockers is an invaluable resource. The Symbol Manager provides you with information about symbols contained and saved only to an open document and also provides User Symbols, an area on the Symbol Manager where you can duplicate a catalogued symbol into any document at any time.

Let's say you've found a great symbol for a layout, you've placed it in your document, and you decide you want to reuse it tomorrow. The steps for cataloguing the symbol and for accessing an *instance* (a duplicate that takes up less saved file space in a document) of it tomorrow follow.

Saving Frequently Used Symbols to Your Own Library

1. With an object selected, choose Object | Symbol | New Symbol.
2. In the Create New Symbol box, type a name you'll remember later in the Name field and then click OK. As you create more and more new files using CorelDRAW, you'll definitely want to stay tidy in your cataloguing work. Cross-referencing is a good practice; in Figure 10-8, the description area on the docker has been filled in with the name of the typeface from which the rocket ship was copied. Later, you can easily look up the name of the font that contains this symbol and use it in a program outside of CorelDRAW.

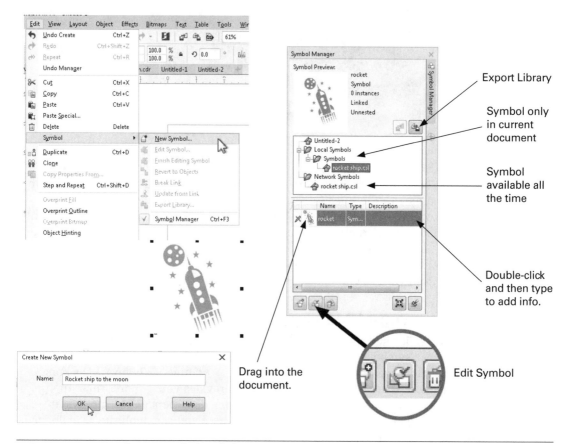

FIGURE 10-8 Define a symbol and then save it to a Symbol library.

3. Open the Symbol Manager and then click the name of your saved document. A thumbnail of the symbol you just saved appears.

4. A tiny Export icon becomes active; click it, it's the Export Library command. This is not much of a library, but you need to start somewhere!

5. In the Export Library dialog, save the new library to the location that CorelDRAW recommends (to better allow the program to locate it in the future; the Symbols folder is a good location). Name the library and then click Save. You're done.

6. In any new document, open the Symbol Manager, click the User Symbols + icon to open the collection, and then click the name of the library you saved in step 5. Now all you need to do is drag the thumbnail into a document, and you have an instance of the symbol you saved.

In Windows 7 and later, your saved Symbol library will be in C:\Users\(your user name)\AppData\Roaming\Corel\CorelDRAW Graphics Suite X7\Symbols. This is good to know when you want to load your collection by clicking Add Library on the Symbol Manager docker to add symbols to a Local document.

Tip With the Pick tool, right-click over any object you create, and you can then choose Symbol | New Symbol and Symbol | Symbol Manager from the context menu.

Symbols saved to a library are always *instances,* and, as such, duplicates you add to a document cannot be edited using the Shape tool or other shape-editing features. You can apply transformations such as scaling and rotating, but you cannot edit the nodes of a shape instance. You can edit the original shape as saved in the library, however, and all future instances you use reflect your edits. To edit a symbol in your library, right-click over the name on the Symbol Manager list and then choose Edit. After you've edited the shape, right-click over the shape in the document window, and then choose Finish Editing Symbol from the pop-up menu. Every instance in every document is updated to reflect your edits.

Tip You can easily tell the difference between an instanced symbol and one that can be edited in any document. Choose the shape using the Pick tool. If the bounding box dots are blue, it's a shape *instance*. If the bounding box handles are black, it's a regular shape, and you can perform any CorelDRAW operation on it.

Managing Symbols (The Abridged Edition for Mortals)

Saving and editing symbols in the future is not quite as easy as playing jump rope. The following bulleted list is a quick reference for symbols that are assigned to different "locations" in a document or as a file on a network, and how to edit and resave them:

- If you save a symbol via the Object menu and Symbol Manager docker, it is saved to the document only, and if you close the document without saving it, the symbol is not saved. The advantage to saving symbols to a single document is that editing them is a breeze, as described earlier. The disadvantage is that every time you want to access a symbol to use in a new document, you have to either open the document in which the symbol is stored, or save this document as a template via the File | Save As Template command. You can delete all the objects on the page, and when you open a document based on the template, all the saved symbols are there from your saved template.

- If you want to save all the symbols in a document into a library (a CSL file), select all the symbols on the list (hold SHIFT and then click them), and then click the icon toward the top of the docker, as shown here. Now with all documents you create in the future, you can load this saved library in the Symbol Manager and have access to all the symbols you saved. Unfortunately, to keep the library intact, you'll see a little pencil with a red slash through it to the left of symbols. This means you cannot edit them directly, as you can with local symbols. The solution to this editing setback (*not* a "problem") is to drag a symbol onto the page from the Symbol Manager's list. This symbol is an instance, a clone of the original, and cannot be edited—or so it seems. But select the instance with the Pick tool and then right-click and choose Revert To Objects. Do your editing and then save the new (edited) symbol.

CorelDRAW's Font Playground: Take a Ride!

To end this chapter on the lighter side, Corel Corp. has added a utility to CorelDRAW X7 that's both useful *and* **fun**. The Font Playground is an onscreen panel that looks like any other CorelDRAW docker, but aside from copying and pasting text, its purpose is *not* to enhance drawings or modify text, but to *preview* and *compare* a phrase or word when set in different font styles.

Type some Artistic Text, something like **FLASH SALE 8 HOURS ONLY!** Then Choose Text | Font Playground. The illustration shown here is a composite of the Font Playground docker, showing multiple views of it to clue you into your options visually.

From left to right, your display options for the font type and the preview you've entered (covered in a moment) are as follows:

- **Single-line Display** Clicking this button displays a phrase once, in as many font styles as you like.
- **Multiline Display** Clicking this button displays an entire phrase you might choose as the display sample, again, in any number of chosen font styles.
- **Waterfall** This button option shows you only the text sample you've clicked on in the preview window, at various increasing point sizes. This option is useful for predetermining whether your chosen font is legible at, say, very small point sizes.

Additionally, you have a Type Size slider toward the top left of the docker. But perhaps the neatest part of Font Playground is the option to copy a phrase into the Playground so you can compare it in several styles and then copy the chosen phrase and typeface to the drawing page.

To put a phrase into the Font Playground preview window, select the text on the drawing page with the Pick tool, press CTRL + C to copy your text selection, and then click an entry in the preview window and press CTRL + V. Remember this shortcut because the docker doesn't have a Paste command or button.

To put your dream font and phrase on the page, all you do is click + drag the desired version of your text from the text entry list on the docker into your CorelDRAW document.

Typography is such a large part of human communications, and type features are such a large part of CorelDRAW, that we can't just say, "Nice lecture, thanks. *Next...*" Paragraph margins, column widths, setting dot leaders for fancy menus, creating bulleted lists—this is all important stuff, too, unless you're certain you can convey any message with your drawings alone. Advanced typesetting features and CorelDRAW's proofing tools are your next stop in Chapter 11, because fancy text layouts just don't cut it if you've used an expensive font, extruded it, colored it magnificently, and the headline reads, "SUPER-SAL 2TODAY ONLY. EVERTHIN MUST GO!"

We can do much better. Turn the page...

11 Intermediate Desktop Publishing and Proofing Tools

After reading Chapter 10, you should be up and running and getting handsome results from *some* of X7's Text tool. But like the child in all of us who wanted to skip the bicycle riding and get straight to Formula 1 racing, this chapter is intended to train you on professional typesetting, desktop publishing, and the proofing tools CorelDRAW offers so what you've written is as easy to understand as the way the writing looks on a page. Bring an idea, bring an open mind, and let's explore some of the more advanced typographic tools CorelDRAW X7 has to offer.

Note Download and extract all the files from the Chapter11.zip archive to follow the tutorials in this chapter.

A Few Paragraphs Covering Advanced Paragraph Features

When you set type in a text-intensive document, you'll certainly have special needs for formatting the text. You might want to set up a number of columns, move sections around to make your article better to read, perhaps you even need a bulleted list like you might find on a fancy restaurant's outrageously priced menu. The following sections take you through the mechanics of accomplishing special formatting requirements with CorelDRAW's tools.

Working with Columns

Although you can manually create flowing columns of Paragraph Text, using the automated Columns feature in CorelDRAW is often less time-consuming. Text columns divide Paragraph Text frames into several vertical columns separated by *gutters* (margins). Multiple columns can be created only in the Column Settings dialog (Text | Columns). The following section describes how to adjust columns with the mouse. Naturally, you need to start with Paragraph Text on a page before creating columns; you diagonally drag with the Text tool to create a Paragraph frame. Also, you must select Paragraph Text with the Text tool to work with columns: the tabs do not show on the rulers using other tools.

Select the frame in which you want to place columns, open the Text | Columns dialog, and then set the number of columns in the Column Settings dialog. It is always a good idea to keep the number of columns balanced, so each column is neither too wide nor too narrow. Here is a good rule of thumb for legibility: each line of text should be no wider than 6 inches or 16 words, but it should be wide enough to have *at least* 4 words per line. Anything else becomes hard for your audience to read and your layout will look unprofessional.

To change the width of the columns and margins, drag the column guides, column-boundary markers, gutter handles, and horizontal-resize handles, as shown in Figure 11-1. When dragging the column guides or boundary markers, if the Equal

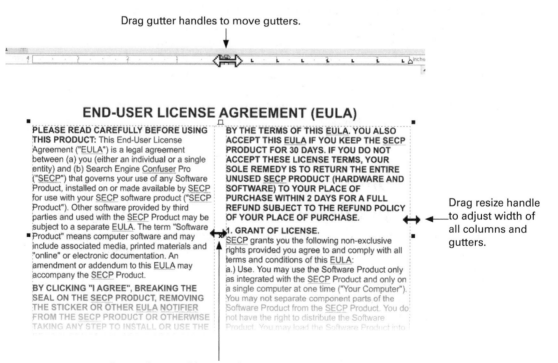

Drag gutter handles to move gutters.

END-USER LICENSE AGREEMENT (EULA)

PLEASE READ CAREFULLY BEFORE USING THIS PRODUCT: This End-User License Agreement ("EULA") is a legal agreement between (a) you (either an individual or a single entity) and (b) Search Engine Confuser Pro ("SECP") that governs your use of any Software Product, installed on or made available by SECP for use with your SECP software product ("SECP Product"). Other software provided by third parties and used with the SECP Product may be subject to a separate EULA. The term "Software Product" means computer software and may include associated media, printed materials and "online" or electronic documentation. An amendment or addendum to this EULA may accompany the SECP Product.

BY CLICKING "I AGREE", BREAKING THE SEAL ON THE SECP PRODUCT, REMOVING THE STICKER OR OTHER EULA NOTIFIER FROM THE SECP PRODUCT OR OTHERWISE TAKING ANY STEP TO INSTALL OR USE THE

BY THE TERMS OF THIS EULA. YOU ALSO ACCEPT THIS EULA IF YOU KEEP THE SECP PRODUCT FOR 30 DAYS. IF YOU DO NOT ACCEPT THESE LICENSE TERMS, YOUR SOLE REMEDY IS TO RETURN THE ENTIRE UNUSED SECP PRODUCT (HARDWARE AND SOFTWARE) TO YOUR PLACE OF PURCHASE WITHIN 2 DAYS FOR A FULL REFUND SUBJECT TO THE REFUND POLICY OF YOUR PLACE OF PURCHASE.

1. GRANT OF LICENSE.
SECP grants you the following non-exclusive rights provided you agree to and comply with all terms and conditions of this EULA:
a.) Use. You may use the Software Product only as integrated with the SECP Product and only on a single computer at one time ("Your Computer"). You may not separate component parts of the Software Product from the SECP Product. You do not have the right to distribute the Software Product. You may load the Software Product into

Drag resize handle to adjust width of all columns and gutters.

Drag column guides to resize columns and gutters.

FIGURE 11-1 Column widths can be edited directly by dragging with the mouse.

Column Width option is selected in the Format Text dialog, all the gutters will be resized together; the gutter handles are available only when this option is not selected.

 Note Columns can be applied only to entire Paragraph Text frames and cannot be applied to individual paragraphs or to Artistic Text.

Column Settings

Once you've created a Paragraph Text object with columns, you can refine and make precise columns and gutter widths through the Text | Columns dialog, shown in Figure 11-2.

To add extra columns, first set the Number Of Columns, and then set the Widths of the columns. The Gutter value is the distance between the selected column and the next one. If Equal Column Width is selected, changing the width of any column

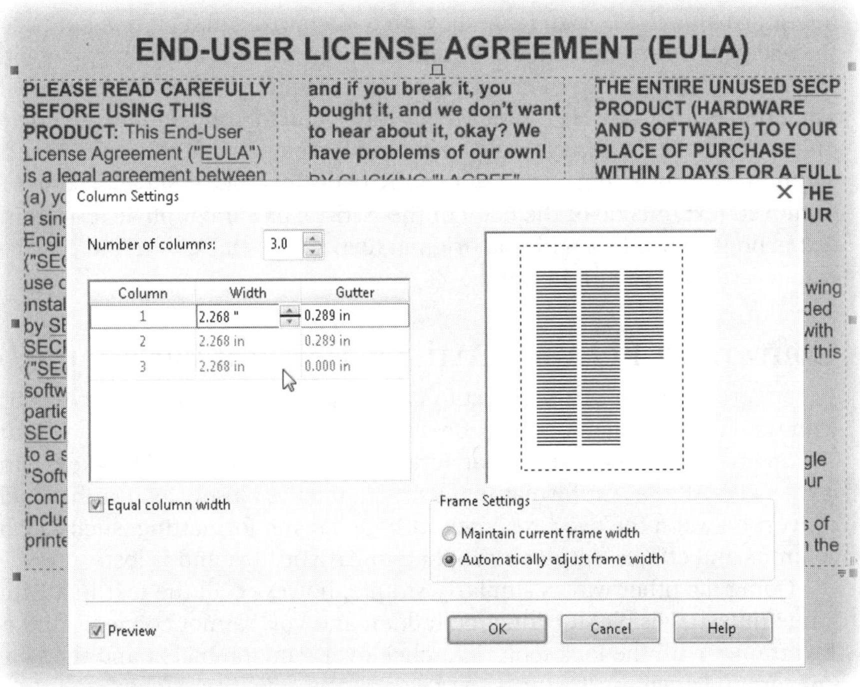

FIGURE 11-2   Under Text | Columns, use the Column Settings dialog to apply columns to paragraph text.

or gutter changes the width of all columns or gutters to the same value. If Maintain Current Frame Width is selected, changing the width of any column or gutter will not change the overall width of the frame, so the other columns and gutters will be resized to accommodate the change. A preview of the column settings is shown in the preview frame on the right side of the dialog.

Text in columns (even if only one column is used) can be justified via the Alignment button on the Property bar, the Text bar, and the Object Properties docker when you click the Paragraph tab.

Tip You'll have more control over columns by laying them out as multiple text frames, each one containing a single column.

Moving Text Within a Paragraph

You can move a selection of text with the mouse by dragging-and-dropping; select the word or phrase you want to move, and then click-and-drag the text to its new location in the current text object—or any other text object—with the primary mouse button. A vertical bar indicates the insertion point at the new location; the cursor becomes the international "no" sign (a circle with a slash through it) if it is not possible to drop the text at the current location. When you drop the text after dragging with the *right* mouse button, a pop-up menu appears, giving you options for working with the text. The options are Copy Here and Move Here (Add To Rollover doesn't do anything unless you have a webpage rollover defined). You can use this editing gesture to copy and move words within Paragraph and Artistic Text, but you can also put the copied or moved text outside of the body of the Artistic or Paragraph Text. In this event, the text is no longer inline with the original text, so use this command (particularly Move) with a *very* good reason in mind.

Converting Between Artistic Text and Paragraph Text

To convert a block of Artistic Text to Paragraph Text, right-click the Artistic Text object with the Pick tool; then choose Convert To Paragraph Text from the pop-up menu. The menu command is Text | Convert To Paragraph Text, and the keyboard shortcut is CTRL + F8. All the text formatting is maintained as closely as possible each time you convert between the two text types, although some formatting, such as Paragraph Text columns and effects, cannot be applied to Artistic Text and is lost.

Going the other way is similarly simple; however, all the text in a Paragraph Text frame must be visible: it cannot be hidden and you cannot convert a linked Paragraph Text frame. With the Pick tool, right-click over Paragraph Text and then choose Convert To Paragraph Text (CTRL + F8 works, too).

The Text Bar and Special Paragraph Formatting

Because of the large-screen resolutions we enjoy today, we can view pages at almost a 1:1 resolution, just as they would print, but this also means we might need to scroll and mouse around a document more than is healthy for the wrists. The solution in CorelDRAW is simple: if you're working extensively with text, you *float* the Text bar close to the area you're fine-tuning in the document. Right-click over any area of the Property bar and then choose Text from the pop-up menu. You can drag the Text bar to hover over any area you like.

The Text bar can be used to edit single characters in Artistic Text and Paragraph Text, but its real strength is in its offering of options for making Paragraph Text look polished and sophisticated. When the Pick tool or Text tool is active, all the features are active and at your disposal. You can make some additional modifications to the available options; these are described a little later in this chapter.

 Tip The Text bar and the Text options on the Property bar when the Pick or the Text tool have selected text are essentially identical. The Text bar is simply a more portable device for working closely to text.

Formatting Bulleted Lists

Bulleted lists are a common necessity for page layouts: restaurant menus, assembly instructions, just about anything that's a list that doesn't need to be a numbered list is a bulleted list! In the following sections, you'll see how not only to create a bulleted list, but also to choose any character you like and even create a hanging indent for the bullet.

Making Bulleted Paragraph Text

Like the toggling Drop Cap, the Show/Hide Bullet button can be your one-click stop for creating bulleted lists; however, you'll surely want a custom bulleted list that looks as artistic as your document layout. On the Text menu, you'll find the Bullets command: it's straightforward and you'll quickly achieve great results. Find or create a list of something and follow along to see how to work the bullet options.

`Tutorial` Creating a Bullet Motif

1. If you'd care to create a specific bulleted list instead of just reading a scenario, open *All-Star Recipes.cdr*. All the content you need to build a finished recipe is there.
2. There's no real harm in simply using the Pick tool to select the Paragraph Text that you want to make a fancy bulleted list. Every line break in the list begins a new bulleted item, so select the text and then click the Show/Hide Bullets button on the Property bar or the Text bar.

3. Choose Text | Bullets, as shown in the illustration.

4. Choose a typeface that contrasts, yet is compatible with ITC Machine, the font used in the extruded headline text. Kabel Book BT comes with the Graphics Suite and is used in these figures. The illustration here is an "All-Star Recipe," and the interiors of the *As* are stars, so a bullet shaped like a star is appropriate.

5. Highlight all the lines of text, because the Bullets feature understands that only the current bullets will be replaced.

6. Microsoft's Wingdings font is installed with every copy of Windows, and it features some nice symbols: choose Wingdings from the Font drop-down list in this example, and then click the Symbol drop-down button and locate a good star shape.

7. Click the Use Hanging Indent Style For Bulleted Lists checkbox to get a polished look for the list.

8. Increase the point size of the bullets by dragging upward in the center of the Size spin box control. Most likely, the baseline of the enlarged symbol won't look right compared to the text in the list (it'll be too high). Drag on the Baseline Shift spin box control until the bullets look aligned.

9. Optionally, if your symbol is crowding into the list text, increase the Bullet To Text spacing. Similarly, the Paragraph Text frame might be too tight to the left

of the bullet; in this case, you increase the Text Frame To Bullet amount. See the following illustration for the completed design.

❂ 3 tbsp virgin olive oil

❂ 1 tbsp red wine vinegar

❂ A dash of ground black pepper

❂ Two twists of ground sea salt

Changing Text Case

Occasionally you'll receive text from a client who doesn't know where the CAPS LOCK key is on the keyboard, or you have a really, really old plaintext file created using a DOS application. In any event, all caps in a text message, unless it's a very brief headline, can be a real eyesore.

To change the case of text you have typed, insert the Text tool cursor in the text and then right-click: choose an option from the Change Case submenu. Changing the case of characters replaces the original characters with new characters of the correct case.

Formatting Paragraph Text

Stepping inside the frame and column formatting of Paragraph Text, CorelDRAW has extensive options for specifying how lines of text look compared to one another, how tightly characters and words are spaced, and how you want individual paragraphs to separate from each other. The following sections cover the Paragraph features on the Object Properties docker.

Paragraph Alignment

The Alignment settings in the Paragraph section of Object Properties affect the spacing for the entire selected paragraph; you can choose the entire Paragraph Text object using the Pick tool, or only pages by highlighting them with the Text tool. You have Left, Right, Center, Full, and Forced as Alignment settings (called *Justification* in the publishing world), and None at far left, which removes the current alignment.

Spacing

Below the Alignment controls for *interline spacing* (*leading*) are options for setting how much space should go before or after a paragraph, intercharacter and interword spacing, and finally Indent preferences. It should be noted here that proper typographical form dictates that separate paragraphs are usually indicated by either a first-line indent or a line space between paragraphs, but not both. You should also understand that character and word spacing apply to the entire paragraph, whether you have only a portion highlighted with the Text tool or not. See the following illustration.

Paragraph and Line Spacing

You might choose to separate paragraphs by using the Before or the After Paragraph spin boxes, but not both. The spacing between paragraphs is measured, by default, as the percent of the character height—the total height of a character in a digital font—which is not always easy to discern, but typically it's about 30 percent taller than a capital letter in the font. However, you can always choose Points or Percentage Of Point Size from the drop-down list. You'll want to experiment with this option, depending on the typeface you're using. Anywhere from 125 percent to 200 percent can work from an artistic standpoint.

Line Spacing is used to let some "air" into paragraph text and is especially nice when you have a font whose ascenders or descenders are unusually tall. You can also use wide Line Spacing to create an artistic effect when starting, for example, a magazine article. It's been fashionable for several years now to use about 300 percent line spacing in the opening paragraph: it lightens the page when using a bold font and also allows the reader to see more of any decorative background you've used.

Language, Character, and Word Spacing

If you're typesetting, for example, an article using an Asian font, Language Spacing will be helpful for spacing non-left-to-right sentences; if not, you have little use for this option. You can set how much extra space is added to the default intercharacter space for the paragraph as a whole by using Character Spacing. The values are a percentage of a normal space character for the current font. You can also modify interword spacing by using Word Spacing—this has the effect of adjusting the width of the space character. As a rule, if you need to adjust typeface kerning to all the contents of a paragraph frame, use Character Spacing in the Paragraph area of Object Properties. If, however, there is only a bothersome line or two in a paragraph, you highlight only those lines and then adjust character spacing with the Range Kerning spin combo box in the Character area of the Object Properties docker.

Tip   Remember the control handles on the bounding boxes of Paragraph Text. Also remember that the Shape tool is the only tool for editing Paragraph Text. They're quick to use and provide a good coarse view of how your layout is shaping up.

Indentation and Margins of Paragraph Text

You can set the sizes of the indents of the left and right margins, as well as the size of the first-line indentation, just as you do in a word processor. You can set them using the triangular markers on the ruler, which are shown here:

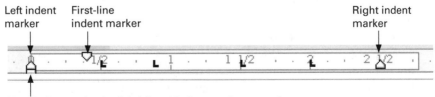

Left indent marker   First-line indent marker   Right indent marker

Handle for moving both left-hand indent markers together

Formatting Tabs

Tab stops for Paragraph Text can be edited either directly on the ruler or in the Text | Tabs dialog, as shown in the following illustration. CorelDRAW supports left, right, center, and decimal tabs, just like most word processors.

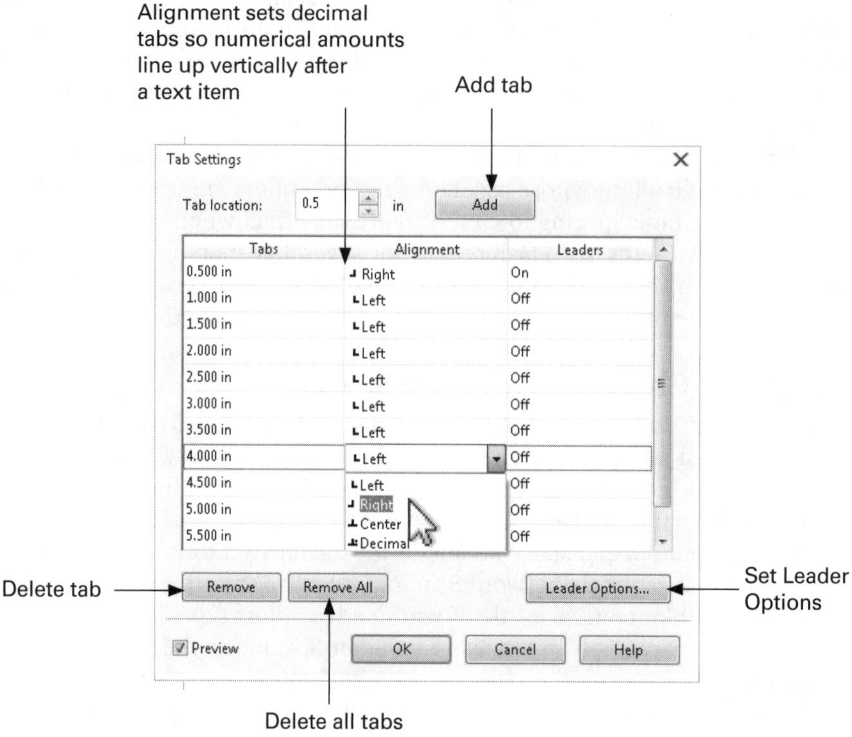

Alignment sets decimal tabs so numerical amounts line up vertically after a text item

Add tab

Delete tab — Remove

Set Leader Options

Delete all tabs

Adding, Moving, and Deleting Tabs from the Dialog

Tabs can be added to the current paragraph from the Text | Tab Settings box by first entering a value in the Tab Location spin box and then clicking Add. To set the type of a new tab, choose it from the drop-down list associated with the tab. Similarly, you can adjust an existing tab by clicking its position (thus opening the value for editing) and then typing in a new value. To delete a tab, select it in the list, and then click the Remove button.

When you create a new paragraph, unless you have modified the default paragraph style, tab stops are positioned every half-inch. To remove all the tabs, click the Remove All button.

Formatting Tab Leaders from the Dialog

You can choose whether text positioned to any tab uses a leader between tab settings in the Leader Settings dialog. You get there by clicking the Leader Options button. *Leading characters* are often used in tabulated lists, such as tables of contents and menus, to join the section titles or menu items on the left with their respective page numbers or prices on the right.

Leaders are usually displayed as a series of dots, but you can change them to any of the characters shown in the Character drop-down list. Unfortunately, you can't make a leader using a font other than the one used in the Paragraph Text. To change the leader character, select a Character from the drop-down list, as shown in this illustration. The distance between the leader characters is set with the Spacing setting: this value is the number of space characters to insert between each leader character.

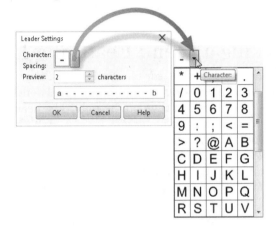

Using the Ruler to Set Tabs

To edit tab stops on the ruler, the ruler must be visible (choose View | Rulers). To view tab characters in the body of your Paragraph Text, press CTRL + SHIFT + C (Text | Show Non-Printing Characters). Before creating new tabs, you should delete all the tabs that are already in place—select Remove All from the Tab Settings dialog.

To create new tabs with the ruler, use the Text tool to select the paragraphs to which you want to add tabs, and then click the horizontal ruler at the point where you want to insert the new tab stop. The type of tab can be set by right-clicking over the tab. You'll also see a selector button, shown in the illustration, where the ruler origin usually is when working with Paragraph Text. Clicking the selector button cycles between the four tab states: left, right, center, and decimal.

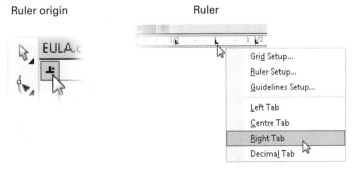

To move a tab, drag it to its new position on the ruler. To delete a tab, drag it off the ruler and into the workspace. To change the tab *type*, you can right-click the tab stop on the ruler to select a new type from the pop-up menu, or change its type in the Tab Settings dialog. Tabs cannot be added to Artistic Text.

Here's a practical example of the value of knowing how to set up tabs: create a folding menu design, and then create Paragraph Text with menu items and their corresponding prices on the same lines (make up anything you like; have fun!). Here's how to create a dot leader so the guests can see the prices at the far right easily, based on the menu items on the far left.

Tutorial   Making a Menu Featuring Dot Leaders

1. Open the *Art Café menu.cdr* file. Notice that the prices are directly after the menu item with no space in-between. This is done deliberately so when you add leaders, the prices will align on the right. The headline text (Gillies Gothic) and all elements except the menu text are locked. With the Text tool cursor inserted in the body of any of the linked text blocks, press CTRL + A to select all the text. Now choose Text | Tabs.

2. Click Remove All; you don't want the default evenly spaced tabs in this menu. If you look closely at the ruler in the tabs region above the document, you'll see the paragraph box is a little more than 4" wide. Therefore, type **3.75** in the Tab Location box at the top and then click Add.

3. The first entry in the list, as shown in the following illustration, is 3.75", but its alignment is, by default, to the left, which is wrong for making a tab leader layout. Click the Left entry in the Alignment column, and it turns into a drop-down list—choose Right from the list. If you haven't checked the Preview box in the Tab Settings dialog, do so now so you can watch live updates on the page as you work. Also, you probably want to turn leaders on; you do this the same way you chose right alignment for the 3.75" tab. See the following illustration.

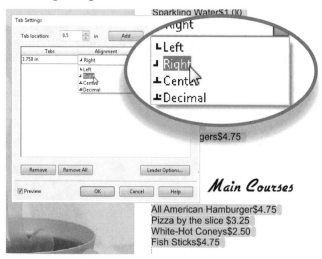

4. Click Leader Options.
5. Choose a period as the character. If you want something fancier, you might try a caret (^) or a tilde (~) instead.

6. Set the spacing for the leader character.
7. Click OK, and then place the Text tool between the price and the menu item, and then press TAB. Figure 11-3 shows the nearly complete, easy-to-read, somewhat-underpriced menu. Notice that your document updates live, so you can preview how your dot leader looks before clicking OK.

FIGURE 11-3 Tab leaders help guide the eye from an item to its price.

Using CorelDraw's Writing Tools

You want your text to look as good as your drawings, and the same powerful grammar and spelling tools offered in Corel WordPerfect Office suite are right inside CorelDRAW. A spell checking system, thesaurus, and grammar checker—in 25 different languages—are at your fingertips. This means you can both compose in CorelDRAW and import writing to CorelDRAW—and be assured your words are perfect.

CorelDRAW also includes the same QuickCorrect feature that's in WordPerfect, for correcting common typos and spelling mistakes *as you type.* This is extremely helpful for words that you commonly mistype and for common extended characters such as © or ™.

Both CorelDRAW and WordPerfect use the same writing tools, dictionaries, word lists, and configurations. If you add a word to your User Word List in WordPerfect, it is there for you in CorelDRAW. If you're a Microsoft Word user, CorelDRAW's proofing tools are as easy to learn as Word's—the dialogs and labels are a little different in appearance, but you'll soon get the idea. It's time now for you to add the title of Literary Wizard to CorelDRAW Design Guru.

Assigning Language Codes

When you install CorelDRAW, choose the languages you are most likely to use, and you are ready to check the spelling and grammar of anything that comes your way. By default, CorelDRAW assigns a language code and checks all text using the proofing tools that correspond to the language your operating system uses. If you use a US English copy of Windows, CorelDRAW automatically installs English–U.S. proofing tools and assigns all text to U.S. English (ENU).

If your document contains text in a language other than the default language, you need to select the foreign language text and assign the proper language code to the text so CorelDRAW will use the appropriate proofing tools. The language currently assigned to selected text is noted by a three-letter code in parentheses next to the font description in the Status bar, for example, by "(ENU)," as shown in most of this book.

To change the language assignment of any character, word, or paragraph of Artistic or Paragraph Text in a document, select the text and then choose Text | Writing Tools | Language. When the Text Language dialog opens, you can choose any one of the 122 different language and language variants that appear in the list. See the following illustration; click OK to make the change.

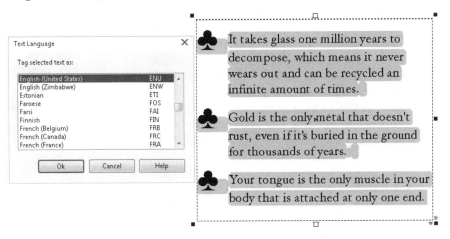

Using the Proofing Tools

To use CorelDRAW's spell checker, thesaurus, or grammar check, select the text with the Pick tool or the Text tool, and then choose the appropriate writing tool from the Text | Writing Tools menu. Alternatively, you can right-click a text object with the Text tool and then choose a proofing tool from the pop-up menu. CTRL + F12 is the shortcut for opening the Writing Tools dialog to the Spell Checker tab, as shown here:

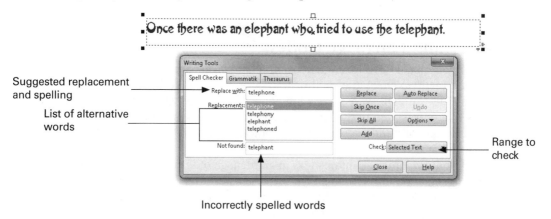

Suggested replacement and spelling

List of alternative words

Range to check

Incorrectly spelled words

Common Buttons

The Spell Checker and Grammatik tools share common buttons in the Writing Tools dialog. These buttons perform the functions described here:

- **Start button**   The Start button starts the Spell Checker or Grammatik. This button is visible only if Auto Start is off—it is on by default. To enable or disable the Auto Start option, click the Options button in the Writing Tools dialog, and make a selection from the drop-down menu.

- **Replace button**   As the check is performed, when a misspelled word or grammatical error is found, the Start button changes to Replace, and the misspelled word or grammatical error is highlighted. Select the suggested correction from the list, and click Replace to apply it. You can also edit the replacement word in the Spell Checker's Replace With box, or type in a new word before replacing it. After the replacement has been made, the checker rechecks the replacement and continues checking.

- **Undo button**   The Undo button reverts the last correction to its previous state.

- **Resume button**   After you correct a mistake, if you move the insertion point— for example, to a different part of the text—the Start button changes to the Resume button. Simply click it to recheck any selected text and to continue checking from the insertion point.

- **Skip Once and Skip All**   If the word or sentence that a checker has queried is actually correct—for example, a brand name such as Pringles or Humvee— you can click one of the Skip buttons to have the checker ignore it. Skip Once causes the check to continue, but future instances of the same problem will stop the checker. Skip All tells the checker to ignore *all* instances of this spelling or grammatical error.

- **Add**   Add allows you to add a word to the current User Word List. Many unusual names and technical terms are not included in the Spell Checker's dictionary, and these can be added to the User Word List for the current language. In the future, these words will not be queried. If a word appears in the Replace With box or in the Not Found box, clicking Add immediately adds the queried word to the default User Word List. Otherwise, if no word appears in either box, clicking the Add button opens an input box, where you can type the word you want to enter into the User Word List.
- **Auto Replace**   If you choose an alternative spelling for a queried word, the Auto Replace button becomes active. Clicking this button will add the misspelled word and its replacement to the default User Word List, *and* if QuickCorrect is enabled, then the next time you type the same mistake, the correct word will be automatically substituted.
- **Options**   The Options button displays a drop-down menu that contains various settings for the current Writing Tool.
- **Range Of Text**   By using the options from the Check drop-down list, you can set the range of text for performing a spell check or a Grammatik check. The available options depend on whether text is selected with the Text Tool or the Pick Tool.

Setting Spell Checker Options

You can click the Options button on the Spell Checker page of the Writing Tools dialog to access various settings that affect how the Spell Checker works.

Using Word Lists

CorelDRAW's writing tools maintain Word Lists that contain all the valid words and phrases for spelling checks. If a word in your document is not in one of the active lists, it is flagged as being incorrectly spelled. CorelDRAW has two types of Word Lists:

- **Main Word Lists**   These lists are provided by Corel and contain the most common words and spellings in each language. One Main Word List exists per language and this list is not editable.
- **User Word Lists**   These lists contain words that are not in the Corel-supplied lists but rather are made up of words you have added during a spell check by clicking the Add button. Words and phrases that are common to an industry are useful to add. You're responsible for ensuring that the words you add to a User Word List are spelled correctly! User Word Lists also contain the QuickCorrect entries for the text's language. Each language has at least one User Word List.

Using Main Word Lists

Although Main Word Lists are predefined by Corel and cannot be edited in CorelDRAW, they can, however, be edited by the WordPerfect suite's Spell Utility if you happen to have a copy. Main Word Lists contain only words used by the Spell Checker—no QuickCorrect word pairs are included.

   Which Main Word List is currently being used changes according to the Language setting. Click the Change button (Writing Tools | Spell Check | Options | Main Word

Lists), choose a different language, and CorelDRAW will use the Main Word List for the new language. Changing which word list CorelDRAW is currently using does not change the language code of the selected text but rather temporarily proofs that text using the new Main Word List.

You can also *add* extra Main Word Lists to a language by using the Add List button. For example, some US English users might want their *US Spell Checker* to include Spanish words. By adding the Spanish word list, the Spell Checker will first check words against the English lists. Then, if the words are not found in the English list, the checker compares words against the Spanish list. Only if the check fails against both lists will the Spell Checker display an error. Using this method, you don't have to set a language code specifically for the Spanish text.

Other Spell Checking Options

Some other options available from the Options drop-down menu of the Writing Tools dialog are described here:

- **Auto Start**   The Spell Checker and Grammatik start the check automatically when the Writing Tools dialog is opened or when that checker's page is opened in the Writing Tools dialog.
- **Check Words With Numbers**   Checks or ignores words that include numbers.
- **Check Duplicate Words**   Flags words that appear twice in succession.
- **Check Irregular Capitalization**   Checks for words that have capital letters in places other than the first character.
- **Show Phonetic Suggestions**   Makes *phonetic* suggestions—replacement words that *sound* like the unrecognized word.

Main Spell Checking Options

The Workplace | Text | Spelling section of CorelDRAW's global Options dialog (CTRL + J) also includes various options that modify how the writing tools work.

- **Perform Automatic Spell Checking**   Check this if you want to check spelling as you type. When it is turned on, unrecognized words are underlined with a red zigzag line while you're editing text with the Text tool.
- **Visibility Of Errors**   Select this option to have all errors underlined in all text objects or just the text object being edited.
- **Display Spelling Suggestions**   You set the number of suggestions to display in the pop-up menu after right-clicking a misspelled word when using the Text tool. The maximum and default number of suggestions is 10.
- **Add Corrections To QuickCorrect**   When checked, CorelDRAW will add a correction pair to the User Word List based on a correction made from the right-click pop-up menu.
- **Show Errors Which Have Been Ignored**   When you right-click a word, the pop-up menu includes an Ignore All command, which tells the Spell Checker to ignore this word. With this option set, CorelDRAW will still show ignored errors, but it will use a blue zigzag line to indicate that they have been ignored.

Using Grammatik

Spelling errors aren't the only proofing goof that can make your work look unprofessional. Poor grammar is a big, red flag that reflects on your education and communication skills. CorelDRAW includes the Grammatik grammar checker, in many of the same languages that spell checkers are available in.

Grammatik is a flexible, powerful tool for checking your work. What Grammatik excels at is calling your attention to parts of your text that *might be* grammatically incorrect; it second-guesses you. Grammatik encourages you to stop and think about what you've written and offers helpful suggestions to fix the problem it *thinks* is a thorn in your rosy prose. The day-to-day operation of Grammatik is not difficult to manage, as you'll see in the next section, where the basics are covered.

Checking and Correcting Grammar

To check your grammar, select the text objects to check with the Pick tool, or select sentences with the Text tool; then in the Writing Tools dialog, open the Grammatik tab, shown in Figure 11-4, by choosing Text | Writing Tools | Grammatik. As with all of the other writing tools, you can also select text and then use the right-click pop-up menu to launch the tool you want to use. It's common to use a word that sounds like the word you want. For example, "affects" is indeed a real word, but it's a homonym—a word that *sounds* like a word you might intend to use such as "effects."

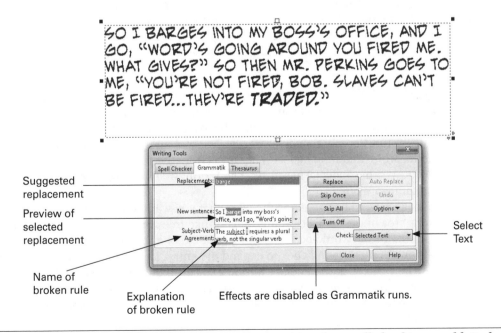

FIGURE 11-4   Grammatik catches errors in your writing that spell checking wouldn't alert you to.

Grammatik highlights potential grammar problems with light blue on the page. Occasionally, when it finds more than one space between words, the white space is underlined. This is very helpful; modern rules of good digital typography call for only one space between sentences and not the two that were required in the days of typewriters.

If Auto Start is enabled, Grammatik will immediately start checking the text; otherwise, you must click the Start button.

If Grammatik finds something that breaks the rules of grammar using the current settings, it displays an explanation of the problem next to the name of the broken rule—the *Rule Class* that has been broken. Grammatik may make one or more suggestions of better grammar, and if you click an option, the new sentence is shown so you can decide if that's what you meant to say. Click Replace to apply the change and continue checking.

Turning Grammatik's Rules On and Off

If you don't want Grammatik to check a certain kind of grammatical error, you can tell it to ignore it. As soon as Grammatik pops up a grammar query, the Add button in the Writing Tools dialog changes to Turn Off. If you click Turn Off, the specific grammar rule that is currently being used will be deactivated for as long as the Writing Tools dialog is open. If you want to turn it back on again, choose Options | Turn On Rules, which brings up the Turn On Rules dialog. Choose those rules that you want to reactivate and click OK. The next time you perform a check, these rules are included.

After you have pared down the rules to the ones you want to keep, you can save this new "profile" for future use: choose Options | Save Rules. The Save Rules dialog opens, and you can either click the Save button to update the current style or click Save As to create a new checking style.

Using the Thesaurus

When the word you're using doesn't convey exactly the right shade of meaning or if you've already used it three or four times, check out the available synonyms with the Thesaurus Writing Tool. Right-click with the Text tool on the word you want to replace with a better word, and then choose Thesaurus from the pop-up menu. Alternatively, choose Text | Writing Tools | Thesaurus. The Writing Tools dialog opens with the word in the look-up word box.

The look-up word box contains the word that you want to look up. The suggestions area of the dialog contains a folder-like tree view list of alternative words and meanings for the word you are looking up. Find one that matches the message you are trying to present and click to expand the entry. If you find the word you want to use, select it and click the Replace button to insert the word into your text. You can also choose *the opposite meaning* of a word in case inverting a sentence is a style of writing you like—*antonyms* are available for the chosen word in the expandable tree in the suggestions area.

If you find a word that is close, but not exactly right, double-click the word to open another area automatically in the dialog that makes suggestions for words that are similar to the selected word. Up to three panes of suggestions are visible at once, but you can keep clicking suggestions and open up more panes that you can navigate through using the left and right navigation buttons at the top of the dialog. To use a word in one of the alternate panes as your replacement word, select it and click the Replace button.

Setting Thesaurus Options

You can set various options for the Thesaurus by first choosing the tab and then clicking the Options button in the Writing Tools dialog. You then click the Thesaurus tab to view the drop-down menu; the most useful options are described here:

- **Auto Look Up**   This option speeds up your work by starting the process right away.
- **Auto Close**   When turned on, it closes the dialog as soon as the Replace button is clicked.
- **Spelling Assist**   When enabled, if the word that you selected to check in the Thesaurus is not recognized, a list of similar words from the Thesaurus is shown. Click the word that best matches the correct spelling of the word you typed, and then click Look Up. The suggestions area will contain alternatives.
- **Synonyms**   This option displays synonyms of the look-up word in the list of suggested alternatives.
- **Antonym**   This option displays antonyms of the word—a lifesaver for those times when you can't think of an opposite for the word you want.
- **Language**   Choose this to change which language's Thesaurus is used for the current session. This does not change the language of the text in your document, but any replacements will be set to the new language. This only works with languages you have currently installed.

Finding and Replacing Text and Special Characters

All too often you may find yourself in the situation of having to find a specific piece of text so you can change the font or formatting or even the content of the text itself. CorelDRAW has terrific tools for searching for and replacing text—and text attributes— regardless of whether your layout is a paragraph or a multi-page document.

Finding Text

To find a word, phrases, and other marks such as dashes, hyphens, and special characters like tabs, paragraph breaks, and spaces, open the Find Text dialog by choosing Edit | Find And Replace | Find Text. In the Find box, enter the word or exact phrase you want to find.

You can include special characters such as an Em or En Space or Dash, a ¼ Em Space, a Non-breaking Space, a Non-breaking Hyphen, a Column/Frame Break, an Optional Hyphen, a Space, a Tab, or a Hard Return in your search. To enter the search tag for a special character in the Find box, click the right arrow next to the Find drop-down, and choose the character you want to include in your search.

If you know the exact character case of the word or phrase, enter it and check the Match Case checkbox—if the Match Case checkbox is cleared, all matching words will be found, regardless of the case of the characters (a case-insensitive search). The Find Text dialog is shown here:

You can include special characters such as an Em or En Space or Dash, a ¾ Em Space, a Non-Breaking Space, a Non-Breaking Hyphen, a Column/Frame Break, an Optional Hyphen, a Space, a Tab, or a Hard Return in your search. To enter the search tag for a special character into the Find box, click on the right arrow next to the Find drop-down, and choose the character you want to include in your search.

Click the Find Next button to find the next instance of the searched text within the document. All the text objects in the document—Paragraph, Artistic, and Fitted Text—will be searched, starting with the current page and working to the end of the document. You will be asked whether you want to continue from the start of the document when you reach the end: Clicking Yes takes the search back to page 1, and it will continue through to the start position, so the whole document is checked once. If the search text is not found, CorelDRAW tells you.

Replacing Text

If you want to replace a word, phrase, or special character in the text with another word, phrase, or special character, use the Replace Text dialog, which is accessed by choosing Edit | Find And Replace | Replace Text.

You enter the word or phrase you want to find into the Find box, and enter the replacement word or phrase into the Replace With box using the same process as described for finding text in the previous section. Click the Find Next button to find the first instance of the search text. When the search text is found, click the Replace button to replace it with the replacement text, or click the Find Next button to skip over the found text and to find the next instance to replace.

If you are sure that you want to replace *all* instances of the Find text in the current document with the Replace With text, click the Replace All button.

Note The ability to search and replace special characters in addition to text is incredibly useful when you are cleaning up imported text, changing five spaces to a tab, and removing column/frame breaks (soft returns). It is also a useful feature if you want to tweak your typography; for example, you can search for a hyphen between numbers and replace it with an en dash. You can also give your text some breathing room and search for all the em dashes in your text and put ¼ em spaces on either side of the em dash.

And this is the last word on typography in CorelDRAW! You now know how to spell check, grammar check, and find and replace text. Our next stop is setting properties for filling objects and outline properties for paths. Let's get your objects—*including* text objects—looking as handsome and as visually captivating as you'd like them to be.

PART V

Attributes for Objects and Lines

12 Options for Filling Objects

A shape without a fill on your drawing page is like a brand-new coloring book. To make a coloring book—and your CorelDRAW artwork—more complete, you need to *fill* your shapes with colors and textures. CorelDRAW has more than a half-dozen types of fills you can apply to your shapes, and these types have hundreds of variations. In computer graphics, you have over 16 million solid shades of color at your disposal; imagine what you can do with *blend*s, *patterns*, and *textures* of colors! The worst part of filling CorelDRAW objects will be deciding on a style of fill. The *best* part, as you explore filling shapes in this chapter, is that it's very difficult to color outside of the lines.

> **Note** Download and extract all the files from the Chapter12.zip archive to follow the tutorials in this chapter.

Examining the Fill Types

Each type of CorelDRAW fill has its own special characteristics:

- *Uniform* fills apply flat, solid color.
- *Fountain* fills make a color transition from one color to another, in different directions—sometimes also called a *gradient fill*. You can also create a fountain fill composed of more than two different colors. CorelDRAW ships with many preset fills, and this chapter demonstrates how to pick and apply them.
- *PostScript* fills are good for repeating patterns. Although PostScript is a *printing* technology, you don't need to print a CorelDRAW document to see a PostScript fill, and you can indeed export a PostScript-filled object to bitmap format and the fill looks fine. PostScript fills support transparency and are ideal for exporting to

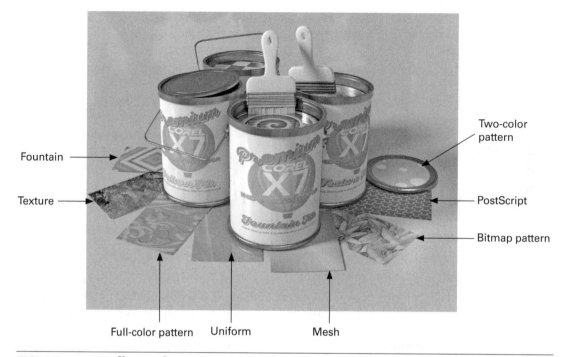

FIGURE 12-1 Fill your shapes in a composition with the fill type that draws attention to your design work.

EPS file format to use in desktop publishing programs. And, naturally, a PostScript fill is valid for printing to a PostScript printer.

- *Pattern* and *texture* fills can fill shapes with bitmaps, including photographs, and a large supply of preset bitmaps is included with CorelDRAW.
- *Mesh* fills take multicolored fills and present you with the option of "smearing" colors within the fill, much like finger-painting.

Every fill type is applied in a slightly different way through the use of onscreen tools, docker windows, or the Interactive Fill and Mesh Fill tool (see Figure 12-1).

Using the Color Palette

For color selection, the color palette is an excellent starting point, and to apply a uniform (solid) fill to a selected object, just select an object with the Pick tool and then left-click a color on the color palette. You can also drag a color swatch from the color palette, drop it onto a shape—which *doesn't* have to be selected—and the object is filled.

You can choose not only a color from the color palette, but also a *shade* or a *tone* of that color. To pick a shade of a color on the color palette, you first select the object you want to fill, click-hold on a color swatch, and a small pop-up menu of shades and tones of that color appears. While holding the mouse button, drag to the exact shade you want, release the mouse button, and the object is filled. This pop-up features shades that vary in *hue* from top to bottom, and in *brightness* from left to right. You have 49 possible colors at your cursor tip when you choose one color.

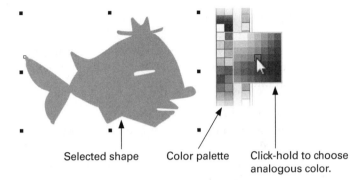

Selected shape   Color palette   Click-hold to choose
                                   analogous color.

Uniform fills can also be assigned to all objects right from the get-go. With no objects selected in the drawing window, left-click a color you want to use for future Artistic Media (such as calligraphic pens), Artistic Text, callouts, dimension lines, graphics, and/or Paragraph Text. CorelDRAW then displays a dialog that asks what sort of object you want filled as it's created from now on. You can cancel out of this operation, but you can choose objects, text, or both.

From Uniform to Non-Uniform Object Filling

The quick way to apply any of the fill types is to use the Fill tool, shown here. You'll find it at the bottom of the Toolbox; to select it quickly, press G. You'll see a hint here that the Fill tool is also a selection tool—the cursor is an arrow cursor with a paint bucket. You don't have to have already selected the object that you want to fill when you use this tool. You can click an unselected, solid-filled object with the Fill tool to select it, and then a click-drag on the object, by default, applies the Linear-style fountain fill, making a transition from the current solid color to white. You can then change the colors used, or choose a different fill type from the Property bar—and here's where version X7 has been reworked to make applying different types of fills easier than ever.

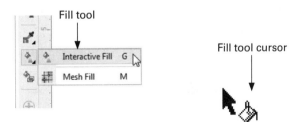

Fill tool

Fill tool cursor

Suppose you just filled an object with the default Linear-style fountain fill. If you've used a previous version of CorelDRAW, you're going to be pleasantly surprised to see more than one control node on the fill: a mini–color and transparency picker pops up when you click over a color node. And all the fill types you can imagine are on the Property bar. Additionally, you can change some controls for the fountain fill parameters, so this streamlined, fortified Fill tool will get you where you need to go in a jiffy. Figure 12-2 shows you what you'll see on your page when you click-drag with the Fill tool to create a linear gradient. The element names and what they do are described in a moment.

- **Start and End color nodes**   In an object filled with a fountain fill (also called a gradient), the fountain fill begins at a Start color node and transitions toward the End color node inside the object. With the Fill tool, you can click either the Start or End node, and then choose a different color for them by using the pop-up mini–Node Color picker, by clicking a color on the color palette, or by click-dragging a color swatch from the palette onto one of the color nodes. In addition to defining a color, the Start and End nodes can be moved like little handles using

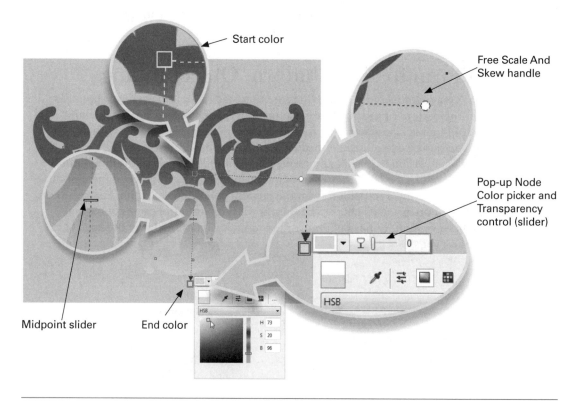

FIGURE 12-2   X7's Fill tool properties include both familiar and new onscreen interactive features.

the Fill tool in a click-drag gesture. Click-dragging the Start node moves the entire gradient; it's repositioned within the object. Click-dragging the End node does two things. If you drag in a circular motion, you change the angle of the fountain fill. If you click-drag toward or away from the begin color handle, you increase or decrease the contrast of the transition between the two colors.

- **Free Scale And Skew handle**   The result you achieve by moving this round node is more obvious with, say, the Elliptical fountain fill style than Linear; see the following illustration. You can now skew and disproportionately scale a fountain fill. One of the most obvious benefits in version X7 is that making an elliptical fill for elliptical objects is a breeze. If you drag the Free Scale And Skew node toward or away from the Start node, fill types such as elliptical and rectangular become obviously disproportional in their fountain fill characteristic; that is, not circular and not perfectly square. If you drag the Free Scale And Skew node in a direction other than a 90-degree angle to the line between Start and End nodes, the fountain fill takes on a skewed appearance. This handle node operates independent from the Start/End nodes. If you drag the End node, the Free Scale node moves with it both distance-wise and rotationally. It stays parallel to the Start node if you move that one, as well.

Free Scale And Skew handle dragged down.
It is shorter now than the fountain fill transition line.

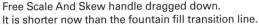

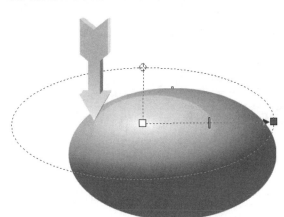

- **Midpoint slider**   You drag this slider toward one color node or the other to establish where, within the filled object, the 50/50 blend of each color has arrived. Therefore, if you want the filled object to feature more of the Start color than the End color, you drag this slider toward the *End* color, so the distance is greater between the Start color and midpoint.
- **Pop-up Node Color picker and Transparency control slider**   An innovation new to version X7, the pop-up Node Color picker and Transparency control slider only appears with fountain fill types of fills. When you click a color node—and an outline appears around it, indicating it's selected and can be changed—you'll see a mini toolbar with a drop-down button that leads to a Node Color picker and a transparency slider to the right. You can now set transparency values every time

you select a color node in a fountain fill. This is definitely a feature you want to explore, because, in addition to an Eyedropper tool on the Node Color picker, you can choose color modes (HSB, CMYK; see Chapter 15 if you're unfamiliar with color spaces), and work with a click-drag color field or enter numerical values for color components.

While you're using the Fill tool, the Property bar displays options that change depending on the type of fill you choose from the Fountain Fill Types selector or which style of fill is the current one (fountain, bitmap, two-color—all covered later in this chapter). If your selected object features no fill color at all, the selector displays the type as No Fill and the Property bar displays no options. On the Property bar shown in Figure 12-3, there are callouts pointing to the fountain fill options; and what they do is discussed next. There are options for fill types *other* than fountain fills, which are also covered in this chapter, but let's learn one type at a time.

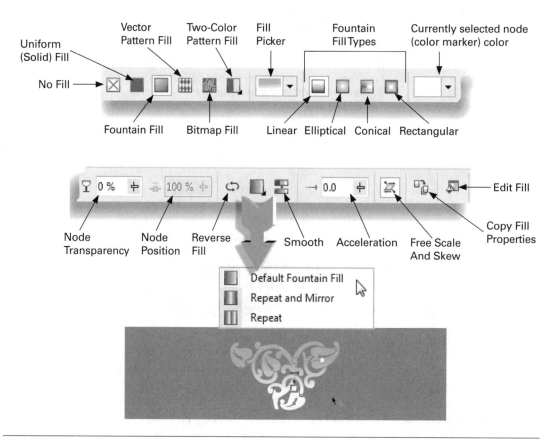

FIGURE 12-3   The properties for fountain fills are available when the Fill tool is active. You can *change* fill types using the Property bar.

Let's walk through the relevant options on the Property bar now for fountain fills, and then practice what you've learned in a tutorial to follow.

- **Fountain Fill button**   Only options for fountain fills are available when this button is depressed. If you click a different fill type, such as Vector pattern fill, fountain fill options disappear from the Property bar. If you select an object that already has a fountain fill and you use the Fill tool to select it, the Fountain Fill button will immediately appear on the Property bar in its depressed (on) position.
- **Fill Picker**   Read Chapter 1 if you're not familiar with Corel's subscription plans and community sharing. If you click the Fill Picker while a fountain fill object is selected, opening the Fill Picker flyout reveals a mind-boggling collection of fills in different categories. You'll notice that most of the fills have no marking or a "C" for Content Exchange marking, which means these fills were created and donated by members of the Corel community. They can be downloaded (they're all part of the Corel Connect implementation for content and might not physically be on your hard drive) by registered Corel Graphics Suite users. Other styles of fills might be marked with an "S," for Standard Membership. You need to create a free Standard Membership to access these fountain fill creations. "P" is for Premium Account (in other words, not free to download), and these fills can only be accessed if you've purchased a subscription from Corel Corp., which can be done through the Help file under Account Settings.

Tip   Because a custom fountain fill doesn't contain a bitmap or vector content—it's just an arrangement of color nodes—there's no real need to save a file you've downloaded. You can simply save an object with this fill and copy the fill at any time in the future. You can save your content locally from Window | Dockers | Tray.

- **Fountain Fill Types—Linear, Elliptical, Conical, and Rectangular**   Figure 12-4 shows the four types of fountain fills, along with callouts for the interactive options available for click-dragging screen elements. The *Linear* style is fairly self-evident: moving the Start node sets the beginning point for the Start color, and moving the End color node changes the angle, the end point, and to a certain extent the acceleration of the fill from one color to the other. Acceleration is covered shortly in this chapter. *Elliptical* fountain fills begin as circular fills, and they can take on the elliptical appearance when you shorten or lengthen the distance between the Start node to the Free Scale And Skew handle. The *Conical* fountain fill is the only type whose Start and End nodes are precisely over one another and this cannot be changed. You can choose to repeat and mirror the fill from the Property bar, and you can also add intermediate color nodes (covered later) to soften the abrupt transition in this fill type. The *Rectangular* fountain fill is closely related to the Elliptical fill except it has four corners within the design. It begins as a square pattern, and you can use the Free Scale And Skew handle to distort and create a rectangular and/or skewed color transition.

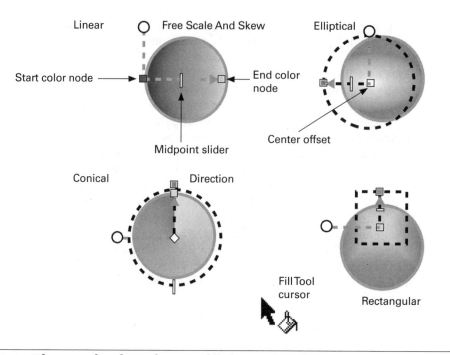

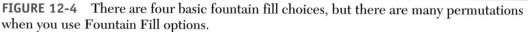

FIGURE 12-4 There are four basic fountain fill choices, but there are many permutations when you use Fountain Fill options.

- **Currently selected node (color node) color** To change the Start or End color in an applied fountain fill, it needs to be selected onscreen using the Interactive Fill tool. Because the color nodes serve more than one purpose—they mark both the color and the position of the color within the object—you'll be unintentionally confused in this *Guide* when the term node is also called *marker, handle,* and, occasionally, Phillip. If you want to change the color when a node is selected, you can use the Property bar or the color palette; if you want to move the node, you need to click-drag it to the desired position.

- **Node Transparency** Corel has gone all-out in this version, so every time you click a color node to alter its color, you can also change its opacity via a transparency slider. You can, in fact, have fountain fills that change opacity from left to right or from center to exterior, as shown next. You can see that the circle, sandwiched between the triangle and the squiggle, is not only lighter in color toward the 11 o'clock position, but it also allows parts of the underlying and obscured triangle to appear through. All you do is drag the pop-up slider from left to right.

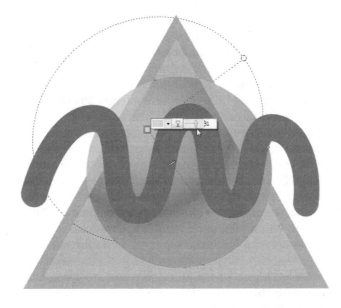

Tip An object that has any of the four fountain fill types can also contain transparencies that are also any of the four fountain fill types. You can, therefore, build an elegantly shaded object by, for example, applying an Elliptical fountain fill to an object and then giving it a Linear transparency property. See Chapter 19 for more details on transparency.

- **Node Position** This combo box is only active when there are more than two color nodes along a fountain fill. When you've created several intermediate color nodes, you select one with the Fill tool, and this box can be used to reposition it precisely.
- **Reverse Fill** If you've created a multicolor elliptical gradient, for example, it would be a royal pain to have to change all the nodes if you wanted to reverse the appearance of the colors. But you don't have to! All you do is click this button on the Property bar to reverse color node order immediately.
- **Smooth** Because fountain fills are mathematically calculated as step progressions from one color to another, occasionally you might see the steps—called *color banding*—if the colors change dramatically over a very short distance. Enabling (depressing) this button makes an attempt to add more intermediate colors to make the steps less visible.
- **Acceleration** Acceleration might be called *contrast*—how fast toward the center of a fountain fill does the 50 percent blending point occur. Corel has called this the *Edge Pad* in previous versions of CorelDRAW. When you need an abrupt change from the Start color to the End color, you increase the acceleration.

- **Free Scale And Skew** This button enables/disables the Free Transform function in fountain (and other) fills. By default, it's on, and you can see and work with the node onscreen within an object. Disabled, the screen element disappears and you're left with only Start and End color nodes (and the midpoint slider).
- **Copy Fill Properties** This option is common to many object fills in CorelDRAW. To use this feature, you have to have a target object (the object to which you want to apply a fancy fill) and an object with the desired fill. You first select the object you want to fill, then choose the Interactive Fill tool, and then click this button. You're presented with an oversized arrow cursor onscreen; click over the object you want to copy the fill from, and the action is completed.
- **Edit Fill** Gone is the dialog you used to have to drill down to by choosing the Fill Properties icon from the Toolbox. Clicking this button provides an onscreen dialog where everything you might want to do using the Property bar is presented to you, but with more options and a more precise way to fill objects through number boxes with fractional amounts out to three decimal places.

Tip If you want to change the fill properties of an object, but you're working with a tool other than the Fill tool, with this object selected, press ALT+ENTER and the Properties docker in version X7 now includes all the features from the Edit Fill dialog.

Customizing Your Fountain Fills

A default fountain fill features two colors, but you can *add* colors to customize any type of fountain fill. When you make multicolored fountain fills, the appearance of your artwork can change dramatically. To add a node, double-click with the Fill tool on the dashed line connecting the Start and End color nodes. The position of added colors is shown by node positions on the dashed line guide joining the two default colors. After you've added color nodes and clicked to select them on the object, the Property bar will display their position and color.

You can add, move, and delete fountain fill colors you've added to a default fountain fill type in several ways, but you *must* have both the object and the Interactive Fill tool selected, or you'll wind up editing the object and not the fill. To explore doing this, follow the steps in this tutorial.

Tutorial Editing a Fountain Fill In-Place

1. Select the object to be filled, choose the Interactive Fill tool (G), and then apply a fountain fill by choosing Linear, Elliptical, Conical, or Rectangular from the Property bar.
2. With this fill applied, double-click a point on the guide between the two existing color nodes where you want to add a color node. Doing this adds a color that is based on an average of two existing node colors, so your custom fountain fill probably looks the same as the default fill.

3. Decide on a new intermediate color (choose one in this example from the color palette), and drag a color from the color swatch (drag the swatch) onto your new node. You have a three-color gradient now.
4. Try a different technique to add a color node position and color at the same time: drag a color swatch directly onto the same fountain fill guide, but at a different location.
5. To reposition an added color, click-drag it along the guide path. As you do this, the color's node position changes, as indicated by the Node Position percentage value on the Property bar.
6. To change any fountain fill color, click to select it, and choose a color from the Property bar selector or click a color swatch on the color palette.
7. To delete an added color, right-click or double-click it on the guide. End and Start color nodes can't be deleted, but they can be assigned different colors and you can make them invisible by choosing 100% transparency from the mini pop-up color mixer.

You can also add color when a color node position is selected; choose from the color selector to the right of the Fountain Fill Types selector on the Property bar.

Although fountain fills are useful and fun, we need to return to uniform colors for a while because color models and color components—and importantly for commercial print designers—standards such as PANTONE colors haven't been addressed yet. The following section takes you way beyond the color palette and into the Edit Fill dialog.

Uniform Color Fill Options on the Property Bar

Uniform fills are like the paint chips at the hardware store; they're solid colors, no variations. A uniform fill floods an object within the boundaries of its outline with the color you choose. The color palette is a fast, easy way to assign a uniform color; however, when you choose the Fill tool, you have several different color models from which to choose. See Chapter 15 for some details on color theory; if you're already familiar with the CMYK printing color model, the intuitive HSB color model, and others, you'll feel right at home using the Property bar to mix up color values and, better still, entering values a client might telephone to you for that big advertising job. Figure 12-5 shows the Edit Fill dialog, and if any of the callouts seem unfamiliar, a plain and frank discussion follows that'll get you from novice to expert in no time.

Tip HSB and RGB color models occupy the same *color space*, the extent to which a color can be expressed onscreen. Therefore, you can arrive at an identical color using either color mode. This means you can switch color models for a filled object, and between RGB and HSB there will be no real color change.

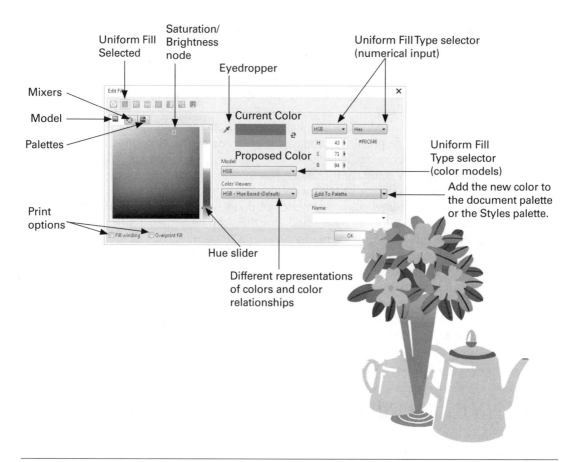

FIGURE 12-5 The Edit Fill dialog is where you specify an exact color and an exact color space for that color, such as printing CMYK and web page RGB models.

When a uniform color is filling a selected object and you enter the Edit Fill dialog, you'll see the following areas and controls:

- **Color Model** In Figure 12-5, the author is working in RGB color mode and, therefore, has chosen HSB from the Model drop-down list, which offers three different views for specifying a color by dragging your cursor through a color field and a color slider. Two additional color selection layouts and two other mixers are covered in this section. In the HSB Hue-Based Color Viewer, colors are specified by first dragging the hue slider to the hue you want, and then dragging a small onscreen puck through the Saturation/Brightness field to the left of the Hue slider.
- **Hue slider** In the HSB configuration for defining a color, the *H* stands for *Hue*, and the Hue slider is offered in the Hue-Based Color Viewer in the Edit Fill dialog.

Hue is the predominantly recognizable aspect of HSB color; red is a hue, orange is a hue, but an exotic home-decorating color such as Pale Salmon is not a hue, but rather a brightness and saturation-altered variation of a red hue. Hues might be described as "pure" colors; they can't get any brighter, and they can't get any more saturated.

- **Saturation/Brightness puck**   This is the small square in the color field when HSB Hue-Based Color Viewer is chosen. Move this around within the field to designate a specific brightness and saturation for the current hue. Dragging the puck to the left makes a hue paler, whereas dragging it to the right makes the hue more saturated. Dragging up and down increases or decreases the brightness of a hue. If you want pure black and forgot that it's on the color palette (I'm kidding here), based on what you've read so far, you'd set the Hue slider to any color you like, and then drag the brightness and saturation puck all the way down (no brightness) and all the way to the left (no saturation).

- **Uniform Fill Type selector (color models)**   This drop-down list, titled simply "Model," offers HSB, RGB, HLS (basically the same as HSB and RGB), CMYK, Greyscale, and other color models. Depending on your work on a specific piece, you might choose Greyscale for final output to a laser printer or CMYK for commercial output. A *color model* defines a space, an expressible perimeter of available colors. For example, the CMYK color space is smaller than LAB color, and that's why an illustration created in LAB color mode looks dull when printed to CMYK colors—some of the LAB colors need to be shifted into a narrower color space and the "closest match" is chosen by CorelDRAW. More on this in Chapter 15. Always choose your color model, and always set up your document when you choose New Document according to your intended final output.

- **Uniform Fill Type selector (numerical input)**   This area is basically the same as the color-picking visual input at the left of this dialog, but you use number values instead of click-dragging to define a color. Not to worry: as you change the values in this area, you *will* see your proposed color to the left. You are shown duplicate fields in this area for a very important reason: you might need to know, for example, what the equivalent of a selected color is in a "different language." For example, your boss told you a specific color for a logo using RGB values. No problem, you typed them into the fields and saved the color to the color palette. However, the commercial printer now wants to know what this logo color is in CMYK values. You can see both set of color components values if you set one field to RGB and the other to CMYK. Take the rest of the day off; that was easy!

- **Different representations of colors and color relationships**   The Color Viewers drop-down list represents different ways to manipulate the components of colors graphically to accommodate the way you work, or the way your client might want you to work. In the next illustration, RGB 3D Additive viewer is selected, and you can see an entirely different way to make up a color, based on red, green, and blue primary color markers that add brightness when dragged away from the center of the hexagon and mix with the other primary colors when dragged toward each extreme. Additionally, a slider controls the brightness of all the RGB markers simultaneously. You have several different views of color relationships; pick the one that makes the most sense to you.

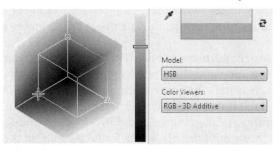

- **Add the new color to the document palette or the Styles palette**   These are your two choices when you click Add To Palette. When you've arrived at the color of your dreams, you might want to add the color to the document palette—the horizontal strip at the bottom of the interface, not the default color palette that's vertically attached outside of the drawing window. Once the custom color is added to the document palette, then you can double-click the newly created swatch on the document palette at the bottom of the window and enter a new name for it. Your other choice, aside from not adding the color to any palette, is to add the color to the Color Styles palette, a vertical strip that pops up to the right of the default color palette when you choose Window | Color Palettes | Color Styles Palette.

- **Color Mixer**   The Color Mixer tab at left in the Edit Fill dialog is an artistic way to define a color, not based on empirical value but instead on how colors compare and relate to one another, as shown in this illustration. You have your choice of the uncomplicated Complementary color arrangement that shows the "color opposite" of the current color along with variations of both colors in a selection box below the arrangement of colors. The Variation drop-down offers Lighter (to define tints of a specific color), Warmer, Darker, and other option. For a more complex arrangement, you can choose Rectangle from the Hues drop-down, and drag any of the white markers at the corner of the rectangle to skew toward a narrower selection of hues and drag the black triangle node around outside of the circle to set the baseline hue to then create variations and other harmonic comparisons of colors. Although initially a challenge, you might grow to love working with harmonies as a color basis because you're choosing colors by emotion— how they impress you—instead of by numerical values.

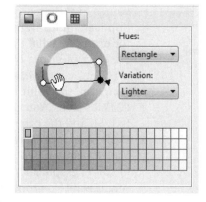

- **Palette options**   There are two checkboxes, Fill Winding and Overprint Fill, that pertain to commercial printing and not web work or personal printing. *Fill Winding* refers to the *Winding Path Rule:* If you follow a combined path, the fill should go to your left. This means that, potentially, a combined path such as a donut could have its inner subpath going in the same direction as its outer path. You might not even notice this, but when printed to PostScript technology, the donut would wind up being filled, and not with raspberry jelly. Checking Fill Winding helps alleviate this potential problem. *Overprint Fill* usually has the opposite effect that artists want when printing artwork. By default, overlapping colors are knocked out—colors printed after the latest color in multicolor printing do not mix together. If you enable Overprint Fill, overlapping colors, cyan and yellow, for example, in CMYK printing, will produce green when areas overlap accidentally or intentionally. Unless you have experience with commercial presses, leave this box unchecked.

- **Current Color and Proposed Color**　This handy feature is for visually comparing the current color you've chosen against the color you've mixed up and intend to use to replace the current color. To the right of these fields is a little recycle icon: it swaps the colors onscreen so you can preview what the object will look like before making a final decision to click OK and apply the new color.

- **Eyedropper**　You will find instances of the Eyedropper tool all over the place in version X7 and it's quite welcome in the Edit Fill dialog because the dialog isn't *modeless*—your cursor can't step out of the box and adjust something on the page. But the Eyedropper tool can be moved anywhere to sample a color in your drawing, on the page, on the interface, and even outside the interface in a different program or on your desktop.

Swatches and Preset CMYK "Color Chips"

If you're unfamiliar with spot colors, spot color is the printing process used to add a color to packages, for example, that cannot be reproduced using standard press inks, such as that reflective silver logo on a box of cereal. The third tab in the Edit Fill dialog is for viewing preset swatches from several preset catalogs, from simple grayscale values to PANTONE. Not all the libraries here are based on the cyan, magenta, yellow, and black (also called the *key* color) color model. If you or your client has specified a color standard color—however, let's pretend it's from a PANTONE Solid uncoated swatch book—using that color in a design is not a brain-teaser:

1. Open the Edit Fill dialog, click the Swatches tab, and then choose the color library from which the color was chosen.
2. Begin typing the number value of the PANTONE color in the Name field; doing this performs an automatic search; in the illustration following these steps, **223** was typed in the Name field, and the swatch book immediately went to that swatch.
3. Solid colors are used as an *additional* color to the cyan, magenta, yellow, and key *process* colors in traditional commercial press printing. They're used as spot colors—a metallic gold burst of pigment that says "New!" on a cereal box, for example. Because spot colors are added as a separate ink in the composition, you can choose a tint of these colors by using the Tint slider to

specify the amount of this color expressed as a halftone screen on the printed page. Again, Chapter 23 has more info on printing than can be presented in this chapter, but the two are related.

Color swatches, similar to those paint chips you see in hardware and home improvement stores, are presented as names in the color field as well; see the following illustration.

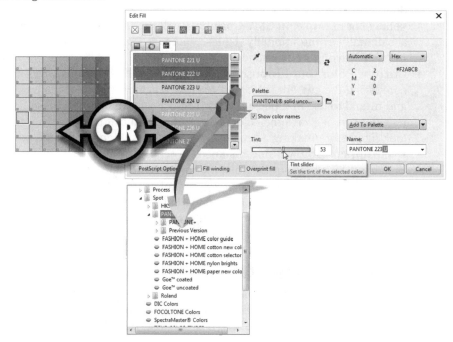

Applying Pattern Fills

Pattern fills are rectangular-shaped tiles that repeat vertically and horizontally to fill a closed-path object completely. They come in three different varieties: Two-Color, Vector, and Bitmap, each with its own unique qualities, shown here.

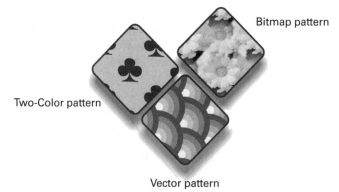

Bitmap pattern

Two-Color pattern

Vector pattern

Two-Color Fills

When you decide a Two-Color fill will suit your object, the Property bar displays a host of options that you can use to apply dramatic changes to the fill's appearance. Figure 12-6 shows what the control handles look like for the pattern fill, and details the options offered on the Property bar for Two-Color fills.

The Property bar offers options for the type of pattern, colors used, and general appearance of the Two-Color pattern. The interactive control nodes around the pattern control the pattern's frequency, degree of rotation, and other things covered right now:

- **Fill selector**   Use this drop-down box to choose from existing pattern fill libraries. Notice that there is a More... button at the bottom of the Selector flyout. Clicking this takes you to a pattern-making utility where you can create an original two-color pattern that you can save and apply later.
- **Color selectors**   When you've selected a two-color pattern, these two selectors let you set colors other than black and white for a pattern.
- **Transform Fill With Object**   When this option is active, transformations applied to your object will also be applied to your fill pattern. This feature is useful when you need to scale an object larger and don't want your pattern to "shrink"! Stretching and squashing a pattern within an object is possible when you specify that the fill should reproportion according to what you do to the object itself.

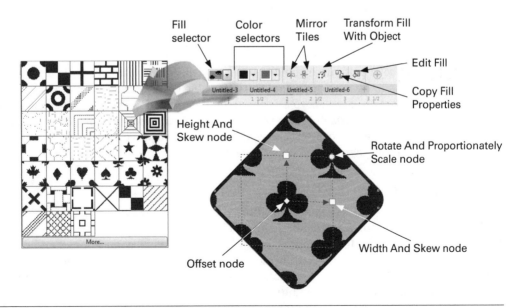

FIGURE 12-6   Two-Color patterns are ideal for filling clothing on cartoons and for simple walls and other structures in drawings.

- **Mirror Tiles** You have your choice of vertical or horizontal mirroring (or both) and the result is most apparent when the two-color design does *not* feature symmetrical objects. The club pattern shown in Figure 12-6 doesn't change significantly when horizontal mirroring is applied because the clubs themselves are symmetrical from left to right. If you choose vertical mirroring, however, every other row of clubs is turned upside down. Mirroring is a good feature for producing symmetrical patterns but also is great when you want a more visually interesting fill than, say, polka dots.

- **Copy Fill Properties** This is a persistent button when the Fill tool is selected, and as with fountain fills, you select an unfilled object, click the Copy Fill button, and then click the cursor over an object on the page whose fill you want to copy to the unfilled object.

- **Edit Fill** As with most pattern-filled options, the Edit Fill dialog has almost identical features to those found on the Property bar, except it has numerical fields for precise size, rotation, skew, and other pattern properties.

- **Offset node** Within the filled shape when using the Fill tool, you drag on this node to establish a center to the design. This feature is terrific if the pattern appears just a little lopsided within the "window" that is your object, through which the pattern peeks.

- **Stretch And Skew node** These two node handles, arranged at right angles to each other, by default, control how much the pattern inside the object is stretched or skewed. Moving one node controls the vertical stretch and skew, and the other controls the horizontal. If only one node is moved away from the default position, the pattern's shape is disproportionally altered. Although they are not true perspective controls, they can be used as a simple way to change a brick-wall fill into a brick road.

Note Two-color patterns are limited to *exactly* two colors, with no additional edge colors to create antialiasing. This means the edges of the design can be harsh if you export your work to a screen resolution of 96 dpi. If you use the default page resolution of 300 dpi when you set up a new page, however, and then export, for example, a TIFF copy of your work, the aliased edges you see onscreen will *not* appear in the exported bitmap image.

Vector Pattern Fills

You have access to scores of beautifully designed vector shapes created by Corel staff and the Corel Community when you click the Vector Pattern Fill selector button on the Property bar. However, the pattern itself already has color applied and cannot be altered. Additionally, these full-color fills cannot be extracted as vector shapes from the pattern. Therefore, when making your own, save a copy of your pattern to CDR file format for editing in the future, and forget about the Break Apart and Convert To Curves commands in an attempt to reduce a full-color pattern to its vector component shapes.

Bitmap Fills

Bitmap patterns are carefully edited bitmaps; some of the presets are taken from photos whereas others are paintings, and all of them are relatively small in dimension. The difference between a full-color and a Bitmap fill is that the vector-based pattern tiles for the full-color fills can be resized without losing design detail, focus, or introducing noise, but enlarging Bitmap pattern tiles carries the same caveat as enlarging any bitmap—the more you enlarge it, the better your chances are that the component pixels will eventually become visible. You can scale bitmaps down, but not up—computers are "smart," but they can't create extra visual data from data that wasn't there to begin with.

Controlling Pattern Fills Interactively

Knowing what you do now about the eminent editablility of patterns when applied to objects, it's time for a little hands-on tutorial to demonstrate how to edit the look of an applied pattern fill by adjusting the interactive markers and using the various Property bar options common to a pattern style.

The interactive handles surrounding a pattern fill help you to set the tile size, offset, skew, and rotation of the pattern. To experience this firsthand, open *Platonic.cdr* and work with the uncompleted group of objects on the left of the page. Use the right-side duplicate of the Platonic geometry as a reference.

Tutorial   Customizing a Pattern Fill

1. Select an object in the group at left, and then choose the Interactive Fill tool (G).
2. Choose Two-Color Pattern from the Fill Type selector. Choose the first sample entry, the polka dot pattern. Because the object you selected was already filled with a uniform color, the polka dot pattern is probably very light gray against white. Don't worry; you'll change this shortly.
3. Click the Front color button on the Property bar, and just so we don't drag this tutorial out until next week, rather than trying to define an appropriate gold polka-dot color with the Node Color picker drop-down, click the Eyedropper tool and then go sample the color used in the corresponding finished design at right. If you have the spare time, experiment with foreground and background colors as applied to your own pattern work.
4. Repeat step 3 with the Back color, choosing a medium purple with the Eyedropper and applying it to your current pattern fill.
5. Drag the Rotation/Size handle toward the center of the selected object until the polka-dot pattern repeats about four times.
6. Drag the diamond-shaped center origin handle slightly in any direction. Notice that the center origin of the pattern changes.
7. Drag the Stretch And Skew node to the right to stretch the polka dots a little, creating perspective within this composition.
8. Use the right Stretch And Skew node to skew the pattern a little to the left, so it is about the same angle as the selected object. Then, use the Scale/Rotate node again to achieve the proper angle for this object.

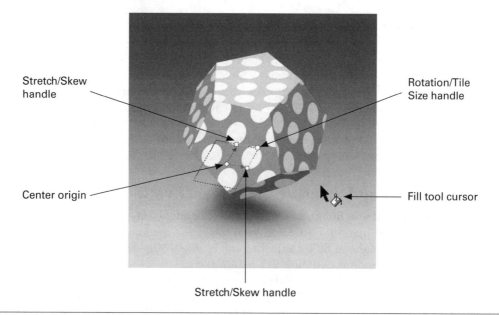

Stretch/Skew handle

Center origin

Rotation/Tile Size handle

Fill tool cursor

Stretch/Skew handle

FIGURE 12-7 The nodes surrounding a Two-Color pattern fill are there for you to control the pattern's colors, size, and skew.

9. That's all you need to know about editing to finish this composition! Repeat steps 3–8, varying the Front and Back colors to complete filling in other objects.

Figure 12-7 shows the node handles around a Two-Color pattern fill.

Tip One important feature found in the Edit Fill dialog that *doesn't* appear on the Property bar is Row and Column Offsets. By default, pattern tiles join to appear seamless. However, you can *intentionally* ruin the pattern (or just create an "interesting" one) by offsetting the pattern seams through either of these two options. To apply an offset, choose either Row or Column as the offset option, and enter a value between 0 and 100 percent.

Create Your Own Two-Color and Full-Color Patterns

Two-color patterns are harder to think up than they are to create, and the details are covered right after this section. Full-color vector or bitmap patterns are created by sampling an area on the page. With your desired pattern created, draw a new object outside of the pattern area and make sure it's selected. Open the Object Properties docker (ALT + ENTER) and click the Fill button at the top. Select either the Vector Pattern Fill or the Bitmap Pattern Fill option. Click the New From Document icon located to the right of the pattern list. Move your cursor into the document and drag a selection around the desired pattern area, but don't include the new object you created. It will have a default fill automatically applied to it when you clicked the Vector or Bitmap Pattern Fill buttons. After the pattern area is selected, click the Accept icon floating underneath the box. If you clicked the Vector Pattern Fill button, you now click the Save As New button in the docker, where you can name it, tag it with keywords, and elect to share it with Content Exchange. If you clicked the Bitmap Pattern Fill button when selecting your pattern, click the floating Accept icon to display a Convert To Bitmap dialog. Here, you can assign resolution, color mode, and more to the pattern. Saving a bitmap pattern is the same as for vector patterns—click the Save As New button in the Object Properties docker. To apply a custom pattern, click either the Vector or Bitmap Fill Pattern buttons and the Fill Picker drop-down list on the Property bar. Click the Browse button at the bottom and navigate to your saved pattern. Saved patterns are located in My Documents\Corel\Corel Content\Fills. Note that both Vector and Bitmap fills are shown, and that your fill type will change to Vector pattern fill if you choose a saved vector file and to Bitmap pattern fill if you choose a bitmap pattern. Both kinds of pattern fills have the same file extension (*.fill), so it might be wise to include the word *vector* or *bitmap* in your filename when you initially save a pattern as either type.

Two-Color patterns, on the other hand, are created using a special editor box displayed by clicking the More button at the bottom of the First Fill Pattern or Color button on the Property bar. As you can see in Figure 12-8, Two-Color patterns are

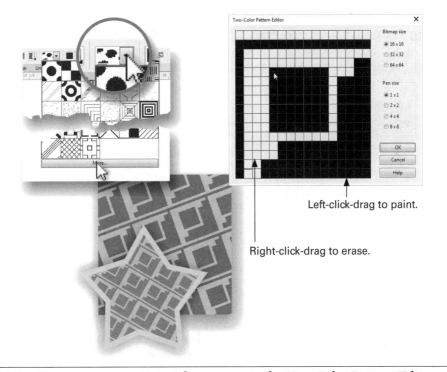

Left-click-drag to paint.

Right-click-drag to erase.

FIGURE 12-8   Create your own Two-Color pattern in the Two-Color Pattern Editor.

created by choosing a tile size, a cursor size, and then left-dragging and/or clicking to set the foreground pattern; right-clicks and right-click-drags act like an eraser. Two-Color patterns you create are immediately applied to a selected object, unlike full-color patterns, which are saved to a *.fill file on hard disk. Although you are creating a black-and-white pattern in the Editor, Two-Color patterns can be any two colors; you apply the pattern and then use the Property bar's mini-palettes to define the two colors.

Tip You can also create patterns by using the Tools | Create | Pattern Fill menu command. This command lets you capture a screen area and use it as a Two-Color or **full-color** pattern. And it is here you can elect to share it with Content Exchange—part of the Corel Community—or not.

Applying Texture Fills

PostScript and (fractal) texture fill types aren't "out in the open" in version X7—they're still available, but you need to click Edit Fill with the Fill tool active to locate these fill types. For users new to CorelDRAW, draw a rectangle, select the Fill tool, apply any type of fill just so the Edit Fill button appears, and click the Edit Fill button on the Property bar. Let's review texture fills. Here's the Edit Fill dialog when the Texture Fill type has been selected, along with a labeled layout of the options.

Tip Although it's one more thing to remember in this feature-filled program, you can also access PostScript and texture fills on the Property bar by click-holding the Two-Color Pattern Fill button.

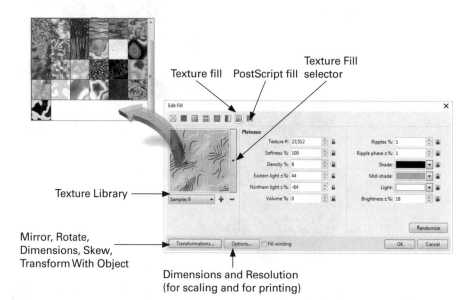

Texture fill   PostScript fill   Texture Fill selector

Texture Library

Mirror, Rotate, Dimensions, Skew, Transform With Object

Dimensions and Resolution (for scaling and for printing)

The strange and wonderful thing about Corel's texture fills is that they are math-based bitmap images that can be scaled without a loss of detail because the math belongs to the *fractal* family of imaging. Fractal fills are resolution-independent in a certain way—the closer you zoom in, the more detail you'll see in any one given shape. The textures are based on more than a hundred different styles ranging from bubbles to clouds.

For the artist, all you really need to know about fractal (texture) fills is that you have an awful lot of customization controls that change as you choose various samples from different collections. In the previous illustration, the "Plateau" preset was originally too dull for the author's taste; I increased the Brightness parameter and changed a dull green to a lively red, and then clicked the plus (+) button—a button common to most content collections in CorelDRAW—to add and save a custom texture or whatever to a collection for later use.

The interactive nodes surrounding a texture fill are the same as those for pattern fills; they're there for you to set the size, offset, skew, and rotation of the texture. If you have experience manipulating pattern fills by click-dragging the control nodes above the object, you'll discover bitmap fills are exactly the same. However, because these are *bitmap-based* textures, rotating or scaling them to a larger size will degrade the image.

Applying PostScript Fills

PostScript fills are vector-based and use PostScript page-descriptor language to create a variety of patterns from black-and-white to full color. Each PostScript fill included with CorelDRAW has individual variables that control the appearance of the pattern, much the same way as you can customize texture fills. PostScript pattern styles come in a variety of patterns, as shown here, and also come as nonrepeating fills.

Like accessing texture fills, you must select a filled object, choose the Fill tool, and then click the Edit Fill button on the Property bar to get access to the PostScript fill type and the available options—presets, line widths, pattern element size, and color options, depending on the specific preset.

The image you see onscreen is an accurate representation of the actual pattern that will be printed; again, PostScript is a printing technology, but Corel Corporation has made the technology viewable in CorelDRAW and printable without the need for a PostScript printer. On that note, it should be mentioned that PostScript fills will print exceptionally well to any PostScript device; that's what the fills are intended for, but you don't necessarily have to use PostScript. However, *you must be using Enhanced View to see it* (choose View | Enhanced).

To apply a PostScript fill, follow these steps:

1. Create and then select the object to apply any PostScript texture fill, and then click-hold the Two-Color Pattern Fill button on the Property bar, the first in a collection of fills immediately fills the object, and you can choose other preset patterns from the PostScript patterns drop-down list.

Tip The Edit Fill dialog can also be accessed by double-clicking the fill icon on the Status bar, toward the right of the bar below the local color palette.

2. Click the Edit Fill button on the Property bar—you can only modify the PostScript fill so much from the Property bar. In the Edit Fill dialog, click the PostScript button.

3. Version X7 has a Refresh button that forces a redraw of the current pattern when you make changes, but you will see an unchanged preset right away when entering this set of options in the Edit Fill dialog, and if you move the Edit Fill dialog to the side, you can see a preview of the fill in the selected object on the page.

4. Notice that each fill has its own set of parameters that can be changed. For example, the GreenLeaves preset is chosen in the next illustration; however, the leaves are too small and there's not enough variation in the greens to suit a specific assignment. The solution is to decrease the number of leaves per square inch, thus increasing each leaf's relative size, and to lower the Minimum Green, so a wider expression of the preset's green color is visible.

5. Click Refresh to refresh the preview, and if it looks good, you click OK and get back to your work!

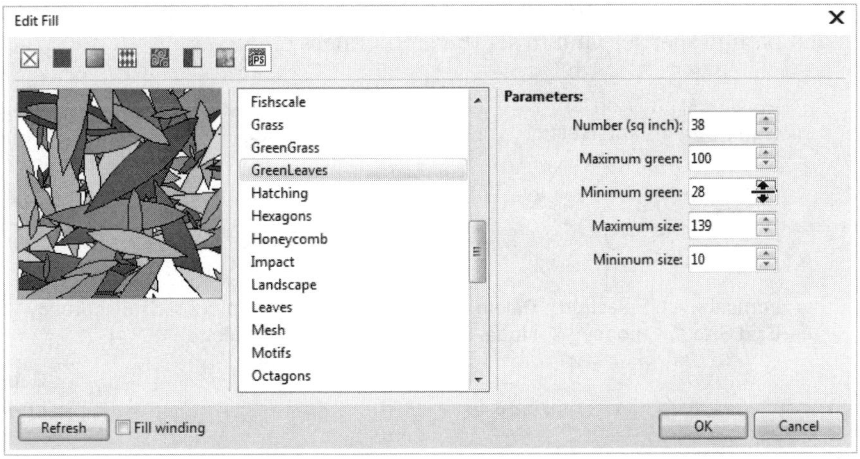

PostScript fills are great for schematic and roadmap illustrations, and if you use no background color when you customize many of the fills, the fills support transparency. So you can actually apply, for example, crosshatching, over a color-filled object to enhance the shading.

Working with Mesh Fills

Mesh fills can be used to create the effect of several blending-color fountain fills over a mesh of vertical and horizontal Bézier curves. Editing a mesh grid creates a sort of fill that doesn't really look like a fountain fill but instead looks very much like a *painting*. Mesh fills make it easy to create, as you'll see in the following illustrations, most of the visual complexity of a reflective sphere—*using only one object and one fill*. Add to the visual complexity the capability to set transparency levels to each patch of a mesh fill individually, and in no time you'll be creating scenes that look like paintings, using a fraction of the number of individual objects you'd imagine. You'll find the Interactive Mesh Fill tool in the Toolbox grouped with the Interactive Fill tool; or press M for speedy selection.

With the Mesh Fill tool selected, the Property bar features a number of options, shown next, for controlling this truly unique fill type. Many of these options will look familiar to those who work with the Shape tool to edit paths because, essentially, a mesh fill defines different color areas in a vector, resolution-independent way. Use these options to set the vertical and horizontal size in the mesh grid, to change node and path properties, and to set the smoothness of curves.

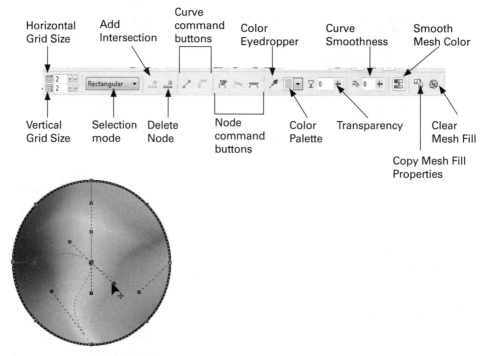

Believe it or not, the circle in the previous illustration has one scalable fill, made up of nine colors that blend into one another according to how the color nodes are moved around the interior of the circle. Acceleration between color nodes is done by dragging on the color node handles. It might not be apparent in the black-and-white edition of this *Guide*, but if you try it out on your copy of CorelDRAW, you'll see and understand the instant complexity of the result!!

Applying a mesh grid to an object is a quick operation. Mesh fills are dynamic, so they can be edited and reedited at any time. Editing the shape and color of a mesh grid can be a little bit of a challenge your first time out, but being able to smear and almost paint on a fill will make the effort worthwhile to you and your work. Node- and curve-editing actions needed to move fill areas are the same as for Bézier curves. For information on how to do this, see Chapter 9.

Mesh Fill Options

On the Property bar, when the Mesh Fill tool and an object are selected, you have control over the following attributes:

- **Frequency of the patches** By default, a new mesh fill is created on an object with two horizontal and two vertical sets of patches. These patches are linked at the edges by paths and at their vertices by nodes. You can use the numerical entry fields or the spin boxes with these fields to increase or decrease the number of columns and rows of patches. Manually, if you right-click a node or a path segment you have the option to create a node or an intersection by choosing from the pop-up menu.

Tip You can double-click a path segment to create a new intersection. This method might be faster for you.

- **Add Intersection/Delete Node**   When you've clicked on a path segment and a node appears, you can add an intersection, either by clicking the Add Intersection button or by pressing + on the numerical keypad. When you add an interception, you add a row or a column to the mesh fill, depending on whether you've added a point to a vertical or a horizontal mesh path segment. You must first select a node to then delete it. Clicking the Delete Node button or pressing DELETE on your keyboard removes both the mesh node and its associated intersecting path segments—reducing the number of columns or rows of mesh patches. Deleting nodes can yield unanticipated results so give some thought before you delete a node.
- **Curve and Node command buttons**   By default, path segments that make up the mesh fill are curves, bound by nodes that have the Smooth property. To change a path segment to a line, you use the Convert To Line command button; click Convert To Curve to create the opposite property. Nodes can be changed to Cusp, Smooth, and Symmetrical properties by clicking the associated Property bar button; the commands can also be found on the right-click pop-up menu when your cursor has selected a node.
- **Curve Smoothness**   Suppose you've added far too many nodes to a path segment and your mesh fill looks like a bad accident in one area. If you marquee-select the nodes that bind this path segment, the Curve Smoothness slider and numerical entry field act like the Node Reduction feature in CorelDRAW. You reduce the number of superfluous nodes (CorelDRAW decides on the meaning of "superfluous"; you yourself have no control) by entering a value or using the slider.
- **Selection mode**   By default, you can select nodes in Rectangular mode, which means you marquee-drag a rectangular shape with your cursor to select nodes and then change their properties such as color, position, and transparency. Your other selection choice is Freehand; in this mode, your cursor behaves like a real-world lasso and you are unconstrained by a selection shape for nodes. Additionally, you can SHIFT-click and select non-neighboring nodes to edit. When using Freehand mode, you can't select patches—selecting patches by clicking within them is only available in Rectangular selection mode.
- **Smooth Mesh Color**   This toggle on/off button can produce smoother color blends in your fill without changing the position or properties of the mesh nodes and curve path segments.
- **Eyedropper**   When a patch or node is selected, you can choose a color anywhere on screen by dragging the Color Eyedropper over to any point.
- **Color Palette**   The mini–color palette flyout on the Property bar lets you select colors for selected nodes and patches. Click the flyout button to access the default color palette or choose from other preinstalled CorelDRAW palettes. Clicking a color swatch on the (regular) color palette applies color, too.

When working with the mesh fill, you'll get far more predictable results if you apply colors to the nodes instead of dropping colors onto patches. Also bear in mind that regardless of how you create a shape, the mesh fill makes the object "soft"—the control nodes that make the closed path of the object are also mesh fill nodes. So, unavoidably, if you want to move a node you've colored in *at the edge* of the object, you're also *moving the associated path segment*. This is fun and creative stuff, actually, and if you need the fill to be soft with the object's original shape intact, you can put your finished object inside a container by using the Objects | PowerClip | Place In Frame feature.

Sampling Fills

Many of us are already familiar with an Eyedropper tool; you click on a color on the page with such a tool and the sampled color immediately becomes the foreground color on the toolbar and you can then use this sampled color somewhere else in your drawing.

CorelDRAW has two eyedropper tools, though, and each one has a specific purpose.

Applying the Color Eyedropper

The Color Eyedropper is your "standard" eyedropper tool, and it operates as you probably anticipate, with one or two notable enhancements that Corel has given it. To sample a color and apply it to one or more other objects, you select the tool from the Eyedropper group on the Toolbox. Now here's where something cool comes into play: bitmap images can have millions of colors, but high-resolution images impress us as having a predominant color in an area, such as tree leaves, when, in actuality, at a pixel level, there are dozens of different green colors that leave the human eye with but a single color impression.

The Color Eyedropper offers Sample Size on the Property bar. You can choose from a precise 1×1 pixel sampling size, a 2×2 pixel average, and a 5×5 pixel average color sample. When sampling from bitmap images and even fountain fills, increase the Sample Size on the Property bar to capture the color your brain sees, not the precise color under your cursor.

With the Color Eyedropper, unlike many other graphics programs, once you've sampled, it's not a one-pop deal to then fill another object. The filling part of the Attributes Eyedropper is persistent—you'll see a bucket icon on the Property bar that stands for "Fill," and you can continue to fill two or a hundred objects on your page until you want to reset the sample color, in which case you click the Eyedropper button to the left of the paint bucket icon.

Using the Attributes Eyedropper Tool

The Color Eyedropper's cousin tool, the Attributes Eyedropper, is used to sample and apply fills such as fountain and texture fills and all the others. Choose the Attributes Eyedropper from the Toolbox, and three drop-down categories are presented to you: Properties, Transformations, and Effects. The default installation of CorelDRAW X7 selects all the Properties, but none of the Transformations or Effects. This means that "right out of the box," you can sample and apply all Outline properties for sampled objects, all fills, and all text attributes if you sample some text. The illustration displays all three categories. As you can see—and imagine—if you dressed up a rectangle with a fountain fill and a dashed outline and a drop shadow, it would take about two clicks to apply all these trappings to a plain ellipse you've created on the page. What a time-saver, eh?

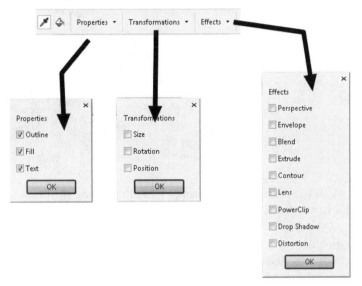

Tip As an alternative to using the Attributes Eyedropper tool, you can drag an object using the right mouse button, and then drop it on top of an object to which you want to apply any fill style. The pop-up menu appears when you've released the right mouse button, and you then choose Copy Fill, Outline, or All Properties. The position of the source object does not move when you use this drag technique.

Here's a brief tutorial to demonstrate the utility of the Attributes Eyedropper.

Tutorial   Drop a Property

1. Open *Fancy Circle.cdr*. You'll note that in front of a small locked bitmap background, there's an elegantly decorated circle to the left of a minimalist star. Your mission, should you decided to accept it, Jim, is to make the star look like the circle without changing its shape.
2. Choose the Attributes Eyedropper tool from the group in the Toolbox.
3. Click the Eyedropper cursor over the circle. Good—the circle's outline and fill properties are copied, look at callout "**a**" in Figure 12-9, and your cursor is now a paint bucket, all set to fill that star.

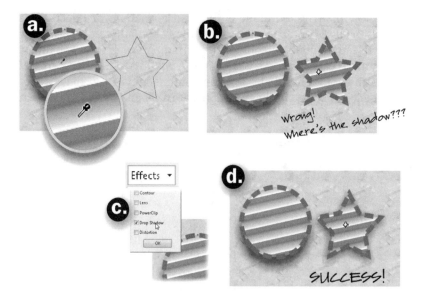

FIGURE 12-9 Use the Attributes Eyedropper to add several different custom properties from one object to another. And another. And…

4. Click over the star. No, wait a moment. That circle has a drop-shadow under it, doesn't it? See callout "**b**" in Figure 12-9. And that's not an Attribute property, but rather an Effect, and Bouton told you earlier that, by default, none of the Effects attributes are checked.

5. Go up to the Property bar and then click the Effects button, marked with callout "**c**" in Figure 12-9. Put a checkmark beside the Drop Shadow entry *and then click OK*. If you don't click OK, the box will close without registering this change in sampling parameters.

6. Well. Darn. Because your list of attributes has changed, you need to go back to Eyedropper mode (click the Eyedropper icon on the Property bar) and sample that circle again.

7. Click over the star shape with the Attributes Eyedropper tool's paint bucket cursor and yep, the star looks related to the circle. You can create new objects and even bold text now and fill them the same way you just dressed up the star with the circle's attributes. Or not. Figure 12-9 shows the steps you've run through here, with the grand finale marked with a "**d**" (for DONE!!!).

If you've had your fill, this is okay…so have your objects. You've learned in this chapter how to tap into CorelDRAW fills, and, hopefully, you've also seen how important fills can be to your drawings. Fills can actually contribute to the visual robustness of a composition more than the shape of objects. Take a cardboard box, for example. The shape of the box isn't that interesting and takes only a few seconds to draw. But the *texture* of a cardboard box is where the object gets its character and mood.

Outline properties and attributes are covered in the following chapter. You can do as much with customizing the thing that goes *around* an object as with the object itself.

13 Applying Strokes to Paths

Chapter 12 covers only half the story about how you can flesh out a visual idea by using CorelDRAW. Although an object can usually live its life just fine without an outline, the attributes you can apply to a path can add a touch of refinement to an illustration. The right outline color can visually separate different objects. Additionally, you can simulate calligraphic strokes without using Artistic Media when you know the options on the Object Properties docker. You can even make a path a dashed line, complete with arrowheads for fancy presentations and elegant maps. In fact, an outline, especially an open outline, can live its life in your work just fine without defining a filled object. You don't have to draw the line with fills and effects in your CorelDRAW artwork. This chapter shows you the ins and outs of properties you apply to your paths, from beginning to end.

Note Download and extract all the files from the Chapter13.zip archive to follow the tutorials in this chapter.

Applying Outline Pen Properties

By default, when you create an open or closed path, it's given a hairline width in black, with square corners and line caps...and no fancy extras. Part of the rationale for this default is that vector paths can't really be seen without some sort of width. In contrast, bitmap artwork, by definition, is made up of pixels, written to screen and file; so when a user draws an outline, it always has a width (it's always visible). Happily, vector drawing programs can display a wide range of path properties, and unlike bitmap outlines, you can change your mind at any time and easily alter the property of an outline.

In CorelDRAW, you can apply a property such as color, stroke width, and other fun stuff to an open or closed path (and even to open paths that don't touch each other but have been unified using the Object | Combine command). The following sections explore your options and point out the smartest and most convenient way to travel in the document window to arrive quickly at the perfect outline. When an open path or an object (which necessarily has to be described using a path) is selected on the page, the Property bar offers many options for outline properties. You can also dig into the Outline Pen dialog—now accessed by double-clicking the Outline box on the Status bar; there is no longer any Toolbox button for this dialog. And you also have the Object Properties docker—accessed from the pop-up menu when you right-click a path; ALT-ENTER also gets you there. Some shortcuts for performing simple property adjustments are covered on the long and winding path through this chapter.

Outline Pen Options and the Property Bar

Although it doesn't offer *all* options for path properties, the Property bar is probably the most convenient route to the most often-needed outline properties. It actively displays a selected path's *current* properties, which you can change when a path is selected and the current drawing tool is still active. Some options are persistent and are available when you choose a drawing tool but have not drawn a path yet, such as the Outline Width box. The Property bar—shown next for the Freehand Pen tool at top, and the Pen tool at bottom—offers outline width, style, and arrowhead options. You can make an open path with a head, tail, two heads—it's up to you. Other options give you control over wrapping text around a path, showing or hiding a bounding box around a path, and items not directly related to the outline's look. Closed paths, naturally, can't have arrowheads, but your options for dashed lines and other attributes are available for rectangles, ellipses, all the polygon shapes, and for freeform closed curves you've drawn by hand. You can see that when using the Pen tool, you have two tool-specific options—Preview mode and the capability to use the tool to add or remove nodes along the path you're drawing. The Freehand tool doesn't have these options, but it does offer the Auto-Smoothing option, which the Pen tool does not (because it is irrelevant).

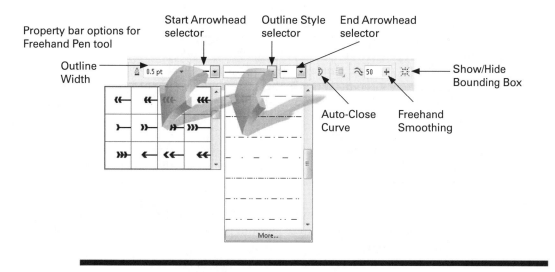

Property bar options for Freehand Pen tool

Start Arrowhead selector

Outline Style selector

End Arrowhead selector

Outline Width

Auto-Close Curve

Freehand Smoothing

Show/Hide Bounding Box

Property bar options for Pen tool

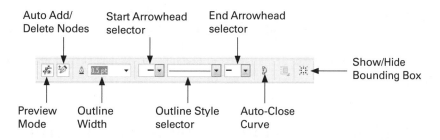

Auto Add/ Delete Nodes

Start Arrowhead selector

End Arrowhead selector

Show/Hide Bounding Box

Preview Mode

Outline Width

Outline Style selector

Auto-Close Curve

In the following tutorial, you'll use the Property bar when you draw a path.

Tutorial Going Long and Wide

1. Choose any drawing tool—the default Freehand Pen tool is fine—just drag a squiggle and then press SPACEBAR to switch to the Pick tool; the path is selected now.
2. On the Property bar, choose an outline thickness using the Outline Width selector, or enter a value and then press ENTER. If you're zoomed out of the drawing page, try choosing 8 points or greater so it's easier to see the effects in the following steps.

3. For arrowheads (on an open path), click the Start or End Arrowhead selectors, and then choose an arrowhead style from the pop-up. The Start option applies an arrowhead to the first node of the path; the End option applies it to the most-recently created. However, this might not be the direction in which you want the arrow to point. If this is the case, you have to perform a little mental juggling; the head of your arrow is always the *last* node on a path you create, not the first.

> **Tip** You can reverse the direction of an open path by choosing the Shape tool (F10), right-clicking over any of the path segments, and then choosing Reverse Subpaths from the contextual pop-up menu.

4. To apply a dashed or dotted-line pattern to the path, click the Outline Style selector, and then choose from one of the presets. Creating custom dashed patterns is covered later in this chapter.
5. Try increasing and decreasing the outline width, and see what happens to dashed line styles and arrowheads; they scale proportionately to the width of the outline.

As you apply outline properties from the Property bar to your object or path, the effect is immediately visible, making this method both quick and convenient to use.

> **Tip** To set the color of a shape's outline quickly, right-click over any color palette swatch.

Outline Tool Features on the Object Properties Docker

You can define a path's properties by accessing three levels of features: The Property bar is always available when you select a line, providing basic outline attributes. The Object Properties docker has taken over most of the duties from your third option, the Outline Pen dialog (formerly the Outline tool). The redesigned Object Properties docker can modify virtually everything about a drawn line except editing the path itself (covered in Chapters 7 and 9). These features, shown in Figure 13-1, are covered in the following sections.

To display the Outline section of the Object Properties docker, right-click over a selected outline on a page or press ALT + ENTER. Make sure the docker is fully extended so you can see all the outline properties.

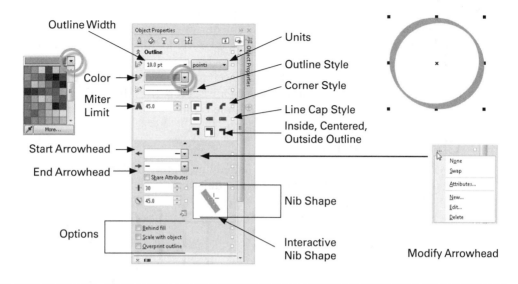

FIGURE 13-1   You have complete control over how an outline looks when you use the Object Properties docker.

Exploring the Outline Pen Features

The Object Properties docker is virtually your one-stop shop for modifying all attributes of a selected path, whether open or closed. Although some of the options for path outlines on the Object Properties docker are self-explanatory, even with Tooltips turned on, other features in CorelDRAW might not strike you immediately as useful. Therefore, a survey is in order, as follows.

Tip   The Color Eyedropper tool can be used to sample and apply outline properties between objects.

Draw a *closed* path (you'll see why in a while) with the tool of your preference. As soon as it's drawn, you can right-click over it with your current drawing tool, and then choose Object Properties on the contextual pop-up menu. This pop-up toggles the visibility of the Object Properties docker, so don't accidentally move to a different page and right-click because it will toggle to *removing* visibility. This can be a source of confusion, so either bookmark this passage, or remember it.

Setting Outline Color

The Pen Color mini flyout on the Object Properties docker affects only the color of the object's path; object *fills* are not changed. Outline color can be set only to CorelDRAW's Uniform colors from the drop-down palette. To access *every* color collection and color model for outlines, click the More button at the bottom of the Pen Color selector in the dialog. The Select Color dialog provides access to all CorelDRAW's color palettes, including custom swatches and the Color Mixer, Model, and Palettes tabs. The Select Color dialog is nearly identical to the one you used for fills, covered in Chapter 12.

If you want color control and don't need to fuss with dashed outlines, arrowheads, or other outline attributes, don't choose Object Properties. Instead, right-click a color swatch on the color palette to set an outline color.

Choosing Outline Styles

For a quick way to apply a dashed- or dotted-line pattern to the path of a selected object, use the Line Style selector, which offers 28 different preset variations.

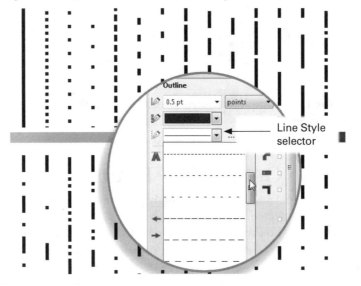

Applying an outline style causes a pattern to appear along the entire path, which is a must for anything you need to suggest visually to readers, for instance, that they should go running for the scissors: coupons, tickets, you name it. *Styles* are repeating patterns of short, long, and combinations of dashes that apply to the entire path. Line styles can be applied to any open or closed path object, as well as to *compound paths*— such as a donut object or an *O*. The quickest way to apply a dashed line style is to use the Pick tool and the Property bar's Outline Style selector when one or more paths are selected, as shown next.

Note Circles, rectangles, and polygons do not show the Outline Style selector on the Property bar. Happily, you can press ALT+ENTER, and edit the properties of these objects using the Object Properties docker.

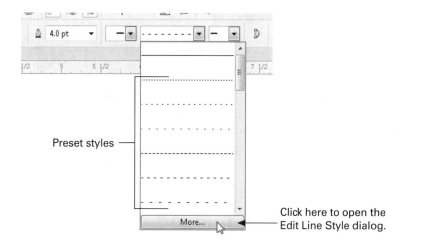

Preset styles

Click here to open the
Edit Line Style dialog.

More...

Tip Once you have a nice custom outline set of properties defined and want to apply all the parameters to a different path, you can copy outline properties from one path to another by right-clicking and dragging one path on top of the target path (this doesn't move your original path; it's a special editing technique). Release the mouse button when a crosshairs cursor appears over the target path. Then choose Copy Outline Here from the pop-up menu.

Creating and Editing Outline Styles

If you're looking for a special dashed-line style, one of your own invention, you can always *build* it. Click the Settings icon directly to the right of the Line Style selector in the Object Properties docker while a curve is selected to open the Edit Line Style dialog, shown here:

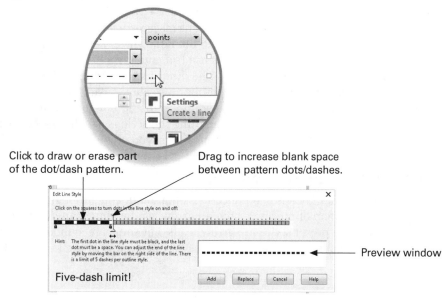

Click to draw or erase part
of the dot/dash pattern.

Drag to increase blank space
between pattern dots/dashes.

Preview window

Five-dash limit!

Creating a custom line style of dots and dashes is a fairly intuitive process, very similar to drawing a line in a paint program; your cursor serves as both a pencil and an eraser—click a black dot to erase it, click a white (space) dot to add to or begin a line. If you practice a little care and patience, you can also click-drag to multiple-draw and erase. Once you save a style by clicking Add, it becomes available throughout CorelDRAW wherever outline styles are offered. Your only limitation—*read the legend at the bottom left of the editor*—is that you can't create a sequence consisting of more than five dashes or dots; adjoining marks count as a single dash.

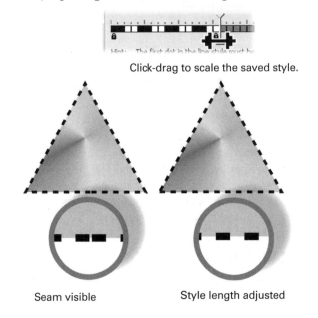

Click-drag to scale the saved style.

Seam visible   Style length adjusted

If the pattern applied to a path doesn't exactly match its length—for example, the pattern is longer than the path it's applied to—you might see a "seam," especially when applying outline styles to closed paths (as shown above). There are two ways to cure the problem. One is to go back to the Edit Line Style editor and increase or decrease the length of the pattern; this is a trial-and-error edit, but it doesn't change the path to which the style is applied. The other method (a desperate measure) is to lengthen the path by using the Shape tool or to scale the path by using the Pick tool. With either of these edits, you change your design and not your custom preset—it's your work so the call is up to you, but editing the style is usually the best way to avoid seams on a case-by-case basis with compositions you create.

Setting Outline Arrowheads

Arrowheads are both heads *and* tails on an open path, and although CorelDRAW has a handsome collection of preset arrows, an arrow can be almost anything you decide to draw. Most of the preset styles are arrowheads, but some are symbols that represent a tail. Here, you can see several of the styles and that many of the tails match the visual style of the arrowheads. When applied, arrowheads can be set to appear at the start and end points of open paths, both ends, one end, or, by default, neither end.

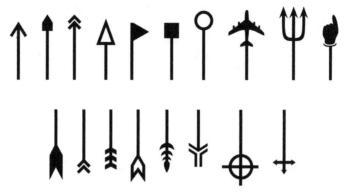

Here's a trick to defining the size of an arrowhead or tail: you increase or decrease the size of an arrowhead by adjusting the outline width using the Property bar or the Outline dialog. The quickest way to apply an arrowhead is by using the Start and/or End Arrowhead selectors on the Property bar when an open path is selected. Incidentally, applying an arrowhead to a closed path has no visible effect unless the path is broken at some point.

Creating Custom Arrowhead Styles

Realistically, CorelDRAW will not always have the ideal arrowhead (and tail) preset for your (and every other user's) assignment—or the preset selector would need a head and a tail itself, from here to the moon! That's why you have the Tools | Create | Arrowhead command—don't choose the command yet; you need to *draw* the arrowhead first, as covered in the following tutorial. The best arrowhead should be simple in its construction and needs to be a single or compound path—fill makes no difference in creating the arrowhead because a finished and applied custom arrow style gets its color from the outline color you use on the selected path in your drawing. The orientation of the arrowhead needs to be in landscape, too, before selecting the Create command. In other words, the top of your custom arrowhead design needs to face right, not the top of the page.

To create a new arrowhead and save it, follow these steps; if you'd like a jump-start, open *Shovel.cdr* first. It contains the elements needed to make both a head and tail.

Tutorial Drawing, Saving, and Editing an Arrowhead Style

1. Give some thought and planning to what would make a good arrowhead and tail. *Shovel.cdr* has a drawing of the ends of a common garden shovel. This design works for garden planning (an arrow pointing to "dig here"), treasure hunts, and certain civil engineering diagrams. Allow about 3" for your arrowhead symbols; this size gets you around the need to edit later. When you've drawn your

arrowhead (a tail is optional for this tutorial), rotate it so it's pointing toward the right of the drawing page.

2. With the shovel head object selected, choose Tools | Create | Arrowhead.

3. Type a name in the upper-left field for future reference. If you like, the Create Arrowhead dialog gives you the chance to set a size for the arrowhead; by default, it's the size of your drawing on the page, as shown in the illustration here. Click OK and your arrowhead is saved at the bottom of the Arrowhead selector list.

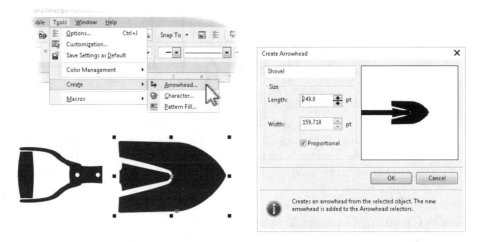

4. If you like, you can perform these steps for an arrowhead *tail* by selecting the shovel handle on the page. Possibly you're done now. Let's check, before calling it a day, to see how the arrowhead shovel looks when applied to an open path.

5. Using the 2-Point Line tool, click-drag a two-node path. Straight is good for checking out the arrowhead, but in the future a curved path might be more visually interesting.

6. With the path selected, on the Property bar, choose the **10 pt.** outline width so you'll have a clear view of the arrowhead you defined (or the shovel head if you used the *Shovel.cdr* file).

7. On the Property bar, choose the arrowhead from the Start Arrowhead drop-down selector. Let's suppose you're not 100 percent happy with the look of the arrowhead; you now access additional options for modifying the saved arrowhead. With the path selected, double-click the Outline Color icon (either the pen icon or the color swatch) on the Status bar to display the Outline Pen dialog. Click the Options button beneath the thumbnail of your arrowhead and then choose Attributes from the pop-up menu.

8. Here's where you can correct a number of problems with your arrowhead; you cannot, however, edit the path of the arrowhead itself. If, for example, your arrowhead is pointing the wrong way, select Mirror | Horizontally. You also have the option to rotate the arrowhead, for corrective or creative

FIGURE 13-2 Edit an arrowhead (or tail) in the Outline Pen dialog.

reasons, as well as to move the head away from its parent line (the Offset options) and to smoosh or stretch the selected arrowhead proportionately or disproportionately. If you made a mistake drawing the arrowhead, you cannot change it in the editor; instead you need to revise your drawing and then redefine the arrowhead. See Figure 13-2 for the visuals for these steps.

9. Click OK to overwrite your saved arrowhead, or rename it to add it to your collection. The Arrowhead Attributes dialog can also be used to modify *existing* preset arrowheads, but only to the extent that you've just modified your custom arrowhead in step 7. End of tour!

Here you can see a few uses for a shovel. Don't be hesitant to mix and match outline styles; in the middle illustration, a dashed outline style happily coexists with a custom arrowhead.

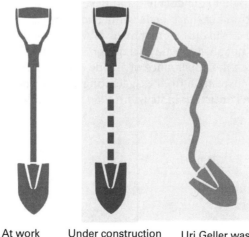

At work   Under construction   Uri Geller was here...

Other Arrowhead Options

Other convenient options are available in the Outline Pen dialog when applying an arrowhead style. Just below each Arrowhead Style selector are two Options buttons. Click either the Start or End Options buttons to open a drop-down menu that features—in addition to Edit and Attributes—the following commands:

- **None**   Choose this command to clear the arrow style you selected from your path. You can also do this from the document window using the Property bar.
- **Swap**   This command switches the styles currently selected for the start and end arrowheads. You can also reverse the path; select the path with the Shape tool, and the Reverse Direction button appears on the Property bar.
- **New**   Choose this command to open the Edit Arrowhead dialog and create a variation on a default style to add to the existing collection. New does *not* offer custom arrowhead creation; you need to use Tools | Create, as you learned earlier, to make a truly new arrowhead.
- **Delete**   While an existing style is applied, choosing this command permanently removes the selected style from the collection.

Note   The Share Attributes checkbox on the Object Properties docker lets you specify that the head and tail should be the same size, offset distance, and orientation.

Setting Corner Shape

You'll frequently create a path whose segments join at a node in a cusp fashion; the connection is *not* smooth—for example, a crescent moon shape has a least two sharp cusp connections between path segments. When shapes have *discontinuous* connections—when a path abruptly changes direction as it passes through a node— you can set the appearance of the node connection through the Outline Pen dialog and the Object Properties docker. The next illustration shows the visual effect of selecting Round, Miter (the default), and Bevel joints on a path with cusp nodes. Notice that at extremely sharp node connection angles, the Bevel joint option produces an area of the outline that extends way beyond the path, an exaggerated effect you might not always want in a design. You can use Corner Style properties creatively to soften the appearance of a node connection (Round works well) and also to keep a severe cusp angle from exaggerating a connection. Mitered corners can often keep a path more consistent in its width than the default corner.

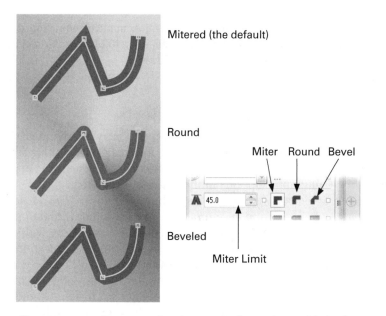

Mitered (the default)

Round

Beveled

Miter   Round   Bevel

Miter Limit

Also, you'll note a num box near the Corner Style settings; this is the Miter Limit angle, which you can set to suit your line needs. By default, if the angle of the line segments meeting at a path node is less than 45 degrees, the Miter connection is automatically replaced by the Bevel connection type. If your *intention* is to have connections that overshoot, you might want to increase this value. Many artists who work with thick lines, however, choose to decrease this Miter Limit setting.

Setting Line Cap Shape

Line caps, the beginning and end of an open path, can look like their counterparts, the corners, covered in the previous section. One of the greatest visual differences you can create is extending the true width of a path using the Round and Extended choices—the outline width overshoots the true path's length, proportional to the width you choose for an outline. Here are visual examples of your Line Caps options.

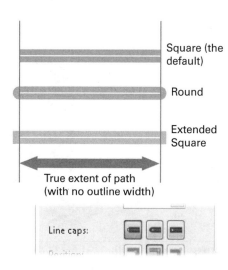

Square (the default)

Round

Extended Square

True extent of path (with no outline width)

Line caps:

Applying Line Caps options to the end points of an open path affects not only the first and last nodes' appearance on an open path, but also dashed and dotted line styles. If you want a string of pill capsules, one way to do this quickly is to make a dotted line with short dashes, widen the line, and then apply the Round line cap.

> **Tip** Line caps are not "mix and match"; for example, if you choose Round, both end caps in a two-node path are rounded—CorelDRAW has no facility for a two-node path that begins Round and ends Square.

Outline Pen Calligraphic Effects

The term *calligraphy* has come to be accepted today as a handwriting craft, the result of which is text and ornaments that have a varying width along strokes due to the popular use of a flat-edged pen nib held at an angle. The same effect can be achieved using the Calligraphic options in the Outline Pen dialog.

Calligraphic options—let's refer to the Object Properties docker here—are applied using a set of options and an interactive preview window to define the shape of the nib that affects a path you've drawn. *Stretch* controls the width of the nib using values between 1 and 100 percent. *Tilt* controls the nib rotation in 360 degrees (the minimum, –180 degrees, produces the same "12 o'clock" stroke angle as the maximum, 360 degrees). Click the Default button to reset these parameters to their original state. Stretch and Tilt values work together to achieve the nib shape. Set them numerically by entering values or better still, interactively, by placing your cursor in the Preview window and then click-dragging to shape the nib. By default, all paths in CorelDRAW are created using a Stretch value of 100 percent and a Tilt value of 0 degrees. As you can see in Figure 13-3, varying the stretch and degree of a calligraphic nib changes the look of an outline, but the *shape* you begin with also has an impact

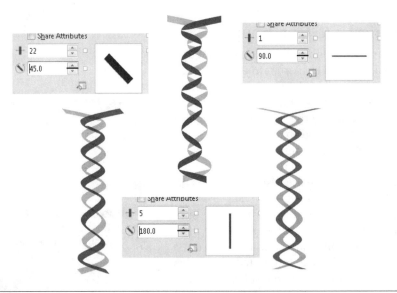

FIGURE 13-3 Calligraphic effects can be used as ornamentations to a piece of work or to imitate handwritten phrases.

on the final look of the design. For example, these three pairs of interwoven B-spine paths are identical, but the one at left is perhaps more visually interesting and elegant with its 45-degree angled nib. The point is that if you have an object you think will look more refined and elegant with a calligraphic stroke, keep changing the angle until you're happy with the finished artwork.

 Tip   The Artistic Media tool—covered later in this chapter—has a Calligraphic style that can be used as a brush; you just drag on the page and it immediately produces angled paths.

Scaling and Behind Fill Options

Two more options for controlling how outlines display in particular design situations are available in the Outline Pen dialog. The following sections explain how Scale With Object and Behind Fill work.

Scale With Object

Choose Scale With Object to increase or decrease the outline width applied to an open path or closed object when you scale the object at any time after the outline width has been applied.

For example, a 2-point outline width applied to a path becomes 1 point if the object is scaled in size by 50 percent. However, if you leave the scale constant (leave Scale With Object unchecked), you can duplicate, for example, 50 stars, arrange them on the page at different sizes, and the design looks good because the outline width is consistent from star to star. The illustration here shows copies of a pretzel shape reduced with and without the Scale With Object option selected.

| Original object | Reduced using the Scale With Object option | Reduced without using the Scale With Object option |

Behind Fill

Behind Fill sets outline properties to print and display in *back* of the object's fill. One of the many practical uses for Behind Fill is in a sign or other simple illustration where you need rounded corners along the outline, but sharp and crisp edges along the fill, the most important and recognizable part of many illustrations. Next, at left, you can see the ubiquitous recycle symbol with a 16-point rounded-corner outline.

The arrows are lost in the design. However, at right, a 32-point outline is used with Behind Fill checked in the Outline Pen dialog. Therefore, the same outline width has been achieved (visually); however, because the outline is behind the fill, the points on the arrows are undistorted, even in weight, and will print crisply.

16-point outline in front of fill: most edges are soft.

32-point outline behind fill: edges are crisp and detailed.

Turning an Outline into an Object

A fancy calligraphic property for an outline, arrowhead, and even for dashed outlines can be made unbelievably more artistically flexible as an *outline* property when you convert an outline to an object. Consider this: an outline is constrained to solid fills, whereas an object that *looks* like an outline, that was originally *based* on an outline, can have any type of CorelDRAW fill. To make an outline into a object, choose Object | Convert Outline To Object—but it will disturb your workflow less if you perform this on a *copy* of the path you slaved over! The shortcut is similar to Convert To Curves; it's CTRL + SHIFT + Q. The path you see in the illustration to follow is fully loaded, using a calligraphic nib, a dashed line, an arrowhead, and a tail. It is about to become a shape that's as editable with Toolbox tools as a rectangle or an ellipse, and will accept all of CorelDRAW's effects, such as contours, fountain, and texture fills; even the Extrude tool can turn this shape into elegant, abstract, or bizarre artwork.

In the next illustration, at left, you can see the path; in the middle, the path is now a shape that will take, in this example, a Linear Style fountain fill—to contrast, you can't fill an open path. At right in this illustration, you can see the arrowhead path is now a shape that can be extruded. To come full circle, the new object based on the path can have an outline; in this figure, a black outline behind the fill is used artistically to separate the linear fill areas visually.

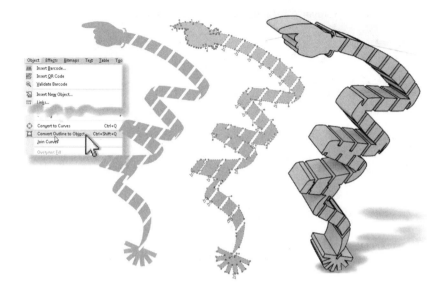

Using the Artistic Media Tool

The Artistic Media tool treats a path as though it's a skeleton to which you can apply any number of CorelDRAW preset "skins": there are five different types of Artistic Media "brushes," and a number of preset variations for the Preset, Brush, and Sprayer Artistic Media types. It helps to get your mind around a "paintbrush" metaphor; by dragging stokes, you can wind up with anything from complex filigree strokes to elegant calligraphic handwriting. The underlying path of an Artistic Media stroke can be altered at any time, changing the corresponding look of the media—and you can see the dynamic changes for accurate visual feedback as you work. You can draw while an Artistic Media effect is enabled, and you can also apply these painterly strokes to existing lines.

You don't have to give up the Pen tools in CorelDRAW to add another dimension to outlines you create. The Artistic Media tool—directly below the Pen Tools group on the Toolbox—can be used by itself as a drawing and painting tool, and the media that comes with CorelDRAW can also be applied to paths you've already created using other drawing tools. Use Window | Dockers | Effects | Artistic Media to go about making more expressive artwork the "manual" way, without the Artistic Media tool itself.

With the Artistic Media tool selected, the Property bar offers five different line-drawing modes, shown in Figure 13-4, each of which has its own options. There are additional options on the Property bar, directly to the right of your choice of Artistic Media, and the options change, depending on the media type selected.

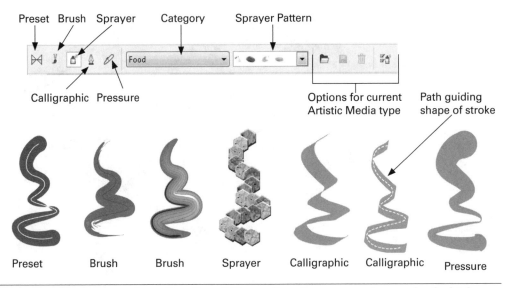

FIGURE 13-4 The Property bar offers five different line-drawing modes, each of which has its own options.

Applying Presets to Lines

Powerlines—elegant strokes found in previous versions of CorelDRAW—are now called *Presets*. When Presets is selected on the Property bar, the Artistic Media tool surrounds your drawn lines with specific preset vector shapes that are dynamically linked to the underlying path. The smoothness and width of the applied effect is set according to the Freehand Smoothing and Width options on the Property bar, as shown here.

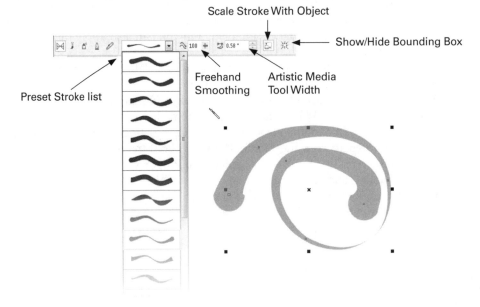

Set the shape using one of the styles in the Preset Stroke list. Smoothing is based on percent values between 0 (no smoothing) and 100 (maximum smoothing). Width can be set on a unit measure within a range of 0.03 to 10 inches. As you draw, a path is created in freehand style and immediately applied to your line.

Ready to take the Artistic Media tool out for a spin? The following tutorial walks you through the completion of an illustration—adding cartoon "reaction lines," the sort of emanations a character has when struck with a revelation—like *you* will be when you discover how the Artistic Media's Preset brush works and feels.

Tutorial   Painting with a Drawing Program

1. Open *Cartoon Guy.cdr* in CorelDRAW.
2. Choose Window | Dockers | Object Manager. From the list, click Add Lines Here to select it as the current editing layer if it's not already highlighted. The underlying layer containing the cartoon is locked so you can't accidentally move it.
3. Choose the Artistic Media tool and then click Preset, the far-left button on the Property bar.
4. Click the Preset Stroke selector and choose a style from the drop-down list. For this example, choose a style that has a rounded head and tapers at the end to a point.
5. Think of how you'd draw a cartoon sun; drag strokes so the "sun" is the cartoon fellow's head. The target width for the strokes is about .35". If your current stroke width is something different, you now have an opportunity to become familiar with Artistic Media features; while the stroke is highlighted, increase or decrease the width on the Property bar.
6. The head of the Preset Stroke starts where you begin your click-drag. If you drew a stroke backward, you can easily fix this. Press F10 to choose the Shape tool, click to select the stroke (you'll see the red underlying path when the stroke is properly selected), and then right-click and choose Reverse Subpaths from the context menu.
7. Click the Artistic Media tool in the Toolbox and you're ready to continue stroking. The Artistic Media tool is persistent—it "remembers" your last-used stroke settings, styles, and all that good stuff.
8. The Preset Strokes you create are a special instance of an object surrounding a path. You can, therefore, recolor the default black fill. With a stroke selected, try clicking a color swatch on the color palette. The cartoon fellow's excitement is now in color on your monitor and in the eBook version of this *Guide*, shown in Figure 13-5.
9. Let's say you want to get adventurous and change the preset for one of the strokes. While the stroke is selected, choose a different Preset Stroke style from the drop-down list ... and every subsequent stroke you make will have that new style. When choosing it, be sure to click *the outer part* of the stroke and avoid *the underlying central path* itself. If you've deselected a stroke and want to change it, choose it with the Pick tool and then use the drop-down list. Alternatively, you can click (don't click-drag, though) on a stroke on the page to select it and then change the Preset Stroke style. Now go answer that doorbell.

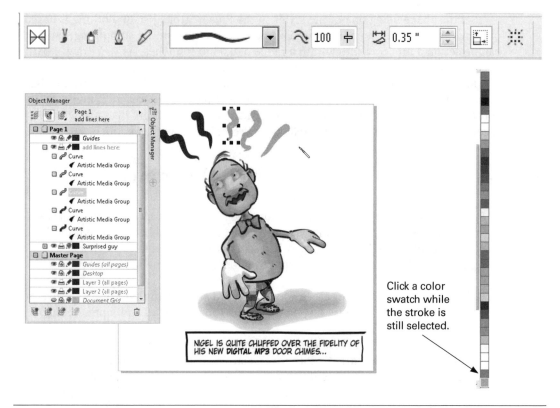

Click a color swatch while the stroke is still selected.

FIGURE 13-5 When a Preset Stroke style is selected, you can change its width, smoothness, and color.

Drawing with Brushes

In Brush mode, you can simulate the look of traditional natural media, which looks very similar to the brushes in Corel Painter, with a notable exception. Beneath an Artistic Media stroke lies a skeleton path, and the strokes you make can be edited ad infinitum. In contrast, bitmap paint programs such as Corel Painter and Adobe Photoshop feature brushstrokes that can't be edited after making them. Like the Presets category, Artistic Media brushes extend the full length of every path you create.

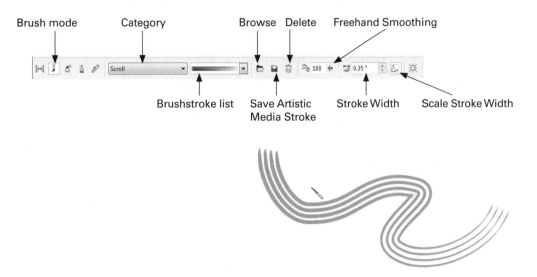

The Brushstroke list offers a variety of different styles; some are shown in the illustration. Freehand Smoothing and Stroke Width options are used to change the appearance of the graphical object—the "skin"—applied to the underlying path.

You can draw using a brush style or, alternatively, apply one to an existing line. To draw using a brushstroke, choose the Artistic Media tool and use the Property bar options to choose a brush style. Begin drawing by click-dragging on your page in a stroking motion. To apply a new brushstroke to an *existing* line, select the line using the Artistic Media tool, choose the Brush mode, and use Property bar options to choose a width and brushstroke style. The important thing with this technique is to *create a change in settings* on the Property bar because there is no Apply button or anything to confirm the changes. However, you can make a slight change to the Stroke Width on the Property bar to apply the effect. You can load saved brushes by clicking the Browse button on the Property bar, and save your own objects as brushstrokes and add them to the existing Brushstroke list.

Tip Custom Artistic Media brushstrokes are saved to Corel's CMX file format, which is a limited subset of its native CDR file format. You don't have unlimited options when creating your own brush, but you *can* use a simplified contour or blend to create a graduated color effect that can stretch when used as a stroke.

Applying the Sprayer

The Artistic Media tool's Sprayer mode is used to pepper the drawing page with a sequence of drawings—your *own* that you save as a brush or by choosing a preset from CorelDRAW's Sprayer collections. Changes to the underlying path and the objects used in a spray can be dynamically changed at any time. The sprayer objects repeat uniformly or randomly across the full length of a path. The Size/Scale, Spray

Order, Dabs, Spacing, Rotation, and Offset values can be set using the Property bar, shown in Figure 13-6.

The Sprayer Property bar options give you control over the following:

- **Object Spray Size/Scaling** Two options control the initial object size of the Sprayer style (that is, the objects that make up a specific Sprayer type) based on a scaled percentage of the original Sprayer object selected. When the Object Spray Size/Scaling option is unlocked, you can set the scaling size of successive objects to be increased or decreased in scale relative to the size of the first object in the Sprayer style. Some Preset Sprays offer scaling, whereas some do not, owing to their construction. The Snowflakes preset, for example, offers successive scaling; it's in the Misc. category. The bottom field is dimmed when you've chosen a preset that cannot be successively scaled.

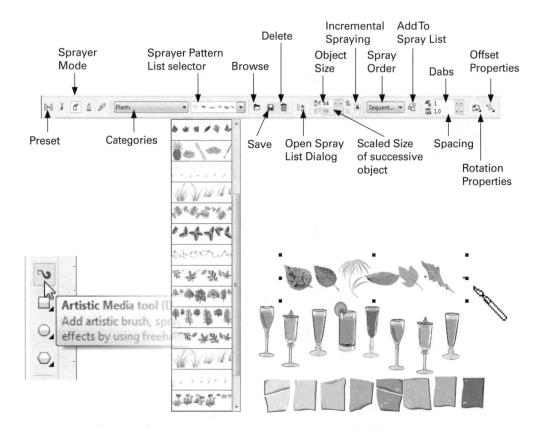

FIGURE 13-6 The Artistic Media Tool's Sprayer mode offers a huge number of design variations.

- **Spray Order** This option lets you set the ordering of the sprayer objects: Randomly, Sequentially, or By Direction. If the Sprayer style features only one object to vary, changing this option has no effect. Try the Mushrooms preset in the Plants category; the Spray presets contain several different objects of different sizes, and you can get various looks by choosing Randomly and By Direction.
- **Dabs and Spacing** These two values set the *number of objects* to be placed along a drawn or existing path and *the distance between* the centers of each object. *Dabs* are the individual objects in the Sprayer style; *Spacing* controls how many objects appear within a given distance. Think of spacing as "population."
- **Rotation** This option sets the angle for the first object in the Sprayer style. The *Increment* option compounds rotation values for each subsequent object. Rotation angles and increment values can be based on the degree measure relative to the page or the path to which the objects are applied. If you need a circular pattern whose objects are oriented toward the center of the circle, for example, the Rotation option is your ticket.
- **Offset** This option sets the distance between the path you click-drag and the Sprayer objects. *Offset* can be set to be Active (the default) at settings between roughly 0.01 and 13 inches. The direction of the offset can also be set to Alternating (the default), Left, Random, or Right. To deactivate the Offset options, uncheck the Use Offset Option in the selector, which sets the Offset measure to 0.

As with other Artistic Media Tool modes, you can draw while applying this effect or apply an Artistic Media stroke to an existing line.

With a Sprayer style applied and the line selected, you can use Property bar options to edit the effect. Doing this edits the style *only as it is applied to your line* and *not* the original style in the Sprayer Pattern List selector.

Tip To create your own Sprayer brush, first open the Artistic Media docker (Window | Dockers | Effects | Artistic Media). Create several shapes—they can be groups of objects, and they can contain any fill you like—and then arrange them horizontally on the page. Select them, and then click the Save button (the little diskette) at the bottom of the docker. You're then asked whether you want to save the selected objects as Brushes (no) or as Object Sprayer (yes). Saving and choosing sprayers is almost identical to the way you save and use brushes.

Calligraphy Pens and Applying Media

The Calligraphy tool mode produces results similar to adjusting the nib shape with any regular Pen tool; however, you can dynamically change the width and angle when you use the Calligraphy tool. Additionally, your artistic approach with this tool is different than drawing paths—you click-drag to produce an entire stroke instead of click-dragging to set a node and a path segment.

You have three options on the Property bar when Calligraphic is selected: Freehand Smoothing (the degree of accuracy when you click-drag), Stroke Width (which sets the *maximum* width because calligraphic strokes are alternately thick and thin), and Calligraphic Angle. Increasing values in this field rotate the stroke evaluated from the vertical in a counterclockwise direction. If you're a mouse user, you'll notice that strokes with the Calligraphy pen might not need any refinement work later. Your success depends mostly on how agile you are with a mouse and your click-drag technique.

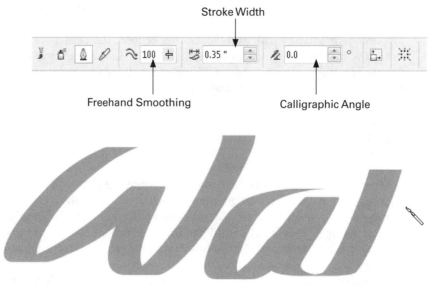

Your experience with using a mouse, however, doesn't have to be an obstacle to creating elegant curves, handsome signatures, and other calligraphic designs. Follow this tutorial to learn how to apply a Calligraphic property—and any Artistic Media except Pressure—to an *existing* path.

Tutorial Defining and Applying Calligraphic Brushstrokes

1. Open the *Calligraphy.cdr* file. You'll see a thin centerline on the top, unlocked layer. The bottom layer is just for reference. Mistal was used as the typeface and is a good example of calligraphic swoops, curves, and turns.
2. With the Pick tool, select the lowercase *a* after the initial *C*.
3. Choose the Artistic Media tool and then click the Calligraphic tool on the Property bar. Do not deselect anything.
4. Here's the trick: click either the up or down elevator button to the right of the Stroke Width field (or type **.2** or **.1** in the field instead of using the elevator buttons). What you've done is get the calligraphic pen to "recognize" that you want to change a value of the selected path's calligraphic width. The change isn't important; it's the *recognition* that applies the calligraphic property to the selected stroke.

Create the value change by clicking the elevator button.

5. Continue to adjust the Stroke Width (**.2"** works well at the path's scale here), and then play with the Calligraphic Angle option—anywhere from 35 to 55 degrees looks good in this example.
6. Because you began with an existing stroke, the calligraphic treatment has an outline and no fill. Click the black color swatch on the color palette, and then right-click the No Fill color swatch to remove the outline.
7. Perform steps 2–6 with the initial *C*, and then with the brush, dot the *i*.

Pressure Mode

The last of the Artistic Media modes was created for digital tablet users; if you own a stylus and tablet, you can set up the drivers for the stylus to apply pressure, and CorelDRAW will read stylus pressure to vary the width of the stroke as you drag across the page. You have Freehand Smoothing, and maximum Width controls on the Property bar.

If you're using a mouse, you can use the up and down keyboard arrows as you drag to (respectively) increase and decrease the width of the stroke. Honestly, don't expect world-class art using the mouse and arrow keys; you might run into a design situation where you need to vary the width of a stroke, but there are other ways to edit an existing stroke that produce more refined results.

This chapter has taken you through the simple assignment of one property to a path to applying several, more complex properties to a path. As you gather more understanding of options in CorelDRAW, you add to your personal, creative wealth of design options. Dashed lines, arrowheads, and calligraphic strokes will come to your rescue during 11th-hour assignment crunches, just as other features will that have been covered in previous chapters.

Blends and contours are the topic of the next chapter; each has their own use. And you can actually take what you know now about filled objects from Chapter 12 and strokes from *this* chapter, and do some ultra-exotic blending and contouring. Will it look weird? Yep, and *interesting*. Just think of it as building on your knowledge!

14 Using Blends and Contours

Although they're different effects, blends and contours share the common trait of creating many shapes based on control shapes. The additional shapes are dynamically linked to the control object, and the "in-between" objects can vary in size, color, and outline shape depending on how you set up the effect. Blends and contours are terrific for shading flat color fills in a way that fountain fills sometimes cannot. Additionally, blend objects can be used to illustrate the transition between two objects of completely dissimilar shape. This chapter takes you through the use of blends and contours so you can create outstanding, intriguing work in addition to what you already know.

Blend and Contour Effects: Similarities with Distinctions

The *blend* effects create a series of objects *between* objects in a number of steps you define—an object can be a closed path, a group of objects, and even a line (an open path). The properties of each step can be determined by the objects used in the blend; more on this later in this chapter. The *contour* effects also create additional objects in steps; however, only one object is used to produce a contour. When you imagine a contour effect, think of a shape surrounded by the same shape radiating outward (or inward) in a concentric pattern, like the circular waves produced when you drop a pebble in a still pond. The following sections explain the properties of the effects you can manipulate, and then you can decide which effect to reach for when you need a complex graphic or a smooth, shaded fill in an illustration.

Blending as Illustration Shading

If you've ever tried to add depth to a drawing and the Mesh Fill tool isn't working and a fountain fill doesn't do the trick, the solution is to blend a large shape through transition objects to a smaller object inside the large one. By making, for example, the outer shape darker than the inner one, you can position a soft-edged highlight on a shiny object. Similarly, a contour can be used to create a highlight; however, the contour object should be symmetrical to achieve the highlight effect, such as an ellipse. Blend effects are used in illustration work for creating photorealistic illustrations, but regardless of whether the visual content of a drawing is real-life accurate or a whimsical cartoon, with blends you can add depth and suggest lighting and the type of material on an object. The left side of Figure 14-1 shows a drawing of a bottle, but something is missing from the illustration. At right, you can see the finished illustration in Enhanced view in CorelDRAW's drawing window after some blends and contours were added; a Wireframe view showing the blend and contour steps is shown at center. You'll see how to do this stuff later in this chapter.

Smooth shading and highlights accomplished by the artistic use of blends create a visual impression of strength, size, and other qualities that help the audience see very quickly, "Oh, that's a *porcelain bottle*! It looks really bright! And it probably contains perfume that's too expensive…" Seriously, the more complexity you build into an object's fill, the more readily the audience will pick up on the complete visual idea and fill in *more* details. And before you know it, you've *sustained your audience's attention.*

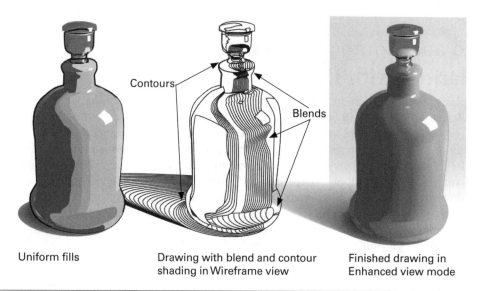

Uniform fills   Drawing with blend and contour   Finished drawing in
                 shading in Wireframe view   Enhanced view mode

FIGURE 14-1   A drawing, especially a perspective drawing of an object, can appear flat until you add shading with blends and contours.

Blends can also be used to create many similar objects very quickly; the trick is to blend between similar objects that are quite a distance apart on the page. The illustration here shows an example of two groups of objects blended to create a bar graph; the reference lines were blended from two identical lines. This graph has an even, upward progression. However, when you need to create similar blend objects that *don't* follow an even progression, you use the Break Apart (CTRL + K) command to break the relationship between the blend control objects and then ungroup the blend group, and finally, you edit the individual blend shapes to create a more random transition from object to object.

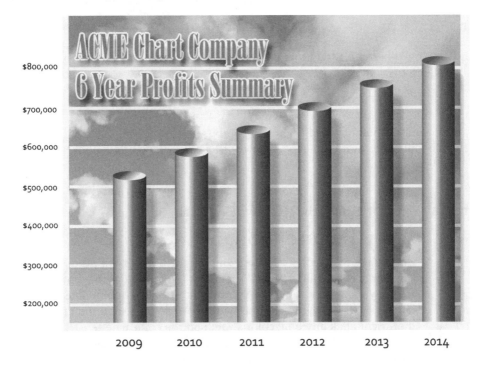

The Interactive Blend Tool and Property Bar

The Blend tool is in the Toolbox, at the top of the Interactive Tools group. When you choose the Blend tool, the Property bar offers options (shown in Figure 14-2) for customizing the effect. By default, 20 intermediate steps are created between two blend control objects.

Creating a Simple Blend Effect

You might want to work with similar objects to create blends that look like repeats—rubberstamped copies of the original objects—but there's another creative use for the Blend tool. You can morph totally dissimilar objects, and the resulting blend will

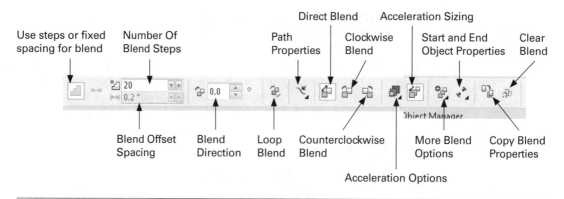

Use steps or fixed spacing for blend · Number Of Blend Steps · Path Properties · Direct Blend · Clockwise Blend · Acceleration Sizing · Start and End Object Properties · Clear Blend

Blend Offset Spacing · Blend Direction · Loop Blend · Counterclockwise Blend · Acceleration Options · More Blend Options · Copy Blend Properties

FIGURE 14-2   When the Blend tool is selected, the Property bar has options to customize your blend effects.

probably contain a lot of interesting and useful transitional shapes. Work through the following tutorial to experiment with a basic blend effect between a star and an ellipse object.

Tutorial A Basic Blend Between Very Different Shapes

1. Choose the Star tool; it's in the group on the Toolbox with the Polygon tool. Click-drag a star that's about 1" in size at the top left of the drawing page. Fill it with yellow from the Color palette, and give it a 4-point blue outline. First, choose **4 pts**. from the Outline Width drop-down box on the Property bar, and then right-click any blue color swatch on the color palette.
2. Choose the Ellipse tool (F7) and then click-drag an ellipse at the top right of the page. Fill it with blue and give it a yellow outline, but keep the outline width at the default of **.5 pts**.
3. Choose the Blend tool from the Toolbox. Your cursor changes and the Property bar's options are all dimmed because a blend doesn't exist yet on the page.
4. Click inside the star and then drag until your cursor is inside the ellipse. Once you release the mouse button, a series of new objects appears, and the Property bar comes to life with almost all options available.
5. Twenty steps is too many for this example: type **2** in the Number Of Blend Steps field on the Property bar, and then press ENTER. As you can see in the following illustration, the blend shapes make an interesting progression; the outline color transitions from blue to yellow; the fill color transitions from yellow to blue; and the intermediate shapes are interesting stars distorted as

they become the ellipse. These intermediate star-like objects are actually a little difficult to make using the standard drawing tools!

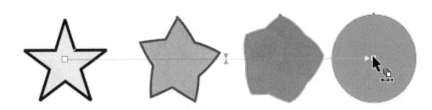

Tip To remove a blend effect, click the blend portion of the effect to select it, and choose Effects | Clear Blend; or, while using the Blend tool, click to select the blend effect portion, and click the Clear Blend button on the Property bar.

Looking at the Components of a Blend

The blend effect you built in the previous tutorial creates a fun composition, but to build on your *knowledge*—so you can create more complex blends—let's now examine what really went on and what properties the objects on your page now have. A two-object blend includes several key components: the original objects become *control objects*; any changes made to either the star or the ellipse will change the blend itself. The effect portion—called the *blend group*—and the *control objects* maintain a relationship as long as the blend exists.

Each of the interactive markers around a blend effect corresponds to an option on the Property bar. Figure 14-3 shows the various parts of a two-object blend.

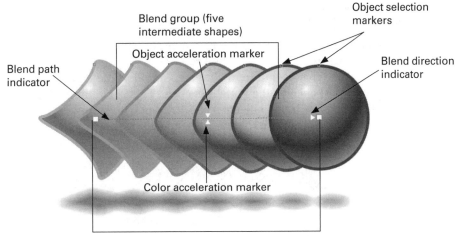

FIGURE 14-3   This blend between two shapes shows the interactive markers controlling the effect.

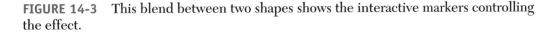

Editing a blend is a little more challenging than making dinner reservations, but significantly less challenging than brain surgery. With the Pick tool, click the blend group to begin editing it using the Property bar options. Single-clicking selects both the blend and its control objects. To select either control object, click only the control object itself. The Status bar tells you that a "Control *Whatever*" (object, curve, rectangle) is selected, confirming the correct object has been selected for editing. Double-click the blend group with the Pick tool to switch to the Blend tool for making adjustments directly to the group. Your cursor becomes a crosshair as you perform an operation. Similarly, when you want to adjust the acceleration, hover your cursor over the central color and object markers until the cursor becomes a crosshair and then you drag.

When you attempt to do something not allowed with the Blend tool cursor (such as move an intermediate blend object), an international "no" symbol appears at the lower left of the cursor.

Editing Blend Effects

You can create a custom blend effect by directly manipulating markers and objects with your cursor, setting specific values for options using the Property bar, and occasionally by using a combination of the two interface elements. The following sections take you through the features you'll use most often; then it's on to useful but less frequently used options. Think of this as a journey from mildly amusing to wonderful and then on to totally bizarre effects as you progress through these sections.

Setting Blend Options

Options controlling a blend effect can impact each intermediate step of the blend itself. You can change the steps' value, rotation, color, and the acceleration of the blend objects, as well as save the effect you've custom-designed as a preset.

Controlling Blend Steps

The number of steps in the blend group can be set within a range of 1 to 999. To set a number of steps, enter a value in the Property bar Blend Steps num box and then press ENTER. Notice that as you set higher step numbers, depending on the closeness of the blend control objects, they might overlap. This is an interesting effect, but if you need intermediate blend objects that don't touch one another, you can resize both blend control objects, or move them farther apart from one another.

5-step blend effect

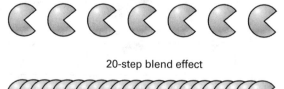

20-step blend effect

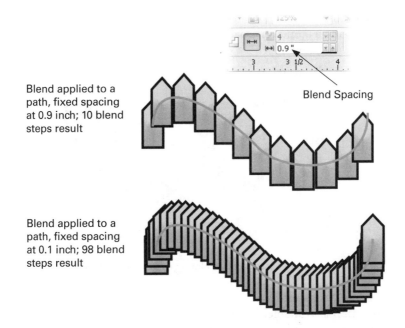

Blend applied to a path, fixed spacing at 0.9 inch; 10 blend steps result

Blend Spacing

Blend applied to a path, fixed spacing at 0.1 inch; 98 blend steps result

FIGURE 14-4   Fixed spacing between blend objects applied to a path can be controlled using the Blend Spacing option on the Property bar.

Specifying Blend Offset Spacing

To set spacing values between blend steps, use the Blend Offset Spacing option, which becomes available *only* if a blend has been applied to a path, as shown in Figure 14-4. This limitation is because the distance between the blend control objects must be fixed by the length of the path. Use the Blend Spacing option on the Property bar; enter the value to a specific unit measure. CorelDRAW automatically calculates the number of objects required to fit the path's length. Blend Spacing works within a range of 0.010 inch to 10.00 inches, in increments of 0.010 inch. To learn how to blend objects along a path, see "Assigning a Blend Path," later in this chapter.

Rotating a Blend

You can rotate the objects in a blend group by fixed degree values using the Blend Direction option, shown here. Enter an angle value (based on degrees of rotation). Positive values rotate the objects counterclockwise; negative values rotate them clockwise. With a rotation value specified, the last object in the blend group is rotated the full angle, with the intermediate steps rotated in even increments starting at 0 degree rotation—the rotation value of the Start blend control object. This feature is handy for suggesting action or even animation. However, rotating a blend cannot be accomplished using a blend on a path.

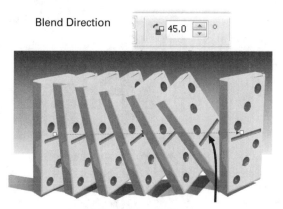

Last object in a blend group rotated 45 degrees

When Blend Direction is set to anything other than 0° on the Property bar, the Loop Blend option is available. Choosing the Loop Blend option has the effect of applying both rotation and path offset effects to the blend group. Looping a blend works in combination with the Blend Direction value, offsetting the objects from their original direction and rotating them simultaneously. If you then modify a blend control object, as done in the illustration here at bottom, you can achieve a different loop effect, sort of like one of those children's toys that never really got the hang of walking down stairs.

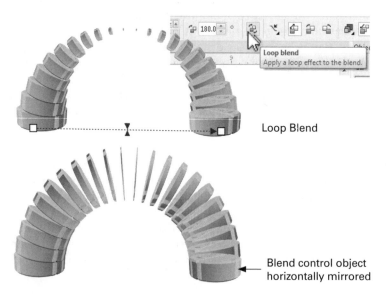

Loop Blend

Blend control object horizontally mirrored

Changing Color Rotation

By default, the object colors in your blend group are blended *directly* from one color to the next to create a smooth color transition. However, you can change this using either Clockwise Blend or Counterclockwise Blend on the Property bar. If you want a rainbow effect, for example, one control object should be red and the other filled with blue so Clockwise Blend and Counterclockwise Blend can cycle through the visible spectrum.

Acceleration Options

Acceleration increases or decreases the rate at which your blend group objects change shape; think of it as "preferring" one control object over the other. When a default blend effect is applied, both of these settings are at the midpoint of the blend; the blend group objects change in color and size evenly between the two control objects. You can change object and color acceleration rates simultaneously (the default) when the two options are linked, or you can make acceleration changes independently of one another by clicking the Unlink Acceleration option between the Object and Color Acceleration buttons on the Property bar. In this illustration, you can see linked acceleration to the right and then to the left control object.

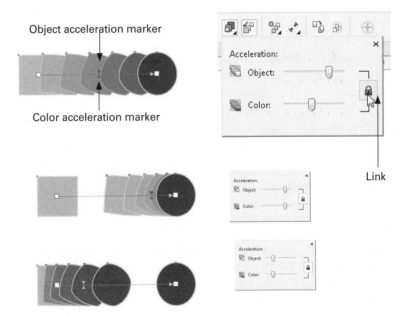

Object acceleration marker

Color acceleration marker

Link

Moving either slider in this pop-out box to the left of the center position reduces (slows) the acceleration from the Start object toward the End object of the blend effect. Moving either of the sliders to the right increases the acceleration. Interactive acceleration markers can also be used to adjust these values. While the two rates are unlinked, changing the Object Acceleration slider affects only the progression of shapes. With the Acceleration sliders unlinked, changing the Color Acceleration slider affects only the change in progression of the fill and outline colors between the two objects. Moving the sliders, or the interactive markers, left or right changes the acceleration of the color change.

Tip Changing the Color Acceleration slider also affects the width properties applied to outline paths of objects.

Using Blend Presets

It's taken up to now to learn how to change blend steps, rotation, color, and acceleration rates; naturally, you want to be able to save an elegantly customized blend so you can apply it to other objects in the future. Saving your hard work as a preset is accomplished through the Blend Preset list when a blend is selected; you can also tap into some nice *existing* presets on the list.

Blend presets are the same as other CorelDRAW preset controls and can be saved and applied to two or more different shapes.

Creating Extraordinary, Complex Blend Effects

More advanced blending can solve illustration challenges when a standard, direct blend can't. The following sections show you how to create *multipoint blends,* how to *map* blend control object *nodes,* and how to apply blends to paths. Yes, this is the "good part" of the chapter!

Creating Compound Blends

A simple, straightforward direct blend from one object to another can be split so that one or more of the child objects in the blend group become another control object. Once you have a "mezzanine" control object between the *original* control objects, you can reposition it on the page—which can make a blend look like Pablo Picasso's idea of a caterpillar—you can recolor the new control object, and you can also edit it with the Shape tool.

You now have *two* different stages of blends within the compound blend object; a transition from the Start point to the point you created, and then a transition between this point and the End point control object. You can achieve the same goal in two different ways when you want to add a transition control point within a simple blend:

- Double-click a blend group object. This method is imprecise, especially when more than 10 blend steps are spaced tightly together.
- Click the More Blend Options pop-up button on the Properties bar and choose Split Blend. Your cursor turns into a targeting cursor, and you can now pick the exact child object in the blend that you want promoted to an intermediate control object.

Here is a visual of both processes:

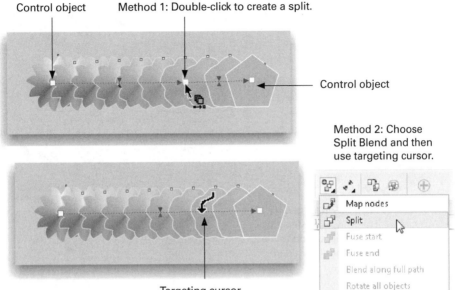

Control object

Method 1: Double-click to create a split.

Control object

Method 2: Choose
Split Blend and then
use targeting cursor.

Map nodes

Split

Fuse start

Fuse end

Blend along full path

Rotate all objects

Targeting cursor

After you've created a split in a blend, you can edit the intermediate control object—change its fill, change its path with the Shape tool, reposition it on the page, scale it, you name it. To perform edits on the new control object, deselect the compound path—choose the Pick tool and then click a blank area on the page—then select the new control object and perform your edits. In the following illustration at top, splitting and then editing the new control object affects all the child group objects on either side of the control object.

You can split a blend in as many places as you have child blend objects. Alternatively, while using the Blend tool, you can add a new shape to the blend by dragging from any new object you've created to any control object on the blend. You'll achieve some wonderfully bizarre effects should you choose to blend between a new object and the middle of a compound blend, but you can do it. In this illustration at bottom, you can see a rounded-corner rectangle being blended to the end of a complex blend.

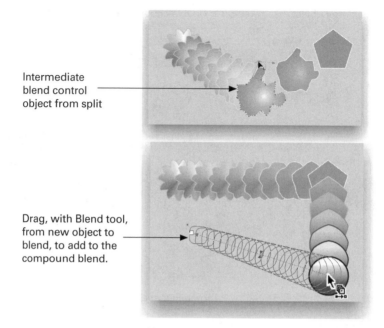

Intermediate blend control object from split

Drag, with Blend tool, from new object to blend, to add to the compound blend.

Fusing a Blend

Fusing, as the term applies to CorelDRAW blends, is the opposite of splitting, and it applies to a complex blend made by adding an object to a direct blend. When you apply a fusing action to a blend, you remove a control object. The resulting blend adjusts to reflect the new lack of a control object and its properties. To remove an intermediate control object that you created by double-clicking with the Shape tool, double-click this marker with the Blend tool and it disappears. To remove, for example, a control object that's part of a complex blend created by adding a control object, you can click the More Blend Options flyout button on the Properties bar and choose Fuse (Start or End), depending on which end of the Blend you added a control object to.

Mapping Control Object Nodes

When a blend is applied, the blend group is built of a series of intermediate objects between the control objects. When you use two completely different shapes as control objects, the chances are they won't have the same number of nodes connecting path segments; additionally, the position on the page of the first node you draw is usually arbitrary, depending on your drawing style. By default, CorelDRAW blends two different objects using *node mapping*: the blend effect assumes the blend should start with the first node on the Start object, and end at the first node on the End object, and that all objects in the blend itself make the transition based on the same node position on the page as the Start and End control objects.

Occasionally you might get a blend that looks like a parade of crumpled sheets of paper, or something similarly nasty—it's interesting, but not what you had in mind. Fortunately, you can match your control objects nodes in a few clicks. To map the nodes in a blend, click the More Blend Options button and click the Map Nodes button. The cursor becomes a targeting cursor—your signal to click the nodes you want matched. Node mapping is a two-step operation: click a node on the Start blend control object (the operation temporarily increases the size of the nodes so you can tell what the targeting cursor wants you to do), and then click the corresponding node on the End blend control object, as shown in this illustration.

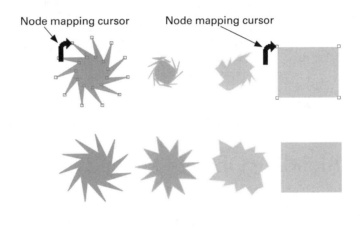

 Note Node mapping is unavailable if a blend effect has been split into a multipoint blend.

Assigning a Blend Path

Objects can be blended along a path: either a path you draw before the blend operation, or by ALT + dragging from one object to another with the Blend tool while nothing is selected on the page. Blend objects on a path can also be rotated, offset from the path, and set to fill the full path or only part of the path.

Here, you can see an example of the ALT + drag technique. If your path is a little shaky or otherwise imperfect, choose Show Path from the Path Properties pop-up on the Property bar. Once you can see the path, you can edit it, just as you would a drawn path, using the Shape tool.

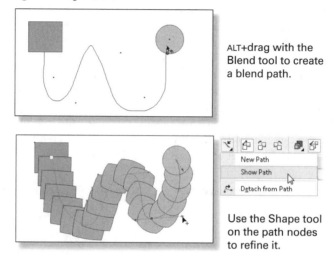

ALT+drag with the Blend tool to create a blend path.

Use the Shape tool on the path nodes to refine it.

The following tutorial takes you through the more studied and precise approach to binding a blend to a path, again using the Path Properties pop-up.

Tutorial Blending Objects Along a Path

1. With a blend effect already created and an open or closed path in view on the page, choose the Blend tool, and then click the blend group portion of your effect to select it, not the control objects on either end of the blend.
2. Click the Path Properties button and then choose New Path. Notice your cursor changes to a targeting cursor.
3. Click the open or closed path with this special cursor; the blend now follows the path you clicked. Notice also that the blend has changed position to align with the path exactly where it's positioned. The blend effect and the new path are featured top to bottom in this illustration.

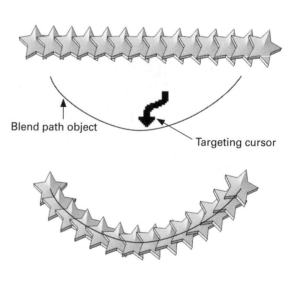

Blend path object

Targeting cursor

Choosing New Path when a blend effect is already applied to a path lets you assign a new and different object as the blend path. To remove a blend effect from a path, use the Detach From Path command. If the blend includes so many steps that the path is hidden—or if the path itself is not visible because it has no outline color applied—use the Show Path command to select and highlight it for editing. Show Path is also a good command for editing a path you created using the ALT + click-drag technique described earlier. Remember: as long as the path is visible (in any View mode), you can change its course by using the Shape tool to edit the path's nodes.

Tip If you don't want a path to be visible in the final effect, set its Fill and Outline colors to None. This way you can edit the path later.

Rotating Blend Objects

Objects set to follow a path do so using their original, unaltered orientation by default. For example, a blend involving vertical lines when blended to a path results in the centers of objects aligning with the path, but their orientation will remain vertical. If you need your blend group objects to *align* with the orientation of the path itself, choose the Rotate All Objects option in the More Blend Options pop-up menu on the Property bar, which is available when a blend on a path is selected.

Doing this applies rotation values to each of the objects in the blend group to align with the direction of the path.

Blend Along Full Path

If the path you've applied your blend effect to is the right size and length to cover your blend completely, you may automatically set the blend group and control objects to cover the entire path. To do this, choose the Blend Along Full Path option from the More Blend Options pop-up. Using this option, you can move the center origins of the control objects in the blend to the State and End nodes of the path. This illustration shows the effect when a blend is applied to an open path.

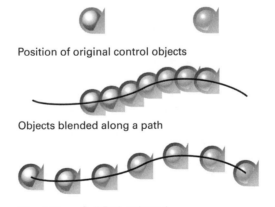

Position of original control objects

Objects blended along a path

Blend Along Full Path selected

Tip Once a blend group is bound to a path, you can manually space the blend objects by click-dragging the Start control object or the End control object with the Pick tool. This technique might not get you where you want to go 100 percent of the time, but this is a good way to visualize how you want spacing to occur in a blend.

Controlling Blend Object Path Alignment

When a blend follows a path, the point at which all objects align with the path is determined by their center origin. The *center origin* is where all objects are rotated during any default rotation. Controlling how a blend aligns to a path is one of those hidden features you won't find in any dialog or on the Property bar. Instead, the center origin is moved manually using the Pick tool, with object rotation and skew handles in view. By moving the center origin, you can control how the objects align to the path.

To perform this alignment operation, you click a blend control object to select it, click again to reveal the center origin and rotation handles, and then move the center origin point. The blend moves in the opposite direction. This trick is a quick way to reshape and move a blend along a path with a minimum number of steps.

Working with Multi-object Blends

Blending between *more* than two objects can produce an effect quite unlike splitting a blend, and it's just as easy to do. You click-drag between different objects on your document page. Each time you do this, a new blend group is created. The dynamic link is maintained between all objects in a multi-object blend, which means you can change control objects and the blends are instantly updated. Figure 14-5 shows two blend effects applied to three different objects with the multi-object blend defined in different directions. The one at left is linear, and the one at right converges from points to the circle object.

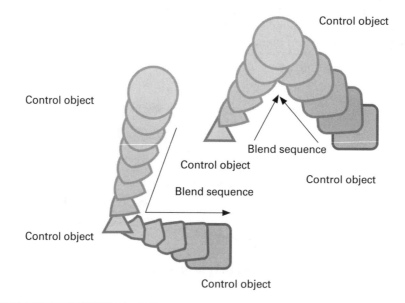

FIGURE 14-5   These three shapes are blended in different sequences.

Tip The order in which objects are created also affects the blend appearance. The object created last will appear on top of the blend group regardless of the click-drag direction. Because of this behavior, you can move an object forward or back one or more positions on its layer (CTRL+PAGE UP, or CTRL+ PAGE DOWN) to alter the blend's appearance.

Each blend of a multi-object blend is considered a separate effect; each has its own control objects with defined Start and End blend objects. You can change the Start and End blend objects using the Start and End Objects Properties pop-out menu commands on the Property bar. The Start and End blend objects are the key to making blends that change shape all over the place in intriguing patterns. And the key to selecting blend groups within blend groups is to hold CTRL and then click a subgroup within the compound object, and then you can access the options on the Property bar.

With a blend selected, you first need to locate the Start or End blend objects—choose either the Show Start or Show End command. Choosing New Start changes the cursor to a targeting cursor, so you can then unlink the blend effect from one object and target a different one. Doing this creates a new effect each time a different object is targeted. Choosing New End works similarly.

After a blend has been made, you might need to dismantle it and break the link between the control objects. You can do this easily, but keep in mind that it can't be reversed without using the Undo command (CTRL + Z). To dismantle a blend, choose the Pick tool, right-click the blend group portion, and choose Break Blend Group Apart from the pop-up menu (or press CTRL + K). The control objects then become separate objects, leaving the blend intermediate objects grouped. To further dismantle the arrangement, select only the blend group by using the Pick tool and then choose Arrange | Ungroup (CTRL + U).

Tip If you prefer working closely to your design on the page, you can use the Blend docker (Windows | Dockers | Effects | Blend). Detach it from the edge of the workspace, and float it near your work.

Tapping into Contour Effects

Contour effects instantly create perfect outlines of shapes or paths by the dozens or even hundreds. The result is similar to viewing a topographical or *contour* map, hence the name.

During a contour effect, dynamically linked shapes are concentrically created outside or inside an object's path. CorelDRAW effectively calculates the shape of each contour step and applies progressive outline and fill colors based on the original object's properties and selected contour options.

While a contour effect is linked to an object, the object itself becomes a control object, and the new shapes created become the *contour group*. Changes made to the properties of the original immediately affect the linked group. While the contour

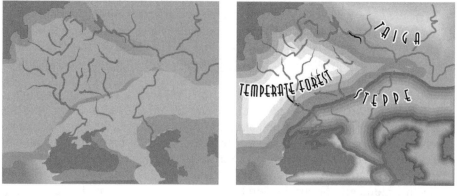

Original filled with solid colors   Finished artwork with contour effects

FIGURE 14-6   Contour effects create a smooth color transition.

group is selected, its properties can be edited at any time—without your having to begin the effect from scratch.

First, let's see what you can do with contour effects. One of the more popular effects is to simulate depth.

Figure 14-6 shows two illustrations of climate zones in the Urals region of Russia. At left, uniform fills (solid colors) occupy the objects; at right, the same objects have contour effects. In the contour version, the control objects still use uniform color, but the contour uses different colors for the outermost and innermost objects. As with blends, intermediate objects are generated from the Start object; however, you don't have to draw the End—the inner object—it's part of the contour effect function. Because many steps are used for a contour effect, you can see a smooth color transition in most of the objects. Also note that some of the objects have a low number of intermediate objects, producing banding, which can be useful in your design work. Just use a low number of steps when drawing a map of the Steppes.

The following illustration shows two versions of the contour effect applied to text. At top, a two-step contour runs inside the word "Opera," creating an engraved look. At bottom, 25 contour steps were used outside the word to create a glowing effect; a duplicate of "Opera" with Linear transparency was put on top of the design as an embellishment. You do not have to convert text to curves to apply a contour effect.

2-step contour effect inside text

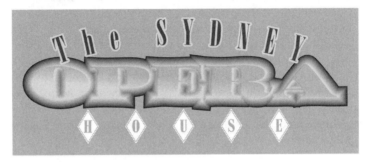

25-step contour effect outside text with transparent overlay

Using the Contour Tool and Property Bar

To apply contour effects, you'll need to use the Contour tool, shown here, in combination with the Property bar. You'll find the tool in the Toolbox, with other interactive tools: Blend, Drop Shadow, Envelope, Distort, Extrude, and Transparency.

While you're using the Contour tool, the Property bar displays options for customizing the effect. These options include contour presets, contour direction, steps and offset spacing, color rotation, outline and fill color, and buttons for copying and clearing the effect, as shown in Figure 14-7.

Let's dig right into using the Contour tool's features.

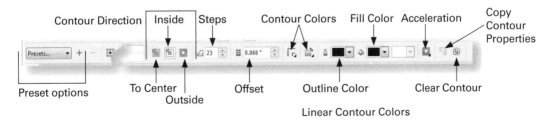

FIGURE 14-7   Use the Property bar to make the fullest use of the Contour tool.

Tutorial Applying a Contour Effect

1. Create an object (a polygon or star shape is a great seed shape for contours); apply a fill and (optionally) outline properties. If you want to go wild with this contour tutorial, try filling the object with a fountain fill—contours produce interesting results with fountain fills.
2. Choose the Contour tool. Notice that your cursor changes and the Property bar now displays Contour tool options.
3. Click the object and drag (click-drag) in the direction you want the contour to be applied. Dragging from the center outward creates outside contours; dragging in the opposite direction creates inside contours. The angle of the drag action has no effect on the contours themselves—only inward and outward count. Notice that as you drag, a silhouette of the final size of the contour effect appears in inverted screen colors.
4. Release the mouse button, and your effect is finished and ready for customizing.

These steps created a contour in its default state. Adjusting the effect to suit your needs takes a little more work with the Property bar options. The contours outside or inside the object can also be controlled using the interactive markers surrounding the effect. The next section explains the use of these markers, their purpose, and how to manipulate them.

Tip To remove a contour effect, click the contour portion of the effect using either the Contour tool or the Pick tool and choose Effects | Clear Contour, or click the Clear Contour button on the Property bar.

Editing Contours Interactively

The easiest way to edit a contour effect is by hand, using the Contour tool to change the interactive markers in combination with adjusting Property bar options. Use the options to adjust the direction, spacing, and offset values of the effect.

The black diamond-shaped marker indicates which object is the effect's control object. The white rectangle marker indicates the End object in the contour group, and its position sets the distance between the control object and the End object in the effect. A slider between these two enables you to adjust the spacing between the contour steps interactively, which, in turn, sets the number of steps by dividing the difference. Figure 14-8 identifies the interactive markers and their purpose.

You'll also notice the Contour tool cursor changes its appearance as you drag outside, inside, or to the centermost point of your selected object, as shown in Figure 14-9. While held over an object, the cursor will also indicate whether you can apply the contour effect to the object.

Tip To quickly edit a contour, double-click the effect portion of an existing contour with the Pick tool.

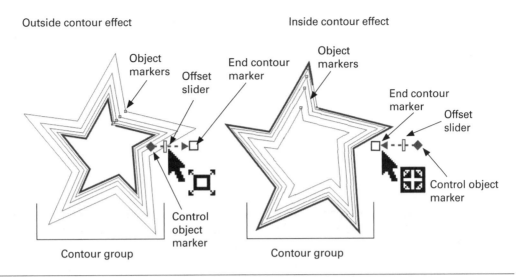

FIGURE 14-8   These two shapes have contours applied in opposite directions.

Choosing Contour Direction

In addition to click-dragging a contour to set its direction, you can also use Property bar options, as shown on the next page. Choosing To Center, Inside, or Outside causes the contours to be applied in the direction relative to the object's outline path. When Inside or Outside is selected, you can set the number of steps and the offset spacing

Object can't be contoured.

Tool cursor in default state

Tool cursor indicates that an outside contour is being created.

Tool cursor indicates that an inside contour is being created.

Tool cursor indicates that a center contour is being created.

FIGURE 14-9   The Contour tool cursor lets you know what's going on.

between the steps by entering values in the Steps and Offset boxes on the Property bar, and pressing ENTER.

To Center   Inside   Outside

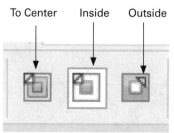

Tip To separate an applied contour and break the dynamic link to the original object, right-click directly on the effect (objects), and then choose Break Contour Group Apart from the pop-up menu.

The effect's contour direction, spacing, and offset values affect one another. In the sections to follow, remember that when you change one parameter's values, a different parameter will probably auto-change.

Inside Contour

With the exception of the 47 clowns who can get out of a Volkswagen, there is a real-world and mathematical limit to how many steps you can create within a shape. For contours, if the offset spacing value you enter in the Offset num box (on the Property bar) exceeds the number of steps the distance allows, the Steps value is automatically reduced to fit. Here, you can see some results of applying inside contours to different objects; as you can see, compound paths produce quite elegant contour steps. Remember: open paths are not eligible for inside contour effects; it can't be done mathematically, and it can't be done in CorelDRAW.

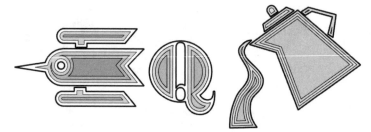

Outside Contour

Choosing Outside creates contours *around* your object, and yes, you can use an open path, as shown in the following illustration with outside contouring. It creates an interesting effect you can use for designing everything from neon signs to expensive paperclips. The Steps value can be set as high as 999, and the Offset values travel within a range from 0.001 to 300 inches.

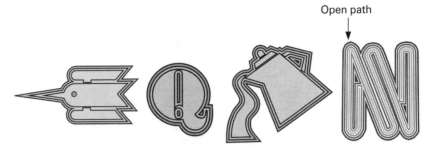

Open path

Contour To Center

The To Center direction creates the contour inside the selected object, but it does so using as many steps as mathematically possible. The number of steps depends on the Offset value (editing the number of steps is not available)—in any case, your object is filled with a contour. This option is terrific for illustrating game mazes—with a little editing after making a contour of a bicycle or a flower in a pot, you could fill a book with games like you see on children's menus in restaurants. Here, the Offset value is the only parameter that can be changed; the number of steps is calculated automatically. This illustration shows contours applied using the To Center option; as with the Inside option, open paths cannot take a To Center contour.

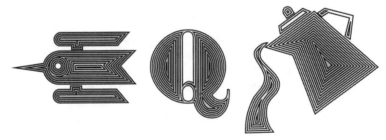

Setting Contour Colors

Controlling the progression of color between your original object and the colors of the contour effect is key to creating great illustrations; CorelDRAW is a wonderful drawing program, but *you* are the artist! You can set color in several different ways, by specifying a *nonlinear color rotation,* control pen and fill colors, and even fountain fill colors for individual contour steps.

Color Rotation Options

A default contour creates fill and outline colors in a steady progression between the base object and the final contour (the End object if contours were blends). However, you can rotate these colors to create rainbow contours and other special effects.

To do this, choose either Clockwise Contour Colors or Counterclockwise Contour Colors, as shown here, which has the effect of applying fill and outline colors based on color positions located around a color wheel—red, orange, yellow...you get the idea!

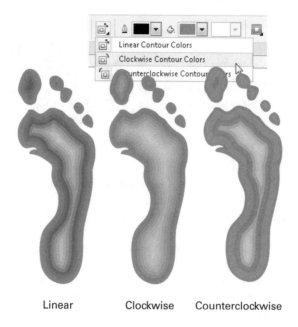

Linear   Clockwise   Counterclockwise

Outline Color

The Outline Color option, the pop-up mini palette directly to the right of the Color rotation options on the Property bar, sets the outline color of the last contour in the effect, meaning the colors change steadily from your original to the End contour object. If your object doesn't have an outline color applied, this option still displays black as the default color, but no color will be applied to your contours. To set the outline color, click the Outline Color selector and choose a color.

Fill Color

If you want to wow your audience, definitely play with the Fill Color option to create significant changes along the steps of a contour. It's the mini-palette directly to the right of Outline Color on the Property bar. If an object doesn't have a fill, although you can set a contour color, the contour will not have a fill. This creates an interesting effect if you have outline width and colors applied to the base object, but with no fill and no outline set for the base object to which you want to apply a contour, it's an exercise in artistic futility. To set the fill color, click the Fill Color selector and choose a color.

Creating Special Effects with Contours

Because contour intermediate steps travel concentrically from the control object to the end of the effect, you can accomplish certain things that would take hours or perhaps not be possible using other tools and effects. For example, a blend effect is simply the wrong choice of tool when you want interior shading in an object, because when you scale an irregularly shaped object (such as the letter Q), it scales disproportionately. As a result, when you blend, say, a Q to a smaller Q you've centered inside the larger Q, the intermediate blend objects scale different areas disproportionately. Therefore, a key to creating smoothly shaded objects is to use a contour effect with many steps and a small offset value. Here's an example recipe: with the Artistic Text tool, type the letter **Q** (uppercase), choose a bold font such as Futura, use black as the fill color, and make it about **200** points in height. With the Contour tool, choose Inside on the Property bar, set the Offset to about **0.001"**, create about 150 steps, and choose white as the fill color. The result is a smoothly shaded piece of artwork that will print beautifully with no banding, because 150 intermediate steps from black to white within relatively small objects is just about the upper limit for laser printers and most inkjet printers.

However, a smooth contour transition might not always be your artistic goal; by using no fill but only an outline width on objects, a small number of steps, and a relatively high Offset value, you can, indeed, design topographic maps, magnetic fields, and other illustrations in the technical vein. In Figure 14-10, you can see an object with the top edge suggesting a landscape—created by using the Roughen Brush. The contour objects are white lines, they have a high Offset value so they're clearly visible, and then the Effects | Add Perspective command was used to suggest contour effects that have depth in the illustration. The text also has a contour effect; a Linear Transparency was then added from top to bottom.

FIGURE 14-10 Make smoothly shaded contour effects or make the effect obvious; the technique you choose depends on the illustration assignment.

Fountain Fill Color

Contour effects also support the use of certain fountain fills in Linear, Elliptical, Conical, and Rectangular modes. If you've applied a fountain fill to your original object, the Color Fill properties of the contour group are also applied with the same fill type. If you've contoured an object that has a fountain fill, use the Property bar to set the end color in the contour fountain fill; if the fountain fill uses multiple colors, the contour fountain fill ignores the transition colors. If an object doesn't include a fountain fill, the *End Color* selector on the Property bar is unavailable.

Controlling Contour Acceleration

Just like blends, Contour Acceleration options have the effect of either increasing or decreasing the rate at which the contour group objects change shape (and color) as they progress between the control object and the final, or end, object. You can choose Object Acceleration and Color Acceleration options on the Property bar when you've selected a contour effect object in the drawing window. When a default contour is applied, both these settings are at a default midpoint—the contour objects change in color and size evenly. Change both acceleration rates simultaneously (the default) while the two options are linked, or change them individually by clicking the Unlink Acceleration option, shown here.

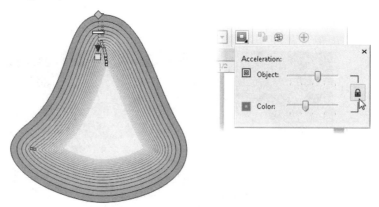

Moving sliders to the left of the center position reduces (or slows) the acceleration rate between the control object and the final contour in the effect. Moving sliders right increases the acceleration. While the two Acceleration options are unlinked, changing the Object Acceleration affects only the progression of shapes in the contour group. Figure 14-11 shows the effects of increasing and decreasing acceleration.

When the Object Acceleration sliders are unlinked, changing the Color Acceleration affects only the change in progression of the fill and outline colors between the control object and the final contour in the effect, leaving the object shape acceleration unchanged. Moving the sliders (or interactive markers) left or right decreases or increases acceleration, respectively, between the control object and the final contour.

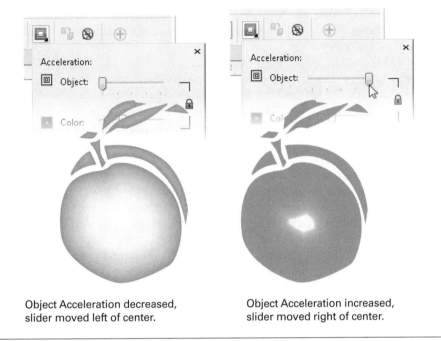

Object Acceleration decreased,
slider moved left of center.

Object Acceleration increased,
slider moved right of center.

FIGURE 14-11   Acceleration rates can dramatically change the look of an object with a contour effect.

Tip   Changing the Color Acceleration slider also affects the color properties applied to the outline paths of objects.

Using the Contour Docker

Although the Contour tool is the most intuitive way of applying contours, you can still apply them using the old Contour docker as an alternative. The Contour docker has been redesigned in CorelDRAW X7 to offer you *all*, not just some, of the Property bar options.

To open the Contour docker, choose Effects | Contour, or choose Window | Dockers | Effects | Contour (CTRL + F9). The docker's options are organized a little differently than on the Property bar, but the same options are found here. One advantage to using the docker is that, as with the Blend docker, you can choose all your options before applying them.

In this chapter, you've seen where to find the options for controlling and customizing blends and contours, so you know where things are, but like operating heavy machinery...

- You don't take prescription medicines an hour before beginning.
- You turn the key and the real fun begins!

Dig into blend and contour effects; add shading to simple objects to make workaday illustration work an inspiring endeavor; and reap the reward of the automation that's possible within CorelDRAW. Blends and contours are one of the best ways to generate scores of similarly shaped objects, so fill your page with a little drawing to make patterns, charts, you name it.

Chapter 15 takes a severe right turn, as we turn to color models: those funny initials CMYK, HSL, and so on, when you begin to define a color using the Window | Color Palettes and the Color Management settings for your document under the Tools menu. After all you've learned so far, and all you intend to create in the future, it's sort of a given that you want the colors you print to be similar to those you see in CorelDRAW's workspace. And you don't want your web graphics to look as though they were taken from the Sunday funny papers. Color management is your next stop in Chapter 15, and it's your insurance that what you create is what you get (WYCIWYG, or something like that).

15 Mixing and Matching with Digital Color Models

Put away those crayons and fling that color wheel out on the front lawn. *Digital* color obeys *none* of the rules we were taught in school, and you use digital color models to fill objects that CorelDRAW, in turn, displays on your monitor. Defining colors, *period,* is an art that even professionals occasionally struggle with. The good news is that version X7 makes applying the color you have in mind as simple as can be, through an extensive collection of industry-standard swatches, intuitive color models, and color mixers that make color definition more like play than work.

If you've ever been faced with picking out a tie to match your shirt at 6:30 a.m. in a dimly lit closet, you'll appreciate the importance of choosing harmonious and intriguing color schemes. Similarly, your color work from CorelDRAW is out there for the public to evaluate; this chapter guides you through the digital process of choosing colors and ensuring that what you print is what you see onscreen. You want your colors to be *consistent* from the screen to the saved file to the final output.

Digital Color Terms and Definitions

Let's say you've created a rectangle on your page; by default, it has no fill. There are two quick ways to fill it. You can left-click on a color on the color palette, which offers a nice selection of preset colors. But let's say you want a specific color. If so, you double-click the Fill icon on the Status bar (either the swatch or the bucket icon), shown in the following illustration, and you can then see (and work in) the Uniform Fill dialog by clicking the Uniform Fill style button at the top of the Edit Fill dialog. You're presented with a combination of interface palettes with tabs for Models, Mixers, and Palettes.

Uniform Fill button

Double-click to display the Uniform Fill dialog.

Palettes are predefined collections of color swatches, pretty self-explanatory. Then you have mixers; this is *not* a self-explanatory area, and it's covered later in this chapter. Finally, you have models, an area worthy of some serious discussion here.

The first set of terms, which sets the stage for color exploration in this chapter, describes digital color and also defines the real-world colors you apply to paper, plastic, and so on, giving you a handle on the seemingly overwhelming variety of attributes that colors have. The terms are somewhat interrelated; when you change a parameter for one, most of the time you change a parameter for another.

Color Model   A *model* is a representation of something that's intangible or too ungainly in other respects to directly manipulate. For example, a child plays with a model airplane because this representation fits in his bedroom better than an actual airplane, and the passengers feel safer. *Color models* are used in CorelDRAW to make dealing with the relationships between colors easy; without a model of the intangible qualities of the light spectrum, choosing the colors you need would be quite a challenge. Additionally, a color model *scales* all the available colors you have when working in CorelDRAW and other programs, in the same way a model airplane can be rotated to see all its sides—a task that's hard to do with a full-sized airplane. Today, using a 24-bit color space, users have at least 16.7 million possible colors from which to choose in design work. There are still more color values if you work with a 48-bit color space, but we're getting off-track here. A color model makes color selection much easier than choosing colors from a palette, for example, containing 16.7 million swatches (if such a thing were possible)!

Color Space   Think of a color model as a piece of architecture: it's a structure. Now, if you were having a house built, your structure would need to take up space, usually on some land. A *color space* is the "land" for your color model "architecture." Different color models require different color spaces. To get off of this analogy kick here, let's say you have a CorelDRAW file to print from your inkjet printer. Inkjet printers use the CMYK color model as the basis for reproducing the colors you've used to fill objects within your document (CMYK color is covered later in this chapter). Unfortunately, digital color, the color you see on your monitor, has its structure in a fairly wide color space; RGB colors have a wider range of expression (more possible colors) than CMYK color space. What can happen (unless you read this chapter carefully) is that some colors you use in your CorelDRAW document look fine onscreen, but they don't print as you anticipate. The reason is that the CMYK color space is smaller than the color space of your monitor, and some of your original design's colors are *clipped* when printed; they've been arbitrarily moved to a color that's *similar* to the color you used, or they just don't print, or you get a nice splotch of muddy brown on the printed page. You certainly want more control over how a CorelDRAW design prints, and that's why CorelDRAW offers a CMYK color picker and also a Gamut Alarm. *Gamut* is a term that means *the expressible range of color*. In other words, colors that fall into a specific color space. When you choose a color that falls out of range of the color space, it's called an *out of gamut* color, and these colors won't print correctly because they are built on a part of the land you don't own.

File Color Capability   If the extent of your CorelDRAW work is to create CDR files, print them, and save them, you have no concerns about a file format that can hold all the colors you've picked and applied to objects. The CDR file format will retain the colors you've used. But if you intend to export a design to bitmap file format, different bitmap file formats have different ceilings of color capability, which relates to color space in many ways. TIFF images, as written by CorelDRAW, for example, can contain 16.7 million unique colors, and this file format can be written to the RGB color model, the CMYK color model, and even some color models, such as Grayscale, which offer no color at all but instead only brightness values. On the other hand, GIF images continue to be used for the Web, and these images can only hold 256 unique colors, pretty meager when compared to 16.7 million colors, so you need to know how to design using only 256 colors, at most.

The sections to follow are a step-by-step guide to understanding the structure of digital color and the space in which color resides, manipulating color models in CorelDRAW to define the colors you want, and matching color values a client gives you over the telephone.

Subtractive and Additive Color Models

Within the world of color models, there are two distinct categories: *subtractive* and *additive* color models. You, the designer, use both: when you print something, you use a device that uses the subtractive color model, and when you design for the Web or an onscreen presentation, you use an additive color model. How these models are similar, how they differ, and how you access these models in CorelDRAW is the subject of the following sections.

Subtractive Color Models

From the moment the first caveman depicted an antelope on his family room wall, humankind has been using a *subtractive* color model for painting. Subtractive color is what many artists were brought up on, mixing physical pigments, and as we all know, when you mix a lot of different pigments together, you eventually get black. This is what the traditional subtractive color model is all about: you *remove* part of the visible spectrum as you overlay one color on another. CMYK is a subtractive color model used in commercial printing, and in theory, if you put cyan, magenta, and yellow pigments together at full intensity, you should get black ... but you don't. Black ink is abbreviated *K* in CMYK. It's shorthand for "key," the color printing plate to which the other colors are registered, or "keyed." In addition to making it possible to obtain a true black color, using black ink instead of heavy mixtures of CMY saves on overall ink costs and speeds ink drying times

The RGB Additive Color Model

The *additive* color model describes color using *light*, not pigments. A combination of the primary additive colors—red, green, and blue—when combined in equal amounts at full intensity, produces white, not black, as subtractive CMYK color does. RGB is a common additive color model, and it is not at all intuitive to use as an artist; however, CorelDRAW has different views of the RGB color model that makes it easy and intuitive to work with.

Because a color model only does one thing—*it shows a mathematical relationship between values that are intangible*—you can use any color model to visualize the relationship among red, green, and blue, with the goal being to make color picking and color relationships as painless as possible to perform! Figure 15-1 shows the default view of the Uniform Fill dialog. When you first install CorelDRAW, it's optimized for print, both with your view of the drawing window and the CMYK color model offered on the Uniform Fill dialog. If you do Web work and no print work, this chapter walks you through how to customize your onscreen display and your color choices for the RGB color model.

Let's look at these controls in Figure 15-1 one at a time. It's quite likely that a color attribute you're looking for right now can be defined in this dialog.

- **Color Model** This selector drop-down list includes CMYK, CMY (as explained earlier, black is more a part of the printing process than a part of the color model), RGB, HSB, HSL, Grayscale, YIQ, LAB, and Registration. These models are covered later in this section. If you're in a hurry: CMYK should be chosen for in-gamut colors for printing, and RGB is the color model for doing nonprinted work.
- **Color field and Hue slider** Here is something tricky, a little confusing, and totally wonderful on the Models tab. A model is a representation of a hard-to-grasp thing or idea. Simply because the default color model is CMYK, there's no real reason to offer a CMYK color picker to accompany the color model: CMYK is an intangible item; a model of it is best represented by what works *for the user*. The *HSB* Color field and slider are a terrific and intuitive mechanism for quickly defining colors, even though you're not *choosing* HSB colors. To manipulate brightness, you drag the little rectangle up or down in the Color field.

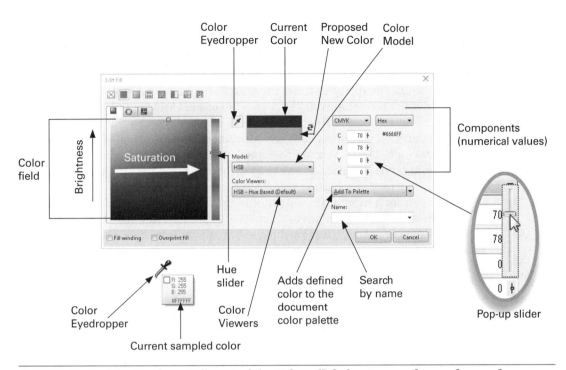

FIGURE 15-1   The Uniform Fill part of the Edit Fill dialog is one of several areas from which you can pick colors in CorelDRAW.

To manipulate saturation, you drag left or right; and obviously you can navigate both brightness and saturation at the same time. The Hue slider to the right of the color field sets the predominant, recognizable attribute of the color you're picking. Users generally set the hue first, and then play with the amounts of saturation and brightness.

- **Current Color/New Color**   The color swatch at the top shows you the current color of the selected object on the page. The bottom color swatch shows you any changes you've made, and the two together provide a convenient way to compare color changes. You can also swap these colors by clicking the little circular arrow pattern icon directly to the right of these fields.
- **Components**   The field at right provides a numerical breakdown of the current color, as expressed in the components of the current color model. Therefore, in Figure 15-1, you can see that the current color is purplish, and if you choose CMYK from the Components area drop-down list, you'll see this color's closest numerical equivalent in CMYK color mode is C: 70, M: 78, Y: 0, and K: 0. However, these values are not static; in fact, when you click the icon to the right of any value (the icon that looks like a slider) a slider does, indeed, pop up, and you can adjust the color by dragging any component value up or down. This gives you a more precise adjustment of the filled object's color; you can also insert your cursor into the number field (it's a live field), double-click to select the entire value, and then type in a new value.

- **Search by name**   The color palette, the strip docked to the right of the drawing window, contains colors that are tagged with names such as Desert Blue and Mint Green. To search quickly for a preset color on the color palette, you can choose from the drop-down list, or begin typing a name in the Name field—as you type more characters, the dialog narrows the search. If you have a custom palette loaded, you can't search it using the Model tab of the Uniform Color dialog; you conduct a search using the Palettes tab, the third tab above the color fields.

- **Add To Palette**   This button adds the current color you've created to the document's color palette. You can then retrieve this color directly from the palette at the bottom of the interface at any time without visiting the Uniform Fill dialog. This is one way to save a custom color; see "Using the Color Styles Docker" later in this chapter for a more feature-filled way to save a custom color.

- **Color Viewers**   This flyout offers a choice of color selection interfaces for your chosen color model. To show the components of color models, the unique structures of the various color models necessarily need to be graphically represented. Some color models such as HSB are blessed with a structure that is intuitive for Mere Mortals to use; others are less intuitive. The illustration here shows the RGB model with various viewers selected. Try the RGB - 3D Additive viewer; you'll hate it—although the model itself is mathematically sound, it just isn't user friendly and a slider is necessary *in addition to* the 3D picking cube because this model is just plain hard to visualize. At top left is the RGB color model, except this time the HSB – Hue Based viewer has been selected from the Color Viewer drop-down list. This viewer is perhaps the best all-purpose color picker from which you can choose colors in any color model. Again, try it; it's very easy to get the color you need quickly. At bottom left is the RGB color model displayed as the HSB – Wheel Based color viewer. A variation of this color picker is used in Corel Painter; it, too, makes defining colors a joy instead of a chore.

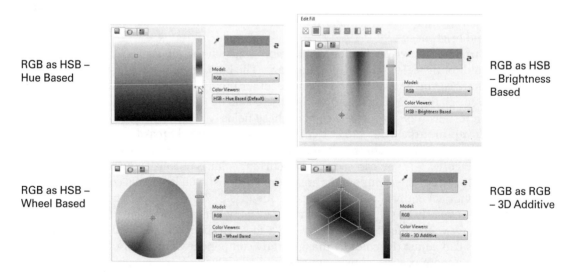

RGB as HSB –
Hue Based

RGB as HSB
– Brightness
Based

RGB as HSB –
Wheel Based

RGB as RGB
– 3D Additive

The HSB Additive Color Model

The HSB color model is to designers what the RGB color model is to software engineers; HSB serves the non-programming community for intuitively choosing colors. HSB and RGB occupy the same color space, but use different components. HSB is the acronym for *hue, saturation, and brightness*. It's occasionally called HSV (the *V* is for *value*) or HSL (*L* for *lightness*), but it all boils down to a user-friendly model for working with digital color. HSB was created by Dr. Alvy Smith, co-founder of Pixar Studios and an accomplished artist. The HSB color model has the same number of colors as the RGB color model. However, HSB organizes the relationship between color differently, and in a friendlier fashion, than RGB. Here are the HSB color components:

- **Hue**   The distinguishing characteristic of color. When you tell a friend, "Oh, that's a very nice blue tie" or "The TV picture is a little orange, isn't it?" you're describing the *hue* component of the color. Hue is usually expressed in degrees on a hue wheel; technically, hue is determined by light wavelength.
- **Saturation**   The presence of color, the purity, the predominance of a hue. We often use the saturation component when we talk about how juicy the colors are in a photograph. If a photo or drawing has a lot of noticeable blues, the blue hue is said to be quite saturated in that color. Conversely, colors you often see on today's household appliances, such as a toaster oven the manufacturer calls *Oyster, Putty, Ivory,* or *Bisque,* are neutral; they have no dominant hue, and they have little saturation. The pages in this chapter have no saturation.
- **Brightness**   The amount of illumination a color has. Brightness, as described in digital color terms, is somewhat elusive, but an analogy from traditional painting with pigments (subtractive color) provides some clarity. When you mix a pure color with white, you increase its brightness; in industries where color description is critical (fashion design, house paints) bright colors are a *tint* of a pure color, also called a *pastel color.* Then there are darker colors: a *shade* is the mixture of a color with black. Mixing with white increases lightness, whereas mixing with black reduces it. In both digital and traditional color, mixing black, white, or a perfectly neutral value in between black and white leaves hue unchanged.

LAB Color

LAB is both a color space *and* a color model. CorelDRAW offers LAB as a color model; however, LAB—the color space—is device-independent, and, therefore, it can be used to describe colors you see in the drawing window, on a physical plastic bottle of soda, or even on a basketball. The Commission Internationale de l'Eclairage (the CIE, the International Commission on Illumination) was established about a century ago as a worldwide body for standardizing and exchanging color specifications. They created the LAB color model. It successfully replicates the spectrum of human vision, and this is why if you check out the color space of CIELAB on a scientific website, you'll note that there is a disproportionately large area of green in LAB color space. This is because the human eye responds to this region of the visible spectrum more strongly than other hues. LAB is modeled after one channel of *luminance*, one color channel (named *A*) that runs from magenta to green, and another channel (named *B*) from blue to yellow. When you use LAB to describe a color, you're (theoretically) assured of color consistency. LAB, the color space, is frequently used by software engineers as a conversion space; when you want, for example, to convert an RGB bitmap to CMYK, the LAB color space is larger than both, and, as a consequence, colors are not driven out of gamut when the pixels in such a bitmap are reassigned new component values.

YIQ

The YIQ color model is similar in its components to LAB color; however, its purpose is for working with designs and text that are video-legal, as defined by the National Television Standards Committee (NTSC). YIQ's components are one channel of luminosity and two of *chromacity* (color). Standard definition TV is brighter than PC monitors, the color range is smaller, and if you get an assignment to draw a logo for a commercial, you'd use this color model.

Grayscale

You use the Grayscale color model (which actually has no hue) if you're designing for one-color commercial printing and for laser-print output. You might find that a color design you've drawn doesn't look right if printed to a laser printer: blue areas seem too faint and reds look much too dark. By using a Grayscale model, you take the influence of hue out of the color equation and what you see onscreen is what you get on paper.

Registration

You do not design with this color model; it's only one color. Registration is used for an object when you want that object to be printed on all commercial press plates, including spot color plates. As the name suggests, Registration applied, for example, to hairline paths around the border of a design helps a commercial pressman to see and keep all the printing plates in registration when he or she reviews progressive proofs of the plates.

The following sections bring relevance to all of these explanations of color; you want to put color to *use* in CorelDRAW, so it's only fitting to move to where the palettes and other features are *located*!

Using Color-Related Dockers

If you've been doing some independent exploring, you might have discovered the Edit Fill dialog and the multitude of fill types, including Uniform. But the Edit Fill dialog is not a persistent part of the interface. The good news is that it's not supposed to be; three dockers—covered next—are used to handle almost all commands that specify uniform color: the Color docker, the Color Styles docker, and the Object Properties docker. Let's take a look at these essential items.

Using the Color Docker

The Color docker, shown next, is extremely convenient to work with; essentially, it's the Uniform Fill dialog, just smaller, dockable, and persistent in the workspace. When an object is selected, you can specify whether the color applies to the outline *or* fill color of the object, and any changes to colors are immediately applied. To open the Color docker, choose Window | Dockers | Color. Unlike Uniform Fill in the Edit Fill box, you don't need to have an object selected to call it.

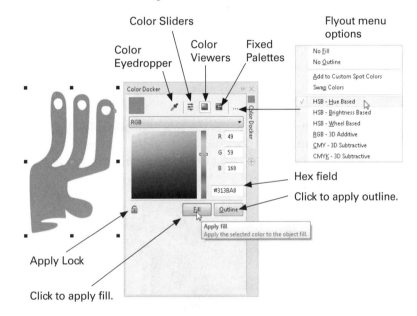

The Color docker is organized into three areas—Color Viewers and Color Sliders, the same as discussed earlier on the Uniform Fill dialog... and Fixed Palettes (actually, they were never broken). You can display each area by clicking one of three buttons at the top of the docker. Each area is geared toward specifying a color using its unique parameters and to then apply that color to the fill and/or outline of a selected object. Here's how each of the three areas is used for specifying color:

- **Color Sliders**   You can mix the components of any color model you choose from the drop-down selector at top by dragging the sliders or entering RGB (red, green, blue) values in the number fields. Notice that the sliders are in color and change dynamically, instantly updating to show you how much of a component affects the overall color, and the relationship between one component and the others.

Note Hexadecimal values are shown under the color component fields for RGB colors. This feature is handy when you or a coder needs to use the hex value of the colors you choose for coding web page backgrounds and such. You can copy the Hex code by swiping to select it in the box, and pressing CTRL+C. Then press CTRL+V to paste the value into a text document.

Color Sliders tab

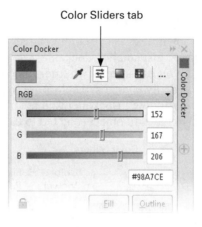

- **Color Viewers** The color viewers (occasionally called *color pickers* in other programs) on the Color docker basically offer the same options as the Color Viewers drop-drop in the Edit Fill dialog when Uniform Fill is chosen.

Color Viewers tab

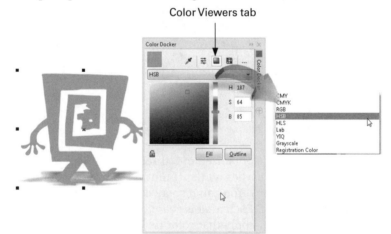

- **Fixed Palettes** Use this area to choose a color from a swatch collection from vendors such as PANTONE, Trumatch, Focoltone, and others from the Palette selector drop-down. Use the flyout options menu to display a color by name; if you have tooltips turned on, the names of the swatches appear when you hover your cursor over them.

The Tint slider at the bottom of this docker is dimmed if you've loaded Uniform Colors or any user or custom palette; this slider is for creating a mathematically precise color tint of an industry-standard solid color, such as any swatches in the PANTONE metallic-coated collection. Solid colors can make use of tints. Tints produce a lighter-appearing halftone of the solid-color ink on paper. Therefore, you can use this Tint slider with solid predefined colors, but not with process colors. Process colors are created in the physical world through separate passes of C, M, Y, and K pigments and, as a consequence, it's impractical to tint the four components. However, CorelDRAW professionals make spot colors for designs by applying a tint to a solid. The technique works because a spot color always requires a separate printing plate. To set up a tint of a solid color quickly, you can click-hold on a swatch and then release the mouse button after the flyout appears. Then you can choose from percentages in 10% increments from solid to white. Tint flyouts appear only from the document palette; click the tint on the flyout, and then click Fill or Outline to apply it.

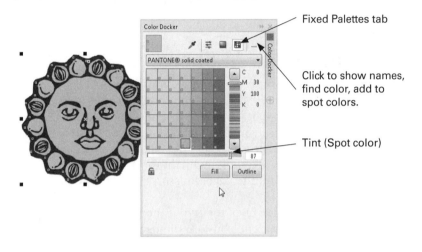

Fixed Palettes tab

Click to show names, find color, add to spot colors.

Tint (Spot color)

Tip Swatches on the Color docker are "drag and drop." You can click-drag a color onto an object, selected or unselected, to instantly fill it. If you have good skills with your mouse or other input device, you can set an outline color for an object by dragging and then dropping a color swatch on the edge of an object, even if the object has no outline attributes; the action of drag-dropping a color forces the object to take on a Hairline outline.

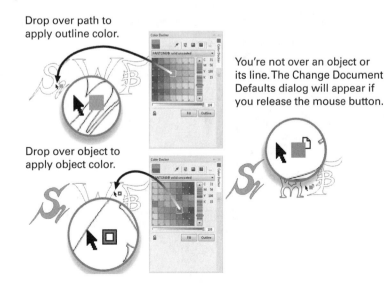

Drop over path to apply outline color.

You're not over an object or its line. The Change Document Defaults dialog will appear if you release the mouse button.

Drop over object to apply object color.

Finding and Applying Fixed Colors (and Tints)

To show you some of the power of the Color docker, the upcoming tutorial shows you how to find a commercial color—specifically a PANTONE color, and if you're familiar with physical swatch books, you know that PANTONE has zillions of unique colors, and an equivalent zillion different sets of numbers to name them.

Open *Fashion Shoes.cdr* now and you'll learn what the fashion color of the year 2014 is, how to find it as a PANTONE swatch on the Color docker, and how to apply both it and a tint to the illustration, effectively recoloring the shoes.

Tutorial   Dying a Pair of Shoes

1. With *Fashion Shoes.cdr* open, choose Window | Dockers | Color.
2. Click the Color Palettes button, and then expand the Palette Libraries drop-down list. Choose Spot | PANTONE, and then choose FASHION + HOME color guide. This is where you look for the latest trends in fashion colors.
3. Note that the number for the Orchid color is typed as editable text on the drawing. With the Text tool, highlight the **18-3224** before the name Radiant Orchid in the text on the page. Press CTRL + C to copy the numbers to the Clipboard.
4. On the Color docker, click the flyout menu—those three dots directly to the right of the Color Palettes button. Choose Find Color, as shown in the next illustration.
5. A pop-up box appears: place the cursor in the field in the box, the cursor becomes a text insertion cursor, and then press CTRL + V. A prefix and suffix are automatically added to denote the exact color specification this number indicates.

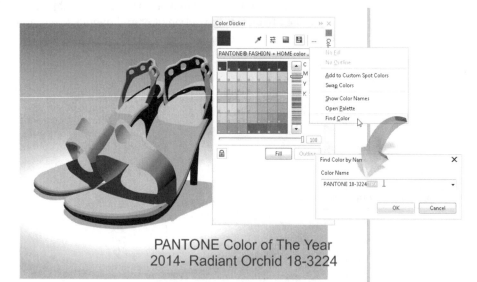

PANTONE Color of The Year
2014- Radiant Orchid 18-3224

6. Click OK, and the swatches on the Color docker move and the exact color you specified is highlighted.

7. Add the current color swatch from the docker to the horizontal document palette at the bottom of the drawing of the shoes by click-dragging it. When you need lighter tones of Orchid for highlights in the drawing, choose the base color, and then use the Tint slider to lighten the color, as shown in the following illustration. From the New Color swatch in the docker, drag a couple of lighter tints to the document palette to add them.

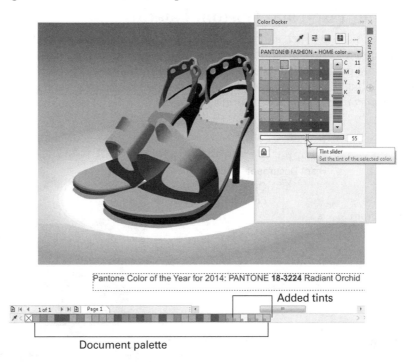

Pantone Color of the Year for 2014: PANTONE **18-3224** Radiant Orchid

Added tints

Document palette

8. Using the new swatches you just added to the document palette at the bottom of the drawing, drag and drop them onto various shapes that make up the shoe. There are a few areas that use a color gradient. To recolor an entire gradient, you need to first click on a color node using the Fill tool to display the color nodes. Drag the appropriate color swatches onto the individual color nodes that make up the gradient.

Using the Color Palette Manager Docker

The Color Palette Manager, shown in Figure 15-2, gives you the option to manage multiple palettes and palette colors. To open the Color Palette Manager docker, choose Window | Dockers | Color Palette Manager. The docker is structured as a tree directory so you can view palettes by folder as your browse, and it includes handy palette command buttons.

As you can see in Figure 15-2, any color palette can be accessed by opening its eye icon (clicking it). By default, the palette will dock to the right, vertically, of the current color palette docked to the right of the drawing window, but you can undock it by dragging just above the flyout arrow at top—three faint dots represent a grip for the palette. Palettes remember their previous configuration, so if you've undocked a palette, closed it, and want to reopen it in a subsequent CorelDRAW session, it will appear as you left it, docked or undocked.

Using Fixed and Custom Palettes

A *fixed* palette—such as the PANTONE palette demonstrated in the previous tutorial—is a noneditable collection of ink colors prepared by an ink manufacturer, such as a specific process or spot color. Fixed palettes are like small color catalogs. Even though you'll likely use only a handful of different fixed palettes, version X7 supports the latest available to support Corel's global community of users.

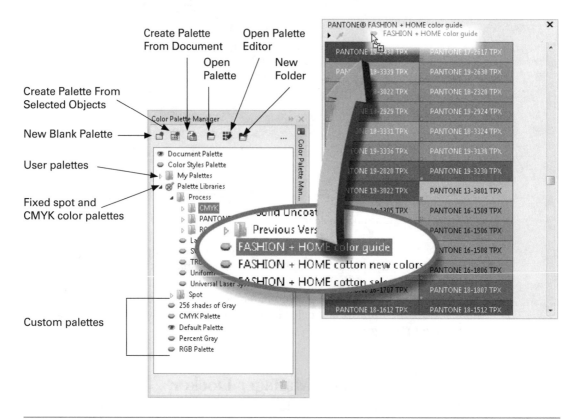

FIGURE 15-2 Choose from a wide selection of palettes with the Color Palette Manager docker.

Using Fixed Palettes

Each fixed palette has its own special characteristics. Some palettes comprise spot and process ink colors, whereas others cater to Web graphics. Using a specific color palette enables you to specify colors within the capabilities of the reproduction or display technique being used.

One of the most commonly used palettes is the spot ink variety. To apply a spot ink color to a selected object, follow these steps:

1. Choose Window | Dockers | Color, and then click the Fixed Palettes tab.
2. Choose a fixed palette type from the Palette Libraries drop-down menu. A listing of colors appears in the main rectangular field, and the vertical selector lets you to navigate through the available colors.
3. Click the color you require from the main selector or choose a specific color name from the Name drop-down menu.
4. Choose a percentage value for your color using the Tint slider. By default, tints of selected colors are set to 100 percent of the ink, but you can specify any value between 0 and 100 percent.

While browsing the fixed palettes within the Palette Libraries drop-down menu, you'll notice that CorelDRAW X7 features an enormous number of choices. Here's a quick rundown on each of the fixed palettes available:

- **SVG Colors**   This palette in the collection is specifically formulated for applying Scalable Vector Graphics (SVG) colors using RGB values according to the standardized W3 consortium. For specific information, visit *http://www.w3c.org/ TR/SVG11/types.html#ColorKeywords*.
- **PANTONE**   PANTONE is perhaps the largest color-matching system in the publishing industry. CorelDRAW includes all of PANTONE's digital ink collections, including coated, uncoated, and matte-color versions for spot inks, as well as process colors. CorelDRAW X7 also features PANTONE's metallic, pastel, and other palettes.
- **HKS**   This palette collection consists of spot ink colors based on CMY combinations varied with black. HKS palettes include HKS Colors, HKS E, HKS Z, HKS N, and HKS K.
- **Focoltone**   This 750-color palette designed by Focoltone reduces the need for color trapping using standardized CMYK screen percentages.
- **Trumatch**   The Trumatch process-color palette comprises more than 2,000 easily printable colors. Trumatch has specifically customized its color matching system to suit the digital color industry using the Computer Electronic Prepress System (CEPS). The palette comprises 40 tints and shades of each hue. Black is varied in 6 percent increments.
- **Web Safe**   The Web Safe palette contains the 216 colors of the Web Safe color model. Colors are defined using the hexadecimal scheme, meaning one of six shades of each color (red, green, and blue) are combined to create each color in the palette.

- **TOYO and DIC** The TOYO and DIC color-matching systems are widely used throughout Asia—especially Japan. Each system contains its own numbering system and collection of different process colors. The TOYO collection of colors has been developed using its own process ink colors.

Creating Custom Palettes

CorelDRAW's custom palettes feature lets you create groups of your own defined colors. By creating a custom palette, you can make these color collections available via your onscreen palette as you work or available for later retrieval.

Tip To create custom color palettes from a selection of objects or from all objects in your document, on the Color Palette Manager docker, choose Create Palette From Selected Objects, or Create Palette From Document, the second and third buttons on the top of this docker. This opens the Save Palette dialog, so you can name and save the colors you've used as a unique palette.

CorelDRAW offers various ways to access custom palettes—via dialogs, the Color docker, or an open color palette. The fastest way is to click the flyout button on an undocked palette and then choose Palette | Open. This opens the Open Palette dialog, and you can now browse through what's available. The pop-up menu where you found Open also includes Save, Save As, Close, and New Palette commands.

In addition to accessing a bundle of fixed color palettes, the Color Palette Manager docker is the ideal place to manage custom palettes. While editing palette colors, you can also access CorelDRAW's other color resources.

To explore this for yourself, use these steps:

1. Open the Palette Editor dialog by choosing Window | Dockers | Color Palette Manager. Choose a palette by first clicking the eye (the visibility) button next to it to display the colors in the palette. You can then double-click a color in the swatches to open the Palette Editor. To edit an existing custom color, select the color and click Edit Color. The Select Color dialog opens to reveal X7's color selection resources.

2. To begin a new palette, click the New Palette button in the Palette Editor dialog to open the New Palette dialog. Enter a name and click Save. Your new palette is automatically opened, but as yet contains no colors.

3. To add colors, click Add Color for access to the Select Color dialog. Proceed by defining your new color and clicking the Add To Palette button. By default, new colors are automatically added.

4. Once your colors have been added, click OK to return to the Palette Editor dialog. If you wish, click to select the new color and enter a unique name in the Name box.

5. To remove a selected color, click Delete Color and confirm your action in the prompt that appears. To reorganize your palette colors, click Sort Colors and choose from Reverse Order, By Name, or By Hue, Brightness, Saturation, RGB Value, or HSB Value.

6. To name or rename an existing color, select the color in the palette, highlight its current name in the Name box, and enter a new name. Existing names are automatically overwritten once a new color is selected.

7. Use the Reset Palette button to restore your palette to its original state before any changes were made, or click OK to accept your changes and close the dialog.

Clearly, there are many ways to mix colors and save them in palettes. Next up is a way to change the *relationship* between colors in an illustration.

Using the Color Styles Docker

InCorelDRAW, the Color Styles docker is the way to create, name, and apply colors and color *relationships* to objects.

 Note Because all styles are associated with individual documents, you must have at least one document open to use the color tools available in the Color Styles docker.

Color styles are managed completely from within the Color Styles docker, shown in Figure 15-3, which is opened by choosing Window | Dockers | Color Styles. The docker is divided roughly into three areas:

- The Color style and Harmony drop-downs for existing colors in the document. You can also mix up a new color with no colors on the page.
- The Color Editor. A style can consist of one or more colors. When only one color needs to be adjusted, use the Color Editor.
- The Harmony Editor. This area is where you can change not only a master color in your document (a color that is a color style), but also the relationship between it and other colors in the document that also have color styles. This is perhaps the most interesting part of the Color Styles docker because, as you'll see in the next tutorial, you can make many variations on a design simply by reassigning a predominant color in a color harmony style.

You won't see the Harmony Editor or the Color Editor before you've added either colors—what the docker calls color styles—to the Color Styles area or the Harmony Styles area. The text in these boxes is self-explanatory—the benefits to your artwork aren't, which is addressed in a moment.

Let's begin with a fairly undemanding tutorial, where you are given a drawing and told to change two colors in it. Because the colors are scattered all over the place in the drawing, it's impractical to select each one, or even to use the Find and Replace Edit command to accomplish this given task. Instead, open *Lots of cubes.cdr*, and the following tutorial walks you through something amazing.

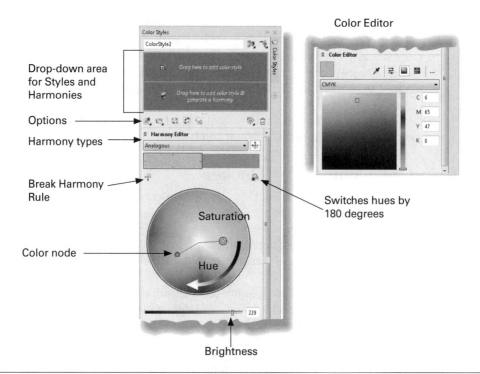

Color Editor

Drop-down area for Styles and Harmonies

Options

Harmony types

Break Harmony Rule

Switches hues by 180 degrees

Saturation

Color node

Hue

Brightness

FIGURE 15-3 The Color Styles docker has commands for creating new styles and harmonies.

Tutorial Making a Color Style and Changing It

1. Open the *Lots of Cubes.cdr*. There is a proliferation of blue, yellow, and red cubes, and guess what? Your boss doesn't like the blue ones. He says, "Make them all yellow or red. Just recolor the blue ones." Bosses like to use the word "just" a lot to belittle the labor of artists; they also like to say, "during your lunch hour," but this is okay. Choose Window | Dockers | Color Styles docker.

2. Click the New Color Style button, the orange square with a green dot at its upper right. Choose New From Document from the menu. This command presents you with a dialog that organizes all the colors in the drawing into harmonic groups of colors. If you want more specific harmony groups, you drag the Less/More slider below the Group Color Styles Into Harmonies checkbox (which should be checked). But in this scenario, you'll see that the blues in this drawing all fall into one tidy style with the diversity slider all the way over to Less.

3. Because the author did this artwork and you didn't, you cannot be sure there are no outlines in this illustration. Click the Create Color Styles From: Both Fill And Outline button. Remember to do this and/or click Object Outline (color) in your own work with the Color Styles docker. Your success depends on whether drawings have outline widths or not. Click OK as shown in this illustration, and it's on to color harmonies next.

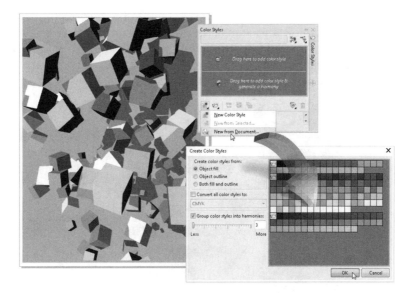

4. Click the Harmony folder that precedes all the swatches on the list, as shown in the following illustration. This is key: The Harmony Editor shows color markers for every color in the style, but, by default, these markers can be moved independently of one another...which makes recoloring all the blue objects to red or yellow a logistic nightmare. However, once the folder icon called out in the illustration is clicked (selected), you can move all the markers to a new location on the color wheel, and each value will be in proportion to the others.

Click the folder button to make sure all the colors are present in the Harmony Editor color wheel.

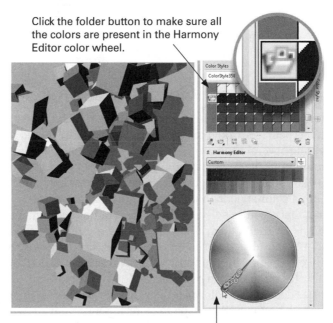

When folder icon above is chosen, you can drag any color marker to move them all.

5. Here's the fun part: drag a marker over to the area on the color wheel slightly between yellow and orange. Impressive, isn't it? Also try moving all the markers to the red hue. In the following illustration, there is no blue in the image, your boss should be happier than he usually appears to be, and *you* learned a new trick to speed up humdrum work!

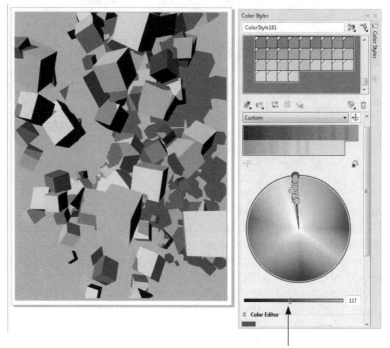

You can elect to brighten all the colors in the style proportionately.

Introducing the New Color Harmony

The parent/child relationship of what used to be called "Master Colors" in previous versions has been reworked to something more intuitive and fast to use. One example of generating several shades of the same color to make a color style group is the new Make Gradient in the New Harmony drop-down in the Options area of the Color Styles docker, shown next. You need to have at least one color harmony swatch to the right of a color style icon in the Harmony Editor to access the Make Gradient command. Once you've selected the Make Gradient command, you're presented with options for the number of colors you want in the style, whether these colors are closely or loosely similar in brightness and saturation or very different (Shade Similarity), and whether you want lighter variations, darker, or both. It depends on your work. It's quite easy to generate three or four gradient styles, and then use the Color Styles docker as a color palette, selecting objects on the page and then dragging a style swatch on top of the shape to color it. Once your drawing is finished, if there's a specific color in the range (the gradient) you don't like, it's easy enough to click that swatch and then change it with the Color Editor. If the entire hue gradient you've used is too warm or the wrong brightness, click the folder icon that precedes the swatches above the Harmony Editor, and then drag all the markers at once to a different hue.

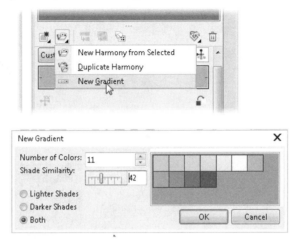

 Tip Dragging the joined markers toward the center of the circle desaturates all of them. Dragging them toward the edge of the circle increases Saturation proportionately.

Color Harmonies for Fashion Design

If you've labored for far too long on an illustration of, say, an informal T-shirt, and you'd like to see how the whole color line of T-shirts this season looks, once again, this is a job for the Color Styles docker, and the steps are similar to, but not exactly like, the cubes you recolored earlier. Very quickly, open *Shirt on hanger.cdr*, and follow along here.

Tutorial   Changing the Color Harmonies of a Monochrome Drawing

1. With *Shirt on Hanger.cdr* and the Color Styles docker open, from the Options area on the docker, click the far left drop-down button and choose New From Document.

2. In the dialog, by default, you'll probably notice that because all the colors in the document are minute differences of brightness and saturation, the Create Color Styles dialog wants to lump all the colors together. You don't want to recolor the shirt hanger to a color similar to any new colored shirt, so drag the Less/More Group Color Styles slider to about **2** in this example. As you can see

in this illustration, the silver of the shirt hanger separates beautifully into its own style group, as do the shirt colors.

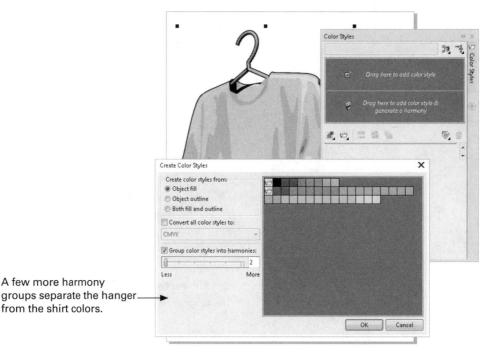

A few more harmony groups separate the hanger from the shirt colors.

3. Click OK, and then click the folder icon that precedes all the purple swatches to select all the swatches.
4. On the Harmony color wheel, click-drag the grouped markers to any color and saturation values and tweak the Brightness slider until you have a variation on the original shirt color.

Changing Groups of Dissimilar Colors

We've had some fun with the amazing Color Styles docker; not many graphics programs can intelligently change the hue of a bunch of colors while slightly tweaking the brightness and saturation so the relationship and the differences between all the colors in a style remain visually constant and eye pleasing.

Here's a true test, though (Spoiler Alert: CorelDRAW wins): you've created a logo whose colors are harmonious, but they are not of the same hue; in fact, some contrast with each other. And you want to experiment with a different color scheme or two for the logo before submitting it. This is *definitely* a job for the Color Styles docker: open the *Breakfast to go logo.cdr* file and get set for some dramatic editing work.

Tutorial   Recoloring a Logo with Color Styles

1. The CDR document contains a logo with several different colors but only a few strong hues. The objective here is to recolor the logo with a *different*, eye-pleasing color combination.

2. Choose Window | Dockers | Color Styles, and then click the New Color Style drop-down. Choose New From Document (callout 1 in Figure 15-4).

3. Make sure the Group Color Styles Into Harmonies checkbox is checked and specify **5** groups. By doing this, you'll have control over every color aspect of the logo when you modify it. See callout 2 in Figure 15-4.

4. The wings in the logo are a Linear fountain fill, and the gold color has its own color harmony group (see callout 3). To dynamically modify this fountain fill, the last color in the fill needs to be in the same group. Drag the purple swatch to the right of the gold one.

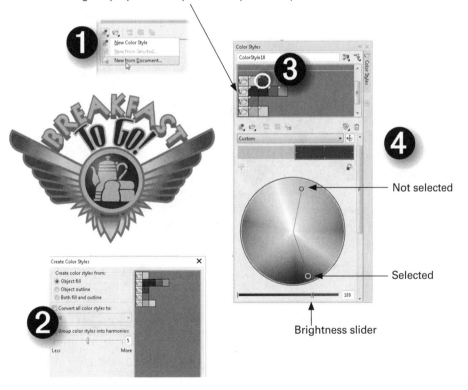

Drag the purple color style to the top Harmony folder.

Not selected

Selected

Brightness slider

FIGURE 15-4   Create harmonies from a drawing so selective color and color relationships can be changed.

As a point of information before continuing, the Color Editor (see callout 4) will display two large colors and markers on the color wheel. When a marker is highlighted, the color is selected and can be changed without changing other colors. Depending on how many colors you've put in a style, each of the color handles can be moved independently of each other. However, when you click the folder icon that precedes the swatches, all the colors change relative to each other when you drag one color marker. You do have control, however, as to *how* the colors change when they move in tandem when you adjust one. You use the Harmony Types drop-down list to choose Analogous colors, or Complementary, or Tetrad, or a host of other color relationships.

5. It's time for you to experiment! Click the top Harmony folder to select the gold and purple, and then in the color wheel, drag either of the selected marker handles around.

6. If and when you're feeling adventurous, click the second-from-top folder to select all the purples and blues in the logo, and then move any of the selected markers around the color wheel. Use your artistic judgment and you'll experience a creative process similar to what's illustrated in Figure 15-5.

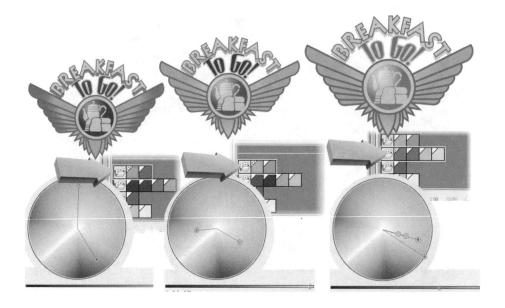

FIGURE 15-5 Changing multiple colors via harmonies can make one design look like a dozen different ones.

Color Relationships

Through color harmonies you can better see the relationships among primary, secondary, and complementary colors. In the additive color model, the primary colors are red, green, and blue. Complementary colors are the color opposites of primaries and lie at 180 degrees in opposition on a color wheel of hues. For example, the complementary color of red is green; the opposite of blue is yellow, and these complements are largely responsible for the A and B color channels in the LAB model, discussed earlier in this chapter. Secondary (additive) colors are the result of a mixture of two primary colors: red+green yields yellow, green+blue produces cyan and red+blue produces magenta, which is the basis for the CMYK (subtractive) color model. It should be noted, however, that color harmonies, relationships that are described based on math, are not necessarily the sort of "harmony" one thinks of when designing a scheme, for example, for the living room. The "color explorer" utilities you can download online typically do exactly what CorelDRAW's mixer does. Usually showing only contrasting colors (color opposites, complementary colors), color mixers have no intelligence; they describe only relationships between hues, and, therefore, can choose, for example, high school and college colors. But you truly have to use your own mind's eye when designing an *eye-pleasing* palette of colors to use in your work.

Adjusting and Transforming Color

In CorelDRAW, you can also alter all colors in a selection of drawing objects at once. Certain color adjustments may be performed either to selected bitmap images or to vector objects via filter commands. All the filters are available when a bitmap is chosen—far fewer commands are available when a vector object is selected. The quick solution is to *make a bitmap copy* of your vector work first, because the next command irreversibly changes your vector work to pixel-based work and your vector copy is gone. Choose Bitmaps | Convert To Bitmap, and then choose the desired options in the dialog, click OK, and the bitmap copy will take all of the filters described here. Choose Effects | Adjust or Effects | Transform to access the available filters for your selection.

- **Brightness-Contrast-Intensity**   Use this to adjust the brightness, contrast, and/or intensity properties of all colors in a selection of bitmap or vector objects. The brightness, contrast, and intensity properties can be adjusted individually based on the visual appearance of the object. Each value can be set between 100 and –100 percent. Choose Brightness-Contrast-Intensity from the Effects | Adjust menu.
- **Color Balance**   The Color Balance filter can be applied to either vector objects or bitmaps and enables you to adjust colors by RGB-CMY values. You can adjust the color balance of Cyan-Red, Magenta-Green, and/or Yellow-Blue colors specifically to the Shadow, Midtone, and/or Highlights, with the added option to Preserve Luminance (brightness). RGB-CMY values range from 0 to 255.

The Color Balance filter values range from –100 to 100. Color Balance is available from the Effects | Adjust menu.

- **Deinterlace** This bitmap-only filter enables you to improve the appearance of bitmaps obtained from the older NTSC standard for video, as opposed to today's progressive video-capturing techniques with digital cameras. You'll find options for reducing either the even or odd horizontal lines seen in video formats. The filter has the effect of optionally filling the tiny gaps between the horizontal lines with either duplicate pixel colors or by averaging the color of surrounding pixels. Deinterlace is located under Effects | Transform.
- **Desaturate** This option-free and instant bitmap-only filter converts your selected color bitmap to grayscale. Desaturate is located under Effects | Adjust.
- **Gamma** This combination vector/bitmap filter changes the range measured between the highest and lowest color values of a selection, enabling you to adjust gamma between 0.10 and 10.00. Gamma is located under Effects | Adjust.
- **Hue-Saturation-Lightness** This combination vector/bitmap filter enables you to adjust color based on the HLS model principles, similar to adjusting color based on color balance—with a twist. Using this filter, the hue, saturation, and/or lightness of colors can be adjusted all at once using the Master option or individually by selecting the Red, Yellow, Green, Cyan, Blue, Magenta, or Grayscale component. You'll find this filter under the Effects | Adjust menu.
- **Invert** This option-free and instantly applied combination vector/bitmap filter changes the colors in a selection to be the "reverse" of the original colors, meaning colors are transposed in relative position across the standard color wheel. Invert is located under Effects | Transform.
- **Contrast Enhancement** This bitmap-only filter enables you to change color contrast by adjusting the levels of the darkest and lightest color shades while automatically adjusting the color values between. Eyedropper tools enable you to sample your image's input and/or output values by color channel. A histogram displays the distribution of pixels according to their color values. The Auto-Adjust option averages colors between the lightest and darkest, or you can manually adjust changes to these colors using the Input Value Clipping slider. The Gamma Adjustment slider enables you to control the resulting midtone values. You'll find this filter under the Effects | Adjust menu.
- **Local Equalization** This bitmap-only filter changes the contrast specifically at the edges to improve image detail. The Width and Height sliders can be set between 5 and 255, enabling you to specify the extent of the equalization effect toward the center of the image. You'll find it under the Effects | Adjust menu.
- **Posterize** This combined vector/bitmap filter limits the number of colors in your selection to as few as 2 or as many as 32 colors using a Level slider control. You'll find it under the Effects | Transform menu.
- **Replace Colors** This bitmap-only filter enables you to substitute one image color with another by choosing old and new colors; specifying hue, saturation, and lightness values; and specifying a color range. Eyedropper tools enable you to perform direct sampling. You'll find it under the Effects | Adjust menu.

- **Sample/Target Balance** This bitmap-only filter takes color replacement a step further by enabling you to sample the color of a point—or an area—of a bitmap image and replace the color with a chosen color or color range. You'll find a complex set of options for sampling highlight, midtone, and/or shadow areas for replacement. Color changes can be adjusted all at once or by individual channel. You'll find this filter under Effects | Adjust.

- **Selective Color** This bitmap-only filter enables you to adjust the color based on changes made to specific color spectrums. Adjust color based on color mode; and/or change reds, yellows, greens, cyans, blues, and/or magentas; and/or change gray levels for shadows, midtones, and highlights. This filter is under Effects | Adjust.

- **Tone Curve** This bitmap-only filter adjusts shadow, midtone, and highlights channels uniformly or selectively or applies a preset tone curve via command buttons. The curve preview can be used to adjust the object's color interactively by click-dragging the curve itself. Clicking one of four Curve Style buttons enables you to apply a preset color adjustment. You can also save your curve or retrieve saved curves, and an Invert button instantly inverts the curve. This filter is found under Effects | Adjust.

Tip You can quickly copy color properties between two objects (including groups) interactively by holding modifiers as you right-drag one object onto another (meaning click and hold the right mouse button to drag an object). Holding SHIFT copies the fill color, holding ALT copies the outline color, and holding SHIFT+ALT together copies both. With each action, your cursor will indicate the property being copied.

You've seen in this chapter how important color is; color sets a mood for an illustration, and the artistic use of color can actually fix an illustration that lacks visual interest or complexity. And you now know how to define and save not only a color you need, but an entire palette. For still more information of color and other CorelDRAW fills, be sure to check out Chapter 12. This concludes the section on colors and fills; from here, we travel to the land of very special effects—take what you've learned, take what you've drawn, and bend it, distort it, in general, make it a unique piece by learning how to sculpt vector shapes.

PART VI

Creating the Illusion of a 3D Composition

16 The Perspective and Extrude Effects

For centuries, traditional artists have studied and sweated, and sometimes failed, to create artwork that conveys a sense of dimension. Perspectives, vanishing points, and angle of view can easily elude all but the most diligent, talented people because the sense of a third-dimension on a 2D canvas is, after all, an illusion.

Fortunately, you don't have to go to school for years and you don't have to break a sweat when you want a little photorealism and dimension the next time you sit down to draw because you have CorelDRAW. In this chapter, you'll learn how to lift your graphical ideas right off the page with version X7's perspective effect and CorelDRAW's legendary Extrude tool.

If you want your audience to be drawn *into* your work and not simply to stare at it, fire up CorelDRAW and read on!

Note Download and extract all the files from the Chapter16.zip archive to follow the tutorials in this chapter.

The Perspective Effect: What Perspective Does to an Object

We've all seen examples of *perspective;* for example, you make sure a train isn't coming, and then you stand on the tracks and look into the horizon. Seemingly, the train tracks converge at the horizon. Naturally, the tracks don't *actually* converge, or it would be difficult to put a train on them. This optical illusion demonstrates the very real optics of the human eye. Any object that has parallel sides (a milk carton, most tables) when viewed at an angle other than face-forward will look as though its parallel sides converge at a point somewhere in the distance. This point, whether you can see it on train tracks or imagine it by mentally extending the parallel lines, is called the *vanishing point,* and CorelDRAW's perspective effect offers an onscreen marker for moving a shape's vanishing point when Effects | Add Perspective has been applied to an object or group of objects.

Depending on the angle at which you view an object—to use a cube as an example—you can see one, two, or three sides of the cube. When you draw a cube, face front, in CorelDRAW, you've drawn a square; there is no perspective, and it's not very interesting. If you can see two faces of the cube, you're viewing from a perspective point; the object is said to have *one-point perspective.* Naturally, you can't see more than three sides of a cube at one time, but when you do see all three front-facing sides, this is called *two-point perspective.* It's visually intriguing to pose an object (or draw one) using two-point perspective; CorelDRAW helps you set up an object for two-point as well as one-point perspective.

Getting a Perspective on Perspective

Now that you understand what a "normal" lens does to perspective, let's take a look at a few abnormal (but artistic and creative) perspectives, beginning with no perspective and working our way up. In Figure 16-1, you can see at left an *isometric* view (also called an *orthographic* view) of the kid's block. Regardless of the term, it's unrealistic because the parallels of the cube do not converge. Isometric views of objects are quickly accomplished in CorelDRAW by putting an object into Rotate/Skew mode (clicking once and then a second time), and then skewing the object by click-dragging a middle control handle. Isometric views are completely the province of computer graphics and geometry. They don't exist in the real world with human eyes, but they are useful in illustration to put equal emphasis on all visible sides of an object. For example, if you want your client to read the side panel of a proposed cereal box design but want the box posed to show more than one side, you'd use an isometric view (occasionally called *isometric perspective*). At right, you can see the same kid's block using a wide-angle perspective. In CorelDRAW, such an illustration is accomplished by putting the vanishing points outside of the drawing page. It's exaggerated mostly because the human eye does not have a field of view as large as 76 degrees, that is, the view is not entirely in focus.

The following illustration goes way over the top; the vanishing points are quite close to the object, and the result is dramatic, unrealistic, and unsuitable for

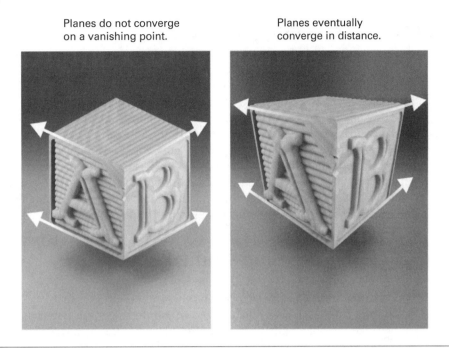

FIGURE 16-1   Example of an isometric view and a fairly wide-angle view of the same object.

presenting a product design. As you read through this chapter, you'll learn that, on some occasions, you want a vanishing point on the drawing page, and on other occasions, you want the "normal" human-eye type of perspective.

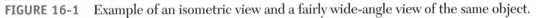
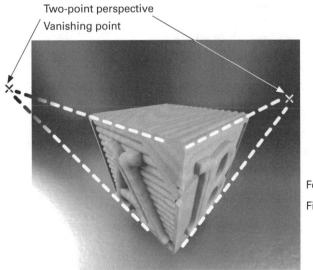

Experiments in Perspective

Experimenting with the perspective effect is a lot more fun and rewarding reading about it. The operations are fairly straightforward, and you'll probably get ideas for future illustrations just by playing with it! Single objects and object groups can be put in perspective; you can change the angle of a perspective shape (or group) by click-dragging any of the four control corners or by click-dragging the vanishing point(s), which changes two of the four control corners at once.

Let's begin with a simple perspective, performed on an object that will immediately give you a reference for what's going on: a 12×12-cell graph paper object. The perspective effect displays subdivisions in red-dotted lines on top of the object you're manipulating, which provides good visual feedback; with a graph paper object, you'll see exactly how the grid corresponds to the visual changes in the graph paper cells.

Tutorial Creating One-Point Perspective

1. Press D, the keyboard shortcut for the Graph Paper tool. On the Property bar, set the number of columns to **12** and the number of rows to **12**.
2. Hold CTRL while you click-drag to constrain the graph paper object to a square. Make the object fairly large, about 7" is good. Because the perspective effect can appreciably shrink one or more sides of an object, it's a good design practice to create objects that are a little exaggerated in size.
3. Click a deep red swatch on the color palette to set the fill for all the cells and then right-click over a pale yellow to set the outline color.
4. Choose Effects | Add Perspective, as shown here. Your object now has control handles around it, and your current tool has changed to the Shape tool. The Shape Tool is used during Perspective creation. Additionally, if you intend to edit a perspective effect while you're working on a different area of a design, all you need to do is choose the Shape tool and then click an object that's in perspective.

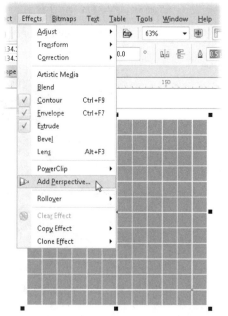

5. Click the top-right handle of the Perspective Effect box surrounding the graph paper object. Hold CTRL to constrain the movement of your cursor to the first direction in which you drag, and then drag down to about the second or third cell in the right column. You've created a perspective effect on the object, as you can see the cells align more or less with the effect's red-dotted overlay reference, and a vanishing point appears directly to the right.

If the vanishing point lies off-screen—which it will when you use a small amount of perspective—press F3 to zoom out so it shows.

6. Click-drag the vanishing point up and then down as long as this is an experiment and not playing for points. Notice what happens: you've defined one-point perspective—this is the right side of a hypothetical cube, and one-point perspectives have only one vanishing point. So the left side of the object is anchored; it doesn't change with the perspective change.

7. Click-drag the vanishing point left and right. The left side is still anchored, and what you're doing is making the hypothetical box's right side deeper and shallower, extending to and from an imaginary horizon on the page.

8. Save this document; you'll work with it in a moment, so don't close it. This is only the beginning of the experiment with suggesting depth in a 2D document!

There *has* to be a practical use for what you've just learned; adding one-point perspective to a graph paper object by itself is about as exciting as watching grass grow. Here, you can see the result of grouping some text with the graph paper object before applying the perspective effect. The real point here is that one-point perspective can establish a *ground plane* for a dimensional composition—a ground has been suggested in this illustration by the effect, the "scene" has depth, and the illustrator obviously can't read signs.

Working with Two-Point Perspective

Using the perspective effect, any 2D drawing can be made to look as though it extends into space, as you proved in the previous tutorial. It's time to up the stakes, however, and create a *second* vanishing point. This second point will make this graph paper object look as though it occupies space, suggesting visually that the grid recedes away from the page and that its depth is traveling in a direction. This tutorial is going to be fun; by the end of the following steps, you'll have created a great high-tech, sci-fi background you can use in several design situations.

Tutorial Creating a 3D Ground Plane

1. With the graph-paper document you saved in the previous tutorial open, choose the Shape tool and then click the object to reveal its Perspective Effect control handles and the vanishing point you defined.

2. Click-drag the top-right control handle up and toward the center of the object, until you see a second vanishing point marker at about 12 o'clock on the page. You might want to zoom out to better see the second vanishing point because it is initially defined quite far away from the object. In the illustration after Step 9, you can see how the graph paper object should look. Notice also that because this two-point perspective is so extreme, the graphpaper outlines are actually curved to accommodate the severely distorted perspective. This is *not* an optical illusion; the lines are indeed curved now.

3. Choose the Pick tool, and with the graph paper object selected, click it to put it into Skew/Rotate mode. Rotate the object about 45 degrees counterclockwise—stop click-dragging when the Property bar reports that you've rotated the object by about this amount. Changing the orientation of the object by only changing the vanishing points' positions would be difficult.

4. Choose the Rectangle tool and then click-drag a rectangle to cover the graph paper object.

5. Choose the Fill tool, and then click-drag from top to bottom on the object so the top is black, fading to white at the rectangle's bottom. Then choose a red from the color palette to fill the Start color indicator of the fountain fill.

6. Choose the rectangle with the Pick tool, and then press SHIFT + PAGE DOWN to put the rectangle on the back of the drawing page, behind the graph paper object.

7. Choose the graph paper object, and then right-click the white color swatch on the color palette. Then double-click the Outline Pen swatch on the Status bar to open the Outline Pen dialog.

8. Type **4** in the Width field, and then click OK to apply this width. You're done and your composition looks like the illustration following Step 9.

9. Left-click the No Fill swatch now while the graph paper object is selected.

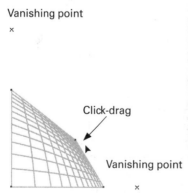

Vanishing point
×

Click-drag

Vanishing point
×

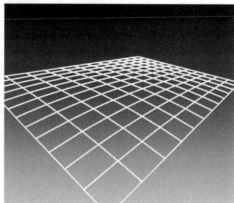

> **Tip** The outline properties of an object possessing the perspective effect do not diminish in width along with the shape of the object. If you need outlines to follow a perspective, you need to first convert the outlines to objects: press CTRL+U, for example, to ungroup a graph paper object, and then choose Object | Convert Outline To Object (CTRL+SHIFT+Q).

Copying Perspective and Creating a 3D Scene

Like many of the features in CorelDRAW, a perspective can be copied from an object and applied to a different object using the options on the Property bar. Being able to instantly copy and match perspective between objects in a composition can turn the entire drawing into a 3D event, as the following tutorial demonstrates.

In the *Commuters.cdr* file that you downloaded, you'll see several characters you can use, or choose to use your own in the following tutorial. The idea is that these fellows are so self-absorbed they're going to miss the train pulling in behind them unless they look to the right a little. So you'll apply a perspective to one guy, copy the instance of the perspective effect to the rest of the gang, and then embellish the composition a little to give the drawing true depth.

Tutorial   Perspective Scenes via Copying

1. Open *Commuters.cdr*. Select the left guy on the page, and then choose Effects | Add Perspective.
2. Click the top-right control handle on the object, and then drag down a little. Then click-drag the bottom-right control handle, and drag up and to the right until the commuter is facing right in perspective, as shown in Figure 16-2. You might not see the vanishing points on the page because this perspective is not severe enough.

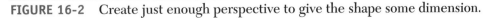

FIGURE 16-2   Create just enough perspective to give the shape some dimension.

3. Choose the Pick tool now. Click the guy with his hat in his hand. Then choose Effects | Copy Effect | Perspective From. Click over the guy at left that has the perspective shown here, and the second object adopts the perspective of the first.

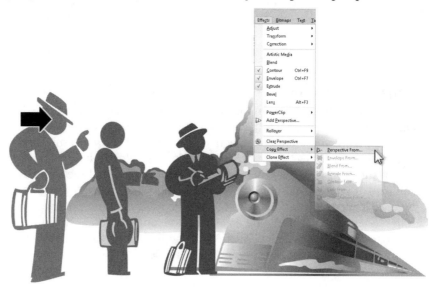

4. Repeat Step 3 for the guy holding the writing pad.
5. Create a graph paper object, and then give it a deep red fill and a white outline. Put it to the back of the illustration.
6. Put the graph paper in perspective to make a ground plane. Next, drag the top-left control handle to the right, and then drag the top-right control handle to the left until you see a vanishing point just above the graph paper object. This object's perspective should be very distorted, suggesting a horizon at about the chest level of the characters.
7. Create a second graph paper object, and then choose Object | Group | Ungroup, and then Object | Combine so the graph paper object is truly a single path.
8. Give it a medium- to light-blue fountain fill, and give its outline a white property exactly like you did with the first object in Step 5. Put it to the back of the drawing (SHIFT + PAGE DOWN).
9. From here, these are the steps to "grounding" the characters on the graph paper below them: click any of the fellows, and then choose the Drop Shadow tool from the Effects group of tools on the Toolbox.
10. Choose Perspective Top Left from the Presets drop-down on the Property bar. With your cursor, click-drag the black control marker for the shadow down and to the right until the shadow looks correct.
11. Repeat Step 9 with the two other commuters. Select a guy, and then choose Effects | Copy Effect | Drop Shadow From, and click the first shadow (not the object casting the shadow) you defined. You can also add a shadow to the train and the cloud group of objects. Additionally, try moving the commuters up or

down from their original position to increase the sense of depth in the scene. Your scene should look like the illustration shown here.

Tip Any object that has the perspective effect can be quickly put into Editing mode when the Pick tool is the current tool by double-clicking the object. And if you want to mirror the perspective effect—to make a symmetrical perspective—hold CTRL+SHIFT while you click-drag a control handle.

Pre-visualizing Designs in Perspective

Often you'll design something, for instance, a pattern, and want to see what it would look like as a garment, giftwrap, or some other physical piece of art before you pay to have the design printed. You can do this in CorelDRAW with the perspective effect. In the following example, you'll create a simple giftwrap pattern; then, using perspective, you'll virtually wrap a package. The package is provided for you as an image on layers in a CorelDRAW document.

Let's use CorelDRAW's Artistic Media tool to create the giftwrap for the present in the following steps.

Tutorial   Pre-visualizing a Design on a Product

1. After creating a new document (choose Landscape orientation), press CTRL + I to import *A present.cdt*. If you get an attention box that says there's a color profile mismatch, click the Convert From Color Profile To Document Color Profile button and then click OK. Now, just click at the upper left of the page to place it to size.

2. Open the Object Manager from the Tools menu. Expand the *A present.cpt* entry to reveal the two image objects.

3. Click the New Layer button at the bottom left of the docker. Doing this creates a new default named "Layer 2."

4. Click-drag the "Bow" entry on the Object Manager and place it on the Layer 1 title. Doing this destroys the list entry "A Present.CPT," and the bow and the present objects now both belong to Layer 1.

5. Drag the object named "Bow" now from Layer 1 to Layer 2. Layer 1 will only contain the "A Present" object now. The bow object is above the present.

6. Create a new layer, by default, named "Layer 3." Click-drag it to below Layer 2. Here is where you'll design the giftwrap.

7. Choose the Artistic Media tool from the Pen Tools group on the Toolbox. Then choose the Sprayer button on the Property bar. You can use any preset you like; one of the festive Food presets.

8. Create a rectangular area by scribbling up and down, like making several *W*s.

9. Choose Object | Break Artistic Media Apart (CTRL + K works, too). With the Pick tool, delete the parent black path that's now visible. See Figure 16-3.

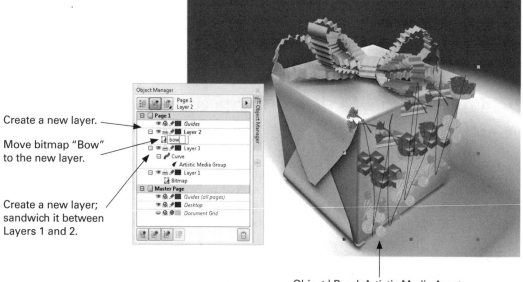

Create a new layer.

Move bitmap "Bow" to the new layer.

Create a new layer; sandwich it between Layers 1 and 2.

Object | Break Artistic Media Apart

FIGURE 16-3 Create a pattern with the Artistic Media Sprayer Tool.

10. Choose Effects | Add Perspective. With the Shape tool, drag, one at a time, the control handles for the effect to match the four corners of the face of the present, as shown here.

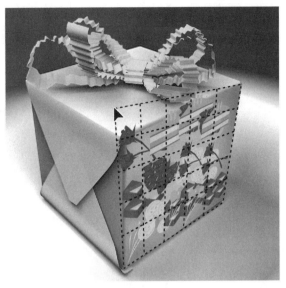

11. Duplicate the pattern (press CTRL + D), and then use the Shape tool to edit this duplicate (which also has the perspective effect), so it matches the four corners of the top side of the present. Because the bow is on the top layer, you're actually adding the top pattern in perspective below the bow so it looks optically correct.

12. Repeat Step 11 to create the left panel of the pattern on the present.

13. The pattern shouldn't look totally opaque, but instead should take on a little of the shading on the blank present. The quickest way to apply transparency to the scores of objects that make up your Artistic Media stroke is to turn it into a bitmap. First, let's check out the resolution of the present image so the conversion of the giftwrap pattern isn't unnecessarily larger than the present or bow images. After choosing the Pick tool, click either the "Bitmap" or the "Bow" entry on the Object Manager list and then look at the Status bar. The correct answer is 96 dpi.

14. Select one of the patterned sides and then choose Bitmaps | Convert To Bitmap. In the Convert To Bitmap dialog, choose **96** in the Resolution box, check the Transparent Background checkbox, and then click OK.

15. With the new bitmap selected, choose the Transparency tool on the Toolbox. On the Property bar, click the Uniform Transparency type, Multiply Style, and then play with the amount of transparency your eye tells you looks best and visually blends the pattern into the present. Repeat Steps 13 and 14 with the other two sides of the gift, be sure to include a card, and then send it to someone who deserves a gift.

This finished pre-visualization provides you and your client with a view of the goods you've designed, as they will appear from the customer's point of view, and perhaps this is the best "perspective" effect of all. This illustration shows a finished version of the tutorial, using the bubbles from the Misc. category of spray patterns.

Extruding Objects: How Extrude Works

Although CorelDRAW is a 2D vector drawing application, the Extrude feature adds a simulated third dimension by adding objects that are shaded and in perspective. This chapter takes you through the rich feature set of the Extrude Tool, offers some creative possibilities for its use, and gets your head around the initial challenges of navigating 3D space in CorelDRAW.

CorelDRAW's extrude effect examines the geometry of an object and then, with your input, creates dynamic extensions to all path segments, suggesting the added objects recede into the distance to a vanishing point. Figure 16-4 shows some finished artwork based on objects that are easy for you to draw in CorelDRAW. The train composition uses *several* extruded objects, and the tabletop was first created by extruding shapes, but then all the shadows you see were manually drawn on top of areas. You need to be imaginative to place the extruded object in context, within a scene, to build a complete graphical idea. The Extrude tool doesn't create "Auto-Art." It's a tool; it needs your creativity to guide it.

When an extrude effect is applied to an object, the original becomes a *control object,* and the extrude effect objects become a dynamically linked group. Any editing you then perform on the properties of the control object, such as fills and edits to the outline of the control object, are immediately updated in the linked extrude group.

Be aware that both lighting and the control object's geometry impact how many extrude group objects are created. Although you don't usually need to concern yourself with how many objects are dynamically created to make an extrude, the sheer number of objects can slow down redraws of your page when you have, for example, hundreds

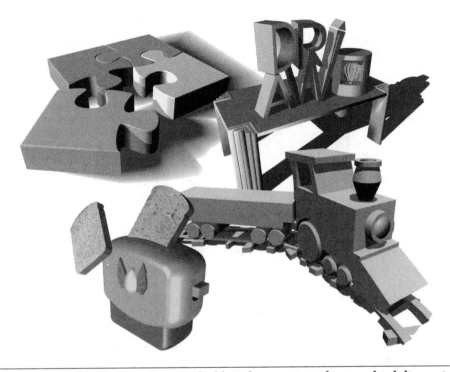

FIGURE 16-4   Imagine what an object looks like when projected into a third dimension, and then manually add what's missing.

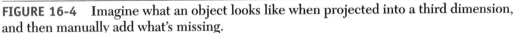

of objects in the extrude group. When CorelDRAW creates an extrude group, it calculates lighting (when you *use* lighting, covered later in this chapter) and creates extrude group objects based on curved path segments in the control object.

Choosing and Applying an Extrude Effect

The extrude effect can be applied interactively using the Extrude tool, which is located in the Toolbox with other effects tools, or you can choose from the Presets list to create a 3D object instantly.

While you're using this tool, the Property bar provides all the options for setting the effect's properties. Browse the Property bar options as shown in Figure 16-5. Options are grouped into areas for saving your applied extrusions as Presets, controlling the shape, depth, vanishing point position, rotation, lighting, color, and bevel effects.

Navigating the Interactive Markers

When you decide to extrude a shape manually, interactive markers appear around the resulting object after you perform the first step in an extrude: you click-drag on the face of the object you want to be the control object. The interactive markers offer you control over the position, depth, and vanishing point position of the 3D object. You'll

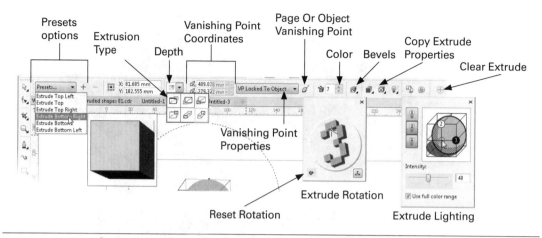

FIGURE 16-5 The Property bar contains all the options for defining and saving the look of an extrude.

create a 3D object by hand in the following tutorial, so familiarize yourself with the elements that surround a 3D extruded shape, as shown in Figure 16-6.

Alternatively, you can apply a Preset extrude effect to get a 3D version of a shape in lightning time; however, you might want hands-on control over creating the extrude effect. Follow this tutorial to get a handle on what some of the Property bar options do to an extrude effect.

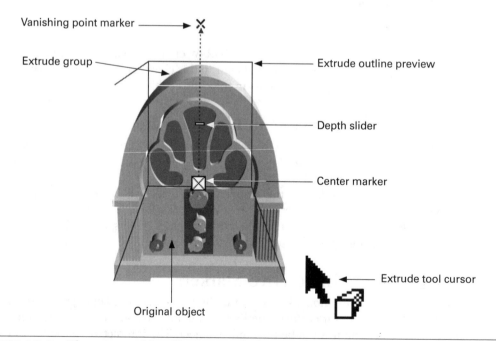

FIGURE 16-6 These control handles are used after an object is initially extruded to change the appearance of the extrude.

Tutorial Going Deep with the Extrude Tool

1. Create an object to be the control object for the extrude. A rectangle produces results that make the relationship between the face of the object and the sides clear, but not very artistic. Try a star shape for more dramatic extrude results. Give the shape a fill (a fountain fill will produce a stunning effect), and give the outline a contrasting color such as white so you can visually track where the extrude objects are created.

2. Choose the Extrude tool, and your cursor changes to the Extrude tool cursor, which is hard to mistake for the Pick or Pen tool. When held over your object, the cursor indicates a Start extrude position by displaying a tiny shape with a direction line below the symbol of an extruded cube.

3. Drag from the center of your object outward in any direction, but don't release the mouse button. The control object now has interactive markers and a Wireframe preview of the front and back boundaries of the extrude; the front of the object is bound by a red outline, and the back of the 3D shape is bound by a blue outline. The preview indicates the length and direction of the extrude effect and the X symbol you're dragging is the *vanishing point*. As discussed earlier in this chapter, a vanishing point is a geometric indicator of where parallel lines on a surface would converge at the horizon if the surface were actually to extend to the horizon. Once you're satisfied with the extrude Wireframe preview, release the mouse button. Now you can edit the extruded object and immediately see the results.

4. Drag the vanishing point X symbol around the page; not only does the preview outline change, but also, more importantly, the view on the 3D object also changes. When the vanishing point is above the control object, you're looking down on the object; similarly, you move your view to expose the side of an object in direct correlation to the position of the vanishing point.

5. As you use the Extrude tool, you define both the direction and depth of the 3D object. Try dragging the Depth slider toward and then away from the control object. Notice how you first make the extrude a shallow one and then a deeper one, all while the sides extend in the direction of the vanishing point. At any time from when you create the object by releasing the cursor, you can also set the object depth by using the Depth spin box on the Property bar.

6. Click outside of the object, and the extrude operation is complete. However, because extrude is a *dynamic* effect, you can change the extrude's appearance at any time in the future by double-clicking either the extrude group or the control object with the Pick tool to once again display the interactive handles.

Using the Extrude Tool and Property Bar

Like other effects, extrusions can be set using the Property bar. However, regardless of your work preferences, version X7's Extrude feature produces the same results whether you use the Property bar controls or the Extrude tool. The following sections walk you through some of the design options you have when you use the Extrude tool.

Setting Extrude Depth

Extrude depth is based on the distance between the control object and the vanishing point. You will get different appearances using the same depth value but different styles, and you can set extrude depth as high as 99. Here, you can see a shallow and a deep extrude, using two different depth values but the same extrude style. You can control object depth manually by dragging the interactive Depth slider on top of the object, or enter values in the Num box on the Property bar (press ENTER after typing a value; the spin-box controls update the object without your needing to press ENTER).

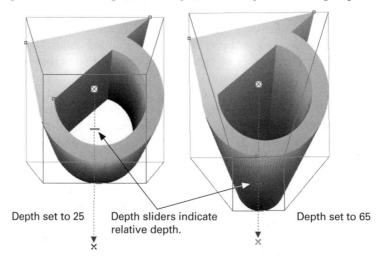

Depth set to 25   Depth sliders indicate   Depth set to 65
                       relative depth.

Setting Vanishing Point Properties

The direction of the vanishing point determines only the point toward which objects diminish; it does not control whether the extruded portion extends from the front or back of the object. Using the Vanishing Point Properties drop-down on the Property bar, you can lock an extrusion's vanishing point, copy vanishing points from an existing extrusion, and share vanishing points between extruded objects.

Here are the options for vanishing points—how they can be set and shared between different extruded objects:

- **Locking to the object**   Choosing the VP Locked To Object option (the default setting) fixes the vanishing point to a position relative to the object, regardless of where the original extruded object is positioned.
- **Locking to the page**   VP Locked To Page offers the option to tack the vanishing point to your page, forcing the extrusion to diminish toward a fixed page position, no matter where the original object is moved. Try this to see for yourself the effectiveness of this setting: Lock the vanishing point of an extruded object to the page, and then move the object using the Pick tool; you'll see that the sides of the extrude dynamically update to always show the object's correct perspective.

- **Copying vanishing point from**   The Copy VP From command doesn't define a vanishing point like the other drop-down choices do; instead, you use it to copy an existing vanishing point. Copying a vanishing point lets you set up several extruded objects on a page, and in a few clicks, the objects all appear to be facing the same direction, at a common point of view from the audience's perspective. Immediately after you choose Copy VP From, your cursor changes to a vanishing point targeting cursor (a really, really large arrow), which you use to target any other extruded object on your document page, with the goal of copying its vanishing point position. For this command to be successful, you must have at least one other extrude effect applied to an object and in view. After the vanishing point has been copied, the Property bar indicates the object's vanishing point as VP Locked To Object, and the vanishing point can now be moved.

- **Sharing vanishing points**   Choosing Shared Vanishing Point lets you share the *same* vanishing point among several objects, but you must have applied at least an initial extrude effect to your objects before attempting to use this command. Immediately after you choose this option, your cursor changes to a vanishing point targeting cursor, so you can now target any other extruded object for the purpose of creating a common vanishing point position for multiple objects. This option creates a similar effect to copying vanishing points, but the overall effect is every object on the page is in the same scene. You can move two or more selected objects simultaneously, and change the perspective of all of them.

- **Setting a relative position for vanishing points**   The V Page Or Object Vanishing Point button on the Property bar is used to toggle the measurement state of object vanishing points between page and object. When the option is inactive (the button is not depressed), the vanishing point position boxes allow you to specify the vanishing point relative to your page origin—a value determined either by the lower-left corner, by default, or by the zero markers on your ruler origin. When the option is active (the button is depressed), the center of your currently selected object is used as the measurement value, which changes according to the object's page position. You will see this most noticeably if you have a depth on an object of more than 40 and you drag the object around the page with the Pick tool. The extrude group actually changes to reflect different vanishing point views.

Setting 3D Rotation

Beginning your extrude adventures with the object facing you is a good beginning point in your 3D experience, but not always the most visually interesting of poses. You can *rotate* extruded objects after extruding them via the Property bar or via the interactive control handles. Create an extrude group of objects and then let's begin with the precise, noninteractive method of rotation you access on the Property bar when you've chosen the Extrude tool and selected an object. VP Locked To Object is necessary for this trick to work.

The Rotation pop-up menu offers a proxy box that you use by click-dragging on the "3" as shown next. As you drag, a faint yellow line appears on the "3," indicating the current rotation of the object and the proposed new rotation once you release the mouse button. You might not always get the exact look you need using this technique because of the position of the object's vanishing point—your experience can be similar to levering an object seesaw-fashion when the pivot point (the fulcrum) is 15 miles away! To avoid imprecision, you can click the toggle button labeled in the illustration. The value fields have spin-box controls that increase and decrease the values by 5; you probably want to enter values manually because a single percent of rotation (from 0 to 100 percent, not degrees) can be quite significant, considering only 100 of them are in this pop-up box. If at any time you find you've gotten too deep in this 3D rotation stuff, clicking the Undo curved arrow icon on the lower left of the selector, as shown here, resets all rotation values to zero.

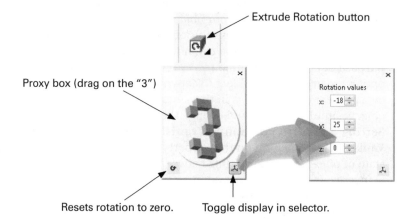

Overall, the best teacher is experience, particularly with manipulating your view of a 3D object in CorelDRAW. Set aside some quality time, and you might even be pleasantly surprised by some of your errors!

Using the Rotation Tools

You don't have to use the Extrude Rotation pop-up box on the Property bar to rotate an extruded object: you can define a degree of rotation along the X, Y, and Z axes of any object by click-dragging the object directly. To do some manual rotation, the object needs to be extruded and first put into Editing mode—you can double-click on the extrude group of objects with the Pick tool to put the object into Editing mode, and then click a second time to expose the control handles shown next.

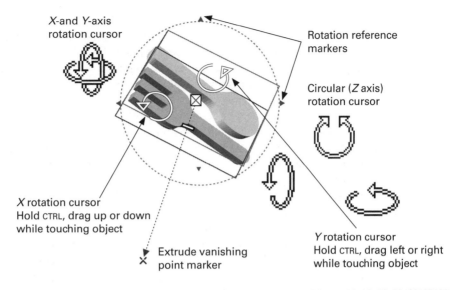

X-and Y-axis
rotation cursor

Rotation reference
markers

Circular (Z axis)
rotation cursor

X rotation cursor
Hold CTRL, drag up or down
while touching object

Extrude vanishing
point marker

Y rotation cursor
Hold CTRL, drag left or right
while touching object

Note If either Back Parallel or Front Parallel is selected, the Extrude Rotation controls are unavailable; parallel extrusions have no vanishing point, so there's nothing to pivot with. Also, when the vanishing point is locked to the page, Extrude Rotation cannot be performed.

When an object is rotated, you can't use the vanishing point controls on the Property bar, mostly because mathematically, the vanishing point is nowhere near your drawing page. If you need to adjust an object's vanishing point, you must work backward; on the Extrude Rotation pop-up panel on the Property bar, click the Reset Rotation icon. Then the vanishing point options and controls become active (and your object is no longer rotated).

Adding Lights

Adding lighting to an extruded object can spell the difference between an effect and a piece of artwork that truly attracts a viewer with its realistic appearance; many of the figures in this chapter use the Lighting option. To access the lighting controls, click the Extrude Lighting button on the Property bar while selecting an extrude effect.

Working with the Options in the Lighting Control Window

Three independent light sources can be activated, positioned, and adjusted for intensity and to set whether all the control object's colors are used in the extrude group (the Use Full Color Range option). These lights perform like bare light bulbs. You can reposition them, but not aim them as you would a real flashlight or spotlight. Light intensity is set on a light-by-light basis between 0 and 100 percent by using the slider control when each light is selected. One of the nice things about setting up light intensity and position is that response is immediate—there is no Apply button and your object's light changes as you make changes in the control window.

When you first open the Extrude Lighting control window, all lights are inactive. To activate a light, click one of the three Light Source buttons—the numbering is for your reference; it's just a label. There is nothing special about light 3 versus light 1, for example, in any of its properties. Once you click a light button, a circle with the light's number inside appears in the front, upper-right position on a 3D grid surrounding a sphere, which represents the extrude object (see Figure 16-7). The lights themselves aren't visible on the drawing page, but the lighting effect you define displays highlights and shaded areas on your extrude object, particularly evident when the sides of the control object are curved. You can pose the light sources by adding them to the grid and then dragging them—there are over a dozen possible positions for lights; some of the positions can create very interesting "edge lighting" on your object.

Every time you activate a new light, it appears on the grid in the default position of front, top, right. This means if you click to activate two or three Light Source buttons in succession without first moving them, you'll stack them on top of each other and wind up with one extremely intense light source on the object. When this happens, drag the individual lights to reposition them at different points.

A *selected* light is shown as a black circle in the preview; unselected lights are shown as white circles. Lights set to brightness levels less than 100 percent appear in shades of gray. As these light sources are dragged around the 3D grid, they

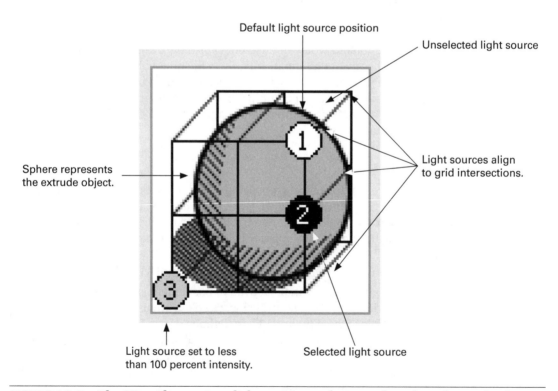

FIGURE 16-7 The 3D grid represents light positions relative to the selected extrude object.

automatically snap to line-intersection points on the grid. You *can* position lights at the back-mid-center or back-center-bottom position—if you're *really* determined and have lots of time to spare—but lights in these positions will not contribute significantly to the shading of the extrude shape.

Note There is no option to set the color of lights; all lights cast white.

The following tutorial obliges you to put on your stagehand cap as you work the lights in a scene, adding them to the extrude object's properties and learning how to position them and turn the wattage up and down.

Tutorial   Working with Extrude Light Options

1. Create a color-filled object and apply an extrude effect to it.
2. Using the Extrude tool, click the Extrude Lighting selector on the Property bar to open the light source option.
3. Click the Light Source 1 button, and a light source symbol appears in the upper-right-front corner of the grid, shown as a black circle numbered *1*. The Intensity slider is activated. Light Source 1 is now active, and the colors of your extrude effect are altered (brightened and possibly a little washed-out) to reflect the new light's contribution to the extrude effect.
4. Drag the symbol representing Light Source 1 to a different position on the 3D grid; notice how the coloring of the effect changes in response to the new lighting position.
5. With Light Source 1 still selected, drag the Intensity slider to the left, approximately to the 50% position, and notice how the color of the object becomes darker and more saturated.
6. Click the Light Source 2 button to activate it. Notice that it appears in the same default position as the first light source, and the symbol representing Light Source 1 is gray, indicating it is not selected and is not at 100% intensity. When an unselected light is at 100% intensity, the symbol is white. Drag Light Source 2 to a different grid position—in classic scene lighting, a secondary light of, say, 50% of the main light's intensity, is usually positioned directly opposite the main light to make objects look rounder, deeper, and more flattering with more visible detail than when using only one light source.
7. Click the activation buttons for Light Sources 1 and 2 to toggle them off, and the color of the extrude object returns to its original state. To finish editing lights, click anywhere outside the Extrude Lighting selector.

Tip Occasionally in your design work, you might like the perspective you've created for the face of an extrude object, but you might not need the extruded side or the extrude group of objects. You can remove an extrude effect from an object and keep its perspective and position on the page by clicking the extruded portion of the effect and choosing Effects | Clear Extrude. You can also use the Extrude tool by clicking the Clear Extrude button on the Property bar.

Controlling Light Properties

Two additional options are available when you use lighting, and they have the following effects on your extruded objects:

- **Lighting intensity** As mentioned in the previous tutorial, the Intensity slider determines the brightness of each light. When a light is selected, you can set the range between 0 and 100%; higher values mean brighter lighting.
- **Full color range** Below the Intensity slider, you'll find the Use Full Color Range option, which directs your display to use the full *gamut* of colors when coloring the surfaces of your original object and its extruded portion. *Gamut* is the expressible range of colors available to CorelDRAW, which depends on the color mode of the original object and the extrusion. When working in CMYK process or RGB color, you might find the shading on an object to have too much contrast; the lighting might look too harsh and might create washed-out surfaces. The remedy is to uncheck Use Full Color Range; the gamut of colors is then limited, and the dynamic range of available colors becomes narrower. You just might wind up seeing areas that are hidden in deeply shaded zones when Use Full Color Range is not checked.

Setting Extrude Color

In addition to shading an extrude group using lighting, you can further embellish and draw out photorealistic qualities by using color options for the extrude. You might need to perform some technical illustration with extrude objects, and you might need cross-hatching in addition to lighting, for example. In these situations, turn to the Color option on the Property bar; you can shade an extrude group in three different ways: object fill color, solid color, or color shading (much like a fountain fill transition from one color to a different color).

Going from left to right on the Color Control window, you'll see the color modes you can use.

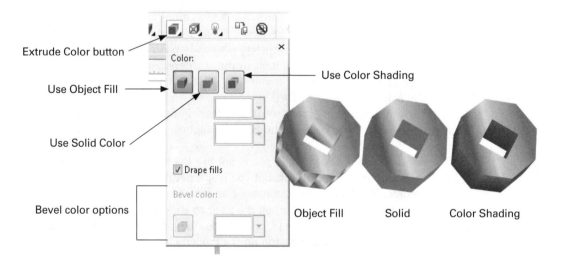

You can achieve effects that range from flat, technical illustrations to highly polished metallic surfaces—which actually can work on their own without your needing to light the object—and it all depends on the choices you make in the Color Control window:

- **Using an object's fill** The Use Object Fill option is the most straightforward to use, but it does not automatically create any sort of shading—if you choose to use the default object fill and the object is filled with a uniform color, give the control object an outline width whose color contrasts with the object fill color. When Use Object Fill is selected, the Drape Fills option also becomes available (and is selected automatically). Drape Fills is discussed shortly; here is an example of a fountain fill control object, with and without Drape Fills.

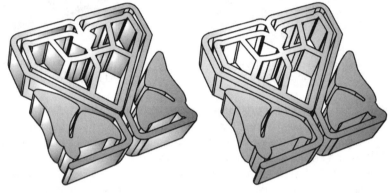

Radial fountain fill control object, Use Object Fill

Radial fountain fill control object, Use Object Fill, Drape Fills

- **Choosing your own solid fill** Choose Use Solid Color to set any uniform color to the extrude portion of your effect, regardless of the fill type currently applied to your object. The secondary color option becomes available only when Use Color Shading is selected.

> **Tip** If an object has no outline width/color applied, you might have difficulty seeing the edges between the original and extruded portions. Applying an outline to your original object might help define the edges of the overall composition.

- **Using color shading** Choose Use Color Shading to add depth by using your object's color as the Start color and black (by default) as the End color. If the object to which you've applied your Extrude effect is already filled with a fountain fill, Use Color Shading is selected automatically. Creating visual separation between the extrude group objects and the suggestion of depth is easy with Use Color Shading.

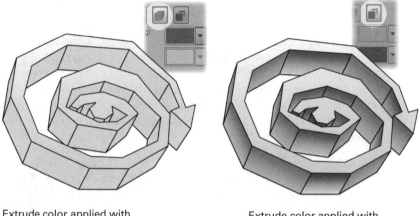

Extrude color applied with
Use Solid Color option

Extrude color applied with
Use Color Shading option

- **Draping your object's fill over the extrude effect**   *Draping,* as used in CorelDRAW's extrude effect, means, "treat each extrude group object's fill as a unique item." Say, for example, you have a patterned piece of cloth, and you drape it over a coffee table: you will see discontinuity in the pattern as each angle of the folds of cloth travels in different directions in 3D space. Similarly, draping creates discontinuity in a pattern and fountain fill that you apply to both the control object and the extrude group of objects, as shown in Figure 16-8. At right, with Drape Fills enabled, the polka-dot shape (with some lighting applied) truly looks dimensional,

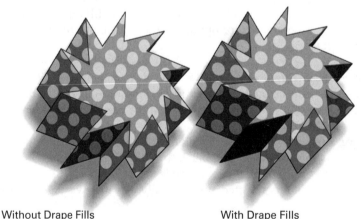

Without Drape Fills
Pattern is continuous (looks hokey).

With Drape Fills
Pattern is discontinuous (looks realistic).

FIGURE 16-8   The Drape Fills options can make or break the realism you're trying to illustrate.

even though the two-color bitmap fill doesn't change perspective (bitmap fills do not take on the rotation angle of extrude objects; they always face forward). At left, with Drape Fills turned off, the pattern proceeds across the object and the extrude group of objects in a continuous pattern, as though it's *projected* onto the surface of the shape instead of *being* the surface of the shape.

- **Using bevel color**   The Bevel Color option becomes available only if you've applied the bevel effect to an extruded shape. Bevel options are located on the Bevels selector on the Property bar (covered in the next section). This option can be used to give the bevel and the front face of an object the same color, while the extrude shapes retain the original type of fills you specified.

Using the Extrude Docker

If you're a longtime CorelDRAW user, you may have grown accustomed to applying extrude effects using a docker; new users will probably find the interactive editing methods and the options on the Property bar more convenient to access, but the Extrude docker is available via Window | Dockers | Extrude. The Extrude docker is organized into five areas: Camera (referring to shape), Rotation, Light, Color, and Bevel.

Although these options are organized differently from the Property bar, the same options are there. Using the docker method for extruding objects lets you choose extrude settings before applying them.

Extruding shapes is something many artists who compete with you for jobs might not be able to offer, especially if they don't own CorelDRAW! However, it's probably not a career-enhancer to use the extrude effect (or any other effect) as a substitute for your own talent as a designer. Use extrude with good judgment. Use it when you're in a design rut and need that certain something to perk up a piece. But don't let yourself get branded as the Extrude King or Queen (it even *sounds* rude!).

Chapter 17 continues *The Official Guide* Effects Extravaganza, with envelopes, lens effects, and additional fun stuff. Learn to take an object or group of objects from being close to what you want to draw to *exactly* what you want. Just rotate this page 180 degrees counterclockwise along your local X axis.

17 Using the Envelope Tool, Lens Effects, and Bevels

When you feel a design needs an element of realism—or even surrealism—to add attention, complexity, and that "certain something" that makes a shining piece absolutely brilliant, you turn to some of the effects CorelDRAW offers—specifically, the ones not covered yet in this book and, more specifically, effects that can add lighting to an object, bend it, twist it, and in general, modify it as though you are sculpting and not drawing.

This chapter reveals the inner workings of the envelope effect—probably the most advanced effect of its kind in any drawing program, and the Lens Effects docker, which provides some pretty wild variations on your artwork by overlaying it with a lens object. To round up this chapter's collection of neat embellishments, you'll also get hands-on experience with creating beveled objects; create anything from an emboss to a 3D starfish shape. These effects are easy to use and apply—the only hard part is deciding the *type* of effect that works best in your illustration!

 Note Download and extract all the files from the Chapter17.zip archive to follow the tutorials in this chapter.

What Does an Envelope Do?

You've probably seen this effect in stores a dozen times: the words "Fresh Fish" are shaped in the silhouette of a fish. In CorelDRAW, conforming objects to a different shape is done with the Envelope tool.

In CorelDRAW, you can start with a fresh envelope around an object, use presets, and copy a shape to use as an envelope of a different shape. Then, you edit the envelope until the shape suits your need. Envelopes are nondestructive; your original artwork can be restored at any time. The Property bar includes a Clear Envelope button when an enveloped object is selected with the Shape tool. Once an envelope has been defined, you edit the envelope exactly as you would a path—you can drag on segments and nodes and change the node control points to your heart's content.

Here are two visual examples of how useful the envelope effect can be. In the top illustration, the Artistic Text object is enveloped, and the envelope is based on an existing shape seen at right. The bottom illustration shows the envelope control segments and nodes in the process of being edited. It's true: the CorelDRAW envelope effect is just like playing with silly you-know-what!

Envelope shape copied from the object

Envelope manipulated

Creating Envelope Effects

When creating envelope effects, you can choose from three different methods. You can shape your envelope from scratch by defining a default envelope and then manually reshaping it. You can copy an envelope shape based on an object on the drawing page, and you can also use a preset shipped with CorelDRAW.

Using the Envelope Tool and Property Bar

Using the Envelope tool along with the Property bar options is the most intuitive way to apply envelopes. You'll find this tool in the Toolbox with the other effects, such as the Extrude and Drop Shadow tools.

With both the Envelope tool and an object selected, the Property bar displays the options shown here:

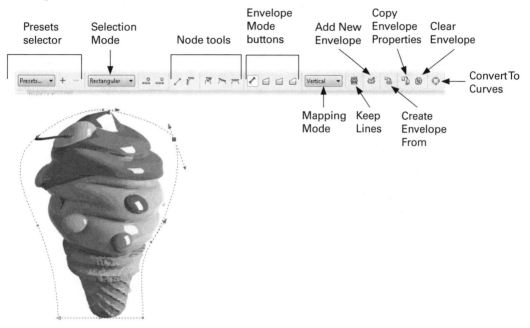

You'll get the best results from the Envelope tool if you follow a sequence of moves in CorelDRAW. Let's work through some basic maneuvers using the following steps.

Tutorial The Envelope, Please

1. Create or open an object (or group of objects) that you feel would make a good target for the envelope effect, and then choose the Envelope tool from the Toolbox. Notice that the Property bar shows Envelope options. The more intricate the object, the more noticeable the effect will be. In general, don't choose a rectangular shape to which you want to apply a rectangular envelope; the effect would be more or less defeated.
2. Click the Envelope Mode button that resembles a square with one corner higher than the other—Straight Line Mode—and notice the markers surrounding your shape.
3. Drag one of the nodes on your object in any direction. Notice the direction of movement is constrained and the shape of your object changes to match the envelope as you release the mouse button.
4. Click the next Envelope Mode button resembling a square with one curved side—Single Arc Mode. Drag any node in any direction, and notice the object shape changes, but this time you have some curvature going on with the edges of the envelope and the object(s) inside. Double Arc Mode provides more distortion, most noticeably when you drag a center envelope node instead of one of the four corner bounding nodes.

5. Notice that you can drag an envelope node to reshape the object, but the direction handles on either side of the node are fixed and won't budge. Click the Unconstrained Mode button, the leftmost Envelope Mode button on the Property bar. Now try dragging nodes and then their direction handles. The following illustration shows the object group in its original state, and then, at right, it's been worked over a little in Unconstrained Mode ... it looks reminiscent of how your packages occasionally arrive on Mondays, doesn't it? Seriously, though, nothing is hard and fixed in a CorelDRAW drawing and no changes are permanent.

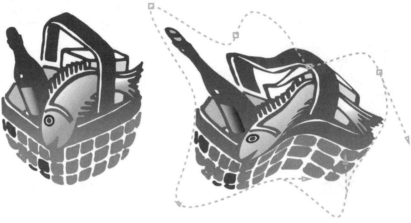

Original   Unconstrained Envelope Mode

Note For most effects in CorelDRAW, the Property bar offers Presets and the ability to add your own preset by clicking the + button; whereas clicking the minus button (-) deletes the currently selected preset on the drop-down list.

Clicking the Clear Envelope button on the Property bar removes the last applied envelope, but don't stop reading here! You can apply an envelope to an object that already has an envelope, by clicking the Add New Envelope button on the Property bar. If you want to return the object to its original state, you must click the Clear Envelope button, which returns you to the Pick tool and only reverts one stage of enveloping. You then have to select the Shape or Envelope tool, reselect the shape, and then click the Clear Envelope button, and *repeat* this somewhat tedious process until you return the object to its original form. A better option is Windows | Docker | Undo Manager; click on a previous saved state, reverting the object completely to its pre-envelope state. One click, nice trick.

Caution There is a limit, particularly with grouped objects in an envelope, to how much you can reshape before the paths that make up an object begin to self-intersect. Self-intersecting is usually an unwanted effect, so either use the tool sparingly on a group, or ungroup the group and apply similar envelope effects to individual objects.

Using the Envelope Docker

The Envelope docker provides an alternative to using the Envelope tool in combination with the Property bar. You can select options before they are actually applied. To open the Envelope docker, choose Effects | Envelope, or press CTRL + F7.

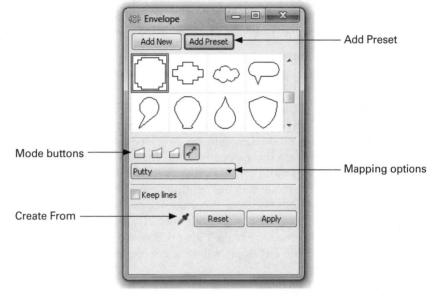

Add Preset

Mode buttons

Mapping options

Create From

Tip For speedy envelope editing, use the Pick tool to double-click any object that has an envelope. The enveloped object is immediately available for editing, and the Pick tool becomes the Envelope tool. A single click with the Shape tool also opens an enveloped object for editing.

Choosing an Envelope Mode

The Envelope mode you choose has no initial effect on the envelope you apply to an object; however, as you begin to move envelope nodes around, the selected Envelope mode offers features and limitations. Depending on the mode, corner and segment nodes take on different properties, which result in different capabilities to edit the envelope, as seen here:

Straight Line   Single Arc

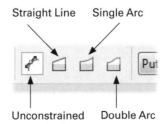

Unconstrained   Double Arc

Envelope modes (shown on the Property bar)

Tip At any time while editing an envelope, you can change its mode just by clicking a button on the Property bar. This capability gives you control over the overall shape you're trying to create. Any previous mode limitation is inherited with existing nodes, but nodes you've not changed inherit the new node property. For example, if your envelope is in Double Arc mode and you drag a node to make a swooping arc, and then you click the Straight Line Mode button on the Property bar, the arc remains an arc, but all the other nodes can now only be edited as connectors to straight lines.

These modes have the following effects during shaping operations:

- **Straight Line** This mode (the default) makes envelope segments into straight lines; in effect, you're manipulating an eight-point polygon when the envelope is in Straight Line mode. Dragging an envelope node creates a different polygon shape, and this mode serves you well for imitating the shape of a traffic sign, a simple house shape, and other outlines you create with straight line segments.
- **Single Arc** This mode sets the resulting envelope segments to curves and sets side nodes to Smooth nodes, and corner nodes to Cusp nodes; you can't change the angle of the Cusp for corner nodes directly, but you can change it when you reposition a side envelope node. Using this mode, dragging corner nodes creates a curved side on the envelope, whereas side nodes align with the path of the resulting curve.
- **Double Arc** This mode creates sine-wave-shaped sides. Behind the scenes, corner points become Cusp nodes, and side nodes become Smooth nodes. However, the curve handles of side nodes remain stationary in relation to the nodes, causing the segments to take on a double-arc shape. The same vertical and horizontal constraint restrictions as with the previous modes apply.
- **Unconstrained** Unconstrained mode gives you complete control over nodes, segments, and control handles for envelope elements; it gives you almost unlimited freedom to reshape an object. You can position either side or corner nodes as if they were vector path object nodes. In this mode, the Shape tool and Envelope tool let you *severely* reshape objects, and nodes can be dragged in any direction to shape the envelope in any way. Unconstrained mode also allows you to add or delete nodes, change any line segment states to straight or curved, or change the properties of nodes to Cusp, Smooth, or Symmetrical using Property bar buttons for these tasks.

Here's a visual example of the four modes, with a faint outline overlay indicating the original shape of the extruded phoenix object:

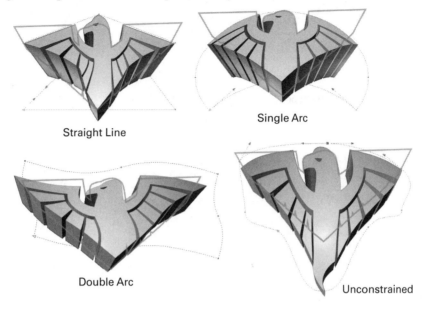

Straight Line

Single Arc

Double Arc

Unconstrained

 Note Modifier keys offer valuable ways to constrain the shaping of an envelope while using *Single Arc* mode. By holding key modifiers, you can quickly shape two sides concentrically or simultaneously. Hold SHIFT and drag any side or corner node to move the corresponding node on the opposite side in the *opposite* direction. Hold CTRL to move the corresponding node on the opposite side of the shape in the *same* direction and by an equal distance.

Choosing Envelope Mapping Options

Envelope Mapping options are available for both the Envelope docker and when using the Envelope tool and Property bar options, which control how the shape of an envelope changes your object's shape (see Figure 17-1). As you can see, Original and Putty mapping provide almost identical results for this particular group of objects and the envelope shape used here, but Horizontal and Vertical mapping give you the design opportunity to ignore the other envelope axis (Horizontal mapping ignores the vertical aspect of the envelope, and vice versa). This option is handy when you want to limit distortion of an envelope but don't have the time (or need!) to create a unique envelope for several different design purposes.

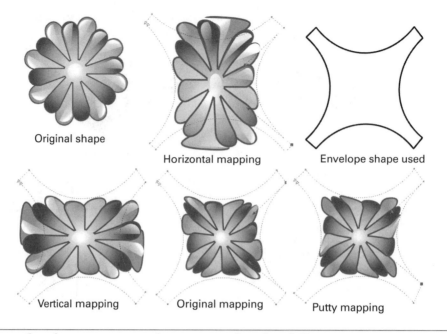

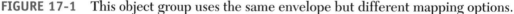

FIGURE 17-1   This object group uses the same envelope but different mapping options.

Mapping options give preference to the shape of your original object's node positions and path shapes. Four types are available: Putty (the default), Horizontal, Vertical, and Original.

The four Envelope mapping options, plus a special option for text and another to preserve lines, are worthy of explanation:

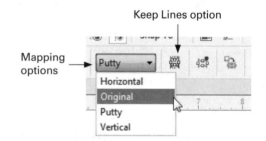

- **Putty**   This option (the default) distorts the shape of your object to match the envelope as closely as possible; the envelope's nodes are given priority over the nodes in the object being enveloped. Putty maps the envelope shape to your object and results in a smoothly mapped effect.
- **Horizontal**   This option maps the lines and node positions in your original object to match the horizontal shape of the envelope, without significantly altering the vertical shape of the original object.
- **Vertical**   This option maps the lines and node positions in your original object to the *vertical* shape of the envelope, with the horizontal shape mostly ignored.
- **Original**   This mapping type is similar to Putty. The main difference is that Original maps *only the outer shape* of your original object to the envelope shape. Corner nodes are mapped to the corner nodes of your original object's shape, whereas node positions and line shapes toward the inside of your object are

mapped using an averaging value. The result can be less distorted. If Putty mapping is too severe, try Original.

- **Keep Lines**   Using this option changes only the node positions in your object to match the envelope shape being applied, leaving any existing straight lines unaffected. If your object is already composed only of curved lines, choosing Keep Lines has no effect. When Keep Lines is *not* selected (the default), all node positions and lines in your original object are reshaped to match the envelope shape—even if this means changing straight lines to curved lines.

- **Text**   This option is the only mapping option available when a Paragraph Text object frame is selected. Text mode applies an envelope to the *frame* properties of a Paragraph Text object; the actual text and line of text are not distorted. This feature presents a wonderful opportunity to walk through a tutorial.

In this tutorial, you'll use the *Violin.cdr* file, which contains a silhouette drawing of a violin and a block of Paragraph Text attributed to Wikipedia. Your task is to fit the text inside the profile of the violin drawing. It's a class act, and this technique can be used for scores of designs. Especially music scores.

Tutorial   Creating a Text Envelope

1. In the *Violin.cdr* document, choose the Paragraph Text object with the Envelope tool.
2. On the Property bar, click the Create Envelope From button, and once your cursor changes to a targeting arrow, click the violin shape.

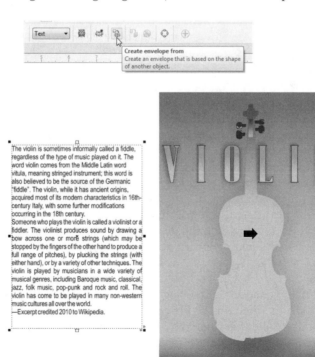

3. What you'll see next appears to be a mistake, but it isn't. There is a blue-dashed outline around the Paragraph Text with nodes and an outline in the shape of the violin, but the Paragraph Text is still a block of text. Click any of the dashed outline nodes and move it ever so slightly. CorelDRAW recognizes this as a change to the Paragraph Text and obligingly pours the text into the violin shape, as shown here.

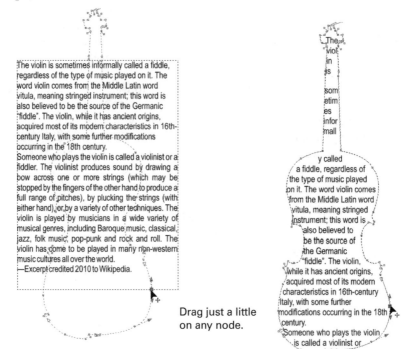

Drag just a little on any node.

4. Choose the Pick tool—the dashed outline is replaced with a red outline—and move the text to fit over the violin drawing. You will probably have to scale the enveloped text up a little. When you do this by dragging on a corner selection handle, try to keep the text just a little to the inside of the violin shape so there is a small margin between the text and the edge of the violin shape. You can also click-drag the object selection handles with the Shape tool to fine-tune the flow of the text.

5. With the Text tool, insert your cursor at the beginning of the paragraph, and then press ENTER to kick the text down so none of it is in the neck part of the violin, which looks awkward, reads terribly, and makes it hard to play the instrument. See Figure 17-2 as a reference for where your composition should be now.

6. Optionally, choose a more elegant typeface than Arial. Select the text with the Pick tool, and then on the Property bar, choose an installed font. In Figure 17-3, Mona Lisa Solid (distributed by ITC) is used. End of exercise—pretty fancy graphic using the Envelope tool!

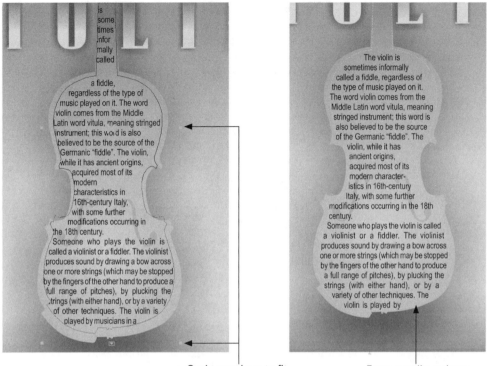

Scale envelope to fit
within violin.

Force text lines down
using Text tool.

FIGURE 17-2   Perform a little manual editing to make the envelope text fit within the
violin drawing.

Tip Once the text has been enveloped, you can add this shape to your Envelope
Presets list. Unfortunately, you cannot add an object as a preset envelope, but
only the product of enveloping an object based on the shape of a different object.

Let's move now from twisting objects to recoloring, magnifying, and, in general,
applying a lens over the object.

Tip You can apply *several* instances of an envelope, an envelope enveloping an
envelope, and so on, if you need a truly gnarly effect. After you've sampled the
envelope, click the cursor over the target shape three or four times until your
laughter subsides.

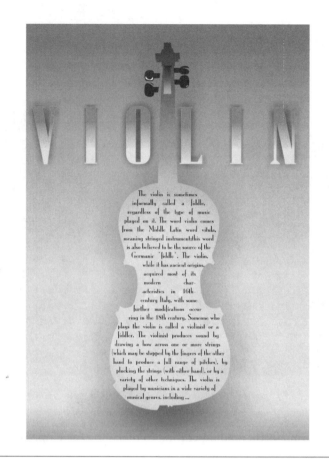

FIGURE 17-3   Create an elegant symbiosis of text as a graphic combined with a simple CorelDRAW drawing.

What's Behind a Lens Effect

Looking at your drawings with a lens effect object on top is like looking through a window or a magnifying glass. What you see is influenced by the *properties* of the glass. For example, tinted glass in the real world makes objects in the distance appear darker—you can easily simulate this phenomenon with the lens effect set to Color Limit applied to a 50 percent black object.

One of the more popular uses of this feature is to overlap a shape partially with a lens effect so you can see both affected and original areas at once. You can also freeze the lens effect object, capturing whatever's underneath the lens, and then move the lens object around, retaining the original view within the object.

Using the Lens Docker

The only way to apply a lens in CorelDRAW is through the Lens docker, opened by choosing Effects | Lens (ALT + F3). Figure 17-4 shows the Lens docker, whose options change depending on the function you choose. Operate the Lens docker by first placing an object—which becomes the lens object—over a *different* object (or several objects, vector or imported bitmaps), choosing a Lens type from the drop-down menu, and then choosing from different property options.

It's easier to understand lens effects if you just do it, as the running shoe manufacturer says. Let's take the Lens docker out for a trial spin.

Tutorial   Working with a Lens Effect

1. Create a rectangle and then with the Fill tool, click-drag to create a default Linear fountain fill from black to white. This rectangle will serve for this demonstration, but you'll most certainly get better effects using artwork of your own.
2. Create an ellipse, and, with the Pick tool, arrange the ellipse so it partially overlaps the rectangle to better see the creative possibilities of applying a lens to the ellipse object.

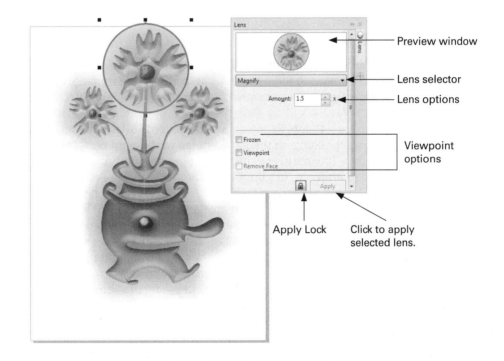

FIGURE 17-4   The Lens docker is where you customize effects to create the specific type of lens you need.

3. With the ellipse selected, open the Lens docker (ALT + F3).
4. Choose Custom Color Map from the docker's Lens selector drop-down list. Choose a deep blue from the From Color picker and then choose a bright green from the To Color picker.
5. The Apply Lock button, when in locked position, auto-applies the effect as you adjust the parameters. If you like to review stuff *before* applying it (like car wax and cosmetic surgery), click the lock icon to unlock the auto-apply state, and then click the Apply button to finalize the effect. The lens effect has remapped deeper shades in the rectangle to blues and lighter shades to greens. But areas of the rectangle not covered by the ellipse are still a black-to-white fountain fill.
6. Move the ellipse around a little to see how the lens effect changes only those areas of the rectangle that the ellipse covers.
7. With the ellipse partially eclipsing the rectangle, click the Frozen checkbox to put a checkmark in it.
8. Move the ellipse around. As you can see, its content colors remain constant, even when you move the ellipse totally away from the rectangle.
9. Show your friends this effect. This is *fascinating* stuff!

Tip The Apply Lock on the Lens docker applies lens effects immediately so you don't need to click the Apply button.

Exploring the Lens Effects

Each lens effect has different properties you set using the docker controls. Each lens type is covered in the sections to follow so you can better judge your starting point when you want to dress up an illustration with a certain type of lens effect.

- **Brighten lens effect**   Colors in objects seen through a Brighten lens can appear brighter *or* darker, depending on the Rate defined in the num box. The Rate can be between 100 and –100; positive values brighten up underlying colors, whereas negative values darken them. Brighten is a handy effect when, for example, part of an illustration you've worked on for days looks under- or overexposed when you print it. The solution is to design an object to use as the lens and place it directly on top, perfectly aligned with the area that prints poorly.
- **Color Add lens effect**   The Color Add lens fills the lens object with the color you choose by clicking the Node Color picker and then combining all underlying colors in an additive fashion—the culmination of the three primary colors being white instead of the real-world physical pigment model of subtractive colors, which eventually produce black when excessive amounts of primary colors are mixed. As an example, if you created an object with a red-to-blue fountain fill, and then put a red Color Add lens object over it, the red areas will look unaffected at all rates, whereas the blue areas will change to cyan. This effect is good for adding a tint to isolated areas of an illustration and imported bitmaps. Any color can be

added within a range of 0 to 100 percent in increments of 5 percent. Higher values add more color; 0 adds no color at all.

- **Color Limit lens effect**   The Color Limit lens produces an effect that looks like the opposite effect produced by the Color Add lens. Color Limit tints underlying areas and decreases brightness in all underlying areas *except* for the hues in the color you choose from the docker. Color Limit can be quite useful, for example, to highlight an object in a composition by deemphasizing all other objects.

- **Custom Color Map lens effect**   This type of lens object looks at the original colors in the underlying objects based on brightness values and then reproduces the design with the remapping colors you specifying on the Lens docker. Usually, you want to choose a deep From color and a light To color; this tints and colorizes a drawing or bitmap in a predictable way. You can also remap your drawing colors in untraditional ways; mapping options include three palette-mapping choices: Direct Palette, Forward, and Reverse Rainbow.

  - Choosing Direct Palette offers two colors (From and To) and maps the colors found in your objects evenly between the brightness values of colors found directly between these two around the color wheel.

  - Conversely, Forward Rainbow has the same effect as Direct Palette, but, in this case, each of the object colors is mapped to *all* colors between your two chosen colors in a clockwise rotation. For example, if you choose red as the From color and green as the To color, instead of a blend between these two colors throughout your illustration, you'll get greens making a transition to magenta and then purple recoloring the underlying design. If you want the entire spectrum of the rainbow, choose red as the Start color and violet (purple) as the End color.

  - The Reverse Rainbow option has the effect of mapping the colors in your object to the RGB brightness values of all colors between your two chosen colors in a counterclockwise direction. If you choose this option after setting up Forward Rainbow colors, you'll get a chromatic inverse of Forward Rainbow color mapping, a highly solarized look, much like what developed physical film would look like it if you opened the back of the camera before rewinding the film.

Tip To swap your selected From and To colors quickly in the Lens docker while applying Custom Color Map Lens effects, click the small button located between the From and To color selectors. You might need to click Apply to make the swap and change what the lens object is doing.

- **Fish Eye lens effect**   A conventional camera "fish eye" lens has a very wide angle of view. CorelDRAW's Fish Eye lens performs the virtual equivalent; you can produce exceptionally distorted artwork, which can be an interesting, if not an everyday, effect in commercial design. Fish Eye is controlled by setting the rate of distortion within a range of 1,000 to –1,000 percent. You'll probably find these extreme values useless in your work. At lower rates, the effect is subtle while retaining a sense of drama and dynamics.

- **Heat Map lens effect**   The Heat Map lens is similar to the Color Map lens effect except the colors are predetermined (there are no specific color options). The effect simulates "black body" physics: a hypothetical object (in space) absorbs all light, and the presumption in this hypothesis is that the body is warm. With the Heat Map lens, colors in underlying objects on the warm side of the color wheel (red, orange, yellow) appear in shades of red or orange. Cool colors (green, blue, and violet) appear in shades of white, yellow, purple, blue, and light blue. You can also offset the color mapping by using the Palette rotation spin box. When you use the Palette rotation spin box, values between 0 and 49 usually make colors appear warmer, and values between 50 and 100 make colors appear cooler.

- **Invert lens effect** The Invert lens applies color inversion to the colors of underlying objects. In this case, colors are directly mapped to colors found on the opposite side of a color wheel. Black areas change to white, light grays turn to dark grays, reds turn to greens, yellows turn to blues, and so on. To make a "day and night" composition follow these steps:

1. Open the *Sundial.cdr* image.
2. Put the black half-circle over the left half of the logo.
3. Choose Invert from the Lens selector list on the Lens docker.

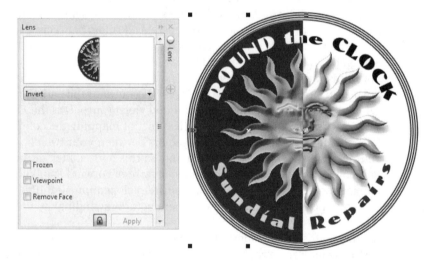

- **Magnify lens effect** Although this lens produces a straightforward and predictable effect, it can make underlying objects larger *or* smaller, depending on the settings you enter for the Rate value. The Rate can be set within a range of 0.1 to 100, where values between 1 and 100·increase magnification and values less than 1 reduce magnification. Try opening *Swamp Water.cdr*, and magnify the 1-point text at the bottom of the bottle so the public can see what's in this "sports drink." Bitmaps are resolution dependent, so you can only magnify the image of the bottle so much. The text in this composition is, however, a pure native CorelDRAW vector. Place the ellipse over the fine print in the image, and then magnify it **8×** or even higher if you like, and the text remains crisp, legible, and, in this example, you'll get a little reminder about what it is you're potentially putting into your system.

- **Tinted Grayscale lens effect**   By default, the Tinted Grayscale lens converts the colors of underlying objects to grayscale values, which is terrific if you're into black-and-white photography, but you can use any color you like, thus tinting photos and drawings just by choosing a color from the Color flyout palette on the docker. Remember that digital images use the additive color model, so the lighter the lens color, the fainter the resulting composition. You might want this effect, however; try light grays and light warm browns to make new photographs look like they were originally taken in the 1940s.

- **The Transparency lens effect**   This lens effect is a simplified version of the effects you can achieve using the Transparency tool on the Toolbox. Blending modes are unavailable, and the object itself becomes transparent—not the underlying objects—to varying degrees based on the rate you set on the Lens docker. The perk to using a Transparency lens effect over the Transparency tool is that you can freeze the effect and then move a partially transparent copy of the underlying area anywhere you like on the page.

- **The Wireframe lens effect**   This lens effect converts the color and outline properties of objects to specific colors; this effect is useful for pointing out the technical details in an illustration. You can set the outline and fill colors of objects beneath the lens to any uniform color you choose by clicking the Outline or Fill flyout palettes on the docker. The fill and outline colors of your objects are replaced with the selected colors, whereas outline properties—such as applied widths and line styles—are ignored; Wireframe produces a fixed-width outline.

Although *Burger.cdr*—the file you'll work with in a moment—is a good illustration, let's say the fictitious client, Mr. Beefbarn, wants to "accentuate" his sixteenth of a pound all-beef special by plumping up the illustration for the advertisement instead of the actual weight of his product. Instead of using the envelope effects (which will not work on imported photographs), in a few mouse clicks, you can create a shape that roughly fits over only the burger in the drawing and then apply the Fish Eye lens.

Tutorial Changing Object Size with the Fish Eye Lens

1. Open *Burger.cdr*; with a Pen tool, draw a shape that roughly matches the shape of the hamburger, just a little larger so the lens effect works. If you want to cut to the chase, creating an ellipse around the burger provides decent results.
2. On the Lens docker, with the object selected, choose Fish Eye. Set the Rate to **65%**. If the Apply button is unlocked, click Apply now to see the results. Try moving the lens object around a little if the illusion that the burger is almost twice its original size isn't perfect.
3. Let's say Mr. Beefbarn gets on a health-food kick and wants you to design a leaner burger. You just crank the Fish Eye lens effect to –90 and then click Apply. In one click and perhaps moving the lens object a little, today's health-conscious culture will buy the advertisement, if not the burger.

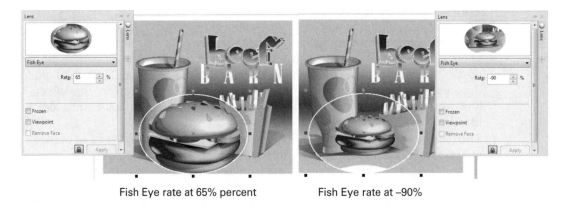

Fish Eye rate at 65% percent   Fish Eye rate at –90%

FIGURE 17-5 Two different Fish Eye lens effects settings are used to bloat and pucker the underlying drawing area.

In Figure 17-5, you can see, at left, the result of an ellipse shape with the Fish Eye lens type defined at a rate of 65%. The burger bulges toward the viewer, and Mr. Beefbarn is happy. At right, a negative rate, –90%, is defined using the same lens object. Happy client and very little editing work needed.

Using Lens Options

Only one option has been discussed so far with the Lens docker: the *types* of effects. You'll gain more control of your effects when the other options on the docker are explained in the following sections. Locking an effect, altering viewpoints, and controlling whether the page background is involved in an effect open extra doors to this docker.

Using the Frozen Option

The Frozen option "freezes" the view seen through any lens effect—even if the lens object itself is moved. You can then apply and freeze the lens object view and use it for other purposes. A Frozen lens effect object can actually be ungrouped to reveal a set of objects based on the lens you've applied. If the effect is applied above a bitmap, the result is often a complete copy of the filtered image area, and it can be exported as a bitmap.

After choosing the Frozen option, the lens object can be ungrouped (CTRL + U). This action converts the effect to a collection of ungrouped vector and/or bitmap objects. Each of the objects representing the complete effect becomes a separate object, including the lens object, the page background, and the objects within the lens view.

Changing a Lens Viewpoint

The Lens Viewpoint option lets you move a lens and keep the view inside the lens constant—like freezing a lens but this option *keeps the effect dynamic*. When you check Viewpoint on the docker, an Edit button appears. You then click-drag interactively to reposition the viewpoint of the lens effect either by using your cursor (indicated onscreen by an *X*) or by entering numeric values in the X and Y page position boxes.

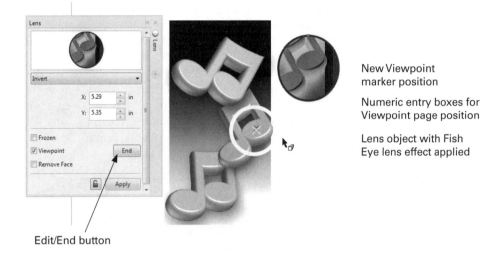

New Viewpoint marker position

Numeric entry boxes for Viewpoint page position

Lens object with Fish Eye lens effect applied

Edit/End button

Tip The view seen through a lens object depends on the object order on a layer—all objects layered below the lens object appear in the lens. When the Viewpoint is repositioned, you may find that an object is not visible. Arranging objects in back of the lens object causes them to be affected; arranging them in front of the lens object prevents the lens effect from changing them.

The default Viewpoint position of a lens effect is always the center of your object, but you can move it anywhere you like. After moving it, click the End button and then the Apply button on the Lens docker to set the new position.

Using the Remove Face Option

Remove Face is available for only a few types of lens effects. It lets you specify whether other objects and the page background participate in the effect. By default, whenever a lens effect is applied, the background—your page, which is usually white—is involved in the effect.

If the lens you are using changes the colors—such as with Custom Color Map—and you *don't* want your background to be changed within the view seen through the lens object, selecting this option leaves the background unaltered. The design idea is to remap only the objects under the lens. Without Remove Face, a background on your drawing page is tinted, but after Remove Face is applied, the page background of your composition is unaffected by the tinting effect.

Using the Bevel Effect

The Window | Dockers | Effects | Bevel docker gives you a way to make objects dimensional, but not as completely three-dimensional as the Extrude tool. The Bevel docker offers two different types of engraving effect: Emboss and Soft Edge. The Emboss mode is an automated routine that creates duplicates of an object, offsets them, and gives them different colors to create the effect of, for example, a seal crimped onto a piece of paper like notary publics used to do. Although you can manually create this emboss effect, the Bevel docker creates a dynamic, linked group whose color and position can change when you define different light intensities and light angles.

Here are visual examples of the emboss effect. If you choose to use Emboss mode, create a background for the object because either the highlight or the shadow object might not be visible against the page background. Usually, a color similar to the background will serve you well for the object color. You can use any fill, including bitmaps and fountain fills, for the object you want to emboss, but the resulting emboss objects will not *feature* the fill, only solid (uniform) colors.

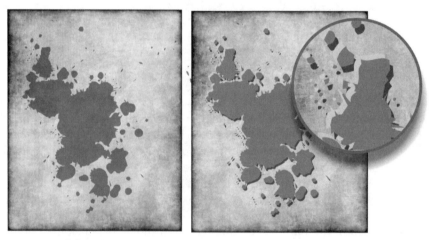

Original   Two offset duplicates create the effect.

Here, you can see the Bevel docker and the options available while applying the Emboss mode.

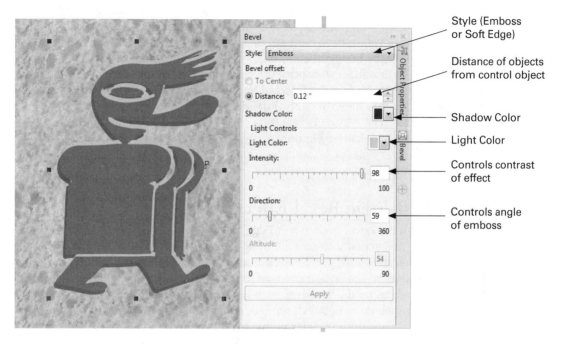

Style (Emboss or Soft Edge)

Distance of objects from control object

Shadow Color

Light Color

Controls contrast of effect

Controls angle of emboss

Here's a rundown of what the options do on the Bevel docker in Emboss mode:

- **Bevel Offset – Distance**   This combination num box and spin box is used to set the distance of the duplicate objects from the original. You don't gain anything visually by setting a high value for an object; rather, this box is used to set a relational distance, depending on the size of the object to which you apply the emboss effect. For example, a 4" object looks embossed if you use a 0.09" Distance setting, but the effect looks a little phony at greater distances. On the other hand, an 8" object will probably not look embossed with a 0.09" Distance setting—0.16", however, scales the effect proportionately to the object and the emboss effect looks good. If you need to resize an object, plan to redefine the Distance setting for the Emboss mode after you scale the parent object.
- **Shadow Color**   The color of the object has a direct influence on the color of the shadow object behind the control object. For example, if you create an emboss effect with a blue object, the shadow object is a dark blue, even if you set the color to black. You can neutralize the shadow color by defining the color opposite the control object; for example, if you have a cyan circle, set the Shadow Color to red, the color complement of cyan. The resulting color is always duller than the color you define because—well, it's a *shadow*! Shadow Color is unaffected by the Intensity option.

- **Light Color**   This controls the color of the highlight object; it affects neither the control object's color nor the color or brightness of the shadow object. Light Color at full intensity displays the color you choose, and as you decrease intensity, the Light Color blends with the object color—Light Color does not depend on any object's color you might have beneath the effect. As light intensity decreases, a bitmap-filled object's highlight color changes from its original color to white.
- **Intensity**   Use this slider to control the contrast of the emboss effect. Although the shadow object's color is not affected by intensity, the highlight object's color is.
- **Direction**   Use this slider to control the direction that light seems to cast on the emboss object(s). A Direction setting of 0° points the highlight at 3 o'clock, traveling counterclockwise. Therefore, if you need a highlight on an emboss effect at 11 o'clock (a very classic lighting position), set the Direction at about 160°.
- **Altitude**   This option is reserved for Bevel mode, covered next.

Creating Soft-Edge Bevel Effects

The other mode on the Bevel docker, Soft Edge, performs many more calculations than the Emboss mode and actually creates a bitmap image, masked by the control object, which you can adjust dynamically. The Shadow Color, Light Intensity (and Color), and Direction options on the docker produce predictable results, much like those you get when using Emboss mode, but because the Soft Edge mode is generated to bitmap format, the results look more detailed, refined, and almost photorealistic in appearance. In addition to having an Altitude slider in this mode, you have To Center as an available option in the Bevel Offset field. Here's what it does and how To Center works.

All soft-edge bevels are produced from the edge of a shape traveling toward its center. If, for example, you've created a circle that's 3" across and then type a Distance offset value in the num box in any amount less than 1.5", you'll see a dimensional, sloping bevel created inside the circle, with a flat top in the shape of the circle in its center. If, however, you type in a value greater than 1.5", the center of the object bevels to a point, and the front face of the object is entirely lost. The reason this happens is that the bevel effect travels toward the interior of the shape, and half of the 3" diameter of this circle is 1.5". Just keep in mind the size of the shape to which you apply a bevel effect to gain total control over the effect. If, on the other hand, you intend for the sides of the bevel to come to a point, you don't need to set values in the Distance field; you choose To Center, click Apply, and CorelDRAW creates the maximum-width bevel, meeting at a point inside the shape. You can create interesting marine creatures such as a starfish by using the Polygon tool to create the silhouette of a starfish. Then you fill the object and choose To Center to auto-create a very lifelike composition.

Here are two different looks for the bevel effect: at top, the Distance is set for Offset, and, at bottom, To Center has been chosen.

Distance: 0.18"   To Center chosen

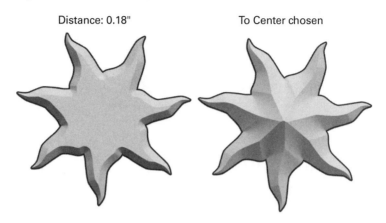

Determining Altitude

Altitude determines the angle of the sun illuminating the bevel effect … if the sun were actually *involved* in creating the effect. Altitude is a simulation that does something a little different than Shadow and Light Color do to increase and decrease the contrast of the effect. At Altitude settings that approach 90 degrees, you lessen the difference in brightness between the darkest and lightest areas in the bevel effect. Think of a coin on the sidewalk at high noon; you can't really see the embossed famous person on the coin because the bulges and recesses on the coin are fairly evenly lit. It's the same with the Bevel Altitude setting; smaller Altitude amounts cast the hypothetical sun closer to the hypothetical horizon, and you get more contrast on the bevel. If you want the bevel effect to have the greatest visual impact on your work, use a moderate Altitude value most of the time.

This chapter has shown you a lot of effects that do more to please than to stun your audience. Envelopes, lens effects, and bevels speak of a quiet elegance that strikes the viewer on a subliminal level. It's well worth your time to become proficient with these effects for the future when you need a touch of photorealism in a drawing, something that strikes the audience without hitting them over the head.

The following chapter is totally twisted—but in a *good* sort of way. Chapter 18 delves into not only the Shape Editing tools in X7 (there's an astounding eight of them), but also three types of Distort options. So you have eleven ways to make a boring object into an interesting one, and an opportunity to treat vector objects more like paint and other liquids. Turn the page and immerse yourself in some funny and fun creativity.

PART VII

Special Effects in CorelDRAW

18 The Shape Editing Tools and Distortions

Once you've created an object, you might want to *edit* it, and that is the theme of this chapter. Whether it's a preset object drawn with the Rectangle tool or manual design work created with the Pen tools, not even a skilled illustrator is always satisfied with her first try. In the pages to follow, you'll learn various techniques to massage that almost-perfect shape into *exactly* the shape you've envisioned. This chapter covers CorelDRAW's tools and features for treating vector objects as though they're malleable in an organic way and vector paths as though they're as linear as a crumbled piece of paper. Often, creating an *approximation* of an object you need is a good Step One. Then with a pull and a tug here and there, bulging an area or roughening an edge, you'll get quicker results than if you had built the object from scratch. You'll also see in this chapter that you can add visual complexity and embellishments that would be hard to achieve using other methods.

 Note Download and extract all the files from the Chapter18.zip archive to follow the tutorials in this chapter.

The Shape Edit Tool Group

Corel has added tools to the Shape Edit group on the Toolbox: Smear, Twirl, Attract, and Repel are incredibly dramatic and powerful tools that will make you feel as though you're dragging your finger through wet paint. Let's begin with a survey from top to bottom in this group; the Shape tool at top is such a fundamentally important tool in CorelDRAW that it's covered in Chapter 9 and several other chapters in this book, but not here. Here's the group; draw an object and get set to have a lot of fun.

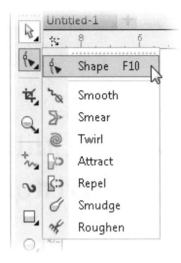

Using the Smooth Tool

New to version X7 is a tool that can undo accidental bumps and curves you've inadvertently created along a path. You can get better results with the Smooth tool than you can selecting nodes with the Shape tool and then using the Reduce Nodes slider, because you might want some areas to remain rough, while smoothing other areas. With the Smooth tool, you have complete control over which areas are smoothed.

Three controls on the Property bar govern how the Smooth tool works:

- **Nib Size**   Determines the size of your cursor.
- **Rate**   Determines how quickly the tool responds. At a fast rate (a high value), scrubbing over a path produces immediate results; the curve is smoother and usually there are fewer nodes. At low rates, you can be more selective and leisurely about smoothing your object.
- **Pen Pressure**   Works only if you are using a tablet or a digitizing stylus. You set how much pressure is applied with the tool, and what result you get when you press harder or lighter. You might want pressure set to determine the *rate* of the Smooth tool.

Here, you can see an example of the purposefulness of the Smooth tool. At upper left is a design that was (unfortunately) drawn with the Freehand tool; the B-Spline tool would have been a better choice. At bottom, you can see the Smooth tool at work over areas that need the most help to create this design of a kidney-shaped retro coffee table. At right, the design is realized.

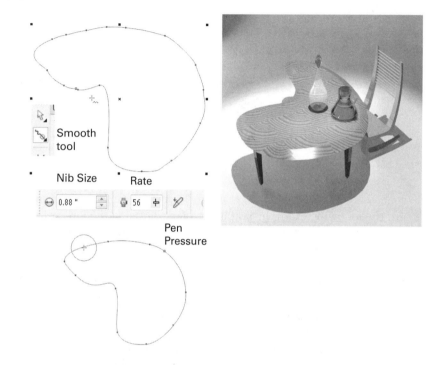

The Smear Tool

The Smear tool behaves like the Smudge tool's big brother (covered later), offering more plasticity to areas you drag over, more control, and with a little practice, a gallery of freeform shapes that look like anything but vector graphics. On the Property bar, you have the following options:

- **Nib Size**   Nib size determines the tool's diameter.
- **Pressure**   Artists who use a mouse can use the num entry box or the flyout slider to set the tool's intensity.
- **Smooth and Pointy Smear buttons**   Use one or the other type of smear to affect the end of a stroke. Smooth is good for natural, freeform distortion, whereas Pointy—an aesthetically severe effect—might be useful for embellishing machined parts and metal band logos.

- **Pen Pressure** Digitizing tablet users should click the Pen Pressure button to use physical pressure to add character to strokes.

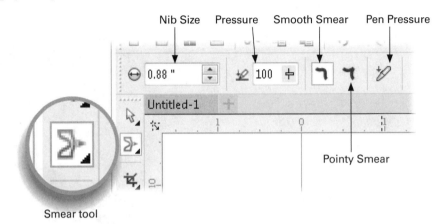

Nib Size   Pressure   Smooth Smear   Pen Pressure

Pointy Smear

Smear tool

In the following example, you'll get a feel for using the Smear tool in Smooth mode to create a stylistic hairdo for a cartoon character who has no hair. Yet.

Tutorial   Adding the Smear to Your Artistic Career

1. Open *Cartoon Guy.cdr*. Most of the drawing is on a locked Layer 1. The top of his scalp is on Layer 2, which is unlocked. Select the scalp object (press CTRL + A, which is the shortcut for Select All).
2. Select the Smear tool; set the size of the tool to about **.75"**, the Pressure to about **85%**, and the style of the smear to smooth by pressing the Smooth Smear button on the Property bar.
3. There is no "right" or "wrong" in this example; you're just experimenting. Try dragging from the fellow's scalp upward. Then try dragging on the area you just dragged. Repetition over an area can lead to quite intricate shapes.

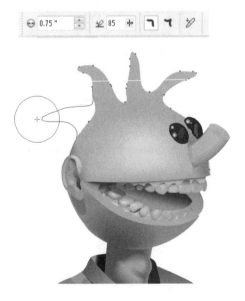

4. Set the pressure lower, say, to 35, and drag from the scalp away toward the top. You might want to drag repeatedly over this area; a pressure of 35 creates a bumpy skull, similar to the author's, as attested to in this illustration.
5. Now press the Pointy Smear button, try setting the Pressure to **100%**, and when the fellow's head is totally messed up, choose the Fill tool (toward the bottom of the Toolbox).

6. Drag from the base of the scalp upward, and then click the Start color node. When the Node Color picker appears, click the down arrow to expand the box, click the Eyedropper tool, and then sample a scalp color very close to where the Start node is located.

7. Repeat Step 6, except choose the End color node and sample a medium mustard color for the hair. Adjust the Start and End colors so a transition between scalp and blonde hair color is created. You can see the result in Figure 18-1. Write your boss's name at the top of the page, and then think twice about printing several copies, especially if you're on a network printer.

The Twirl Tool

The Twirl tool has clockwise and counterclockwise direction features on the Property bar, in addition to options for setting the pressure and size of the tool. Depending on the size and pressure, you can create just about anything from a sink drain to a gentle swash on a typeface character. You can also get creative and apply a twirl to objects that you've already modified with other Shape Edit group tools.

An unobvious technique to use with the Twirl tool—*and* the other Shape Edit tools— is to click, drag, and then hold the mouse button at the end of a stroke. Doing this increases the distortion at the end of the affected object and provides a novel effect.

Try this tool out to create a pinwheel effect in the following tutorial.

FIGURE 18-1   The Smear tool can quickly change parts of a path without the need to use the Shape tool.

Tutorial Creating a Stylized Sun

1. Open *Suntoon.cdr*. The sunbeam object behind the face is a polygon object whose outer points were dragged inward with the Shape tool, in case you'd like to build one in the future.
2. Select the polygon object, and then choose the Twirl tool from the Toolbox.
3. Set the Nib Size to **3/4"** (.75") so it scales with the drawing, set the Pressure to about **60**, and it's your call whether to twirl the sunbeams clockwise or counterclockwise.
4. Drag in a circular direction around the sunbeam object, as shown in the following illustration. If you want to create a little solar flare action, remain over an area (don't drag, just hold) for a moment or two.

The Attract and Repel Tools

These two tools in the Shape Edit group could also be called the Pull and the Push tools, for this is what they do when you drag them over a selected object. To add to their versatility, for example, the effect you get with the Attract tool depends on whether you begin on the inside, dragging outward, or on the outside, dragging inward. Either approach is valid with the Repel tool as well. There's an additional trick you can perform with either tool: click, drag just a little to start the tool's effect, and then *hold* over an area of an object. Doing this sort of turns the Attract tool into a "Pucker tool"—especially visible on corners of rectangles and other sharp turns in paths, and the Repel tool becomes a "Bloat tool."

Try this simple tutorial to get an idea of the power of the Repel tool on a star shape. You'll turn it into an asterisk,

Tutorial Repelling a Polygon Object

1. Choose the Polygon tool from the Object group on the Toolbox.
2. Hold CTRL to constrain the shape to symmetrical, and then drag a shape that's about 3" across.

3. Press F10 to get the Shape tool, and then drag the node that's at about 1 o'clock toward the center of the object until it looks like a very spiky star. Fill it with any color. See callout 1 in Figure 18-2.

4. Zoom in, and then choose the Repel tool. Set the size of the nib to about ½" (.5"), and the pressure to about **56%**.

5. Position the cursor carefully so it's inside the tip of the top point of the star. Then click-hold the mouse button until the preview outline of the intended effect doesn't get any larger. See callout 2 in Figure 18-2.

6. Repeat Step 5 with the other four points. Then find a sentence that claims a new car will get 500 miles per gallon, put the asterisk after that statement, and then give the copywriter the bad news.

Using the Smudge Brush

The Smudge brush is sort of a paint tool in a drawing program: you can dramatically alter shapes in a natural, painterly fashion, with results that would take hours using any other method. You move areas of a vector object by dragging from a starting point inside the object and dragging outward, or starting outside and dragging inside the object. The result is a little like the Eraser tool if you move object areas inward, and if you drag from the inside out, the result might remind you of dripping paint.

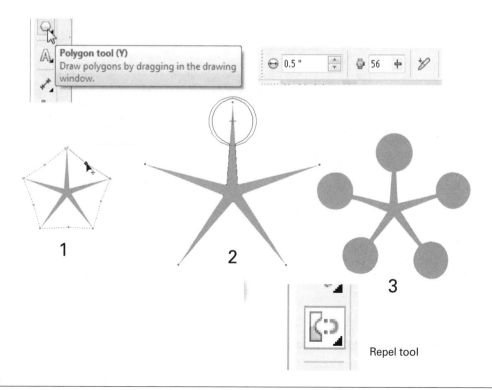

FIGURE 18-2   The Repel tool can make a bulbous area on a sharp-cornered object.

Applying Smudge to Shapes

Using the Smudge brush, you can alter the outline shapes of open or closed paths by click-dragging across the outline path, in either an outward direction (to add to the object) or an inward direction (to create a recess in the object). As you drag, the path is altered according to your drag action and the Smudge Brush cursor's shape settings. The following illustration shows a creative example of using the Smudge brush: the rectangle is almost a puzzle piece now, the editing took less than five seconds, and the resulting path can be refined using the Shape tool or other CorelDRAW features.

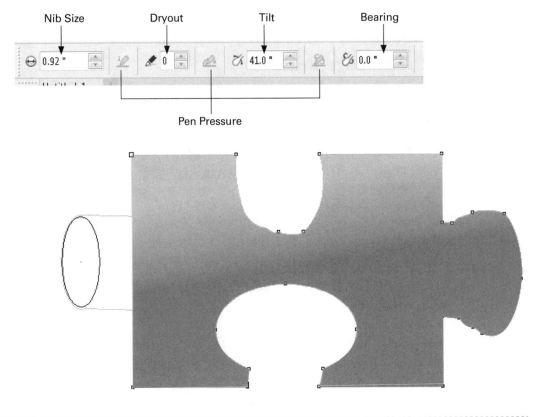

Nib Size   Dryout   Tilt   Bearing

Pen Pressure

> **Tip** Smudging cannot be applied to groups of objects, bitmaps, or mesh-filled objects. It will work on objects that have been altered using effects (blends, extrudes, drop shadows) but can be unpredictable used with effects like envelopes, distortions, and some contours.

Choosing Smudge Brush Property Bar Options

The Smudge brush works quite differently from other tools. You can control how the Smudge brush effect is applied by varying tool properties such as the tilt, angle, and size of the nib; by adjusting how quickly the effect diminishes; or by using optional pressure settings, which are unavailable unless you are using a stylus and tablet.

While the Smudge brush is selected, the Property bar offers these options for controlling the shape and condition of your Smudge Brush cursor:

- **Nib Size**   Nib Size can be set between hundredths of an inch up to 2 inches.
- **Use Pen Pressure**   If you have a digitizing tablet and stylus that supports pressure, choose this option so the Smudge brush will react to pressure you apply, increasing the width of the nib.
- **Dryout**   This option sets a rate for the effect of gradually reducing the width of a smudge according to the speed of your click-drag action and can be set between −10 and 10. Higher values reduce the width of your smudge more quickly (as shown next), whereas a setting of 0 deactivates the Dryout effect. Interestingly, with negative Dryout values, your stroke begins small and eventually widens as you click-drag.
- **Tilt**   The Tilt value controls the elliptical shape of the Smudge brush nib. Tilt is measured in degrees set between 15 (a flat-shaped nib) and 90 (a circular-shaped nib), as shown next. Tilt and Bearing values work in combination with each other to control the Smudge nib shape.
- **Bearing**   Bearing lets you set the angle of the cursor in circular degrees (0 to 359). The effects of changing bearing are most noticeable at lower Tilt values—such as 12 degrees, as shown here. It's the rotational angle of a *noncircular* tip.

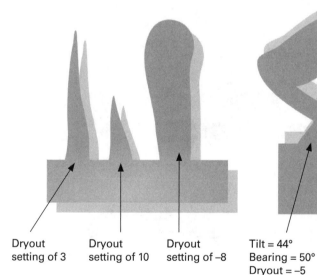
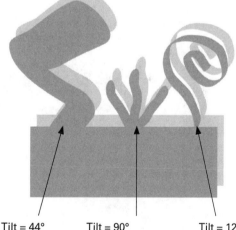

Dryout setting of 3

Dryout setting of 10

Dryout setting of −8

Tilt = 44°
Bearing = 50°
Dryout = −5

Tilt = 90°
Bearing = irrelevant
Dryout = 0

Tilt = 12°
Bearing = 130°
Dryout = 0

The Roughen Brush

To add a touch of character and imperfection to ultraprecise objects, you have the Roughen brush.

The Roughen brush alters the course of an outline path on an object, and depending on the setting you use on the Property bar, you can achieve effects that range from lightning bolts to really gnarly lines to zigzag patterns, just by dragging on the edge of a shape. The options that are available when using the Roughen brush can be seen here on the Property bar. They're similar to those of the Smudge brush.

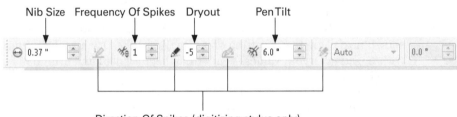

- **Nib Size** This sets the size of the Roughen brush. Scale the nib in proportion to the selected object you want to roughen. By default, the scale of the nib is measured in inches.
- **Frequency Of Spikes** You'll see that the Roughen brush creates irregularity on an object edge that is similar to the peaks and valleys of a mountain

range—it varies the object outline in an "in and out" fashion. At low frequency values, the roughened object outline features large, varying areas. At high frequency settings, you attain a zigzag effect. The range of frequency is from 1 to 10 (10 produces zigzags).

- **Dryout**   Like the Smudge brush, the Roughen brush can "dry out" at the end of a stroke you drag with the cursor. The range of dryout effect is from −10 (the stroke tapers in the opposite direction in which you click-drag) to 10 (the stroke tapers and fades). At 0, the stroke remains consistent. The greater the dryout setting, negative or positive, the more natural a roughened appearance you can achieve.

- **Pen Tilt**   This property can be used in combination with stroking over areas that have already been roughened. At 0 degrees, you increase the irregularity of the spikes, often to a point of abstract, amateurish artwork. At high Tilt settings (such as 90 degrees), however, dragging over an area that's already roughened can smooth out some of the jaginess and add a subtle, organic feel to a path segment.

- **Direction Of Spikes**   This feature is, by default, set to Automatic; it is not editable unless CorelDRAW is told (in Options) that you are using a digitizing tablet that supports pressure/direction. In default mode, spikes run perpendicular to the path you modify with the tool.

Try this basic tutorial to get a feel for the Roughen brush and a creative way to use it.

Tutorial   Adding Character with the Roughen Brush

1. Open *Jack O Lantern.cdr*. All objects except for the crescent moon smile are locked on Layer 1, and Layer 2 is selected and unlocked.

2. Select the smile object by pressing CTRL + A (Edit | Select All), which selects the smile and switches you over to the Pick tool, saving you the step of switching to the Pick tool manually.

3. Choose the Roughen brush and then on the Property bar, set the Nib Size to ½" (for shark-scaled teeth—use a smaller size for less intimidating jaws). Set the Frequency Of Spikes to **1**, Dryout to **0**, and Tilt to about **8** degrees, in case you want to modify the toothy smile after you've completed the next step.

4. Drag the cursor over the top edge of the smile object, but start about ½" from the absolute left and end ½" before the right side. The Roughen brush tends to mess up path areas where there is a sharp change in direction.

5. Perform Step 4 on the bottom smile object. Optionally, you can duplicate the smile object (select it and then press CTRL + C and then CTRL + V), fill it with yellow from the color palette, press SHIFT + PAGEDOWN to put the object behind the black smile, and then use the nudge keys up and left to offset its position, creating a highlight to the carved effect, as the pumpkin's eyes display in Figure 18-3.

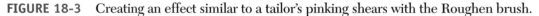

FIGURE 18-3 Creating an effect similar to a tailor's pinking shears with the Roughen brush.

Mastering Distortion Effects

The Distort tool in the Effects group on the Toolbox has three modes of operation, each producing a different effect you can also customize, plus the Property bar has a Preset selector to introduce you to some wild effects. The Distort tool and options are also *dynamic,* which means they create distortion without ruining your original. Distortion properties can be edited at any time, and they can be cleared from your shape, just like envelopes. This undoable property makes the Distort tool unlike the Shape Edit tool group discussed at the beginning of this chapter.

Distortion effects also change your object without affecting its other properties such as outline width and fill. Using distortion, the curve values and node properties are dramatically changed, and the more complex your object is to begin with, the more dramatic the distortion effect will be. Adobe Illustrator users will feel right at home; although distortions are similar to Punk & Bloat, they go beyond this effect in variety and complexity, and when you're using CorelDRAW distortions, you can restore your objects at any time. Distortion effects are great for a number of illustration challenges, including organic-type effects. You can create flower shapes, zippers, swirly galaxies in space—not even the sky's the limit.

Using the Distort Tool and the Property Bar

Apply your distortions using the Distort tool, shown next, which is found in the Toolbox grouped with other Effects tools and is used together with these Property bar options.

Property bar options for distortion

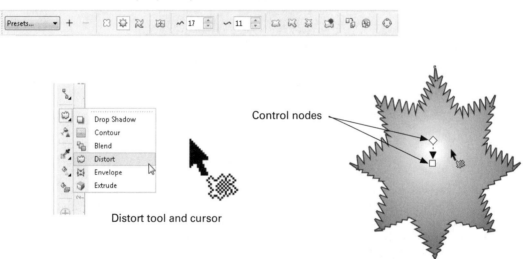

Distort tool and cursor

Control nodes

You'll notice three distortion modes on the Property bar in the next illustration: Push And Pull, Zipper, and Twister. With each mode, a different set of parameters is available. Amplitude and Frequency values can be varied in combination with certain other options (covered next) controlled interactively or by setting values on the

Property bar. Let's first take a look at the Property bar when Zipper mode has been selected. By reviewing Zipper mode, you'll get a handle on many of the options.

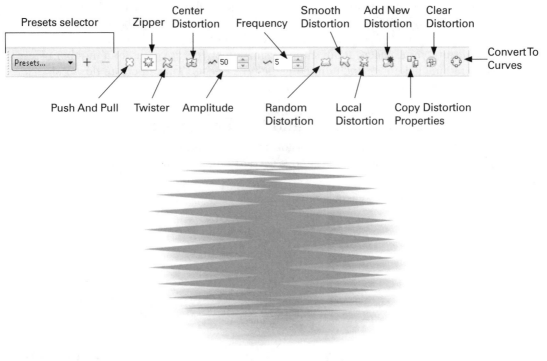

(This originally was a circle.)

If you've tried using this distortion effect, even just a little, you probably have a newfound appreciation for "steering"—it's akin to slipping into a Ferrari right after your dad took the training wheels off your bike. However, the Distort tool will grow on you, and the intimidation factor will dwindle.

During a distortion session, interactive nodes (markers) provide much of the control over this effect. The nodes vary by the mode you've selected. The Distort modes are covered in the sections to follow in digestible, easy-to-assimilate, fun-size servings.

Push And Pull Distortion

Push And Pull distortions can inflate or deflate the slope of your shape's curves by amplitude. The *amplitude* value affects the *extent* of the effect, moving the curves of paths from an object's original path, from shallow at low settings to severe at high settings. Think of an oscilloscope when you use these effects—it's all amplitude and frequency.

Amplitude can be set from 200 to –200 percent. Negative values distort the path away from the center origin of the object, which creates the "push" condition of the distortion. Negative values (which you can also define interactively with the Distort tool—it's fun and creatively therapeutic) can be used to illustrate flower petals, a cartoon splash into a pond, a thought balloon—all from beginning with a rectangle shape. Positive Amplitude values distort the path toward the object's center origin, the "pull" condition. Again, if you use a rectangle as the target shape, you can almost instantly produce anything from a diner sign from the 1950s to a sleek, aerodynamic auto or airplane to a nice 3D visualization of a TV tube viewed in perspective. At an amplitude of 0, there is no distortion. Here you can see the effects of both negative and positive Push And Pull Amplitude settings.

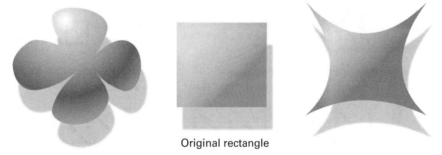

Push and Pull at positive amplitude   Push and Pull at negative amplitude

Original rectangle

Zipper Distortion

Zipper mode distorts the paths in your object to resemble a zigzag or stitching pattern. Here, Amplitude can be set between 0 and 100 percent and can be used together with a Frequency value and options for Random, Smooth, or Local Distortion, as shown here.

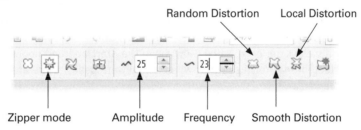

Random Distortion   Local Distortion

Zipper mode   Amplitude   Frequency   Smooth Distortion

Interactive nodes are made up of an End node controlling the amplitude and a slider controlling frequency, which enables you to set the number of zigzags within a given distance. Both can be set within a range of 0 to 100 percent. You can see the dramatic effects of various amplitude and frequency values while applying a Zipper distortion in the next illustration. When beginning to work with the distortion effects, you might prefer to use only the Property bar to define an effect, but as you grow more comfortable with the Distort tool, you'll surely want hands-on control by dragging the control nodes directly with your cursor.

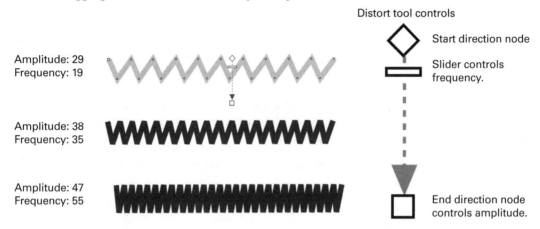

After the effect has been created, you can slant the zipper line by dragging the Start direction node vertically, left or right, as shown here.

Tip You can invert the direction of the zigzags on a line or closed shape by repositioning the control nodes for the effect. For example, begin by placing the Start and End nodes so they bisect the line that is affected. Then arrange the nodes so both the Start and End nodes are above the line; notice where the peaks and valleys are on the line. Now move the Start and End nodes so they're below the affected line. You'll see that where there were peaks, there are now valleys, and vice versa.

In addition to Amplitude and Frequency, three additional options are available for setting the shape and size of the zigzags. Each can be toggled on or off, so you can mix and match to create the following effects:

- **Random Distortion** Choosing Random Distortion causes the zigzag zipper distortion on your object's path to vary randomly between the current Amplitude values and zero. This creates the appearance of nonrepeating frequency and varied wave size, creating an uncontrolled distortion appearance. In this illustration, you can see two examples of Random Distortion, set at 25 and then at 74. Notice where the interactive frequency marker is on the controls just above each object. You can slide this control instead of entering values on the Property bar.

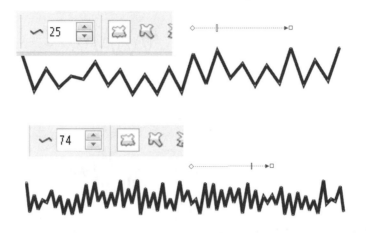

- **Smooth Distortion**   When the Smooth Distortion option is selected, the cusps of the zigzag zipper distortion become rounded, instead of the default sharp corners. This option is great if you need to simulate sound-wave frequencies and equipment monitors in hospitals. The next illustration shows *constant* (Random is toggled off) amplitude and variations in frequency when the Smooth Distortion option is active.

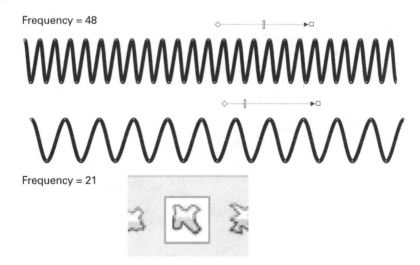

Frequency = 48

Frequency = 21

- **Local Distortion**   Using the Local Distortion option has the effect of varying the Amplitude value of your distortion effect around the center origin. At the center of the distortion effect, amplitude is at its maximum value. Amplitude then tapers to 0 as the distortion emanates from the center origin of the effect. The results of applying the Local Distortion option with varied frequency is shown here:

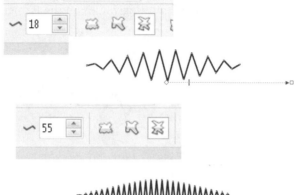

Tip To clear a distortion effect, click Clear Distortion Effect on the Property bar or choose Effects | Clear Distortion. If you've applied successive distortions, each distortion is cleared individually in order, from the last distortion applied to the first, so you can step out of the effect incrementally.

To bring all this Zipper talk down to a practical level, the following illustration shows two creative, commercial uses for Zipper mode. At left, the zipper distortion is used as a coupon border. The only finessing needed was to apply a dashed Outline Pen Style. At right, the diagram of a sewing pattern is gussied up a little by making the cut marks look as though real pinking shears were used.

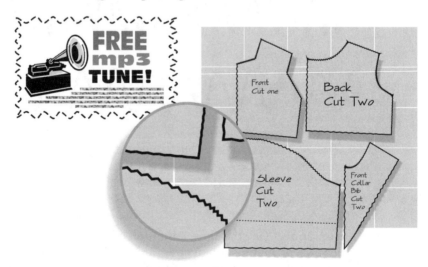

Twister Distortion

Twister distorts the outline paths and nodes of objects by rotating the outer areas around the center (which is largely undistorted), either clockwise or counterclockwise, to achieve an effect much like a child's pinwheel toy. Twister options on the Property bar include Rotation Direction, Rotation Amount, and Degree Of Additional Rotation.

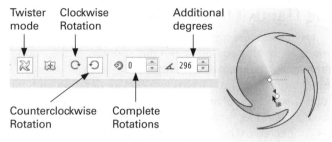

(This used to be a rectangle.)

   Controlling a twister distortion is simple; rotation can be clockwise or counterclockwise, but increasing the rotation really dramatizes the effect of this mode. Whole rotations can be set to a maximum of 9; additional rotations can be added up to 359 degrees—nearly another full rotation. Figure 18-4 shows some of the widely differing effects that can result—it all depends on the number of rotations and the object used as the target for the effect.

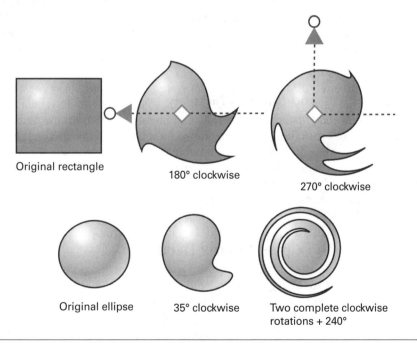

FIGURE 18-4   Using simple objects and the Distort tool's Twister mode creates wild, organic shapes.

Note Objects applied with a distortion effect can't be edited using the Shape tool unless the effect is cleared. You can *convert* a distorted shape to curves (CTRL+Q), however, and then edit away to get the shape you need.

Getting Hands-On with the Distortion Tool Markers

The best way to shape a distortion is interactively by dragging directly on the Distort tool markers with your cursor. Depending on which distortion mode you're using, these interactive markers serve different purposes.

There are different interactive markers, depending on which mode (Push And Pull, Zipper, Twister) you've chosen, but basically you have a Start direction handle shaped like a diamond, which sets the center of the distort effect. The Start direction handle is connected to the End direction handle, which is used to define the direction of the effect and also the *amplitude* (with the Push And Pull and Zipper modes). Generally, interactive markers involve a center marker and at least one other, each joined by a directional guide. When Zipper mode is being applied, a small extra slider appears between these two markers and controls the *frequency* applied. In the case of Twister distortions, the End marker serves as a handle for determining the degree angle and amount of rotation you apply to an object.

Note To realign the center marker (the Start control node) with the center of the distortion, click the Center Distortion button on the Property bar while the Distort tool and the distorted objects are selected. It's the button with the + symbol, to the right of the Twister mode button.

Changing Push And Pull Interactively

Push And Pull mode distortions are controlled using two markers: a diamond shape indicates the center of the distortion, and a square marker controls amplitude. The center marker can be moved around the object, but the Amplitude marker movement is constrained to left or right movement. Dragging the Amplitude marker left of center changes the negative amplitude values, causing the push effect. Dragging it right of the center marker changes the positive values, causing the pull effect. Figure 18-5 shows the effects of different marker positions.

Working with the Zipper Control Handles

Using Zipper mode, the movable diamond marker represents the center origin, and the square marker to the right controls the amplitude value. Use the small rectangular slider on the dashed blue centerline to set the frequency by moving it left or right. Dragging it right increases the frequency, adding more zigzag shapes to your object's path, whereas dragging it left does the opposite. You also have the opportunity with

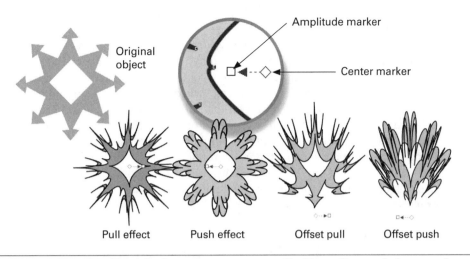

Pull effect   Push effect   Offset pull   Offset push

FIGURE 18-5   Push And Pull mode distortions are controlled by a diamond shape and a square marker onscreen.

Zipper, unlike the fixed positions of the markers in Push And Pull mode, to move the amplitude handle to slant the zigs and zags in a direction:

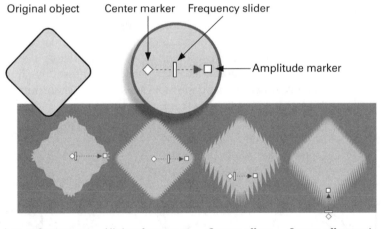

Lower frequency   Higher frequency   Center offset   Center offset and
                                                          Amplitude marker rotated

Tip   As with envelopes, the distortion effects can be copied using the Toolbox's Eyedropper tool. First, choose the Attributes Eyedropper from the Toolbox. Next, on the Property bar, click Effects and check the Distortion box. Click the object with the distortion desired, and then after clicking to copy the distortion, the cursor automatically turns into a paintbucket shape—and then click the new object to be distorted.

Changing Twister Interactively

Controlling Twister mode distortions by dragging with your cursor over the markers is the most productive (and fun) way to apply this distortion mode since one click-drag enables you to set two properties at once, both of which have a dramatic effect on the distortion. The markers when using Twister mode are a diamond-shaped center marker and a circular-shaped rotation handle. Dragging the rotation handle around the center marker causes distortion based on the angle of the guide between the center and rotation markers and the number of times the rotation marker is dragged completely around the center marker. You'll also see a dashed blue line connecting the markers, which provides a quick visual reference of the beginning angle of the twister effect and the current angle of distortion you define. Figure 18-6 shows examples of Twister mode distortions and positions of the markers.

> **Tip** To copy a distortion to a new object, select an object, click the Copy Distortion Properties button on the Property bar, and use the cursor to target an existing distortion.

Exploring Distortion Presets

The Property bar Presets selector for the Distort tool gives you the power to apply, save, and delete saved distortions. Use the options on the Property bar when the Distort tool is active, exactly as you use the Presets selector with other effects in CorelDRAW.

When the Distort tool is selected, choosing a Preset from the list immediately applies a new distortion effect to a selected object. If you've created a really awesome distortion effect and you want to save the effect while the distorted shape in your document is selected, you can add it as a new Distortion preset by clicking the Add button. The Delete button *permanently* removes a selected Distortion preset from the list; therefore, think twice about ever clicking this button.

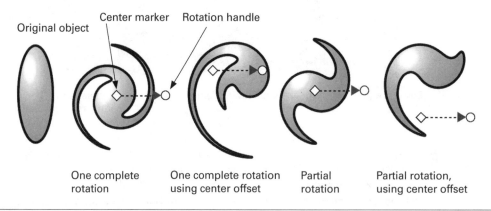

FIGURE 18-6 Use the control handles to create twister distortions.

Between the Shape Edit and the Distort tools covered in this chapter, you should be well on your way to massaging an object or object group from being close to what you like to being *exactly* what you like. Remember, these are dynamic effects and as such, you don't permanently change that shape you've worked on for hours. And if you need to exchange data with a client or coworker who doesn't own CorelDRAW:

- Take pity on them.
- Convert *a copy* of your effects work to curves (CTRL + Q), and then export the distorted or enveloped object to any number of file formats CorelDRAW supports. Effects are proprietary to CorelDRAW, but vector information can be used in other vector design programs and modeling programs or exported as typefaces—you name it.

This chapter has taken you through several processes by which you can create minor and big-time alterations to just about anything you draw; additionally, many of the operations apply to bitmaps you bring into the workspace. Use the command that best suits the task you have in mind, and use your judgment as to which operation will get you to your goal fastest. Personal computers are productivity enhancers: you do not need to labor over something when CorelDRAW and your PC can do it for you in less time.

Shadows and transparencies are the topic of the next chapter, each with their own way to make objects look a little more photorealistic. Got a drawing of a cube? Why not put a shadow under it so it's in the page and not on top of it? Got a drawing of a glass of lemonade or other semitransparent and nutritious liquid? Make areas partially transparent! Get ready for adding effects to make your drawings look more like they're made out of actual materials. Steps are right around the corner, to your right.

19 Transparencies and Shadows

In our endeavors to make drawings more complete—to give the audience as detailed an illustration as possible—we rely on not just the silhouette of an object and its fill and texture, but also how an object *interacts* with its surroundings. There's more than meets the eye when it comes to replicating a scene or even a simple object. Wherever you have a light source, a solid object on a solid surface casts a shadow in the opposing direction. Even partially transparent objects leave their mark on a surface when illuminated from a direction. Similarly, what would our world be like if everything was 100 percent opaque? Sunglasses would be an impossibility, a room with a view would be false advertising, and even ice cubes would look suspicious! This chapter takes you through the CorelDRAW tools that assist you in creating transparent shapes and shadows cast by objects.

The Importance of Objects Interacting with the Scene

Here are a couple of illustrations to sell you on the importance of real-world phenomena. In the illustration here (*glass cube.cdr* if you'd like to see how it was created), you can see a cube that is being illuminated from the right. There are no surprises, nothing of special interest, nothing being said artistically about a cube resting on a surface. In fact, the most interesting thing about this illustration is the cube's shadow—its softness contrasts with the hard lines of the cube, but you can do a *lot* better than this.

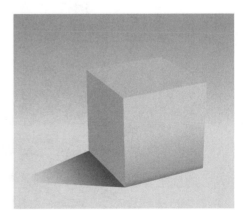

Here's the same cube, but it's made out of something; it's not simply covered with a texture (which is not necessarily a bad thing; see Chapter 12)—it's a material through and through, and you can see this. It might not be immediately obvious, but when you create a partially transparent object, you can see both its front and its back side, thus providing you with a more complete image of what you've drawn. If you create your drawing in a ¾ view, looking slightly downward, you can see all six faces of the cube. With solid cubes, the maximum number of sides viewable from a single angle is three.

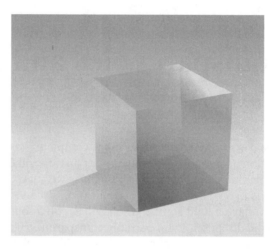

Notice also that even a semitransparent object casts shadows. And shadows, in turn, aren't always 100 percent opaque; you can usually see details in the surface beneath the shadow. Shadows anchor a shape to the ground; they give you a visual clue as to where they are located relative to other objects in the scene. In the illustration here, the ball is not casting a shadow. No, it's not a vampire, but it's not a very complete illustration of a graphical idea, either. Is the ball floating? How close is it to the wall?

The answers to both these questions is immediately solved in this next illustration, where one of CorelDRAW's drop shadow effects was broken from the control object, converted to curves, and then split so the two pieces could give a reference point for the ball on both the floor and the wall. You can take a look at the pieces that make up the illustration by opening *Shadows.cdr*.

If the author has done his job, you're now sold on exploring how to create transparent shapes and shadows in CorelDRAW using this chapter.

Clearing Things Up with the Transparency Tool

Transparency is an effect CorelDRAW users have leveraged for many years to illustrate scenes that have a very photorealistic look. The Transparency tool is quite different to use than the Transparency lens, as is the effect you achieve. You have *directions* for transparency such as Linear and Elliptical and also various operators (styles of transparency) available on the Property bar to set how a partially transparent object interacts with object below it.

One thing to keep in mind when working with transparency in a design: this is the way you blend colors between objects. That's it; your work doesn't benefit from a totally transparent object—there has to be *some* influence from the object to which you apply transparency, and it's usually color. In a way, to think about transparency is to think about color blending.

One of the keys to creating amazing artwork using the Transparency tool is *the fill* that a semitransparent object has; in addition to uniform fills, fountain and pattern fills can also take on transparency. You put fills and transparency together, and you're talking seriously sophisticated compositions! Another key lies in how you approach a drawing in which you plan to feature partially transparent objects. To illustrate a real-world object, you need a few *nontransparent* objects in such a drawing, so don't overindulge in transparency when only certain parts of an illustration need the effect. In the next illustration, you can see what is today a fairly common button for a web page; it suggests glass. At left, you can see a Wireframe view—not many objects went into a fairly convincing drawing of a glass button.

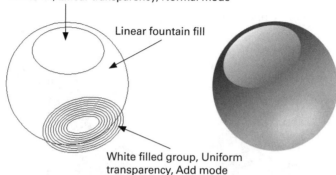

Using the Transparency Tool and Property Bar

The transparency effects discussed next are applied using the Transparency tool located in the Toolbox; the icon looks like a wine glass, and in version X7, it's a lone button and is not grouped with other effects.

While the Transparency tool is selected, the Property bar displays all options to control the transparency effect. These options, as shown in Figure 19-1, can be used

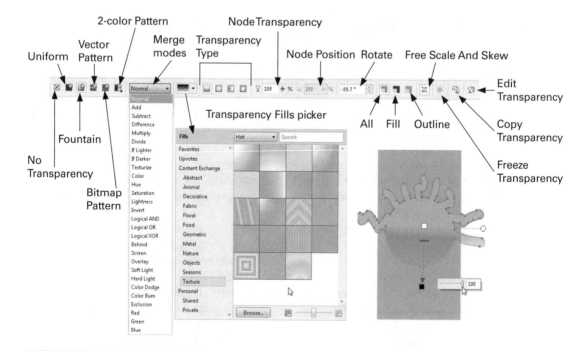

FIGURE 19-1 Use the Property bar to customize a transparency object.

along with the object's interactive markers to produce phenomenally complex and fascinating compositions.

Often, the most rewarding way to discover and gain control over a feature in CorelDRAW or any program is to dive straight in. The following tutorial might seem a little challenging because an explanation of the transparency options is provided on the fly, sort of like getting directions *while* you're driving, but you might want the power of transparencies at hand *right now,* as we all do with valuable stuff. Follow along here to create a fairly realistic composition of a child's marble; transparency will take care of the shading and the highlights. This might remind you a little of Chapter 3's example, but the following tutorial is more of a comprehensive study of *how* transparency works in CorelDRAW. You can check out the *Marble.cdr* document to see and take apart the components at any time.

Tutorial Creating a Dimensional Drawing Through Transparency

1. Create a circle; choose the Ellipse tool and then hold CTRL while you drag. Click the Edit Fill button directly to the left of the Customize button on the Property bar, which displays the Edit Fill dialog, where fractal fills can be found (the button is not located on the Property bar). Click the Texture Fill button (next to the last button on the right). Click the drop-down button to the right of the blue sky preview area, and then choose the third from the left thumbnail. The texture is a pink agate-style fractal texture, perfect for making a kid's marble. Click OK, the Edit Fill box disappears, and you now have an agate-style fill in the circle.

2. With the Pick tool, select the circle. Press CTRL + C and then CTRL + V to copy a duplicate of the circle directly above the original. Click the black color swatch on the color palette to give this duplicate a Uniform black fill.

3. Choose the Transparency tool. Click the Fountain Transparency button on the Property bar.

4. Choose Elliptical Fountain transparency from the Property bar, and then choose If Darker from the Merge Mode selector on the Property bar. (In Figure 19-1, it says Normal, which is the default state on the Property bar for Merge modes.)

5. Click-drag the white transparency node (the Start node) a little toward 10 o'clock. Now, this transparency is going exactly the opposite as intended: a white node represents 100% opacity and you need 0% opacity (a black-colored node). Fortunately, if you click over the black transparency node, a mini pop-up with a Transparency slider saves you the trip to the Property bar. Drag the slider from its current position at far left to far right: 100% transparency.

6. Click-drag the other node (the End node) to a position at about 5 o'clock on the edge of the circle object. Hover the cursor for a moment, and when the pop-up appears, drag its slider to the left arriving at zero (0) transparency. Check out the illustration following Step 10 to get a better idea of where you should be now. The illustration shows the steps, but not directly in place in this example, so you can better see the individual steps. You'll see that the marble drawing is taking on some dimension and depth with this fountain-transparent object over it.

7. Create a circle that's about a tenth of the size of the original circle. Give it a white fill and no outline.

8. Set the Transparency Type to Fountain and the transparency to Elliptical Fountain transparency. Leave the Merge mode at the default of Normal.

9. The Start node should be in the center of the circle; click-drag it there if it's not, and it should be totally opaque (0% transparent)—indicated by white. Use the pop-up slider to make it **0%** transparent using the slider.

10. Drag the End node to just inside the circle object; doing this ensures the object is 100% transparent at its edges, creating a perfect highlight object. Put it at the upper left of the marble drawing, and consider this a frenetic tutorial well done! See the following illustration if you haven't peeked ahead yet.

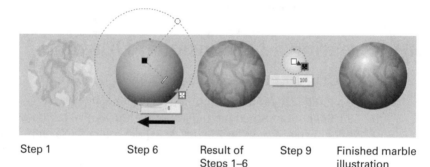

Step 1   Step 6   Result of   Step 9   Finished marble
                                Steps 1–6   illustration

Setting Transparency Properties

If you have experience with CorelDRAW's Fill tool, you're 99 percent of the way to mastering the Transparency Fill Types with the Transparency tool. Because transparency isn't the same as an object's fill, the following sections take you through some unique properties. You can leverage wonderful design potential by choosing your transparency type according to what you need to design.

Uniform Transparency

Uniform transparency is the default for objects to which you assign this trait; the object will feature a flat and even transparency value. The way this semitransparent object blends with underlying objects is completely predictable. For example, if you assign a red rectangle and then a blue rectangle with 50% (the default) transparency and overlap them, yep, you'll see violet in the intersection.

Tip The Uniform transparency type has no Start or End nodes over the object as other types do.

Fountain Fill Transparencies

Transparent objects that use any of the Fountain fill direction types are an exceptionally powerful tool for illustration, as you'll see in a moment. What governs the degree of transparency at the Start and End points are the control nodes, not only their position relative to the object underneath but also *the brightness value* of the markers. Fountain fill transparencies are driven *by any of 256 shades, from black to white.* Let's use the Linear transparency type; you understand this type and all the others (Elliptical, Conical, and so on) will become obvious. When you click-drag using Linear transparency on an object, the Start node is white, indicating full opacity, and the End node is black, indicating no opacity at all.

Here's Trick Number One in creating an elegant Fountain fill transparency: you can change the degree of opacity at the Start and End points using three methods:

- Reposition the Start and End nodes using the Transparency tool. If you position the markers way outside of the object, the transition between full and no opacity will be gradual and the outermost parts of the transparent object will be neither completely opaque nor completely transparent if you do this.
- Change the brightness; the nodes can have any of 256 shades of black. Let's say you have the Start and End nodes exactly where you want them; you like the angle of the Fountain fill transparency. But you don't want the End (the black node) to be 100% transparent. You click-drag a deep shade of black from the color palette and then drop it onto the black End node. The end of the transparency then becomes mostly but not 100% transparent.
- Use the mini pop-up controls that appear next to a selected transparency node to change the transparency value, by dragging from 0 (opaque) to 100 (transparent).

Trick Number Two is to choose the transparency object's color— any color is acceptable, but because this physical *Guide* is in black and white, black, gray, and white are used here to influence the objects visually below the transparency object. Here's an illustration: some black Paragraph Text is on the bottom of the drawing page. On top of it is a rectangle. At left, the rectangle is filled with white and a Linear Fountain fill transparency is click-dragged from top to bottom. The text appears to be coming out of a fog. In the center, a 50% black fill is then applied to the rectangle and a different visual effect is achieved—the Paragraph Text still looks like it's in a haze, but more of it is legible toward the top. At right, black is the fill for the rectangle and now the top of the text is as illegible as the white rectangle example, but a different artistic sense of drama has been achieved. You now know two different methods for shading with Fountain-type transparency fills: change the position of the transparency nodes, and change the color of the transparency object.

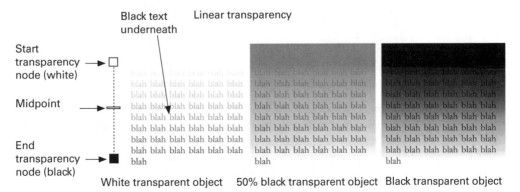

White transparent object   50% black transparent object   Black transparent object

---

Tip Although the transparency nodes can only be shades of black and white, the object taking the transparency can certainly be in color, or have any of the available fills in CorelDRAW, including bitmap patterns and fountain fills.

New Controls and Locations for Transparency Options

You still have two approaches to modifying an object's transparency in CorelDRAW X7—using the Property bar controls and the interactive markers (or nodes) on an object—but users of previous versions might be a little disoriented when trying to go through the same old moves to accomplish something. And for new users, the additional transparency effects were designed to be intuitive and easier to use than in previous versions. Here are a few of the more frequently used modification features, what they do, and where they are located:

- **Midpoint slider** This slider controls where the 50% point in a transparency is located. It does *not* indicate where an object is 50% transparent, but it instead sets a relative 50% breakpoint because, as mentioned earlier, you can set the Start and End nodes to any brightness value you like. The midpoint slider is located on the Start-End line on the transparency object when selected. This feature is no longer on the Property bar, but you can access by clicking the Edit Transparency button on the Property bar, and then you can click-drag the midpoint, as shown in this illustration, to any point between the Start and End points.

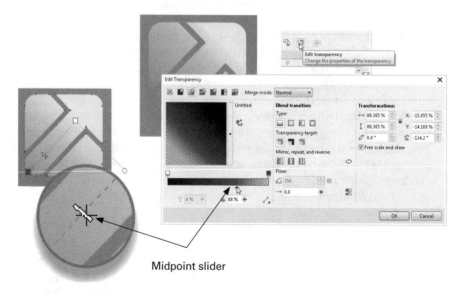

Midpoint slider

Tip If no object is selected and you want to make any object partially transparent, the Transparency tool is a selection tool in addition to controlling the transparency nodes. With the tool selected, click once to select the object to which you want to apply transparency, and then click-drag to create a Linear Fountain transparency that can then be modified using the Property bar controls.

- **Rotate**   Some, but not all, transparency types will show any difference when you rotate their orientation. For example, a Linear Fountain transparency creates a different look when you rotate its orientation, but a perfectly circular Elliptical transparency, or 2-color transparency, will definitely look different when you rotate it. You can rotate a transparency in three ways: by directly dragging on the End node above the object in the workspace, by changing the value in the Rotate spin box on the Property bar, and in the Transformations area of the Edit Transparency dialog. See the following illustration.

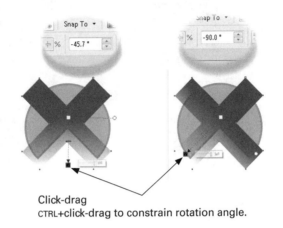

Click-drag
CTRL+click-drag to constrain rotation angle.

Tip   By default, when you hold CTRL and drag a control marker for a Fountain type transparency, you constrain the angle you're setting in 15-degree increments. You can also straighten a crooked Fountain transparency you've manually defined by CTRL+click-dragging.

- **Free Scale And Skew**   As with the fill controls on objects, the transparency control nodes operate in 90-degree opposition to one another...*except* when you decide to activate the Free Scale And Skew button on the Property bar, which adds a third handle and a white control node that can govern one dimension of a transparency while the End node controls the other. Free Scale And Skew can set the angle between, for example, an Elliptical transparency to anything in addition to the default 90 degrees. This next illustration shows the difference between a default applied transparency and the same type of transparency after messing with it using the Free Scale And Skew feature. Dragging the Free Scale And Skew node away from the Start transparency node converts an Elliptical transparency type in its default circular state to an oval, and dragging in a circular direction around the Start node rotates the elliptical transparency.

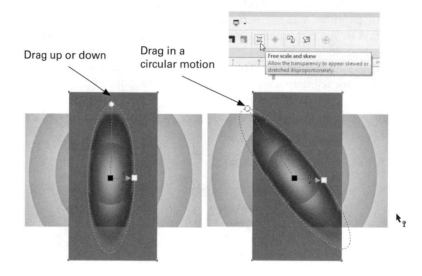

Drag up or down

Drag in a circular motion

Free scale and skew
Allow the transparency to appear skewed or stretched disproportionately.

The Free Scale And Skew feature can also be applied using the Edit Transparency dialog, but it's not as much fun as dragging the interactive nodes around.

- **Mirror, Repeat, and Reverse**   These options—exactly like the Fill options for fountain fills—are not located on the Property bar as the Fill options are. You access them by selecting a transparent object and then clicking the Edit Transparency button on the Property bar. You have a terrific visual of the proposed transformation in the Edit Transparency dialog, and the options are fairly self-explanatory. The biggest difference between Repeat and Repeat And Mirror is that the mirror function tends to create "tubes" of transparency, whereas the simple Repeat function makes objects look like anything from shingles on a roof to a splash screen to a cartoon.

You can set the number of repeats within an object by dragging the End transparency node; when you click the Free Scale And Skew button on the Property bar, you can also set the angle of distorted repeats in an object by dragging on the Free Scale And Skew node (the third, round node between the Start and End nodes).

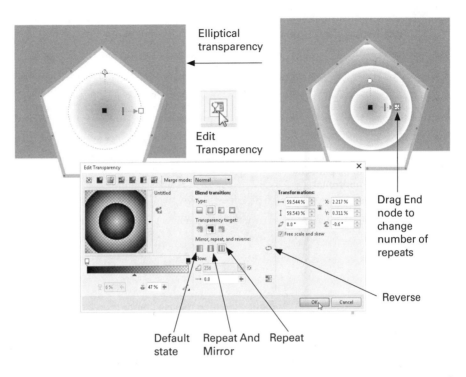

Let's kick back for a moment, and run through some steps that demonstrate the practicality of a Linear transparency used in an illustration to imitate the "glass icon" reflective look.

Tutorial   Creating a Reflection on a Shiny Surface

1. Get out *The X7 files.cdr*. The background checkered surface is locked and all you need to do is play with the file, which is a group of objects.
2. With the Pick tool, select the file, and then hold CTRL while holding the top, center selection handle—you're going to drop a copy of this file, but you're going to place the copy directly below the original, so both bottoms of the files line up perfectly.
3. Drag down on the selection handle, and then as soon as you can see the preview of where the duplicate is going to go, press the right mouse button

and then release CTRL and the mouse buttons. The action is mapped out in the following illustration.

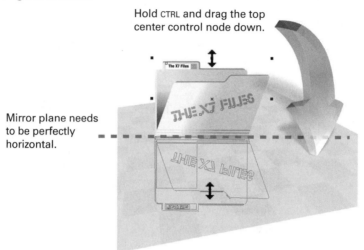

Hold CTRL and drag the top center control node down.

Mirror plane needs to be perfectly horizontal.

Right-click, then release CTRL to drop a mirrored copy.

4. Choose the Transparency tool, and then select the bottom, mirrored file (you can do this with the Transparency tool) and then beginning at the very top of the upside-down file, drag down so that the 0% transparent area of this Linear transparency is at top and the bottom is 100% transparent. Neat effect, eh? You're not quite done yet.

5. You neither want the top to be totally opaque nor the bottom totally transparent. The default for the Transparency tool can and should be modified to convey a little more convincing scene than opaque to transparent—that's not how you see reflections. Click the Start transparency node to reveal the pop-up slider and change the value to about **23**. Then click the End transparency node and make the value about **96**. See the following illustration.

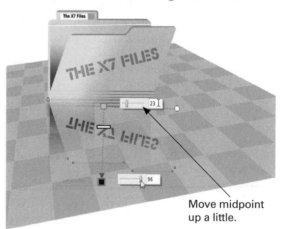

Move midpoint up a little.

6. Remember earlier we talked about moving the control nodes to change the transparency effect. You might want to do this to make the effect seem more real to you (and your audience), but the alternative—moving the midpoint slider—is quicker and gets the task completed, as shown in the illustration. Just drag the slider up a little and you've got yourself a file reflected in the floor.

 Tip For best results on your own with the preceding tutorial, create an object whose bottom side is perfectly horizontal. Making a tilted folder resting on its corner with a convincing reflection is hard.

Additional Fountain Transparency Types

You also have Elliptical, Conical, and Rectangular Fountain transparency types at hand when you design something you need to look more dimensional. The Elliptical transparency effect is fantastic for making spectacular highlights—brilliant but soft-edged highlights you commonly see when sunlight hits a highly polished metal or smooth plastic object. A Conical transparency is good to use when you need a pie-wedge-shaped area, and this, too, is good for simulating highlights and reflections. The Rectangular transparency type might not prove to be useful on a day-to-day basis, but it's great for creating soft-edged highlights to use as window panes and other right-angle geometric areas you want to emphasize visually.

Let's take a detour in this documentation to explain *transparency operations*. Also called Merge modes and Blend modes, these operations have an additional effect on all objects with a transparency effect.

Using Transparency Operations (Merge Modes)

The Property bar has a list of *modes* so you set how your transparency colors interact with the colors of underlying objects. These options further the visual complexity of semitransparent objects. For example, a red plastic drinking glass on a yellow tablecloth will show some orange through it due to the nature of colors that mix as light passes through the glass. But the shadow cast by the nontransparent areas of the glass will not be the same shade of orange as the light we see through the glass—light in the real world is subtractive, and the shadow in such a scene would be almost brown. However, you don't have to calculate light properties or material properties when you choose the best Merge mode for your illustration.

The following definitions of Merge modes describe the effect you can expect with each mode; let's use "source" to refer to the top object that takes the transparency effect and "target" to refer to one or more objects below the transparency object that are overlapped by the transparency object. The "result" is the color you see in your drawing in the overlapping areas:

- **Normal**   Normal Merge mode is the default whenever a new transparency effect is applied to an object. Choosing Normal at 50% opacity usually produces predictable color blends between the source and target objects; for example, a pure yellow object at 50% Normal opacity over a pure red object yields orange as a result in overlapping areas. Similarly and in traditional physical painting, a white source object produces a *tint* result over a pure color object (a pastel color), whereas a black source object produces a *shade* of the target object's color (if you're shopping for house paints, the salesperson will love this jargon).

- **Add**   The Add(itive) mode applies transparency in a similar fashion to Normal mode, except it whitens and brightens the result, seriously! In English, there's a subtle but distinct difference between "plus" and "added to"; similarly, Additive Merge mode moves the combined result of the target and source object colors in a positive direction in brightness value. The artistic result is good for adding subtle shading to composition areas; this is something painters through the centuries could not do without the added step of applying pure white because inks and pigments use the real-world subtractive color model.

- **Subtract**   This mode ignores the brightness value in the source object and is similar to mixing physical pigments. If you use Subtractive transparency mode on green and red objects and overlap then with a target blue object, the result color will be black.

- **Difference**   Remember color opposites on the color wheel? This is what Difference Merge mode does: it moves the result color to the difference (on the color wheel) between the source and target colors. For example, a red Difference transparency object over a yellow target object produces green areas. You'll see the Difference Merge effect most clearly if you put the object over an empty area of the drawing page. A red Difference object will cast cyan as the result on the page. This blending mode is for creating dramatic lighting effects—for example, you can shine a Difference Merge mode drawing of a shaft of theater spotlight on an object and get truly wonderful and bizarre lighting effects.

- **Multiply**   Multiply always produces a darker result color from merging the source and target objects. Its effect is similar to wood stain or repeatedly stroking a felt marker on paper. Several objects in Multiply Merge mode, when overlapped, can produce black, and this is perhaps the best mode for artists to re-create real-world shadows cast on objects. If the source object's color is lighter than the target object, the result is no change.

- **Divide**   The Divide mode produces only a lighter result color if neither the target nor source objects are black or white. Use this Merge mode to bleach and produce highlights in a composition by using a light color for the transparency object such as 10% black. Divide is also occasionally called Difference, Exclusion, and Subtract mode.

- **If Lighter**   If the target color is lighter than the source transparency color, the area is replaced with the transparency object's (the source) color. If the target color is darker than the source transparency shape, the result is this region shows no change in color.

- **If Darker**   The opposite effect of If Lighter. If the bottom (target) object's color is darker than the source object, this area takes the color of the top (the source, the transparency) object. There is no visible change if the target object is lighter than the source object.

- **Texturize**   This mode will not produce much of a change unless you fill the source object with a bitmap or pattern fill. However, if you fill the transparency object with a bitmap fill, the result is a shaded and patterned area. This mode removes the hue and saturation from the bitmap fill, leaving only brightness values, in effect, making your target object a shaded version of the original, sort of like merging a grayscale photograph over an object. This is a useful Merge mode when you do not want the target object to influence the result colors with any distinct hues. You can also use this mode to build up texture quickly and simulate real-world complexity in your composition.
- **Color**   This mode uses the hue and saturation values of the source color and the lightness value of the target color to create a result. This is the opposite of the Lightness Merge mode.
- **Hue**   The Hue Merge mode changes the result color to the hue of the target color, without affecting saturation or brightness in the result. This mode is useful for tinting compositions and the target object colors are ignored in the result.
- **Saturation**   The Saturation Merge mode can be used to remove color from the result; it's quite nice at making black-and-white photographs from color images. This mode ignores hue and brightness components in the result. Try using shades of black as the transparency object's fill. Highlight saturated target and source objects will produce no change in the result.
- **Lightness**   The target object's lightness values are calculated, ignoring hue and saturation. This is a great mode for brightening the result colors because the target object's colors are never changed, just the *lightness* (also called *value* and *brightness*).
- **Invert**   This Merge mode creates a result color that is the chromatic inverse of the target color. You can occasionally reproduce the look of a color negative using this mode—it moves the result color 180 degrees on the color wheel. Using Invert Merge mode on the same colored target and source objects produces gray.
- **Logical AND, Logical OR, and Logical XOR**   The AND function includes similarity between the source and target objects; for example, two red ellipses that overlap and both have the AND transparency Merge mode appear not to be transparent at all but instead display 100% red where they overlap. This is a useful mode when you want only a color result in overlapping areas because AND creates no change outside of the overlapping result area. The OR operator is an exclusive operator; it excludes stuff: this is a good mode for clipping a color change, thus limiting it to areas only where the target and source objects overlap. You'll see nothing outside the overlapping areas when the target object has the OR operator. XOR is a Boolean math statement, based on something called a Truth Table where certain conditions must be met to produce a result. You might not find a use for this transparency mode unless you use more than two objects in a design area; if either or neither object in an XOR operation is similar, you'll get no result color. This operation only works if there is one differently colored object in the color calculation operation.
- **Behind**   You need two objects that have transparency for Behind Merge mode to work. Wherever the target object on bottom contains transparency, the source

object with Behind mode fills the transparent bottom areas with its color(s). Therefore, the source object will appear invisible in areas where the target object has no transparency. Use this mode in your design work to fill in missing areas (transparent ones) in the target image without being apparent in areas that do not contain source object transparency.

- **Screen** This Merge mode always returns a lighter color, or the source object is invisible if it is darker than the base object or if it's black. Screen is similar to, but less intense an effect than, Add Merge mode; the effect looks like bleach applied to a colored garment.

- **Overlay** This mode examines the brightness value of the base color. If the result of combining the source with the base is greater than 128 on a brightness scale of 256, the result is a screened area. If the result is not as light as 128, the area is color multiplied. Highlights and shadow areas are preserved in the base image when you use this mode. You almost always achieve a result that has more visual contrast than the original when you use Overlay.

- **Soft Light** Akin to Overlay Merge mode, except instead of screening and multiplying areas, the result is lightening and darkening, a less intense effect.

- **Hard Light** Very similar to the screening and multiplying effect of the Overlay Merge mode, except highlight and shadow regions are *not* preserved. Use this mode if Overlay doesn't prove to be an intense enough effect for merging two color objects or images.

- **Color Dodge** The base colors are brightened based on the colors used in the source object. Black produces no effect when used as a source color, whereas white can produce a near-white. The effect could be compared to adjusting the exposure of the base image by brightening and tinting the base image simultaneously while reducing overall contrast.

- **Color Burn** The inverse effect of Color Dodge. White in the source object produces no effect above the base object; colors are reduced in exposure, increased in contrast, and black and darker shades of color in the source object appear to stain the base object.

- **Exclusion** Similar to the Difference Merge mode, but instead of subtracting either the source or the base color (whichever is brighter) to arrive at a darker color, Exclusion Merge mode removes the color of the transparent areas in the resulting blend. When white is used in the source object, it inverts the underlying colors in the base object. Using black produces no effect.

- **Red, Green, and Blue** Each of these merge modes filters out a respective (RGB) channel and the native color of the source object is ignored. This is a useful transparency mode for color correcting photographs you import to CorelDRAW; for example, if you put a Green transparency mode object over a portrait, and then play with the amount of transparency on the Property bar, you can sometimes correct for harsh indoor (particularly cheap fluorescent) lighting.

Creating Multistage Transparencies

You might find you need a transparency object that's more complex than the Fountain types offered on the Property bar; for example, a lens flare can add photorealism to an illustration, and this option doesn't seem to be on the Property bar. But now, in version X7, the first place you might want to look for an exotic, complex multistage transparency is on the Transparency Fills picker on the Property bar. (You can see the Transparency Fills picker in Figure 19-1).

If you don't find what you envision, CorelDRAW's Transparency tool's power can be used to build a multistage fountain fill for an object, and then you can use the Transparency tool in a Merge mode operation that hides certain colors in the fountain fill. For example, if you want to create bands of transparency in an object, you drag shades of black from the color palette and drop them onto the marker connector, alternating with white markers. Remember, darker shades represent transparency, and lighter shades stand for opacity. You might want to reposition the new markers once you've added them; this is done by click-dragging with the Transparency tool. If your drop point for a new marker isn't exactly over the marker connector (the blue-dashed line), your cursor will turn into an international "no can do" symbol.

Pattern Transparencies

Pattern transparencies can create intricate detail by combining the transparency object and all the objects below it. The Transparency Type buttons on the Property bar include Vector Pattern, Bitmap Pattern, and 2-color Pattern transparency types. With any of these selected for the transparency type, the starting Transparency (the "Start") slider controls the percentage of transparency applied to brightness values in the chosen bitmap that lie above 126 on a brightness scale of 0–255 (256 shades); the ending (the "End") Transparency slider controls the percentage of transparency applied to brightness values in the chosen bitmap that fall below 128.

Note The Texture Transparency type is still available, except you must go to Edit Transparency to locate and use it.

Figure 19-2 shows *Hawaiian shirt.cdr*, a file you should feel free to experiment with, along with the options on the Property bar when the Transparency tool is selected and the control nodes above the target object; you work with scale, rotate, and skew in addition to setting the midpoint for the transparency a little differently than you do the Fill tools, but you'll pick up the Rotate And Scale node—which looks like the Free Scale And Skew node in Fills—quick enough. Clearly, CorelDRAW provides you not only with a robust feature set, but also with enough Hawaiian shirt patterns to last you several months vacationing.

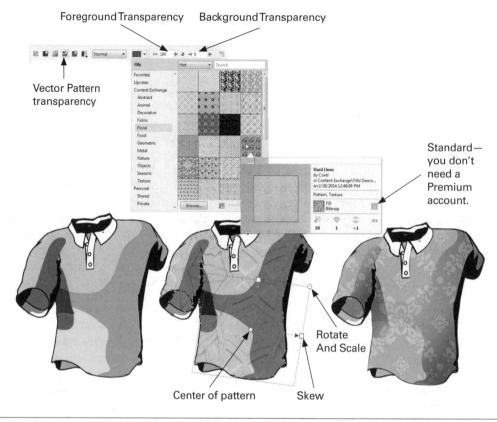

FIGURE 19-2 Use patterns as the basis for transparency to add visual complexity, simulating a woven texture, a painted one, or other engraved and embossed effects.

You don't need a tutorial to make a shirt decorated with a custom transparency. You select the light solid part of the shirt, you open the Transparency Fills picker, and then drag your choice of fills to the selected object. CorelDRAW might inform you that your choice of transparency fills is free as long as you've registered your product—in which case, the swatch is marked with an "S," but unless you have a Premium account (there's a little "M" next to the texture when you open it), you can't use this transparency fill.

Using Transparency Freeze

In addition to the options on the Property bar that are almost identical to the Fill tool's options—Copy Transparency, Apply To Outline, Fill, or All, and Edit Transparency—we have the option to Freeze Transparency, which is much like freezing a lens effect. When you freeze a transparency object, the object captures the composite of the object's properties combined with whatever was beneath the object before using the Freeze Transparency button on the Property bar.

Tip Deactivating the Freeze Transparency option (without ungrouping it) returns a transparent object to its current and active state. This means if you freeze the object, move it, and then unfreeze it, its interior will display whatever is *currently* under it.

Using the Drop Shadow Effect

With the Drop Shadow tool and the options available on the Property bar when this is the active tool, you can create both shadows and glows, in drop shadow and cast shadow fashions (explained shortly). Although this section walks you through several variations, basically you have three different types of effects at hand when you use the Drop Shadow tool, as shown in Figure 19-3.

- **Drop shadows**   This shadow type creates the impression that you're viewing an object from the front and that the object is basically lit from the front. Drop shadows are a popular effect; however, they don't always bring out depth in a composition because the drop shadow suggests a face-front orientation of a scene—a viewpoint usually reserved for driver's license photos and wanted posters in the post office. However, drop shadows will indeed perk up a web page, because the audience expects a face-front orientation since we all tend to face the front of our monitors.

| | | |
| Drop shadow | Perspective (cast) shadow | Glow |

FIGURE 19-3   The drop shadow effect can add perspective and be used to light up a scene, not simply to make things cast shadows.

- **Cast shadows** This effect is sometimes called a *perspective shadow* in CorelDRAW. The effect suggests a shadow casting on the ground and diminishing in size as it travels to a scene's vanishing point. It visually suggests that the audience is looking *into* a scene from a perspective point and is not looking *at* an object placed *on* a scene, as drop shadows tend to do.
- **Glows** All effects created with the Drop Shadow tool are dynamically updated bitmaps, and, as such, they can look soft as shadows do on overcast days; they can also be put into Merge modes. Therefore, you take a blurry bitmap, put it in Multiply Merge mode, and you have a re-creation of a shadow. However, if you take that same blurry bitmap, give it a light color, and then put it in Normal or Add Merge mode, you have a glow effect. This is part of what CorelDRAW does when you use a Glow preset, and you have a lot of manual control over creating a shady or glowing look that perfectly suits a piece of work.

Like other effects in CorelDRAW, drop shadows maintain a dynamic link; any changes to the control object automatically update the shadow. A shadow's look—its position, color, opacity, and feathering—can be customized, plus you can manipulate the angle, stretch, and fade properties of shadows and glows.

Using the Drop Shadow Tool and Property Bar

The Drop Shadow tool—located and clearly marked in the Effects flyout on the Toolbox—is about as hard to use as click-dragging, and after you click-drag to create a custom shadow, you'll see a series of Property bar options. The tool is found in the Toolbox with other interactive tools.

After an initial click-drag to add a drop shadow to an object, you'll notice the Property bar lights up, and you now have a ton of options for refining what amounts to a sort of "default" drop shadow effect. Drop shadows can take one of two states: flat (drop) or perspective (cast). Depending on which state you use, the Property bar options will change. Figure 19-4 handsomely illustrates a look at the Property bar when applying a flat shadow.

Here's an introduction to shadow-making through a tutorial intended to familiarize you with the Property bar options as well as with a little interactive editing. As with most of the effects in CorelDRAW, the onscreen markers for click-dragging to customize a shadow are very much like the markers for the Extrude fountain fill and other tool control handles.

Tutorial Working the Property Bar and Shadow-Making Markers

1. Create an interesting object to which you want to apply a shadow, and finish applying its fill and outline properties. If you deselect it, this is okay—a click on the object with the Drop Shadow tool selects it.
2. Choose the Drop Shadow tool, and notice that your cursor changes to resemble the Pick tool with a tiny Drop Shadow icon in its corner. If you don't do

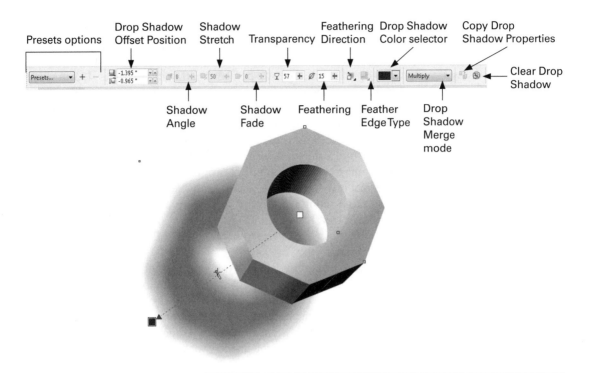

FIGURE 19-4   You might be a shadow of your former self after sifting through all the drop shadow options!

anything with the tool, the only option on the Property bar is the Presets drop-down selector at the moment.

3. Click-drag from roughly the center of the selected object; continue holding down the mouse button so you can see some of the mechanics of this effect. Notice that a preview outline appears that matches your object. This indicates the position of the new shadow once you release the mouse button. Notice also that a white node has appeared in the center of the object, and that another node has appeared under the cursor as you drag it. A slider control has also appeared at the midpoint of a dotted guideline joining the two nodes.

4. Release the mouse button and boing! A drop shadow appears. This is a default shadow, colored black, and it has default properties.

5. Drag the slider control on the guideline between the two square-shaped nodes toward the center of your original object. This reduces the shadow's opacity, making it appear lighter and allowing the page background color—and any underlying objects—to become more visible.

6. To change the shadow color, click the Color selector on the Property bar and then select a color. Notice that the color is applied; you can do some wild stage-lighting stuff by choosing a bright color for the shadow, but the opacity of the shadow remains the same.

7. Drag the white node to the edge of one side of the original object. Notice the shadow changes shape, and the node snaps to the edge. This action changes a drop shadow to a perspective shadow.

8. Using Property bar options, change the default Feathering value to **4**, and then press ENTER. The shadow edges are now more defined. Increase this value to a setting of **35**, and notice that the shadow edges become blurry; you've gone from a sunny-day shadow to an overcast-day shadow.

9. Click the Fade slider control and increase it to **80**. Notice that the shadow now features a graduated color effect, with the darkest point closest to the original object becoming a lighter color as the effect progresses farther away from your object. This is not only a photorealistic touch, but it also helps visually integrate a shadow into a scene containing several objects.

10. Click the Drop Shadow Stretch slider and increase it to **80**. The shadow stretches further in the direction of the bottom node, and you've gone from high noon to almost dusk in only one step.

11. Click a blank space on the page to deselect the effect, or choose the Pick tool, and you're done. Take a break and hang out in the shade for a while.

Tip To launch quickly into the editing state of an existing drop shadow effect while using the Pick tool, click the shadow once to display Property bar options, or double-click the shadow to make the Drop Shadow tool the current tool.

Manually Adjusting a Drop Shadow Effect

After applying the drop shadow effect, you'll notice the interactive nodes that appear around your shape. You'll see a combination Offset Position And Color node joined by a dotted line featuring an Opacity slider. If you're new to interactive controls, this illustration identifies these markers and indicates their functions.

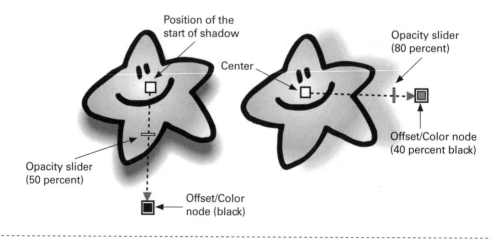

Tip To change a selected drop shadow's color, click-drag any color swatch from the onscreen color palette onto the shadow's Color node.

Shadows as Glow Effects

CorelDRAW's drop shadow effect is not limited to making shadows; if you think about it, a blurry bitmap can also represent a glow effect by using a different Merge mode and color.

By default, whenever a new shadow is created, black is automatically the applied color. You can reverse this effect by applying light-colored shadows to dark-colored objects arranged on a dark page background or in front of a darker-colored object. Here, you can see a black compound path (the cartoon light bulb) on top of an Elliptical fountain-filled rectangle (black is the End color and 30% black is the Start color at center) with a light-colored shadow effect applied. The result is a credible glow effect; there are also Glow Presets on the Property bar when you use the Drop Shadow tool to give you a jump-start on creating glows.

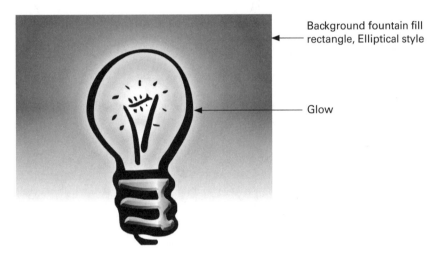

Background fountain fill rectangle, Elliptical style

Glow

This chapter has shown a lot of non-special effects—transparencies and shadows that aren't supposed to "wow" your audience, but rather speak of a quiet elegance that strikes the viewer on a subliminal level. It's well worth your time to become proficient with these effects for the future when you need a touch of photorealism in a drawing, something that strikes the audience without hitting them over the head. Speaking of photorealism, the next chapter takes you into a land where pixels and vectors happily coexist. No, this not the intro to a cheesy sci-fi flick—it's all about what you can do with photographs you import into CorelDRAW. You'll be amazed at first, and then you'll be amazing to others.

PART VIII

Bitmaps and Photos and How to Use CorelDRAW Graphics Suite to Work with Them

20 Working with Bitmap Images in CorelDRAW

Because people seldom photograph an object or a scene with exactly the elements they want in a composition, the field of retouching has thrived since the day a professional had something to sell using a photograph! This is why professionals trim photographs, and so can you, using the CorelDRAW features covered in this chapter. As objects, photographic areas that have been carefully cut out can be composited with other photos and vector shapes to add a whole new dimension to your posters, flyers, and fine art. Additionally this chapter demonstrates Corel PowerTRACE, part of CorelDRAW; you'll learn how to create a vector version of a bitmap so you can scale and rotate it, edit it, and never lose details or resolution as bitmap images are prone to do.

Note Download and extract all the files from the Chapter20.zip archive to follow the tutorials in this chapter.

Cropping a Placed Photograph

You can perform two types of cropping on placed photos: destructive (permanent) and nondestructive (you can undo what you've done). The Crop tool on the Toolbox performs destructive cropping. Unless you press CTRL + Z to undo a crop you don't like, you're stuck with your crop, and no exterior areas beyond the cropped image remain that you can expose later. Cropping a photo involves several steps:

1. You define the area you want to crop by click-diagonal-dragging the Crop tool from one corner to the opposite corner.
2. You can redefine the crop by click-dragging the resulting bounding-box markers. The corner markers scale the proposed crop area proportionately,

whereas the center markers are used to resize the proposed crop area disproportionately.

3. You can rotate the crop box, if, for example, you need to straighten a horizon. To do this, make a crop and then click inside the crop to put the crop into Rotate mode. You then drag on a corner double-headed arrow marker to rotate the crop. This doesn't rotate the photo itself, but rather the crop area.

4. You double-click inside the crop area to finish the crop. Figure 20-1 shows the elements you work with onscreen to crop a bitmap image.

Tip To see the resolution of a placed bitmap image quickly, with the bitmap selected, look at the Status bar, which names the file, tells you its color mode, and its current resolution. The rule is: as you increase bitmap dimensions, resolution decreases proportionately.

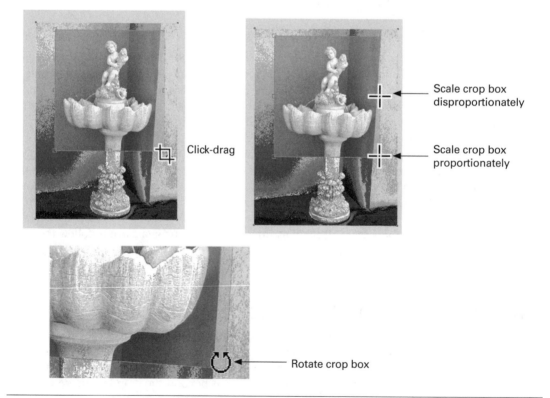

Click-drag

Scale crop box disproportionately

Scale crop box proportionately

Rotate crop box

FIGURE 20-1 The Crop tool eliminates the exterior image areas of your defined crop area.

Nondestructive Cropping

In a nutshell, if you want to hide an area of a photo and not delete it as you do with the Crop tool, you use the Shape tool. Try this out with the *Statue DSCN6562.jpg* image by following the steps here.

Using the Shape Tool to Crop

1. Create a new (default-sized) document with landscape orientation. Place the image of *Statue DSCN6562.jpg* in a new document by clicking the Import button on the Property bar and then selecting the image from the location you downloaded it to. With the loaded cursor, click-diagonal-drag to place the image so it fills most of the page.

2. This image needs to be rotated ever so slightly, so the light portion of the wall at right doesn't sneak into the crop you'll perform. Also, the left pedal that supports the kid holding the really large fish is higher than the petal at right. Drag a horizontal guide out of the top ruler and place it at the very top of the left petal.

3. Choose View | Simple Wireframe. You'll still be able to see a ghost of the image, but the reason you're doing this is so you can see the center rotation point of the photo so you can move it.

4. Using the Pick tool, select the image and then click it to turn the scaling handles into rotation handles.

5. Click-drag the center rotation marker over to the top of the left petal, as shown in this illustration.

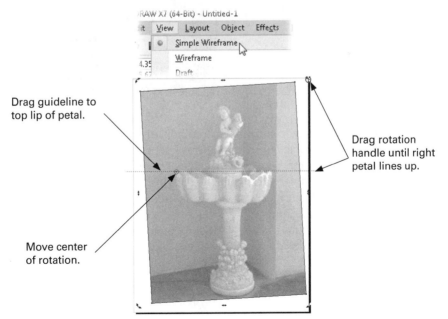

Drag guideline to top lip of petal.

Drag rotation handle until right petal lines up.

Move center of rotation.

6. Click drag the upper-right rotation handle until the right petal's top touches the guideline. You'll also notice that the edge of that wall has straightened up, too. You can go back to View | Enhanced now and deselect the photo.

7. Choose the Rectangle tool from the Toolbox, and then click-drag a rectangle over the top portion of the statue, including the petals and the child, but excluding the artistically trivial base. You do this because the image is rotated and you need a guide to perform a rectangular crop using the Shape tool.

8. Give the rectangle a white outline by right-clicking on the white color swatch on the color palette and then give it a 2-point outline using the num box on the Property bar—just so you can see the rectangle when you edit the underlying photo. Right-click over the rectangle and then choose Lock Object from the pop-up context menu; see the next illustration.

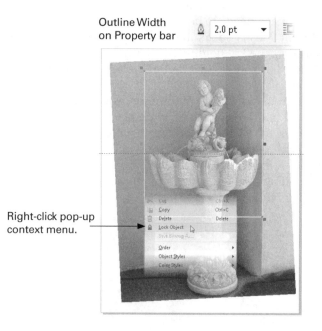

Outline Width on Property bar

Right-click pop-up context menu.

9. Choose the Shape tool from the Toolbox, and then click the photo to select it. The photo now has control node markers at each corner. These nodes behave and operate exactly like control nodes on vector shapes.

10. On the Standard bar, click the Snap To drop-down list and then choose Objects by placing a check to the left of the name.

11. Select one corner node of the photo and then drag it to the corresponding corner of the white rectangle, as shown in the next illustration. Like magic, the corner node of the photo magnetically aligns itself precisely with the corner of the rectangle.

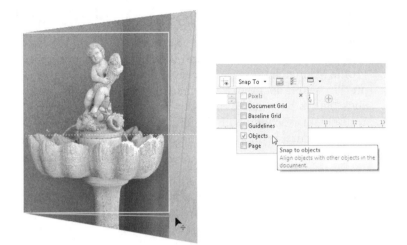

12. You're home free! Click-drag the remaining three corners to their corresponding positions around the rectangle. You can unlock and delete the rectangle now, and you have a clean, expertly executed, nondestructive crop. At any time, you can take the Shape tool and drag the image's four corner nodes way out until the original image is visible.

Masking Through Nondestructive Cropping

Go to the head of the class if you've already discovered that you can *add* control nodes to a placed photograph with the Shape tool! CorelDRAW "sees" a bitmap as an object that has a fill—specifically a bitmap fill. Therefore, this object can be shaped and reshaped by adding nodes and also by changing the segment property between nodes. The following sections take you through some advanced bitmap editing to trim around a photograph so it becomes a floating object in a composition.

Trimming Away Unwanted Image Areas

What you'll learn in this section goes way beyond the simple cropping of an image. You're going to trim the background away from an image of a bust of classical composer Johann Sebastian Bach, put a new background behind the bust, and by the end of this section, you'll have designed a concert poster. There are two nondestructive methods for removing the background from a photo's subject, and both techniques are described in this section. The elements of the poster have already been created for you, and shortly you'll see how to make a design with elements in front of and behind each other, just like you do with vector shapes, but using *photographs*.

To begin this poster design (call it the overture), you need to create a new document (portrait orientation, default page size) and import the image of Bach—a little smaller than the page size, but he can be scaled at a later time when needed. Then you use the Shape tool to trim the background.

Tutorial Background Removal, Technique 1

1. Click the Import button on the Property bar, and then in the Import dialog, locate *JS Bach.tif*, select him, and then click Import. If you receive a Color Profile Mismatch message, you should let CorelDRAW assign the image the color profile of your document, which is the default action, and all you need to do is click the OK button. See the following NOTE.

2. Your cursor is loaded with the image: click-drag, and then release the mouse when the cursor reports that the height for the placed image is about 9 inches.

Click-diagonal drag to size and place.

JS Bach.tif
w: 6.34 in, h: 8.942 in

Note If you get a Color Profile Mismatch message here or when working through other tutorials in this chapter, it's because your New Document settings are not the same color space as the photo, which is unavoidable sometimes. Click OK if this box appears, and the image's color profile will be compatible with your document now.

3. Choose the Shape tool. Begin by clicking the top-right node of the image, and then click-drag it toward the center of the image until the top and right edges touch the bust of Bach, as shown next. Clearly, you're not going to get where you want to go with only four control nodes because the geometry of the bust

is far from perfectly rectangular. This is okay; you'll add nodes to the outline of the image in the following step.

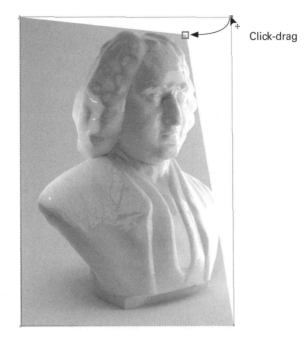

Click-drag

4. With the Shape tool, click a point on the outline of the photo where you want to change the direction of the line; Bach's powdered wig near his forehead is a prime area. Now, either double-click the segment, press the keyboard plus (+) key, or click the Add Node button on the Property bar to add a node. While you're in the vicinity of Bach's forehead, add several more points. A quick way to add points in-between existing points is to click a point repeatedly and press the + key.
5. Click-drag points so they visually coincide with the vertices of Bach's wig. It's okay if the lines between the nodes hide areas you want exposed.
6. Click a straight line segment that should curve away from the photo. Then click the To Curve button on the Property bar. The segment can now curve; click-drag the segment away from the photo, as shown next, until you can see

Bach's locks. You can also right-click a segment and choose To Curve from the pop-up menu.

Add Node

To Curve

7. That's it; all it takes now is about 10 minutes of your time to work around the profile of the bust, hiding areas and creating curved segments where needed. Yes, it's a lot of work, but so is putting on a tuxedo or gown to go and collect an industry award for outstanding design work (*prompt, hint, encouragement!*).

A good thing to do once you've trimmed away the nonessential Bach, because the default color of the page is white, is to put a colored vector shape behind your work to check your edge work. Make a rectangle, fill it with a dark color, and then press SHIFT + PAGE DOWN to place the rectangle to the back.

If you'd like to confirm the fact that the editing you performed is nondestructive, take the Shape tool and marquee-select several control nodes. Then drag them away from the center of the photo, as shown here. Then press CTRL + Z to undo this nondestructive *and unwanted* edit!

Boolean Operations as a Trimming Technique

You'll exert an equal amount of effort, but you might have an easier time visualizing the nondestructive photo-trimming process by drawing the outline of the image object you want to isolate and then use the Shaping commands to slice out the area you want to use. If you have Bach trimmed now, you don't have to follow this tutorial, but *do* read the steps because you might find this technique easier than editing the control nodes.

Tutorial   Background Removal, Technique 2

1. Using any of the Pen tools with which you're the most comfortable and experienced (the author uses the Bézier pen), draw a silhouette around the object you want to isolate in the photo, as shown here. It usually helps if you choose a contrasting outline color as you progress; you right-click, in this example, on white on the color palette *after* you've begun tracing. Choosing outline and fill colors *after* you've begun drawing a shape avoids triggering the attention box asking whether all new objects should get a white outline.

2. After you've closed the shape, choose Object | Shaping | Shaping to display the docker for performing an Intersect Boolean operation. You *could* use the Property bar Shaping buttons to perform this operation, but the Property bar Shaping buttons, by default, leave a copy of the target and source objects after the operation, a minor hassle to clean up later. You also must have both the outline and the photo selected, or the Shaping tool buttons won't appear on the Property bar, so let's go easy on these steps.
3. Select the object you just drew. Choose Intersect from the drop-down selector, and then uncheck both Leave Original... boxes if they are checked. Click Intersect With, click the region of the photograph that is outside of the white outline you just drew, and you're home free, as shown in Figure 20-2.

FIGURE 20-2 Use the Intersect Shaping command to remove all regions of the photo outside of the shape you drew.

Compositions with Mixed Media

Creating the poster is going to be fun—you're going to go beyond arranging and moving both bitmap and vector objects to laying out a finished art composition. What you'll see in the *Concert poster.cdr* file are two image objects: the background night image is locked on the bottom layer, and the gold title is an *alpha-channel masked image,* something covered a little later in this chapter.

Work through the following steps to duplicate your Bach trimming work to the concert poster document (an unlocked layer is active, so duplicating takes only one step). Then you'll add a vector shape to the composition to create an air of elegance ... it's a piece of *chorale* sheet music, actually, not an *air.*

Tutorial Composing a Design Using Vector and Image Shapes

1. Open *Concert poster.cdr*, and then choose Window | Tile Horizontally so you have a view of both your Bach work and the tutorial *.cdr* file. This is one of the rare occasions when the new tabbed document feature in X7 doesn't work for duplicating objects as quickly or precisely as the old-fashioned Windows cascading windows configuration.

2. Hold CTRL and then drag your trimmed bust of Bach into the Concert poster.cdr window, as shown in Figure 20-3. This duplicates your work; it doesn't move it. You can save and then close your Bach image as a CDR file now.

3. Choose Window | Dockers | Object Manager and make sure your copy of Bach is on Layer 1 (not hard because the "Bachground" layer is locked) and that the "Bach Text.png" image is below the Bach bust you just duplicated to this document. Drag the entries on the Object Layer around so they are in the correct order.

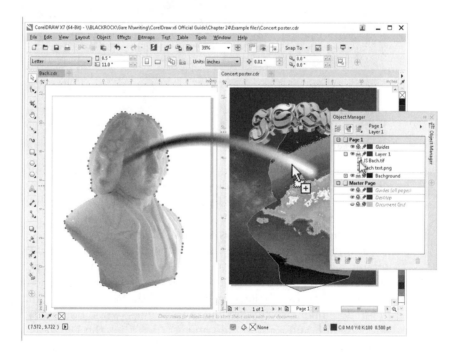

FIGURE 20-3   Duplicate your work in the *Concert poster.cdr* window.

4. Click the Import button on the Property bar, and then choose the *Bach 4 part Chorale.cdr* file from your hard drive. Click Import; your cursor is now loaded with the imported file. You can click anywhere to place it at its original size, but, for this example, click-drag beginning about ¾" from the left edge of the page until the legend at the bottom right of the cursor reads approximately **w: 7.5 in**.

5. With the music notes selected, click the white color swatch on the color palette.
6. Choose Window | Dockers | Object Manager. Click-drag the title "Bach 4 part Chorale.cdr" (the music notes), and then release the mouse button when the title is below the "JS Bach.tif" object.
7. Let's make the music sort of swell behind its composer. Choose the Envelope tool from the Effects group on the Toolbox. You're working in Putty mode by default, a good place to start; now, let's customize the envelope for a specific distortion. First, click the Add New button...because you're adding a new envelope (that was obvious, wasn't it?). With the Shape tool, marquee-select the middle nodes on the top and bottom lines; while holding SHIFT, marquee-select the left and right middle nodes. Then click the Delete Nodes button on the Property bar; see top left, Figure 20-4. Click the left side of the Envelope

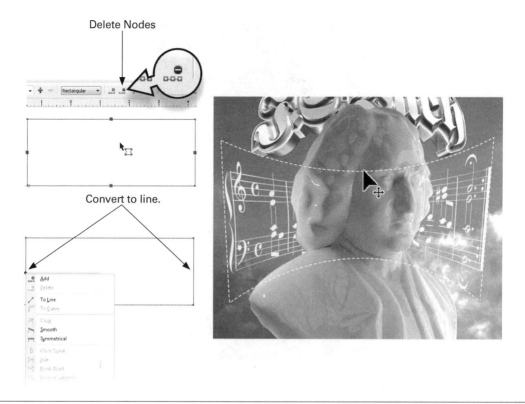

FIGURE 20-4   Shape the music so it appears to extend around the bust toward the audience.

bounding box, and then right-click and choose To Line from the pop-up menu. Then perform the same edit on the right side. The top and bottom default properties for Putty mode envelopes are curved segments—they need no editing. See the top left screen capture in Figure 20-4.

8. With the Shape tool, one at a time, click the control nodes that bound the music notes, and then drag the top ones up a little and the bottom ones down a little. Then click-drag the bottom line up and the top line down. Use your artistic eye and Figure 20-4 to guide you. Bach's compositions are stirring; the music notes should visually reflect this.

9. A time and place for this concert would help sell it; read Chapter 10 if you haven't done so already for good text-composition techniques. As you can see in Figure 20-5, the completed poster looks handsome, and most of its visual success is because you now know how to isolate an important subject from a fairly boring background.

FIGURE 20-5 When you can move image objects around on a page as easily as vector shapes, new design opportunities open up for you.

Working with Alpha Channels and Image Transparency

The following sections explain how you can trim your subject out of an image background, why certain file types are imported with transparency, and what transparency really means in your CorelDRAW work. More features than you might imagine are available for working with bitmaps directly in CorelDRAW; for *exceptionally* tricky image-editing assignments, Chapter 22 covers some of Corel PHOTO-PAINT.

Working with Partial Transparency

Both Alpha Channel transparency and Image Layer transparency offer more than simply 100 percent opaque or 100 percent transparent areas. With 24-bit images, you can have 256 levels of opacity in any area of the image, and this leads to some fascinating visual effects that you can create. You'll work shortly with an image that has semitransparent areas, but right now, you'll learn how to *build* semitransparent areas into an image that has none but should have them. Bob's Beer, a fictitious micro-brewery, has an image of a bottle in PNG file format that is surrounded by transparency. Let's say Bob wants the bottle to sit in front of a background that has his name repeated far too many times. Visually, his name should partially show through the neck of the bottle where there's only tinted glass and no beer.

The following tutorial shows you how to trim away the top quarter of the bottle, the most transparent part. Then you'll see how to make this area only partially opaque so some of the background shows through. And to top it off, you'll see how to build a cast shadow from the bottle onto the "ground" in the composition.

Tutorial   Creating a Photorealistic Glass Effect

1. Open *Bob's Background.cdr*, and then click the Import button and choose *Bob's Beer.png*; it's a domestic beer, but you'll import it anyway. Click Import and then with the loaded cursor, click-diagonal-drag until the bottle is placed in the image as shown here.

2. With a Pen tool (the Bézier pen works fine in this example), create a shape that fits in the top part of the glass, from the fill line to the bottle's lip, staying slightly inside the neck of the beer bottle so the edge is not part of the trimming operation you'll perform in a moment. You should fill the shape after creating it to better see what you're doing in the following steps—any color is fine.

3. Select the shape but not the bottle. Choose Object | Shaping | Shaping to display the Shaping docker. Choose Intersect from the selector drop-down list, and then check Leave Original Target Object. Click the Intersect With button, and then click the bottle. The shape is deleted because it's the source object, and you didn't choose to leave it. Apparently the bottle has not changed, but there is a perfect cutout duplicate of the top of the bottle resting on top of an

unchanged bottle; you're halfway there—you need to trim away part of the bottle using the new intersect shape now.

4. Click the spot formerly occupied by your drawn object to select the product of the intersect operation in Step 3 (don't worry; it's hard to see that it's a separate object). Choose Trim from the Shaping docker's drop-down list, check Leave Original Source Object, and uncheck Leave Original Target Object. Click the Trim button and then click the bottle, and the beer bottle is now actually two separate pieces. See the following illustration for the docker settings for Steps 3 and 4. Now it's on to transparency.

Separate object (but not obvious)

5. Select the top part shape, and then choose the Transparency tool from the Toolbox; the icon with the little wine glass that's about to tip over. Click the Uniform Transparency button on the Property bar, and then drag the Opacity slider on the Property bar to about **50%**. As you can see next, your editing work results in a quite convincing illustration. You can see Bob's logo in the background peeking through semitransparent glass; the background is even tinted a little from the green of the object on top of it.

Uniform
transparency

6. Here's the *pièce de résistance*: with the bottle selected, not the semitransparent piece, choose the Drop Shadow tool. Click toward the bottom of the bottle image to define an anchor for the shadow and then drag up and to the right.

7. Click-drag the End marker of the shadow so the shadow ends closer to the bottle. Then, because the bottle should be casting a deep green (not black) shadow, click the Shadow Color flyout on the Property bar, and then you might want to click More so you can choose from the Select Color dialog. Hex value 20800D works pretty well in this case, so you can type in the value, and then click OK to get back to your work. Also consider increasing the opacity of the shadow by dragging the Drop Shadow Opacity slider on the Property bar up to **70%** or so.

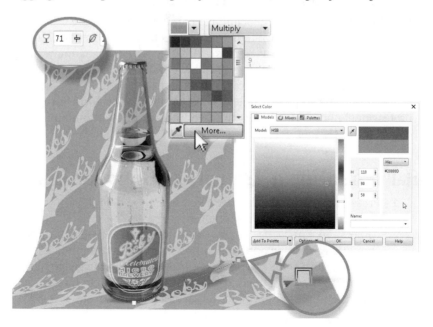

8. Well, oops. The area you trimmed in Step 4 is not part of the shadow—there's a hole in the shadow where there should be a lighter green because a shadow cast by green glass through beer would be a little darker than a shadow cast through green glass alone. No problem; you draw a fill shape for the missing part of the shadow, as shown here, fill the shape with a lighter green than the bottle shadow's color, and then give it about **60** to **69%** Uniform transparency.

Blending Photos with Transparency

Let's imagine in the tutorial challenge coming up next that the *Tree.png* file you'll work with in the following steps was created by masking everything except the tree in the photo, and then you saved it as a PNG file with transparency using PHOTO-PAINT.

You know now that an image can have transparent areas, and you know you can use CorelDRAW's Transparency tool to make any object on a page *partially* transparent. The steps that follow show you how to perform surreal, completely professional photo retouching with two images you graft onto one another with only one CorelDRAW tool.

Tutorial Creating a Transition Between Two Images

1. Press CTRL + N to create a new file. Accept the default standard letter page size, and define it as Portrait orientation.
2. Import *ThumbsUp.jpg*. Accept the Color Profile Mismatch message's suggestion—should the message appear at all—to convert from embedded color profile to the document color profile; just click OK. JPEG images do not retain resolution information, so you need to click-drag the loaded cursor after clicking Import to scale the imported image to the 11" height of the page.

3. Import *Tree.png*. PNG files can (in some cases) retain image-resolution information, so all you need to do is click the loaded cursor on the page.
4. With the Pick tool, position the tree so its trunk fits over the thumb in the underlying photo.
5. Choose the Transparency tool from the Toolbox.
6. Click-drag downward, starting from around the thumbnail area in the underlying photo to just above the trunk on the tree. You should see the amazing transformation between the guy's thumb and the trunk of the tree. If the Start and End points for this Linear transparency aren't perfect, you can adjust the Start and End points with the Transparency tool cursor. Because you performed this edit interactively, you'll see that the Property bar states this is a Fountain transparency style and that the Linear Transparency button is depressed automatically.
7. Unfortunately, the guy's thumb doesn't taper toward the top like the tree trunk does; some of the thumb is visible, ruining the special effect. Choose the Bézier pen tool from the Toolbox, and then draw a closed shape whose right edge matches the contour of the tree trunk's left side. Fill it with the same color as the background of the thumb photo—choose the Color Eyedropper tool from the Toolbox, click over the background, and then click the paint bucket cursor on the shape you drew. See Figure 20-6 for the exact location of this edit in the photo.

FIGURE 20-6 Create a blend between two photos to present unique and visually arresting imagery.

8. Perform Step 7 on the right side of the thumb, after drawing a second shape.

9. Remove the outline of both shapes (select them both) by right-clicking the No Fill color swatch on the color palette.

10. With both shapes selected, press CTRL + PAGEDOWN to put them behind the tree, yet in front of the thumb photo.

11. Read Chapter 10 on working with text because this image would make a terrific magazine cover.

Bitmaps to Vector Art: Using PowerTRACE

You can export both vector art and bitmaps to bitmap file format, but once in a while, you'll need to go the other way: taking a bitmap and making vector art from it. Many design professionals are faced daily with clients who want to use their logo for a truck sign or a high-resolution print ad, but all they can provide the designer is a really pathetic GIF copy from their web page.

Fortunately, designers don't have to reconstruct logos by hand—Corel PowerTRACE is a highly accurate utility that often produces a vector equivalent of a placed bitmap that requires no hand-tweaking afterward. What PowerTRACE does is simple: it creates a vector version of the selected bitmap. *How* PowerTRACE does this is not easy to explain, but if you understand the "how," you'll be better prepared to choose the right option before making a vector copy of an imported bitmap. In a nutshell, PowerTRACE examines the bitmap based on the criteria you specify in the dialog and then seeks edges in the bitmaps that show a clear and marked difference in color and/or brightness between neighboring pixels. PowerTRACE then creates a vector line at this neighboring region, continues to create a closed path (with the Centerline option chosen, it creates open paths), and fills the path with the closest color match to the pixels inside the area it creates. The following sections take you through the operation of PowerTRACE and offer suggestions on settings and when and why you'd use this handy feature.

Bitmap Conversions for Logo Alterations

Sometimes you'll want to use PowerTRACE to rework an existing logo that's in bitmap format. Suppose *SilverSpoon.png*—a good, clean graphic—is the logo for a caterer that was bought out yesterday by Phil Greasy, and Phil likes the logo but wants the name changed to… you guessed it. You use PowerTRACE to make a vector conversion of the logo, covered in the following section, but this is a prime example of the importance of knowing general looks of popular fonts and acceptable substitutions. Many times tracing typography in a logo is a futile endeavor: recasting the text using the same or a similar font is much easier and provides cleaner results.

Pretouching: Use PHOTO-PAINT for Cleanup Before Tracing

The Silver Spoon logo that PowerTRACE will convert so you can alter the logo for the new owner is a detailed and complex one. The logo has four or five areas that you need to assist PowerTRACE with by manually editing the logo before auto-tracing it. Your own artistic eye is hooked up to your brain, and it can discern the edge between the black outline around "Silver" and the black background checkerboard. PowerTRACE, on the other hand, doesn't have eyes and doesn't have a brain (these features are expected in CorelDRAW XX19). Therefore, you will make life a lot easier if you use Corel PHOTO-PAINT to erase the areas—working to the outside of the outline around "Silver"—so there is a gap and so PowerTRACE can create separate objects for the word "Silver" and the checkerboard background.

This logo is probably the hardest one you'll encounter professionally to use PowerTRACE on for cleanup work and alterations. If you succeed at this fictitious example, your paying gigs will be a charm. These steps are really quite easy, and shortly, you'll see how little sweat you have to break to alter the logo dramatically:

Tutorial   Working Between CorelDRAW and PHOTO-PAINT

1. In a new document in CorelDRAW, import the *Silver Spoon.png* image. Click the loaded cursor to place the bitmap at its original size.
2. Click Edit Bitmap on the Property bar. In a moment, PHOTO-PAINT loads with *Silver Spoon.png* displayed in a document window.
3. Choose the Eraser tool from PHOTO-PAINT's Toolbox. On PHOTO-PAINT's Property bar, type **10** in the Size field to set the diameter of the Eraser tool. Leave the Feather amount at its default value. Doing this gives you a small, hard tool for erasing areas to the default white background color.

4. The bottom right of the *S*, the dot over the *i*, the upper left of the *l*, the top and bottom left of the *e* where it touches the outline of the spoon, and the bottom and right portions of the *r*, all touch what you can see as black background areas. Refer to the illustration here, and carefully erase areas outside of these characters, creating a white gutter between background elements touching the black border around the letters in "Silver."

5. When you're finished, click the Finish Editing button on PHOTO-PAINT's Standard bar. Click Yes to save changes, PHOTO-PAINT closes, and you're returned to CorelDRAW with your edits made to the copy of the logo you imported.
6. With the bitmap selected, click Trace Bitmap (the button on the Property bar when a bitmap is selected), and then choose Outline Trace | High Quality Image. It's not time to trace yet; it's time to *explore your options* before tracing.

PowerTRACE Options

After you import and select the bitmap, you have the option to Quick Trace the bitmap or to get more specific about the final traced object's quality and fidelity. This logo has no dithering and no aliased edges. Therefore, the PowerTRACE can be set for less smoothing and greater precision. As you can see in Figure 20-7, the logo has a transparent background because Options | Remove Background has been checked.

Type of bitmap/quality of original bitmap   Produces objects or lines

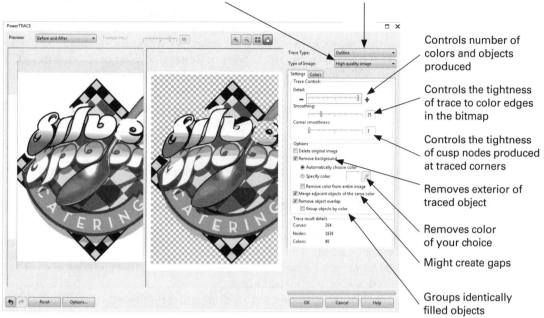

Controls number of colors and objects produced

Controls the tightness of trace to color edges in the bitmap

Controls the tightness of cusp nodes produced at traced corners

Removes exterior of traced object

Removes color of your choice

Might create gaps

Groups identically filled objects

FIGURE 20-7 Use the features and settings in PowerTRACE to create an optimized group of vector objects based on the bitmap.

The final product, therefore, will include a little something special with no extra time spent by you removing the white background by hand. Once you are in the interface for tracing, there's some ground to cover regarding the options you set, which will definitely impact the quality of the trace.

- **Trace Type** In addition to Quick Trace, you can choose Outline or Centerline from this drop-down. Outline is the method that produces objects based on areas of similar color in the bitmap. Centerline is a good option when your source bitmap is calligraphy or a technical drawing; this option generates open paths to which you can assign different widths and styles after the trace is placed on the page.
- **Type Of Image** Both Centerline and Outline trace have options—you'll be using Outline Trace, which has the most options for helping PowerTRACE understand what type of graphic is to be traced—that govern accuracy, image noise, and other criteria. Depending on your choice for Type Of Image—from Line Art to High Quality Image—PowerTRACE renders a few objects or hundreds. You can customize an image type's setting by altering parameters, and you can also use an "inappropriate" setting for your imported image. No two images are alike, and you might be surprised at the hi-fi rendering of a piece of clipart you trace using the Line Art setting, for example.

- **Colors**   On this tab, you can set the number of unique colors PowerTRACE evaluates, from 1 (which renders a stencil of your original) to a varying maximum of unique colors, which you can limit by typing in a value. You can specify the color mode for the trace; choose CMYK, for example, if you need a trace that can be sent as an EPS file to a commercial printer. Generally, your best bet is the RGB color mode. You can also sort the colors to be used by how frequently they appear in the original bitmap or by similarity. Additionally, if you intend to replace a color when you edit the traced result, you can do so by clicking a color swatch and then clicking Edit.

- **Settings**   This tab defines how tightly and accurately you want PowerTRACE to render the bitmap as a vector object.

  - **Detail**   You set the overall complexity of the trace with this slider. Higher values instruct PowerTRACE to evaluate the bitmap carefully, whereas lower Detail settings can produce a stylized, posterized trace with fewer colors and much fewer groups of objects.

  - **Smoothing**   This setting controls both the number of nodes along paths and, to a lesser extent, the number of objects the trace yields. A higher smoothing value is good when your bitmap import is a GIF image that contains a lot of noise, dithered colors, and jagged edges.

  - **Corner Smoothness**   Use this setting depending on the visual content of your imported bitmap. For example, a photo of a sphere probably doesn't require any corner smoothness. However, a photo of a bird's feather will certainly have a lot of abrupt color and geometry changes—you use a very low Corner Smoothness setting to represent accurately the sharp turns and corners that make up a feather.

  - **Remove Background**   Usually you'll want to check this box. When an imported image such as this logo is floating in a background of white, Remove Background doesn't make the background a huge white rectangle. Optionally, any color can be removed from the final trace by clicking the Specify Color button and then using the Eyedropper to choose a color from the preview window.

  - **Merge Adjacent Objects Of The Same Color**   This option makes one object instead of several if the bitmap contains areas of almost identical color in neighboring regions.

  - **Remove Object Overlap**   Most of the time, you'll leave this box unchecked. If you do choose to enable Remove Object Overlap, there might be visible gaps between the resulting grouped vector shapes, making it hard to put a solid background behind your trace without the background color or texture peeking through. You must choose this option before you can use Group Objects By Color.

  - **Group Objects By Color**   This is a handy feature that automatically groups identically colored objects after you click OK to make the trace. You can then choose a different color and apply it to the entire group or delete an entire group of objects identically filled, so you don't have dozens of objects that can be accidentally moved lying all over the page.

- **Trace Result Details**   This area on the dialog predicts how many objects (Curves), how many nodes, and how many different colors are produced. As a guideline, if the results show more than 200 objects will be created, think twice. That's a large number of objects to edit, and the resulting trace could possibly be a challenge to work with.

Let's put all this knowledge into practice in the next section.

Performing a Trace

You're almost set to click OK and have PowerTRACE convert the *Silver Spoon.jpg* logo into a set of vector objects.

The original logo's text was cast in Motter Fem; if you don't own this font, it's okay. Open this chapter's zip file, and install *Candid.ttf* through the Start menu | Control Panel | Fonts before you begin the tutorial. Candid is not a complete typeface; it's missing punctuation marks and numbers, and it was created after the Candy font by URW. It similar to Motter Fem, and Candy is a great packaging design font you might seriously consider purchasing for your collection—*Candid.ttf* is an author-cobbled knockoff whose purpose is solely to get you through the techniques in the following steps.

Tutorial   Reworking a Logo Using Vectors

1. In the PowerTRACE box, set the Detail slider all the way to the right lower setting to ignore details such as the "Catering" text because the text is made up of only a few pixels in character width. Set Smoothing to about **25%**; the logo is already fairly smooth and will not benefit from the averaging PowerTRACE would make in defining paths.
2. Set the Corner Smoothness slider to the far left (no corner smoothing). You want cusp nodes and sharp corners rendered to keep the checkerboard pieces and serifs on the typefaces sharp. Then, check Remove Background, check Merge Adjacent Objects Of The Same Color, and then look over the Trace Curve Results field just as a matter of practice.
3. Click the Colors tab and then set the Number Of Colors to **30**—there really aren't more colors than 30 in the image; more colors will create superfluous additional objects. These settings should yield about 200 separate objects, so click OK.
4. Move the objects away from the bitmap original; you want to keep the original on the page for reference. Ungroup the group of objects, and then delete what's left of the word "Silver." This will leave a hole in the background in a few places.
5. With the Text tool, type **Greasy**, and then apply Candid from the Font selector drop-down on the Property bar.
6. Apply a white fill to the text, and then press ALT + ENTER to display the Object Properties docker. Click the three dots (Outline Settings) to the right of the Outline Weight list to display the Outline Pen dialog. Set the outline to **8** points, and check Behind Fill. This makes the apparent outline width 4 points, but areas are filled in within the characters to give the text a bold look.

7. Choose the Envelope tool from the Effects group on the Toolbox, and then perform the same steps as you did earlier with the music notes in the Bach composition. Use the Shape tool to massage the text to look arced like the original text. If your design now looks like the one shown here, you're in good shape with only a step or two to go.

Delete unnecessary logo objects.

Apply an envelope effect around new text to copy the style of original text.

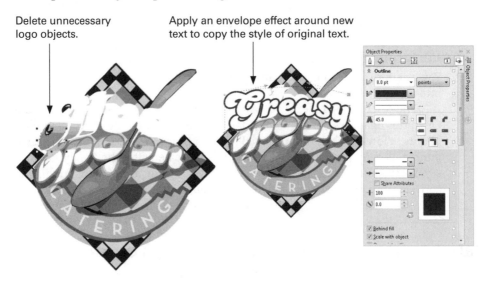

8. Create rectangles that match the color of the missing checkerboard in the logo, rotate them to the correct diamond-shaped orientation as the original logo, position them accordingly for your patchwork, and then send them to the back of the page by pressing SHIFT + PAGEDOWN.
9. With the Shape tool, edit the characters in the word "catering" to make them look more refined. At small image sizes, CorelDRAW does its best to render approximations of small text, but the images often need a little human intervention!

Create background replacement pieces.

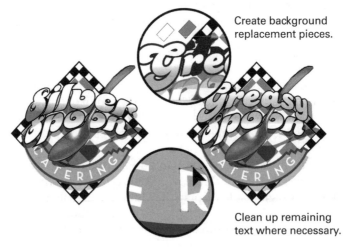

Clean up remaining text where necessary.

10. You can embellish the revised logo by adding a drop shadow to the new owner's name, as it appears in the original logo, and you can smooth out the posterized edges on the spoon by overlaying an object that uses a fountain fill with the same colors. But, as you can see here, the new logo is pretty faithful to the original, and with the help of PowerTRACE, it took ten steps. Think of how many steps and lost nights of sleep you'd have without an auto-tracing utility.

Tip To get superfluous objects out of a finished PowerTRACE quickly, use Edit | Find And Replace | Find Objects, and set the criteria for the search to specific unwanted colors. Then you can delete all the selected objects at once.

PowerTRACE for Traditional Artists

Many different types of users are attracted to CorelDRAW. Logo and other graphic designers are one category of visual communicators. However, CorelDRAW's tracing feature also appeals to artists who come to the digital world of illustration after years of work with physical pens, pencils, and inks.

If you have a scanner, and have, for example, a pen-and-ink cartoon, PowerTRACE makes child's play out of re-creating your cartoon as scalable vector art, to which you can apply color fills with a smoothness and precision that enhances your cartoons and can elevate them to the status of Fine Art. Seriously!

Cartoon sneaker drawing.png is a fairly high-resolution scan to get you started with a specific workflow you can adopt with scans of your own drawings. One important issue is removing pencil or other marks on the physical paper before you scan; use a kneaded eraser, and even if the paper doesn't come completely clean, the following steps show you a novel way to use PowerTRACE to remove stray marks.

Here's how to create a digital cartoon suitable for exporting as either vector or bitmap art to any size you need; this is a perk you don't have when working with only physical tools.

Tutorial Digi-tooning

1. In a new document, select Landscape orientation, click the Import button on the Standard bar, and then choose *Cartoon sneaker drawing.png*. Place it by click-dragging the loaded cursor so it fills the page.
2. Click Trace Bitmap, and then choose Outline Trace | Line Art. You'll receive an attention box that the bitmap size is too large and that, if you choose not to resize the bitmap, the trace process might be on the slow side. This is your artistic call: if you want the pen strokes to look extremely faithful to the author's original cartoon, click Keep Original Size. If you're in a hurry, click Reduce Bitmap.
3. In the PowerTRACE window, choose a medium amount of detail, about **25%** Smoothing, no Corner Smoothing, check Remove Background, and then click the Colors tab. Set the number of colors to **2**. Doing this generates almost entirely black objects with the exception of one or two areas that are totally

enclosed, which should produce a white fill inside a black object. Check Remove Color From Entire Image to get rid of superfluous white areas. Check Delete Original Image, click OK, and you'll see that the pencil marks that are not entirely a black color disappear from the trace.

4. Choose Window | Dockers | Object Manager. Create a new layer and then drag its title on the list to below Layer 1. You can rename these layers **Coloring** and **Trace** by clicking to select the name and then clicking a second time to open the title for editing—type anything you like in the field. Lock the tracing layer.

5. Using the Pen tool you're most comfortable with for creating freeform shapes, create objects that represent the different areas of the cartoon you'd like to color in. For example, the treads of the sneaker would look good in several different shades of warm gray. The solution would be to use the Mesh fill on this object you draw—see Chapter 12 for thorough documentation of object fills. The top of the sneaker could be an interesting Linear fountain fill,

traversing from deep orange at bottom to a bright yellow at top. Another great thing about coloring your work digitally is that you never have to decide on a final color.

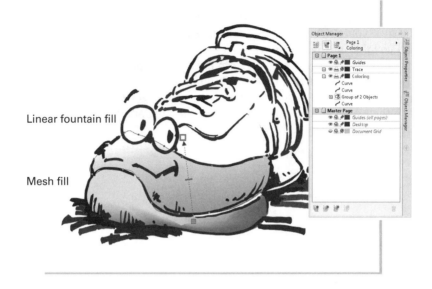

Linear fountain fill

Mesh fill

6. You continue this process until you've "colored inside the lines" and filled as much of the drawing as you see fit artistically. You can see a logo mockup here for a children's footwear store. Clearly the drawing has an organic sense about it, the opposite of the sterile and flawless "computer art" we see occasionally, and yet this is CorelDRAW computer art, with a little ingenuity added to create a symbiosis between the physical and traditional elements.

You can take a look at how this drawing was completed if you open *Sneaky kids finished.cdr*.

This chapter has been an introduction to how imported bitmaps can happily coexist and help enhance your vector work in CorelDRAW. As you move on to Chapter 21, you're going to graduate to *Advanced* Bitmap and Vector Integrator. You'll see how all the stuff you've learned in this chapter can be applied to advanced design compositions, and you'll gain experience with a trick or two on image resolution and color space that will make your work stand out from the crowd. And to top it off, you'll work a little with CorelDRAW's filters that can turn ho-hum photography into oh-wow eye-catchers. You might even exceed your *own* expectations after getting the lowdown on bitmaps and how they can complement your vector drawing and text design work. Set your sights high, and let's move on!

21 Understanding and Working with Pixel-Based Images in CorelDRAW

You'll occasionally want to set aside the Bézier pen tool and fountain fill. Your layout for a brochure, for example, is all done, and now you want to add a photograph of your product. The good news is that CorelDRAW can import just about any bitmap file you have. Whether a photo from your camera, a scan of a photo, or a painting you created in PHOTO-PAINT—you can crop, rotate, and perform enhancements on it within CorelDRAW. This chapter takes you first through the structure of *pixel-based images* (bitmaps). You'll learn how you can get them to print well, what you can and cannot do with them, their special properties, and the difference between this type of graphic and vector artwork. Then you'll work with some photographed and created bitmap images to learn how to edit and enhance your images.

This chapter delivers the goods on the whats, whys, and whens for bitmap importing, finessing, and integration to make your documents come alive and communicate.

> **Note** Download and extract all the files from the Chapter21.zip archive to follow the tutorials in this chapter.

The Properties of a Pixel-Based Image

We all tend to take a photograph with our multi-megapixel camera, and then we text it or post it on social media and that's the end of the story. We don't question the *structure* of a digital image at all.

If you want to do something with a digital image, however, such as incorporate it into a flyer, crop it, resize it, or put something else into it within a CorelDRAW composition, this is the beginning of the story of pixel-based images and their manipulation that you should heed. Without a cursory understanding of how pixel-based images are structured, you won't be able to do as many things successfully as you'd like to do with them in CorelDRAW. Therefore, the following sections dig a little into what goes into a pixel-based image, so you can get more out of them as covered in the rest of this chapter.

Pixel Artwork vs. Vector Artwork

Although you can work with two fundamentally different types of graphics on a personal computer—vector graphics and pixel graphics—actually 100 percent of what you see onscreen is a *pixel-based graphic.* Your computer monitor has no easy way to display vectors as vectors, so even when you work with paths in CorelDRAW, what you're seeing onscreen is a pixel-based representation that CorelDRAW draws to your screen on-the-fly. So now is a good and appropriate time to think more about pixels as an art form and as a tool.

Vector artwork, the kind of art you create in CorelDRAW, is *resolution independent,* a term you hear a lot, particularly if you're around programmers. Resolution independent means that the art you create in CorelDRAW can be scaled up and down, rotated and distorted every which way, and it still retains its crispness and structural integrity. Vector artwork can be boiled down to a direction a path travels in, the width of its outline, its fill color—regardless of how complex you make a drawing, it can be explained and saved to a file in math terms. And because math can be divided and multiplied without discarding the values you put into an equation, scaling a vector drawing doesn't change its core values. For example, $150 \times 2 = 300$ is an equation that results in twice the 150 value, but the 150 value isn't really altered to produce a result of 300.

Pixel-based graphics, on the other hand, are *resolution dependent.* This means a finite number of pixels go into what you see onscreen, and they cannot be increased or decreased without making a visible, fundamental change to the structure of such a graphic. Pixel-based images aren't truly as flexible as vector artwork, and until you understand the term *resolution,* you can irrevocably damage a pixel-based image. You could throw a digital photo out of focus or add artifacting (explained in a moment). However, the positives of pixel images outweigh any negatives: Although taking a snapshot is easy, drawing something that looks exactly like a photograph, using vectors, is quite hard. Pixel-based images can have depth of field, exposure, a source of scene lighting, and other properties. Although many talented artists have created CorelDRAW pieces that look almost like a photograph, not many of us can invest the time nor do we have the sheer talent to "make photographs" using CorelDRAW. Fortunately, this chapter shows you the easy way to make CorelDRAW more photographic in nature: you just import a *photograph!*

Artifacts and Anti-aliasing

You can take resolution-dependent bitmap images and make them larger, artificially increasing the size (and the saved file size) of the final image. You cannot add *detail* to an existing photograph by enlarging it, however: when a computer application is told to add pixels to an image, it has no real way of telling what color pixels should be added to the photograph. Not CorelDRAW, not Adobe Photoshop, nor any other application (except those phony forensic computers you see on TV shows) can intelligently, artistically, or accurately add, for example, detail to a photo of the getaway car so the license plate instantly becomes crisp and legible.

What you get when you perform any "make this photo larger" command is "fake resolution"; the program averages pixel colors neighboring the original pixels to create more, similarly colored pixels. This can often lead to *artifacting,* what we commonly describe as "there's some junk in the upper left of this photo near my aunt's face." Artifacting can be introduced to a digital photograph at any stage of photography: your camera didn't write the file correctly; the image became corrupted when you copied it to your hard drive; and or you tried to enlarge a resolution-dependent image. The cure for the last reason is don't resample important images; instead, print a copy of the image at its original size and see how it looks. From there, increase its size, check for visible artifacts in your print, and if there's visible corruption, go back to your original or seriously consider reshooting the image.

One of the methods CorelDRAW, PHOTO-PAINT, and other programs that can import bitmaps use to lessen and occasionally eliminate visible artifacting from a resampled photo is called *anti-aliasing,* and you have some control over this method, discussed later in this chapter. Anti-aliasing is a math calculation that performs averaging in a resulting photo that's been altered in areas where there is visual ambiguity (some of the pesky pixels are traveling under an alias). For example, suppose you could photograph a checkerboard plane that extends from your feet way out to the horizon. You look down toward your feet and clearly see black squares and white squares. You look at the horizon, and you do not see clear edges of the black-and-white squares: actually you see a lot of gray, as your mind blends black and white together because your eyes don't have photoreceptors fine enough to resolve the very distant black-and-white squares. Similarly, our computers cannot reconcile black-and-white areas in a digital image that are smaller than the size of the pixels in the image, so when you resample the image, they create—inaccurately—little black-and-white squares where they shouldn't be. The inaccuracy means the black-and-white squares are traveling as an *alias* and presenting themselves falsely.

(continued)

Anti-aliasing comes to the designer's rescue by *averaging* pixel colors when you resample such a checkerboard photo, or any photo. The anti-aliasing technique examines, in this example, areas that include both a white square and a black one, understands that both colors can't be assigned to only one pixel, and so writes a blend of colors—gray—to the new pixel color value. At left in this illustration, you can see some unwanted patterning toward the horizon—this image was not anti-aliased when it was resampled to produce a larger image. At right, the same image was resampled using anti-aliasing; at 1:1 viewing, you can see the smooth transition as the checkerboard extends into the distance—and the close-up shows the result of good anti-aliasing (some applications anti-alias poorly)—gray is substituted for black and white when it's a tossup for a single pixel color.

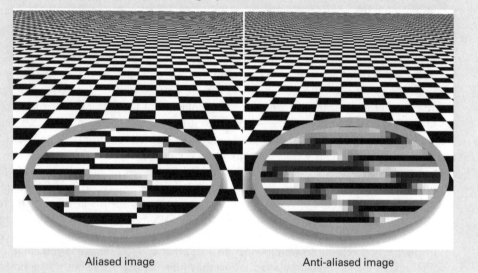

Aliased image   Anti-aliased image

Bytemaps and Pixels

Programmers and users alike are accustomed to calling a pixel-based image a *bitmap*. However, the term "bitmap" is a little like the term "dial phone." Telephones haven't had dials in two decades or more, and similarly, a bitmap—literally a map of bits of information—is inadequate to describe a pixel-based image, but "bitmap" is used as the term for non-vector graphics in this chapter anyway. We're comfortable with the term and "bitmap" is shorter to write than "pixel-based image."

Let's say you have onscreen a JPEG fresh off your camera. What are you seeing? You're seeing a finite number of placeholders for color, and the sheer *number* of placeholders for color is so large that your mind integrates the placeholders into a familiar image. That's the "map" part of the term "bitmap"; this map could also be called a *mesh,* a *grid,* or a *canvas.* All the bitmap images you take with a camera or paint in a paint program are composed of information units all lined up in a grid. You don't *see* the grid (or the *map* part of a bitmap); it's only a figurative expression—it's the *structure* for the visual information. The finer the grid, the less likely you are to see the individual color elements, instead of your mind blending the elements into a photograph. The "bit" part of the term "bitmap" is actually a *byte* of color information: a bit of information can only have two possible values (usually on or off); the graphics that artists work with today have a byte (8 bits) of information (sometimes more) per color channel with which to express a color value. The term "bitmap" was coined in the days when a monitor could truly only display a color or no color, thus the term "bitmap"; and the term has stuck with us for more than 30 years.

To extend this explanation further, this unit of information lodged in a map is called a *pixel,* short for *pic*ture *el*ement, the smallest unit of color you can see in a bitmap image. A pixel is only *a placeholder for a color value;* it is *not* a unit of measurement, and it doesn't even have to be square (digital movie cameras take rectangular-proportioned movie pixels), and it has no fixed size. Other things a pixel is *not* include

- **A dot**   Even professionals lapse into describing the resolution of a digital image in terms of dots per inch once in a while. This is okay if they're using the term "dot" as slang to mean a pixel, but this jargon is confusing. Printers print dots of toner and other pigment onto a surface (usually paper); a 1,200 dpi printer, for example, renders 1,200 dots of toner per inch of paper, but it is not rendering 1,200 pixels per inch of toner! In fact, a 1,200 dpi laser printer is incapable of rendering 1,200 pixels per inch (ppi). A pixel is *not* a dot of toner or ink, nor is a dot of ink equal to a pixel—pixels that are not part of a physical dimension ratio do not have a size.
- **A screen phosphor or LED**   Pixels that make up an image do not usually correspond 1:1 to whatever the elements on your monitor are made of. With high-quality images, there are many more pixels per inch than there are light units (phosphors, LEDs, and so on) on your screen. This is why CorelDRAW and paint programs such as PHOTO-PAINT and Adobe Photoshop offer zoom tools, so you can get a better look at image areas, mapping small amounts of pixels to your screen, which has a finite number of light-emitting elements. As resolution is discussed later in this chapter, it's good to know that the most frequently used resolution for web graphics is 72 ppi (pixels per inch), even though a Retina displays a staggeringly beautiful 220 ppi, and local (non-Internet) desktop monitor resolution is typically estimated at 96 ppi. Therefore, if the resolution of an image is, let's say 96 ppi, this means when you view it at 100 percent viewing resolution, what your screen's light-emitting elements are mapping is 1:1 to the image resolution. You're viewing a bitmap graphic exactly as the creator of the bitmap intended it.
- **Any sort of ratio**   The measurement commonly used in bitmap evaluation is *pixels per inch,* which is a ratio, like mph is a ratio—miles (one unit) per hour (a different unit). A pixel is a unit, but not a ratio. Therefore, if someone says they have an image that's 640 by 480 pixels, they've told you how many pixels are in the image, but not its resolution and not its size. A pixel is a unit and needs to be contextualized—for example, 120 pixels per inch or 300 pixels per centimeter— before the unit becomes meaningful and useful to a printer or designer. If you

told friends you were driving your car down the Autobahn at "200 miles," they probably wouldn't be impressed because you haven't contextualized this unit into something meaningful such as a measurement. But "200 miles per hour" tells your friends something—that they probably don't want to ride with you!

Color Depth

In addition to being color value placeholders, pixels also have "depth," not "depth" as you'd measure a swimming pool, but rather a color "density," color capability, or the range within which the image format can express a given number of unique colors. For example, GIF images have a maximum color depth of 256 unique values; grayscale images have a brightness depth of 256 shades.

Because 256 unique colors can't truly express the beauty we capture with a digital camera (even dull scenes can contain tens of thousands of unique colors), programmers decided early on in the digital imaging game to structure high-quality images into components, the most common structure being red, green, and blue— your computer monitor is based on the RGB color model. These three components are usually called *color channels*: by adding the brightness values of these three channels together, you get the composite view of digital photos and other bitmaps. Channels are an efficient method for storing bitmap color information—in contrast, GIF images store image colors as explicit color table values, and this is one of the reasons why GIF images are limited to 256 unique colors. By assigning the red, green, and blue color channels in a bitmap image an 8-bit per channel color capability, this equals 2^8, meaning the red, green, and blue channels can each have one of 256 possible brightness values with which to contribute color to the RGB composite image. Eight bits per channel times three color channels adds up to 24-bit images—BMP, PNG, TIFF, TGA (Targa), and Photoshop PSD being the most common file formats that can hold this color information. So 24-bit images have a maximum unique color capability of 16.7 million colors.

However, color depth doesn't stop at 24-bit (8 bits per channel); although most affordable monitors today can only display 24-bit image depth, camera manufacturers anticipate that this will change eventually, with the increasing popularity of high dynamic range (HDR) displays and higher-definition monitors. Today, many of the middle-range digital cameras can write photos to the Raw file format, whose specifics vary from manufacturer to manufacturer as do the file extensions. Happily, CorelDRAW can import most digital camera Raw files. *Raw files* (covered later in this chapter) are "unprocessed film": they contain exposure settings, f-stops, and other camera data, but they also provide a lot of flexibility when you import such an image. CorelDRAW has a little utility called Camera Raw Lab where you can color-correct and change image exposure—all after the photo is taken. You can do this because Raw images can contain 16 bits per color channel, to offer a 48-bit image—more than 281 trillion possible colors ... we're talking a *very* large crayon box.

Consider it a given that because CorelDRAW can handle such mega-information and has some very good processing tools for imported bitmap images, the compositions you create using bitmaps along with vector designs will print splendidly. Now it's time to discuss image resolution as it relates to outputting your work.

Printing Resolution and Resolution-Dependent Images

As mentioned earlier, resolution is expressed as a fraction, a ratio between units (pixels) and space (inches, usually). As you'll see later in Table 21-1, a few image file types such as PSD and TIFF can store image resolution information, and this is good. For example, let's say you need to inkjet-print a brochure, and the front page needs a photograph. A photograph of insufficient resolution is going to print lousily, pure and simple. However, if the photographer saved the digital photo to PSD, TIFF, PNG, or Raw camera file format (and knows about image resolution), you can import the image and know before you print whether the image needs to be *resized* (the opposite of *resampling*). The rule is that an image's resolution should be in the neighborhood of your printer's resolution. Let's say you've imported a photo and you know, by looking at the Bitmap page of Object Properties, that it's 4" wide, 3" tall, and 250 pixels per inch in resolution. Your next move is to check the printer manufacturer's documentation: although manufacturers tend to tap dance around specific printer resolutions, a good working guide is that an inkjet prints about one-third of the stated overall resolution on the box. Image resolution for day-to-day printing, without giving yourself a headache over empirical values, should be anywhere between 240 to 300 pixels per inch.

There is a way to tell the resolution of image file formats that cannot hold resolution information, so don't worry if you have a bunch of JPEG images you want to use in a composition you need to inkjet-print. As you progress through this chapter, working tutorial files will demonstrate what you want to do and when.

Resolution vs. Image Size

Another digital-image reality that makes many designers pull their hair out is that image resolution is inversely proportional to dimension: this is another cold and hard fact about bitmap resolution. When you make an image larger in dimension, its resolution decreases. Now, viewing resolution and image resolution display the same thing onscreen, but changing *viewing resolution*—zooming in and out of an image—is nondestructive, whereas changing *image resolution* is destructive editing and often irreversible. Here's an example that demonstrates the resolution-dependence properties of bitmaps. Figure 21-1 shows a desktop icon; it's 128×128 pixels, and the largely adopted resolution convention is that screen pixels are 96 per inch. At 1:1 viewing resolution, this icon looks fine, but when you zoom into it to 10:1 viewing resolution, it begins to look coarse. The same thing would be visible if you actually were to change the resolution of the image. Bitmap images are resolution dependent; the pixels you capture of a scene with a camera can't be added to later to increase detail—no application can guess what the extra detail and extra pixels would be. At right in Figure 21-1, you can see an extreme enlargement of the icon, and the pixels are so clearly visible that you can't make out what the design is!

Take advantage of the unique property of bitmap images—that they accurately portray a photographic scene—but you need to take a photo that is *high resolution*: 3,264 pixels × 2,448 pixels is average for an 8-megapixel camera, a little larger than 10 × 8 at 300 ppi. CorelDRAW can resize an image; for example, this same 8-megapixel

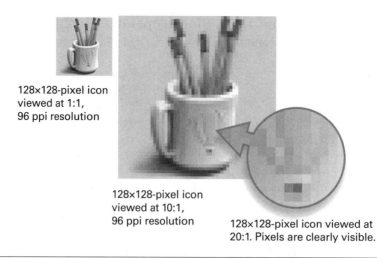

128×128-pixel icon
viewed at 1:1,
96 ppi resolution

128×128-pixel icon
viewed at 10:1,
96 ppi resolution

128×128-pixel icon viewed at
20:1. Pixels are clearly visible.

FIGURE 21-1   With resolution-dependent bitmaps, the larger the image, the fewer pixels per inch.

image could also be expressed as 20" × 15" at 163 ppi without changing any visual information. CorelDRAW can also resample an image, and this is the *destructive* type of editing; you change original pixel colors when you resample, so generally resizing is good, but only resample as a last resort when adding photos to a CorelDRAW composition.

Importing Bitmaps into a Document

As a CorelDRAW user, you have at your fingertips a vast collection of bitmap import filter selections. And some of the import options apply specifically to bitmaps and are explained here; you'll definitely find them useful if your work requires photographs and graphics from the Web. Table 21-1 does not list the bitmap types CorelDRAW can import the way that the Files Of Type drop-down list does in the Import dialog. Although it's terrific to have a billion different file types available for import, particularly if you have legacy file formats, you probably only use a handful of image types in everyday work. Therefore, Table 21-1 lists the most common file types first; more exotic and legacy file formats appear toward the bottom of this table. The asterisk after the file extension indicates that a file type can retain resolution information; this is a *capability*—it doesn't necessarily mean the person who saved the file actually saved resolution information.

If you intend to print a CorelDRAW composition you've created that features a bitmap photo or painting, Step 1 is to set up the color management of the document. You can access settings for your document's color profile through Tools | Color Management | Document Settings.

TABLE 21-1   CorelDRAW's Importable Bitmap Formats

Bitmap Type	File Extension
Adobe Photoshop	PSD*
JPEG and JPEG 2000 bitmaps	JPG*, JP2, JPEG, JFF, and JTF
Adobe Portable Document File	PDF
TIFF bitmap	TIF*, TIFF, TP1
Portable Network Graphic	PNG*
Targa bitmap	TGA* (Enhanced mode, export only), VDA, ICB, VST
Raw image file format	CRW, CR2 (Canon), MRW (Minolta), NEF (Nikon), ORF (Olympus), DNG (Adobe), PTX (Pentax), ARW, SRF, SR2 (Sony), MRW, THM, RAF, DCR, KDC, PEF, RAW, MOS, SRW, NRW, RW2
Corel PHOTO-PAINT	CPT*
CompuServe bitmap	GIF
GIF animation	GIF
Windows bitmap	BMP* (DIB, RLE)
CALS compressed bitmap	CAL
Computer graphics metafile	CGM
Corel (and Micrografx) Picture Publisher	PP4
Gem Paint file	GEM, IMG
GIMP image	XCF*
Lotus Pic	PIC
Macintosh PICT	PCT, PICT
MACPaint bitmap	MAC
OS/2 bitmap	BMP
Painter 5 and higher	RIF*
PC Paintbrush bitmap	PCX*
Scitex CT bitmap	SCT, CT
Windows Icon Resource	ICO, EXE, DLL
WordPerfect graphic bitmap	WPG

The following steps aren't a tutorial but rather a checklist, a workflow based on your need to bring a copy of a photo into a CorelDRAW composition:

1. After launching CorelDRAW, press CTRL + N (File | New) *if* you've clicked the checkbox Do Not Show This Create A New Document After Launch dialog again. It's at the bottom left of the dialog.

2. Define the color settings after you've specified page size, resolution, and other parameters. Your *color settings*—the color space within which everything on the page "resides"—is not an "Oh, yes! I know the answer!" sort of conclusion or decision you make lightly. Generally, you're safe choosing sRGB IEC6 1966-2.1 because many digital cameras and scanners use this color profile. If, however, after importing a photo, the photo looks dull or lacks contrast, then the color space of the photo doesn't match the color settings of your CorelDRAW document. You can change this later; let's continue the workflow here...

3. Before importing a photo, choose Tools | Color Management | Default Settings. Check both the Warn On Color Profile Mismatch and the Warn On Missing Color Profile boxes. Do this both in the Open and in the Import and Paste sections. You're all set to import a photo now.

4. When you choose File | Import (or press CTRL + I), you have the opportunity to scale an image before placing it on the page. More experienced users might want to simply drag an image file into the workspace when CorelDRAW is not maximized. Using either technique, when you import an image, if it has a color profile that doesn't match your current document—or has no color profile at all—you'll get a message box where you have the opportunity to choose the color space for the imported image.

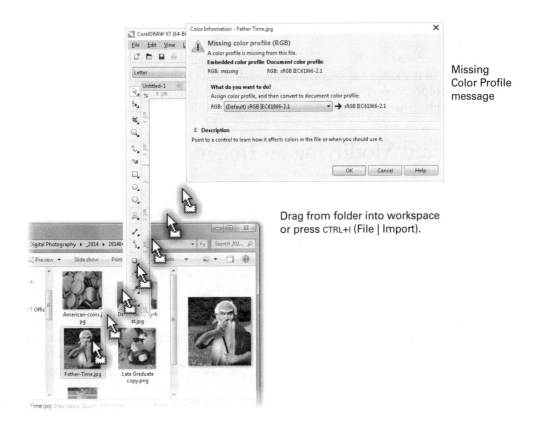

Missing Color Profile message

Drag from folder into workspace or press CTRL+I (File | Import).

5. Generally, you want to choose the same color space as the document's color space. However, if you set up your document incorrectly—for example, your client specified Adobe RGB, you had soap in your ears and thought he said "sRGB"—import the photo using the Adobe RGB choice from the drop-down list. Then choose Tools | Color Management | Document Settings, and choose Adobe RGB from the RGB drop-down list in the Edit Document Settings area.

Because the method of dragging an image file into the workspace doesn't afford scaling options, you might want to stick with CTRL + I for importing. File | Import also gives you the chance to filter for the file types you seek in a Windows folder. Choose your bitmap format from the All File Formats drop-down list in the Import dialog.

After the Import dialog closes, your cursor changes to an import cursor that has three functions:

- With it you specify the upper-left corner of your new bitmap using a single-click, which, in turn, imports the image onto a document page at its original size—whatever dimensions, whatever its original saved resolution.

- Pressing ENTER instead of using a mouse click imports the image to the center of the page.
- Click-dragging the cursor scales the imported photo to the dimensions you need. When you try out this technique, you'll notice the cursor keeps the image scaled proportionately—it doesn't distort photos by allowing independent vertical and horizontal motion when you import and scale the image.

Placing and Modifying an Image

The best way to get the hang of inserting an image into a CorelDRAW composition is by example: open *Wally's Wheels.cdr*, and in the tutorial to follow you'll place a picture of an auto and then perform a little manual cropping.

You're going to place and proportionately scale the imported image by click-dragging diagonally, as described in the third technique of the previous section. After you specify the size this way, the bitmap is imported and automatically resized to fit the defined area closely with the original *proportions* of the bitmap preserved, but the resolution will not be the original's. As you drag, the cursor changes orientation and the image's bounding box appears, showing the space the new image will occupy. While importing during either operation, the original filename and the image dimensions are displayed beside the cursor. Your goal in the next steps is to place *Expensive car.jpg* at the top of the 5" × 7" riser card layout. As you work through the steps, you'll note the document's color space isn't the same as the JPEG image, but you already know how to correct this. The native dimensions of the JPEG are also larger than the CorelDRAW page layout, which affords the perfect opportunity to try out this importing and scaling stuff.

Tutorial   **Putting a Picture into a Car Advertisement**

1. Click the Import icon on the Standard bar or press CTRL + I to import *Expensive car.jpg*. Locate it on your hard drive, select the file, and then click Import.
2. You'll now see the message box that tells you the *Expensive car.jpg* is not tagged with the same color space as the *Wally's Wheels.cdr* file. Click Convert From Embedded Color Profile To The Document Color Profile radio button, and then click OK. There is often a noticeable color difference in the image you view on the page when you choose to ignore the color profile (the first option in this message box), instead of allowing CorelDRAW to convert it to the document's color space. Another good reason not to ignore a color profile is if you send this file to a commercial printer with two different color spaces in the document, the commercial printer is not likely to thank you for the time and paper the two of you have wasted. One document requires one color profile for all of its contents.
3. Begin your click as close as possible to the top-left point on the rulers, and then drag down and to the right; don't release the mouse button yet. When you believe you're very close to the right edge of the layout, look at the cursor. If the dimensions it reports are close to 5 inches, you're good to release the

mouse button. In the illustration here, if you can read the cursor, it reports a height and width of 4.981 inches, which is close enough for government work. Move your pointing device up and down on the page just a fractional amount until you're close to 5", and then release the mouse button.

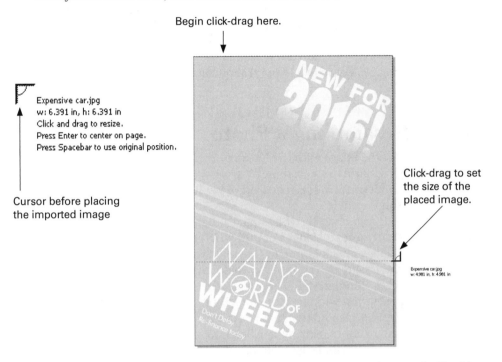

Begin click-drag here.

Expensive car.jpg
w: 6.391 in, h: 6.391 in
Click and drag to resize.
Press Enter to center on page.
Press Spacebar to use original position.

Cursor before placing
the imported image

Click-drag to set
the size of the
placed image.

Expensive car.jpg
w: 4.981 in, h: 4.981 in

4. If you want this image (or one in your own assignment) to be *exactly* 5" wide, now choose Object | Transformations | Size. Click the top-left checkbox below the Proportional checkbox to set the direction in which the image should be scaled (the Proportional checkbox *has* to be checked to enable the direction boxes, and you want to, anyway), and then type **5** in the W field, press ENTER, and you've accomplished precision placement and scaling.

5. Save this file to disk and keep it open for the sections to follow.

Switching from Resizing to Resampling

If you had right-clicked over the *Expensive Car.jpg* image in the Import dialog box earlier, and then chosen Properties | Details, Windows would have told you the image is 1,700 × 1,700 pixels at a resolution of 266pixels/per inch. Any bitmap's resolution can be discovered this way, within the Import box, and anywhere in Windows where you can open a folder. However, if you click the image as placed now, the Status bar tells you that *Expensive car.jpg* on Layer 1 is currently about 340pixels/inch in resolution. The reason why is that *image resolution is inversely proportional to image dimensions*—you make one smaller and the other one becomes larger, as discussed earlier. This is a function of resizing; by default, CorelDRAW doesn't change the number of pixels in an imported photo.

However, an imaging service bureau or commercial printer might request a specific resolution for an image placed in a CorelDRAW file—many services that make full-color business cards, for example, want 300 ppi images in files and often reject or charge extra for processing fees if an image has a higher resolution. Changing the number of pixels in an image is not resizing; instead it's *resampling,* and you're basically altering the visual content of the copy of the image in your CorelDRAW document.

Let's pretend this auto advertisement needs to be sent to a commercial printer with the image at exactly 300 ppi. Follow these brief steps to prep this file for proper printing.

Tutorial Resampling a Photo

1. Select the image with the Pick tool.
2. Choose Bitmap | Resample.
3. With Identical Values checked, type **300** in either the Horizontal or the Vertical Resolution field.
4. Check Anti-aliased (which makes the reduction of the image smooth and basically undetectable from the original image), check Maintain Aspect Ratio, but do *not* check Maintain Original Size. If you maintained the original size of the image, no resampling would take place; instead, the image would be resized. Compare the before and after file size in this dialog; this not only provides you with an estimate of how large your saved CorelDRAW file will be, but it's also intellectual reassurance that you're down-sampling the photo and not simply resizing it. Click OK and you're finished. Keep the file open because the layout isn't done. Yet.

Nonrectangular Cropping in a Jiffy

This mock advertisement clearly is designed on the diagonal, but the car image—like most bitmap images—is rectangular, somewhat spoiling the look of the ad as it's currently placed. This isn't a big design challenge; it's an opportunity to explore CorelDRAW's features. CorelDRAW offers a Crop tool on the Toolbox, which, as discussed in Chapter 20, performs *destructive* editing.

CorelDRAW considers any placed bitmap image to be an object with four control nodes, one at each corner of the rectangle. Moreover, these control nodes can be moved (inward because there's nothing outside the boundary of a bitmap) to change the shape of a bitmap without removing areas of the bitmap—CorelDRAW simply hides them for you. Work through the following steps to hide a triangular area of the Expensive Car–placed jpeg image and complete the design:

Tutorial   Cropping with the Shape Tool

1. With the Pick tool, select the image and then press CTRL + PAGEDOWN to put the image behind the text at top.
2. Choose the Shape tool from the Toolbox.
3. Click the image to reveal the control nodes.
4. One approach to removing the slice of the image that's covering Wally's name is to hold CTRL (to constrain the direction in which you'll drag the node) and then click-drag the bottom-left control node up to about the 5" tick on the vertical ruler so you can see the underlying stripes first. Then, while holding CTRL, drag the control node down so it meets the bottom of the top diagonal stripe in the design. Then perform the same action on the bottom-right control node.
5. Nodes can be nudged: try saying that three times fast! You can use your UP and DOWN keyboard arrow keys to nudge a selected image control node up or down. Begin with the Pick tool and no objects selected on the page. You then set the nudge distance on the Property bar, click a node using the Shape tool, and you're ready to nudge nodes. If you choose this method, it offers precision, and you don't have to hold CTRL. You can also use the Super Nudge option and

hold SHIFT while keystroking the UP and DOWN arrow keys. By default, if you hold SHIFT, your nudges are 2× the value you set.

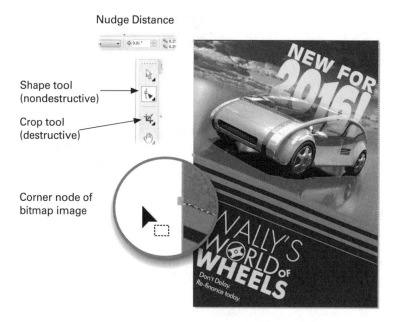

Importing Nonstandard Bitmaps

A bitmap image that contains several layers—the layers themselves surrounded by transparency—isn't your everyday BMP or TIFF bitmap image. Adobe Photoshop and Corel PHOTO-PAINT both can write image files that contain layers; you'll see the advantages to using a layered bitmap image shortly. When you choose File | Import and then choose PSD, PHOTO-PAINT's CPT, or even Corel Painter's RIF file format, any layers in these file types are imported and nested within an entry on a CorelDRAW layer. You can unnest the layers, move them, or delete them, and one of the most useful properties of layered image files is that the file's creator probably did so to include partially transparent areas within the bitmap composition.

Let's say fictitious guitar teacher Tom Pastor asked a friend to design an eye-catching 4" by 3" leave-behind card for his business, knowing his buddy is an expert with 3D graphics and metallic surfaces and stuff. Sadly, Tom's pal went way over the top: Tom teaches classical acoustic guitar, and his buddy created something that screams metal-head mayhem. However, the guitar is nice, it's on its own layer, and Tom is reading this book along with you. Let's see how to separate elements imported as a PSD file and whether a few of CorelDRAW's features can't tone down the card.

Tutorial   Working with Layered Bitmaps

1. Create a new document. In the Create A New Document dialog, the Primary Color Mode should be set to RGB, making the image appropriate for an inkjet printer. Make the dimensions about 4.5" wide and 3.5" high to give a little wiggle room for composing a 4×3 card. Document size can be changed at any time.

2. Click the Import button on the Standard bar, and then in the Import dialog box, scout out *Tom Pastor guitarist.psd*. Select it, and then click Import.

3. With the cursor loaded and ready to place a copy of the file, press ENTER to place the file at full size, centered on the page.

4. Choose Window | Dockers | Object Manager. Click the + icon to the left of the Layer 1 title to expand it, and then click the + to the left of the *Tom Pastor Guitarist.psd* entry to open its nest of layers.

5. Click the "Gold Notes Background" layer item on the list to select it in the document window. This file was thoughtfully prepared; the layers were named in Photoshop. In your own work, you might not be so fortunate if the creator of the layered file didn't name the layers. Therefore, always check out what's selected in the drawing window before proceeding.

6. You're sure the "Gold Notes Background" is selected? Then click the trash icon to delete this layer. It's a neat 3D picture, but it's overbearing and distracting and will fight any reasonable attempt to promote Tom's name and phone number.

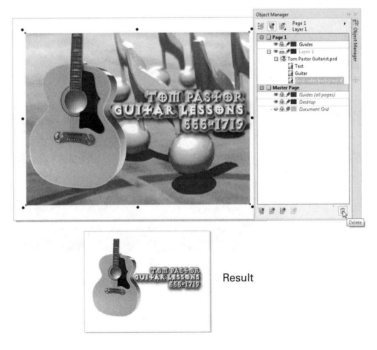

Result

7. Choose the Rectangle tool from the Toolbox, and then drag a rectangle that's about the same size as the Background layer you deleted.

8. On the Object Manager, click-drag the Rectangle entry down; this will put it in the Layers group of bitmaps you imported, so a second drag down to below the "Guitar" entry will put the Rectangle to the back of the composition. Alternatively, you could press SHIFT + PAGEDOWN with the rectangle selected to put it to the back of the layer.

9. Choose the Fill tool from the Toolbox. With the rectangle selected, drag from the bottom to the top to put default black at the bottom and white at the top of this Linear fountain fill.

10. Click the bottom fountain fill node to get the Node Color picker to appear and then specify a dark warm gray, not black, but something like **#6E6D68** as expressed in hexadecimal (which the Node Color picker allows you to enter directly). You need to be in RGB color mode to access the Hex value box.

11. Click the top fountain fill node and then enter a light warm gray value such as **#DEDDD3**.

12. With the Fill tool, drag the top color node down to about the height of the ghastly text in the composition. Then take the midpoint slider and drag this down to midway between the bottom of the guitar and the guitar's bridge—that horizontal bar where the strings terminate. See the following illustration. What might be nice to strive for here is the effect of a lit studio seamless paper sweep. All that's missing is a shadow beneath the guitar being cast on the paper sweep.

From gradient color node

Midpoint slider   Start gradient color node

13. Select the guitar masked photo, and then choose the Drop Shadow tool from the Toolbox. Click-drag, as shown in the following illustration, from the base of the guitar upward, at about a 2 o'clock angle. Optionally, once you've created the shadow, you might want to decrease its opacity using the slider on the

Property bar. The choice is yours as the artist; however, a black shadow against a dark but not exceptionally dark background looks a little intense.

Drop Shadow Opacity

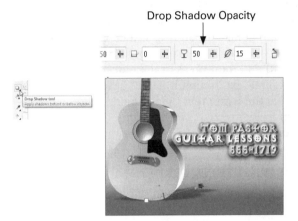

14. The logo layer can simply be deleted *after you've typed out the text.* The original typeface is way too Goth for the tone of this new composition, and there are plenty of typefaces that convey art in a strong, legible style. For example, Exoct350 (you can find it in Corel's Fonts collection in the "E" folder; its industry standard name is Peignot) goes in and out of style, and it might be back in style in 2014. Type out the name, profession, and telephone number with hard breaks at the end of each line. For this example, 28 to 30 points in font height will work; with the Pick tool, you can select the text and then use the Justification drop-down on the Standard bar (with the text selected) to right-justify the text. Make sure your transcription is accurate. See the following illustration.

15. The text is large, but one of the wonderful things about typography is you can tone down large text not only by making it smaller, but also by keeping the size and using a paler color. Try 50 to 60% black on the text.

16. Finally, to make the text "pop" a little, you can use a classic and simple technique to fake an emboss effect. Choose the text, and then press CTRL + C and then CTRL + V to make a copy directly on top of the original text. Give it a white fill and then press CTRL + PAGEDOWN to put the duplicate one step below the original text, hiding it. Don't deselect it—use the keyboard nudge keys now to nudge the white text twice down and twice to the right. The finished card is shown in Figure 21-2. Now *this* guy, I'd take guitar lessons from, and I'll bet he wouldn't give me "In A Gadda Da Vida" for homework.

Working with Raw Images

Camera Raw is the new generation of high-fidelity imaging: it's affordable; most cameras you *don't* buy at a drugstore can write a Raw file format; and as with any comparatively new technology, there's a small learning curve, which we'll tackle in this section.

A Raw image is similar to an unprocessed physical piece of camera film; although it contains a lot of data about exposure, light temperature, f-stop, lens, and other conditions, the Raw image does *not* have locked data about pixel colors. Raw offers the ultimate in flexibility—if the light was too low or the wrong temperature, you can adjust for these and other flaws through CorelDRAW's Camera Raw Lab. The Camera Raw Lab appears after you choose to import a Raw camera image; a Raw image cannot

FIGURE 21-2 Combine CorelDRAW objects in a layered bitmap file to edit layouts extensively.

be placed in a CorelDRAW composition before it passes through the Lab (even if you choose not to do anything to the image). Depending on your camera settings, you'll most likely be working with a 48-bit image, 16 bits per channel; this offers a color space of several trillion unique colors and is part of the reason why Raw images can be adjusted to make dramatic lighting changes while retaining high image fidelity.

Working with the Camera Raw Lab

Working with the Camera Raw Lab in CorelDRAW is an experience you won't want to miss. If you don't have a Raw image handy, or if your camera cannot take Raw file format images, a small DNG file is in the zip archive you downloaded for this chapter.

Because no two manufacturers could agree on a file extension, a Raw image can have .CRW, .DNG, or any of over a dozen other file extensions. The good news is that CorelDRAW doesn't care about the file extension—you just choose All File formats (*.*) from the drop-down list in the Import dialog and then navigate to the location of a Raw image, in the following example, *Bookends.dng*. The *better* news is that CorelDRAW can import Raw images from a *three-page list* of manufacturers—just short of photos on a View-Master reel, you're assured that CorelDRAW can import most Raw files.

Let's dig right into the features and options available to you when you import a Raw image. Follow these steps and guidelines to import the image, and then perform minor processing enhancements. There's nothing truly wrong with the image, but this tutorial is instead an opportunity to gain hands-on experience with the Camera Raw Lab features.

Tutorial Raw Image Color Correction

1. Choose File | Import, or click the Import button on the Standard bar.
2. Choose All File Formats (*.), and then choose *Bookends.dng* from the folder you downloaded the file to. Click Import or press ENTER.
3. The Camera Raw Lab interface appears. The very first thing to do is to check the properties of this unprocessed photograph. The Properties tab tells the day and date of the photo, the camera, whether flash was used, aperture, and ISO-equivalent film speed. If you're familiar at all with cameras, the information shown here will give you a clue to what, if anything, needs adjusting in the image. For example, the photo was made as ISO 100 using an aperture of f/3.4 and a shutter speed of 1/61th of a second, which the Properties tab confirms.

Also, because a flash wasn't used, when you get to the Color tab, you can rule out Flash as a choice from the White Balance options.

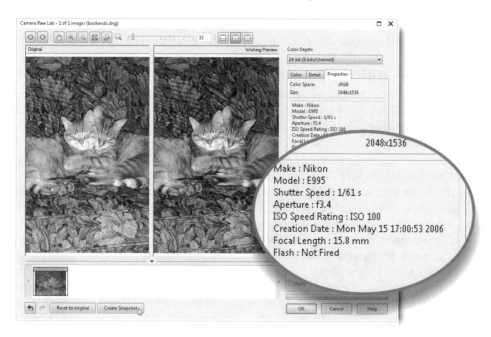

4. The Detail tab has a slider for sharpening the image as well as sliders for reducing luminance noise and overall color noise. This photo doesn't require these enhancements. The Hints area at the bottom of the tab is a handy context-sensitive reminder of what each slider does. Before you take your next Raw image, it's good practice to "get it right in the camera." You get less noise in a photo generally if you set your camera to slower ISO speeds. The ISO of 100 in this example image produces an acceptably small amount of visible noise (noise is similar to *grain* in traditional physical film). Using an ISO setting of, say, 400 or higher, in dim indoor light when a good depth of field is needed would, indeed, have required noise reduction using the Detail sliders.

5. Click the Color tab; here's where the fun begins. Follow the callout letters in Figure 21-3 to guide you through which features do what.

- The *A* area is for rotating the Raw image before placing the copy into your CorelDRAW document. Raw camera data can also include portrait and landscape orientation, so you might never need to use these buttons if your camera saved orientation info.

- *B* marks your navigation tools for previewing the image. From left to right, you have tools for panning the window (you click-drag when your cursor is inside the preview window), Zoom In and Zoom Out, Fit To Window, 100% (1:1) viewing resolution, and finally there's a slider to zoom your current view in and out.

- *C* marks the Split Pane view so you can compare the original image to any corrections you make.

- *D* marks Color Depth. You'd be ill-advised to change this from 48-bit because only a high-depth image can be adjusted extensively without taking on banding and color clipping (explained shortly). The only reason you'd choose 24-bit from the selector list is if the image were flawless and you wanted to get down to work by placing it in your document and saving space on your hard disk.
- *E* marks the White Balance selector. You have many choices that influence the color casting of the Raw image. Ideally, you want the placed image to be color-balanced; the grays in the image contain no hues, and the photo looks neither too warm nor too cold. You have selections such as Tungsten, Cloudy, and other lighting conditions that influence the color cast of images. As Shot is the default setting.
- *F* is the White Balance Eyedropper tool, which is used to define a completely neutral area in the preview window to better set and possibly neutralize color casting. The cursor for this tool gives you an RGB readout of the current area

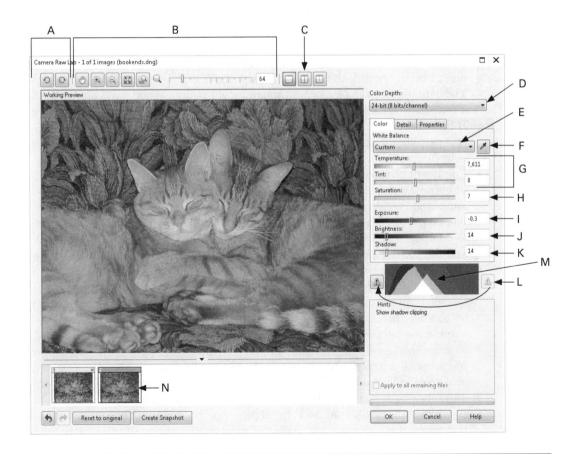

FIGURE 21-3   Use the Camera Raw Lab to color- and tone-correct high-quality digital images.

in the preview photo; this is the true color over a pixel, not the "ideally neutral color." You click over an area you believe *should* contain equal amounts of red, green, and blue components (R:64, G:64, B:64, for example), and this action remaps the image to reflect the color casting in the image based on where you clicked. Although a useful tool, you might not have a photo that contains a perfectly white or a perfectly neutral gray area; if this is the case, don't use this tool.

- *G* marks color Temperature and Tint, perhaps the least intuitive of Raw digital image properties. The values in the Camera Raw Lab's color Temperature controls run from low at the left of the slider (cools down warm images) to high at right (warms cool images). The Temperature controls, specifically values you enter in the numeric field, are *not* degrees of Kelvin; they are correction values only for you to refer to and compare with other settings and other images. However, it *is* correct to *think* of color temperature, in general, as measured in degrees Kelvin. You might want to "uncorrect" a perfect image to make it warmer or colder. The Tint slider is the color complement of the color Temperature control; a neutral temperature displays a band on the Tint slider from magenta at left to green at right. You always use Tint after you've set Temperature because Tint varies according to temperature. This photo needed just a little more red, so the Temperature slider was dragged a little to the right. The Tint *appeared to* be okay, although ginger tabby cats on a red tapestry sofa is a little hard to calibrate mentally. Your Tint options are from Magenta to Green.

- *H* is the Saturation control, which is mostly self-explanatory—it's used to compensate for dull photographs (you increase saturation) or for overly colorful images (you desaturate by dragging to the left with the slider).

- *I* marks the Exposure control. Exposure is not the same as, for example, the brightness/contrast controls on a TV set or the Levels command in image-editing applications. Exposure is the *total light that falls on a scene,* and it is set when you take a picture by setting the ISO value. Therefore, it's always a good idea to double-check the information on the Properties tab: if the ISO is a low value and the picture looks dark or muddy, then Exposure probably needs adjusting.

- *J* marks Brightness, which you should play with only after setting the best exposure. If you drag the Brightness slider to the right with this image, you'll see the upper ranges of the image become brighter, but not the shadow areas. So you use this slider to bring out detail in the midranges in an image without ruining the deeper tones.

- *K* is the Shadow slider, and this option is used only to make deeper areas more pronounced without affecting the midtones and highlights. Shadows might also be called *contrast;* dragging the slider to the right does indeed create a difference between the lighter and darker areas of the overall image.

- *L* marks both the Shadow and Highlights clipping regions. These two buttons that frame the histogram (*M*) display a bright red color overlay in the preview window in areas where the brightest brights have fallen out of range (they can't be accurately displayed onscreen, and they can't be accurately printed), and the deepest shadows display a green-tinted overlay. If you see a tint in areas, this means the Shadow, the Exposure, or the Saturation adjustments you've made are too intense. The solution is to choose lower values for any of these options until the tint disappears in the preview window.

- *M* is the histogram of the current photograph. A *histogram* is a visual representation of how many pixels of what color are located at what brightness in the image. A well-toned image has a lot of color pixels in the midregion of the histogram—this is where the most visual detail is apparent in digital photographs. If the histogram shows too many pixels, your image needs less shadow or more exposure—in the lower regions in this example, you see a hump in the histogram curve toward the left.

- *N* is the area where you can create snapshots. When you arrive at a good exposure for an image you want to copy into a page, click the Create Snapshot button and a thumbnail appears at bottom left. Snapshots are not saved—they are for comparison purposes—and ultimately, you choose one you'll import.

6. Once you've made your adjustments, you click OK, and you're then presented with a loaded cursor for placing and scaling the imported image, as discussed earlier in this chapter.

An Everyday Bitmap-Oriented Workflow

Once you're finished working on a composition, whether it's vector, bitmap, or a combination of these two elements, you probably want to pop a copy of your work off to a friend or a client. The following sections take you through the four stages of CorelDRAW design work; in the process, you'll grow quite comfortable with all this "bitmap stuff" and appreciate CorelDRAW's power to bring different media together for both your import and export needs.

Creating a Catalog Cover

LUM, a fictitious candle manufacturer, needs a new catalog cover for 2015. As to be expected, they have no money to take a new picture for the cover, but they've heard that your copy of CorelDRAW ships with some really cool filters that might put a new spin on an old image. Follow along in the next sections' steps to take a tour of the Image Adjustment Lab, the Bitmap effects CorelDRAW offers, and as a grand finale, you'll breeze through the Export options for the JPEG file format so you can send a comp to the fictitious client.

Working in the Image Adjustment Lab

For "normal" photographs—photos in JPEG, TIFF, and file formats other than Camera Raw—the Bitmaps menu in CorelDRAW offers a fairly comprehensive Image Adjustment Lab to make practically every *global* adjustment (but not pixel-level editing adjustments) you'll find in PHOTO-PAINT. The Image Adjustment Lab makes photo-correcting imported bitmaps easy—you can integrate them into a composition without ever leaving CorelDRAW; better still, the features are almost identical to those in the Camera Raw Lab.

Let's work through the mock assignment now: first, you'll import and place an image in the layout that's been designed for you.

[Tutorial] Adjusting a PNG Image in the Lab

1. Open *LUM catalog.cdr*. Choose the Object Manager docker (Window | Dockers | Manager). Click the "Put The Photo On This Layer" title on the Object Docker to make it the current layer (the Background layer with the text is locked).

2. Choose File | Import (CTRL + I), and then choose *LUM candles.png* from the location where you downloaded it. Click Import.

3. Your cursor is loaded with the image now, and it's much larger than the place reserved for it within the layout, so you'll scale the image as you place it. First, make sure Snap To Guidelines is checked on the Snap To list on the Standard bar. Click an insertion point at the top left of the guides intersection and then drag down until the right edge of the image meets the right guide. You've scaled and placed the image now, as shown in the illustration here.

4. With the photo selected, choose Bitmaps | Image Adjustment Lab.

5. In Figure 21-4, you'll see many of the same navigation controls as you did in the Camera Raw Lab, but with slightly different features for color and tone adjustments. Select the Split Pane view now to make the adjustments easier to compare to the original photo. Always shoot for tone correction for exposure, and then work on the color if necessary.

   - *A* marks Auto Adjust, a one-step routine that adds contrast to an image; let's skip this feature—automated routines don't give "one-off" assignments the custom attention they need, and you don't learn anything from automated routines.

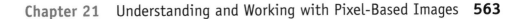

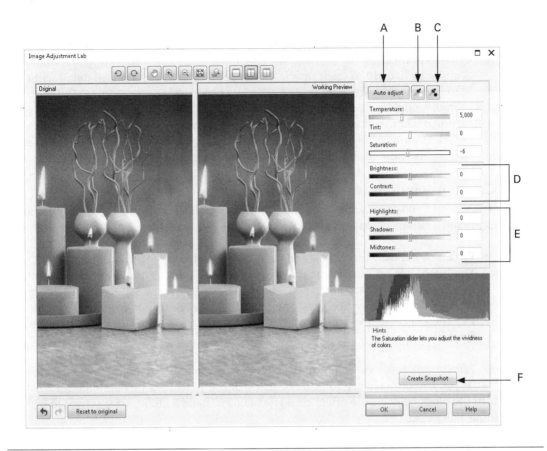

FIGURE 21-4   Color and tone correction can be performed on photographs with CorelDRAW.

- *B* marks the White Point Eyedropper tool, used to define in the preview window the lightest area that should be in the picture. Click in the center of one of the candle flames (presumably the whitest white in the image) to see if the Lab adjusts the other tones and snaps up the image.
- *C* marks the Black Point Eyedropper tool, which redefines the darkest point in the image based on where you click in the preview window. This step is optional; hover your cursor over the top left of the background in the image. Your cursor will tell you that the background toward the top is almost black with a little red tossed in. Click this point with the Black Point Eyedropper tool; your artistic judgment might tell you the preview pane at right shows a better, snappier image. If you disagree, click the Reset To Original button at bottom left.
- *D* marks the Brightness and Contrast sliders. They basically do what you'd expect, but brightness and contrast don't always make an image better. Skip these controls for this assignment.

- *E* marks the area the professionals use to snap up a photo: Leave the Highlights slider alone in this assignment; this brightens the brighter areas in the image without affecting the midtones or shadow areas. However, do drag the Midtones slider to 10 or 12 to open up the darker regions to provide image detail without messing up the shadows region, which is fine as is.

6. Finally, click the Create Snapshot button (*F*). This creates an entry on the Undo docker in case you want to reverse a correction after exiting the Lab. Click OK and your adjusted image is now placed in the layout. Keep the file open, and now is also a good time to Save (press CTRL + S).

Create Alterations with Photo Effects

If you need to do something dramatic to a photo, such as bowing the image so it looks as though a fish-eye lens was used, these options are available:

- Put an object over the photo, and then use lens effects, covered in Chapter 17. You might not get exactly the effect you want with a lens; therefore, the advantage to this method is that the change isn't made directly to the photo—a lens effect can be deleted at any time, restoring the normal appearance of objects beneath it.
- Use the effects on the bottom of the Bitmaps menu, as you'll do in the following tutorial.

Effects you apply via the Bitmaps menu are permanent changes; the bad news is that you can only choose to Undo or use Window | Dockers | Undo Manager to turn the clock back on the effect step after you've made a change if it proves to be unpleasing.

The good news is that all effects are applied only to an image you've imported—your original photo is safely tucked away somewhere on your hard drive. Effects filters in CorelDRAW are divided into categories, and you'll only be using two from the Color Transform and Art Strokes categories in this assignment. You should feel free and set aside some time to experiment with the various filters on an image you believe has the potential to look more interesting after a little Distortion or Trace Contour filtering.

Any filter you apply to a photo removes original image information and occasionally supplies altered image information. Therefore, you need to make a creative and qualitative judgment as to whether an image looks "better" after applying one or more filters. There is no such thing as "instant art"; you yourself need to use your artistic taste when applying a filter to change the original image's data, and don't dismiss the possibility that an original image might look better and be more appropriate than a filtered one in a paying assignment.

In general, you might want to reach for the Bitmaps menu's filters on two occasions:

- When a photography session isn't possible to provide a new photo for a new catalog or brochure. You or the client have to use an older photo, but you want it to look a little different than last year's photo.

- When a photo is visually boring. Not a bad photo, but just an uninspired photograph whose composition, geometry, and colors are very staid and simple. The LUM candle image isn't a bad image; its problems in this example are that it was used last year and the geometry in the scene is exceptionally simple so it looks like any still photo of a bunch of cylinders.

To use a Bitmaps effect, you need to first select an imported bitmap. The bitmap has to be either an 8-bit (Grayscale mode, for example) or 24-bit image in either RGB or CMYK color mode. Raw images you import—if they are higher than 24-bit—need to be changed to a *bit depth* that the effects can work with. In English, if the Effects menus and submenus are dimmed, choose Bitmaps | Mode and then convert the selected image to RGB 24-bit, and life is good. Working with an effect is easy and intuitive: specific effects have different options and sliders, but to use an effect, you work in three key areas of the dialog that appears when you choose one:

- **Preview**   Even at an effect's default settings, you need to click Preview to see what the effect will look like on the page.
- **Reset**   Clicking this button removes all changes you've made to the sliders and other controls for all effects.
- **Apply**   Click OK to apply the effect using the options you've defined; the dialog then closes.
- **The controls**   To customize an effect, you drag sliders, enter values in number boxes, and/or drag other controls such as the direction of an effect. Once you've made changes to the effect's values, click Preview to update the page preview, and when you're satisfied with the customized effect, you click Apply.

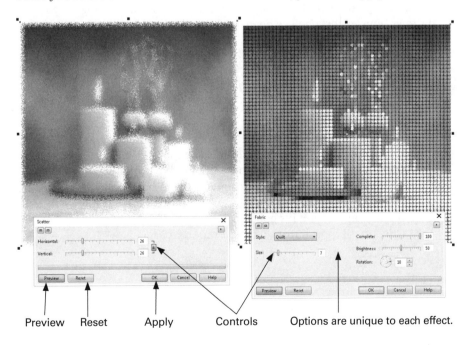

Preview   Reset   Apply   Controls   Options are unique to each effect.

> **Tip** If you duplicate an image and then apply two different effects, you can create something exceptionally interesting if you apply 50% Uniform Transparency to the top image. Experiment, for example, with totally desaturating an image, applying Find Contours to the other, and blend them together via transparency. This is one way to make effects of your own that aren't presets and no one would think to imitate.

Keep *LUM catalog.cdr* open, whether you've created a bitmap effect or not. It's now time to export the work and to demonstrate how the text, which is entirely vector (it was converted to curves from a font called Avant Garde), is seamlessly merged with the bitmap image in an entirely new bitmap image.

Exporting Your Composition to Bitmap Format

One of the terrific things about designing using a computer application is that you can repurpose a good design. A good design such as the front cover of this catalog can yield several different uses from only one investment in time—and from knowing how to export the design.

CorelDRAW is a vector drawing program, but it *can* create a bitmap copy of photographs, a bitmap from photos combined with vectors, and it can also export vector art only—text, graphics, anything is fair game. When vectors are copied out of CorelDRAW as bitmaps, a process called *rasterizing* is performed. CorelDRAW examines the vector artwork at the size and resolution you specify and then uses anti-aliasing (unless you specify no anti-aliasing) to create a bitmap that looks as good as what you see onscreen in your CorelDRAW document.

Let's say you want to feature the front cover of this catalog on your website. This narrows your export choices down to GIF, PNG, and JPEG. Let's briefly run through exporting the composition to JPEG now.

Tutorial Saving a Bitmap Copy of Your CorelDRAW Composition

1. In the Object Manager, unlock the layer titled "This One's Locked" by clicking the pencil icon to remove the red slash mark. With the Pick tool, drag a marquee from outside the top left of the design to the bottom right. Doing this is simply good practice for exporting designs: if there had been a hidden object or one outside of your workspace view, CorelDRAW's Export filter will not include it in the bitmap version it's going to render.

2. Click the Export button on the Property bar.

3. In the Export dialog, choose JPG-JPEG Bitmaps as the Save As Type from the drop-down list. Check the Selected Only checkbox, type a name in the File Name field, use the directory pane to choose a location for the export, and then click Export.

4. You have the option to select a preset export for JPEGs by choosing from the Preset list at top right, but this doesn't teach you anything. First, set the Color Mode to RGB—JPEGs are increasingly used today for commercial printing, but it's the wrong color mode for the Web and e-mail attachments.

5. For starters, set the Quality to **80%** (the High setting). Choose the Hand tool and use your mouse scroll wheel to zoom in or out of the preview window. To produce a smaller file, choose **50%** (Medium) quality—which is reported at the bottom left of the dialog. This image shows some JPEG artifacting (noise and corruption) at 50% but not very much at 80%.

6. Check to Embed Color Profile. Doing this costs about half a kilobit (K) of file transfer size, but today's web browsers, such as Safari, Firefox, and Internet Explorer 9 and up, have color management features. This means what you see on your monitor (if it's calibrated) will appear on the Web, with colors as expected.

7. Check Optimize to save on a few K of exported image.

8. Extend the folded-up Transformation area so you can access Units. Choose Pixels as the unit, and then choose **96** as the Resolution for export. The resolution is meaningless for screen documents, but 96 provides you with a benchmark by which you can calculate the absolute height and width of the exported image—in pixels. The layout's original size is a little large for the Web and for the reading pane in mail readers such as MS Outlook; type **700** in the Height field to reduce both the height and width of the export.

9. The estimated download time shown at bottom left is calculated based on a hypothetical Internet connection you specify by selecting from the drop-down list toward the bottom center of the dialog. By default, it's set to fast dial-up, which represents an estimated 75 percent (and shrinking) of the United States, but Europe and many other counties are almost entirely on broadband today. ISDN (dial-up) essentially plays to the lowest common denominator—it's the *worst* speed you can use to estimate how your audience receives your image files. Therefore, 4.4 seconds—and certainly less time for most audiences—is acceptable; most will see the image in less than 2 seconds. Depending on the

exact size of the image, you might get a little better or a little worse download time estimate. Click OK and your work is exported to JPEG file format.

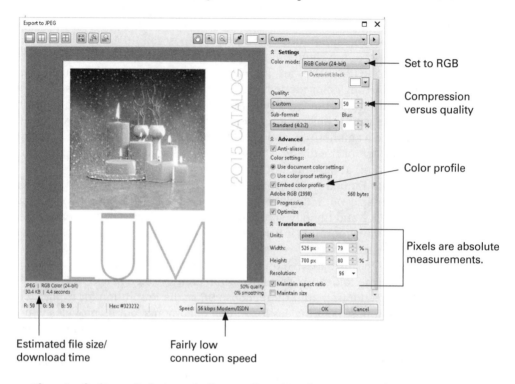

- Set to RGB
- Compression versus quality
- Color profile
- Pixels are absolute measurements.
- Estimated file size/ download time
- Fairly low connection speed

If you're feeling a little jazzed after reading this chapter, get a friend to pat you on your back, because you deserve it. You've taken a serious detour in your "CorelDRAW is a drawing program" education and vaulted right into the arena of design professionals who integrate photos and vector artwork on a daily basis. You now know how to scale an image, to check to see whether its resolution is sufficient to pull a good print, to color-correct both Raw images and regular ones, and how to export your work so friends you'd like to send an e-mail attachment to can see it without necessarily owning CorelDRAW—and the composition is Web-worthy, to boot.

This is not the complete story of the Corel Graphics Suite, however. If you really want to get into bitmap editing, and pulling off some special effects, the next chapter is right up your alley...if you happen to be standing in an alley. Read on and see how to create exactly the effect you need for tomorrow's assignment at work using PHOTO-PAINT.

22 Common Image-Editing Techniques Using PHOTO-PAINT

Photography tells a different story than the vector graphics you create in CorelDRAW. Although vector drawings can look crisp, powerful, and brilliant in coloring, photographs typically mirror more of a literal human story. Digital images deliver emotional content through soft tones, an intricate latticework of highlights and shadows, and all the photorealistic qualities that portray the world as we're accustomed to seeing it. Understandably, the tools you use to edit a digital photo or other bitmap image are different than those you use to edit paths in CorelDRAW. This is where PHOTO-PAINT enters the scene to round out your creative tool set.

This chapter introduces you to the fundamentals of *bitmap images*—how to measure bitmaps, how to crop them to suit a specific output need, and ultimately how to make your original photo look better than when it came off the camera.

Note Download and extract all the files from the Chapter22.zip archive to follow the tutorials in this chapter.

The Building Block of Digital Photos: The Pixel

We all use the word occasionally in a humorous context in conversations, but seldom is an explanation or *definition* of a *pixel* provided in a way that is useful when you need to alter a digital photograph. A *pixel*—an abbreviation for *picture element*—is the smallest recognizable unit of color in a digital photograph. It is *not* a linear unit of measurement; a pixel doesn't have to be square in proportions; and it's not any specific color. Now that you know what a pixel *isn't*, read on to learn what a pixel *is*, and how understanding its properties will help you work with PHOTO-PAINT's tools.

569

Pixels and Resolution

A pixel is a *placeholder* in a bitmap image; as such, it has no fixed size we can measure the same way as you'd measure the length of a 2 by 4 piece of wood (which is usually 2" by 4"). It's hard to discuss a pixel with a friend or co-worker without any sort of *context* because these pixel units cannot exist unless they're within a background, which is usually called the *paper* or the *canvas*. The *paper* in PHOTO-PAINT is an imaginary grid into which you assign units of colors with the Paint tool or the Fill tool. When you open a digital photograph, the paper is predefined by the capability of the digital camera; the *resolution* of your photographs are of a fixed size.

Resolution is expressed as a fraction, a ratio: how many *pixels per inch* expresses image resolution in the same way that *miles per hour* expresses speed. We often call this resolution *dpi* (*dots per inch*) owing to the visual similarity between dots of ink on a printed page and the pixels of color we see on a monitor. Bitmap images are also called *resolution-dependent* images because once a photo has been taken or a paper size defined for a PHOTO-PAINT painting, you cannot change the resolution without distorting the visual content of the picture. Here's an example that shows the use of resolution when you press CTRL+N or choose File | New.

1. In the Create A New Image dialog box, you're offered a Preset Destination of PHOTO-PAINT default size, which, as you can see here, is 5 inches in width by 7 inches in height. However, this is not a *complete* description of how large default paper size is in real-world units. How many *pixels* will be created per inch? Without knowing the resolution, the paper size is as meaningful as how many grapefruits per inch will fit on the page! Fortunately, below the Height and Width fields, you see the Resolution field, set to the default of 72 dpi.

5"×72 (dpi) = 360 pixels
7"×72 (dpi) = 504 pixels

2. Aha! Now we can discover the number of pixels in the new document. Knowing this can be important for website work because you always presume a fixed screen resolution with the audience, and therefore images are always measured in absolute number of pixels in width and height for graphics. In this example, 504 pixels wide might make a good logo at the top page of a website; in 2014 many people who browse the Web run a screen that displays 1280×1024 pixels or higher, so this default image size is a little more than 1/3 the width of an audience's screen.

Image Resolution

Any PHOTO-PAINT document resolution can be great for web graphics, but *not* so good for printing. The finite number of pixels in the resolution-dependent bitmap image can be the culprit. Figure 22-1 shows, at left, a CorelDRAW illustration of a child's paint box. In this book, the drawing looks crisp around the edges and smooth in its transitions from neighboring tones. It was a graphic suitable for printing as a bitmap because it was exported at a high resolution (300 dots per inch) for printing in this book. At right, however, is an illustration of the same paint box, with the imaginary bitmap grid shown, but it was exported at desktop icon size (about 19 by 19 pixels), and the loss of image detail is evident at its resolution of 72 pixels per inch.

Resolution, Pixel Count, and Printing

It's a frequently asked question, and one whose answer is not precise: what is the resolution needed for a photograph to make a good print?

Scanning a physical photograph doesn't provide the best sampling of color pixels to produce a terrific photograph, but it *does* ensure that you have a *sufficient* number of pixels (an image's *pixel count*) to print the scanned photo.

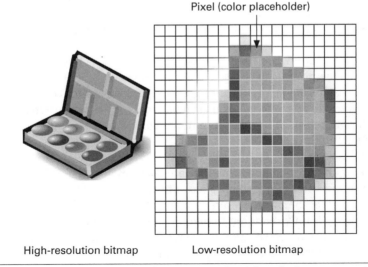

Pixel (color placeholder)

High-resolution bitmap   Low-resolution bitmap

FIGURE 22-1   The number of pixels in a bitmap, combined with the image's resolution, determines whether an image is suitable for printing.

The most direct way to acquire a photo and manipulate it in PHOTO-PAINT is by using a digital camera. Today's digital cameras are capable of taking full-frame pictures that can be printed to inkjet printers at 12" by 18" in high quality. Digital cameras measure the number of pixels in width and height of the picture's frame in *megapixels (MP)*: a million pixels equal a megapixel. As a benchmark for prosumers today, the Nikon D90 can take 12.3 megapixels—its sensor array captures 4288 pixels along one dimension and 2848 pixels along the other, therefore, $4288 \times 2848 = 12.2$ (plus a fractional amount) of megapixels.

Depending on the make and model of your digital camera (price plays a deciding factor here), you can take photos that vary in maximum print size. The following table provides the maximum printable dimensions for different megapixel-capable cameras:

Camera	Maximum Print Size
12.3MP	12"h×18"w
10.1MP	10.8"h×16.2"w
9MP	10.2"h×15.3"w
8MP (most smartphones)	8"h×10"w
6MP	8.3"h×12.5"w

Print size at 1 to 1 resolution can be far greater than computer screen resolution, and that's why digital photos can be enlarged to a great extent while retaining focus and clarity. Even the largest computer monitor resolution of 2560×1440 pixels yields a megapixel count of only 3.67 megapixels.

There is even the Nokia Lumia 1020—a smartphone—that can take a staggering 41MP image. To give you a down-to-earth comparison, a large monitor running 2560×1440 resolution has less than a 4MP count when viewing images at 1 to 1 resolution.

The maximum print sizes listed in the previous table are not hard-and-fast dimensions, but are guidelines for print output for two reasons:

- The dots that inkjet printers render are imprecise. They are more like *splats* than dots as the print head sprays color onto the page.
- There is flexibility when printing to home inkjet printers because *image dimensions are inversely proportional to image resolution*. All the resolutions listed in the table presume an image resolution in the neighborhood of 250 pixels per inch, a typical inkjet output resolution.

The math for calculating maximum resolution goes like this: most affordable inkjet printers offer a high-quality resolution of about 720 dpi. The documentation might claim that the printer offers "enhanced resolution of 1440 dpi," but usually this enhancement is only rendered in one direction, height or width, depending on your print layout. The *true* resolution is always the lower number when two are offered in the inkjet printer's documentation. Manufacturers of inkjet printers, makers of inks, and other printing experts agree that the ideal resolution for printing—in dots per inch—requires about 1/3 this number—in pixels per inch—for the image to be printed, so 720 dpi divided by 3 is 240 dpi.

The good news is that you can change the resolution of an image, thereby changing its real-world dimensions, without changing the pixel count—which tends to sharpen an image when it's made smaller, but blurs it when it's enlarged. For example, a photo that is 3" by 3" at 300 pixels per inch (ppi) is *exactly equal* to the image at 6" by 6" at a resolution of 150 ppi. Both images have the same number of pixels, but the print dimensions and resolution have been changed.

Let's walk through an example of how to determine a photo's resolution and then adjust it for printing.

`Tutorial` Resizing a Photograph

1. In PHOTO-PAINT, open *Late Graduate.png*, a photo that has been somewhat contrived to demonstrate a technique in this chapter.
2. Let's say you need to print this photo at inkjet high quality. This means at least 240 pixels/inch are required. To check the resolution of the current foreground document, with the Object Pick tool, right-click over the document and then choose Document Properties from the context menu.

Tip To display rulers around the edges of a document, press CTRL+SHIFT+R. To hide rulers, press CTRL+SHIFT+R again to toggle them off. If the rulers don't display the units you need, right-click over either ruler and then choose Ruler Setup from the context menu.

Well, oops. This photo is a nice 8" by 11", but it's of insufficient resolution to print at the required 240 ppi, as shown here. It *can* print with high quality and great image fidelity, but the physical output dimensions need to be decreased to *increase* the resolution.

3. Right-click over the photo and then choose Resample from the context menu. The Resample (Image menu item) box does more than resample an image; it can also *resize* an image, and the two terms are very different. *Resizing* is the action of decreasing or increasing image resolution, affecting image dimensions inversely, and the result is an image that has the same number of pixels. *Resampling* (covered in this chapter) involves changing the number of pixels in the image. Original pixel colors are moved around the grid—some are duplicated, some removed—and the resulting color pixels are a new color based on an average of neighboring original color pixels. Resampling changes original image data and occasionally blurs or creates unwanted harsh edges in image areas.

4. Click to check the Maintain Original Size box, and make sure the Maintain Aspect Ratio box is checked, and then type **7** in the Height field. Because the photo was doctored for this example, the photo is now a perfect 7" by 5", smaller than its original dimensions. As the dimensions decreased, as shown in Figure 22-2, its resolution increased and is now more than adequate in resolution for inkjet printing. Save the file if you like ducks, or college, or both, and then print it to see what image resolution does for digital images: it *improves* them.

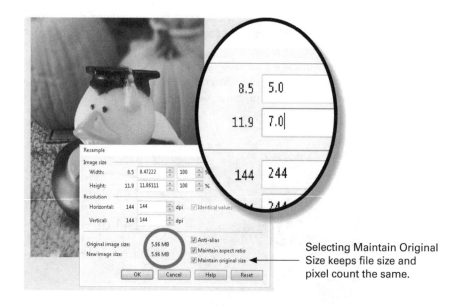

Selecting Maintain Original Size keeps file size and pixel count the same.

FIGURE 22-2   Resolution is inversely proportional to image dimensions.

> **Note** There is a little disagreement in the imaging community about screen resolution: whether it should be measured at 72 or 96 pixels per inch, the standard that Microsoft put forth with Windows 95. The answer to this disagreement is: when you're measuring pixels for screen display, it makes absolutely no difference. Screen resolution, regardless of how you measure it, is a fixed size, so a 300-pixel-wide bitmap might look larger or smaller depending on the screen resolution you use for display, but it neither changes the number of pixels in width, nor the total pixel count of a bitmap when you display it on your monitor.

Resampling and Resizing Photos

At times, you absolutely *have* to upscale a photo; you might not have a better image and you can't retake the scene or person's portrait. When you increase the number of pixels in a photo, you're not increasing image detail—all the details in the scene were captured when you took the photo. PHOTO-PAINT adds pixels by duplicating existing pixel colors and then averages the colors a little to make a smooth photo transition between neighboring pixels in the resampled photo *if* you leave Anti-alias checked in the Resample dialog.

How much larger you can make a photo before the individual pixels become apparent depends on the visual content of the photo. Pictures of intricate machinery and images of lots of differently colored small objects such as leaves do not upsample nearly as well as, say, a photo of soft clouds on an overcast day. If you need to make a photo 150 percent of its original size, usually you can get away with this without taking any additional steps. However, if, for example, you need to print a picture from the Web that's only 300 pixels wide, you have two things going for you in this endeavor:

- Inkjet printers tend to smooth out small rough areas in a digital image because ink spreads on the printed page, blending flaws together. Don't count on this factor; it's an assistant, but a small one.
- PHOTO-PAINT can sharpen edges in the resampled photo while keeping large areas of similar colors smooth in appearance.

> **Tip** PHOTO-PAINT has several sharpening filters under Effects | Sharpen. PHOTO-PAINT's Help system provides a good general explanation of the Sharpen filters; launch any of them and then click the Help button in the filter dialog box. Generally, when in doubt, choose Unsharp Mask to add some crispness to resampled photos. Unsharp Mask provides good sharpening without an overwhelming number of options you need to learn. Click the Preview button in any of the filter dialogs to toggle the effect on and off within the document window for comparison.

Figure 22-3 shows a small JPEG photograph; let's pretend for the purposes of working through a tutorial that you own this condo and want to time-share it. And you want to print postcard-size images to hand out in addition to your website's image.

350 pixels wide   Zoom to 800%

FIGURE 22-3 Unless some corrective steps are taken, this small photo would print with huge, clearly visible color pixels.

Tip The Zoom tool (z) affords you the opportunity to get in very close to an image area to view and edit. However, if you're not familiar with resolution-dependent bitmap editing, a zoomed-in view of a photo might look coarse and your instinct might be to soften the image. Periodically check the document title bar: after the name of the file, there's an "@" symbol followed by your current viewing resolution. If the zoom factor is greater than 100 percent, this document is not displaying as your audience will see it. To quickly zoom a document to 1:1, 100 percent viewing resolution, double-click the Zoom tool on the Toolbox.

The following set of steps are a "worst-case" scenario—you will almost certainly be able to enlarge photos so they become printworthy by resampling up to 150 percent or so; you won't have to make the *gross* sort of enlargement and image corrections shown in these steps. However, as you'll soon see, the High Pass effect you'll use does, indeed, enhance a copy of the small JPEG photo to a usable state.

Tutorial Making a Thumbnail Image Suitable for Printing

1. Open *Hollywood-5203.jpg* in PHOTO-PAINT. With the Object Pick tool, right-click over the image and then choose Resample from the context menu.
2. In the Width field, type **7**, and then click an insertion point in the Resolution | Horizontal field. Make sure the Maintain Aspect Ratio and Anti-alias checkboxes are checked, and then type **240** in the box. Click OK to resample the photo.

3. At 100 percent viewing resolution, clearly the photo needs a little edge sharpening without sharpening the larger smooth areas of the photo. Press CTRL + F7 if the Object Manager docker isn't docked to the window or isn't visible. You're going to duplicate this image and put the copy on top of the original. This is an unusual thing to do, and *to be able to do,* but PHOTO-PAINT has advanced image-editing features that let you change and merge image areas (called *objects*) so the pixels in objects can have different colors but are aligned to the imaginary grid in the document identically.

4. With the Object Pick tool, drag the thumbnail labeled Background, as shown here, so it's on top of the New Object button on the Object Manager docker and then release the mouse button. Doing this duplicates the image, creating the new object directly on top of the original.

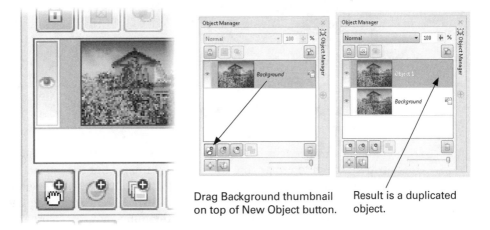

Drag Background thumbnail on top of New Object button.

Result is a duplicated object.

5. Click the Object 1 thumbnail on the Object list to select it—you want to edit this, not the Background object.

6. Choose Effects | Sharpen | High Pass. Wherever sharp transitions between pixel colors appear in the photo, edge details are retained and strengthened. Wherever there is little color difference between neighboring pixels (called *low-frequency* areas), the visual information is filtered out, leaving a neutral gray. The higher the percentage you specify (use **100** in this example), the less original color is retained. The greater the radius (use about **12** in this

example), the greater the distance this filter examines from neighboring pixels to filter out areas of little detail difference. Click OK to apply these settings.

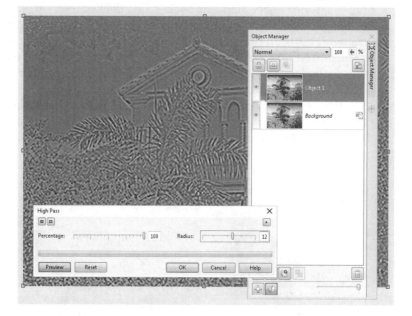

7. Beyond the strong edges in Object 1, this object doesn't look as though it will contribute much to enhancing this enlarged image, but the correct answer is, "Yes, it will!" Here's a simple explanation of why Overlay mode will turn this largely gray object into a perfect "lens" to sharpen the underlying Background photo. The brightness values in a photo (the tones, not the colors) are usually calculated on a scale from 0 to 255, 255 representing the brightest area (pure white has a brightness of 255). Overlay Merge mode can be thought of as a filter: Overlay mode objects that have a brightness greater than 128 lighten (bleach, screen) objects under them, whereas brightness pixel values less than 128 darken (multiply) the underlying pixels. The High Pass filter made most of the pixels in this object neutral gray—which has no effect in Overlay mode on the underlying pixels. However, the *edge details* in Object 1 are darker and lighter than the underlying, corresponding Background areas. Choose Overlay from the Merge Mode drop-down list.

8. Objects do not have to be 100 percent opaque. This Overlay mode object contributes a little too strongly to the overall picture; click the Transparency combo box at the top right of the Object Manager docker to reveal the slider and then drag the slider left to about **29%**, or whatever value looks best in the document window.

9. You can choose to save this file right now as a PHOTO-PAINT (CPT) or Adobe Photoshop (PSD) document, and the objects will retain their order using these special image file formats. And you can now print the composition. However, if you'd like to standardize the image so it can be saved to practically any

Without High
Pass object

High Pass object
in Overlay mode

FIGURE 22-4   Use **PHOTO-PAINT** filters and objects to strengthen and smooth image areas selectively.

file format (PNG, JPEG, TIFF, and others) and thus shared with most other computer users, with the Object Pick tool, right-click on either object on the Object Manager docker and then choose Combine | Combine All Objects With Background.

As you can see by way of comparison in Figure 22-4, without the High Pass copy of the image in Overlay mode, at left, the pixels dominate the image in visual importance. At right, however, with the duplicate object you filtered and merged with the original, it's a fairly photogenic image...given that you enlarged it to almost *23 times* its original file size!

Automation: Recording Your Cropping and Resampling

It's almost a foregone conclusion that if you work at a small- to medium-size business, you have dozens if not hundreds of photos that need some sort of alterations and uniformity so they'll look consistent in size when you make a catalogue or web page. Cropping is a separate process from resizing photos in PHOTO-PAINT, but the good news is that if your collection of photos are even remotely similar in subject matter, you can record your cropping and resampling moves and then play this recorded script back on an entire folder of images. No errors, no recalculations, and you might have a free hand to eat your sandwich as you work through lunch.

Evaluating a Crop Area for a Collection of Photos

PHOTO-PAINT's Crop tool does only one thing perfectly well: it eliminates areas of a picture outside the crop rectangle you drag before double-clicking or pressing ENTER to finalize the crop. You are free before finalizing to reposition, reset, and move the crop rectangle. The Crop tool resizes an image area, and depending on whether you've chosen Custom on the Property bar, the Crop tool can possibly resample an image, but you might not be happy with an up-sampled photo. Therefore, if you want to enlarge or decrease the number of pixels in the finished version, you must perform the additional step of resampling *before* saving a copy of the photo.

The imaginary company in this scenario (leading up to a tutorial) specializes in exotic minerals—no common quartz or hematite to be found on their website—and the photographer took seven pictures whose visual content is more or less all in the same position from photo to photo. Your mission is to crop out the bottom pedestal and place a card in all the photos to favor the mineral itself. You also want to reduce the size of all the pictures, all sized to exactly the same dimensions, so the collection of minerals can be featured on a web page. Because Windows 7 and 8 can display large thumbnails of common image file formats such as PNG, you can easily preview the contents of an entire folder of images to better see which individual photo needs the most height or width to then apply a suitable crop for all the images.

Figure 22-5 is a view of the folder of mineral pictures as seen from the File | Open An Image window in PHOTO-PAINT, with Extra Large Icons chosen from the drop-down list. The overlay of the dotted line shows that the Fliakite.png image requires

FIGURE 22-5 Out of the many images you need to resample and crop, choose the one that requires the loosest cropping as the basis for your automation recording.

the greatest width of all the files—this is something you can detect by eye. Therefore, when you begin the tutorial, you'll begin by choosing Fliakite.png as the image on which you'll record your cropping and resampling edits.

Tutorial Recording Your Edits

The following set of steps guides you simultaneously through recording and editing the resampling and cropping process. Playing the saved recording back on a folder is quite simple and covered in a following section. If you have a real-world need to crop and resample scores of images, and your boss or client wanted them yesterday, you're going to have your solution and the images completed sooner than anyone might imagine! Locate the images you downloaded at the beginning of this chapter: put only the mineral PNG files in a unique folder.

1. Choose Windows | Dockers | Recorder (CTRL + F3).
2. Choose File | Open (CTRL + O), and then open Fliakite.png from the folder to which you copied the seven PNG files.
3. Click the red button on the Recorder docker; you're recording now. Choose the Crop tool from the Toolbox.
4. Drag a rectangle around the top of the image, excluding the glass pedestal from your crop.

Crop tool

5. Press ENTER to finalize the crop (double-clicking inside the document does the same thing).
6. Press o (Object Pick tool), and then right-click over the image and choose Resample.
7. Three or possibly four thumbnails across a conservatively sized web page of 800 pixels wide means the width to resample this image should be about

200 pixels. Choose Pixels from the Image Size units drop-down list, and then type **200** in the Width field. The height will automatically scale down in proportion.

8. Because you're not measuring in real-world units, but instead in number of pixels, you don't have to specify 72 or 96 dpi for the resampled image. On the Web, a screen pixel is an absolute, unchangeable size. Additionally, if you change the dpi setting now, you'll need to go back and respecify the width as 200 because you've changed the resolution value. If the percentage field reads 32%, you're good to go—click OK to apply.

![Resample dialog box]

9. Double-click the Zoom tool to move your view to 100%. The resampled image could use just a touch of Effect | Sharpen | Sharpen, a good choice for extremely small images. Set the Edge Level to about **26%**; this is the degree of sharpening with emphasis on neighboring pixels that have dissimilar colors. Set the Threshold to **0** (zero)—the lower the value, the more pronounced the sharpening effect. Click OK to apply the filter.

10. Click the square Stop button on the Recorder docker.

11. Click the Save button on the Recorder docker, name the script, and then choose a location on your hard disk where you keep important files.

 Note The Save icon on the Recorder and other dockers is of a floppy disk. Floppy disks were once used to store digital media before DVDs, CDs, air travel, and horses were invented.

You can close the Fliakite file without saving changes. In the following section, you'll run the recorded script on this image and save it, so your work that's not done yet will be automatically done for you in a moment.

The Fun Part: Playing Back Your Script

The following steps will seem anticlimactic; the bulk of the work you have ahead of you is accomplished merely by filling out a few fields in the File | Batch Process dialog and clicking Play.

1. Choose File | Batch Process.
2. Click Add File. Navigate to where you stored the minerals image. Select all of them; click on one file to place your cursor inside the file box; press CTRL + A to select all; and then click Import.
3. Click Add Script. Look at the default path where PHOTO-PAINT saves scripts at the top of the box. The default location is under your *user account* | Appdata | Roaming | Corel ... if you lose a file in the future. Click the name of the script you saved in the previous tutorial, and then click Open.
4. In the Options field, click the drop-down list and then choose On Completion: Save As New Type.
5. Save To Folder is an important choice if you want to find the processed images later! Because you'll be saving to JPEG, it's okay to save the processed images to the same folder as the originals, which are in the PNG file format, and will not be overwritten by the batch process.
6. You'll probably want the JPEG file type for the resampled photos if this is a website display. Click the Save As Type drop-down list and then choose JPG-JPEG Bitmaps.

Batch Process   ✕

List of files to batch process:

```
:ample files\Minerals\Calamarium.png                    Add File...
:ample files\Minerals\Fliakite.png
:ample files\Minerals\Hysterium.png                     Remove File
:ample files\Minerals\Memorandom.png
:ample files\Minerals\Pompomogranite.png
:ample files\Minerals\Russettite.png
```

List of scripts:

```
22\Example files\Minerals\Web Gallery.csc               Add Script...

                                                        Remove Script
```

Options

On Completion: Save as new type

☑ Close file after batch process

Save to folder: Browse...   C:\Users\Gare\Pictures

Save as type: JPG - JPEG Bitmaps

Play   Cancel   Help

7. Click Play. Done!

Back in CorelDRAW, use the Extrude tool for a fancy website banner. As you can see here, when you select the multiple files for import into CorelDRAW from the destination folder to which you saved your batch processing, you can simply click the page to place the images, one at a time, at 100 percent their size, and in no time you either look like a miracle worker to your boss, or if you're self-employed, you can look in your bathroom mirror and say, "Darn, I'm good!" (this is a PG book).

Flipping Images…with a Twist

Let's cover one more common imaging need. A problem can occur when you try to accomplish something seemingly as simple as mirroring a photograph. This is going to be your first step into the league of the pros with invisible image retouching.

Many objects that you photograph in the real world, in particular, portraits of people, are bilaterally symmetrical—when you look in the mirror, you recognize yourself because even though your image is horizontally flipped, the right and left side of your face looks pretty much the same. This reality usually allows us to flip a photograph when you need, for example, your subject looking to the right instead of the left. The fly in the ointment, however, is when your subject is wearing a garment that has text on it; similarly, when a building in the background has a sign, or there's only one shirt pocket on a garment—these flipped images will have something in them that looks clearly wrong to the audience.

The following steps venture into the area of PHOTO-PAINT objects: how you can lift an area, copy it to a new object, and then flip the background but not the new object—which in this example is the text on a child's T-shirt. Retouching is not this simple; you will have a little edgework to clean up before considering the task completed, but with a little guidance, you'll learn a technique now that can be applied to a number of different retouching needs down the road:

1. Open *Two Kids.tif* in PHOTO-PAINT. On the Object Manager docker, you need to convert this "normal" bitmap image into an object-capable one so the objects can be flipped independent of one another. Click the From Background icon at the right of the thumbnail, and the name of the item now changes to "Object 1,"

as shown here. Once a photo is an object, you can perform many PHOTO-PAINT feats not possible with a standard JPEG or other image file.

Click to turn a
Background
into an Object.

2. Choose the Freehand Mask tool from the Toolbox; if it's not visible, click + hold on the third from top icon on the Toolbox (usually the Rectangle Mask tool) to reveal the entire group of Masking tools, and then choose the Freehand tool.

3. On the Property bar, set the Feathering value to about **6** pixels. Feathering softens a selection, so inside and outside the edge of a selection mask there are pixels that are *partially* selected. To have an area partially selected might sound strange (like an egg being partially broken), but the effect ensures smooth and seamless retouching work.

4. Drag around the word "Julian" on (Julian's) T-shirt to select it; double-click when you're done, and the image area is now available for editing. If you don't include the entire name on your first try, click the Additive Mode button on the Property bar and use the Freehand Mask tool to add to the existing mask.

5. Right-click inside the dashed indicator lines for the mask area, and then choose Copy From Mask from the context menu. On the Object Manager docker, you'll now see a new thumbnail at the top of the list of objects, titled "Object 2"; see Figure 22-6.

Tip   Pressing CTRL+SHIFT+H reveals and hides an object marquee onscreen. CTRL+H alternately hides and shows mask marquees, not the same thing as the dotted lines running around objects.

6. Click the Object 1 entry on the Object list to make it the current editing object. Then, choose Object | Flip | Horizontally.

7. Click the Object 2 entry on the Object Manager docker, choose Lightness Merge mode from the Object Manager's drop-down list—a good mode for making underlying areas fade away only if the top affecting object has lighter corresponding pixels—and then move the object over Julian's chest at left on the image with the Object Pick tool.

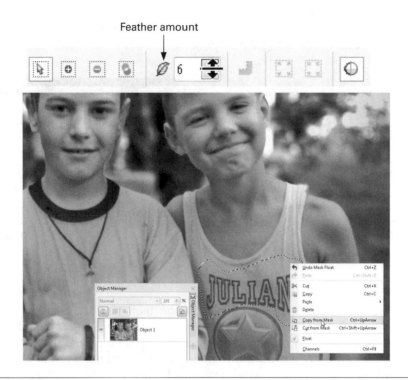

FIGURE 22-6 Copy the image area that you don't want to flip to a new object in the document.

8. Evaluate the composition for a moment. What needs to be done now is to remove some of the backward text on Object 1 to keep it from showing through. A straight paint color won't do the job because the image area has varying tones of color from the texture of the T-shirt. Choose the Clone tool from Toolbox; it's the Toolbox icon with the two brushes.

9. The Clone tool picks up an image area you define by right-clicking and then applies the image area to a different area when you drag, based on the diameter and hardness you set for the tool. On the Property bar, choose Medium Soft Clone from the drop-down list.

10. Click on Object 1 to choose it for editing, and then hide Object 2 by clicking the Visibility (the eye) icon to the left of its thumbnail.

11. Right-click with the Clone tool just below the name on Julian's T-shirt. You're choosing a sampling area that's close in tone and color to the area you want to hide.

12. Drag, ever-so-slowly, slightly, and carefully over the backward lettering on the T-shirt, to get a feel for the Clone tool. When you release the mouse button, the sampling point for the Clone tool snaps back to its original position. Therefore, release the mouse button when you see that the traveling sampling point is getting mighty close to an undesired area for sampling. Work from the outside inward, resampling frequently to match the original tones of the light shirt. Periodically, unhide Object 2 to see how much work you need to do and what areas are not necessary to clone away. See Figure 22-7.

13. When you think you're finished cloning, restore the visibility of Object 2. You might be done, but you might want to refine the edges of Object 2 with the Eraser tool. If so...

14. Click Object 2, to select it for editing. Choose the Eraser tool, and then on the Property bar, choose a soft tip from the Presets drop-down list, and set the size to about **35** pixels in diameter.

Clone tool

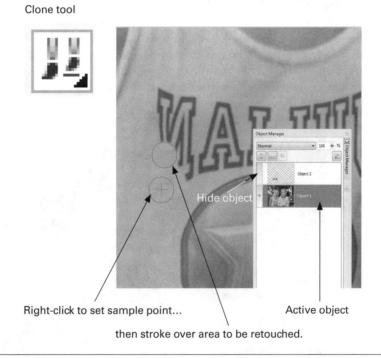

Right-click to set sample point...   Active object

then stroke over area to be retouched.

FIGURE 22-7   Use the Clone tool to visually integrate the areas in Objects 2 and 1.

15. Zoom into the editing area, and then drag over any areas whose brightness doesn't match the edge of the object. The work in progress and the illusion shown here looks pretty convincing.

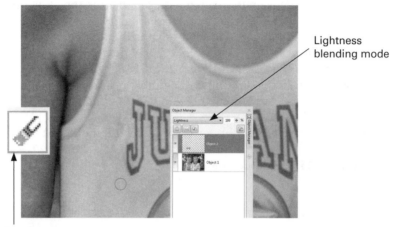

Lightness blending mode

Eraser tool

16. Optionally, you can standardize this image's data by combining all objects—as you did in the Hollywood condo example. Right-click over either object title on the Object Manager docker and then choose Combine | Combine All Objects With Background.

Consider what you've learned in this chapter: you now know how to repeat actions on an entire folder of images, you can scale, crop, flip pictures, and you have a basic handle on all the sophisticated editing you can perform using transparency, objects, and merge modes. But the biggest payoff is an ironic one: a good photo retoucher's work should go unnoticed!

PART IX

Getting Your Work in the Public Eye

23 Professional Output: A Primer on Prepping Your Work for Print

Print is alive and well today, thank you, in almost every enterprise. *Outputting* your work so your clients can hold it in their hands is just as much an art as *designing* a piece in CorelDRAW. This chapter takes you through *professional* output—CorelDRAW's features that extend *beyond* the familiar File | Print command—and what it takes from CorelDRAW and you to make every dot of ink on a page look exactly like every pixel you designed on the screen.

Printing a Document to a Personal Printer

Let's suppose you want to print a "one off," perhaps to see if everything is arranged on the page correctly before packing off a copy to a commercial press. If your artwork is for black and white (you used no color, only shades of black in the design), you might print to a laser printer. Laser printers don't really have any color-critical settings, so you're probably as ready to go as you'd be if you were printing a text document. If you're printing to an inkjet, most of today's inkjet circuitry does an automatic conversion from RGB color space and the color ink space (usually CMYK, although many affordable printers use six inks), and again, you really don't have to jump through any hoops if you've designed a document that uses RGB, LAB, or CMYK color spaces to define the colors you filled objects with.

Here's a tutorial that covers the basics for outputting your work to a personal printer. Before you begin, make sure the layers you want to print are visible on the Object Manager docker and that printing is enabled for the layers; a tiny red international "no" appears on disabled layer properties—click the "no" symbol to enable the layer property.

Tutorial Printing Single- and Multiple-Page Documents

1. Open the document you want to print, and then choose File | Print (CTRL + P), or click the Print button on the Standard bar. Any of these actions opens the Print dialog, shown here. Pay attention to the orientation of the page with respect to the *orientation of the paper* as it will print. The Page drop-down offers to match the orientation of the page, or to use the Printer default orientation settings.

Quick Preview button   Quick Preview

2. On the General tab, choose your printer from the Printer drop-down menu, and then click Preferences to set any printer properties such as the print material page size, orientation, and so on. Keep in mind that any special features specific to your printer might override any CorelDRAW-specific features, in particular, color management (discussed later in this chapter). In general, it's *not* a good idea to have a color management feature enabled on your printer when CorelDRAW color manages the document. Two color management systems will contend with each other, and what you see onscreen will *not* be what you get on the printed page.

3. Click the Quick Preview button to expand the dialog to show a preview window if you want to check the document for position on the printable page. A dashed line appears in the preview window, indicating document areas that are close to or that go over the printable page margin. If you see this, you

might want to cancel the print operation and rework your page. Alternatively, you can click the Layout tab and then check Fit To Page, although doing this scales the objects in your document, so forget about the business cards aligning perfectly to that micro-perforated paper.

4. If you have more than one document open in CorelDRAW, you can choose which document to print by clicking the Documents radio button in the Print Range area; *make certain* that all documents you want to print have the same portrait or landscape orientation before printing. In a multi-page CorelDRAW document, choose the page(s) you want to print from the Print Range area, and then enter the print quantity in the Number Of Copies box.

5. Before you click Print, check to see whether there are any Issues on the Issues tab. If the tab reads "No Issues," proceed to step 6 and collect $200. If there's an issue, however, you should address it (or them) first. Issues come in two varieties: showstoppers, indicated by a triangular traffic sign with an exclamation mark, and trivial stuff, indicated by an info (*i*) icon. A common example of trivial stuff is printing blank pages; you can easily correct this by changing the Pages value in the Print Range area of the General tab. Showstoppers require careful reading of the explanation provided on the Issues tab; the remarks and explanations are quite clear—such as attempting to print a low-resolution image to a high-resolution printer—and your best bet is to cancel the print job and read the rest of this chapter...and save paper and ink. Here's what the Issues icons look like:

Life is good; click Print.   Minor inconvenience; check Print Range.   Possible showstopper: read the info, and then consider canceling the print job.

6. Click Print, go get your favorite refreshment, wait a moment, and then get your printout.

The Quick Preview deserves a little more coverage here. After clicking the Quick Preview button, you're shown a preview window and page browsing controls. While you're previewing, you can right-click to access invaluable commands from the pop-up menu: Show Image, Preview Color, Preview Separations, and to toggle the view of Rulers. When you want to print a multi-page CorelDRAW file, you can quickly turn pages in Quick Preview to make sure you're printing within page boundaries and that all the pages contain what you want to print. To print the preview page at the current settings, choose Print This Sheet Now from the pop-up menu.

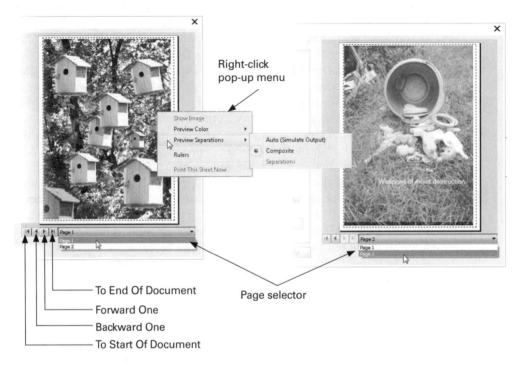

Setting Print Options

The tabbed areas of the Print dialog more or less follow from left to right a progression from personal printing options to more ambitious endeavors such as printing separations for process *color composite* (commercial) printing. Some of the areas on the tabs are device dependent and appear only after CorelDRAW evaluates your printer's capabilities; Use PPD (PostScript Printing Description), for example, is dimmed on the General tab until you've chosen a printer that is PostScript capable, or choose to output to a PDF file, increasingly popular with commercial printers today. This is why your first step is to select your printing device. Depending on the printer defined, you'll see tabbed areas for General, Color, Composite, Layout, Prepress, PostScript, and Issues.

Setting General Options

The General tab of the Print dialog, shown next, offers control over some of the most common printing options.

Here's a description of what each area on the General tab controls:

- **Destination** This area displays feedback provided by the printer driver used with your selected printer. It shows the Printer name, Status, Location (local port or on a network), and Comment information. Direct, network, or spooler printers are indicated according to their connection status. If CorelDRAW cannot find a printer connected directly or remotely (through a network) to your computer, you'll need to pay a visit to the Windows Start menu | Devices And Printers, and then choose Add A Printer. The good news is this is a wizard-style process and Windows ships with just about every conceivable print driver for popular makes and models. You might be prompted for a specific print driver, so have the manufacturer's disk handy or download the latest driver from the website. Clicking the Preferences button provides control over printer-specific properties and output material sizes. Choosing Use PPD lets you assign a PostScript Printer Description file; checking this box displays the Select PPD dialog, where you locate and then select an appropriate PPD file. Unless you're already familiar with what Print To File does, *don't* check this box in your everyday printing.
- **Print Range** This area contains options to select pages from the file you have maximized in the drawing window—or from *any* document you have open in CorelDRAW. Click the Documents button to see and choose what's open. Choose Current Page to print the page currently in view in your CorelDRAW document, or enter specific page numbers in the Pages box. If you have one or more objects selected when you open the Print dialog, the Selection option is available so you can print *only* your selection; this option is quite handy for printing only a part of your document. Choose Even & Odd from the drop-down menu to print only certain pages. By default, both Even and Odd pages are printed.
- **Copies** This area has two options for setting the Number Of Copies to print either collated or not. When Collate is chosen, a picture appears indicating the

effect of collating. Collating is a great timesaver when you don't want the hassle of reordering pages as they come out of the printer.

Tip To print consecutive pages of a document, in the Print Range area's Pages box, enter the page numbers separated by a hyphen (for example, type **6-8** to print pages 6, 7, and 8). To print noncontiguous pages, for example, pages 6, 8, and 16, type commas between specific page numbers—**6, 8, 16** in this example. You can also combine these two conventions by separating each entry by a comma. For example, entering **6-8, 10-13, 16** will print pages 6, 7, 8, 10, 11, 12, 13, and 16.

Using Print Styles

Print Styles remove the repetitive task of setting up the same (or similar) printing parameters by letting you save all the selected options in the Print dialog in one tidy Print Style file. If your printing options have already been saved as a style, open the Print Style drop-down menu on the General tab, and choose the style from the list.

To create a style that includes all the currently selected settings, follow these steps:

1. On the General tab, click Save As to open the Save Settings As dialog, shown here. As you can see, this dialog includes a Settings To Include tree directory listing the categorized print options and checkboxes according to current settings.

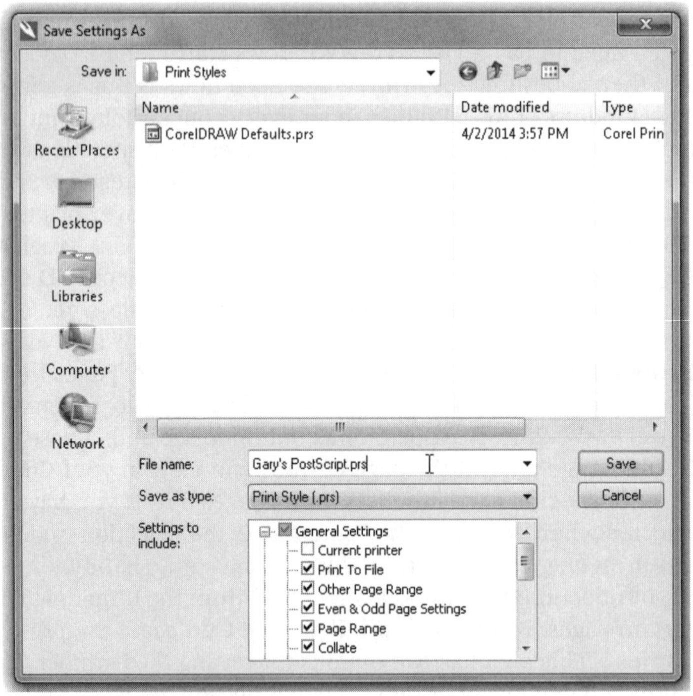

2. Click to select the options you want to save with your new style, enter a unique name for your style, and then click Save to store the settings, after which they are available from the Print Style drop-down list.

Using the Color Tab Settings

When outputting to color, you'll find all options relating to Color on this single tabbed menu. The following sections document color-related operations.

Print Composite/Print Separations

At the top of this tab is the area where you choose to print color separations (covered in "Printing Separations," later in this chapter) or to print a composite—the standard way most designers print color documents to a home inkjet printer. If you choose separations, the Composite tab in the Print dialog changes to Separations options, and vice versa.

Document/Color Proof Settings

Your either/or choice by clicking one of these buttons determines whether you'll print using your current document color settings—found under Tools | Color Management—or disregard color settings you've made in the file and use the settings you pick in the Print dialog.

Color Conversions Performed By

This drop-down list lets you convert the color space of the document using CorelDRAW's features or you can choose to let your printer handle the conversion from your monitor's color space to the slightly smaller and duller color space of physical pigments. If you're undecided, it's a safe bet to let CorelDRAW handle the conversion if your printer is an inkjet and not a PostScript printer. When a Postscript printer is defined, the alternative options to CorelDRAW is a Device Independent PostScript file—or different options depending on a specific printer. PostScript is PostScript, so the specific make and model of the printer is not relevant.

Output Colors As

When you're printing to a personal, non-PostScript device such as an inkjet, your options are only RGB and Grayscale, which is fair enough: laser printers can only reproduce grayscale halftones, and inkjets usually use the RGB color space to then convert colors to the color space of CMYK. When you select a PostScript device, your options are

- **Native**   CorelDRAW handles the reconciliation between any color models you've used when filling objects and the colors in any imported bitmap images.
- **RGB**   The file is sent to the printer using the RGB color model. Use this option when you're printing a composite image (not separations).

- **CMYK**   Use this mode when you want to proof your work so you have a good idea of how your colors will print when sending a file to a commercial printer (Composite printing). Similarly, if you're printing separations, CorelDRAW forces all colors in your document into the CMYK color space using the Rendering Intent you've selected (see Chapter 1).
- **Grayscale**   Choosing this mode sends all color information to the printer as percentages of black. When choosing this option, you will also see a Convert Spot Colors To Grayscale, something you might *not* want to choose if you want to print a plate of your spot colors.
- **Convert Spot Colors To CMYK**   If for some reason your budget doesn't allow a spot color, clicking this checkbox will force any spot color plates to be rendered as CMYK process color equivalents. Forget about color fidelity and accuracy, but the option is available.

Correct Colors Using

When printing to a non-PostScript device, you have the option to correct colors to the color profile of a specific printer, or to choose from the list of available ICC color profiles installed on your computer.

 Tip You might be surprised at the lush colors you'll render to a home inkjet printer by choosing sRGB IE6C 1966-2.1 as the color correction option instead of relying on your printer's color correction. sRGB is a widely used color space for today's consumer-level scanners and printing devices.

When you've defined a PostScript printer as your target device, you can choose from several presets defined from many different imagesetting manufacturers, or choose a predefined color space, the same as for a non-PostScript printer.

Note You have four options for choosing how CorelDRAW handles converting from one color space to another. See Chapter 1 for thorough documentation on color conversion and choosing the best Rendering Intent to suit a specific document.

Choosing a Layout

Options on the Layout tab give you control over how the page is laid out on the printing material you've loaded into your rendering device. Although the options are set to defaults for the most common print tasks, you can customize options in each area.

Setting Image Position and Size

Image Position And Size options control the layout of each page. These settings will override settings you've defined in Printer Properties (your system's printing preferences, which aren't related to CorelDRAW). The following options are available:

- **As In Document**   This option (the default) leaves the current layout unchanged.
- **Fit To Page**   Choose this to enlarge or reduce your page layout to fit exactly within the printable area for your selected output material. Understand that choosing this option immediately ruins as a print any precise measurements you've created in your file. If you run into this problem, hang on and check out the Print Tiled Pages option covered shortly. Below the Fit To Page area is the Include Marks And Calibration Bars checkbox. This option is almost entirely meant for a commercial printer and not for printing your own separations. Basically, it keeps color separations aligned if you scale down your work to fit the page.
- **Reposition Images To**   Choose this option to change the position of images as they print relative to how they're arranged on your CorelDRAW page. By default, images are automatically positioned to Center Of Page on your printing material. However, you can align images to the top, left, right, and bottom corners of the printing material page size—a convenient way to save paper and to make trimming a printed piece easier. Use the Position, Size, and Scale Factor boxes to enter specific values. Unlocking the horizontal/vertical lock by clicking the nearby lock icon gives you the opportunity to set the horizontal and/or vertical scale factor separately for nonproportional scaling, although you might not want a distorted print.
- **Settings For page**   This set of options lets you change settings based on a page you want to print that is not the same size or number of tiles as other pages you're printing.
- **Imposition Layout**   *Imposition* is the orientation and position of multiple pages to create a book signature—pages are ordered and rotated so a commercial press can print a large page, and then the pages can be trimmed and bound so the book looks like a finished product. If you intend to print to high-resolution output, this option must be set exactly according to the specifications given to you by the printing service or other vendor you are using. It's always wise to talk with press operators (or their boss) before an expensive print job because the owners of the press know the characteristics of it better than you do. Clicking the Edit button opens a preview feature where you can customize the imposition requirements; you can rotate pages, move gutters, and even reorder pages at the last minute. However, Imposition Layout is also an important feature even if you're home printing a single copy of a booklet from your inkjet printer. Here, you can see a layout defined from a four-page CorelDRAW document; a template was *not* used

to set up the file, and yet by choosing from the Imposition Layout drop-down, you ensure the pages will indeed be printed in book fashion.

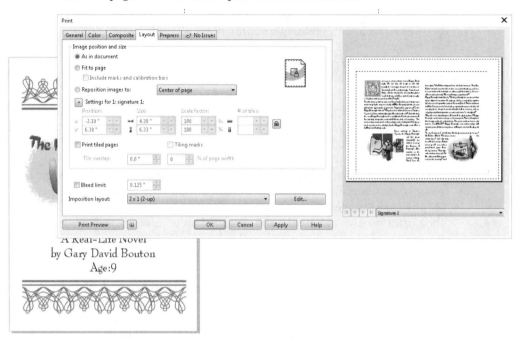

Tiling Your Printed Document

Often you'll need to print a piece that is much larger than the maximum output size of a personal printer: a bake sale banner, for example, or other display that exceeds even the output dimensions of today's wide-format inkjet printers. This calls for using the Print Tiled Pages option. After printing, you get a utility blade, a metal ruler, some adhesive, and a cutting surface, and you're in business. The options for setting how each tile is printed are as follows:

- **Print Tiled Pages** Choose this option to print pages in portions. Once selected, the # (Number) Of Tiles, Tiling Marks (you want to use Tile Overlap if you use this to avoid showing the marks in your finished project), and Tile Overlap options are available. The # Of Tiles option lets you print your document in vertical or horizontal tiles, up to 24 portions for each. Setting the Tile Overlap option gives you control over how much image portion is repeated around the edges of each tile, based on unit measure or a percentage of the original page width. By default, Tile Overlap is set to 0 inches.
- **Tiling Marks** Choose this to have crop-style marks print around your tiles, making it easier to realign the tile pages when you put the tiles together.
- **Tile Overlap** This option adds an extra printed portion around each tile to make aligning the tiles for your large sign easier. Overlap can be set from 0 through 2.125 inches.

- **% Of Page Width** Use this to specify the tile overlap as a percentage of the page size between 0 and 25 percent.
- **Bleed Limit** Choosing this checkbox lets you use a portion of the area surrounding your document page. For example, if certain objects overlap the page border of a document, this option lets you print a portion outside the limits of the page. Bleed Limit can be set within a range of 0 to 40 inches, the default of which is a standard 0.125 inch.

The illustration here shows dashed lines (which would not be in the finished banner) where the single sheets tile in the bake sale banner, only one of scores of needs for tiling a print when your budget prohibits extra-extra-large-format prints.

Printing Separations

If you know what color separations are and you work at a commercial printer, this next section is for you. If you *hire* a commercial printer when you have a color job, and only have a working understanding of process color and separations, read on to learn a little more, but *don't* provide a commercial press operator with your own color separations! CorelDRAW creates terrific color separation work, but you really need to output to a high-resolution (expensive, you don't buy them at a department store) imagesetting device that can render to film or other reproduction medium. You need to know as much about the printing characteristics of a printer as you do about color separations to prepare your own job for printing presses—for example, trapping margin of error, undercolor removal, ink characteristics, and other factors. You probably wouldn't practice brain surgery on yourself—similarly, don't do your own separations ("seps") if you're inexperienced in the field of standard web-offset printing.

If you're a silk screener or know a commercial press inside-out, when Print Separations is selected on the Color tab of the Print dialog, you have control over how each ink color prints.

Choosing Separation Options

Here is the rundown on your color separation options as shown in the dialog in Figure 23-1:

- **Print Separations In Color** This option is available only if the printer you've defined is a color printer such as a personal inkjet, which prints a simulation of a coated printing plate, each plate reproduced in its respective color. This option is sometimes used for printing progressive proofs, checking registration, and

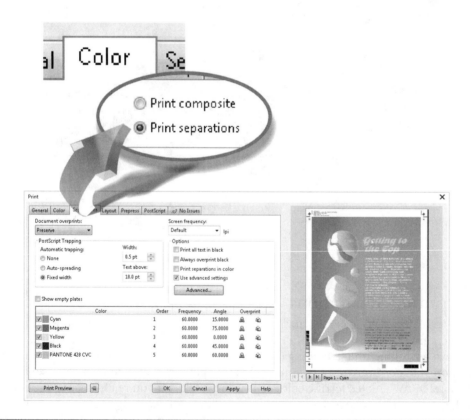

FIGURE 23-1 Use the Separations tab options to specify ink colors and trapping preferences.

checking color accuracy. Understand that if you use this option on a personal inkjet printer, you'll print several pages, each containing a single color; this could use a lot of ink, particularly if your CorelDRAW is dense with colored objects! Printing separations in color results in a good test for separations, but it's nothing you would want to frame and hang in the den later.

- **Convert Spot Colors To Process** This option is important, but it's on the Color tab, *not* Separations. Choosing this option is often a wise choice in non-color-critical printing, when you can't afford to print a fifth plate using a spot color. This option converts non-CMYK colors such as fixed-palette, spot-ink colored objects to the closest process color equivalent when printing. You can usually get away with this if your spot color *is not* a special ink, such as a metallic. Letting CorelDRAW convert a metallic, fluorescent, or other specialty spot ink to process will dull the final print job; the results will look amateurish at best.

- **Show Empty Plates** While unchecked (the default), this option causes pages without any objects to be skipped during printing to avoid printing blank pages. To include the blank pages, check this option. This can save you time, for example, if you only have a spot color on one page but not others in a multi-page document.

Frequency and Angle and Overprint Options

When you've selected separations to print, the ink colors used in your document are listed at the bottom of the Separations tab. Each ink includes options for choosing if and how they will be printed. You'll see a series of columns that show how each ink color is set to print, with its color reference, ink Color name, screen Frequency, screen Angle, and Overprint options. The inks ultimately print in order from top to bottom as you see them on the list.

Don't change the Frequency or line Angle values unless you're a professional—the default values are standard among the printing community. To change the Frequency and/or Angle of a specific ink color, first check the Use Advanced Settings checkbox, and then click directly on the value and then enter a new value. To change overprinting properties of a specific ink color, click directly on the Overprint symbols for text and/or graphic objects to toggle their state. The following list explains what each of these options controls:

- **Order** Use the selector for each ink to set the order in which separations are printed based on the number of available ink colors.

- **Frequency** This option sets the output resolution in *lines per inch (lpi)*; high-resolution imagesetters that speak PostScript organize dots for printing into lines. A typical line frequency for high-quality printing is 133 lpi, which results in color process prints of 2,500 dots per inch and higher. In comparison, a home laser printer, the 1,200 dpi variety, is only capable of rendering 80 lines per inch—you would not get magazine-quality prints using 80 lpi for color separations. Screen frequency values are automatically set to the default values of the imagesetter or printer selected on the General tab. Screen frequency values are also controlled by settings in the Advanced Separations Settings dialog.

- **Angle** This option sets the angle at which the rows of resolution dots align. When separating process color inks, the following standard default screen angles are set automatically: Cyan = 15 degrees, Magenta = 75 degrees, Yellow = 0 degrees, and Black = 45 degrees. When separating fixed-palette ink colors such as Pantone, Toyo, DIC, and so on, all colors are set to the default 45 degree value. You occasionally need to check the Issues tab when custom inks are used for spot-color plates to ensure the spot plate is not at the same or even similar angle to the process-plate screen angles. Change the angle if necessary; an incompatible spot-color screen angle can result in moiré patterning in your print, an effect similar to laying a screen window on top of another one at a certain angle.
- **Overprint** Click directly on the symbols for text (the *A* symbol) and/or objects (the page symbol) to set whether text and/or objects for each ink are printed. Both states toggle on or off when clicked, and a gray overscore above the icons confirm your alterations

The Use Advanced Settings option is always dimmed unless you have a PostScript printer selected. You click the Color tab and make sure Print Separations is clicked. When it's enabled, the Composite tab changes to Separations and you click this tab. Advanced settings will override settings on the Separations tab. Clicking the Advanced button displays the Advanced Separations Settings dialog, shown here.

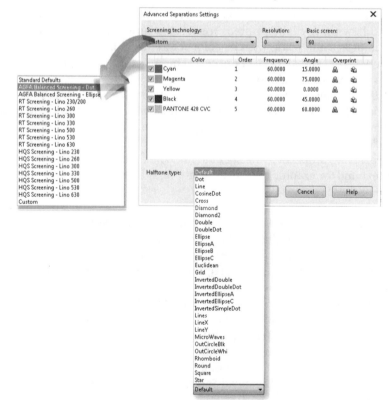

Here are the options in this dialog:

- **Screening Technology**   This selector drop-down contains scripts for specific printing technologies such as Agfa and Linotronic imagesetting devices. When Standard Defaults is used as the Screening Technology, other options are set according to settings for your specific printer driver, accessed through Properties on the General tab.
- **Resolution**   This displays the output resolution of your printed material, the default value of which is set according to the Screening Technology selected. A service bureau or your print vendor will know the specifics.
- **Basic Screen**   This option sets the resolution as measured in lines per inch of the screens rendered in your output material. Check with your print vendor for the exact setting needed. If you need to adjust this value manually, it's done right here.
- **Halftone Type**   The Halftone Type selector sets the shape of the actual dots that compose the screens in the final output. Using this drop-down menu, you can choose such shapes as the default (Dot), Line, Diamond, Elliptical, Euclidean, Lines, Grid, Microwaves, Rhomboid, and Star. If you're just getting into commercial printing, anything other than a dot halftone shape is used either because the print press pulls better prints or because you really know what you're doing and want to create an effect in the finished print job. Elliptical and Star shapes can be used to sharpen the output of a print and, therefore, are more of an enhancer than a special effect.

Setting Trapping Options

Trapping involves either spreading or overprinting portions of colored objects to avoid printing inaccuracies, the most common one being paper white showing at the edge between two color objects. Overprinting causes one ink color to print over another, resulting in two layers of ink—it's a technique used to work around precise ink alignment. Overprinting can be set in three ways: directly in your document for each object, on the Separations tab from the Document Overprints drop-down list, or by setting the Automatic Trapping option below the Document Overprints drop-down— just click the button that applies to your need.

To set the overprinting of fills and outlines applied to objects directly in your document, cancel out of the Print dialog and return to the open document. Then with the Pick tool, right-click one or more objects, and choose Overprint Fill or Overprint Outline from the pop-up menu options.

Where options have been set manually in your document or for each ink color, overprinting operates on a three-level hierarchy, which creates a condition where one overprinting setting overrides another one as follows:

1. When printing, the objects in the drawing are first examined for any selected fill and/or outline overprinting properties. Applying overprint properties directly to an object in a drawing overrides all other overprinting functions.

2. Next, ink color overprinting options are examined. If an ink color is set to overprint and no object fill or outline overprint properties are applied, the ink color overprints the objects beneath it.
3. Finally, the PostScript Trapping options you have chosen on the Separations tab of the Print dialog are examined. If no other options are set, the automatic settings are used.

Automatic trapping and Document Overprints options on the Separations tab have the following effects on how colors in your document are printed:

- **Document Overprints Preserve** This option (enabled by default) preserves the overprint options applied directly to your drawing objects, regardless of the settings selected elsewhere. Your other option, Ignore (on the drop-down list), lets you work with the settings in the Separations tab, and any custom overprinting you've applied directly to objects in your document is ignored.
- **Always Overprint Black** When this option is selected, all objects that have color tints between 95 and 100 percent black will overprint underlying ink colors. Usually, you want black to overprint; black is the key plate for all the fine details, particularly necessary if you're using a bitmap image in part of your design.
- **Auto-Spreading** This option causes CorelDRAW's print engine automatically to create an overprinting outline of identical ink color around objects where they overlap other ink colors. When the option is selected, you can set the Maximum width of the spread within a range of 0 to 10 points (0.5 point is the default, a little wider than a hairline). Automatic width values vary according to the difference between the color being overprinted and the underlying color. Choose Fixed Width to set the Auto-Spreading width of the outline to a constant width regardless of this color difference. When Auto-Spreading is selected, choosing the Text Above option makes CorelDRAW ignore text sizes below a certain size; small text is often distorted by the spread effect. Choose a size between 0 and 200 points; the default is 18 points.

In-RIP Trapping Settings

If your output device is equipped with its own In-RIP trapping software, you can use this option. The term *RIP* stands for *raster image processor,* the process of converting mathematical chunks of information to a map where dots of ink go on the page to represent what you see onscreen. Many high-end imagesetters are equipped with internal software with which certain In-RIP trapping makes the whole trapping process faster and more efficient.

This option is dimmed unless the output device defined on the General tab is PostScript compatible, PostScript 3 is selected on the PostScript tab, and Print Separations is *disabled* on the Color tab. With the feature enabled, on the Composite tab, click the PostScript Level 3 In-RIP Trapping box, and then click the Settings button to open the In-RIP Trapping Settings dialog, shown next.

Here, you'll find an ink listing similar to the one on the Separations tab, plus other options for setting these items:

- **Neutral Density** This value is based on an ink color's CMYK equivalents, ranging from 0.001 to 10.000. Default values often work, or the value can be set according to advice from your print vendor. Most third-party ink swatches list the neutral density values for each ink color.
- **Type** You choose the Type for an individual ink by clicking its type in the top list to reveal an options drop-down. Although Neutral Density is the default for Image Trap Placement, this option becomes available when you have a specialty ink defined for a spot plate, such as a spot varnish. You can choose from Neutral Density, Transparent, Opaque, or Opaque Ignore. Opaque is often used for heavy nontransparent inks such as metallic inks, to prevent the trapping of underlying colors while still allowing trapping along the ink's edges. Opaque Ignore is used for heavy nontransparent inks to prevent trapping of underlying color *and* along the ink's edges.
- **Trap Width** This option controls the width of the overlap value, where due to imprecise printing tolerances and ink impurities, a plate's ink might spread. This used to be known as "choking" (choking compensates for spreading); the term has fallen into disuse.
- **Black Trap Width** This option controls the distance that inks spread into solid black, or the distance between black ink edges and underlying inks. It is used when the amount of black ink reaches the percentage specified in the Black Limit field (in the Thresholds area).
- **Trap Color Reduction** Use this option to prevent certain *butt-aligned colors* (areas on different plates that meet one another) from creating a trap that is darker than both colors combined. Values less than 100 percent lighten the color of the trap.

- **Step Limit**   This option controls the degree to which components of butt-aligned color must vary before a trap is created, usually set between 8 and 20 percent. Lower percentages increase sensitivity to color differences and create larger traps.
- **Black Limit**   This value controls the minimum amount of black ink required before the value entered in the Black Trap Width field is applied.
- **Black Density Limit**   This option controls the neutral density value at, or above, the value at which the In-RIP feature considers it solid black. To treat a dark spot-color as black, enter its Neutral Density value in this field.
- **Sliding Trap Limit**   This value sets the percentage difference between the neutral density of butt-aligned colors at which the trap is moved from the darker side of the color edge toward the centerline. Use this option when colors have similar neutral densities to prevent abrupt shifts in trap color along a fountain fill edge, for example.
- **Trap Objects To Images**   Choosing this option lets you create traps between vectors and bitmaps.
- **Image Trap Placement**   This option sets where the trap falls when trapping vector objects to bitmap objects to either Neutral Density, Spread, Choke, or Centerline in this option's drop-down list. Neutral Density applies the same trapping rules used elsewhere in the printed document. Using this option to trap a vector to a bitmap can cause uneven edges because the trap moves from one side of the edge to the other. Spread produces a trap in areas where bitmaps meet vector objects. Choke causes vector objects to overlap the bitmap (the bitmap is choked). Centerline creates a trap that straddles the edge between vectors and bitmaps.
- **Internal Image Trapping**   This option creates traps *within* the area of a bitmap, which is useful when very high contrast and posterized images are part of a design.
- **Trap Black-And-White Images**   Choosing this option performs trapping between vectors and black-and-white (monochrome) bitmaps.

Note   Much of this trapping information should be left to a press operator; most CorelDRAW owners are designers and shouldn't have to master trapping.

Setting Prepress Options

The term *prepress* is used to describe the preparing of film for various printing processes. Choosing the Prepress tab displays all options controlling how your printing material will be produced and which information is included on the page, as shown next.

Here are the options offered on the Prepress tab:

- **Paper/Film Settings** These two options specify negative/positive printing and on which side of the film the light-sensitive emulsion layer appears. Choose Invert to print your output as a negative; choose Mirror to print the image backward. Ask the press operator or service bureau which way its imagesetter is set up for film.
- **Print File Information** A Job Name/Slug Line text box is printed on each separation to better visually identify each printed sheet. The path and filename of your document is used, by default, but you can enter your own information. Choose Print Page Numbers to print page numbers as defined in your CorelDRAW document; choose Position Within Page to print this information *inside* the page boundaries—outside is the default.
- **Crop/Fold Marks** Crop marks help locate your document's page corners; fold marks indicate folds for a specific layout. Choose Crop/Fold Marks to print these markings. When this is selected, you can also choose Exterior Only to print the marks only outside the page boundaries on your printing material, which produces a more polished final presentation. Both options are selected by default.
- **Registration Marks and Styles** Registration marks help to align each separation plate; the film print is used to make the plate, and the plates need to be precisely aligned when your piece is printed or you get a "Sunday Funny Pages" finished output. Choosing Print Registration Marks (selected by default) includes these marks on your output. Use the Style selector to specify a specific mark shape; the selector includes a preview of both positive and negative versions.

Note If a commercial press operator tells you not to bother with registration marks, listen to them. Many houses do their own registrations because they know the presses a lot better than you do, unless you *are* a press operator.

- **Calibration Bars and Densitometer Scales** These two options enable you to include color calibration bars and densitometer scales outside the page boundaries of your printed material. Calibration bars help you evaluate color density accuracy by printing a selection of grayscale shades that may be used for measuring the density—or blackness value—of film or paper output.
- **Marks To Objects** Choosing this option positions your selected prepress marks to align with the imaginary bounding box of your objects, not the page bounding box. These marks appear regardless of whether the Crop/Fold Marks option is selected to print.

Choosing PostScript Options

The previous information on separations and advanced trapping features will be meaningless if your chosen output is not to a PostScript device. If you don't currently see the PostScript tab, shown in Figure 23-2, you need to define a different print driver. Options in this tab area offer control over PostScript options that use a specific type of page description language, Level 2 (older digital format), Level 3, the type of device (imagesetter, plain paper PostScript personal printing, other manufacturers' devices that claim to handle PostScript Level 3), and so on.

You set the following options on the PostScript tab:

- **Compatibility** In most cases, the printer and the PPD (PostScript Printing Description) file you choose are automatically set with the Compatibility option, which determines which PostScript features the output device is capable of handling. Older printers may be limited to PostScript Level 1 or 2 technology;

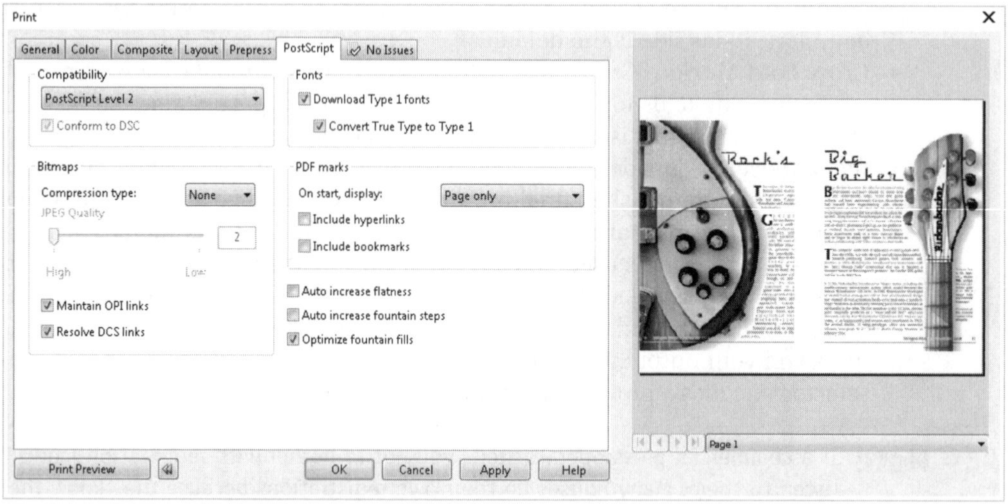

FIGURE 23-2 Use these options to control how PostScript options are made, but only after you've defined a PostScript printer as your output device.

most new models are compatible with Level 3. If you're unsure which to choose, check out the manufacturer's FAQ area on its website or the physical printer documentation.

- **Conform To DSC**   *Document Structuring Convention (DSC)* is a special file format for PostScript documents. It includes a number of comments that provide information for *postprocessors.* Postprocessors can shuffle the order of pages, print two or more pages on a side, and perform other tasks often needlessly performed by humans.

- **Bitmaps**   Selecting Level 2 or 3 PostScript-compatible printers gives you the option to Use JPEG Compression, in the drop-down list to the right of Compression Type. The JPEG option reduces printing time if you have bitmap images in your document. When this option is selected, the Quality Factor slider is available for setting the quality of the bitmaps being printed. Keep in mind that JPEG is a *lossy* compression standard: some of the original image information is discarded, quality is compromised, and at high compression settings, a photograph can take on visual noise. The other two compression options, LZW and RLE, are lossless—they don't change data like JPEG lossy compression does, and as a consequence, there is no noise in the files you compress, but LZW and RLE don't save as much space as JPEG.

- **Maintain OPI Links**   This option preserves links to server-based bitmap images, provided you have imported temporary low-resolution versions using the Open Prepress Interface (OPI) option when you created your CorelDRAW document. Using OPI, you can store high-resolution bitmap images in a printer's memory and work temporarily with an imported low-resolution version. When your document is printed, the lower-resolution version is swapped with the higher-resolution version. By default, this option is selected.

- **Resolve DCS Links**   Desktop Color Separation (DCS) technology is similar to OPI; you use placeholders that link to digitally separated images for use in process or multi-ink printing. When this option is enabled, the linked images automatically replace the placeholder images at print time. By default, this option is selected. If this option is not selected, a prompt will appear while the document is being printed, so you can relink the files manually through directory boxes.

- **Fonts**   PostScript printing devices can print both Type 1 and True Type fonts. Type 1 fonts are often preferred because the font data is written in PostScript language. CorelDRAW's options let you control which fonts are used during printing. Downloading the fonts to the printing device is more reliable; this speeds printing and produces better-looking text. To enable this feature, select Download Type 1 Fonts. If this option is disabled, fonts are printed as curves, which can take a lot of printing time when you have a lot of text on a page. When you select the Download Type 1 Fonts option, the Convert True Type To Type 1 option becomes available (and selected by default).

- **PDF Marks**   If your document is being prepared for printing as a composite to an Adobe PDF distiller, these options are available. You can specify how your PDF file initially displays when viewed in Adobe Acrobat Reader or a third-party reader by using options in the On Start, Display selector. Choose Page Only, Full Screen, or Thumbnail view. You can also choose whether to Include Hyperlinks and/or Include Bookmarks in the resulting PDF file. If you're preparing a PDF to send to a service bureau for high-resolution output, *don't* use hyperlinks; they mess up the appearance of your printed piece, and how does your intended audience click a piece of paper to visit a website?

- **Auto Increase Flatness**   This option lets you simplify the printing of curves by decreasing the number of straight vector lines that describe the curve. This option can be used as a last resort if you run into problems printing highly complex shapes in your CorelDRAW document, usually a printer memory problem, as in *not enough* memory.
- **Auto Increase Fountain Steps**   This option makes the print engine examine your document for opportunities to increase the number of fountain steps in an effort to avoid fountain fill banding. *Banding* is the visible effect of not having enough sequential steps in a fountain fill; with banding, you see bands of gradually changing color instead of a smooth transition from one object area to another. Increasing the number of steps that describe a fountain fill will make your fountain fills appear smoother, but it will also increase printing complexity and output time.
- **Optimize Fountain Fills**   This option works in reverse of the previous option by setting the print engine to *decrease* the number of fountain steps set for objects in your document to the number of steps your printer is capable of reproducing.

CorelDRAW's Printing Issues Tab

The process of verifying that every last detail in your document will print as expected is often called *preflight,* and the good news is the Issues tab is your flight attendant. CorelDRAW checks out the contents of your document and the printing options you've selected and then compares them to the capabilities of your selected printer and output material. Printing snafus are found automatically and flagged by warning symbols. Figure 23-3 shows the Issues tab, which is divided into two sections; with Print Preview turned on, it's both documented and visually obvious what this proposed print has going against it.

The top half of the Issues dialog lists the preflight issues detected with a brief explanation. The bottom half explains the causes, identifies the exact problems, and offers suggestions and recommendations for correcting them.

The Issues tab will not prevent you from printing your document. If you want, you can deactivate the feature by selecting the found issue in the upper portion of the tab and choosing Don't Check For This Issue In The Future at the bottom of the tab. This disables the detection of the issue in the Preflight Settings dialog. Clicking the Settings button opens this dialog, which also lets you save and load current settings for future use.

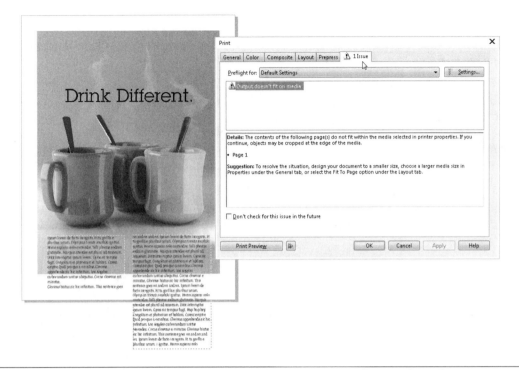

FIGURE 23-3   If CorelDRAW detects printing problems, they'll be explained in this dialog.

Previewing Your Printed Document

CorelDRAW's Print Preview feature is a great way to view your document and perform minor touchups, and it's fully integrated with CorelDRAW's print engine. To open the Print Preview feature, click the Print Preview button from within the Print dialog. Print Preview also is available in the File menu.

Print Preview (see Figure 23-4) is a separate application window and includes its own command menus, toolbars, Property bar, Status bar, and Toolbox. When Print Preview is open, CorelDRAW is still open in the background. You'll also find that nearly all of the options that can be set while viewing your document in the Print Preview window are available, except they provide a higher level of control.

Tip   The first thing you'll want to do in Print Preview is examine how your printed pages will look. Across the bottom of the Print Preview window, you'll find page controls—they are located and appear the same as the page controls in the workspace—so you can browse each printed page. Use the arrow buttons to move forward or backward in the sequence. As you do this, you'll discover each printed page is represented—including individual ink separation pages for each page in your document when you're printing separations.

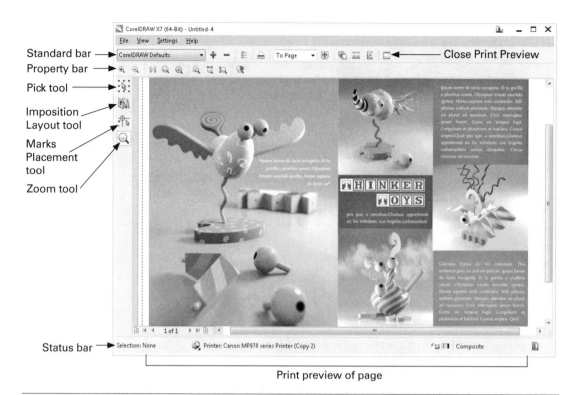

Standard bar — Property bar — Pick tool — Imposition Layout tool — Marks Placement tool — Zoom tool — Status bar — Close Print Preview

Print preview of page

FIGURE 23-4 Print Preview is a program within a program, with its own interface, tools, shortcuts, and commands.

Print Preview Tools and the Property Bar

The key to using Print Preview to its fullest is learning where all the options are located, what each tool does, and what print properties are available while using each. The Toolbox contains four tools—the Pick tool, Imposition Layout tool, Marks Placement tool, and Zoom tool—each of which is discussed in the sections to follow. The Standard bar, shown next, contains printing options, viewing options, and shortcuts you can use to open print-related dialogs.

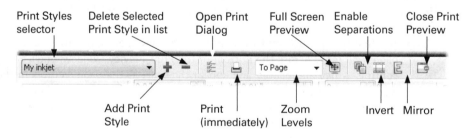

Print Styles selector — Delete Selected Print Style in list — Open Print Dialog — Full Screen Preview — Enable Separations — Close Print Preview — Add Print Style — Print (immediately) — Zoom Levels — Invert — Mirror

First is the Print Styles selector, which is used to choose all printing options according to a saved set of print parameters. As with other CorelDRAW Presets features, you can select, save, delete, or modify Print Styles in the selector. Choose an existing Print Style, use the current unsaved settings on the current print job, or choose Browse to access the Open dialog so you can work with a saved Print Style. To delete a selected Print Style, click the Delete (–) button. To save a Print Style, click the Add (+) button (or use the F12 shortcut) to open the Save Settings As dialog. Use the Settings To Include options to specify which print options to save with your new style, and click Save to add the Print Style to the selector.

The remaining options on the Standard bar have the following functions, many of which are covered earlier in this chapter:

- **Print Options**   This option opens the Print dialog.
- **Print button**   This option immediately sends the document to the printer using the current options. Use CTRL + T or CTRL + P as a shortcut.
- **Zoom Levels**   Select a predefined zoom level from the list to change the view magnification level.
- **Full Screen Preview button**   This option is self-explanatory. Press ESC to return to Print Preview. You can also use CTRL + U as a shortcut.
- **Enable Color Separations button**   This option sends the printing of color separations to the output device using color selected on the Separations tab of the Print dialog.
- **Invert button**   This option inverts the printed image to print in reverse. This is for film using an imagesetting device.
- **Mirror button**   This option flips the printed document to print backward to set emulsion orientation on imagesetting devices. You can also use this to print to T-shirt transfers.
- **Close Print Preview button**   Pressing this (or using the ALT + C shortcut) returns you to the current CorelDRAW document.

Pick Tool Property Bar Options

The Pick tool in Print Preview is used in much the same way that it's used in the drawing window; with it, you select and move (by click-dragging) whole pages. While the Pick tool and objects on a page are selected, the Property bar features a variety of printing options, shortcuts, position settings, and tool settings, as shown here:

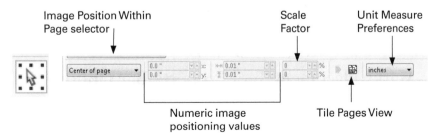

Many of these options are for positioning and scaling the contents of whole pages in relation to the printed output page size that your printer is currently set to use. You can click-drag to move whole pages or enter numeric values in Property bar boxes. Click-dragging the page object control handles lets you scale the objects interactively.

Imposition Layout Tool Property Bar Options

The Imposition Layout tool provides control over the print layout. Only certain imagesetters are capable of printing multiple pages in signature formats, so check with the person doing your print job *before* making changes using the Imposition options.

When the Imposition Layout tool is selected, the preview displays imposition-specific properties. This tool has four separate editing states, each of which is chosen on the Edit Settings selector. Options accessible on the Property bar while Edit Basic Settings is selected, shown here, give you control over imposition layout options. Choosing Edit Page Placements, Edit Gutters & Finishing, or Edit Margins from this selector displays a set of imposition options for each state.

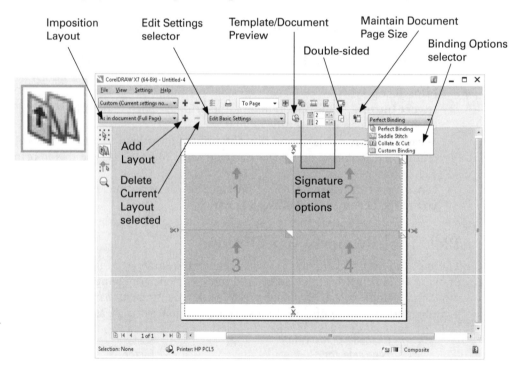

Marks Placement Tool Property Bar Options

The Marks Placement tool lets you alter the position of crop and fold marks, registration marks, color calibration bars, printing information, and Density Scale positions.

When the Marks Placement tool is selected, the Property bar features options for positioning and printing certain mark types, as shown here.

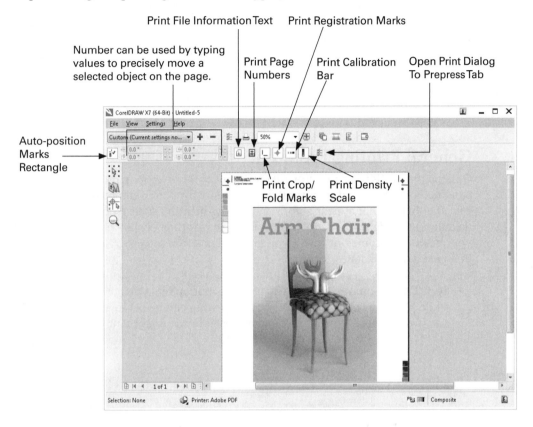

To move registration marks, page number indicators, file information text, and color calibration bars, click-drag the top, bottom, or sides of the rectangle defining their position, or enter values in the Property bar boxes.

Zoom Tool Property Bar Options

The Zoom tool in the Print Preview window is used much the same way as the Zoom tool in CorelDRAW. You can increase or decrease the view of your Print Preview. Many Zoom tool functions are performed interactively or by using hot keys. While the Zoom tool is selected, the Property bar features all Zoom options and magnification commands.

You can also change Zoom settings by choosing View | Zoom (CTRL + Z) to open the Zoom dialog to choose among all Zoom tool functions.

Setting Printing Preferences

Once you're familiar with the ocean of printing options, what your output device is capable of, and what you want from a specific print job, Printing Preferences can be your one-stop shop for most of the items covered in this chapter. Choose Settings | Printing Preferences (CTRL + F is the shortcut) while in the Print Preview window to open the Printing Preferences dialog, shown in Figure 23-5. Preferences are subdivided into General, Driver Compatibility, and Preflight options. To change any of the options, click a Setting title; a drop-down selector appears, and then you make your change.

General Printing Preferences

Options on the General tab provide control over fonts, crop mark color, driver banding, and so on, and they set the parameters for potential preflight issues or warning dialogs that appear before and during printing. These options are set, by default, to the highest fault tolerance for most printing jobs; 99 percent of the time your prints will come out fine if you don't change the settings. Here's a list explaining the most common states:

- **Spot Color Separations Warning** This option lets you control the warning state while printing color separations. The warning can be set to appear if more than one, two, three, or any spot colors are used in the document being printed.

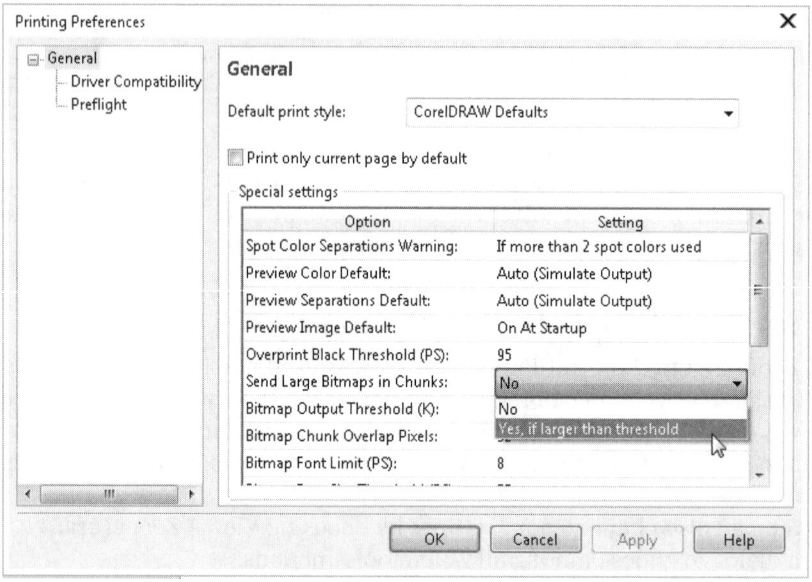

FIGURE 23-5 The Printing Preferences dialog offers comprehensive control over output settings.

- **Preview Color Default**   This option sets the initial color display of your printed document when the Print Preview window is first opened. Choose Auto (Simulate Output), Color, or Grayscale.

- **Preview Separations Default**   This option sets the initial color display of your separations when the Print Preview window is first opened. Choose Auto (Simulate Output) or Composite.

- **Preview Image Default**   This option controls whether your document image is automatically set to show when the Print Preview window first opens. Choose On At Startup (the default) or Off At Startup.

- **Page**   This drop-down offers Match Orientation, in which case CorelDRAW matches the output to the current printer settings, or Use Printer Default—CorelDRAW lets you know, parenthetically, what the current printer setting is.

- **Overprint Black Threshold (PS)**   During overprinting, CorelDRAW sets a default value for overprinting black objects only if they contain a uniform fill of 95 percent or more black. The Overprint Black Threshold setting can be changed using this option, so you can further customize the global overprinting function. The threshold limit can be set between 0 and 100 percent black.

- **Send Large Bitmaps In Chunks**   This option works in combination with the Bitmap Output Threshold setting and can be set to Yes, If Larger Than Threshold (referring to the Bitmap Threshold value), or No, The Default.

- **Bitmap Output Threshold (K)**   When printing to non-PostScript printers, this option lets you set a limit on the size of bitmaps, as measured in kilobytes, sent to the printing device. By default, this value is set to the maximum, but you can set it to specific values within a range of 0 to 4,096 (the default). This is a good option to change if your non-PostScript printer doesn't have a lot of memory and you're pulling prints that are unfinished owing to lack of RAM for processing the image.

- **Bitmap Chunk Overlap Pixels**   If a printing device has insufficient memory or another technical problem processing very large bitmap images, you can have CorelDRAW tile sections of the bitmap. The Overlap value is used to prevent seams from showing between "chunks" of the large image. When you're printing to non-PostScript printers, this option lets you define the number of overlap pixels within a range of 0 to 48 pixels. The default is 32 pixels.

- **Bitmap Font Limit (PS)**   Usually, font sizes set below the Bitmap Font Size Threshold preference are converted to bitmap and stored in a PostScript printer's internal memory. This operation can be time-consuming and usually increases the time your document takes to print. You can limit the number of fonts to which this occurs, forcing the printer to store only a given number of fonts per document. The default setting here is 8, but it can be set anywhere within a range of 0 to 100. Unless your document is a specimen sheet of all the fonts you have installed, 8 is a good number for this option.

- **Bitmap Font Size Threshold (PS)**   Most of the time CorelDRAW converts small sizes of text to bitmap format when printing to PostScript printers, such as 4-point legal type on a bottle label. This option lets you control how this is done, based on the size of the font's characters. The default Bitmap Font Size Threshold is 75 pixels, but it can be set within a range of 0 to 1,000 pixels. The actual point size converted to bitmap varies according to the resolution used when printing a document. The threshold limit will determine exactly which font sizes are affected. For example, the equivalent font size of 75 pixels when printing to a printer resolution of 300 dpi is roughly 18 points, whereas at 600 dpi it's about 9 points. The higher the resolution, the lower the point size affected. A number of provisions determine whether these controls apply, including whether the font has been scaled or skewed, and whether envelope effects, fountain or texture fills, or print scaling options such as Fit To Page have been chosen.

- **Image Resolution Too Low (Preflight)** This option alerts the user in the Issues area if the resolution of an element in the document is below the resolution limit set here. The range is 70 to 400 pixels per inch. The default is 96.

- **Composite Crop Marks (PS)** This useful feature is for setting the pen color of crop marks either to print in black only or in process (CMYK) color, making the crop marks print to every color plate during process color separation printing.

- **PostScript 2 Stroke Adjust (PS)** The PostScript Level 2 language (introduced in 1991) has a provision particularly useful for graphics programs such as CorelDRAW. Stroke Adjust produces strokes of uniform thickness to compensate for uneven line widths due to the conversion of *vector* artwork to *raster* printed graphics, which is what all printers do. The PostScript 2 Stroke Adjust option *should not* be used for older printers that are not compatible with PostScript Level 2 or Level 3 technology. Most recently manufactured printing devices are at least PostScript Level 2 compatible. If you are not sure what level your printing device is, leave this setting Off or consult the docs that came with the device.

- **Many Fonts** This setting controls a warning that appears if the document you're printing includes more than ten different fonts. If you're new to CorelDRAW and are experimenting with all the cool fonts that came with the program, your file can easily exceed this limit. If your printer's memory and/or your system resources are capable of handling large numbers of different fonts, consider increasing this value. The Many Fonts warning option can be set within a range of 1 to 50 fonts. Tangentially related to this option is a creative design issue: very few professionals use more than ten different typefaces in a design; five can express an idea using text quite well in most situations.

- **NT Double Download Workaround (PS) (Default Is On)** Under certain circumstances some fonts may be downloaded more than one time in an NT system. Although this is not a Corel-related issue, this is provided as a workaround.

- **NT Bookman Download Workaround (PS) (Default Is On)** The Bookman font is downloaded to printers even though the font is present in the printer in Windows NT. Although this is not a Corel-related issue, this is provided as a workaround.

- **Render To Bitmap Resolution** This option, by default, is set to Automatic, which causes bitmaps to be output at the same resolution as vector objects and text in your document. For example, if you have a bitmap that is 150 dpi under a lens, with an active Transparency effect, the bitmap portion of the document will be printed at 150 dpi while the rest of the document will be printed at the maximum printer resolution.

Driver Compatibility

The Driver Compatibility area isn't on the Print tabbed menu at all, but under Tools on CorelDRAW's main menu, under Options, under Global | Printing | Driver Compatibility. Driver Compatibility provides control over specific driver features for *non-PostScript* printers. Choose a Printer from the drop-down menu, and then choose specific options in the dialog to make changes. Clicking OK saves and associates your changes with the selected driver.

Printing Issues Warning Options

You can customize issues found by CorelDRAW' s built-in preflight feature using options on the Preflight page of the Printing Preferences dialog (CTRL + F), which can be accessed only from within Print Preview by choosing Settings | Printing Preferences and clicking Preflight in the tree directory.

This comprehensive list covers specific issues ranging from mismatched layout sizes to spot colors with similar names. Use the checkbox options in the list to activate or deactivate each option, or use the Don't Check For This Issue In The Future option, located at the bottom of the Issues tab of the Print dialog when an issue is discovered.

Using the Collect For Output Wizard

CorelDRAW has a wizard that collects all the information, fonts, and files required to display and print your documents correctly if you don't own an imagesetter or other high-end output device and need to send your document to press.

Corel has a service bureau affiliate program, and service bureaus approved by Corel can provide you with a profile to prepare your document with the Collect For Output Wizard. This profile can also contain special instructions that a service bureau needs you to follow before sending your files. Check with your vendor to see whether it is a *Corel Approved Service Bureau (CASB)*.

To launch the wizard, choose File | Collect For Output. From there, the wizard guides you through a series of question-and-answer pages that gather the information you need to upload or put on a disk to deliver to a printer or service bureau. When you finish the process, all necessary files are copied to a folder you define, and optional documents specifying your required output are included, depending on your wizard option choices. You'll experience a succession of wizard dialogs from the beginning to the end of the process. At the end, CorelDRAW offers a final screen with a summary; click Finish.

Print Merge

Print Merge gives you the design and business opportunities to merge database information with specific fields of your CorelDRAW documents at print time, so you can print personalized documents with only a click or two. If you create mailing labels, short runs targeted at a specific audience, or marketing documents, this feature will be invaluable. By creating special fields, you can merge specific database information into your document and set properties such as color, font style, and so on. This feature also lets you use ODBC Data Sources from database management systems that use Structured Query Language (SQL) as a standard.

Follow these steps when you need to create a Print Merge:

1. Choose File | Print Merge | Create/Load Merge Fields. Choosing this command opens the Print Merge Wizard, and you either create a database from scratch or choose an existing one.

2. If you need to create a custom merge document, choose the Create New Text option and then click Next. Create fields for your custom database by entering unique names in the Text Field and/or Numeric Field, shown in Figure 23-6, and then click the Add button. As you build your field list, you can change the order of the fields by clicking to highlight a field in the Field Name list, and then clicking the Move Up and Move Down buttons. You can also edit the fields you've created by using the Rename and Delete buttons to change or remove a selected field. Choose the Continually Increment The Field Data option while a field is selected in the list to number each entry in the field automatically. If you need numeric data, enter the value in the Numeric Field; when this option is used, new fields display, letting you specify the numeric sequence of your data and formatting. You can also choose the Continually Increment The Numeric Field checkbox to save time making your field entries. Once your list is created, click Next to proceed.

FIGURE 23-6 Create your custom database fields by typing in the Text and/or Numeric Field box and then click Add.

3. The next page of the wizard, shown in Figure 23-7, gets you right into building your database by entering values to build sets of field entries. To begin a new entry, click the New button, and then fill in the fields with the appropriate data; click the spreadsheet-like box to highlight it, and then type your entry. Click in any field in a record to edit it. To delete an entire record, select any field and click the Delete button. Browse your database entries using the navigation buttons, or search for specific entries by clicking the Find button. Once your database is complete, click Next to proceed.

4. The final wizard page is where you save your database to reuse and update in the future. Choose the Save Data Settings As box, and then browse your hard drive for a location to save the file in Windows Rich Text Format, Plain Text, or File With A Comma Used As A Delimiter (CSV Files). You probably also want to save the Incremental field data to make looking up a record easier in the future. Click Finish to exit the wizard and automatically open the Print Merge

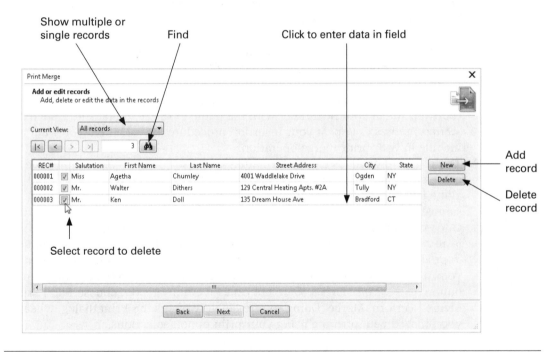

FIGURE 23-7   Use this page of the wizard to begin building your field entry sets.

toolbar, shown here. The Print Merge toolbar can also be displayed using Window | Toolbars.

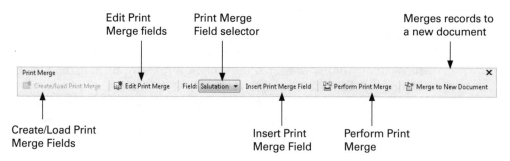

5. By default, the toolbar opens with your newly created database open and the individual fields it includes listed in the Print Merge Field selector. To load your fields from a different database, click the Create/Load Print Merge Fields button to relaunch the Print Merge Wizard.

6. By inserting fields, you're creating a link from entries in your database to insertion points in your document. To insert a field into your document, make a selection from the Print Merge Field selector, and then click the Insert Selected Print Merge Field button. Use the Text tool cursor to define an insertion point in your document with a single click. As you insert a field, a code appears in your document with the name of the field bracketed, such as < *Street Address* >. Repeat your insertion procedure for each field you want to include in your print merge operation.

7. The print merge fields can be formatted as Artistic Text, so you can include color, alignment, font, size, style, and so on. Fields can be inserted as stand-alone text objects, inserted into Paragraph Text, or simply typed using the same code format.

8. Once your fields have been placed and formatted, the print merge document is all set up, and you might want to click the Merge To New Document button to proof the different pages with the data entered. When it comes to merging your printed document with the Print Merge feature, you must use the Print button *on the Print Merge toolbar,* not CTRL + P. Alternatively, choose File | Print Merge | Perform Merge. Doing so immediately opens the Print dialog, where you proceed with printing using your print option selections.

This chapter has shown you where the print options are for both PostScript and non-PostScript output, how to check for errors and correct them before you send your CorelDRAW file to an output device, and how to make your work portable so someone with more expensive equipment than mere mortals own can print your work to magazine quality.

However, you can *still* publish from your office or home, never leaving the comfort of your computer when you understand the basics of page layout and creating documents for the Web. Save time, save a tree, and save your sites publishing to the Web, coming up next!

24 Basic HTML Page Layout and Publishing

Whether it's for personal pleasure or selling your wares, the Web is a connection between your ideas and your business and social contacts. It's far less expensive than other publication media such as television and print, and the really great thing about it is it's *hot*. You don't have to be a rocket scientist to get media up on your website using CorelDRAW. Once you've designed a piece for print, it's practically ready to go on the Web. Create once, publish many times!

In this chapter, you learn about the many tools and features at your disposal in CorelDRAW for perfecting your work for the Web, about how to create web page elements such as rollover buttons, and about optimal file dimensions and file sizes, font choices, and more.

 Note Download and extract all the files from the Chapter24.zip archive to follow the tutorials in this chapter.

Web Page Navigation Buttons and Hotspots

What makes the Web a *web* are the links that connect pages to other pages. The World Wide Web is engineered by connecting *this* bit of this page to that bit of *that* page on the same site—or on any other website in the world. The engine that performs all this interconnecting magic is actually the text-based *hyperlink*. Although text-based hyperlinks are the foundation of the Web, text links are about as attractive as a foundation, and the links themselves often are just a bunch of letters and numbers that mean something to a computer, but mean nothing to a human.

However, if you put a graphic *face* on a link—perhaps one that changes as a visitor hovers or clicks it—you have a link that speaks well of your artistic skills. You also get a chance to communicate nonverbally, which plays to a worldwide audience, many of whom might not speak your native tongue. With a graphic, you can clearly point out that Area X is a link and not part of your text message. Using a graphic also gives you the opportunity to provide a visual clue about where the link goes. How about the humble shopping cart icon? Virtually everyone with a computer and a web connection knows that clicking a shopping cart button takes them to a page that will let them buy something. That's a pretty all-encompassing message using only a few pixels.

Creating and applying attractive, well-thought-out navigational aids to a web page is a must in the competitive online marketplace. The following sections take a look at how you can use CorelDRAW's tools in combination with your input and ingenuity to create web pages worth a thousand words.

CorelDRAW's Internet Toolbar

You'll find several web tools and resources located throughout CorelDRAW, but the *central* location for many of these resources is the Internet toolbar. Here's a look at the toolbar; you choose Window | Toolbars | Internet or right-click any visible toolbar, and then choose Internet from the pop-up menu. The buttons on this toolbar are dimmed unless you have an object or two on the current drawing page; now is a good time to create a few button-shaped graphics for tutorial steps you can follow a little later.

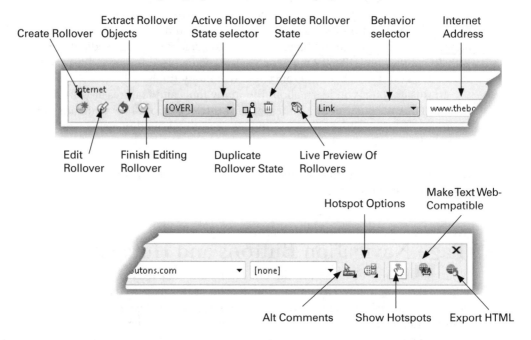

From the Internet toolbar, you can apply web-specific properties to objects, such as hyperlinks, rollover effects, and image maps. *Hyperlinks* are links to existing web pages (or to bookmark links applied to objects in your CorelDRAW document). *Rollovers* are objects that can change their appearance and perform an event in response to a visitor's cursor action over the object. *Image maps* are objects that have one or more linked areas to web page destinations. Rollovers are unique object types (that this chapter shows you how to make); however, hyperlinks can be applied to *any* single object or to specific characters in a Paragraph Text object.

 Caution Arial, Verdana, Times New Roman, and several other typefaces are web-compatible; when CorelDRAW exports one of these fonts, it will appear as editable text in the audience's browser. Be sure to click the Make Text Web-Compatible button before exporting your HTML, or you'll see that CorelDRAW will export the text as a JPEG graphic when you get to the Images tab while exporting. See "Web Text Options" later in this chapter.

The Internet toolbar provides a convenient hub for applying nearly all web object properties. Many of these properties can also be found and applied elsewhere in CorelDRAW, but using the Internet toolbar is more convenient. Making your graphics actually perform the duties you've assigned to them (by applying web properties) requires that a matching piece of HTML code be added to the web page HTML. CorelDRAW will write this code for you when you export your Corel document. You *will* need to give the HTML along with the graphic to your client or to the webmaster so the interactive graphics you've created do what they're supposed to do. In the sections to follow, you'll learn what options are available and where they are located.

Creating Rollover Buttons

Almost any object you draw can be made into a rollover that reacts to cursor actions, so you can liven up your published document with simple animated effects and hyperlinks. *Cursor actions* are events such as when a user holds or passes a cursor over the object or clicks the object by using a mouse.

When you're creating rollovers, you can define three basic states: Normal, Over, and Down. The *Normal state* sets how an object appears in its "static" state—when the cursor is not over or clicked on the object on the web page. The *Over state* sets the appearance of the object whenever a cursor is over it. The *Down state* sets how the object appears when being clicked, when the visitor's mouse button is clicked down on an object. By varying what the graphic looks like in these states, you can create interesting visual effects and give your users meaningful feedback related to their cursor movement.

 Note Consider your audience. Smartphone and users of popular tablets such as the iPad do not have the facility to respond to an "Over" rollover button state. The only states that count if your audience is primarily mobile are Normal and Down.

This is fun stuff and deserves a tutorial. The following steps show how to make a region interactive when an object (or group of objects) is displayed on a web page. Although the button will react to cursor actions when you've completed the tutorial, the actions will not link to anything; linking a button is covered later in this chapter—let's concentrate on the *art* for the button first. Let's suppose you want a button that tells the visitor that something is for sale: a button with a $ symbol plays in several countries, or use a currency symbol of your preference in this example. To continue the concept here, the action a visitor takes would be to click to buy the item; therefore, when visitors hover their cursor over and/or click the button, the button should change to a different look. In this example, its text will change from a $ symbol to an official-looking "SOLD" message. Yep, as ambitious as this might seem, all you need to do is to follow these steps...

Tutorial Creating Different Looks for Rollover States

1. Create a button object, make it as fancy as you like (Effects | Bevel is a classic web effect), but keep the size of the button to approximately the size you'd want on your web page—under an inch is fine for this example. Then with the Text tool type **$** and give the symbol a fill color that contrasts with the button color.
2. Select all the objects (CTRL + A), and then click the Create Rollover button on the Internet toolbar to let CorelDRAW know this is going to be a rollover button once you've finished, as shown here.

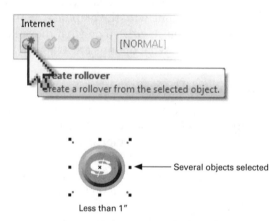

3. With the object now defined as a rollover object, all the states on the Active Rollover State selector display the same group of objects you selected...and it's time to create a change now. Click the Edit Rollover button to enter the editing state, as shown here, and then choose Over from the selector list.

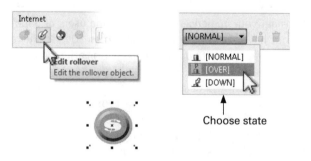

4. Edit your button; in the next illustration, the embossed circle has actually been replaced with a polygon object. You *can* replace objects, change the fill, do just about anything you like because this editing state is not a "normal" page view in CorelDRAW's drawing window. Some tricky stuff is going on behind the scenes, and if you choose to delete a shape and replace it now, you haven't really deleted it. You remove an object from a state's *view,* in this case from the Over state, but in the Normal state all your original objects are still there. Similarly, delete the $ and then with the Text tool type **SOLD** in an interesting font.

Replacement objects

5. For the sake of testing all these features, let's suppose that the Over state, the SOLD button, is also good for the Down state, the state that occurs when the visitor clicks the button. By default, the Normal state is assigned to all three available states when you first made the collection of objects a rollover button. First, click the Rollover State selector and choose Down; a view of the Normal state object appears.
6. Trash the contents of the Down state by clicking the Delete Rollover State trashcan button.
7. Choose Over from the selector, and then click the Duplicate Rollover State button. The Over state now duplicates the following unassigned state (Down).
8. You're finished! Click the Finish Editing Rollover button (shown here), and save this file to CDR file format.

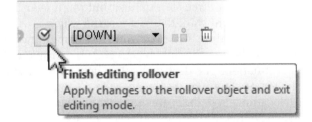

9. Oh, *yeah*; you want to see your creation *in action*! CorelDRAW will preview your interactive button right on the drawing page. Click the Live Preview Of Rollovers button; before you move your cursor over the button, it should look like it did when you set it to Normal—your original group of objects. Move

your cursor over the button, and it should show the Over state, as it will in the Down state (when you click the button) because you duplicated Over to Down in the tutorial. After previewing the effect, click the Live Preview Of Rollovers icon again to deactivate the live preview, because live drawings can be a little disconcerting.

Look at *rollover.cdr* and take it apart to better see the wealth of creative possibilities in your own work. This setup has three different states, and when you click the button, it changes shape and sort of squishes away from you. Just about any edit you can perform on objects, including totally replacing them, can be used in a rollover button.

The Internet toolbar also has other rollover-related commands, as follows:

- **Edit Rollover** This option was covered earlier, but you should know that even after you think you're finished, rollovers can be edited a week or a year from now.
- **Extract All Objects From Rollover** This is a *destructive* edit! Think about this command twice before you undo all your rollover work. Depending on the replacement objects you've built into a rollover, use this button to view and edit everything CorelDRAW has hidden while the document was a rollover. The objects will be stacked on top of each other, so you will have to change the stack order or drag them apart to see them.
- **Duplicate Rollover State** Covered briefly in the tutorial, this button is used to copy the Normal state to Over and Down states if you have deleted them using the command button, discussed next.
- **Delete Rollover State** This option deserves a little more quality time here: while editing any rollover state, you can delete the object(s) representing it by clicking this button. After a state has been deleted, there will be no object to represent it, so the rollover state will appear blank. If needed, use the Duplicate Rollover State button to create an exact copy of the Normal state back into a blank state to avoid having to re-create the object(s) used for this state. If you've deleted a state, be sure to set the Active Rollover State list back to Normal, or your button will be blank during an action once you put it on a web page.

You've just created a three-step rollover button! It is an interesting graphic effect, and sometimes you might want to use it just the way it is—a sort of graphic hide-and-seek game. Most of the time, however, you want something additional to happen; you want the action of clicking the link to activate a hyperlink and the user to be taken to the link's destination. The destination can be a bookmark location on the current page, like the top or bottom of the page, or the destination might be another web page or URL location altogether. How to make the rollover or any other element do something is presented in the following section.

Setting Internet Object Behavior

While any individual object or rollover state is selected, you can set its behavior as a web object to either a URL or an Internet bookmark using options in the Behavior selector on the Internet toolbar, shown next.

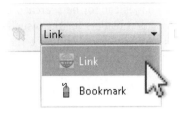

Adding URL Behavior

You can apply hyperlinks to any object using this option. For example, Corel's URL is http://www.corel.com. Internet addresses must be preceded with the correct Internet protocol prefix (such as *http://*, *https://*, or *ftp://*). For example, if you're linking to www.corel.com, the format must be http://www.corel.com. You can also use a "mailto" protocol to link to an email address, such as by entering **mailto:*someone@ somewhere.com***. This is a great way to get, for example, a potential client to write to you. By default, the *http://* protocol is automatically added to precede your URL, but you can edit it as needed.

> **Tip** Don't mistake what you type in a browser to go to a website, with what you enter as HTML code for the URL to a webpage. More and more you will see, for example, carpenters.com painted on a truck, with no http or slashes at the beginning. You can enter **carpenters.com** or something similar in most web browsers and go to the site, but when you are *coding* in HTML, you *have* to be explicit and type **http://www.carpenters.com**.

To set a URL as the behavior for your web object, click to select the object, and use the Behavior selector on the Internet toolbar to specify the URL. With this option selected, type the actual URL in the Internet Address box, pressing ENTER to apply the address link. Once a URL has been applied, the Internet toolbar displays other options. Here are the URL-specific things you can define:

- **Target Frame**   Use this option to specify an optional browser window location for the new page to open into. Unless you specify differently using this drop-down, the page that is called by the assigned URL address will open in the current browser window, replacing the page that contained the link. This produces the same results as the Default [None] setting in the Target Frame list. Choosing the *_blank* option from the list causes a new web browser window to open to display the linked page.

  If your web page uses frames for its display, you can specify where in the frameset the new content will open. Choosing *_self* opens the new URL in the same frame where the web object is located. The *_top* option opens the new URL in the full body of the window, and all frames are replaced with a single frame containing the new document. The *_parent* option opens the new document in the current frame's Parent frameset. You can also enter custom frame names by typing them in the Target Frame combo box.

> **Note** Frame-based web pages cannot be searched by most search engines such as Google's, and onscreen readers for the visually impaired cannot read the contents of frames. Think carefully if you choose a frame-based web document, and consider the audience you might lose and annoy.

- **Alt Comments** Use this option to add Alt (alternative) text to your web object. Alt text is a text description that is displayed either until the web object downloads or while your web user's cursor is held over the object. It is both polite and professional to add meaningful Alt Comments text to all graphics for accessibility reasons. Because page-reading software usually prefaces the reading of Alt text with an announcement of what kind of object the Alt text belongs to, such as a graphic or a hyperlink, don't repeat the link URL or enter the words "graphic" or "link." Instead describe the function or content the link leads to, for example, "Home Page," or "CorelDRAW Forums," or "send email to this terrific guy or gal." If you don't enter Alt comments for an URL, reading software will probably read or spell out the URL to your visitor; this is not a considerate way to treat visitors to your site.
- **Hotspots** A hotspot in a graphic can be a great way to create one graphic and yet tag several different areas to different links. Once you've entered a link for an object, click this icon to choose whether an object's shape or its bounding box will define the clickable area. Choose either object Shape or Bounds in the selector, as shown. You can choose the Cross-Hatch and Background colors if the currently set colors are difficult to distinguish from other colors in your document. These don't show on your published web page; they're only a visual convenience while you work in CorelDRAW.

- **Show Hotspots** This option in the middle of the toolbar can be toggled on or off, and it can activate or deactivate the display of the crosshatch pattern, which indicates hotspots applied to web objects, as shown next.

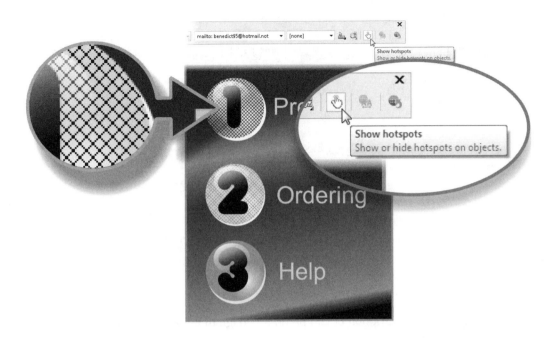

Adding Bookmark Behavior

Assigning a bookmark to a graphic object gives users a convenient way to navigate between web pages on your site. For example, you can use a bookmark if you want your audience to click a button or other link and return to the first page of your site from another page in your site. This is a two-step process. In the first part of the process, you define a fixed location to which one or more URL links can point. The fixed location is an anchor or bookmarked object. The second step in the process is to create a button or text link elsewhere that points to the object's bookmark. Let's walk through the process.

Tutorial   Creating Bookmark Links

1. Select an object that you want to serve as the anchor or bookmark, for example, a graphic at the top of your first page. The object that is bookmarked *must be a graphic, not text.*
2. From the Behavior selection on the Internet toolbar choose Bookmark.
3. In the Internet Bookmark box, enter a descriptive name for the bookmark, such as **home _page** or **bottom_of_page_4** and press ENTER, as shown in Figure 24-1. HTML must not have spaces in names; you can mix upper and lower case in HTML names, but use an underscore or a hyphen to separate words—or the code won't work.
4. Select another object or button or piece of Paragraph Text on the same page or on another page in your document. When this object is clicked on, it will take your user to the object you previously bookmarked.

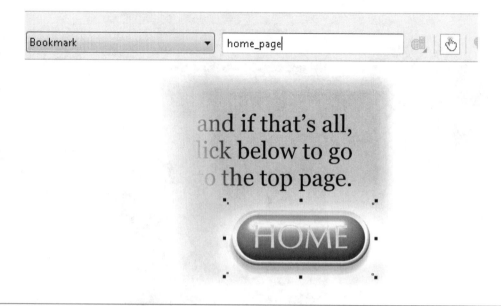

FIGURE 24-1 A bookmark object can be on any page of a multi-page document you want to publish as a website.

5. From the Behavior selector on the Internet toolbar, choose Link.
6. From the Internet Address drop-down list, choose the Bookmark name you gave to the object in step 3. For example, if "home_page" was the bookmark name you used, you would see an entry like this: _PAGE1#home_page, as shown in Figure 24-2.

You can also enter a fully qualified URL in the Internet Address field to link to the bookmark. The URL would take the form of the web page's address, followed by a pound (#) sign and then the bookmark name. For example, a website's home page is usually named index.html. So a bookmark named "picture" on the index.html page would be typed in as **http://www.mysite.com/index.html#picture**.

Tip If you are not familiar with how to write valid HTML hyperlinks and link anchor names or IDs (called *bookmarks* in CorelDRAW), consult your favorite HTML manual or the World Wide Web Consortium (W3C) page on Links and Anchors at http://www.w3.org/TR/html4/struct/links.html#h-12.2.1.

FIGURE 24-2   Use the target for the bookmark you find on the Internet Address drop-down selector.

Using the Links And Bookmarks Docker

Use the Links And Bookmarks docker to view, name, and apply preexisting bookmarks to objects. To open the docker, shown in Figure 24-3, choose Window | Dockers | Links And Bookmarks.

Purely for convenience, this docker automatically lists the currently applied bookmarks and includes commands for linking, selecting, and deleting existing bookmark links. The bookmarks themselves can only be created using the Bookmarks option in the Behavior selector on the Internet toolbar. You will find this docker most useful if you are trying to find a particular bookmarked graphic in a multi-page document that contains a lot of bookmarked items.

To find a bookmark in your document, open the Links And Bookmarks docker, and then double-click an entry in the Name column. You're automatically taken to the page and the bookmarked object is selected.

To create a link to a bookmark, first select the object to which you want to link a bookmark, click the New Link button, and then type the name in the open field on the Name list.

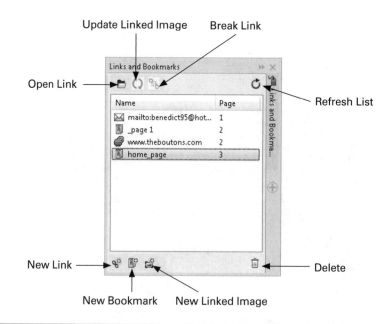

FIGURE 24-3 The Links And Bookmarks docker provides a convenient way to manage bookmarks applied to objects.

Applying a Page Background

If the background of your web page design calls for something other than white, you'll need to apply a unique background color or tiling background pattern. Page background is applied using the Page Setup pane of the Options dialog, shown in Figure 24-4. To access this dialog quickly, click to expand the listing under Document, and then click Background in the tree directory to view the available options.

Although it might seem logical to create a separate background object for your page and to apply your background properties to it, doing this can cause problems when it comes time to export your page. The background should be chosen in this dialog as No Background (the default), Solid, or Bitmap. Choose Solid to access the color selector for choosing a uniform color. Choose Bitmap and click the Browse button to select a bitmap image as the tiling background.

When you select Bitmap and specify a bitmap file, the Source and Bitmap Size options in the dialog become available. The Source option lets you link to and embed the bitmap with your document, but it has no bearing on how exported web pages are created. The Bitmap Size options let you use either Default Size (the inherent size of the original bitmap) or Custom Size. By default, the Print And Export Background option is selected, and should be so it's included as one of your web page elements.

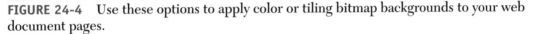

FIGURE 24-4   Use these options to apply color or tiling bitmap backgrounds to your web document pages.

Publishing Web Documents

You use the Publish To The Web command to export your CorelDRAW document to web page file format. To access this command, choose File | Export For | HTML or click the Export HTML button on the Internet toolbar. Both open the same Export To HTML dialog, shown in Figure 24-5, which has options for setting exactly how your web page content will be exported. The tabbed dialog looks like and is arranged similarly to CorelDRAW's Print dialog.

You'll find everything you need to save your web page and images. You can also use options to upload your page and the image content to a web server. The dialog itself is divided into six option areas ranging from General to Issues. You can also view a detailed Summary of the exported content and any web export preflight issues that CorelDRAW detects on the Issues tab. Use the Browser Preview button to check the appearance of your web page; by default CorelDRAW launches Internet Explorer for previews. The sections that follow provide a close look at all the options available.

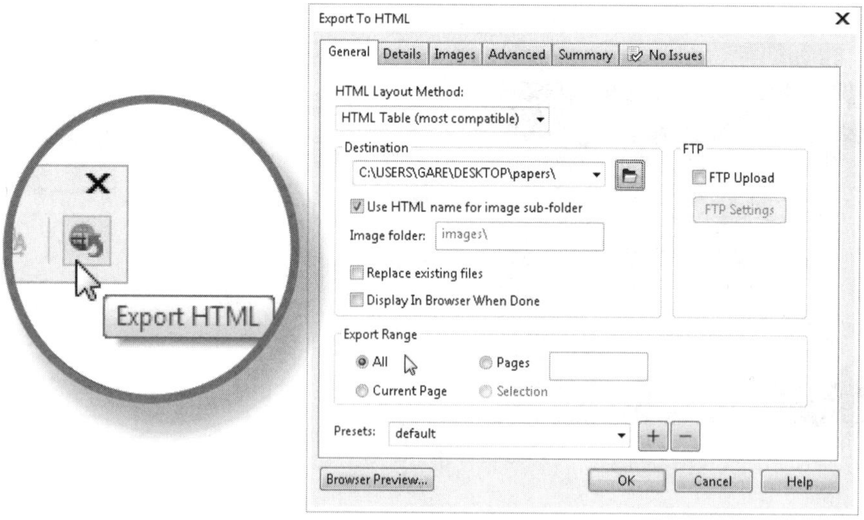

FIGURE 24-5   You can use these options for total control over how your page content will be exported.

Setting General Options

Use the General tab to set options such as the destination folder for your exported files. You can specify a separate subfolder for your graphics or remove the default subfolder name (images\) to have the graphics saved in the same folder as your HTML document. To give the graphics subfolder the same name as the HTML document, select Use HTML Name For Image Sub-Folder.

As for the HTML Layout Method area, the best choice for the majority of users is the HTML Table (Most Compatible) method. If you're using the export filter only to export the HTML code for an image map (rather than for an entire web page), you should select Single Image With Image Map.

Examining Web Page Details

The Details tab, shown next, provides information regarding exactly what you selected for export and what the exported file(s) will be named. If you want, you can apply unique page titles and/or HTML filenames to your exported web pages by clicking the existing fields and typing in new names.

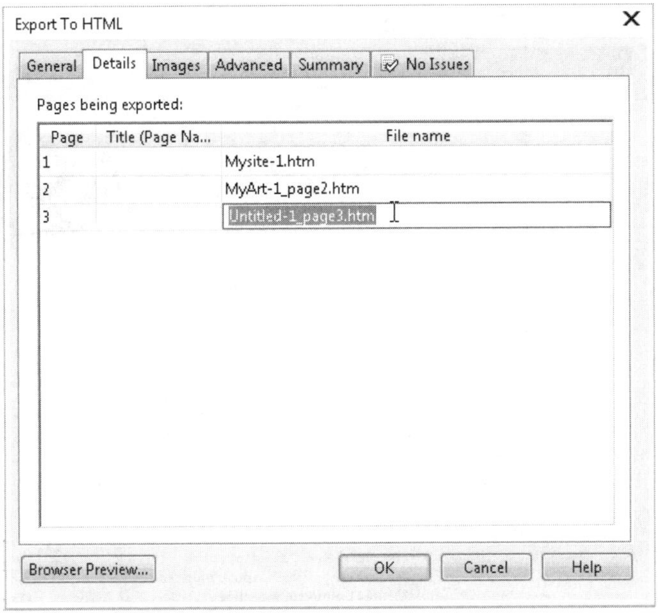

Reviewing Web Images

The Images tab, shown next, provides a detailed list of the images that will be exported and their default filenames. For a thumbnail preview of each image, click the Image Name. To change the type of format an image is exported to, click the field adjacent to the Image Name under the Type heading.

To change the settings used for each type of exported image, click and then choose a setting from the Type drop-down list. This is where you choose an export format for GIFs, JPEGs, and PNGs.

Setting Advanced HTML Options

The Advanced tab provides options for maintaining links you may have made to external files, including JavaScript, in your HTML output, and for adding cascading style sheets (CSS) information in your web page. If you're using rollovers, be sure to choose the JavaScript option.

Browsing the Web Page Export Summary

The Summary tab, shown next, provides information on the total size of your web page and how long it will take users to download your page at various modem speeds. The information is then itemized for each HTML page and image, so you can see if something in particular (such as a large image) might cause an unnecessarily long download time.

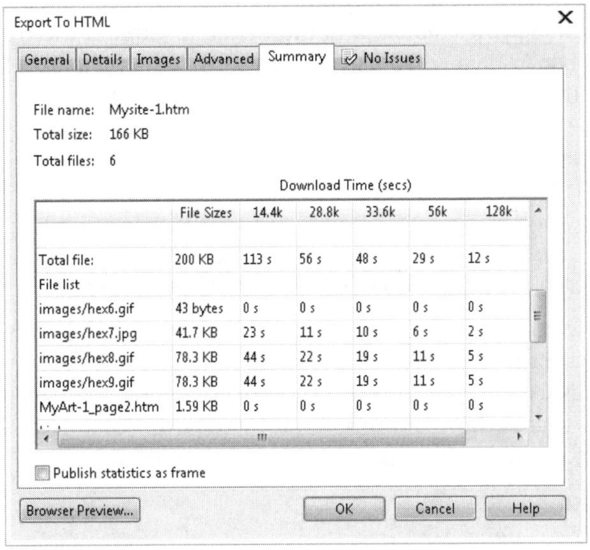

Preflight Web Issues

The Issues tab, shown in the following illustration—where an object that's off the web page has been flagged—detects and displays potential HTML export problems by using a series of preflight conditions. Preflight issues are found and displayed according to the options set throughout the Export To HTML dialog, most commonly regarding issues surrounding color model use, text compatibility, and image size and resolution. The top portion of the dialog tab lists any issues found, whereas the bottom portion offers suggestions for correcting the problems.

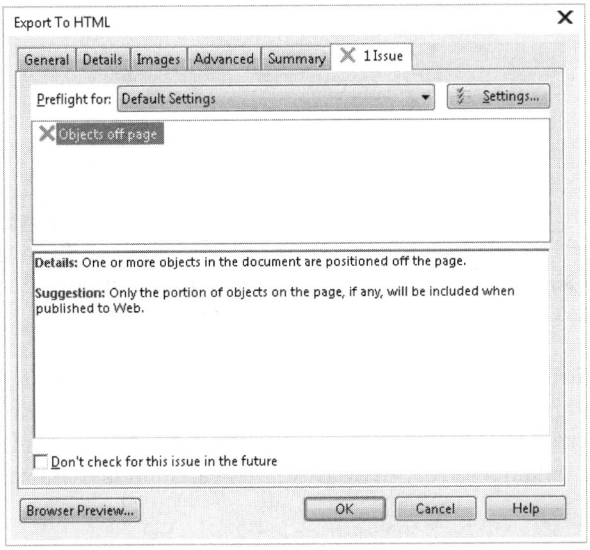

To change the issues the preflight feature detects, click the Settings button to open the Preflight Settings dialog, and then click to expand the tree directory under Issues To Check For. You can also use options in this dialog to Add (+) saved preflight issue sets or to Delete (–) existing issue sets in the list. HTML preflight rules are a function only of the web document HTML that you are exporting. If you have, for example, more than three issues flagged, make a mental note of the problems, cancel out of the Export HTML dialog, and then manually correct the issues in your drawing.

Setting Web Publishing Preferences

CorelDRAW gives you control over your personal web publishing preferences by letting you set Export To HTML options. These options let you predetermine many of the settings used when your documents are exported to HTML format, as described earlier. To access these options, open the Options dialog (CTRL + J), click to expand the tree directory under Document, and click Export To HTML, shown here.

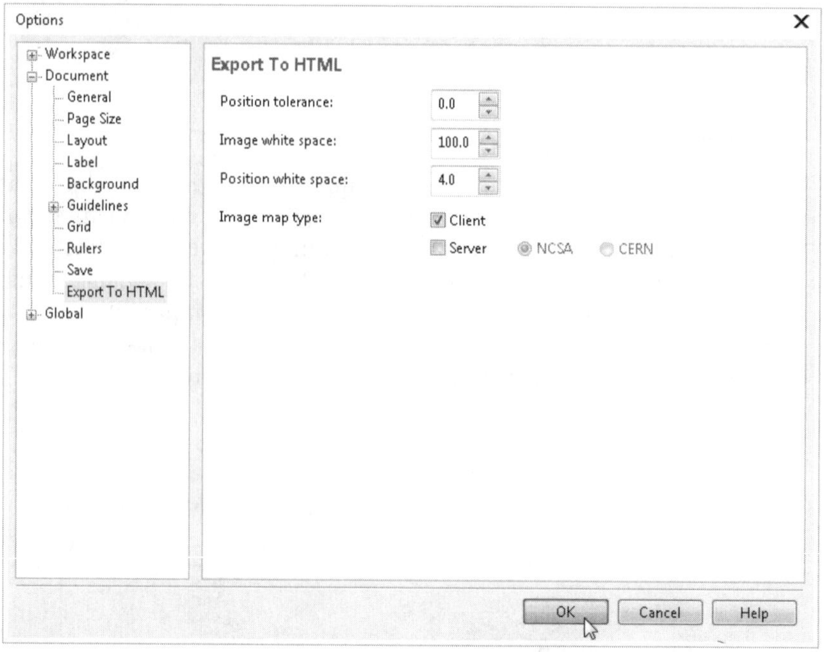

You'll see three options for setting conditions under which object position and white space are handled when your web page is exported:

- **Position Tolerance**   Here, you specify the number of pixels that text objects can be nudged to avoid creating very thin rows or narrow columns when the page is converted to HTML during export. Position Tolerance can be set within a range of 0 (the default) to 100. Increasing this value adds extra space.

- **Image White Space**   Here, you specify the number of pixels an empty cell may contain before being merged with an adjacent cell to avoid unnecessary splitting of graphic images.
- **Position White Space**   This option controls the amount of white space to be added to simplify your exported HTML document.
- **Image Map Type**   Choosing Client for the Image Map is the best choice because client image maps provide faster interaction with your user than server image maps. Only select Server if your provider specifically requests it.

Exporting Images for the Web

Although you can specify PNG, GIF, and JPEG file formats for images in your HTML page, you don't have access to nearly the variety of compression types or transparency options unless you pass your images through File | Export For | Web. This process is separate from Export To HTML, and to get images that feature transparency so they "float" against a page background, you follow these steps:

1. Export your HTML document and allow images to be exported to the Images folder CorelDRAW creates.
2. Export images you want to treat as special elements—such as PNGs and GIFs with transparent backgrounds—using File | Export For | Web.
3. Save these files and then replace the ones in the Images folder with your new files, using the same filenames as the ones in the Images folder.

Now create a graphic you'd like to appear on a web page against a background, and follow these next steps to learn how to export the graphic with transparency:

Tutorial   Exporting a Graphic with Transparency

1. Select the graphic on the page with the Pick tool. If the graphic has a background, don't select the background and you'll save a step.
2. Choose File | Export For | Web.
3. In the Export For Web dialog, shown in Figure 24-6, choose GIF from the Format drop-down list.
4. Click the Eyedropper tool to select it, and then click over the background in the GIF preview pane, not the one marked "Original" at its bottom.
5. Click the Make The Selected Color Transparent button; in a moment, you'll see the preview of the graphic with a checkerboard background indicating the transparent areas of your intended export.
6. Because GIF images can drop out only one color and not a range of colors, if the background of your document isn't black, consider using one of the matte colors, selected from the Matte mini-palette. If, for example, your web page is solid blue, choose solid blue. Choosing a matte color has nothing to do with the drop-out color you selected, but instead has to do with fringing. Choose a compatible background color from the Matte drop-down mini-palette colors to disguise aliased edges around your graphic.

7. Set the unique number of colors for the export. By default, it's 256, but to save transfer time, many simple graphics look fine using 128 or even 32 colors. You specify the number of colors from the Number Of Colors drop-down below the preview of the color palette, or you can type a value in the box.

8. If you need to resize the graphic, use the Percentage boxes in the Transformation field of this dialog, not shown in Figure 24-6 as it's at the bottom of the dialog and you need to scroll down to see it. But *think twice about this:* your HTML page *won't display the image properly* if you're replacing, for example, a 400 × 300 pixel GIF that CorelDRAW just exported to the Images folder with a new graphic that's 375 × 285 pixels.

9. Click Save As, and after you're done, replace the original exported image with this one, renaming the file to match the original filename. See Figure 24-6 for the location of the features used in this tutorial.

Replacing graphics in an HTML page has to be done with precision. The filename, the file type, and image dimensions have to be identical because the image dimensions are written into the HTML code. And very few artists want to edit to backward correct an HTML document!

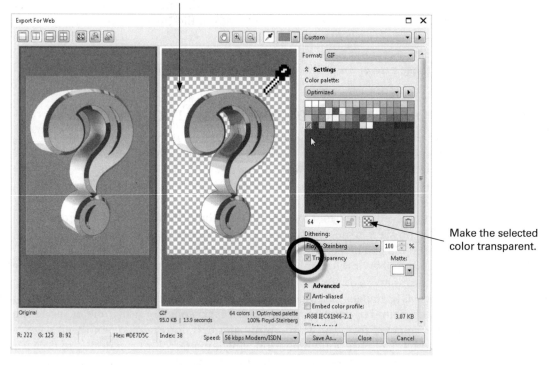

FIGURE 24-6 Export at the file size and with the options you need with Export For Web.

Web Text Options

Recently, web fonts have become a popular, slightly nonstandard way to use any font that can be embedded in a document on a web page. Unfortunately, the method to embed web fonts is outside of this chapter's scope, and *standard* W3C-compliant typeface use on web pages is this chapter's topic.

 Note Unfortunately, this version of CorelDRAW cannot implement web fonts—fonts on a server that are downloaded as a preload for a web page. You need to use the fonts listed in the following section.

The Web has no true "default" font—font display depends on the HTML, the web browsers your visitors use, and the fonts that are installed on their system. Over the years, though, Microsoft has quietly provided your system—and tens of millions of others—with system fonts that you can be basically assured reside on more than 90 percent of all computers used to surf the Web. Here are the current "Web safe" typefaces.

Arial is a web-safe font.
Comic Sans MS is a web-safe font.
Courier New is a web-safe font.
Georgia is a web-safe font.
Impact is a web-safe font.
Lucida Sans is a web-safe font.
Palatino Linotype is a web-safe font.
Tahoma is a web-safe font.
Times New Roman is a web-safe font.
Trebuchet is a web-safe font.
Verdana is a web-safe font.

On the Web, posting long sections of text as bitmap graphics is considered discourteous: visitors can't copy or bookmark the text and it violates the rules of accessibility—text-to-speech readers can't decipher text-as-graphics, and indexing services will ignore what might be valuable information. Therefore, when you create Paragraph Text for a web page, you should use one of the typefaces listed in the previous illustration, for at least two more important reasons:

- Your web page will load more slowly with text displayed as a graphic instead of as editable text.
- Small text, such as 10 point, probably will not be legible. Consider that a screen pixel is approximately 1/72nd of an inch, and a typographic point is approximately equal in size to one pixel. Ten-point text, then, has to be rendered to screen using only ten pixels in height. That's the size of the font previews on CorelDRAW's Fonts drop-down list, and many of the fancier fonts are not legible at this size as bitmap renders.

Figure 24-7 is an example of a web page layout, and as you can see, the text for the business hours is small and formatted as Paragraph Text. This text needs to be exported as text and not as a bitmap. On the other hand, the name of the fictitious spa and the elegant headlines above business hours can be exported as bitmap graphics, especially if the designer wants to retain the typeface style.

Follow these steps with any web page layout you have that contains text, to learn how to make the document conform to web standards for text:

Tutorial Formatting Text for the Web

1. Format any text you want to be editable text on the web page using the fonts listed earlier.

2. The first thing to do is to check to see that any text you want displayed as text on the web page is *Paragraph Text*. Select any text in question with the Pick tool, and then choose Text from the menu. If the command Convert To Paragraph Text is available, choose this command. If it's not available, the text is already Paragraph Text. It's easy to spot on the page because you should see a nonprinting frame around Paragraph Text.

FIGURE 24-7 Text that uses a distinctive typeface has to be exported as a bitmap to retain that look on the Web.

3. Conversely, any headlines or other ornate, large, short text entries should be Artistic Text. With the Pick tool, select any text that's Paragraph Text but needs to be Artistic Text, and then choose Text | Convert To Artistic Text.

4. Choose Window | Toolbars | Internet. Select a Paragraph Text block, and then click the Make Text Web-Compatible button. Do this again for any remaining Paragraph Text blocks.

5. Use Styles in the HTML Layout Method when exporting to ensure your web page has real text, and not a bunch of graphics for Paragraph Text.

6. If there is nothing left to link on your web page, click Export HTML.

You will not see Paragraph Text change in any way on your CorelDRAW page; the Make Text Web-Compatible button is a toggle—you can select tagged text and then turn off its web compatibility. This compatibility is just an instruction on how CorelDRAW writes the HTML. You need to look at the finished HTML page in a web browser—*on a computer other than your own*—to see how the web-compatible Paragraph Text looks. Because web browsers examine your installed fonts, you have no other way to see the text as the rest of the world will see it unless you go through the unpleasant process of temporarily uninstalling several typefaces from your own computer.

Use Alt Tags

The Alt Comments button on the Internet toolbar—popularly known as *Alt tags*—is used to provide descriptive information about a graphic for those in your audience who either are surfing with graphics disabled (it's a fast way to perform text searches) or have a visual impairment. It's just plain considerate to label graphics on a web page with an Alt tag, particularly if your logo is a graphic and it's the only time it's seen on a web page. Applying Alt tags takes only a second. Here's an example: the fictitious Spa-Di-Dah Health Club's logo is a special typeface and, therefore, has to be posted online as a bitmap graphic. Here, the logo is selected, the Alt Comments button is clicked, and a description of the graphic is typed in.

SVG: Export as Vector Objects

The Scalable Vector Graphic (SVG) is a web object that CorelDRAW can both import and export. Since 1999, the SVG file format has been under development by the W3C. SVG is based on the text-based Extensible Markup Language (XML) for describing two-dimensional vector graphics. All current Web browsers can directly render an SVG web page element to screen.

One of the most useful properties of an SVG graphic is that it is scalable, with no loss of image detail. This means you can post a graphic, for example, of directions as a map, and if the SVG file is coded properly for a page, a visitor to your site can enlarge or decrease the size of the map to find exactly where a location is. Also, SVG files are very small because they are text-based, and if a friend or client doesn't own CorelDRAW, SVG is an ideal medium for sharing graphics—and a good alternative to the PDF file format.

Open *Map.cdr* in CorelDRAW now, and follow these next steps to see how to export a graphic to the SVG file format:

Tutorial Exporting Vectors as Vectors for the Web

1. Select the graphic with the Pick tool or press CTRL + A to Select All.
2. Choose File | Export (or click the Export button on the Standard bar). Choose SVG Scalable Vector Graphic (*.SVG), pick a filename and location, and then click Export.
3. Choose SVG 1.1 from the Compatibility drop-down, unless your site absolutely needs to conform to the older standard, perhaps for an enterprise intranet. Choose Unicode-UTF-8 as the encoding method. This produces a smaller file than UTF 16 because it encodes words to 8 bits, eliminating some multilingual parameters used in non-Latin text. See the following illustration.

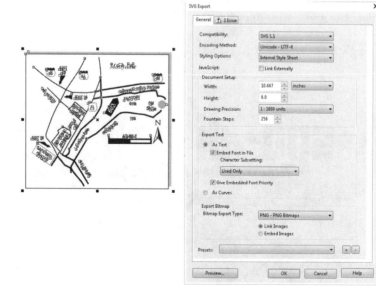

4. In the Export Text area, you can choose to export any text in the selected objects as text or as curves. If you chose UTF 8, you should export as curves. If you've used non-Latin characters such as those available in fonts such as Arial and Georgia, Asian and Greek glyphs are present in Unicode fonts.

5. In the Styling Options list box, you can choose to embed a style sheet (a cascading style sheet, or CSS) internally or externally with the exported SVG file. If you choose an external style sheet, it's linked to the graphic and can help a webmaster embed the graphic in a web page.

6. You can also make the SVG part of a rollover button if you check the Link Externally box in the JavaScript area.

7. Choose to embed fonts if you're using a typeface that's not web-compatible.

8. You can create smooth fountain fill steps by increasing the value using the Fountain Steps box. Doing this increases the saved file size, however.

9. Choose the dimensions at which you want the SVG graphic to display in a browser window. It makes no sense, in this example, to make it a small graphic, so choose a width of 900 pixels.

10. Export Bitmap is only a relevant field if objects you've selected cannot be interpreted as vectors. Choose this option if you've used drop shadows, mesh fills, texture fills, and any effect such as lens effects. You can embed or export the bitmaps as linked files. Embedding the bitmaps makes the SVG file much larger; if you choose to do this, JPEG—a highly compressed image file type—is probably a smarter choice than PNG.

11. Click OK to export the SVG file. If you have Firefox, Safari, Opera, or Internet Explorer version 9 or better, try dragging the SVG file into an open browser window to see the results.

Exploring SWF Files

There has been a little confusion in recent years over mobile devices and the general decision not to support Flash, an Adobe product that has been used on the Web to play exceptionally compressed, but high-quality video. A Shockwave file (a file with the .swf extension) is not a Flash file, not strictly speaking. A Shockwave file can contain bitmap images, but it's usually impractical to do this (to save on the file size). There are two types of SWF files: animations and still images. CorelDRAW can export only still SWF files, but the overall attractive thing about SWF artwork is that it can be scaled with no loss in image quality, and you might find that an SWF piece of artwork might be smaller than the same size graphic exported as an SVG file.

CorelDRAW can add some fill and outline properties to objects that the Shockwave format doesn't support. Like SVG files, if an SWF file can't write a vector, a bitmap copy of the graphic is included in the exported file. Exporting bitmaps within an SWF file defeats the purpose of this compact vector-enabled file type, so a review of what can export as vector objects, and what cannot, is called for here.

> **Note** The Mac OS does, indeed, support SWF file on the Web. It's *Flash* files, highly compressed movies, that will not play on mobile devices and the iPad.

Objects and Fills that SWF Supports

The good news is that everything that an SWF file can handle, CorelDRAW can create. The following list describes what you should and shouldn't use when making a drawing destined for SWF export:

- **Outline properties** Standard SWF export supports outline width and color, but only rounded line caps and joins; CorelDRAW's export filter can convert straight end caps to rounded if you choose High Quality-Optimized from the Presets drop-down list. The Export dialog also offers to convert only dashed outlines to be compatible with SWF.
- **Fill properties** SWF will render Uniform color fills, plus Linear and Radial fountain fills. A gradient can contain up to eight color transitions (color stops).
- **Transparency** If you apply transparency to a gradient-filled shape, you are limited to the Uniform transparency type. When a shape is filled with a flat (solid) color, however, you can use Linear and Radial transparency types.
- **Text** You can use any typeface you have installed, as long as you uncheck Text As Text before exporting so the text is converted to curves. A visitor's computer must have the same font installed as you do to read text as text.
- **Bitmaps** Photos and digital paintings can be exported to a Shockwave file, but they cannot be as efficiently compressed as vector shapes. Make a copy of high-resolution images at the size you intend to use in JPEG file format.
- **Effects** All effects—contours, blends, and envelopes—applied to shapes can be exported; using these effects is a good workaround to certain types of fountain fills that don't work as Shockwave vector objects.

Open *Solutions Graphic.cdr* in CorelDRAW now. Here's the procedure and your options for exporting an SWF file.

Tutorial Making a Single-Frame SWF File

1. Select all the objects using the marquee selection technique around the objects. They are on different layers, so CTRL + A doesn't work here.
2. Click the Export button on the Standard bar, and then choose SWF-Adobe Flash (.SWF) from the Save /As Type drop-down list. Choose a location for the saved file and name it, and then click Export. The Flash Export dialog appears.

3. On the General tab, Bitmap settings are only of relevance when objects have fills that the export engine cannot recognize. In your own exporting adventures, use JPEG with no or 10 percent compression to preserve the appearance of vector objects that have texture or other nonacceptable fills.

4. Click Objects in the Bounding Box Size area; you selected the objects in Step 1, so this option is the smart one.

5. Check Convert Dashed Outlines just as a matter of practice. Use Default Fountain Steps is a handy option if your objects only have subtle fills or less than eight color transitions. Unchecking this box can create larger files, but unchecking this box might cause visible banding when you look at the Flash file.

6. The HTML tab really only contains one item of interest: Image Size. If you want to export this graphic at any size, select the size using the spin boxes or by typing a specific value here.

7. If the Issues tab reports that there are non-RGB colors in the selection, dismiss it. Click OK to export the graphic as a Flash media object.

8. Some older web browsers require JavaScript to display an SWF file directly in a web browser, but if you have a copy of Firefox or IE 9 or later, you can drag the SWF file into its browser pane and you'll see the graphic full screen. Also, Adobe's Flash Player 10.*x* will display the file if you've downloaded the player; chances are good some application has already fetched it for you and made the file association. Just double-clicking the file icon might bring up Flash Player.

This chapter has shown you how to take just about any media on a CorelDRAW page—be it a drawing, a photo, or text—and make your design web-page compatible.

As you might note, there are more pages under your left thumb than under your right, unless you're reading this on a Kindle, in which case, the left side is heavier than the right side. And this means this book must draw to a close. Your own story with CorelDRAW is just beginning, however. Use this *Guide* in combination with CorelDRAW's online manual to draw compositions to please your client or to please yourself, and you will probably also draw some attention.

Index

Symbols and Numbers

- (minus) key, 179
+ (plus) key
    adding nodes with, 179
    drag/drop copies with, 40
    generating new nodes, 220
    inserting pages with, 93
3-Point Callout tool, 194–195, 200–201
3-Point Curve tool, 166, 170–173
3-Point Ellipse tool, 118–119
3-Point Rectangle tool, 115
3D grid, 424–425
3D ground plane, 410–411
3D rotation, 421–422

A

Absolute Colorimetric rendering
    intent, 13
acceleration
    blend color, 355–356
    controlling contour effect,
      372–373
    fountain fill, 299
    markers for blend, 351, 355
acceleration handles, 69–70
accounts for CorelDRAW, 8
additive color models, 377, 378, 381
adjusting text spacing, 249–250
Adobe Flash, 649–651
Adobe Photoshop, 552
Advanced Separations Settings dialog,
    604–605
aligning
    blend object path, 362
    nodes, 181
    objects, 104–106
    paragraphs, 272
Alignment and Dynamic Guides
    docker
      illustrated, 105
      Intelligent Dimensioning
        option, 105, 106
      Intelligent Spacing option, 105,
        106
      options of, 104–106
      using Dynamic Guide options,
        107–110
      working with margins, 107
Alpha Channel transparency,
    520–521

ALT (alternatives) key
    marquee-selecting objects
      with, 136
    selecting covered objects with
      ALT-click, 137
    using, 37
Alt comments, 632, 647
Altitude option (Bevel docker), 452
amplitude
    changing Push And Pull
      distortion, 476, 477
    of Zipper distortion,
      470–471, 472
anchor point. *See* center origin
    marker
angles
    constraining Bézier, 177
    constraining for rotated
      transparencies, 489
    creating and saving custom,
      109–110
    Free Transform mode for, 46
    resolution dot, 603, 604
    saving Dynamic Guide custom,
      109–110
    setting default increments
      for, 108
anti-aliasing, 83, 539–540
antonyms, 284, 285
Application Launcher (Standard bar),
    43, 45
application window, 14–19
arcs
    creating with Ellipse, 116,
      117–118
    discovering nodes for, 170
    drawing with 3-Point Curve,
      170–173
arrowheads
    adding to open paths, 169
    applying to callouts, 200, 201
    customizing, 329–332
    Outline Pen options for, 332
    setting for outlines, 328–329
    specifying same attributes for
      head/tail, 332
    using for connector lines, 202
artifacting, 539
Artistic Media tool, 337–346
    Calligraphy mode for, 343–345
    drawing with brushes, 338,
      340–341

location of, 165
pre-visualizing Sprayer design,
    413–416
Pressure mode, 345–346
Property bar options for,
    337–338, 340, 341, 342
Sprayer mode for, 341–343
uses for, 337
using Preset strokes, 338–340
Artistic Text
    adjusting text spacing for,
      249–250
    changing to Paragraph Text, 268
    columns unavailable for, 267
    combining and breaking
      apart, 250
    converting to curves, 250
    creating with Text tool,
      238–239
    entering and editing,
      239–242
    Paragraph Text vs., 250–251
assigning language codes, 279
attitude for bevel effects, 453
Attract tool, 462
Attributes Eyedropper tool, 147–148,
    318–319, 477
Auto-Close On Cut mode
    (Knife tool), 228
Auto-Join option (Freehand/Bézier
    Tool pane), 184
auto-spreading option, 606
automatic spell checking, 282

B

B-Spline tool cursor, 166
Back Minus Front command, 210,
    213, 214
Back One command, 154
backgrounds
    adding behind shape, 70–72
    applying web page, 636–637
    bitmap images as, 81, 82–83
    choosing solid page, 91
    creating external links to, 81–82
    exporting page, 83
    making object, 52–53
    masking, 511–514
    removing tracing, 530
    sampling, 63, 64
    specifying color for, 81–83